Accountants' Guidebook

A Financial and Managerial Accounting Reference

Second Edition

Steven M. Bragg

For more information about AccountingTools® products, visit our Web site at www.accountingtools.com.

ISBN-13: 978-1-938910-34-0

Printed in the United States of America

Table of Contents

iii

Preface

The accounting profession requires that the accountant have a broad knowledge of many topics. Systems must be installed for the recordation of information, accounting standards used to properly classify transactions, and financial statements issued. In addition, the accountant must be able to manage several functions, while also having a sufficiently deep knowledge of operations and finances to issue cogent financial analyses. The *Accountants' Guidebook* addresses all of these areas by discussing such issues as the chart of accounts, general ledger, procedures, Generally Accepted Accounting Principles, closing the books, management reports, payroll management, budgeting, and much more. As examples of the topics covered, the *Accountants' Guidebook* provides answers to the following questions:

- What techniques are available for reducing the chart of accounts?
- How do I close the books in the most efficient manner?
- Which reports must be filed by a publicly-held company?
- How do I assemble a comprehensive company-wide budget?
- Which tactics should I use when attempting to collect an overdue invoice?
- What are the disclosure requirements for investments?
- How do I compile the cost of inventory?
- Which depreciation methods are available for fixed assets?
- How do I account for a stock split?
- How do I account for payroll?
- How do I account for transactions stated in foreign currencies?
- Which ratios are most useful for interpreting the results of a business?

The *Accountants' Guidebook* is intended for anyone involved in the accounting profession, such as accounting staff and managers, consultants, analysts, and students. The book also provides extensive references to the author's popular Accounting Best Practices podcast, which provides additional coverage of many accounting topics. As such, this book may earn a place on your book shelf as a reference tool for years to come.

Centennial, Colorado
June 2014

About the Author

Steven Bragg, CPA, has been the chief financial officer or controller of four companies, as well as a consulting manager at Ernst & Young. He received a master's degree in finance from Bentley College, an MBA from Babson College, and a Bachelor's degree in Economics from the University of Maine. He has been a two-time president of the Colorado Mountain Club, and is an avid alpine skier, mountain biker, and certified master diver. Mr. Bragg resides in Centennial, Colorado. He has written the following books and courses:

Accountants' Guidebook
Accounting Controls Guidebook
Accounting for Inventory
Accounting for Investments
Accounting for Managers
Accounting Procedures Guidebook
Budgeting
Business Ratios
CFO Guidebook
Closing the Books
Corporate Cash Management
Cost Accounting Fundamentals
Cost Management Guidebook
Credit & Collection Guidebook

Financial Analysis
Fixed Asset Accounting
GAAP Guidebook
Human Resources Guidebook
IFRS Guidebook
Inventory Management
Investor Relations Guidebook
Lean Accounting Guidebook
Mergers & Acquisitions
New Controller Guidebook
Nonprofit Accounting
Payroll Management
Revenue Recognition

On-Line Resources by Steven Bragg

Steven maintains the accountingtools.com web site, which contains continuing professional education courses, the Accounting Best Practices podcast, and hundreds of articles on accounting subjects.

The *Accountants' Guidebook* is also available as a continuing professional education (CPE) course. You can purchase the course (and many other courses) and take an on-line exam at:

www.accountingtools.com/cpe

Chapter 1
The Role of the Accountant

Introduction

This book is designed to give the accountant a practical knowledge of how to complete many accounting tasks, as well as impart an understanding of the more critical accounting standards. Before engaging in these tasks, it is necessary to first address the concept of accountancy, and how this book addresses each of the accountancy concepts. We also cover the differences between financial and managerial accounting, describe the various accounting positions, note the responsibilities of the accounting department, and finish with a discussion of how the department is organized. In total, these topics provide an overview of the role of the accountant.

> **Related Podcast Episodes:** Episodes 87, 123, 140, and 157 of the Accounting Best Practices Podcast discuss the chief financial officer, controller, cost accountant, and senior accountant positions, respectively. You can listen to them at: **accounting-tools.com/podcasts** or **iTunes**

The Accountancy Concept

Accountancy is the practice of recording, classifying, and reporting on financial transactions for a business. These tasks are expanded upon as follows:

- *Recordation.* The recording of accounting transactions usually involves several key business transactions that are handled on a repetitive basis, which are issuing customer invoices, paying supplier invoices, recording cash receipts from customers, and paying employees. These tasks are handled by the billing clerk, accounts payable clerk, cashier, and payroll clerk, respectively. There are also a number of accounting transactions that are non-repetitive in nature, and so require the use of journal entries to record them in the accounting records. The fixed asset accountant, general ledger clerk, and tax accountant are most likely to be involved in the use of journal entries.
- *Classification.* The results of the efforts of the preceding accountants are accumulated into a set of accounting records, of which the summary document is the general ledger. The general ledger consists of a number of accounts, each of which stores information about a particular type of transaction, such as product sales, depreciation expense, accounts receivable, debt, and so on. Certain high-volume transactions, such as customer billings, may be stored in a sub-ledger, with only its totals rolling into the general ledger. The ending balances in the general ledger may be altered with adjusting

entries each month, mostly to record expenses incurred for which no supplier invoices have yet been received. The information in the general ledger is used to derive financial statements, and may also be the source of information used for internal management reports.

- *Reporting.* The reporting aspects of accountancy are considerable, and so have been divided into smaller areas of specialization, which are:
    - *Financial accounting.* This area is the province of the general ledger accountant, controller, and chief financial officer, and is concerned with the accumulation of business transactions into financial statements. These documents are presented based on sets of rules known as accounting frameworks, of which the best known are Generally Accepted Accounting Principles (GAAP) and International Financial Reporting Standards (IFRS).
    - *Management accounting.* This area is the province of the cost accountant and financial analyst, who investigate ways to improve the profitability of a business and present their results to management. Their reports may be derived from the main system of accounts, but may also include separate data accumulation systems. Management accounting is not governed by any accounting framework – the structure of the reports issued to management can be tailored to the needs of the business.

Financial and managerial accounting are addressed at greater length in the next section.

In short, the full range of accountancy tasks involve the recordation, classification, and reporting of business transactions. We can translate these three general areas of accountancy into a number of more specific activities and knowledge areas, which are noted in the following table, along with the chapters in which additional information is located:

Accountancy Basic Activities

Accountancy Area	Type of Activity or Knowledge Area
Recordation	The chart of accounts (Chapter 2)
	The general ledger and trial balance (Chapter 3)
	Accounting procedures (Chapter 4)
Classification	Accounting for receivables (Chapter 5)
	Accounting for investments (Chapter 6)
	Accounting for inventory (Chapter 7)
	Accounting for property, plant, and equipment (Chapter 8)
	Accounting for intangibles (Chapter 9)
	Accounting for equity (Chapter 10)
	Revenue recognition (Chapter 11)
	Accounting for payroll (Chapter 12)
	Accounting for stock-based compensation (Chapter 13)

Accountancy Area	Type of Activity or Knowledge Area
	Accounting for income taxes (Chapter 14)
	Accounting for business combinations (Chapter 15)
	Foreign currency matters (Chapter 16)
	Accounting for leases (Chapter 17)
	Accounting for changes and error corrections (Chapter 18)
Reporting	Closing the books (Chapter 19)
	The financial statements (Chapter 20)
	Public company financial reporting (Chapter 21)
	Management reports (Chapter 22)

In addition, there are practical operational aspects to accountancy that should be considered. The accountant is likely to be judged on the efficiency and effectiveness with which certain accounting tasks are completed. Also, the accountant will likely be expected to provide some interpretation of the financial statements, and to apply basic analysis skills to the results and financial position of a business. The following table notes the specific activities and knowledge areas, as well as the related chapters that apply to these additional concepts:

Accountancy Additional Activities

Accountancy Area	Type of Activity or Knowledge Area
Operations	Cash receipts management (Chapter 23)
	Collection tactics (Chapter 24)
	Payroll management (Chapter 25)
Analysis	Budgeting (Chapter 26)
	Capital budgeting (Chapter 27)
	Business ratios (Chapter 28)
	Cost object analysis (Chapter 29)

Financial and Managerial Accounting

In general, *financial accounting* refers to the aggregation of accounting information into financial statements, while *managerial accounting* refers to the internal processes used to account for and improve upon business transactions. There are a number of differences between financial and managerial accounting, which fall into the following categories:

- *Aggregation.* Financial accounting reports on the results of an entire business. Managerial accounting almost always reports at a more detailed level, such as profits by product, product line, customer, and geographic region.
- *Efficiency.* Financial accounting reports on the profitability (and therefore the efficiency) of a business, whereas managerial accounting reports on specifically what is causing problems and how to fix these issues.

- *Proven information.* Financial accounting requires that records be kept with considerable precision, which is needed to prove that the financial statements are correct. Managerial accounting frequently deals with estimates, rather than proven and verifiable facts.
- *Reporting focus.* Financial accounting is oriented toward the creation of financial statements, which are distributed both within and outside of a company. Managerial accounting is more concerned with operational reports, which are only distributed within a company.
- *Standards.* Financial accounting must comply with various accounting standards, whereas managerial accounting does not have to comply with any standards when it compiles information for internal consumption.
- *Systems.* Financial accounting pays no attention to the overall system that a company has for generating a profit, only its outcome. Conversely, managerial accounting is interested in the location of bottleneck operations, and the various ways to enhance profits by resolving bottleneck issues.
- *Time period.* Financial accounting is concerned with the financial results that a business has already achieved, so it has a historical orientation. Managerial accounting may address budgets and forecasts, and so has a somewhat greater orientation toward the future.
- *Timing.* Financial accounting requires that financial statements be issued following the end of a reporting period. Managerial accounting may issue reports much more frequently, since the information it provides is of most relevance if managers can see it right away.
- *Valuation.* Financial accounting addresses the proper valuation of assets and liabilities, and so is involved with impairments, revaluations, and so forth. Managerial accounting is not concerned with the value of these items, only their productivity.

There is also a difference in the accounting certifications typically earned by accountants working in these areas. People with the Certified Public Accountant designation have been trained in financial accounting, while those with the Certified Management Accountant designation have been trained in managerial accounting.

Types of Accountants

The following is a list and brief description of the more commonly recognized types of accountants:

- *Billing clerk.* This position is responsible for invoicing customers, submitting the invoices to customers by whatever means are required, issuing credit memos, and keeping billing records up-to-date.
- *Bookkeeper.* This position originates accounting transactions and compiles the information into financial statements. It also reconciles general ledger accounts. This position is responsible for, and likely personally handles, the invoicing of customers, processing of cash receipts, payment of suppliers, and tracking of fixed assets. The bookkeeper also handles sales and income

taxes. The bookkeeper position is only found in a small accounting department.

- *Budget analyst.* This position is responsible for coordinating the assembly of the annual budget, loading it into the accounting software, comparing it to actual results, and reporting on variances.
- *Cashier.* This position handles and properly records incoming and outgoing cash, including the processing of bills, coins, credit cards, and debit cards. This can involve the use of a cash register. Accurate cash recordation is emphasized.
- *Chief financial officer.* This is the top-level accounting position in a business. This position is responsible for the accounting, taxation, and treasury staff, as well as for maintaining a proper system of controls, strategic planning, risk management, fund raising, investor relations, and investments.
- *Collections clerk.* This position collects cash related to overdue accounts receivable by whatever means are most efficient and legally allowed, and will also recommend the recordation of some receivables as bad debts.
- *Controller.* This position manages the accounting department. In that role, the position is responsible for all transactions, controls within the accounting department, and the production of financial statements and other financial reports.
- *Cost accountant.* This position reports on the cost of activities, products, and processes. The position can involve participation in target costing teams, reviewing inventory, analyzing proposed product or services prices, and many other tasks.
- *Credit manager.* This position is usually found in mid-size to larger firms, and is responsible for reviewing and granting customer credit requests, with the goal of maximizing revenues while minimizing bad debts.
- *Fixed asset accountant.* This position records the cost of fixed assets as acquired and altered over time, as well as their subsequent depreciation and disposition; also includes the recordation of asset retirement obligations and impairment charges.
- *Forensic accountant.* This position is involved with the examination of financial records when there is a suspicion of fraud, as well as the reconstruction of destroyed or damaged financial records. Thus, the position tends to be a third-party consultant that moves from job to job as required. This is considered a senior-level position, and should have an excellent grounding in audit engagements.
- *General ledger clerk.* This position records all journal entries in the general ledger, and reconciles all accounts. This person may also prepare several disclosures that accompany the financial statements.
- *Payables clerk.* This position records incoming supplier invoices, ensures that they have been approved for payment, possibly with three-way matching, and pays suppliers.

- *Payroll clerk.* This position collects and aggregates timekeeping information, calculates gross pay, subtracts payroll deductions to arrive at net pay, and issues payments to employees. This position usually requires an in-depth knowledge of payroll regulations, as well as the operation of payroll software.
- *Project accountant.* This position monitors the progress of projects, investigates variances from the project budget, and ensures that project billings are issued and payments collected.
- *Tax accountant.* This position collects the information needed to complete tax forms, ensures that tax reports are filed in a timely manner, and researches tax issues as requested, advising management on the impact of different corporate strategies.

Responsibilities of the Accounting Department

The accounting department is responsible for a broad range of activities, which are sometimes performed in conjunction with other departments. In this section, we describe the main accounting activities, as well as those areas in which responsibility may be shared with or handed off from other departments. The key responsibilities are:

Customer-oriented Responsibilities

- *Credit.* Customers requesting credit from the company are reviewed to see if any credit will be granted, and the terms under which payments will be made to the company. This involves the deployment of a set of policies and procedures governing how to process customer invoices where credit is involved, and how to determine the amount of credit to be granted. This responsibility is sometimes split off into a separate department that is administered by the treasurer.
- *Billings.* When goods are shipped, the accounting staff is notified and issues an invoice to the customer, based on shipping documentation and the related sales order. When services are provided, the accounting staff compiles the hours spent on a job, ensures that there is sufficient customer-authorized funding available, and then issues an invoice. The billing staff may also be involved in the issuance of credits to customers for various product returns or sales allowances.
- *Collections.* A separate group within the department typically specializes in the collection of overdue invoice payments from customers. This group is trained in collection techniques and interfaces with an outside group of collection attorneys and collection agencies. In a small organization, this may be a part-time job for one of the accountants.
- *Cash receipts.* When cash is received from customers, the accounting staff applies the cash to outstanding invoices and then transports the cash to a bank. There are several variations on this basic task, such as handling large

amounts of bills and coins in a retail environment, or shifting the cash handling task to a bank by using a lockbox. If a lockbox is used, the treasurer may be responsible for maintaining it.

Supplier-oriented Responsibilities

- *Payables.* The accounting staff receives invoices from suppliers, ensures that the invoices are authorized for payment, and records the payments in the accounting system. The accounting staff also records recurring payments for which there may not always be invoices from suppliers.
- *Payments to suppliers.* The staff identifies payables that are due for payment, verifies the existence of sufficient cash to support the payments, and issues payments. The payments may be in a variety of forms, including petty cash, checks, and electronic payments. This activity may sometimes be handled by the treasury department.

Employee-oriented Responsibilities

- *Time tracking.* The accounting staff maintains a time tracking system for those employees paid on an hourly basis, which may be highly automated or paperwork-intensive. The staff also reviews submitted time reports for errors, and has supervisors sign off on unusual amounts, such as overtime.
- *Payroll calculations.* The staff updates the payroll database for pay rate changes, employee addresses, and so forth. Hours worked information is periodically entered, and gross wages calculated. The staff then determines applicable taxes and other deductions from pay to arrive at net pay for all employees.
- *Payments to employees.* The staff uses the preceding payroll calculations to create payments to employees, which may be in the form of cash, checks, or electronic payments.

Financial Statements

- *Account reconciliation.* The accounting staff conducts an ongoing examination of the contents of all balance sheet accounts, to ensure that the items recorded as assets can be validated, and that all liabilities are properly recorded.
- *Fixed asset tracking.* If a company is asset-intensive, the accounting staff maintains records of all expenditures designated as fixed assets, regularly evaluates them for impairment, and calculates depreciation.
- *Inventory valuation.* The cost accountant verifies the accuracy of inventory records, and assigns costs to inventory items based on a cost-flow methodology, such as the first in, first out method. Inventory items are also examined to see if their costs should be reduced for obsolescence or if their recorded costs should be adjusted downward to their market values.

- *Close the books*. The department staff engages in a variety of activities to produce financial statements, including ensuring that all revenues and expenses have been recorded, and that all transactions have been posted to the general ledger.
- *Public company reporting*. If a company is publicly-held, then the accounting staff is involved in the production of a variety of reports, such as the quarterly Form 10-Q and annual Form 10-K, which are filed with the Securities and Exchange Commission. These tasks may be fully or partially outsourced to a public company reporting specialist.
- *Government reporting*. It may be necessary to file reports with various government entities. Since the accounting staff usually has the most knowledge of the information required for these reports, it is called upon to complete the reports on an ongoing basis.
- *Audit support*. If a company has its financial statements audited, the accounting staff is called upon to provide a large amount of information to the auditors in the form of supporting schedules, as well as researching specific documents.
- *Tax returns*. Since tax returns are based on financial transactions, the accounting staff is in the best position to complete tax returns. The preparation of these returns may sometimes be outsourced to third party tax specialists, or handed off to a separate tax department.

Analysis

- *Project monitoring*. If a company constructs assets on behalf of its customers, a large part of the department's staff time may be allocated to the review of expenditures as they are incurred, and the allocation of these costs to the appropriate projects. There is also likely to be a cost allocation review for general overhead costs that are assigned to specific projects, as well as the reporting of costs to customers. This responsibility may be shifted to a separate project management department.
- *Budgeting*. The staff coordinates the production of a budget, which may be updated at varying intervals. This responsibility includes a great deal of coordination with department managers, as well as the examination of preliminary budget versions for problems. The staff then loads the final version of the budget into the accounting software, for use in comparing actual to budgeted results. This responsibility may be shifted to a separate budgeting department.
- *Capital budgeting*. The staff reviews submitted proposals for the acquisition of capital goods. This analysis may include the use of cash flow and bottleneck analysis. The staff also coordinates the flow of reviews and approvals for each proposal. This responsibility may be handled by a separate financial analysis staff.

- *Target costing.* The cost accountant participates in product design teams, with the role of examining on-going design changes for their impact on the eventual cost of completed products.
- *Metrics and variance analysis.* When financial statements are released, management may require the accounting staff to prepare a set of measurements and variance analyses that highlights areas in which company results have varied from expectations. This task may be shifted to a separate financial analysis group.

In short, the accounting department is responsible for an extraordinarily broad set of activities. In order to accomplish all of these tasks, a number of specialist accountant positions must be closely coordinated. In the next section, we describe how to do so with various types of organizational structures.

Organizational Structure of the Accounting Department

When a business is quite small, there is little need for a formal organizational structure for the accounting department, since it is comprised of just one or two bookkeepers and perhaps an outside accounting specialist who advises the staff. However, as the company becomes larger and the trickle of business transactions turns into a flood, it will be necessary to devise a formal structure for the department. Initially, this will require the hiring of a corporate controller, who manages a small staff of general-purpose accountants. Over time, additional positions will be added, until the organizational structure comes close to the configuration noted in the following exhibit.

Single Entity Accounting Organization

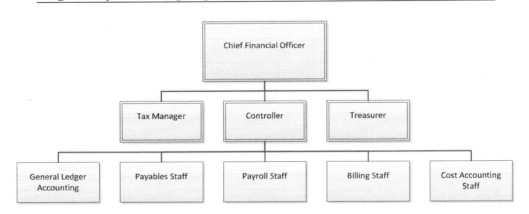

In the preceding exhibit, several activities have been split away from the controller's management area and aggregated under the direction of a tax manager and treasurer, with a chief financial officer presiding over the entire group. Some areas of responsibility can vary between the controller and treasurer, including the cashier, credit, and payment functions. Also, the payroll function may sometimes be placed under the control of the human resources manager.

If a company splits its operations into several subsidiaries (or acquires subsidiaries), then it must decide whether to adopt a decentralized or centralized accounting structure. Under a decentralized structure, the handling of all normal business transactions is handled at the level of the subsidiary, with a small number of corporate-level positions that address such issues as parent-level taxation, budgeting, and transfer pricing. The advantage of this configuration is that the accounting staff is highly knowledgeable about local subsidiary activities. However, this approach also means that a number of positions are duplicated across the company, and that there is no way to take advantage of economies of scale. A typical decentralized accounting organization is shown in the following exhibit.

Decentralized Accounting Organization

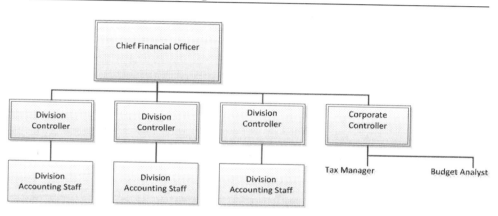

An alternative approach is to centralize nearly all accounting operations. By doing so, a company can take advantage of economies of scale, thereby driving down the cost of processing transactions to the lowest possible level. Also, there is no duplication of accounting positions across the various subsidiaries. However, there is a tendency for the accounting staff to lose touch with the needs of the subsidiaries, so it can make sense to retain an on-site division bookkeeper; this person is responsible for those transactions over which the local subsidiary managers want to maintain a higher level of control. A sample structure is shown in the following exhibit.

Centralized Accounting Organization

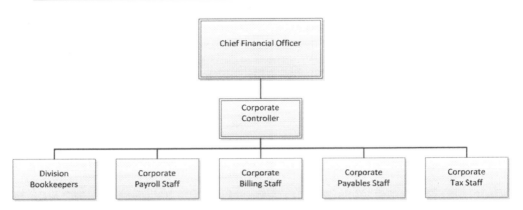

There is no ideal organizational structure that will work for all accounting departments. Instead, the structure should match the conditions that an organization encounters. For example, an acquisition may only be possible if the local management team is given control over its accounting function – if so, a decentralized structure is the only possible option. Alternatively, a chain of retail stores may find that a local bookkeeper is always needed to process cash receipts, with all other functions being handled from a central location. As a third example, a consulting firm with locations around the world may find that it must centralize the billing function in order to ensure that contract funding levels are properly monitored, while allowing local branches to process their own payroll. As a final example, if a company operates under the strategy of being the low-cost leader, it may be compelled to reduce its accounting costs to the bare minimum by centralizing all functions in a single, massive accounting operations center.

Summary

This chapter gave an overview of the role of the accountant. The key concept to be gained from this chapter is the enormously broad range of activities for which the accountant is responsible. There are few tasks anywhere in an organization in which the accountant is *not* going to be involved. This means that accountancy should not be considered a merely clerical activity, but rather one that is essential to the ongoing conduct of business operations. Without a well-trained accounting staff, a company is at considerable risk of failure.

In the following chapters, we turn to the training of that accounting staff, by focusing on all areas of accountancy – recordation, classification, and reporting, as well as the ancillary operations and analysis activities.

Chapter 2
The Chart of Accounts

Introduction

The chart of accounts defines how accounting information is stored. A properly structured chart of accounts makes it much easier to accumulate and report on information, so the account structure is an area of considerable interest to the accountant. In this chapter, we give an overview of the chart of accounts and the most common accounts used, and then address the account coding structures for successively more complex types of organizations. We finish with a discussion of methods for reducing the complexity of the chart of accounts.

> **Related Podcast Episode:** Episode 163 of the Accounting Best Practices Podcast discusses the chart of accounts. You can listen to it at: **accounting-tools.com/podcasts** or **iTunes**

Overview of the Chart of Accounts

The chart of accounts is a listing of all accounts used in the general ledger, usually sorted in order by account number. The accounts are typically numeric, but can also be alphabetic or alphanumeric. The account numbering system is used by the accounting software to aggregate information into an entity's financial statements.

Accounts are usually listed in order of their appearance in the financial statements, starting with the balance sheet and continuing with the income statement. Thus, the chart of accounts begins with cash, proceeds through liabilities and shareholders' equity, and then continues with accounts for revenues and then expenses. Many organizations structure their chart of accounts so that expense information is separately compiled by department; thus, the sales department, engineering department, and accounting department all have the same set of expense accounts. Typical accounts found in the chart of accounts include:

Assets

- *Cash.* Contains the amounts of petty cash and bank account balances.
- *Marketable securities.* Contains the valuations of any investments in marketable securities.
- *Accounts receivable.* Contains the balances of trade and non-trade receivables. Trade receivables are with customers, and non-trade receivables are with everyone else, such as employees.
- *Allowance for doubtful accounts.* Contains a reserve against expected future losses on accounts receivable. The account contains a negative balance.

- *Prepaid expenses.* Contains the unconsumed balances of any payments made, such as prepaid rent.
- *Inventory.* Contains the balances of raw materials, work-in-process, and finished goods inventory.
- *Fixed assets.* Contains the amounts paid for fixed assets, such as machinery, furniture and fixtures, and computer equipment.
- *Accumulated depreciation.* Contains the grand total accumulation of depreciation charged against fixed assets over time. The account contains a negative balance.
- *Other assets.* Contains all other assets that do not fit into the descriptions for the preceding asset accounts.

Liabilities

- *Accounts payable.* Contains the complete set of all payables owed to suppliers, based on invoices submitted by the suppliers.
- *Accrued liabilities.* Contains estimated liabilities for which no documented supplier invoices have yet been received.
- *Taxes payable.* Contains the liabilities for all types of taxes owed, including sales and use taxes, property taxes, payroll taxes, and income taxes.
- *Wages payable.* Contains the estimated amount of wages owed to employees that have not yet been paid.
- *Notes payable.* Contains the remaining balances of loans owed to lenders.

Stockholders' Equity

- *Capital stock.* Contains the amount of funds received by a business in exchange for the sale of its stock to investors.
- *Retained earnings.* Contains the accumulated amount of any earnings generated by a business.

Revenue

- *Revenue.* Contains the gross amount of all sales recognized during the reporting period.
- *Sales returns and allowances.* Contains the amount of any credits granted to customers for sales returns and allowances. This account balance offsets the revenue account.

Expenses

- *Cost of goods sold.* Contains the cost of all direct labor, direct materials, and factory overhead associated with the sale of goods and services.
- *Advertising expense.* Contains the recognized cost of advertising expenditures.

- *Bank fees*. Contains the fees charged by a company's bank to process transactions.
- *Depreciation expense*. Contains a depreciation charge that reflects the consumption of assets over time.
- *Payroll tax expense*. Contains the cost of all taxes associated with the payment of salaries and wages.
- *Rent expense*. Contains the cost of the rent associated with the facilities used by a business.
- *Supplies expense*. Contains the cost of all supplies consumed by a business.
- *Utilities expense*. Contains the aggregated cost of all utilities, which may include water, heat, electricity, waste disposal, and so forth.
- *Wages expense*. Contains the cost of salaries and hourly wages incurred by a business to compensate its employees.
- *Other expenses*. Contains a variety of incidental expenses that are individually too small to warrant the use of a separate account.

There are a number of ways to structure the chart of accounts, as noted in the following sections that describe three-digit, five-digit, and seven-digit charts of accounts.

The Three-Digit Chart of Accounts

A three-digit chart of accounts allows a business to create a numerical sequence of accounts that can contain as many as 1,000 potential accounts. The three-digit format is most commonly used by small businesses that do not break out the results of any departments or divisions in their financial statements. A sample three-digit chart of accounts is shown below:

Account Number	Description
010	Cash
020	Petty cash
030	Accounts receivable
040	Reserve for doubtful accounts
050	Marketable securities
060	Raw materials inventory
070	Work-in-process inventory
080	Finished goods inventory
090	Reserve for obsolete inventory
100	Fixed assets – Computer equipment
110	Fixed assets – Computer software
120	Fixed assets – Furniture and fixtures
130	Fixed assets – Leasehold improvements
140	Fixed assets – Machinery
150	Accumulated depreciation – Computer equipment
160	Accumulated depreciation – Computer software

Account Number	Description
170	Accumulated depreciation – Furniture and fixtures
180	Accumulated depreciation – Leasehold improvements
190	Accumulated depreciation – Machinery
200	Other assets
300	Accounts payable
310	Accrued payroll liability
320	Accrued vacation liability
330	Accrued expenses liability – other
340	Unremitted sales taxes
350	Unremitted pension payments
360	Short-term notes payable
370	Other short-term liabilities
400	Long-term notes payable
500	Capital stock
510	Retained earnings
600	Revenue
700	Cost of goods sold – Materials
710	Cost of goods sold – Direct labor
720	Cost of goods sold – Manufacturing supplies
730	Cost of goods sold – Applied overhead
800	Bank charges
805	Benefits
810	Depreciation
815	Insurance
825	Office supplies
830	Salaries and wages
835	Telephones
840	Training
845	Travel and entertainment
850	Utilities
855	Other expenses
860	Interest expense
900	Extraordinary items

In the example, each block of related accounts begins with a different set of account numbers. Thus, current liabilities begin with "300," revenue items begin with "600," and cost of goods sold items begin with "700." This numbering scheme makes it easier for the accounting staff to remember where accounts are located within the chart of accounts. This type of account range format is also required by the report writing module in many accounting software packages.

The Five-Digit Chart of Accounts

A five-digit chart of accounts is used by organizations that want to track information at the departmental level. With a five-digit code, they can produce a separate income statement for each department. This format duplicates the account codes found in a three-digit chart of accounts, but then adds a two-digit code to the left, which indicates specific departments. The three-digit codes for expenses (and sometimes also revenues) are then duplicated for each department for which management wants to record information. A sample of the five-digit chart of accounts format follows, using the accounting and production departments to show how expense account codes can be duplicated.

Account Number	Department	Description
00-010	xxx	Cash
00-020	xxx	Petty cash
00-030	xxx	Accounts receivable
00-040	xxx	Allowance for doubtful accounts
00-050	xxx	Marketable securities
00-060	xxx	Raw materials inventory
00-070	xxx	Work-in-process inventory
00-080	xxx	Finished goods inventory
00-090	xxx	Reserve for obsolete inventory
00-100	xxx	Fixed assets – Computer equipment
00-110	xxx	Fixed assets – Computer software
00-120	xxx	Fixed assets – Furniture and fixtures
00-130	xxx	Fixed assets – Leasehold improvements
00-140	xxx	Fixed assets – Machinery
00-150	xxx	Accumulated depreciation – Computer equipment
00-160	xxx	Accumulated depreciation – Computer software
00-170	xxx	Accumulated depreciation – Furniture and fixtures
00-180	xxx	Accumulated depreciation – Leasehold improvements
00-190	xxx	Accumulated depreciation – Machinery
00-200	xxx	Other assets
00-300	xxx	Accounts payable
00-310	xxx	Accrued payroll liability
00-320	xxx	Accrued vacation liability
00-330	xxx	Accrued expenses liability – other
00-340	xxx	Unremitted sales taxes
00-350	xxx	Unremitted pension payments
00-360	xxx	Short-term notes payable
00-370	xxx	Other short-term liabilities
00-400	xxx	Long-term notes payable
00-500	xxx	Capital stock
00-510	xxx	Retained earnings
00-600	xxx	Revenue
00-700	xxx	Cost of goods sold – Materials
00-710	xxx	Cost of goods sold – Direct labor
00-720	xxx	Cost of goods sold – Manufacturing supplies
00-730	xxx	Cost of goods sold – Applied overhead
10-800	Accounting	Bank charges

Account Number	Department	Description
10-805	Accounting	Benefits
10-810	Accounting	Depreciation
10-815	Accounting	Insurance
10-825	Accounting	Office supplies
10-830	Accounting	Salaries and wages
10-835	Accounting	Telephones
10-840	Accounting	Training
10-845	Accounting	Travel and entertainment
10-850	Accounting	Utilities
10-855	Accounting	Other expenses
10-860	Accounting	Interest expense
20-800	Production	Bank charges
20-805	Production	Benefits
20-810	Production	Depreciation
20-815	Production	Insurance
20-825	Production	Office supplies
20-830	Production	Salaries and wages
20-835	Production	Telephones
20-840	Production	Training
20-845	Production	Travel and entertainment
20-850	Production	Utilities
20-855	Production	Other expenses
20-860	Production	Interest expense
00-900	xxx	Extraordinary items

The preceding sample chart of accounts shows an exact duplication of accounts for each department listed. This is not necessarily the case in reality, since some departments have accounts for which they are the only probable users. For example, the accounting department in the example has an account for bank charges that the production department is unlikely to use. Thus, some accounts can be avoided by flagging them as inactive in the accounting system. By doing so, they do not appear in the formal chart of accounts.

The Seven-Digit Chart of Accounts

The seven-digit chart of accounts is needed by larger organizations in which management wants to track information about departments within divisions. The seven-digit coding structure requires the coding used for a five-digit system as its baseline, plus two additional digits that are placed to the left of the five-digit codes to designate company divisions. In those cases where a business also wants to track its assets and liabilities by division, it will also be necessary to apply the additional two digits to balance sheet accounts. The following seven-digit chart of accounts could be used:

The Chart of Accounts

Account Number	Division	Department	Description
10-00-010	Boston	xxx	Cash
10-00-020	Boston	xxx	Petty cash
10-00-030	Boston	xxx	Accounts receivable
10-00-040	Boston	xxx	Allowance for doubtful accounts
10-00-050	Boston	xxx	Marketable securities
10-00-060	Boston	xxx	Raw materials inventory
10-00-070	Boston	xxx	Work-in-process inventory
10-00-080	Boston	xxx	Finished goods inventory
10-00-090	Boston	xxx	Reserve for obsolete inventory
10-00-100	Boston	xxx	Fixed assets – Computer equipment
10-00-110	Boston	xxx	Fixed assets – Computer software
10-00-120	Boston	xxx	Fixed assets – Furniture and fixtures
10-00-130	Boston	xxx	Fixed assets – Leasehold improvements
10-00-140	Boston	xxx	Fixed assets – Machinery
10-00-150	Boston	xxx	Accumulated depreciation – Computer equipment
10-00-160	Boston	xxx	Accumulated depreciation – Computer software
10-00-170	Boston	xxx	Accumulated depreciation – Furniture and fixtures
10-00-180	Boston	xxx	Accumulated depreciation – Leasehold improvements
10-00-190	Boston	xxx	Accumulated depreciation – Machinery
10-00-200	Boston	xxx	Other assets
10-00-300	Boston	xxx	Accounts payable
10-00-310	Boston	xxx	Accrued payroll liability
10-00-320	Boston	xxx	Accrued vacation liability
10-00-330	Boston	xxx	Accrued expenses liability – other
10-00-340	Boston	xxx	Unremitted sales taxes
10-00-350	Boston	xxx	Unremitted pension payments
10-00-360	Boston	xxx	Short-term notes payable
10-00-370	Boston	xxx	Other short-term liabilities
10-00-400	Boston	xxx	Long-term notes payable
10-00-500	Boston	xxx	Capital stock
10-00-510	Boston	xxx	Retained earnings
10-00-600	Boston	xxx	Revenue
10-00-700	Boston	xxx	Cost of goods sold – Materials
10-00-710	Boston	xxx	Cost of goods sold – Direct labor
10-00-720	Boston	xxx	Cost of goods sold – Manufacturing supplies
10-00-730	Boston	xxx	Cost of goods sold – Applied overhead
10-10-800	Boston	Engineering	Bank charges
10-10-805	Boston	Engineering	Benefits
10-10-810	Boston	Engineering	Depreciation
10-10-815	Boston	Engineering	Insurance
10-10-825	Boston	Engineering	Office supplies
10-10-830	Boston	Engineering	Salaries and wages
10-10-835	Boston	Engineering	Telephones
10-10-840	Boston	Engineering	Training
10-10-845	Boston	Engineering	Travel and entertainment
10-10-850	Boston	Engineering	Utilities
10-10-855	Boston	Engineering	Other expenses
10-10-860	Boston	Engineering	Interest expense
10-20-800	Boston	Sales	Bank charges
10-20-805	Boston	Sales	Benefits
10-20-810	Boston	Sales	Depreciation

The Chart of Accounts

Account Number	Division	Department	Description
10-20-815	Boston	Sales	Insurance
10-20-825	Boston	Sales	Office supplies
10-20-830	Boston	Sales	Salaries and wages
10-20-835	Boston	Sales	Telephones
10-20-840	Boston	Sales	Training
10-20-845	Boston	Sales	Travel and entertainment
10-20-850	Boston	Sales	Utilities
10-20-855	Boston	Sales	Other expenses
10-20-860	Boston	Sales	Interest expense
10-00-900	Boston	xxx	Extraordinary items
20-00-010	Omaha	xxx	Cash
20-00-020	Omaha	xxx	Petty cash
20-00-030	Omaha	xxx	Accounts receivable
20-00-040	Omaha	xxx	Allowance for doubtful accounts
20-00-050	Omaha	xxx	Marketable securities
20-00-060	Omaha	xxx	Raw materials inventory
20-00-070	Omaha	xxx	Work-in-process inventory
20-00-080	Omaha	xxx	Finished goods inventory
20-00-090	Omaha	xxx	Reserve for obsolete inventory
20-00-100	Omaha	xxx	Fixed assets – Computer equipment
20-00-110	Omaha	xxx	Fixed assets – Computer software
20-00-120	Omaha	xxx	Fixed assets – Furniture and fixtures
20-00-130	Omaha	xxx	Fixed assets – Leasehold improvements
20-00-140	Omaha	xxx	Fixed assets – Machinery
20-00-150	Omaha	xxx	Accumulated depreciation – Computer equipment
20-00-160	Omaha	xxx	Accumulated depreciation – Computer software
20-00-170	Omaha	xxx	Accumulated depreciation – Furniture and fixtures
20-00-180	Omaha	xxx	Accumulated depreciation – Leasehold improvements
20-00-190	Omaha	xxx	Accumulated depreciation – Machinery
20-00-200	Omaha	xxx	Other assets
20-00-300	Omaha	xxx	Accounts payable
20-00-310	Omaha	xxx	Accrued payroll liability
20-00-320	Omaha	xxx	Accrued vacation liability
20-00-330	Omaha	xxx	Accrued expenses liability – other
20-00-340	Omaha	xxx	Unremitted sales taxes
20-00-350	Omaha	xxx	Unremitted pension payments
20-00-360	Omaha	xxx	Short-term notes payable
20-00-370	Omaha	xxx	Other short-term liabilities
20-00-400	Omaha	xxx	Long-term notes payable
20-00-500	Omaha	xxx	Capital stock
20-00-510	Omaha	xxx	Retained earnings
20-00-600	Omaha	xxx	Revenue
20-00-700	Omaha	xxx	Cost of goods sold – Materials
20-00-710	Omaha	xxx	Cost of goods sold – Direct labor
20-00-720	Omaha	xxx	Cost of goods sold – Manufacturing supplies
20-00-730	Omaha	xxx	Cost of goods sold – Applied overhead
20-10-800	Omaha	Engineering	Bank charges
20-10-805	Omaha	Engineering	Benefits
20-10-810	Omaha	Engineering	Depreciation
20-10-815	Omaha	Engineering	Insurance
20-10-825	Omaha	Engineering	Office supplies

Account Number	Division	Department	Description
20-10-830	Omaha	Engineering	Salaries and wages
20-10-835	Omaha	Engineering	Telephones
20-10-840	Omaha	Engineering	Training
20-10-845	Omaha	Engineering	Travel and entertainment
20-10-850	Omaha	Engineering	Utilities
20-10-855	Omaha	Engineering	Other expenses
20-10-860	Omaha	Engineering	Interest expense
20-20-800	Omaha	Sales	Bank charges
20-20-805	Omaha	Sales	Benefits
20-20-810	Omaha	Sales	Depreciation
20-20-815	Omaha	Sales	Insurance
20-20-825	Omaha	Sales	Office supplies
20-20-830	Omaha	Sales	Salaries and wages
20-20-835	Omaha	Sales	Telephones
20-20-840	Omaha	Sales	Training
20-20-845	Omaha	Sales	Travel and entertainment
20-20-850	Omaha	Sales	Utilities
20-20-855	Omaha	Sales	Other expenses
20-20-860	Omaha	Sales	Interest expense
20-00-900	Omaha	xxx	Extraordinary items

Chart of Accounts Reduction

The typical chart of accounts contains hundreds or even thousands of accounts, with most of the accounts concentrated in the area of expenses. Most departments have roughly the same accounts, which are copied forward into any new department that a company creates. This leads to the following issues:

- *Incorrect account usage.* It is quite common for an expense to be charged to the wrong account within a department, which is discovered when the first draft of the financial statements are printed and reviewed. The result is that someone must create a journal entry to move the incorrect charge to a different account.

- *Immaterial balances.* The majority of all accounts contain small balances that have little impact on the reader's understanding of a business. Instead, readers tend to focus on just a small number of accounts that contain the bulk of all transactions.

- *Training.* New accountants may require extensive training before they are comfortable with recording transactions into the correct accounts.

- *Audit cost.* It takes longer for outside auditors to audit a lengthy chart of accounts, which can increase the cost of an audit.

- *Financial statement links.* If there are many account numbers, it can be difficult to map these accounts into a coherent set of financial statements. The result may be financial statements that incorrectly reflect the contents of the general ledger.

It may be possible to drastically shrink the number of expense accounts in use. In particular, consider using just the following mega-accounts:

- *Direct costs.* This account contains the cost of materials and supplies used in the production process, as well as freight costs, and not a great deal more.
- *Allocated costs.* The major accounting frameworks require that overhead costs be allocated. Therefore, have a single account that contains all factory overhead costs that are to be allocated. The account would include production labor, since this cost is not a direct cost of goods or services in most companies.
- *Employee compensation.* This account contains an aggregation of hourly wages, salaries, payroll taxes, and employee benefits.
- *Business operations.* This account contains all of the expenses required to operate a company on a day-to-day basis, such as non-factory rent, utilities, legal fees, and office supplies.

In addition, there may be a need for a small number of accounts in which information is aggregated for tax reporting or other specialized purposes, such as entertainment expenses.

When reducing the number of accounts, be aware that this makes it more difficult to compare a company's financial statements to its historical financials. For example, an account may have been merged into another one that is now located in a different line item in the financial statements than was previously the case. This is a particular problem if accounts are being closed part way through a fiscal year, so that financial statement line items no longer show consistent results within the year. There is no easy workaround for this issue, other than only closing down accounts at the beginning of each fiscal year.

The concept of a massive reduction in the number of accounts might trigger cries of outrage from those accountants who are accustomed to breaking down expenses into a multitude of buckets, which makes expenses easier to analyze. However, consider these points:

- *Usage of account analysis.* Once the accounting staff has provided a detailed variance analysis to management of the contents of each account, does anyone act on the information? Usually, they do not.
- *Help or hindrance.* How much time is spent by the accounting staff in reviewing accounts and reporting variances to management, and how much time is spent by management in investigating these items without taking any significant remedial action? In other words, is account analysis really a continual cycle of uncovering "issues" and then explaining them away?
- *Requirements of accounting standards.* Accounting standards do not require a broad range of accounts. On the contrary, the standard-setting organizations have largely kept away from the business of requiring the use of certain accounts.

Even if these points are not sufficiently persuasive to result in a wholesale reduction in the number of accounts, at least use them as discussion points whenever anyone wants to *increase* the number of accounts – hopefully, these concepts will prevent the chart of accounts from becoming more bloated than its current state.

Alphanumeric Account Coding

The typical account code structure uses a code that describes a primary account, and possibly also a specific department or division. Historically, this code has been stated in a numeric format, as shown in the previous sections. When entering an account code for a journal entry or some other type of transaction, an employee must understand which department or division codes to use, which are not overly clear. Though the accounting software may state an account name somewhere on the computer screen, the employee may not see it. If so, there is a considerable risk that a transaction will be charged against the wrong account code, which means that it may be charged against the wrong department or subsidiary.

An excellent technique for avoiding incorrect account coding is to associate specific expense codes with each supplier, as well as by employing pre-built journal entry templates on a repetitive basis. Nonetheless, there is still a significant risk that unique or rarely-used transactions will be coded incorrectly.

A possible solution to coding errors is to use alphanumeric account codes. Doing so allows the accountant to assign a meaning to an account code. For example, the name of a department can be contracted into a three-digit code, such as ACC for the accounting department or MAR for the marketing department. Doing so makes it much easier for the accounting staff to understand which account codes they are using. For example, account 10-830 may be the salaries and wages account for the accounting department; by instead using ACC-830, the accounting staff is much more likely to correctly charge expenses to the accounting department, rather than to some other department. In short, using alphanumeric coding allows for the use of account codes that have unique meanings, and which are therefore less likely to be coded incorrectly.

Summary

The accountant should exercise a high degree of control over the chart of accounts. Accounts should not be added or subtracted without first considering how these changes will impact the recordation of transactions, the structure of the financial statements, and how information is compared between periods. The likely result is that changes to the chart of accounts are only made with considerable caution, and in an incremental manner over a long period of time.

Chapter 3
The General Ledger and Trial Balance

Introduction

The primary source of information in an accounting system is the general ledger. Information can also be restated into the trial balance report from the general ledger, for further use in constructing the financial statements. This chapter addresses how financial information is entered into the accounting system and eventually appears in the general ledger and trial balance. We also note the different trial balance formats and the uses to which they can be put.

The Ledger Concept

A *ledger* is a book or database in which double-entry accounting transactions are stored or summarized. A *subsidiary ledger* is a ledger designed for the storage of specific types of accounting transactions. The information in a subsidiary ledger is then summarized and posted to an account in the *general ledger*, which in turn is used to construct the financial statements of a company. The account in the general ledger where this summarized information is stored is called a *control account*. Most accounts in the general ledger are not control accounts; instead, transactions are recorded directly into them.

A subsidiary ledger can be set up for virtually any general ledger account. However, they are usually only created for areas in which there are high transaction volumes, which limits their use to a few areas. Examples of subsidiary ledgers are:

- Accounts receivable ledger
- Fixed assets ledger
- Inventory ledger
- Purchases ledger

In order to research accounting information when a subsidiary ledger is used, drill down from the general ledger to the appropriate subsidiary ledger, where the detailed information is stored. Consequently, if you prefer to conduct as much research as possible within the general ledger, use fewer subsidiary ledgers.

As an example of the information in a subsidiary ledger, the inventory ledger may contain transactions pertaining to receipts into stock, movements of stock to the production floor, conversions into finished goods, scrap and rework reporting, and sales of goods to customers.

> **Tip:** Subsidiary ledgers are used when there is a large amount of transaction information that would clutter up the general ledger. This situation typically arises in companies with significant sales volume. Thus, there may be no need for a subsidiary ledger in a small company.

The following chart shows how the various data entry modules within an accounting system are used to create transactions which are recorded in either the general ledger or various subsidiary ledgers, and which are eventually aggregated to create the financial statements.

Transaction Flow in the Accounting System

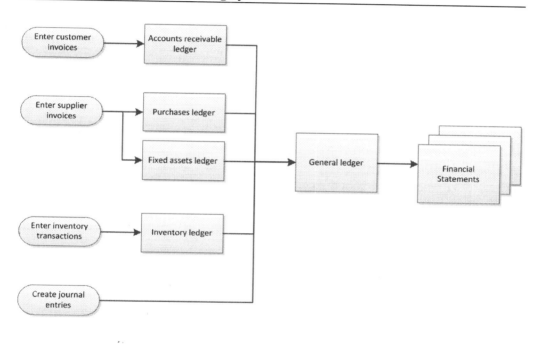

Part of the period-end closing process is to post the information in a subsidiary ledger to the general ledger. This is usually a manual step, so you need to verify that all subsidiary ledgers have been appropriately completed and closed before posting their summarized totals to the general ledger. It can be quite a problem if you forget to post the totals from a subsidiary ledger to the general ledger, since that means you are creating financial statements that may be missing a batch of crucial transactions.

> **Tip:** If you are using subsidiary ledgers, include a step in the period-end closing procedure to post the balances in all subsidiary ledgers to the general ledger, as well as to verify that the subsidiary ledgers have been closed and shifted forward to the next accounting period.

General Ledger Overview

A general ledger is the master set of accounts in which are summarized all transactions occurring within a business during a specific period of time. The general ledger contains all of the accounts currently being used in a chart of accounts, and is sorted by account number. Either individual transactions or summary-level postings from subsidiary ledgers are listed within each account number, and are sorted by transaction date. Each entry in the general ledger includes a reference number that states the source of the information. The source may be a subsidiary ledger, a journal entry, or a transaction entered directly into the general ledger.

The format of the general ledger varies somewhat, depending on the accounting software that you are using, but the basic set of information presented for an account within the general ledger is:

- *Transaction number.* The software assigns a unique number to each transaction, so that you can more easily locate it in the accounting database if you know the transaction number.
- *Transaction date.* This is the date on which the transaction was entered into the accounting database.
- *Description.* This is a brief description that summarizes the reason for the entry.
- *Source.* Information may be forwarded to the general ledger from a variety of sources, so the report should state the source, in case you need to go back to the source to research the reason for the entry.
- *Debit and credit.* States the amount debited or credited to the account for a specific transaction.

The following sample of a general ledger report shows a possible format that could be used to present information for several transactions that are aggregated under a specific account number.

Sample General Ledger Presentation

Trans. No.	Trans. Date	Description	Source	Debit	Credit
Acct. 10400		Acct: Accounts Receivable	Beginning balance		$127,500.00
10473	3/22/xx	Customer invoice	ARL	93.99	
10474	3/23/xx	Customer invoice	ARL	47.80	
10475	3/24/xx	Credit memo	ARL		43.17
10476	3/25/xx	Customer invoice	ARL	65.25	
18903	3/26/xx	Cash receipt	CRJ		1,105.20
			Ending balance		$126,558.67

It is extremely easy to locate information pertinent to an accounting inquiry in the general ledger, which makes it the primary source of accounting information. For example:

- A manager reviews the balance sheet and notices that the amount of debt appears too high. The accounting staff looks up the debt account in the general ledger and sees that a loan was added at the end of the month.
- A manager reviews the income statement and sees that the bad debt expense for his division is very high. The accounting staff looks up the expense in the general ledger, drills down to the source journal entry, and sees that a new bad debt projection was the cause of the increase in bad debt expense.

As the examples show, the source of an inquiry is frequently the financial statements; when conducting an investigation, the accounting staff begins with the general ledger, and may drill down to source documents from there to ascertain the reason(s) for an issue.

We will now proceed to brief discussions of the accounts receivable ledger and purchase ledger, which are representative of the types of subsidiary ledgers that can be used to compile information within the accounting system.

The Accounts Receivable Ledger

The accounts receivable ledger is a subsidiary ledger in which you record all credit sales made by a business. It is useful for segregating into one location a record of all amounts invoiced to customers, as well as all credit memos issued to them, and all payments made against invoices by them. The ending balance of the accounts receivable ledger equals the aggregate amount of unpaid accounts receivable.

A typical transaction entered into the accounts receivable ledger will record an account receivable, followed at a later date by a payment transaction from a customer that eliminates the account receivable.

If you were to maintain a manual record of the accounts receivable ledger, it could contain substantially more information than is allowed by an accounting software package. The data fields in a manually-prepared ledger might include the following information for each transaction:

- Invoice date
- Invoice number
- Customer name
- Identifying code for item sold
- Sales tax invoiced
- Total amount billed
- Payment flag (states whether paid or not)

The primary document recorded in the accounts receivable ledger is the customer invoice. Also, if you grant a credit back to a customer for such items as returned goods or items damaged in transit, then you also record a credit memo in the ledger.

The information in the accounts receivable ledger is aggregated periodically and posted to a control account in the general ledger. This account is used to keep from cluttering up the general ledger with the massive amount of information that is typically stored in the accounts receivable ledger. Immediately after posting, the balance in the control account should match the balance in the accounts receivable ledger. Since no detailed transactions are stored in the control account, anyone wanting to research customer invoice and credit memo transactions will have to drill down from the control account to the accounts receivable ledger to find them.

Before closing the books and generating financial statements at the end of an accounting period, complete all entries in the accounts receivable ledger, close the ledger for that period, and post the totals from the accounts receivable ledger to the general ledger.

The Purchase Ledger

The purchase ledger is a subsidiary ledger in which you record all purchases made by a business. It is useful for segregating into one location a record of the amounts the company is spending with its suppliers. The purchase ledger shows which purchases have been paid for and which ones remain outstanding. A typical transaction entered into the purchase ledger will record an account payable, followed at a later date by a payment transaction that eliminates the accounts payable. Thus, there is likely to be an outstanding account payable balance in the ledger at any time.

If you were to maintain a manual record of the purchase ledger, it could contain substantially more information than is allowed by an accounting software package. The data fields in a manually-prepared purchase ledger might include the following information for each transaction:

- Purchase date
- Supplier code (or name)
- Supplier invoice number
- Purchase order number (if used)
- Identifying code for item purchased
- Amount paid
- Sales tax paid
- Payment flag (states whether paid or not)

The primary document recorded in the purchase ledger is the supplier invoice. Also, if suppliers grant a credit back to the business for such items as returned goods or items damaged in transit, then you also record credit memos issued by suppliers in the purchase ledger.

The information in the purchase ledger is aggregated periodically and posted to a control account in the general ledger. The purchase ledger control account is used to keep from cluttering up the general ledger with the massive amount of information that is typically stored in the purchase ledger. Immediately after posting, the balance in the control account should match the balance in the purchase ledger. Since no detailed transactions are stored in the control account, anyone wanting to research purchase transactions will have to drill down from the control account to the purchase ledger to find them.

Before closing the books and generating financial statements at the end of an accounting period, complete all entries in the purchase ledger, close the ledger for that period, and post the totals from the purchase ledger to the general ledger.

Overview of the Trial Balance

The trial balance is a report run at the end of an accounting period. It is primarily used to ensure that the total of all debits equals the total of all credits, which means that there are no unbalanced journal entries in the accounting system that would make it impossible to generate accurate financial statements. Printing the trial balance to match debit and credit totals has fallen into disuse, since accounting software rejects the entry of unbalanced journal entries.

The trial balance can also be used to manually compile financial statements, though with the predominant use of computerized accounting systems that create the statements automatically, the report is rarely used for this purpose.

When the trial balance is first printed, it is called the *unadjusted trial balance.* Then, when the accounting team corrects any errors found and makes adjustments to bring the financial statements into compliance with an accounting framework (such as GAAP or IFRS), the report is called the *adjusted trial balance.* Finally, after the period has been closed, the report is called the *post-closing trial balance.*

The Trial Balance Format

The initial trial balance report contains the following columns of information:
1. Account number
2. Account name
3. Ending debit balance (if any)
4. Ending credit balance (if any)

Each line item only contains the ending balance in an account, which comes from the general ledger. All accounts having an ending balance are listed in the trial balance; usually, the accounting software automatically blocks all accounts having a zero balance from appearing in the report, which reduces its length. A sample trial balance follows:

Sample Trial Balance

Account Number	Account Description	Unadjusted Trial Balance	
		Debit	Credit
1000	Cash	$60,000	
1500	Accounts receivable	180,000	
2000	Inventory	300,000	
3000	Fixed assets	210,000	
4000	Accounts payable		90,000
4500	Accrued liabilities		50,000
4700	Notes payable		420,000

Account Number	Account Description	Unadjusted Trial Balance	
		Debit	Credit
5000	Equity		350,000
6000	Revenue		400,000
7200	Cost of goods sold	290,000	
7300	Salaries expense	200,000	
7400	Payroll tax expense	20,000	
7500	Rent expense	35,000	
7600	Other expenses	15,000	
	Totals	$1,310,000	$1,310,000

The adjusted version of a trial balance may combine the debit and credit columns into a single combined column, and add columns to show adjusting entries and a revised ending balance. An adjusting entry is a journal entry that is used at the end of an accounting period to adjust the balances in various general ledger accounts to meet the requirements of accounting standards. This format is useful for revealing the derivation of the line items in financial statements.

The following sample shows adjusting entries. It also combines the debit and credit totals into the second column, so that the summary balance for the total is (and should be) zero. Adjusting entries are added in the next column, yielding an adjusted trial balance in the far right column.

Sample Adjusted Trial Balance

Account Description	Unadjusted Trial Balance	Adjusting Entries	Adjusted Trial Balance
Cash	$60,000		$60,000
Accounts receivable	180,000	50,000	230,000
Inventory	300,000		300,000
Fixed assets (net)	210,000		210,000
Accounts payable	-90,000		-90,000
Accrued liabilities	-50,000	-25,000	-75,000
Notes payable	-420,000		-420,000
Equity	-350,000		-350,000
Revenue	-400,000	-50,000	-450,000
Cost of goods sold	290,000		290,000
Salaries expense	200,000	25,000	225,000
Payroll tax expense	20,000		20,000
Rent expense	35,000		35,000
Other expenses	15,000		15,000
Totals	$0	$0	$0

The Extended Trial Balance

An extended trial balance is a standard trial balance to which are added categories extending to the right, and in which are listed the account totals for the balance sheet and the income statement. Thus, all asset, liability, and equity accounts are stated in a balance sheet column, and all revenue, expense, gain, and loss accounts are stated in an income statement column.

The extended trial balance is useful for creating a visual representation of where each of the accounts in the standard trial balance goes in the financial statements, and may be useful for detecting anomalies in the trial balance that should be corrected (as discussed further in the next section). A sample of an extended trial balance is shown below. It uses the same trial balance information used to describe the adjusted trial balance format.

Sample Extended Trial Balance

	Unadjusted Trial Balance	Adjusting Entries	Adjusted Trial Balance	Balance Sheet	Income Statement
Cash	$60,000		$60,000	$60,000	
Accounts receivable	180,000	$50,000	230,000	230,000	
Inventory	300,000		300,000	300,000	
Fixed assets (net)	210,000		210,000	210,000	
Accounts payable	-90,000		-90,000	-90,000	
Accrued liabilities	-50,000	-25,000	-75,000	-75,000	
Notes payable	-420,000		-420,000	-420,000	
Equity	-350,000		-350,000	-350,000	
Retained earnings				-135,000	
Revenue	-400,000	-50,000	-450,000		-450,000
Cost of goods sold	290,000		290,000		290,000
Salaries expense	200,000	25,000	225,000		225,000
Payroll tax expense	20,000		20,000		20,000
Rent expense	35,000		35,000		35,000
Other expenses	15,000		15,000		15,000
Totals	$0	$0	$0	$0	-$135,000

Any computerized accounting system automatically generates financial statements from the trial balance, so the extended trial balance is not a commonly generated report in computerized systems.

Note: The information in the balance sheet and income statement columns in an extended trial balance do not necessarily match the final presentation of these reports, because some of the line items may be aggregated for presentation purposes.

Trial Balance Error Correction

There may be a number of errors in the trial balance, only a few of which are easy to identify. Here are some suggestions for how to find these problems:

- *Entries made twice.* If a journal entry or other transaction is made twice, the trial balance will still be in balance, so this is not a good report for finding duplicate entries. Instead, you may have to wait for the issue to resolve itself. For example, a duplicate invoice to a customer will be rejected by the customer, while a duplicate invoice from a supplier will (hopefully) be spotted during the invoice approval process.

- *Entries not made at all.* This issue is impossible to find on the trial balance, since it is not there. The best alternative is to maintain a checklist of standard entries, and verify that all of them have been made.
- *Entries to the wrong account.* This may be apparent with a quick glance at the trial balance, since an account that previously had no balance at all now has one. Otherwise, the best form of correction is preventive – use standard journal entry templates for all recurring entries.
- *Reversed entries.* An entry for a debit may be mistakenly recorded as a credit, and vice versa. This issue may be visible on the trial balance, especially if the entry is large enough to change the sign of an ending balance to the reverse of its usual sign.
- *Unbalanced entries.* This issue is listed last, since it is impossible in a computerized environment where entries must be balanced or the system will not accept them. If you are using a manual system, the issue will be apparent in the column totals of the trial balance. However, locating the exact entry causing the problem is vastly more difficult, and will call for a detailed review of every entry, or at least the totals in every subsidiary journal that rolls into the general ledger.

Whenever you correct an error, be sure to use a clearly labeled journal entry with supporting documentation, so that someone else can verify your work at a later date.

After reviewing the error correction issues in this section, you may have noticed how poor a role the trial balance plays in the detection of errors. In fact, it is nearly impossible to detect an error solely through this report. Instead, you almost always have to use other, more detailed reports to determine the real cause of an error.

The Post-Closing Trial Balance

A post-closing trial balance is a listing of all balance sheet accounts containing balances at the end of a reporting period. The post-closing trial balance contains no revenue, expense, or summary account balances, since these temporary accounts have all been closed and their balances moved into the retained earnings account in the balance sheet. A temporary account is an account used to hold balances during an accounting period for revenue, expense, gain, and loss transactions. These accounts are flushed into the retained earnings account at the end of an accounting period.

The post-closing trial balance contains columns for the account number, account description, debit balance, and credit balance. In most accounting systems, this report does not have a different report title than the usual trial balance.

The post-closing trial balance is used to verify that the total of all debit balances equals the total of all credit balances, which should net to zero. Once you have ensured that this is the case, begin recording accounting transactions for the next accounting period.

A sample post-closing trial balance is shown in the following sample. Notice that there is no column for adjusting entries, and that there are no temporary accounts, such as revenue and expense accounts.

Sample Post-Closing Trial Balance

Account Number	Account Description	Debit	Credit
1000	Cash	$105,000	
1500	Accounts receivable	320,000	
2000	Inventory	500,000	
3000	Fixed assets	2,000,000	
3100	Accumulated depreciation	-480,000	
4000	Accounts payable		$195,000
4500	Accrued liabilities		108,000
5000	Retained earnings		642,000
5500	Common stock		1,500,000
	Totals	$2,445,000	$2,445,000

Evaluation of the Trial Balance

We have described the layout of the trial balance and how it can be used – but do you really need it? The answer depends upon whether you are using a computerized accounting system or a manual one. In a computerized environment, the system automatically generates financial statements for you, literally at the touch of a button. In this situation, there is no particular need for a trial balance. The user of a computerized accounting system is more likely to go directly to the general ledger to review the details for each account than to first print out a trial balance to see where a problem *might* lie, and *then* go to the general ledger to spot the problem. In short, a computerized system renders the trial balance unnecessary.

The situation is quite a bit different for the user of a manual accounting system. In this case, you would shift the account balances in the general ledger to the trial balance, and then manually create the financial statements from that information. In essence, the extended trial balance noted in an earlier section becomes the primary tool for constructing financial statements.

The only case in which the user of a computerized accounting system might find it necessary to print a trial balance is when the outside auditors request a copy of it. They copy the trial balance into their auditing software, and use it as the basis for subsequent auditing procedures.

Summary

When researching transactions, you will find that it is not overly efficient to switch back and forth between the subsidiary ledgers and the general ledger. Consequently, we recommend that you keep the number of subsidiary ledgers to a minimum, so that as many transactions as possible are available within the general ledger. This also reduces the risk that you will not post the balance in a subsidiary ledger forward into the general ledger, and thereby produce financial statements that may be inaccurate.

The trial balance is essentially a summary of the account balances for a business as of a point in time. It was heavily used in an era when financial statements were generated by hand, but has since fallen out of use as computerized systems have taken over the production of financial statements. Nonetheless, we include it both to provide a historical perspective on closing the books, and also because it is still used for the manual creation of financial statements. At a minimum, the trial balance is likely to remain on the list of standard computerized accounting reports, so the accountant should be familiar with the information on it, and how it is used.

Chapter 4
Accounting Procedures

Introduction

This chapter provides you with a large number of sample accounting procedures. Before doing so, we will first lay the groundwork for a system of procedures. We discuss the nature of procedures, why we need them, and how many to develop (a crucial point), as well as how to construct and use them. By the end of this chapter, you should have developed an understanding of the work required to create, maintain, and enforce a system of procedures, in addition to learning about the core procedures to be employed in an accounting operation.

> **Related Podcast Episode:** Episode 161 of the Accounting Best Practices Podcast discusses when to write a procedure. You can listen to it at: **accounting-tools.com/podcasts** or **iTunes**

The Nature of a Procedure

A procedure documents a business transaction. As such, it lists the specific steps required to complete a transaction, and is very useful for enforcing a high degree of uniformity in how those steps are completed. A procedure frequently incorporates one or more controls, which are designed to mitigate the risk of various types of losses. In some cases, an entire procedure is intended to *be* a control. Procedures may also be used to instruct new employees in how a company does business. Thus, a procedure has three purposes:

- To encourage uniformity in the completion of business transactions
- To enforce the use of controls
- To train employees

From the perspective of the management team, the first purpose (uniformity) is the most important, since it leads to greater efficiency. However, an auditor or risk manager may be more concerned with the second purpose (control), since they have a great interest in mitigating any number of risks to which a business is subjected. Further, the human resources staff has a great interest in the third purpose (training), since it is involved in training new employees. Thus, there are multiple constituencies within a business that have a considerable interest in the construction and maintenance of a set of procedures.

We will expand upon the nature of the procedure in the next section, where we address the specific issues that procedures can remedy.

The Need for Procedures

Procedures are needed to ensure that a company is capable of completing its objectives. For example, the primary purpose of a consumer products company is to place reliable and well-constructed products in the hands of its customers. In order to sell goods to those customers, it must be able to complete the following tasks consistently, time after time:

- Log in a customer order
- Pick the goods from stock
- Assemble them into a complete order that is ready for shipment by the promised date
- Reliably issue an accurate invoice to the customer

A procedure is needed to give structure to these activities. For example, one procedure could instruct the order entry staff regarding how to record order information from a customer into a sales order (which is used to process an order within a company), which errors may arise and how to deal with them, and where to send copies of the sales order.

It is certainly possible for very experienced employees to handle these tasks without a formal procedure, because they have been with the company long enough to have learned how to deal with most situations through experience. However, such an approach relies upon the verbal transfer of information to more junior employees, which is an unreliable approach that gradually leads to the use of many variations on a single procedure.

Imagine a situation where there are no formal procedures in a company that operates multiple retail stores. Each store develops its own methods for handling business transactions. Each one will have different control problems, different forms, different levels of efficiency, and different types of errors. Someone trying to review the operations of all the stores would be overwhelmed by the cacophony of different methods.

You can see from this example that procedures are of great value in providing structure to a business – they define how a business *does* things. In more detail, we need procedures because:

- *Best practices*. When a business routinely examines its operations with the intent of creating procedures, the documentation process often brings to light questionable or inefficient practices. If brought to the attention of management, there may be an opportunity to use best practices to upgrade the company's processes to a more efficient and effective level.
- *Efficiency*. It is much easier for the accounting staff to process business transactions and issue financial statements when there is a regimented approach to dealing with each type of transaction.
- *Errors*. It takes far more time to correct a transaction error than it takes to complete the transaction correctly the first time. Therefore, error avoidance is an excellent reason to use procedures.

- *Computer systems.* An accounting or enterprise-wide system typically works in conjunction with a set of procedures. If there is not a consistent set of procedures surrounding the system, employees may have difficulty entering information, and may not know the sequence of events needed to process transactions through the system.
- *Controls.* When it becomes evident that there is a control weakness in a company, the system of procedures can be adjusted to correct the problem.
- *Handoffs.* Many processes involve handing off work to someone in a different department. Any handoff involves a considerable risk that work will not be transferred correctly, resulting in a transaction lapse that may ultimately impact a customer. A procedure states exactly how a handoff is to be completed, and so reduces the risk of a transaction lapse.
- *Governance.* In a business that has a top-down organizational structure, procedures are needed to ensure that the decisions made by management are carried out properly.
- *Roll out consistency.* It is vastly easier to roll out a business concept when every location uses exactly the same set of procedures.
- *Training.* Procedures can form the basis for employee training manuals that address the basic functions of a business.

The sheer volume of reasons presented here should make it clear that there is a resounding need for procedures. However, we do not need a set of procedures for *everything*, as discussed in the next section.

The Number of Procedures to Develop

Even a smaller business may have a large number of processes. How many of them really need to be documented in a formal procedure? If a business documents all of them, it may find that it has spent an inordinate amount of time and money on some procedures that are rarely used, and which must now be updated from time to time. To keep from making an excessive expenditure on procedure development, consider the following factors when deciding whether to create a procedure:

- *Auditor concern.* If the auditors have indicated that there are control problems in a particular area, you will almost certainly have to develop a procedure that incorporates any controls that they recommend. Otherwise, the issue will have an impact on the auditors' control assessment of the business, which may require them to employ additional audit procedures that increase the price of their audit. In short, an auditor finding essentially mandates the creation of a procedure.
- *Risk.* If there is no procedure, is there a risk that the company will suffer a monetary or reputational loss? If this loss is significant, a procedure is probably called for, even if the procedure will be rarely used. Conversely, a procedure may not be necessary if there is little underlying risk associated with it.

- *Transaction efficiency.* There may be multiple ways in which a business transaction can be completed, of which one is clearly more efficient. If so, create a procedure that directs employees to use the most efficient variation. If there is only one way to complete a transaction, there is less need for a procedure.
- *Transaction volume.* As a general rule, there should be a procedure for the 20% of all transactions that comprise 80% of the total transaction volume in which a business engages. These procedures cover most of the day-to-day activities of a business, and so can be of considerable assistance in defining the jobs of new employees, as well as for ensuring that the most fundamental activities are followed in a prescribed manner.

The last point, transaction volume, is a key determinant of the need for a procedure. There are many low-volume activities where it simply makes no sense to engage in any documentation activities at all. Instead, allow employees to follow their best judgment in deciding how to complete a lesser activity.

Once you have used these criteria to decide which transactions should be documented with a procedure, consider using the next section as a guide for their construction.

The Mechanics of Procedure Production

A typical company will operate with anywhere from several dozen to several hundred procedures. It is of some importance that procedures be produced in the same manner and be issued in the same format, to prevent confusion among employees that may (for example) find one procedure to be excessively detailed and another so general as to be utterly unworkable. The following steps are useful for attaining the appropriate level of consistency.

Procedure Production Steps

The following steps show the sequence of events needed to construct a new procedure. Some smaller procedures can be constructed using a compressed production process, but the full set of operations will be required in most cases.

1. *Determine need.* The most important question to address when producing a procedure is whether the procedure is needed at all. There are many situations where a new procedure is not necessary or cost-effective. You might consider requiring the approval of the controller or chief financial officer before initiating work on a new procedure.
2. *Define boundaries.* Determine where the procedure documentation is to begin and end, since it is possible that only a portion of a process requires a procedure.
3. *Conduct interviews.* Schedule and complete interviews with the people who are currently involved in the process being documented.

4. *Create draft.* Create a first draft of the procedure, using the company's standard procedure template, along with sample forms (if any) and a flowchart.

5. *Review by users.* Have all interviewed people review the procedure for accuracy. If someone wants to make a documentation change, ask the other interviewees about the change to see if it accurately represents the existing process.

6. *Reiterate.* Issue a new version of the procedure that incorporates the changes indicated by the interviewees. Have the interviewees review the document again. There may be several iterations of this step.

7. *Approve.* The series of reviews should result in an accurate procedure. Nonetheless, the approval of the department manager(s) impacted by the procedure should also be obtained, since they will be responsible for following it.

8. *Distribute.* A procedure is useless if it is not distributed to those people most in need of it, and in a timely manner. Consequently, develop a list of positions to which procedures should be distributed, and update it regularly. Procedures should be released to those employees indicated on the list as soon after approval as possible.

Tip: It is much better to have a distribution list by employee title than by employee name, since normal employee turnover would soon render a name-based distribution list obsolete. Employee titles change less frequently, which makes a title-based distribution list less subject to updates.

Formatting Steps

The following bullet points are not really "steps" needed to format a procedure, since they can be used in any sequence. Instead, they show the general layout to be used for a procedure. The points are listed in order as they would be found on a procedure, from the top to the bottom of a procedure document.

- *Procedure header block.* There should be a consistently-applied block of information at the beginning of each procedure that clearly identifies it. In a smaller organization, the procedure title is probably sufficient. In a larger organization, the following more detailed set of information might be required:
  - *Title.* The name of the procedure.
  - *Identification number.* A unique number that identifies the procedure. It may begin with a contraction of the name of the department in which it is primarily used, followed by a sequential number.
  - *Version number.* The number of the most recent version of the procedure. The release date (see next) can substitute for the version number.
  - *Release date.* The date on which the procedure was released for use. The version number can substitute for the release date.

- *Procedure summary.* A brief description of the procedure, and why it is used.
- *Procedure steps.* A clear description of the actions to be taken to complete each procedure step. Use a consistent outlining structure for all procedures that employs only a few levels of indentation.
- *Responsible party.* The person(s) responsible for completing each indicated step.
- *Control issues.* Control issues related to the procedure that an employee should be aware of.
- *Cross references.* If there are similar procedures, list them, as well as any unique identification numbers assigned to them.
- *Forms.* Any forms used in a procedure. Forms can be described in considerable detail, including brief descriptions of each field in a form, and sample forms that have already been completed.
- *Reports.* Any reports used in a procedure. A sample printout may be provided, along with a description of the information in each field on a report.
- *Flowchart.* A flowchart is extremely useful for giving a visual representation of how a procedure is supposed to operate. It usually makes references to any forms and reports used in a procedure. A case could be made for limiting their use to the more complicated procedures with many decision points, but we have found that some readers prefer them to a purely text-based procedure. Consequently, consider including one in most procedures.

Tip: Flowcharts can be especially useful in a multi-lingual workplace or where employee turnover is high, since they present an easy-to-understand overview of a process.

Procedure Design Tips

This section contains a number of design tips that can assist you in creating tightly-constructed procedures that present information in a clear and readily understandable manner. The points are:

- *Avoid excessive detail.* Some procedure writers have a tendency to wallow in extraordinary levels of detail, such as how to fill in each field on a computer screen. Instead, present a level of detail where only the key information needed to complete a procedure is stated. Otherwise, an employee will see a procedure that spans several dozen pages, and not even attempt to read it.
- *Streamline the header section.* Some procedures contain an abundance of material in the header section, detailing the background for the procedure, why it is needed, related policies, and so forth. This level of detail gets between the reader and the actual procedure that they need. Where possible,

only include a brief description of the procedure, and dispense with any extra material.

- *Use the outline format.* A procedure written in paragraph format is too dense to follow, especially if it involves numerous steps. A better approach is to use the outline format, where each step is numbered and sub-steps are indented. For example:

1. Complete matching of accounts payable documents.
    - Compare price on purchase order to price on supplier invoice.
    - Compare units received on receiving report to units on supplier invoice.

2. If a unit variance of greater than 2% is found, complete these steps:
    - Contact the purchasing manager with the details of the variance.
    - Record the supplier invoice in the accounts payable module at a price adjusted for the amount of the units received.
    - Issue an adjustment letter to the supplier.

This approach clearly separates each step in a procedure, making it much easier to understand than a procedure written in a paragraph format.

- *Simplify flowcharts.* The intent of a flowchart is to clarify a procedure. Therefore, the flowchart should contain less information than the procedure, so that only the highlights of the basic process steps are revealed. This means stripping out minor steps and limiting the number of shapes used. It is generally sufficient to use only the following shapes:

Symbol	Discussion
	Process: This is the primary symbol used in a business process flowchart. State each step within a process box. It is possible that a simplified process flowchart may contain no other shapes.
	Decision: This is used when a decision will result in a different process flow. The decision symbol can be overused. Try to restrict its usage to no more than two per flowchart. Otherwise, the flowchart will appear overly complex. If more decision symbols are needed, subdivide a procedure into multiple procedures.
	Document: This symbol is particularly useful for showing where an input form is used to collect information for a process, though it can also represent a report generated by a process.

Symbol	Discussion
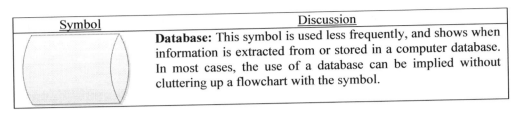	**Database:** This symbol is used less frequently, and shows when information is extracted from or stored in a computer database. In most cases, the use of a database can be implied without cluttering up a flowchart with the symbol.

- *Number pages within each procedure.* If you are issuing procedures in a loose-leaf format (see the next section) or as separate files, state the page numbers on each procedure in the "Page 1 of 2" format, so that readers can see how many pages are supposed to be included in the procedure.

Whatever set of design concepts you choose to adopt, be sure to apply them consistently across the company's entire set of procedures. Rolling out a design revision can require a considerable amount of reformatting work, especially if a company has hundreds of procedures. This is a good reason why there tend to be few design changes that are implemented only at long intervals.

Dissemination of Procedures

Once a set of procedures has been developed, how do you disseminate them throughout a business? The simplest approach is to assemble them into a single integrated document, and issue a replacement version of it at regular intervals. Each version should state the following information in the beginning of the document:

- All procedures that have been deleted
- All procedures that are entirely new
- Which procedures have been modified, and the reasons for the changes
- Any effective date for the procedural changes (usually as of the release date of the new version)

These notifications tell users if they should delve further into the document to clearly understand any updates, or if the changes have minimal impact on them.
But what if a company is a large one, with many procedures that span multiple volumes? In this situation, it may be cost-prohibitive to completely replace the entire set of procedures on a regular basis. In this case, there are two approaches to incremental changes, which are:

- *Binder updates.* Issue procedures in loose-leaf format, with instructions to store them in three-ring binders. When a procedural update is issued, only those pages pertaining to the change are distributed, with a cover page stating which existing pages should be eliminated and/or replaced with the new version. This approach mandates the specific identification of each page with a procedure identification number and revision date.
- *Central storage with notification.* Store all procedures in a server that is accessible by all authorized employees. Then issue an e-mail, stating which pages have changed and the file number on the server to be accessed if em-

ployees wish to print those pages. This approach minimizes the distribution of excess documentation, since employees will only print those documents that they intend to use.

> **Tip:** A variation on the central storage concept is to post the procedures manual on a central file server, and encourage employees to use it instead of retaining a private copy. If you use this approach, be sure to continue to issue notifications of procedural changes, so that employees will know if they need to look up a procedure modification on the file server.

A special issue regarding the dissemination of procedures is the new employee. The human resources staff should have an action item on its new employee checklist, notifying the person in charge of distributing procedures that a new employee has started work. This notification includes the job title of the new employee and the person's inter-office mailing address and e-mail address, so that a copy of the relevant procedures can be sent to the employee.

> **Tip:** If management wants to reinforce the importance of procedures with new employees, schedule a training session for new hires, during which procedures are distributed and their importance discussed.

Procedural Updates

Procedures should be released on a schedule that coincides with changes in the underlying processes that they document. This means that some procedures may not change for years, while others may be updated every few months. There will be a greater need for updates when a company is implementing best practices, has just discovered control problems, or is involved in an acquisition. In all three cases, processes will likely be changed, and written procedures must be altered along with them.

Thus, there may be no fixed schedule to follow in updating procedures. Instead, maintain close contact with the department managers who are responsible for processes, since they can provide information about prospective process updates. Also, talk to the internal audit manager regularly about the results of internal audits, which may uncover undocumented process changes. At a minimum, schedule an annual meeting with each process owner or department manager, to briefly discuss each existing procedure to see if any updates are required.

When updating a procedure, it may be sufficient to simply adjust the one or two parts of the document that have been altered, along with the accompanying adjustments to forms and flowcharts. However, if it becomes apparent that a number of alterations have been made, it is better to have the process users review the entire procedure to ensure that the document still accurately reflects how the process works. Without these reviews, a number of inconsistencies will eventually creep into procedures, which increases the impression among employees that the procedures can no longer be relied upon.

> **Tip:** Minor procedural updates can be handled with a minor notification and replacement e-mail or mailing. However, consider the introduction of a new procedure or the complete replacement of an existing one to be similar to a product launch, with a correspondingly greater level of marketing within the company; doing so improves the probability that it will be perused in detail and followed.

Enforcement of Procedures

A company can develop a flood of procedures, but they are completely useless if employees do not follow them. It is especially difficult to enforce the use of procedures in environments where procedures are updated in a halfhearted manner, and especially where management has displayed little interest in them. The following activities can be of use in improving the situation, and are divided into "carrot" and "stick" methods:

"Carrot" Activities

The following four activities are designed to proactively assist employees with up-to-date procedures that are closely tied to the needs of the business:

- *Link to systems development staff.* Build a working relationship between the procedures development staff and those employees tasked with making alterations to the company's systems. With this connection in place, the procedure developers will be made aware of any system alterations being contemplated, and so can issue procedural revisions at the same time that the changes are implemented.
- *Link to auditors.* If the internal or external auditors review the company's systems and find control problems, the procedures development staff should be aware of the nature of those problems, so that they can develop procedural remedies.
- *Issue rapid updates.* Create a system that issues procedural updates on a regular basis. Doing so gives employees the impression that management is willing to keep employees up-to-date with the latest changes in company operations.
- *Conduct training.* Provide training as needed regarding procedural changes, especially where an entirely new procedure is being installed. This is especially useful for new employees who are least familiar with the company's systems.

"Stick" Activities

The following four activities are designed to bring compliance failures to the attention of management, which may lead to problems for those people with a long history of not following procedures:

- *Report on procedural failures.* The accountant will probably become aware of instances where procedural breakdowns caused any number of problems.

These issues should be documented and issued to the management team. The chief executive officer enforces remediation of each failure, with follow-up actions to ensure that targeted improvements were implemented.

- *Request internal audits.* Request that the internal audit staff engage in an ongoing series of reviews to determine the extent to which employees are following procedures (or not). If there is no internal audit staff, consider hiring a systems analysis consultant for this work on an ongoing basis. The result of these reviews should be a report that is sent to the management team, pointing out areas of noncompliance with procedures.
- *Create audit committee.* Have the board of directors create an audit committee, comprised of board members, which reviews the results of any audits by internal and external auditors. This group can pressure the chief executive officer to enforce greater compliance with the company's official set of procedures.
- *Integrate into evaluations.* Convince the chief executive officer and human resources manager to include procedural compliance in the periodic reviews of employees. Serious non-compliance could even be grounds for dismissal from the company.

Adopting the preceding list of activities still requires the active approval and support of the management team, which is not always forthcoming. However, management is more likely to lend its support, if only grudgingly, if the outside auditors point out control breaches. Further, a robust system of controls (and therefore procedures) is an important certification that company management makes to its shareholders when a business is publicly held; in this case, complying with the rules for a public company will require managers to implement the preceding set of activities.

Deviations from Procedures

Since we have just addressed the enforcement of procedures, it is also worth discussing when to *allow* deviations from procedures. An extensive set of procedures can be considered a straitjacket that is imposed on employees in order to force them to do business in a certain way. An excessively strong level of enforcement leaves little room for employee creativity, explorations of alternative methods, or responses to unusual situations. For example, a retail establishment might consider empowering its customer service staff to respond to customer complaints in any way they believe will most satisfy customers, rather than following a rigid procedure. This type of deviation might even be encouraged, as long as it meets a company objective, such as achieving greater customer satisfaction.

However, deviations from stated procedures are not practical or safe in many situations. For example, the procedure for creating a wire transfer should be rigidly enforced, since there is a high risk of loss if someone circumvents the approvals that are normally built into this procedure. Similarly, a fast food chain with many stores needs to have a food preparation procedure that is absolutely identical across all of its restaurants, so that food preparation can be achieved in the most efficient manner possible.

In short, most organizations will find that there are a small number of procedures that can be considered advisory, rather than mandatory. In most cases, however, it is better to roll out changes in a carefully planned and tested manner, which does not allow for any ad hoc deviations. The manner in which a business is operated will dictate which procedures will fall into each of these two categories.

Presented Procedures

Through the remainder of this chapter, we describe a series of procedures that form of the core of the typical accounting system. The first cluster of procedures is centered on the customer, and describes the examination for customer credit, shipping, billing, and the processing of received payments. We then turn to a set of procedures that focus on the supplier, addressing purchasing, supplier invoice processing, and check payments. The intent is to provide the general process flow for each procedure, which the accountant can modify to meet the specific needs of his or her systems. Other procedures that tend to be more system-specific, such as payroll, are not described.

The Credit Examination Procedure (Manual System)

The credit department may receive paper copies of sales orders from the order entry department, documenting each order requested by a customer. In this manual environment, the receipt of a sales order triggers a manual review process where the credit staff can block sales orders from reaching the shipping department unless it forwards an approved copy of the sales order to the shipping manager. The credit examination procedure for a manual system is outlined below. A primary assumption of this procedure is that a *new* customer is placing an order; the procedure also shows alternative steps for returning customers (for which a separate flowchart is shown at the end of this procedure).

1.   **Receive sales order.** The order entry department sends a copy of each sales order to the credit department. If the customer is a new one, the credit manager assigns it to a credit staff person. A sales order from an existing customer will likely be given to the credit person already assigned to that customer.
Responsible party: Credit manager

Tip: It may be possible to grant a small default amount of credit to new customers. By doing so, the credit staff can reserve its analysis time for larger credit requests.

2.   **Issue credit application.** If the customer is a new one or has not done business with the company for a considerable period of time, send them a credit application and request that it be completed and returned directly to the credit department.

Responsible party: Credit staff

3.   **Collect and review credit application.** Upon receipt of a completed credit application, examine it to ensure that all fields have been completed, and contact the customer for more information if some fields are incomplete. Then collect the following information, if necessary:

- Credit report
- Customer financial statements
- Contacts with customer credit references, including information about average and maximum credit granted, as well as slow payments, discounts taken, and bad debt situations
- Contacts with bank references concerning the existence of bank accounts, the size range of account balances, and how long the customer has done business with each bank
- Any previous ordering, payment, bad debt, and dispute history with the company

Responsible party: Credit staff

Tip: If a sales order is for a small amount, it may not be necessary to collect some of this information. In particular, it may not be cost-effective to obtain a credit report for a small order, nor may some customers be willing to forward their financial statements.

Tip: It can take some time to assemble the information needed for a credit application, which may drive an impatient customer to a competitor. To keep the credit review process from being prolonged, the credit staff should review the status of all unapproved sales orders every day.

---

4.   **Assign credit level.** Based on the collected information and the company's algorithm for granting credit, determine a credit amount that the company is willing to grant to the customer. The following are all valid approaches to granting credit:

- Assign a minimum credit amount in all cases; or
- Assign credit based on the item being ordered (where higher credit levels are allowed for items being cleared from stock); or
- Assign credit based on estimated annual sales volume with the customer; or
- Assign credit based on the credit score listed in a third party's credit report; or
- Assign credit based on a decision table developed from the company's overall credit experience; or
- Assign credit based on an in-house credit granting algorithm

It may also be possible to adjust the credit level if a customer is willing to sign a personal guarantee.

Responsible party: Credit staff

5.   **Hold order** (optional). If the sales order is from an existing customer and there is an existing unpaid and unresolved invoice from the customer for more than $___, place a hold on the sales order. Contact the customer and inform them that the order will be kept on hold until such time as the outstanding invoice has been paid.
Responsible party: Credit staff

> **Tip:** Always inform the sales manager before placing a hold on a sales order. The customer will probably contact the sales manager once it learns of the hold, so the sales manager should be prepared in advance for this call.

6.   **Obtain credit insurance** (optional). If the company uses credit insurance, forward the relevant customer information to the insurer to see if it will insure the credit risk. The result may alter the amount of credit that the credit staff is willing to grant.
Responsible party: Credit staff

> **Tip:** It may be possible to bill the customer for the cost of the credit insurance.

7.   **Verify remaining credit** (optional). A sales order may have been forwarded from the order entry department for an existing customer who already has been granted credit. In this situation, the credit staff compares the remaining amount of available credit to the amount of the sales order, and approves the order if there is sufficient credit for the order. If not, the credit staff considers a one-time increase in the credit level in order to accept the order, or contacts the customer to arrange for an alternative payment arrangement.
Responsible party: Credit staff
Control issues: The credit manager should review and approve larger one-time credit extensions.

8.   **Approve sales order.** If the credit staff approves the credit level needed for a sales order, it stamps the sales order as approved, signs the form, and forwards a copy to the shipping department for fulfillment. It also retains a copy.
Responsible party: Credit staff
Control issues: It may be necessary to maintain control over the credit approval stamp, since someone could use it to fraudulently mark a sales order as having been approved.

> **Tip:** If the customer has agreed to bear the cost of credit insurance, notify the billing department of the additional amount to be billed to the customer.

9.   **File credit documentation.** Create a file for the customer and store all information in it that was collected as part of the credit examination process. This information is useful for future reference, either during periodic reviews or when a customer requests a change in credit level.

Responsible party: Credit staff

> **Tip:** If there are many customers, it may make sense to use a standard methodology to create a unique customer index number for filing purposes. Doing so will reduce the risk that multiple files will be created for the same customer.

The following exhibit shows a streamlined view of the credit procedure for a manual system, excluding most optional steps, and assuming that sales orders are being processed only for new customers.

Credit Process Flow (Manual System for New Customers)

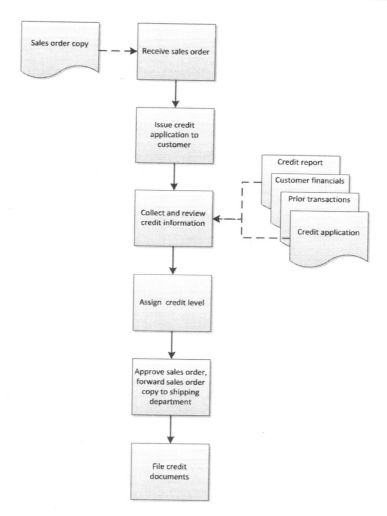

The following exhibit shows a streamlined view of the credit procedure for a manual system, excluding most optional steps, and assuming that sales orders are being processed only for existing customers. In this case, the procedure can be considerably shortened if there is a sufficient amount of unused credit already available to accommodate a sales order.

Credit Process Flow (Manual System for Existing Customers)

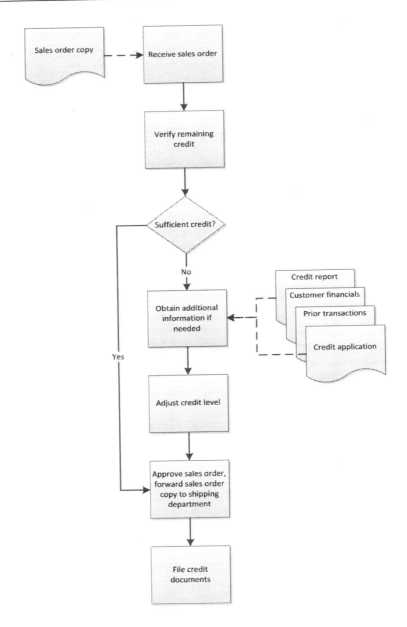

The Shipping Procedure (Manual System)

In many organizations, the shipping department is not linked to the computer systems resident in other departments. This situation requires the use of paper-based notifications of customer orders to the department, as well as a considerable amount of subsequent paperwork to document the picking and shipment of each order. The shipping procedure for a manual system is outlined below.

1.   **Verify sales order.** When a sales order arrives in the shipping department, review it to verify that it is authorized for shipment. This means that there is either a credit authorization stamp on it, or the amount to be shipped is of such a small dollar amount that it bypasses the credit department as per the company's credit policy. If the sales order is not authorized for shipment, send it to the credit manager.
Responsible party: Shipping manager
Control issues: Having an unauthorized sales order arrive in the shipping department is a serious breach in company procedures, so it may make sense to also notify the controller and/or internal audit manager of the issue.

2.   **Issue picking document.** Make a copy of the sales order and forward it to a stock picker. Note on the retained version of the sales order the name of the stock picker to whom a copy was given. This person picks the goods listed on the sales order and brings them to the shipping area. If not all items were on hand, the picker notes this on his copy of the sales order. The stock picker gives the marked-up copy of the sales order to the shipping manager, who matches it to his copy of the document.
Responsible party: Stock picker
Control issues: The shipping manager should run a daily verification of all sales orders for which the picking version has not yet been returned, and follow up with the stock pickers assigned to these sales orders.

> **Tip:** It is also possible to copy all picking information from the sales order to a separate pick list. However, there is some risk in a manual environment that the information will be transcribed incorrectly, leading to an incorrect pick.

3.   **Issue backorder notification** (optional). If some items listed on the sales order were not in stock, ensure that they are clearly noted on the sales order, and send a copy back to the order entry department (a separate backorder form may also be used). The order entry staff may want to contact the customer about the shipping delay, and may attempt to persuade the customer to buy an alternative product. Another copy should go to the materials management staff, who schedule the backordered goods to be produced or procured. The shipping manager retains a copy of the sales order in a backorders file, and periodically has the stock pickers review the inventory to see if the indicated items have arrived.
Responsible party: Shipping manager

Control issues: It is possible for items on backlog to be lost in an entirely manual system. One way to spot missing items is for the billing clerk to note on his or her copy of the sales order any items not yet invoiced, and periodically consult with the shipping manager regarding these missing items.

4. **Prepare goods for shipment.** Package the goods for shipment, and prepare shipping information based on the "ship to" address listed on the sales order. Contact the shipper to arrange a pickup.
Responsible party: Shipping staff
Control issues: If there is a history of incorrect inventory picks, it might be reasonable to have someone other than the inventory picker compare the picked items to the sales order prior to shipment.

5. **Complete shipping documents and ship.** Complete the bill of lading document. Verify that it matches the contents of the shipment. Then sign the document and have the shipper sign it, as well. Retain a copy of the bill of lading. Also print a packing slip, detailing the contents of the shipment. Affix a copy to the outside of the shipment, and retain a copy.
Responsible party: Shipping staff
Control issues: A copy of the bill of lading should always be retained, so that the company can prove that goods were shipped, as well as the date of shipment.

6. **Complete shipping log.** Use the information on the bills of lading or packing slip to complete the shipping log. This log is a summary of all shipments made, sorted by date.
Responsible party: Shipping manager
Control issues: To ensure that the shipping log is complete, periodically match it to the bills of lading retained by the department, and update it for any bills not listed in the log.

7. **Remove from inventory records.** Remove the shipped items from the inventory records for finished goods.
Responsible party: Shipping staff
Control issues: If this step is missed or completed improperly, it can be a major cause of inventory record inaccuracies, so use periodic inventory counts to verify inventory levels. Also, assign inventory record-keeping to a well-trained person, and prohibit all other employees from accessing the inventory records.

8. **Forward shipping documents.** Send a copy of the bill of lading or packing slip to the billing clerk. It may make sense to send the bills of lading, packing slips, and the daily shipping log together as a batch for an entire day of shipping activity, so that the billing clerk can compare the detail documents to the shipping log. If the company bills its customers for shipping charges incurred, note the type of shipping used for each delivery. This information initiates the preparation of a customer invoice.

Responsible party: Shipping manager

Control issues: From an accounting perspective, this is the most critical part of the shipping process, since unforwarded documents will prevent invoices from being generated. An easy control is to have the billing clerk go to the shipping department to request these documents if they do not arrive by a specific time each day.

Tip: Require the shipping department to forward shipping documents to the billing clerk at least twice a day, so that the company can issue invoices as soon after shipments as possible. This practice tends to improve the speed with which customers pay their invoices.

---

9. **File documents**. Attach the bill of lading to the sales order, and file it by date within the shipping department. Also retain the original shipping log within the shipping department. This information may be accessed by auditors to verify that shipments were made, and may also be useful to the billing clerk for investigations of customer invoices.

Responsible party: Shipping manager

Control issues: Consider storing this information in a locked cabinet, since it can be quite useful for investigative purposes at a later date.

The following exhibit shows a streamlined view of the shipping procedure for a manual system.

Shipping Process Flow (Manual System)

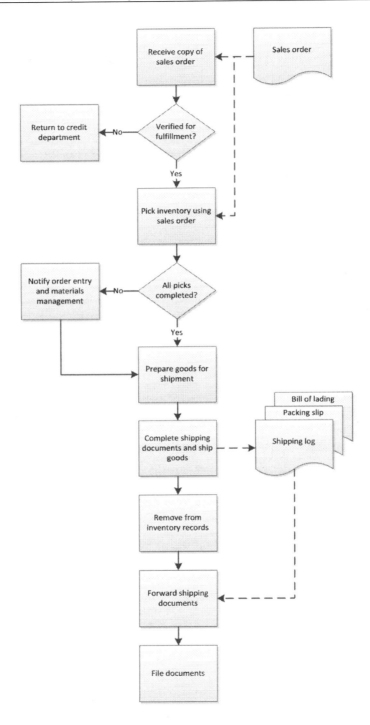

The Billing Procedure

The general process flow for creating a customer invoice is that a packet of information arrives from the shipping department, which the billing clerk verifies and converts into an invoice. There are numerous other steps involved before the shipping department ever sends this information to the billing clerk, including order entry, credit approval, production scheduling, and shipment.

Perform the billing procedure every day. Customers are supposed to enter the invoice date in their computer systems when logging in supplier invoices, so that the computer pays each invoice after the correct number of days, as listed in the payment terms on the invoice. However, many data entry employees do not go to the trouble of entering this date, and instead use the default date, which is the current day. Invoices entered in this manner will be paid later. Thus, you need to process invoices as soon as possible in order to be paid as soon as possible.

The detailed billing procedure, including responsibilities and basic controls, follows:

1. **Access shipping documents.** In a fully computerized system, this will be a screen in the accounting system. In a manual system, this is a document sent from the shipping department that states what has been shipped to a customer. It is frequently a copy of the bill of lading or packing slip.
Responsible party: Billing clerk
Control issues: The person shipping goods cannot be the same person who creates the invoice. Otherwise, an employee could ship goods to a company that he controls and then modify the invoice to contain fewer items shipped or lower prices than normal.

2. **Access the customer order.** In a computerized system, you can access an on-line form that itemizes all customer order items shipped. Then, verify that you want to print an invoice for all flagged items. If there is no automated linkage from the shipping department to the accounting software, you will need to locate the sales order, of which a copy should have been sent from the customer service department to the accounting department when each customer originally placed an order.
Responsible party: Billing clerk
Control issues: In a non-computerized system, it is possible to lose customer sales orders. The order entry staff should always store a backup copy of each sales order, which is usually stapled to any customer purchase order that it may also have received. These documents are usually filed by customer name. If the order entry staff wants to keep two copies of the sales order, then pre-number the forms and file the second copy by number. Though probably overkill, this later approach reduces the risk of a lost sales order.

3. **Verify prices** (optional). In a computerized system, the customer service staff should have already verified pricing when they created the sales order, so there is nothing more to be done. When customer orders are placed manually, compare the

prices listed on the sales order to the standard price list, and flag any items that vary from the standard rates. There should not be too many prices on orders that contain non-standard prices. If there are, consider periodically compiling these orders to see if certain salespeople are allowing nonstandard pricing, or if the marketing department is running undocumented discounts, and so forth.

Responsible party: Billing clerk

Control issues: There can be significant control problems with pricing when the marketing department is constantly running promotions at varying discount rates. The simplest control is to restrict the number of promotions. If that is not possible, then ensure that both the order entry and accounting departments are on the mailing list for all special promotions, and give the marketing department immediate feedback if it does not rigidly adhere to this distribution.

Tip: A company may change its official price list at regular intervals, such as once a year. If so, it is quite possible that a customer may have placed an order when earlier prices were in effect. In such cases, match prices to the price list that was in effect on the date when the order was placed. In addition, consider having a policy to give customers whichever price is lower – the old one or the new price. This may call for some invoice adjustments, but it can create customer goodwill, especially if there is a prominent note on the invoice that explains the reason for the price reduction.

---

4.   **Calculate shipping.** This can be a time-consuming part of invoicing, because not all forms of shipping charges are easily automated in a computerized system. Here are several examples of shipping calculations:

- *Customer pickup*. The customer comes to the company to retrieve his order. This needs to be established at the time of order placement, and either flagged in the computer system or stamped on the order.
- *Price based*. This is typically an increasing price that is based on the price of the order, not its cubic volume or shipping weight. Many order-taking systems contain this feature.
- *Promotional rate*. This is usually free shipping if customers order by a certain date or in an amount greater than a set order size.
- *Prepaid*. If the initial customer order states that shipping is prepaid, do not charge any freight on the invoice.

Responsible party: Billing clerk

Control issues: Unusual shipping requests, such as overnight delivery to a distant location, can cause losses, since these charges may be inordinately high, and the company may underbill the customer for them. If so, either require the customer to pay the delivery company itself, or forbid such deliveries, or forbid them only when the company is uncertain of the full amount of the shipping charge that it will eventually be billed by the transportation firm.

Tip: If you want to have a fairly automated invoicing process, try to standardize the shipping calculation as much as possible, with very few variations from the standard calculation. The simplest approach is to offer free shipping. The next simplest is to use a standard shipping charge based on the total size of the order – this involves a simple table lookup, and is easy for a computer system to accomplish. From the standpoint of simplicity, a customer-specific shipping rate is a bad idea, since it usually calls for a manual override of the computer-generated shipping rate.

5.   **Charge sales tax**. Charge the sales tax rate for the government entity in which the customer is receiving the goods. This tax rate should be included in the accounting software, so the software automatically applies it. If you are creating invoices by hand, keep the sales tax information in a summary sheet for easy reference.

Responsible party: Billing clerk

Control issues: The sales tax code is usually set up in a separate file in the accounting software, which in turn is referenced in the customer master file for each individual customer. If the sales tax code is incorrect, or the customer master file incorrectly references the wrong sales tax code, you will either collect sales taxes for the wrong government entity, or in the wrong amount. This problem can be difficult to spot. One option is to have a second person cross-check all changes to computer records involving sales taxes. Another possibility is to have an internal auditor review these records periodically.

Tip: Governments usually mail out updates to their sales tax rates near the end of each calendar year. Have the person in charge of the mail route all of these notifications to you, so that you can update them in the computer system.

6.   **Print invoice**. If you are using a pre-printed invoice form, make sure that it is positioned properly in the printer, conduct a test print if necessary, and print the invoice. If the computer requires you to print invoices in batch mode, then print all of the invoices that you have selected.

Responsible party: Billing clerk

Tip: Consider using a color printer, so that you can use colors to highlight specific fields on an invoice, such as the amount of an early payment discount or the due date of the invoice.

7.   **Burst invoice** (optional). If using multi-part forms, then you need to burst the copies apart. If it is a two-part form, then you usually file the extra copy by customer name. If it is a three-part form, then you typically file the third copy by invoice number. These extra copies are useful for cross-referencing information at a later date, if you have to research an invoice.

Responsible party: Billing clerk

> **Tip:** The impact printers used to create multi-part invoices are far more likely to jam than laser printers, so consider moving away from this form of printing.

8.   **Proofread the invoice** (optional). If an invoice is unusually complex or is for a large amount, consider having someone else proofread it. You do not want unnecessary delays caused by customer protests at an inaccurate billing, so proofreading may be prudent. The original billing clerk should not conduct this review, since the person who creates a document is less likely to see errors.
Responsible party: Second billing clerk

> **Tip:** Do not use proofreading for routine invoices, since these items rarely contain errors, and proofreading can delay invoice delivery.

9.   **Mail invoice.** Stuff the completed invoices into mailing envelopes, and stamp each envelope with an "Address Correction Requested" stamp, so that the post office will notify you if a customer changes its address.
Responsible party: Billing clerk
Control issues: As noted in this procedure step, it is important to keep track of customer addresses, since you may inadvertently mail an invoice to an old address. To avoid this, have the mail room staff forward all change of address forms received from customers to the accounting department.

> **Tip:** It may be necessary to use different types of mailings to get an invoice into the hands of the correct person at a customer. For example, you may need to use registered mail if customers continually claim that they never receive invoices. Other customers prefer e-mail delivery, or that you enter the invoice into an electronic invoicing portal. In order to be reminded about which mailing method to use, create a code in the customer master file that indicates a specific form of delivery, and have this code appear in a unique box somewhere on the invoice.

10.   **File invoice copy** (optional). If you have created an extra copy of an invoice, file it in the customer's file, along with the sales order and customer purchase order (if any), and the proof of shipment. It is better to use a fastener file folder for storing invoices, so that you can affix them to the folder securely. This reduces the risk of losing documents, and keeps the invoices in order by date. If you created another copy, file it by invoice number in a separate binder.
Responsible party: Accounting clerk (does not have to be the billing clerk)
Control issues: It is not uncommon to lose invoices simply by filing them under the wrong customer name. This has become a relatively minor control issue, since you can still access electronic records of invoices through the computer system. However, if you use the computer as the primary method of access to accounting records, keep records available in the computer for several preceding years – do not archive them for as long as possible.

Tip: Do you need to print or file a copy of an invoice at all? As long as the backup method for the accounting system is first-rate, you can always print the invoice at a later date if you need it. An alternative is to print the invoice and then scan it into an electronic document management system, along with all other documents related to the invoice, such as evidence of shipment and the customer's original order. This results in an easy source of all information about an order, which can be accessed from any computer terminal, and is very useful for the customer service staff, which may have to respond to customer queries.

11. **Retain extra sales order copy** (optional). If the sales order has not been entirely fulfilled, make a copy of it, circle the remaining items that have not yet been shipped, and store it in a pending file. This is eventually matched to the shipping documents for the backordered items when they are shipped.

Responsible party: Billing clerk

Control issues: Review the sales orders for backordered items periodically, and investigate those that are quite old. This can serve as a useful reminder for the order entry staff, who can follow up with customers to see if they want to buy alternative products.

The following exhibit shows a streamlined view of the standard billing procedure, including a few of the more common optional steps. This process flow assumes that a computer system exists that links the order entry, shipping, and accounting departments.

Standard Billing Process Flow

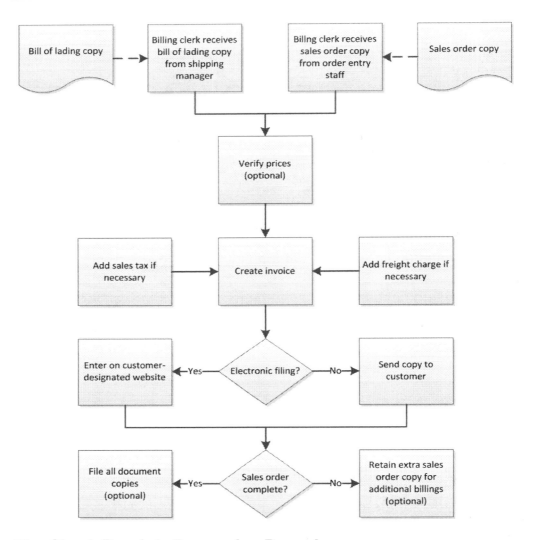

The Check Receipts Processing Procedure

The task of processing checks is loaded with controls. They are needed to ensure that checks are recorded correctly, deposited promptly, and not stolen anywhere in the process. The procedure for check receipts processing is outlined below:

1.   **Record checks and cash.** When the daily mail delivery arrives, record all received checks and cash on the mailroom check receipts list. For each check received, state on the form the name of the paying party, the check number, and the amount paid. If the receipt was in cash, state the name of the paying party, check the "cash?" box, and the amount paid. Once all line items have been completed, enter

the grand total in the "total receipts" field at the bottom of the form. Sign the form, and state the date on which the checks and cash were received. Also, stamp "for deposit only" and the company's bank account number on every check received; this makes it more difficult for someone to extract a check and deposit it into some other bank account.

Responsible party: Mailroom staff

Control issues: Where possible, have two people record incoming checks and cash. Otherwise, someone could easily abscond with any payments received before they have been recorded in the company's accounting systems.

2. **Forward payments.** Insert all checks, cash, and a copy of the mailroom check receipt list into a secure interoffice mail pouch. Have it hand-delivered to the cashier in the accounting department. The cashier matches all items in the pouch to the mailroom check receipt list, initials a copy of the list, and returns the copy by interoffice mail to the mailroom. The mailroom staff then files the initialed copy by date.

Responsible party: Mailroom staff, mail courier, and cashier

Control issues: These steps ensure that the payments are securely shifted to the cashier, and that the cashier officially acknowledges receipt of the funds. Responsibility for the funds has now shifted to the cashier.

Tip: There may need to be an additional reconciliation step if the cashier finds that the checks and cash in the mail pouch do not match the amount listed on the mailroom check receipt list.

---

3. **Apply cash to invoices.** Access the accounting software, call up the unpaid invoices for the relevant customer, and apply the cash to the invoices indicated on the remittance advice that accompanies each payment from the customer. If there is no indication of which invoice is to be credited, record the payment either in a separate suspense account, or as unapplied but within the account of the customer from whom it came.

Responsible party: Cashier

Control issues: It is of some importance to apply cash to open accounts receivable at once, thereby reducing the amount of receivables that the collections staff should pursue. Once all cash received for the day has been applied, another control possibility is to print the cash receipts journal for the day, compare it to the mailroom check receipts list, and reconcile any differences.

4. **Record other cash** (optional). Some cash or checks will occasionally arrive that are not related to unpaid accounts receivable. For example, there may be a prepayment by a customer, or the return of a deposit. In these cases, record the receipt in the accounting system, along with proper documentation of the reason for the payment.

Responsible party: Cashier

Control issues: The controller may want to review the treatment of these payments, to ensure that they have been properly recorded within the correct account.

5.   **Deposit cash.** Record all checks and cash on a deposit slip. Compare the total on the deposit slip to the amount stated on the mailroom check receipts list, and reconcile any differences. Then store the checks and cash in a locked pouch and transport it to the bank.

Responsible party: Cashier and additional reviewer (see the following control issue)

Control issues: An extra level of control is to have a second person compare the total on the deposit slip to the total on the mailroom check receipts list, which prevents the cashier from absconding with funds. This second person should not report to the cashier.

Tip: Cash application should be completed on the day of cash receipt, if only to ensure that no cash is held on the premises overnight. If it is not possible to apply cash to receivables that fast, make photocopies of the receipts that were not applied, so that cash can still be deposited at once.

---

6.   **Match to bank receipt.** Upon receipt of the checks and cash, the bank issues a receipt for it. Someone other than the cashier compares this receipt to the amount on the deposit slip, and reconciles any differences.

Responsible party: Accounting clerk

Control issues: This step is used to prevent the theft of cash while in transit to the bank. Since the person transporting the cash is also returning with the receipt, it is quite possible that this person will deliberately lose the receipt. A missing receipt is therefore a possible indicator of fraud.

The following exhibit shows a streamlined view of the check receipts processing procedure.

Check Receipts Process Flow

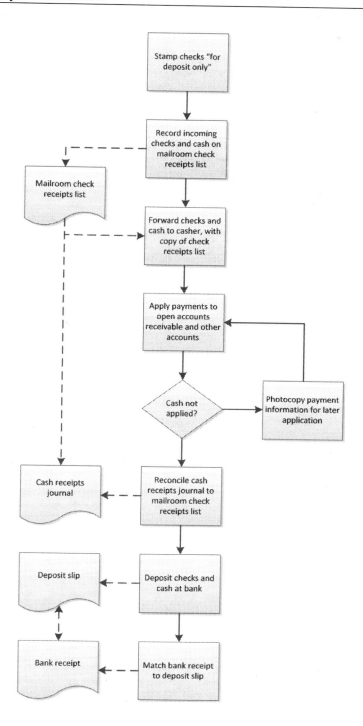

The Purchasing Procedure

The classic approach to ordering goods and services is the purchase order. It is a formal approach to buying that involves the issuance of a legal document, the purchase order, to a supplier. The purchase order identifies the items being ordered, as well as the price and other conditions under which a company is willing to make a purchase. Though the issuance of purchase orders is usually well-controlled, it also requires a considerable amount of time to complete. For this reason, it is generally restricted to more expensive purchases. The purchasing procedure is outlined below:

1.   **Obtain pricing**. When the purchasing staff receives a purchase requisition, it needs to ascertain pricing in order to determine the level of authorization needed by the requesting party.

Responsible party: Purchasing staff

Control issues: It is very time-consuming to obtain multiple prices for the items listed on every purchase requisition, so the purchasing manager should set rules for allowing purchases from a small number of designated suppliers, with multiple bids only needed for larger purchases.

2.   **Match against authorization table.** Once the purchasing staff has obtained preliminary pricing estimates, compare the amounts requested to the company's authorization table. If the requesting person represents sufficient authorization to approve the purchase, then proceed with the ordering process. If not, retain a copy of the purchase requisition and send the original to the person whose approval is required. An example of an authorization table follows.

Sample Purchase Authorization Table

	Department Manager	Division Manager	Chief Operating Officer	Chief Executive Officer	Board of Directors
<$25,000	✓				
$25,000-100,000	✓	✓			
$100,001-250,000	✓	✓	✓		
$250,001-1,000,000	✓	✓	✓	✓	
$1,000,000+	✓	✓	✓	✓	✓

Responsible party: Purchasing staff

Control issues: The purchasing staff should routinely review its copies of unapproved purchase requisitions, and follow up with approvers regarding their status.

Tip: It may be more efficient for the purchasing department to shift this task onto the requesting person, so that all purchase requisitions contain the required approvals. However, this approach may not work if the requesting person is not sure of the prices of items being requested.

---

3. **Obtain additional documentation** (optional). If the item being requested exceeds the company's capitalization limit, send the purchase requisition back to the requesting person with a request to complete a capital request form.
Responsible party: Purchasing staff
Control issues: This step essentially terminates the purchasing process, so there is no need to retain a copy of the purchase requisition.

4. **Prepare purchase order.** Complete a purchase order, based on the information in the purchase requisition or bid results. Depending on the size of the order, it may be necessary for the purchasing manager to approve and sign the purchase order. Retain a copy of the purchase order in a pending file, stapled to the department's copy of the purchase requisition, and send the original to the supplier. Additional copies go to the receiving department and accounts payable staff. Though not necessary, another copy could be sent to the person who placed the requisition, as evidence that the order was placed. If the purchasing system is computerized, then only a single copy is printed and sent to the supplier.
Responsible party: Purchasing staff
Control issues: If purchase orders are prepared manually, have them prenumbered, track all numbers used, and store unused purchase orders in a secure location. This is needed to keep someone from removing a purchase order and using it to order goods or services that have not been authorized.

5. **Obtain legal review** (optional). If the purchase order contains terms and conditions that are not the standard ones normally used in purchase orders, route the document to the legal staff for review.
Responsible party: Corporate counsel
Control issues: It can be difficult to determine what constitutes a reasonable exception from the normal terms and conditions, which would require legal review. Also, a legal review slows down the purchasing process. For both reasons, the purchasing staff may be reluctant to obtain a review. This issue can be detected after-the-fact with a periodic investigation by the internal audit team.

Tip: You can avoid a legal review for recurring contracts whose terms were approved by corporate counsel in an earlier version, but only if the terms and conditions have not subsequently changed.

---

6. **Monitor change orders** (optional). If change orders are issued, keep track of the resulting change in the cumulative total authorized to be spent. If the cumulative total exceeds the original authorization level noted in the authorization table, obtain the higher authorization level needed for the new expenditure level.
Responsible party: Purchasing staff
Control issues: This step requires a considerable amount of monitoring, which the purchasing staff will be reluctant to do. It can be made easier by modifying the purchase order form to include a field for the cumulative dollar total, which the purchasing staff updates for each successive change order.

7. **Monitor purchase acknowledgments** (optional). For the more important items being purchased, it may make sense to ensure that purchase orders have been received by suppliers and acknowledged. This can be a simple phone call to the supplier, or it may be a formal written acknowledgment. Another option is to include a "confirm to phone number" field in the purchase order, as was shown earlier in the sample purchase order template. If the company is issuing purchase orders by electronic means, the supplier's computer system may automatically send back an acknowledgment message.

Responsible party: Purchasing staff

Control issues: This step is probably of least use when dealing with long-term business partners, but could be of considerable importance when ordering from new suppliers where the purchasing department has no idea of supplier performance levels.

8. **Monitor subsequent activity**. Following the due date of the purchase order, remove the department's copy from the pending file and verify with the receiving department that the related goods were received. If not, contact the supplier to determine the status of the order. If complete, file the purchase order by supplier name. If the purchasing system is computerized, the receiving department will flag purchase orders on-line as having been fulfilled, which effectively eliminates this step.

Responsible party: Purchasing staff

Control issues: For more important items, the purchasing staff might consider contacting suppliers *in advance of* the due date to ensure that items were shipped on time.

Tip: If the purchasing staff finds that small residual balances were not fulfilled on a purchase order, and the company no longer requires the residual amount, they should issue a notification to the supplier that the order for the remaining amount has been cancelled.

---

9. **File documents**. When all activity associated with a purchase order has been completed, file the purchasing documents by supplier name for the current year. This will certainly include the purchase order and purchase requisition, and may also include a cancellation notice that terminates any residual unfulfilled balances on a purchase order, as well as any purchase order acknowledgments received from suppliers.

Responsible party: Purchasing staff

The following exhibit shows a streamlined view of the purchasing procedure, not including the optional steps to obtain additional documentation, conduct a legal review, or monitor change orders.

Purchasing Process Flow

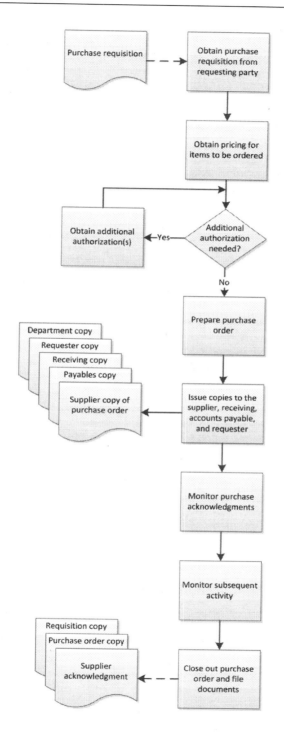

The Supplier Invoice Processing Procedure (Manual System)

Though most companies operate with a computer-based accounting system, it is considerably less likely that they coordinate the information between the accounting, purchasing, and receiving databases. When there is no inter-linking of this information, use the following procedure to process supplier invoices:

1.   **Store purchase order.** When the purchasing department creates a purchase order to authorize the purchase of goods or services, they send a copy of the purchase order to the accounts payable staff. Upon receipt, the accounts payable staff stores the copy in an unmatched purchase orders file, probably sorted by supplier name.
Responsible party: Accounts payable staff

2.   **Store receiving report.** When a supplier delivers goods to the receiving dock, the receiving staff completes a receiving report that references the supplier name, purchase order number, and number of units received, and sends a copy (sometimes including a copy of the bill of lading) to the accounts payable staff. Upon receipt, the accounts payable staff stores the copy in an unmatched receiving reports file, probably sorted by supplier name.
Responsible party: Accounts payable staff

3.   **Review supplier invoice.** When a supplier invoice is received, examine it to ensure that it contains the following information:
   - Supplier pay-to address
   - Payment terms
   - Purchase order reference number (optional)
   - List of services provided (for service contracts)
   - List of hours worked (for service contracts)

If the required information is not listed, obtain it from the supplier and add it to the invoice.
Responsible party: Accounts payable staff

> **Tip:** A payment can also be initiated by a check request form, which must be signed by the person whose budget will be impacted by the resulting expense. The form should contain payment information, the reason for the expenditure, and the appropriate approvals for the expenditure level required.

4.   **Conduct three-way match.** Match the invoice with the receiving report issued by the receiving department and the purchase order issued by the purchasing department. If there is no receiving report or purchase order, contact the issuing department to see if there is a missing document. If the price stated on the supplier invoice does not match the price stated on the purchase order, contact the purchasing department for further instructions. If the quantity stated on the supplier invoice does

not match the amount stated on the receiving report, contact the receiving department for further instructions.

Responsible party: Accounts payable staff

Control issues: The three-way matching process will probably uncover a number of small variances between the various documents. To keep three-way matching from being an excessively onerous control, consider allowing invoice payment without further review, as long as the variances are within predetermined limits.

> **Tip:** If some suppliers persistently submit incorrect billing information, the accounting staff may need to discuss the issue with them. This takes time, but is more efficient over the long-term if payment problems can be eliminated. Thus, there may need to be an additional step following the matching process, to contact suppliers about problems found.

> **Tip:** Three-way matching can be a very good control, but it is also very inefficient. A more cost-effective alternative is to only require it for supplier invoices that exceed a certain dollar amount. It is also not needed for such ongoing payments as taxes, utilities, insurance, legal and accounting fees, and royalties.

5.   **Obtain approval** (optional). If there is no purchase order for a supplier invoice, or if the invoice is an expense report from an employee, or if the invoice is for services (and therefore no receiving report), send the invoice to the person whose budget will be impacted by it and ask for an approval signature. It is customary to first make a copy of the invoice before sending the document to the approver, to ensure that the invoice will not be lost. It may also be useful to maintain a log of all invoices that have been sent out for approval, and cross them off the list as they are returned. The accounts payable staff can use the log to follow up on any unapproved invoices.

Responsible party: Accounts payable staff

Control issues: This is a difficult control to follow, since many supervisors consider invoice authorizations to be an annoyance, and therefore delay returning approved documents to the payables department. One option is to use *negative approvals*, where supervisors are notified that invoices will be paid unless they say otherwise. This means that the payables staff can immediately enter invoices in the accounting system, rather than waiting for approval.

> **Tip:** Approvers may not know why they were sent an invoice, or may not know where to write their approval on the document. To mitigate these issues, create an approval stamp that contains an approval line, and use this stamp on all invoices before sending them out for approval.

6.   **Create vendor master file record** (optional). If the company has not done business with a supplier before, create a vendor master file record for it in the

accounting system. This record contains such information as the supplier's payment address, tax identification number, contact information, and payment terms.
Responsible party: Accounts payable staff

7.   **Obtain Form W-9** (optional). Check the Form W-9 file to see if there is a completed form for the supplier. Alternatively, check the vendor master file to see if a tax identification number has been listed for the supplier. If not, contact the supplier and request that a form be sent. Upon receipt, file the form in the Form W-9 file.
Responsible party: Accounts payable staff

Tip: The Form W-9 is the source document for the tax identification number used in the Form 1099 that is sent to qualifying suppliers at year-end. The company is in the best position to obtain this document when it can withhold payments from suppliers, so be sure to tell suppliers that no payment will be forthcoming until a completed form is received.

8.   **Enter invoice.** Enter the invoice into the accounting system for payment. Set the invoice date in the system at the invoice date noted on the invoice, rather than the current date (otherwise it will be paid late). Also, set the system to take advantage of any early payment discounts allowed by the supplier.
Responsible party: Accounts payable staff
Control issues: It may be advisable to enter invoices into the accounting system before any of them are sent out for approvals (see the preceding step concerning invoice approvals). Doing so eliminates the risk that an invoice is not entered into the system in time to be paid by its due date.

Tip: When invoices contain no unique invoice number, there is a significant risk of paying them twice, since the accounting software cannot uniquely identify them. To avoid this issue, enforce a policy for creating invoice numbers. Such a policy typically converts the invoice date into an invoice number.

9.   **Issue adjustment letter** (optional). If the amount to be paid differs from the amount stated on the supplier invoice, consider sending an adjustment letter to the supplier, stating the amount of and reason for the difference. This can keep the supplier from charging late payment fees and pestering the accounts payable staff with questions about the unpaid difference.
Responsible party: Accounts payable staff

The following exhibit shows a streamlined view of the supplier invoice processing procedure in a manual environment. It only includes those optional steps most likely to occur on an ongoing basis.

Supplier Invoice Process Flow

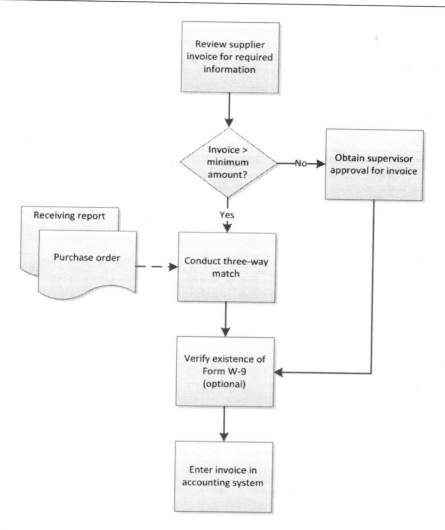

The Check Payment Issuance Procedure

The predominant mode of payment to suppliers is to print a check, though the use of direct deposit and wire transfers is also common. The check payment issuance procedure is outlined below.

1.   **Print payment due dates report.** Any accounting software package includes a standard report that itemizes the invoices that are now due for payment. The accounts payable staff should print this report prior to the next scheduled date on which it makes payments. This report only works if the accounting staff has previously entered the standard payment terms for each supplier in the vendor

master file in the accounting software. The system should automatically present invoices that are available for early payment discounts.

Responsible party: Accounts payable staff

Control issues: It is important not to miss due dates, so running the due dates report should be on the daily schedule of activities in the accounting department.

Tip: If you are operating a manual accounts payable system, store supplier invoices in folders that are organized by due date.

---

2. **Approve payments.** The accounts payable manager or controller should review the report to see if any prospective payments should be delayed. If so, cross out these items.

Responsible party: Accounts payable manager or controller

Control issues: To ensure that only the approved items are paid, consider crossing out line items in ink, initialing the crossed-out items, and later matching printed checks to the report.

3. **Select payments.** Access the payments module in the accounting software and select all approved invoices listed on the payment due dates report. Print a preliminary check register and match it against the approved payment due dates report to ensure that only approved invoices are being paid.

Responsible party: Accounts payable staff

Control issues: The matching process noted here is quite important; otherwise, the software may automatically pay *all* invoices that are currently due for payment.

4. **Obtain check stock.** Go to the locked cabinet where check stock is stored, and extract a sufficient number of checks for the check run. Re-lock the cabinet.

Responsible party: Accounts payable staff

Control issues: It is critical to keep unused check stock locked up at all times. We will return to this issue later, when we log out the range of check numbers used. Also, if there is a check stamp or plate, store it in a different locked location, which makes it more difficult for someone to fraudulently create a check payment.

5. **Print checks.** Enter the beginning check number for the unused checks into the accounting software. Print the checks. Verify that the checks were properly aligned and that all checks were printed. If not, re-print the batch of checks. Otherwise, accept the check run in the software and print a final check register.

Responsible party: Accounts payable staff

Control issues: It is useful to match the final check register to the approved payment due dates report, to ensure that the accounts payable staff has only paid authorized invoices.

> **Tip:** It is customary to retain a copy of the final check register, but there is no particular reason to do so, since the accounting system stores this information and can usually print a replacement report on demand.

6.   **Return unused checks.** Return all unused checks to the locked cabinet. Note in a check usage log the check number range that was used. This step is used to uncover cases where checks may have been fraudulently removed from the stock of unused checks.

Responsible party: Accounts payable staff

Control issues: The check usage log should be stored in a locked location, so that no one can both steal unused checks and modify the log to hide the theft.

7.   **Sign checks.** Attach all supporting documentation to each check. Then schedule a check signing meeting with an authorized check signer. Be available during the meeting to answer any questions posed by the check signer. The check signer should examine the supporting materials for any check where there is a concern about the payment. If the check is for an unusually large amount, consider requiring an additional signature on the check, thereby providing an additional level of authorization.

Responsible party: Accounts payable staff and authorized check signer

Control issues: Check signing is a control, but may not be necessary in cases where the purchasing department has authorized a payment in advance with a signed purchase order. If so, a signature stamp or plate can be used instead of a check signer.

8.   **Issue checks.** Attach any required remittance advices to checks, and mail them to recipients. Then attach the company's copy of remittance advices to supporting documents, and file them by supplier name.

Responsible party: Accounts payable staff

Control issues: In a purely manual payables environment, there is a risk of paying an invoice more than once, so a reasonable control is to stamp each paid invoice, or even perforate it, with a "paid" stamp. This control is not needed in a computerized environment, where the accounting system tracks the payment status of all invoices.

9.   **Issue positive pay file** (optional). If the company uses a positive pay system, compile information about the newly-printed checks into a file and send it to the bank. The bank then matches submitted checks against this file and rejects those not listed in the file.

Responsible party: Accounts payable staff

Control issues: The positive pay notification must encompass manual checks. Otherwise, a special check may be written outside of the normal check printing process, and then be rejected by the bank because no positive pay file was submitted for it.

The following exhibit shows a streamlined view of the check payment issuance procedure, not including the optional use of positive pay.

Check Payment Issuance Process Flow

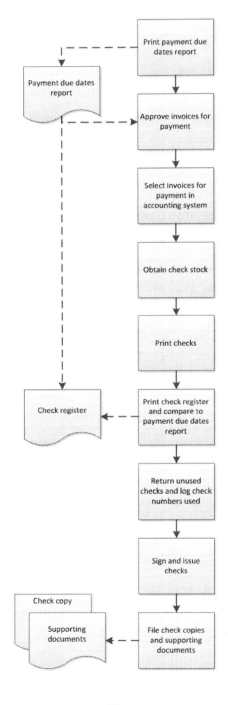

Summary

This chapter is quite large, and yet does not begin to encompass the amount of procedural groundwork that the accountant should engage in before attaining a fully-functioning system of procedures. There are many additional procedures to be considered besides the core ones noted in this chapter, such as how to treat petty cash transactions, how to calculate the cost of ending inventory, and the many steps involved in the payroll process. Also, some of the procedures in this chapter were presented under the assumption that the accountant is operating a largely manual accounting system, which may not be the case. For a more comprehensive treatment of accounting-related procedures, as well as procedures designed for computerized accounting systems, see the author's *Accounting Procedures Guidebook*, which is available at www.accountingtools.com.

A final comment about procedures: it is easy to go too far and create an excessively large number of detailed procedures. If many procedures are created, the accountant will find that too much time is being spent on maintaining the related paperwork, and in setting up controls to enforce compliance with the procedures. Instead, consider maintaining a reduced set of the most critical procedures. This topic is addressed in the podcast episode noted at the beginning of this chapter.

Chapter 5
Accounting for Receivables

Introduction

Receivables are a key part of the accounting for any business that grants credit to its customers. Receivables can take many forms, including trade receivables, loans, notes, and other types of financial instruments. Receivables may also be transferred between parties, such as when a business has a put option that requires a third party to purchase its receivables. Debts can also be sold individually or in groups by one party to another. In this chapter, we discuss the accounting for these and other arrangements, as well as the extensive disclosure requirements associated with certain types of receivables.

Accounting for Billings

When you sell services to a customer, you normally create an invoice in the billing module of the accounting software, which automatically creates an entry to credit the revenue account and debit the accounts receivable account. When the customer later pays the invoice, you debit the cash account and credit the accounts receivable account. For example, if a business invoices a customer for $10,000 in services, the entry generated by the billing module would be:

	Debit	Credit
Accounts receivable	10,000	
Revenue - services		10,000

If you were to sell goods to a customer on credit, then not only would you record the sale and related account receivable, but you would also record the reduction in inventory that was sold to the customer, which then appears in the cost of goods sold expense. For example, if a business were to conclude a sale transaction for $15,000 in which it sold merchandise having an inventory cost of $12,000, the entry would be:

	Debit	Credit
Accounts receivable	15,000	
Revenue - products		15,000
Cost of goods sold	12,000	
Inventory		12,000

There is an issue with the timing of the preceding sale transaction. If the sale is made under *FOB shipping point* terms (where the buyer takes delivery of goods being shipped to it by a supplier once the goods leave the supplier's shipping dock), the seller is supposed to record both the sale transaction and related charge to the cost of goods sold at the time when the shipment leaves its shipping dock. From that point onward, the delivery is technically the responsibility of either a third-party shipper or the buyer.

If a sale is made under *FOB destination* terms (where the buyer takes delivery of goods being shipped to it by a supplier once the goods arrive at the buyer's receiving dock), then the seller is supposed to record these transactions when the shipment arrives at the customer; this is because the delivery is still the responsibility of the seller until it reaches the customer's location.

From a practical perspective, most companies record their sale transactions as though the delivery terms were FOB shipping point, because it is easiest to initiate a sale transaction in the accounting system as soon as the goods are shipped.

If you offer customers a discount when they pay early, and they take advantage of the offer, they will pay an amount less than the invoice total. Eliminate this residual balance by charging it to the sales discounts account, which can be treated as either a reduction of sales or an expense. For example, if a customer takes advantage of a $100 early payment discount on a $2,000 invoice, the following entry would be used to record the payment:

	Debit	Credit
Cash	1,900	
Sales discounts	100	
Accounts receivable		2,000

Accounting for Sales Taxes

You are required to charge customers a sales tax on certain types of sales transactions if you have nexus in the territory of the government entity that charges the sales tax. Nexus is the concept that you are doing business in an area if you have a place of business there, use your own vehicles to transport goods to customers there, or (in some cases) have employees situated or living there.

If the company does not have nexus where a customer is located, then the company does not have to charge a sales tax to the customer; instead, the customer is supposed to self-report a use tax to its local government. Use tax is the same as sales tax, except that the party remitting the tax to the applicable government entity is the buyer of taxable goods or services, rather than the seller.

All accounting software includes a billing feature that allows you to include the sales tax at the bottom of each invoice, after the subtotal of line items billed. When you charge customers the sales tax, you eventually collect it and then remit it to the state government, which in turn pays it out to the various local governments.

When a customer is billed for sales taxes, the journal entry is a debit to the accounts receivable account for the entire amount of the invoice, a credit to the revenue account for that portion of the invoice attributable to goods or services billed, and a credit to the sales tax liability account for the amount of sales taxes billed.

At the end of the month (or longer, depending on your remittance arrangement), you fill out a sales tax remittance form that itemizes sales and sales taxes, and send the applicable government the amount of the sales tax recorded in the sales tax liability account. This remittance may take place before the customer has paid the sales tax to the company.

What if the customer does not pay the sales tax portion of the invoice? In that case, issue a credit memo that reverses the amount of the sales tax liability and eliminates the unpaid taxes from the accounts receivable account. It is quite likely that you will have already remitted this sales tax to the government, so the customer's non-payment becomes a reduction in your next sales tax remittance to the government.

EXAMPLE

Milagro Corporation issues an invoice to The Cupertino Beanery for $1,000 of goods delivered, on which there is a seven percent sales tax. The entry is:

	Debit	Credit
Accounts receivable	1,070	
Revenue		1,000
Sales tax liability		70

Following the end of the month, Milagro remits the sales taxes withheld to the state government. The entry is:

	Debit	Credit
Sales tax liability	70	
Cash		70

Later in the following month, the customer pays the full amount of the invoice. The entry is:

	Debit	Credit
Cash	1,070	
Accounts receivable		1,070

When a company bills its customers for sales taxes, those taxes are not an expense to the company; they are an expense only to customers. From the company's perspective, these sales tax billings are liabilities to the local government until remitted.

Tip: Consider setting up a separate sales tax liability account for each government entity. If the company has nexus in multiple jurisdictions, this makes it much easier to reconcile the accounts, and is essentially mandatory if there is a sales tax audit.

The Allowance for Doubtful Accounts

The allowance for doubtful accounts is a reduction of the total amount of accounts receivable appearing on a company's balance sheet. It is listed as a deduction immediately below the accounts receivable line item. This allowance reflects your best estimate of the amount of accounts receivable that the company will never be paid by its customers.

There are several possible ways to estimate the allowance for doubtful accounts, which are:

- *Risk classification.* Assign a risk score to each customer, and assume a higher risk of default for those having a higher risk score. Here are the steps to follow to create a risk-based bad debt forecast:
  a. Periodically obtain new risk scores for all current customers, excluding those with minimal sales.
  b. Load the scores for each customer into an open field in the customer master file.
  c. Print a custom report that sorts current customers in declining order by risk score.
  d. Divide the sorted list into fourths (low risk through high risk), and determine the bad debt percentage for the previous year for each category. The result is shown in the following sample report:

Sample Bad Debt Analysis Based on Customer Risk

Risk Category	Current Receivable Balance	Historical Bad Debt Percentage	Estimated Bad Debt by Risk Category
Low risk	$1,100,000	0.8%	$8,800
Medium low	606,000	1.6%	9,696
Medium high	384,000	3.9%	14,976
High risk	110,000	7.1%	7,810
Totals	$2,200,000		$41,282

The risk classification approach can be expensive to update, since you may need to buy credit risk reports for all major customers. To avoid this expense, consider using the next approach, which can be developed entirely with internally-available information.

- *Time bucket percentage.* If a certain percentage of accounts receivable became bad debts in the past, then expect the same percentage in the future. This method works best for large numbers of small account balances. Here are the steps to follow to create a bad debt expense based on historical percentages:
  a. Print the accounts receivable aging report.
  b. Assign the historical bad debt percentage applicable to each 30-day time bucket.

c. Multiply the ending receivable balances in each 30-day time bucket by the applicable bad debt percentage to arrive at the total amount of the allowance for doubtful accounts. The result is shown in the following sample report:

Sample Bad Debt Analysis Based on Time Buckets

	0-30 Days	31-60 Days	61-90 Days	90+ Days
Ending balance	$1,500,000	$562,000	$108,000	$30,000
Estimated bad debt percentage	1.0%	2.5%	6.2%	30.0%
Estimated bad debt amount	$15,000	$14,050	$6,696	$9,000

At a less precise level, you can also calculate the allowance based on a simple percentage of the entire amount of outstanding accounts receivable, but that can be notably imprecise, especially if the proportion of older receivables to total receivables varies constantly.

- *80/20 analysis.* Review the largest accounts receivable that make up 80% of the total receivable balance, and estimate which specific customers are most likely to default. Then use the preceding historical percentage method for the remaining smaller accounts. This method works best if there are a small number of large account balances.

You can also evaluate the reasonableness of an allowance for doubtful accounts by comparing it to the total amount of seriously overdue accounts receivable, which are presumably not going to be collected. If the allowance is less than the amount of these overdue receivables, the allowance is probably insufficient.

Review the balance in the allowance for doubtful accounts as part of the month-end closing process, to ensure that the balance is reasonable in comparison to the latest bad debt forecast. For companies with minimal bad debt activity, a quarterly update may be sufficient.

If the company is using the accrual basis of accounting, you should record an allowance for doubtful accounts, since it provides an estimate of future bad debts that improves the accuracy of the company's financial statements. Also, by recording the allowance at the same time that you record a sale, the company is properly matching the projected bad debt expense against the related sale in the same period, which provides an accurate view of the true profitability of a sale.

EXAMPLE

Milagro Corporation records $2,000,000 of sales to several hundred customers, and projects (based on historical experience) that it will incur 1% of this amount as bad debts, though it does not know exactly which customers will default. The controller records the 1% of projected bad debts as a $20,000 debit to the Bad Debt Expense account and a $20,000 credit to the Allowance for Doubtful Accounts. The bad debt expense is charged to expense right away, and the allowance for doubtful accounts becomes a reserve account that offsets the account receivable of $2,000,000 (for a net receivable outstanding of $1,980,000). The entry is:

	Debit	Credit
Bad debt expense	20,000	
Allowance for doubtful accounts		20,000

Later, several customers default on payments totaling $4,000. Accordingly, the controller credits the accounts receivable account by $4,000 to reduce the amount of outstanding accounts receivable, and debits the allowance for doubtful accounts by the same amount. This entry reduces the balance in the allowance account to $16,000. The entry does not impact earnings in the current period. The entry is:

	Debit	Credit
Allowance for doubtful accounts	4,000	
Accounts receivable		4,000

A few months later, a collection agency succeeds in collecting $1,500 of the funds that the controller had already written off. He can now reverse part of the previous entry, thereby increasing the balance in the allowance account. The entry is:

	Debit	Credit
Accounts receivable	1,500	
Allowance for doubtful accounts		1,500

Finally, the controller records the receipt of cash from the collection agency for the $1,500 receivable, net of a collection fee of $500. The entry is:

	Debit	Credit
Cash	1,000	
Collection expense	500	
Accounts receivable		1,500

The only impact that the allowance for doubtful accounts has on the income statement is the initial charge to bad debt expense when the allowance is initially funded. Any subsequent write-offs of accounts receivable against the allowance for doubtful accounts only impact the balance sheet.

Notes Receivable

One of the key aspects of notes receivable is how to recognize them in the accounting records. The following points describe the major issues to consider when initially accounting for a receivable of this type:

- *Notes acquired for cash.* When you receive a note in exchange for cash, record the note at the amount of the cash paid.
- *Notes acquired for noncash consideration.* When you receive a note in exchange for any type of consideration other than cash, the present value of

the note is the fair value of the consideration paid. Alternatively, if similar notes are exchanged in an open market, market prices can provide evidence of the present value of the note. If neither option is available and the interest rate on the note does not match the market rate, use an imputed interest rate to arrive at the discounted present value of the note (subsequent changes in prevailing interest rates can be ignored).

Subsequent to the initial recordation of a note receivable, the following issues may arise that require accounting treatment:

- *Loan impairment.* A loan is considered to be impaired when it is probable that not all of the related principal and interest payments will be collected.
- *Impairment documentation.* Any allowance for loan impairments should be fully documented with the appropriate analysis, and updated consistently from period to period.
- *Impairment allowance.* An impairment allowance can be based on the examination of individual receivables, or groups of similar types of receivables. The creditor can use any impairment measurement method that is practical for the creditor's circumstances. When loans are aggregated for analysis purposes, use historical statistics to derive the estimated amount of impairment. The amount of impairment to recognize should be based on the present value of expected future cash flows, though a loan's market price or the fair value of the related collateral can also be used.
- *Impairment accounting.* The offset to the impairment allowance should be the bad debt expense account. Once actual credit losses are identified, subtract them from the impairment allowance, along with the related loan balance. If loans are subsequently recovered, the previous charge-off transaction should be reversed.

> **Tip:** It is possible that there is no need to establish a reserve for an impaired loan if the value of the related collateral is at least as much as the recorded value of the loan.

As a result of impairment accounting, it is possible that the recorded investment in a loan judged to be impaired may be less than its present value, because the creditor has elected to charge off part of the loan.

In the following bullet points, we note several more specialized recognition practices for several types of receivables:

- *Delinquency fees.* Recognize delinquency fees when the fees are chargeable, as long as the collectability of the fees is reasonably assured.
- *Factoring arrangements.* When receivables are transferred to a factor, the factor should account for them as a purchase of receivables.
- *Interest income on receivables.* It may be necessary to impute interest on receivables, even if there is no stated interest rate associated with those receivables.

- *Loan syndications.* When there are several lenders involved in a loan syndication, each lender separately accounts for the sums owed to it by the borrower. In cases where the lead lender is collecting repayments from the borrower, the lead lender's role is that of a loan servicer, so it would be inappropriate for the lead lender to recognize the aggregate loan as an asset.
- *Loans not previously held for sale.* When the decision is made to sell loans that had not previously been classified as held for sale, report these loans at the lower of cost or fair value. If the loan cost exceeds value at the time of the transfer to the held for sale classification, record the difference in a valuation allowance.
- *Loans receivable held to maturity.* If management intends to hold loans receivable until their maturity, report these loans at their outstanding principal, adjusted for charge-offs, allowances for loan losses, deferred costs, and unamortized premiums or discounts.
- *Nonmortgage loans held for sale.* Report nonmortgage loans that are being held for sale at the lower of their cost or fair value.
- *Prepayment fees.* Do not recognize prepayment penalties until the related loans or receivables are prepaid.
- *Purchase of credit card portfolio.* If a portfolio is purchased for an amount greater than the sum of receivables due, allocate the premium between the loans acquired and the cardholder relationships acquired (which is an intangible asset). Amortize this premium over the life of the loans.
- *Rebates on accrued interest income.* There is no impact on the accrual of interest income on installment loans or trade receivables when there is a prospect of issuing rebates. Any impact is recognized in income when the loans or receivables are paid or renewed.
- *Standby commitment to purchase loan.* When there is a standby commitment to purchase a loan where the settlement date is not within a reasonable period, or the business cannot accept delivery without selling assets, account for the commitment as a written put option, where the fee received is a liability (value the liability at the greater of the initial fee or the fair value of the put option). Otherwise, it is considered part of the normal production of loans, where the fee received is recorded as an offset to loans purchased.

Acquisition, Development, and Construction Arrangements

The guidance in this section only applies to situations where a lender participates in the expected residual profits or cash flows of a property transaction for which the lender is providing funding, either through profit sharing or above-market interest rates or fees. The following characteristics suggest the presence of such an arrangement where the lender takes on the role of an investor:

- *Delinquency.* The debt is structured to avoid foreclosure by not requiring payments until project completion.
- *Fees.* The lender pays for the commitment or origination fees by including them in the loan.

- *Funding.* The lender provides substantially all of the required funding.
- *Interest.* The lender rolls substantially all of the interest and fees during the loan term back into the loan balance.
- *Recourse.* The lender only has recourse to the acquisition, development, and construction project.
- *Repayment.* The lender will only be repaid if the property is sold, refinanced, or begins to generate enough cash flow to service the loan.

Conversely, there are situations where the lender has not taken on the role of an investor, and is merely financing property. The following characteristics suggest the presence of a simple lending arrangement:

- *Borrower investment.* The borrower has a substantial equity investment in the project that is not funded by the lender. The value of the borrower's efforts (sweat equity) in the property development is not to be considered when evaluating the borrower's investment.
- *Collateral.* The lender has recourse to significant other assets of the borrower besides the project, and which are not also pledged as collateral elsewhere, or the lender has an irrevocable letter of credit from a third party for a substantial amount of the loan.
- *Net cash flow.* There are sufficient noncancelable sale or lease contracts from third parties to provide the cash flow needed to service the debt.
- *Profit participation.* The profit participation of the lender is less than half of the expected residual profit.
- *Take-out commitment.* The lender has obtained a take-out commitment for the full amount of its lending arrangement from a third party.

The existence of a personal guarantee is not usually considered sufficient for classifying a lending arrangement as not being an investment. However, this may be the case if the guarantee covers a large part of the loan, the payment ability of the guarantor can be reliably measured (as represented by assets placed in escrow, an irrevocable letter of credit, or financial results), enforcing the guarantee is possible, and there is a demonstrated intent to enforce the guarantee.

When judging the financial statements of a guarantor, place particular emphasis on the presence of sufficient liquidity to fulfill the guarantee, and whether the guarantor has other contingent liabilities.

Also, the initial determination of investment or loan status for the lender may change over time, if the underlying terms of an arrangement are altered. Consequently, reassess the accounting treatment whenever loan terms are altered. The following situations that alter a lending scenario can impact how a lending arrangement is classified:

- *Risk reduction.* If the lender's risk diminishes significantly, an initial classification as an investment or joint venture might be reclassified as a loan.

- *Risk increase.* If the lender's risk increases (such as by releasing collateral) or the lender assumes a greater percentage of expected profits, an initial classification as a loan might be reclassified as an investment.

The initial accounting by a lender in an acquisition, development, and construction project is to be accounted for in one of two ways:

- *As an investment.* If the lender expects to receive more than 50% of the expected residual profit from a project, then any income or loss from the arrangement is to be accounted for by the lender as a real estate investment.
- *As a loan.* If the lender expects to receive 50% or less of the expected residual profit from a project and there is a qualifying personal guarantee (as just described), then the arrangement is to be accounted for as a loan. If the guarantee is not present, then account for the arrangement as a real estate joint venture.

If a lender were to subsequently sell its share of any expected residual profits, there are two ways to account for the sale:

- *As an investment.* If the arrangement has been accounted for as an investment, the lender can account for the sale as a gain.
- *As a loan.* If the arrangement has been accounted for as a loan, the lender should recognize the proceeds from the sale as additional interest over the remaining term of the loan.

Nonrefundable Fees and Other Costs

This topic relates to the nonrefundable fees, origination costs, and acquisition costs relating to lending activities. The fees addressed by this topic have many names, including points, placement fees, commitment fees, application fees, and annual credit card fees; to save space, we will refer to them all as loan origination fees.

The accounting for nonrefundable fees and other costs and revenues is as follows:

- *Loan origination fees.* Defer the recognition of all loan origination fees, and recognize them over the life of the loan as interest income or expense. These costs can include labor, travel costs, phone calls, and mileage reimbursement. Examples of activities considered to relate to loan origination are loan counseling, application processing and credit analysis, asset appraisals, loan approval processing, and loan closing.
- *Loan origination labor.* The direct costs of loan origination can be deferred, which includes the labor associated with the successful production of loans. The cost of bonuses may be deferred if they directly relate to the successful production of loans.
- *Other lending-related costs.* Charge all other lending-related costs to expense as incurred. This includes advertising and solicitations, loan servicing, unsuccessful loan origination activities, idle time, service bureau fees, and administrative costs.

- *Commitment fees.* If the lender receives a commitment fee to originate or purchase a loan, defer recognition of the fee, and offset against it the related loan origination costs. The following scenarios may apply:
  - *Net cost, no exercise.* If the result is a net cost and the likelihood of the commitment being exercised is remote, charge the net amount to expense at once.
  - *Net cost, exercised.* If the result is a net cost and the commitment is likely to be exercised, recognize it over the life of the loan as a reduction in loan yield.
  - *Net revenue, no exercise.* If the result is net revenue and the likelihood of the commitment being exercised is remote, amortize recognition of the net amount on a straight-line basis over the period covered by the commitment as service fee income. If some amount remains unamortized when the commitment expires, recognize it in income as of the expiration date.
  - *Net revenue, exercised.* If the result is net revenue and the commitment is likely to be exercised, recognize it over the life of the loan as an increase in loan yield.
- *Credit card fees.* Fees charged to the holders of credit cards should be deferred, and recognized on a straight-line basis over the period that the card fee entitles the card user to use the card. If there are any credit card origination costs, net them against credit card fees, which are then amortized as just noted. If the business pays a fee to acquire credit card accounts, net this payment against any credit card fees.
- *Lending fees unrelated to loans.* A lender may charge a fee for lending transactions apart from loan originations. Examples of such transactions are for the extension of the maturity date on a loan, or switching a variable-rate loan to a fixed-rate loan. Account for these fees as a yield adjustment over the remaining life of the loan with which the fee is associated.
- *Loan syndication fees.* The entity that constructs a loan syndication should recognize the loan syndication fees earned by it when the syndication is complete. However, if the syndicator retains a portion of the loan, it should defer a portion of the fees and recognize that portion over the term of the retained loan. The amount deferred should result in a loan yield that is not less than the average yield on the loans issued by the other participants in the syndication.
- *Loan purchase.* Defer the cost of fees paid to the seller of a loan or group of loans, and account for it as a yield adjustment over the life of the loan; if prepayments occur or some of the purchased loans are then sold, recognize a proportional amount of the deferred fees in income. Charge all other costs to expense that are incurred in connection with purchased loans or commitments to purchase such loans; these costs are not origination fees, since the loan has already been originated by the seller of the loan.
- *Loan refinancing or restructuring.* Account for a loan refinancing or restructuring as a new loan if the terms are at least as favorable for the lend-

er as the terms associated with comparable loans where there is no refinancing or restructuring (such as when the effective yield on the new loan is similar to the same yield on comparable loans). If there are any unamortized fees or costs associated with the original loan, recognize them within interest income at this time. If the restructuring or refinancing does not meet these conditions or the modifications are minor, carry forward any unamortized fees or costs to the new loan.

- *Revolving line of credit.* When there is a revolving line of credit, recognize the associated net fees or costs in income on a straight-line basis over the period of the line of credit. If the borrower cannot reborrow from the line of credit upon paying off the line, recognize all remaining net fees and costs as of the payment date. If the line of credit includes a payment schedule, account for the remaining net fees and costs as a yield adjustment over the remaining life of the loan.

EXAMPLE

Currency Bank enters into a one-year line of credit arrangement with a borrower, where the borrower can elect to convert the line of credit into a three-year term loan. Currency amortizes the net fees and costs associated with the line of credit over the combined period of the line of credit and term loan. The borrower elects to let the line of credit expire and pays off the remaining balance, without converting to a term loan, so Currency then recognizes the remaining unamortized net fees and costs as of the expiration date.

- *Third party fees.* Fees paid to a third party in regard to portfolio management, investment consultation, or loan origination activities are charged to expense as incurred.

Any loan origination costs related to a loan in process can be deferred until such time as the loan is closed or declared unsuccessful, at which point it is accounted for based on the loan outcome.

If there is a period during which the interest income on a loan is not being recognized, due to concerns about the ability of the borrower to pay, do not amortize any deferred net fees or costs during that period.

Tip: It may be more efficient to defer loan origination fees based on a standard costing system, rather than compiling actual loan origination costs during every accounting period.

Whenever GAAP requires that fees or costs be amortized using the effective interest method, the intent is to use an interest rate that creates an interest differential from the stated interest rate on a loan that recognizes the fees or costs over the life of the loan. The following example illustrates the concept.

EXAMPLE

Currency Bank purchases a loan that had been issued by another bank, at a stated principal amount of $100,000, which the debtor will repay in three years, with three annual interest payments of $5,000 and a balloon payment of $100,000 upon the maturity date of the loan.

Currency acquired the loan for $90,000, which is a discount of $10,000 from the principal amount of the loan. Based on this information, Currency calculates an effective interest rate of 8.95%, which is shown in the following amortization table:

Year	(A) Beginning Amortized Cost	(B) Interest and Principal Payments	(C) Interest Income (A × 8.95%)	(D) Debt Discount Amortization (C – B)	Ending Amortized Cost (A + D)
1	90,000	5,000	8,055	3,055	93,055
2	93,055	5,000	8,328	3,328	96,383
3	96,383	105,000	8,617	3,617	100,000

In a situation where the lender can demand payment of a loan at any time, recognize any remaining net fees or costs as an adjustment of yield on a straight-line basis under the remaining period as agreed to by the lender and borrower, or (if there is no agreement), the lender's estimate of this period. Review the remaining duration at regular intervals, and alter the adjustment of yield if the estimated duration varies.

If the lender has a number of similar loans, considers prepayments of those loans to be probable, and can estimate the timing and amounts of prepayments, it can incorporate prepayment information into its effective yield calculations. If so, and there turns out to be a difference between actual and anticipated prepayments, recalculate the effective yield to take into account the actual amount of prepayments, and adjust the net investment in loans accordingly. Prepayment tracking can be used for a group of loans, or for individual loans; whichever approach is used must be maintained through the life of the loans.

Loans and Debt Securities Acquired with Deteriorated Credit Quality

There are cases where a company will acquire loans that have already displayed evidence of deterioration in their credit quality prior to being acquired. The acquirer presumably pays less for this batch of loans, in expectation of being unable to collect all of the payments associated with the loans. The accounting for loans and debt securities acquired with deteriorated credit quality is as follows:

- *Interest income.* The loan acquirer should recognize the excess of cash flows expected from acquired loans at the acquisition date from the initial investment as interest income over the life of the loans, which is called *accretable yield*; it will result in a higher effective interest rate. Do not recognize interest income if the resulting net loan investment increases above the loan payoff amount. Subsequently, if the expected cash flows increase further, recalculate the accretable yield for the remaining life of the loan, which is a change in estimate. Alternatively, if the loan acquirer is not accounting for the loan as a debt security and expected cash flows increase further, you should first reduce any remaining valuation allowance and then recalculate the accretable yield for any remaining excess cash flows.

- *Income measurement.* Continue to estimate expected cash flows over the life of each loan or group of loans. If the fair value falls below its amortized cost and the decline is other than temporary, treat the loan as an impaired security.

- *Valuation allowances.* Any valuation allowance created for purchased loans should be based on only those losses incurred *after* acquisition. This is the difference between the present value of cash flows expected at the acquisition date and expectations at later dates of what will actually be received.

- *Pool of multiple loans.* Only remove a loan from a pool of loans if the loan is written off, paid off, foreclosed, or sold. Do not remove a loan from a pool of loans if the loan is refinanced.

- *Loans acquired for collateral ownership.* If the loan acquirer purchases loans with the intent of using the acquired collateral in its own operations or improving the collateral for resale, do not accrue any income related to the loans.

- *Variable rate loans.* If the interest rate upon which loan payments are calculated changes over time, then calculate the contractually required payments on the interest rate as the rate changes over the life of the loan. The result is a change in yield over time. Do not project future changes in the interest rate.

EXAMPLE

Currency Bank acquires a loan with a principal balance of $10,000,000 and accrued delinquent interest of $600,000. Currency acquires the loan at a discount, due to concerns that the credit quality of the debtor has declined since the origination of the loan. Currency Bank pays $7,500,000 for the loan on December 31, 20X1. The contractual interest rate is 7% per year. In addition to the delinquent interest, annual payments of $2,300,000 are due in each of the five remaining years to maturity. Currency Bank's analysis staff concludes that it is probable that the bank will not collect the full amounts due, but rather $1,928,193 per year for five years. Based on this information, Currency Bank initially records the acquired loan at a net carrying amount of $7,500,000, and constructs the following table to document the remaining cash flows and interest income:

Year	(A) Beginning Carrying Amount	(B) Cash Flows Expected to be Collected	(C) Interest Income*	(B – C) Reduction of Carrying Amount	(A – D) Ending Carrying Amount
20X2	$7,500,000	$1,928,193	$675,000	$1,253,193	$6,246,807
20X3	6,246,807	1,928,193	562,213	1,365,980	4,880,827
20X4	4,880,827	1,928,193	439,274	1,488,919	3,391,908
20X5	3,391,908	1,928,123	305,272	1,622,921	1,768,987
20X6	1,768,987	1,928,123	159,209	1,768,984	3
		$9,640,965	$2,140,968	$7,499,997	

Calculation of nonaccretable difference:

Contractually required payments receivable (including delinquent interest)	$12,100,000
Less: Cash flows expected to be collected	-9,640,965
= Nonaccretable difference	$2,459,035

Initial calculation of accretable yield:

Cash flows expected to be collected	$9,640,965
Less: Initial investment	-7,500,000
= Accretable yield	$2,140,965

* Note: the effective interest rate for all of the years in this example is 9%, which is the rate that equates all cash flows expected to be collected with the purchase price of the loan.

Troubled Debt Restructurings by Creditors

When a creditor grants a concession under the terms of a debt agreement or receivable because of the financial difficulties of a debtor, the debt may be classified as a troubled debt restructuring. Examples of troubled debt restructurings are payment in the equity of the debtor, reducing the stated interest rate, and reducing the face amount of the debt. In essence, a concession has been granted when the creditor no longer expects to collect all amounts due, and any additional guarantees or collateral received do not offset the amount of the expected loss. When a restructuring results in an insignificant payment delay, this is not considered a concession.

The accounting for troubled debt restructurings is as follows:

- *Restructuring.* Account for a restructured loan as an asset impairment. When calculating the present value of the cash flows expected from a restructured loan, base the effective interest rate used for discounting present values on the original contractual rate, not the rate stated in the restructuring agreement.
- *Receipt of assets.* If the debtor transfers assets to the creditor as partial satisfaction of a debt, reduce the recorded amount of the receivable by the

fair value of the assets received. If the assets received are in full satisfaction of the debt, record a loss in the amount of the remaining balance of the loan.

- *Foreclosure.* When the creditor forecloses on a loan and takes possession of the debtor's assets, it should record the possessed property at the lower of the net amount of the receivable or the fair value of the property.
- *Legal fees.* When the creditor incurs legal fees as part of a troubled debt restructuring, charge them to expense as incurred.

Receivables Presentation

There are a number of requirements regarding the proper presentation of receivables information in the financial statements. Given the number of these requirements, we are stating them separately from the disclosures in the following section, which are usually included in the notes that accompany the financial statements. The presentation requirements are:

- *Acquisition, development, and construction arrangements.* Separately report arrangements in the balance sheet that are classified as investments from those that are classified as loans.
- *Allowances.* Always pair asset valuation allowances with the assets to which they relate on the balance sheet.
- *Bad debt expense.* Report any changes in the observable market price or the fair value of collateral for an impaired loan as a change in bad debt expense.
- *Commitment fees.* Classify loan commitment fees as deferred income in the balance sheet. Report amortized commitment fees as service income in the income statement.
- *Foreclosed or repossessed assets.* It is permissible to either separately state foreclosed or repossessed assets on the balance sheet, or include them in other asset classifications and then disclose them in the accompanying notes. If there is an intent to use repossessed assets in the business, do not classify them separately as foreclosed or repossessed assets.
- *Loan fees.* Include the unamortized balance of loan fees and costs in the balance sheet as part of the loan balances with which these items are paired.
- *Loans or trade receivables.* Present loans or trade receivables in the balance sheet in aggregate. If any of these receivables are classified as held for sale, aggregate them into a separate line item. If there are major categories of loans or trade receivables, separate presentation is encouraged.
- *Receivables classified as current assets.* Trade receivables are classified within the current assets section of the balance sheet, as long as they are expected to be realized in cash during the operating cycle of the business or one year.
- *Receivables from officers, employees, or affiliates.* Separately state all notes or accounts receivable from officers, employees, or affiliates. Do not aggregate them with other notes receivable or accounts receivable.

- *Unearned discounts.* Report unearned discounts, finance charges, and interest stated on receivables as a deduction from the paired receivables line item.
- *Yield adjustments.* Include all interest yield adjustments for loan-related fees and costs as part of interest income.

Receivables Disclosures

There are quite a number of disclosures related to receivables, but many relate to very specialized topics that may not relate to a company's line of business. Consequently, be mindful of which of the following disclosure requirements actually apply to your business, and ignore the rest. The disclosures are:

- *Policies.* State the following policies related to receivables, if applicable:
  - The basis for accounting for loans, lease financings, and trade receivables
  - The policy for charging off uncollectible trade receivables that have a maturity of less than one year, and which arose from the sale of goods or services
  - The policy for charging off financing receivables that cannot be collected
  - The policy for deciding upon past due or delinquency status
  - The policy for discontinuing the accrual of interest on receivables, and the policy for resuming the accrual of interest
  - The policy for recognizing interest income on impaired loans, as well as how cash receipts are recorded
  - The policy for recording payments received against nonaccrual loans and trade receivables
  - The policy for recognizing interest income on loan and trade receivables, related fees and costs, and for amortizing net deferred fees and costs
  - The policy for incorporating prepayments into the interest method for determining loan yield, as well as related assumptions
  - The policy for accounting for credit card fees and costs, both for originated and purchased credit cards
- *Allowance for credit losses related to loans.* Disclose the following information by portfolio segment, relating to the allowance for credit losses related to loans:
  - The methodology used to estimate the allowance for credit losses, including a discussion of the historical losses and existing economic conditions that influenced management's judgment
  - The risk characteristics of each portfolio
  - Any changes in accounting policies from the prior period, the rationale for the change, and the effect of these changes on the current period provision

- o The activity in the allowance for credit losses, including provisions, write-downs, and recoveries during the period
- o The amount paid for significant purchases of financing receivables, by reporting period
- o The amount of significant sales of financing receivables or reclassifications into the held for sale category, by reporting period
- o A breakdown of the ending balance in the allowance for credit losses, by impairment method
- o Match the ending investment in financing receivables to the allowance for credit losses, subdivided by impairment methodology used

- *Allowances.* Disclose the amount of all allowances related to credit losses, as well as unearned income and unamortized premiums and discounts. Also disclose the methodology used to estimate the allowance for losses on the various types of receivables; this may include a discussion of the risk elements relevant to certain categories of financial instruments.

- *Asset basis.* Describe the method used to determine the lower of cost or fair value for any nonmortgage loans held for sale.

- *Credit card fees and costs.* Disclose the net amount of credit card fees and costs capitalized, and the amortization period for these items.

- *Credit quality information.* Provide sufficient information for readers to understand how the company monitors the credit quality of its financing receivables, and the risks arising from the credit quality of those receivables. This information should include the credit quality indicator for each class of receivables, as well as the investment in these receivables by credit quality indicator, and the date range when the information was updated for each credit quality indicator.

- *Debt securities.* State the outstanding balance of debt securities at the beginning and end of the reporting period, and a reconciliation of accretable yield during the period.

- *Financing receivables.* Separately disclose the investment in financing receivables for those receivables on nonaccrual status, and for those receivables that are past due by 90 days or more and still accruing.

- *Impaired loans.* Disclose the accounting for and amount of impaired loans for each class of financing receivable, as well as the amount of related allowances. Also note the amount of the recorded investment for which there is no related allowance for credit losses. Further, disclose the average investment in impaired loans during each presented period, the related amount of interest income recognized, and the related amount of interest income recognized under the cash basis of accounting (if practicable to do so).

- *Interest income.* Describe the method for recognizing interest income on loans and trade receivables, as well as related fees and costs, and how net deferred fees are amortized.

- *Internal risk ratings.* If the business uses internal risk ratings regarding credit quality, discuss how the ratings relate to the likelihood of loss.

- *Loan fees and costs*. Report unamortized net loan fees and costs within the relevant loan categories on the balance sheet.
- *Loans acquired*. Disclose the contractually required payments receivable, expected cash flows, and fair value (at the acquisition date) of loans acquired during the period.
- *Loans not accounted for as debt securities*. If there are any loans not accounted for as debt securities, disclose the impairment losses, any reductions in the associated valuation allowance, and the amount of the allowance for uncollectible accounts at the beginning and end of the period.
- *Non-recovery situations*. Clarify the classification and method of accounting for assets that may be settled such that the holder may not recover its investment.
- *Off-balance-sheet exposures*. State the procedures used to determine the company's off-balance-sheet credit exposures (such as for standby letters of credit and guarantees) and the charges related to those exposures, including a description of risks and those factors influencing management's judgment.
- *Prepayments*. Describe how prepayments are factored into the calculation of loan-related contractual and expected cash flows.
- *Receivables analysis*. Disclose an analysis of the age of past due financing receivables as of the end of the reporting period.
- *Troubled debt restructurings*. Disclose how each class of financing receivable was modified as part of troubled debt restructurings, and the financial effects of those modifications. Also note for each portfolio segment how these modifications were incorporated into the calculation of the allowance for credit losses. Further, disclose the amount of any commitments to lend additional funds to debtors that currently owe receivables to the creditor that have been modified through troubled debt restructurings.

EXAMPLE

Currency Bank provides the following disclosure about its credit quality indicators:

Currency Bank
Credit Quality Indicators
As of December 31, 20X5 and 20X4

Corporate Credit Exposure
Credit Risk Profile by Creditworthiness Category

(000s)	Commercial		Commercial Real Estate	
	20X5	20X4	20X5	20X4
AAA – A	$15,400	$14,200	$9,100	$8,900
BBB – B	3,900	3,600	2,300	2,200
CCC – C	1,000	900	600	500
D	200	200	100	100
Total	$20,500	$18,900	$12,100	$11,700

Consumer Credit Exposure
Credit Risk Profile by Internally Assigned Grade

(000s)	Residential (Prime)		Residential (Subprime)	
	20X5	20X4	20X5	20X4
Grade:				
Pass	$83,000	$74,000	$25,000	$20,000
Watch list	17,000	15,000	13,000	10,000
Substandard	9,000	8,000	7,000	5,000
Total	$109,000	$97,000	$45,000	$35,000

Consumer Credit Exposure
Credit Risk Profile Based on Payment Activity

(000s)	Finance Leases		Consumer Auto	
	20X5	20X4	20X5	20X4
Performing	$35,000	$24,000	$60,000	$52,000
Nonperforming	5,000	3,000	10,000	8,000
Total	$40,000	$27,000	$70,000	$60,000

EXAMPLE

Armenian Consumer Finance (ACF) extends loans to the Armenian immigrant community. ACF provides the following disclosure about its impaired loans:

Armenian Consumer Finance
Impaired Loans
For the Year Ended December 31, 20X5

(000s)	Recorded Investment	Unpaid Principal Balance	Related Allowance	Average Recorded Investment	Interest Income Recognized
With no related allowance recorded:					
Consumer – Credit cards	$110,000	$116,000	$0	$125,000	$19,000
Consumer – Auto	180,000	189,000	0	193,000	15,000
Consumer – Other	40,000	42,000	0	46,000	7,000
With an allowance recorded:					
Commercial – Real estate	190,000	205,000	18,000	180,000	14,000
Residential – Prime	261,000	263,000	2,000	270,000	22,000
Residential – Subprime	156,000	130,000	26,000	145,000	11,000
Total:					
Consumer	$330,000	$347,000	$0	$364,000	$41,000
Commercial	190,000	205,000	18,000	180,000	14,000
Residential	417,000	393,000	28,000	415,000	33,000

EXAMPLE

Currency Bank provides the following disclosure about its troubled debt restructurings:

Currency Bank
Debt Modifications
As of December 31, 20X2

	Number of Contracts	Pre-Modification Outstanding Recorded Investment (000s)	Post-Modification Outstanding Recorded Investment (000s)
Troubled debt restructurings:			
Consumer – Auto	140	$4,000	$3,200
Commercial – Real estate	15	71,000	53,000
Residential – Prime	180	38,000	30,000
Residential – Subprime	48	6,000	3,000

	Number of Contracts	Recorded Investment (000s)
Troubled debt restructurings that subsequently defaulted		
Consumer – Auto	28	$1,000
Commercial – Real estate	4	12,000
Residential – Prime	54	10,000
Residential – Subprime	32	2,000

EXAMPLE

Currency Bank provides the following disclosures concerning loans acquired with deteriorated credit quality:

> Currency Bank has acquired loans that it accounts for as debt securities, for which there was evidence of deterioration of credit quality prior to their acquisition. As of the acquisition date, it was probable that not all contractually required payments for these loans would be collected.

> The carrying amounts of these loans are included in the balance sheet at December 31. The outstanding balance and carrying amounts of these loans are as follows, where the outstanding balance represents amounts owed to the company:

(000s)	20X5	20X4
Held-to-maturity debt securities:		
Outstanding balance	$29,400	$30,900
Carrying amount, net	23,100	27,200
Available-for-sale securities:		
Outstanding balance	$37,700	$39,800
Carrying amount, net	31,500	33,300

(000s)	Held-to-Maturity Securities	Available-for-Sale Securities
Accretable yield:		
Balance at December 31, 20X3	$5,050	$6,130
Additions	520	730
Accretion	-910	-1,380
Balance at December 31, 20X4	4,660	5,480
Additions	790	1,340
Accretion	-870	-1,250
Balance at December 31, 20X5	$4,580	$5,570

Summary

The bulk of the material in this chapter was concerned with the accounting for loan-related activities, and so may not apply to many businesses that do not extend long-term credit to other parties. However, some of the information in this chapter is more generally applicable when accounting for debt securities purchased as an investment, and when dealing with trade receivables that must be restructured due to financial problems afflicting a business partner.

Chapter 6
Accounting for Investments

Introduction

The guidance in this chapter is almost entirely concerned with the proper classification of various kinds of investments, and how to initially and subsequently account for them. This includes the treatment of valuation impairment, as well as the use of the equity method under certain circumstances.

Overview of Investments – Debt and Equity Securities

When a business acquires debt or equity securities for investment purposes, it must be cognizant of how these investments are to be classified, since the classification drives the accounting treatment. In this section, we address not only investment classifications and the related accounting, but also how to deal with investment impairment, and several related issues.

Accounting for Investments

When a business acquires an investment, it must classify the investment into one of the following categories:

- *Trading securities.* This is a security acquired with the intent of selling it in the short-term for a profit.
- *Held-to-maturity securities.* This is a debt security acquired with the intent of holding it to maturity, and where the holder has the ability to do so. This determination should be based not only on intent, but also on a history of being able to do so. Do not classify convertible securities as held-to-maturity.
- *Available-for-sale securities.* This is an investment in a security that is not classified as a trading security or a held-to-maturity security.

Once these investments have been acquired, the subsequent accounting for them is as follows:

- *Trading securities.* Measure trading securities at their fair value on the balance sheet, and include all unrealized gains and losses on these holdings in earnings.
- *Held-to-maturity securities.* Measure all held-to-maturity debt securities at their amortized cost in the balance sheet. Thus, there is no adjustment to fair value.
- *Available-for-sale securities.* Measure available-for-sale securities at their fair value on the balance sheet, and include all unrealized gains and losses

on these holdings in other comprehensive income until realized (i.e., when the securities are sold). However, if these gains or losses are being offset with a fair value hedge, include the amounts in earnings.

EXAMPLE

Armadillo Industries buys $150,000 of equity securities that it classifies as available-for-sale. After six months pass, the quoted market price of these securities declines to $130,000. Armadillo records the decline in value with the following entry:

	Debit	Credit
Loss on available-for-sale securities	20,000	
(recorded in other comprehensive income)		
Investments – Available-for-sale		20,000

Three months later, the securities have regained $6,000 of value, which results in the following entry:

	Debit	Credit
Investments – Available-for-sale	6,000	
Gain on available-for-sale securities		6,000
(recorded in other comprehensive income)		

GAAP mandates that you review the appropriateness of how each investment is classified, and to then alter the classification (and related accounting) as necessary. Whenever there is a transfer between classifications, the investment is recorded at its fair value. If there is an unrealized holding gain or loss on the date of reclassification, use the following table to determine the appropriate accounting.

Accounting for Holding Gains and Losses on Reclassified Investments

Event	Related Accounting
Transfer out of trading classification	All unrealized gains and losses have already been recognized in earnings; do not change
Transfer into trading classification	Recognize all unrealized gains and losses in earnings
Transfer into available-for-sale classification from held-to-maturity	Recognize all unrealized gains and losses in other comprehensive income
Transfer into held-to-maturity from available-for-sale classification	Retain all unrealized gains and losses in other comprehensive income, but amortize it over the remaining life of the security as a yield adjustment

Impairment of Investments

If a security is classified as either available-for-sale or held-to-maturity and there is a decline in its market value below its amortized cost, determine whether the decline is other than temporary. This analysis must be performed in every reporting period. If market value is not readily determinable, evaluate if there have been any events or circumstances that might impact the fair value of an investment (such as a deterioration in the operating performance of the issuer of a security). Several rules regarding the determination of other-than-temporary impairment are:

- *Debt security.* If the business plans to sell a debt security, an other-than-temporary impairment is assumed to have occurred. The same rule applies if it is more likely than not that the company will have to sell the security before its amortized cost basis has been recovered; this is based on a comparison of the present value of cash flows expected to be collected from the security to its amortized cost.
- *Equity security.* If the business plans to sell an equity security and does not expect the fair value of the security to recover by the time of the sale, consider its impairment to be other-than-temporary when the decision to sell is made, not when the security is sold.

If an impairment loss on an equity security is considered to be other-than-temporary, recognize a loss in the amount of the difference between the cost and fair value of the security. Once the impairment is recorded, this becomes the new cost basis of the equity security, and cannot be adjusted upward if there is a subsequent recovery in the fair value of the security.

If an impairment loss on a debt security is considered to be other-than-temporary, recognize a loss based on the following criteria:

- If the business intends to sell the security or it is more likely than not that it will be forced to do so before there has been a recovery of the amortized cost of the security, recognize a loss in earnings in the amount of the difference between the amortized cost and fair value of the security.
- If the business does not intend to sell the security and it is more likely than not that it will not have to do so before there has been a recovery of the amortized cost of the security, separate the impairment into the amount representing a credit loss, and the amount relating to all other causes. Then recognize that portion of the impairment representing a credit loss in earnings. Recognize the remaining portion of the impairment in other comprehensive income, net of taxes.

EXAMPLE

Armadillo Industries buys $250,000 of the equity securities of Currency Bank. A national liquidity crisis causes a downturn in Currency's business, so a major credit rating agency lowers its rating for the bank's securities. These events cause the quoted price of Armadillo's holdings to decline by $50,000. The CFO of Armadillo believes that the liquidity crisis will end soon, resulting in a rebound of the fortunes of Currency Bank, and so authorizes the recordation of the $50,000 valuation decline in other comprehensive income. The following entry records the transaction:

	Debit	Credit
Loss on available-for-sale securities	50,000	
(recorded in other comprehensive income)		
Investments – Available-for-sale		50,000

In the following year, the prognostication abilities of the CFO are unfortunately not justified, as the liquidity crisis continues. Accordingly, the CFO authorizes shifting the $50,000 loss from other comprehensive income to earnings.

Once the impairment is recorded, this becomes the new amortized cost basis of the debt security, and cannot be adjusted upward if there is a significant recovery in the fair value of the security.

Once an impairment has been recorded for a debt security, account for the difference between its new amortized cost basis and the cash flows you expect to collect from it as interest income.

If any portion of the other-than-temporary impairment of a debt security classified as held-to-maturity is recorded in other comprehensive income, use accretion to gradually increase the carrying amount of the security until it matures or is sold.

If there is a subsequent change in the fair value of available-for-sale debt securities, include these changes in other comprehensive income.

It is not acceptable under GAAP to create a general allowance for unidentified impairments in the value of an investment portfolio. Instead, impairments must be determined at the level of each individual security.

Restricted Stock

Ideally, you should initially (and subsequently) measure restricted stock based on the fair value of the quoted price of an unrestricted security issued by the same entity that is identical to the restricted stock in all other respects.

Dividend and Interest Income

If there is any dividend, interest income, or amortization of premium or discount associated with investments, recognize these amounts in earnings.

The Equity Method

When a company owns an interest in another business that it does not control (such as a corporate joint venture), it may use the equity method to account for its ownership interest. The equity method is designed to measure changes in the economic results of the investee, by requiring the investor to recognize its share of the profits or losses recorded by the investee. The equity method is a more complex technique of accounting for ownership, and so is typically used only when there is a significant ownership interest that enables an investor to have influence over the decision-making of the investee.

The key determining factor in the use of the equity method is having significant influence over the operating and financial decisions of the investee. The primary determinant of this level of control is owning at least 20% of the voting shares of the investee, though this measurement can be repudiated by evidence that the investee opposes the influence of the investor. Other types of evidence of significant influence are controlling a seat on the board of directors, active participation in the decisions of the investee, or swapping management personnel with the investee.

The investor can avoid using the equity method if it cannot obtain the financial information it needs from the investee in order to correctly account for its ownership interest under the equity method.

The essential accounting under the equity method is to initially recognize an investment in an investee at cost, and then adjust the carrying amount of the investment by recognizing its share of the earnings or losses of the investee in earnings over time. The following additional guidance applies to these basic points:

- *Dividends.* The investor should subtract any dividends received from the investee from the carrying amount of the investor's investment in the investee.
- *Financial statement issuance.* The investor can only account for its share of the earnings or losses of the investee if the investee issues financial statements. This may result in occasional lags in reporting.
- *Funding of prior losses.* If the investor pays the investee with the intent of offsetting prior investee losses, and the carrying amount of the investor's interest in the investee has already been reduced to zero, then the investor's share of any additional losses can be applied against the additional funds paid to the investee.
- *Intra-entity profits and losses.* Eliminate all intra-entity profits and losses as part of the equity method accounting, as would be the case if financial statements were being consolidated.
- *Investee losses.* It is possible that the investor's share of the losses of an investee will exceed the carrying amount of its investment in the investee. If so, the investor should report losses up to its carrying amount, as well as any additional financial support given to the investee, and then discontinue use of the equity method. However, additional losses can be recorded if it appears assured that the investee will shortly return to profitability. If there is a return to profitability, the investor can return to the equity method only after its share of the profits has been offset by those losses not recognized when use of the equity method was halted.
- *Other comprehensive income.* The investor should record its proportionate share of the investee's equity adjustments related to other comprehensive income. The entry is an adjustment to the investment account, with an offsetting adjustment in equity. If the investor discontinues its use of the equity method, offset the existing proportionate share of these equity adjustments

against the carrying value of the investment. If the result of this netting is a value in the carrying amount of less than zero, charge the excess amount to income. Also, stop recording the investor's proportionate share of the equity adjustments related to other comprehensive income in future periods.

- *Other write-downs.* If an investor's investment in an investee has been written down to zero, but it has other investments in the investee, the investor should continue to report its share of any additional investee losses, and offset them against the other investments, in sequence of the seniority of those investments (with offsets against the most junior items first). If the investee generates income at a later date, the investor should apply its share of these profits to the other investments in order, with application going against the most senior items first.
- *Share calculation.* The proportion of the investee's earnings or losses to be recognized by the investor is based on the investor's holdings of common stock and in-substance common stock.
- *Share issuances.* If the investee issues shares, the investor should account for the transaction as if a proportionate share of its own investment in the investee had been sold. If there is a gain or loss resulting from the stock sale, recognize it in earnings.
- *Ownership increase.* If an investor increases its ownership in an investee, this may qualify it to use the equity method, in which case the investor should retroactively adjust its financial statements for all periods presented to show the investment as though the equity method had been used through the entire reporting period.
- *Ownership decrease.* If an investor decreases its ownership in an investee, this may drop its level of control below the 20% to 25% threshold, in which case the investor may no longer be qualified to use the equity method. If so, the investor should retain the carrying amount of the investment as of the date when the equity method no longer applies, so there is no retroactive adjustment.

EXAMPLE

Armadillo Industries purchases 30% of the common stock of Titanium Barriers, Inc. Armadillo controls two seats on the board of directors of Titanium as a result of this investment, so it uses the equity method to account for the investment. In the next year, Titanium earns $400,000. Armadillo records its 30% share of the profit with the following entry:

	Debit	Credit
Investment in Titanium Barriers	120,000	
Equity in Titanium Barriers income		120,000

A few months later, Titanium issues a $50,000 cash dividend to Armadillo, which the company records with the following entry:

	Debit	Credit
Cash	50,000	
Investment in Titanium Barriers		50,000

EXAMPLE

Armadillo Industries has a 35% ownership interest in the common stock of Arlington Research. The carrying amount of this investment has been reduced to zero because of previous losses. To keep Arlington solvent, Armadillo has purchased $250,000 of Arlington's preferred stock, and extended a long-term unsecured loan of $500,000.

During the next year, Arlington incurs a $1,200,000 loss, of which Armadillo's share is 35%, or $420,000. Since the next most senior level of Arlington's capital after common stock is its preferred stock, Armadillo first offsets its share of the loss against its preferred stock investment. Doing so reduces the carrying amount of the preferred stock to zero, leaving $170,000 to be applied against the carrying amount of the loan. This results in the following entry by Armadillo:

	Debit	Credit
Equity method loss	420,000	
Preferred stock investment		250,000
Loan		170,000

In the following year, Arlington records $800,000 of profits, of which Armadillo's share is $280,000. Armadillo applies the $280,000 first against the loan write-down, and then against the preferred stock write-down with the following entry:

	Debit	Credit
Preferred stock investment	110,000	
Loan	170,000	
Equity method income		280,000

The result is that the carrying amount of the loan is fully restored, while the carrying amount of the preferred stock investment is still reduced by $140,000 from its original level.

Investment Disclosures

Any investments in available-for-sale and trading securities must be separately reported in the balance sheet. This can be done either by stating their fair value and non-fair-value carrying amounts on two separate lines, or by stating their aggregate amount in a single line, plus a parenthetical disclosure of the fair value amount included in the line.

For those securities classified as available-for-sale, disclose the following information by major type of security:

- Amortized cost basis
- Aggregate fair value

- The security-related total other-than-temporary impairments, total gains, and total losses reported in accumulated other comprehensive income
- The contractual maturities of the securities, which may be presented by group

For those securities classified as held-for-sale, disclose the following information by major type of security:
- Amortized cost basis
- Aggregate fair value
- Gross unrecognized holding gains and losses
- Net carrying amount
- The total amount of other-than-temporary impairment reported in accumulated other comprehensive income
- The gross gains and losses reported in accumulated other comprehensive income for any hedges of the forecasted acquisition of held-to-maturity securities
- The contractual maturities of the securities, which may be presented by group

If there are any other-than-temporary impairments of investments that have not yet been recognized in earnings, disclose the following information:
- Present in tabular form the aggregate fair value of investments with unrealized losses and the aggregate amount of the unrealized losses. Segregate this information for investments that have been in continuous unrealized loss positions for less than 12 months, and for 12 months or longer.

EXAMPLE

Armadillo Industries presents its impaired investment information in the following tabular format:

(000s) Securities Description	Less than 12 Months		12 Months or Greater		Total	
	Fair Value	Unrealized Losses	Fair Value	Unrealized Losses	Fair Value	Unrealized Losses
Corporate bonds	$500	$6	$200	--	$700	$6
Equity securities carried at cost	170	30	--	--	170	30
Marketable equity securities	80	10	--	--	80	10
Mortgage-backed securities	600	20	300	$10	900	30
U.S. Treasury obligations	2,010	5	1,400	3	3,410	8
Total	$3,360	$71	$1,900	$13	$5,260	$84

- Discuss the reasoning behind the conclusion that impairments were not other-than-temporary, which could include the nature of the impairments, the number of applicable unrealized loss positions, the severity and duration of the impairments, performance indicators, guarantees, sector credit ratings, and so forth.

- If only the portion of an impairment related to a credit loss was recognized, disclose (by major type of security) the reasoning and information used to measure the amount of the credit loss.
- Present a roll forward of the recognized amount of credit losses in the following format:

=	Beginning balance of credit losses on debt securities for which a portion of the other-than-temporary impairment is recognized in other comprehensive income
+	Amount of credit losses for which other-than-temporary impairments were not previously recognized
-	Reductions related to securities sold during the period
-	Reductions related to securities for which impairment recognized was shifted from other comprehensive income to earnings because of an intention to sell or likelihood of selling
+	Additional increases in the amount of credit losses, where there is no intent to sell the security or likelihood of doing so
-	Reductions related to increased cash flows expected to be collected
=	Ending balance of credit losses on debt securities for which a portion of the other-than-temporary impairment is recognized in other comprehensive income

If there were any sales or transfers of investments during the period, disclose the following information:

For all investments sold or reclassified	The basis on which investment costs or the amounts shifted from other comprehensive income to earnings were derived (such as by specific identification or an averaging method)
For available-for-sale securities	The proceeds from any sales, as well as the related amount of gross realized gains and gross realized losses recorded in earnings
For available-for-sale securities	The net unrealized holding gain or loss included in accumulated other comprehensive income, as well as the amount of gains and losses shifted from accumulated other comprehensive income and into earnings during the period
For trading securities	The amount of trading gains and losses for securities still held at the reporting date
For transfers from available-for-sale to trading classification	The amount of gross gains and gross losses recorded in earnings as a result of the transfer
From the held-to-maturity classification	The net carrying amount sold or transferred, the net gain or loss in accumulated other comprehensive income for hedges of the forecasted acquisition of held-to-maturity securities, the realized or unrealized gain or loss, and a discussion of the circumstances causing the decision to sell or transfer the securities.

When an investor uses the equity method to account for an investment, it should state the investment as a single line item in the balance sheet. Similarly, the investor should report its share of any investee gains or losses as a single line item in the income statement. The only exceptions to reporting investment information on a separate line are:

- Accounting changes
- Extraordinary items
- Other comprehensive income items (to be combined with the investor's own other comprehensive income items)

An investor using the equity method to account for an investment should disclose the following information:

- *Identification*. The name of each investee and the investor's ownership percentage in it.
- *Market value*. The value of each investment at its quoted market price (if such a price is available).
- *Policies*. The investor's policies regarding its investments in common stock, including cases where the investor owns a 20% or more interest in a business but does not use the equity method. Also describe any situations where the investor uses the equity method despite owning less than 20% of an investee. Further, note any difference between the carrying amount of an investment and the amount of underlying equity in net assets.
- *Change in ownership*. If there is a potentially material impact on the investor's share of reported investee earnings from the conversion of convertible securities, the conversion of warrants, or similar transactions, disclose this information.

Summary

The accounting for and disclosure of the three types of investments clearly differ, and so it would initially appear that a considerable amount of detailed investment monitoring is required to ensure that the related accounting will be correct. However, the situation can be made considerably less complex as long as you minimize the need to transfer investments between classifications and develop a clear procedure for the treatment of each class of investment. The situation can be further clarified by restricting all investments to just one or two of the three allowed classifications. Following these rules can result in greatly simplified accounting for debt and equity investments.

Chapter 7
Accounting for Inventory

Introduction

Inventory is one of the most important asset classifications, for it may represent the largest asset investment by a manufacturer or seller of goods. As a major asset, it is imperative that inventory be properly valued, as well as those goods designated as having been sold. This chapter discusses the surprisingly brief GAAP requirements for inventory, and then expands upon them with discussions of inventory tracking systems, costing methodologies, and a variety of related topics.

Related Podcast Episodes: Episodes 56, 66, and 119 of the Accounting Best Practices Podcast discuss inventory record accuracy, obsolete inventory, and overhead allocation, respectively. You can listen to them at: **accounting-tools.com/podcasts** or **iTunes**

Overview of Inventory

In general, inventory is to be accounted for at cost, which is considered to be the sum of those expenditures required to bring an inventory item to its present condition and location. There are three types of costs to apply to inventory, which are:

- *Direct costs.* If a cost was directly incurred to produce or acquire a specific unit of inventory, this is called a direct cost, and is recorded as a cost of inventory.
- *Variable overhead costs.* If there are any factory costs that are not direct, but which vary with production volume, they are assigned to inventory based on actual usage of a company's production facilities. There are usually not many variable overhead costs.
- *Fixed overhead costs.* If there are any factory costs that are not direct, and which do not vary with production volume, they are assigned to inventory based on the normal capacity of a company's production facilities.

The accounting for fixed overhead costs is particularly critical, given the large amount of fixed costs that are allocated in many production facilities. The basic GAAP rules for fixed overhead allocation are:

- *High production.* During periods of abnormally high production, the overhead allocation per unit should be reduced in order to keep from recording inventory above its actual cost.

- *Low production.* During periods of abnormally low production, the overhead allocation per unit is *not* increased.
- *Overhead expense recognition.* If there is any residual fixed overhead that is not allocated to inventory, the unallocated amount is recognized as expense in the period incurred; there is no delay in expense recognition to a later period.

GAAP specifically requires that overhead costs must be allocated to inventory, and that the allocation must be consistently performed from period to period.

> **Tip:** Though GAAP requires that overhead be allocated to inventory, this does not mean that you should spend an inordinate amount of time compiling an exquisitely designed allocation system. Instead, focus on a simple and efficient allocation methodology that allows you to close the books quickly.

Several other rules have been developed regarding inventory costs, most of which are designed to keep certain costs from being allocated to inventory. They are:
- *Abnormal expenses.* If unusually high costs are incurred, such as abnormal freight, spoilage, or scrap charges, they are to be charged to expense in the period incurred.
- *General and administrative expenses.* General and administrative costs can only be allocated to inventory when they are clearly related to production. In nearly all cases, these costs are charged to expense as incurred.
- *Selling expenses.* All costs related to selling are charged to expense as incurred; they are never allocated to inventory.
- *Stating inventory above cost.* Inventories can only be stated above cost in exceptional situations. In all cases where the cost is stated at the sale price, the cost is to be reduced by any expected disposal costs. Stating inventory above cost is specifically allowed by GAAP in the following situations:
  - Gold and silver, where there is a government-control market at a fixed price
  - Inventories of agricultural, mineral, and similar products that have the following criteria:
    - Immediate marketability at a quoted market price
    - Units are interchangeable
    - An inability to determine an appropriate per-unit cost

Once costs have initially been apportioned to inventory, GAAP requires that any decline in the utility of goods below their cost result in the recognition of a loss in the current period. This decline in utility is most commonly caused by the deterioration or obsolescence of inventory items. The Accounting for Obsolete Inventory section describes how to account for this type of loss. A decline in utility may also be caused by a decline in the price of inventory items. The Lower of Cost or Market Rule section describes how to calculate and account for this type of loss.

In addition, if a company has a firm purchase commitment to acquire goods and the utility of the items to be acquired has declined, the company should recognize a loss in the current period for these future purchases; loss recognition is not required when the items to be purchased are also protected by firm sales contracts or similar arrangements.

The *inventory cost flow* assumption is the concept that the cost of an inventory item changes between the time it is acquired or built and the time when it is sold. Because of this cost differential, a company needs to adopt a cost flow assumption regarding how it treats the cost of goods as they move through the company.

For example, a company buys a widget on January 1 for $50. On July 1, it buys an identical widget for $70, and on November 1 it buys yet another identical widget for $90. The products are completely interchangeable. On December 1, the company sells one of the widgets. It bought the widgets at three different prices, so what cost should it report for its cost of goods sold? There are many possible ways to interpret the cost flow assumption. For example:

- *FIFO cost flow assumption.* Under the first in, first out method, you assume that the first item purchased is also the first one sold. Thus, the cost of goods sold would be $50. Since this is the lowest-cost item in the example, profits would be highest under FIFO.
- *LIFO cost flow assumption.* Under the last in, first out method, you assume that the last item purchased is also the first one sold. Thus, the cost of goods sold would be $90. Since this is the highest-cost item in the example, profits would be lowest under LIFO.
- *Weighted average cost flow assumption.* Under the weighted average method, the cost of goods sold is the average cost of all three units, or $70. This cost flow assumption tends to yield a mid-range cost, and therefore also a mid-range profit.

The cost flow assumption does not necessarily match the actual flow of goods (if that were the case, most companies would use the FIFO method). Instead, you can use a cost flow assumption that varies from actual usage. For this reason, companies tend to select a cost flow assumption that either minimizes profits (in order to minimize income taxes) or maximizes profits (in order to increase share value).

In periods of rising materials prices, the LIFO method results in a higher cost of goods sold, lower profits, and therefore lower income taxes. In periods of declining materials prices, the FIFO method yields the same results.

The cost flow assumption is a minor item when inventory costs are relatively stable over the long term, since there will be no particular difference in the cost of goods sold, no matter which cost flow assumption is used. Conversely, dramatic changes in inventory costs over time will yield a considerable difference in reported profit levels, depending on the cost flow assumption used. Therefore, be especially aware of the financial impact of the inventory cost flow assumption in periods of fluctuating costs.

In the following sections, we describe the more commonly-used methods for inventory costing, several of which are based on cost flow assumptions. First, however, we address the two main record-keeping systems needed to accurately track inventory, which are the periodic inventory system and the perpetual inventory system.

The Periodic Inventory System

The periodic inventory system only updates the ending inventory balance when you conduct a physical inventory count. Since physical inventory counts are time-consuming, few companies do them more than once a quarter or year. In the meantime, the inventory account continues to show the cost of the inventory that was recorded as of the last physical inventory count.

Under the periodic inventory system, all purchases made between physical inventory counts are recorded in a purchases account. When a physical inventory count is done, you then shift the balance in the purchases account into the inventory account, which in turn is adjusted to match the cost of the ending inventory.

The calculation of the cost of goods sold under the periodic inventory system is:

Beginning inventory + Purchases = Cost of goods available for sale

Cost of goods available for sale – Ending inventory = Cost of goods sold

---

EXAMPLE

Milagro Corporation has beginning inventory of $100,000, has paid $170,000 for purchases, and its physical inventory count reveals an ending inventory cost of $80,000. The calculation of its cost of goods sold is:

$100,000 Beginning inventory + $170,000 Purchases - $80,000 Ending inventory

= $190,000 Cost of goods sold

The periodic inventory system is most useful for smaller businesses that maintain minimal amounts of inventory. For them, a physical inventory count is easy to complete, and they can estimate cost of goods sold figures for interim periods. However, there are several problems with the system:

- It does not yield any information about the cost of goods sold or ending inventory balances during interim periods when there has been no physical inventory count.
- You must estimate the cost of goods sold during interim periods, which will likely result in a significant adjustment to the actual cost of goods whenever you eventually complete a physical inventory count.
- There is no way to adjust for obsolete inventory or scrap losses during interim periods, so there tends to be a significant (and expensive) adjustment for these issues when a physical inventory count is eventually completed.

A more up-to-date and accurate alternative to the periodic inventory system is the perpetual inventory system, which is described in the next section.

The Perpetual Inventory System

Under the perpetual inventory system, an entity continually updates its inventory records to account for additions to and subtractions from inventory for such activities as received inventory items, goods sold from stock, and items picked from inventory for use in the production process. Thus, a perpetual inventory system has the advantages of both providing up-to-date inventory balance information and requiring a reduced level of physical inventory counts. However, the calculated inventory levels derived by a perpetual inventory system may gradually diverge from actual inventory levels, due to unrecorded transactions or theft, so you should periodically compare book balances to actual on-hand quantities.

EXAMPLE

This example contains several journal entries used to account for transactions in a perpetual inventory system. Milagro Corporation records a purchase of $1,000 of widgets that are stored in inventory:

	Debit	Credit
Inventory	1,000	
Accounts payable		1,000

Milagro records $250 of inbound freight cost associated with the delivery of widgets:

	Debit	Credit
Inventory	250	
Accounts payable		250

Milagro records the sale of widgets on credit from inventory for $2,000, for which the associated inventory cost is $1,200:

	Debit	Credit
Accounts receivable	2,000	
Revenue		2,000
Cost of goods sold	1,200	
Inventory		1,200

Milagro records a downward inventory adjustment of $500, caused by inventory theft, and detected during an inventory count:

	Debit	Credit
Inventory shrinkage expense	500	
Inventory		500

Inventory Costing

Several methods for calculating the cost of inventory are shown in this section. Of the methods presented, only the first in, first out method and the weighted average method have gained worldwide recognition. The last in, first out method cannot realistically be justified based on the actual flow of inventory, and is only used in the United States under the sanction of the Internal Revenue Service; it is specifically banned under international financial reporting standards. Standard costing is an acceptable alternative to cost layering, as long as any associated variances are properly accounted for. The retail inventory method and gross profit method should be used only to derive an approximation of the ending inventory cost, and so should be used only in interim reporting periods when a company does not intend to issue any financial results to outside parties.

The First In, First Out Method

The first in, first out (FIFO) method of inventory valuation operates under the assumption that the first goods purchased are also the first goods sold. In most companies, this accounting assumption closely matches the actual flow of goods, and so is considered the most theoretically correct inventory valuation method.

Under the FIFO method, the earliest goods purchased are the first ones removed from the inventory account. This results in the remaining items in inventory being accounted for at the most recently incurred costs, so that the inventory asset recorded on the balance sheet contains costs quite close to the most recent costs that could be obtained in the marketplace. Conversely, this method also results in older historical costs being matched against current revenues and recorded in the cost of goods sold, so the gross margin does not necessarily reflect a proper matching of revenues and costs.

EXAMPLE

Milagro Corporation decides to use the FIFO method for the month of January. During that month, it records the following transactions:

	Quantity Change	Actual Unit Cost	Actual Total Cost
Beginning inventory (layer 1)	+100	$210	$21,000
Sale	-75		
Purchase (layer 2)	+150	280	42,000
Sale	-100		
Purchase (layer 3)	+50	300	15,000
Ending inventory	= 125		

The cost of goods sold in units is calculated as:

100 Beginning inventory + 200 Purchased − 125 Ending inventory = 175 Units

Milagro's accountant uses the information in the preceding table to calculate the cost of goods sold for January, as well as the cost of the inventory balance as of the end of January.

	Units	Unit Cost	Total Cost
Cost of goods sold			
FIFO layer 1	100	$210	$21,000
FIFO layer 2	75	280	21,000
Total cost of goods sold	175		$42,000
Ending inventory			
FIFO layer 2	75	280	$21,000
FIFO layer 3	50	300	15,000
Total ending inventory	125		$36,000

Thus, the first FIFO layer, which was the beginning inventory layer, is completely used up during the month, as well as half of Layer 2, leaving half of Layer 2 and all of Layer 3 to be the sole components of the ending inventory.

Note that the $42,000 cost of goods sold and $36,000 ending inventory equals the $78,000 combined total of beginning inventory and purchases during the month.

The Last In, First Out Method

The last in, first out (LIFO) method operates under the assumption that the last item of inventory purchased is the first one sold. Picture a store shelf where a clerk adds items from the front, and customers also take their selections from the front; the remaining items of inventory that are located further from the front of the shelf are rarely picked, and so remain on the shelf – that is a LIFO scenario.

The trouble with the LIFO scenario is that it is rarely encountered in practice. If a company were to use the process flow embodied by LIFO, a significant part of its inventory would be very old, and likely obsolete. Nonetheless, a company does not actually have to experience the LIFO process flow in order to use the method to calculate its inventory valuation.

The reason why companies use LIFO is the assumption that the cost of inventory increases over time, which is a reasonable assumption in times of inflating prices. If you were to use LIFO in such a situation, the cost of the most recently acquired inventory will always be higher than the cost of earlier purchases, so the ending inventory balance will be valued at earlier costs, while the most recent costs appear in the cost of goods sold. By shifting high-cost inventory into the cost of goods sold, a company can reduce its reported level of profitability, and thereby defer its recognition of income taxes.

EXAMPLE

Milagro Corporation decides to use the LIFO method for the month of March. The following table shows the various purchasing transactions for the company's Elite Roasters product. The quantity purchased on March 1 actually reflects the inventory beginning balance.

Date Purchased	Quantity Purchased	Cost per Unit	Units Sold	Cost of Layer #1	Cost of Layer #2	Total Cost
March 1	150	$210	95	(55 × $210)		$11,550
March 7	100	235	110	(45 × $210)		9,450
March 11	200	250	180	(45 × $210)	(20 × $250)	14,450
March 17	125	240	125	(45 × $210)	(20 × $250)	14,450
March 25	80	260	120	(25 × $210)		5,250

The following bullet points describe the transactions noted in the preceding table:

- *March 1.* Milagro has a beginning inventory balance of 150 units, and sells 95 of these units between March 1 and March 7. This leaves one inventory layer of 55 units at a cost of $210 each.
- *March 7.* Milagro buys 100 additional units on March 7, and sells 110 units between March 7 and March 11. Under LIFO, we assume that the latest purchase was sold first, so there is still just one inventory layer, which has now been reduced to 45 units.
- *March 11.* Milagro buys 200 additional units on March 11, and sells 180 units between March 11 and March 17, which creates a new inventory layer that is comprised of 20 units at a cost of $250. This new layer appears in the table in the "Cost of Layer #2" column.
- *March 17.* Milagro buys 125 additional units on March 17, and sells 125 units between March 17 and March 25, so there is no change in the inventory layers.
- *March 25.* Milagro buys 80 additional units on March 25, and sells 120 units between March 25 and the end of the month. Sales exceed purchases during this period, so the second inventory layer is eliminated, as well as part of the first layer. The result is an ending inventory balance of $5,250, which is derived from 25 units of ending inventory, multiplied by the $210 cost in the first layer that existed at the beginning of the month.

Before you implement the LIFO system, consider the following points:

- *Consistent usage.* The Internal Revenue Service states that a company using LIFO for its tax reporting must also use it for its financial reporting. Thus, a company wanting to defer tax recognition through early expense recognition must show those same low profit numbers to the outside users of its financial statements.
- *Layering.* Since the LIFO system is intended to use the most recent layers of inventory, you may never access earlier layers, which can result in an administrative problem if there are many layers to document.
- *Profit fluctuations.* If early layers contain inventory costs that depart substantially from current market prices, a company could experience sharp changes in its profitability if those layers are ever used.

In summary, LIFO is only useful for deferring income tax payments in periods of cost inflation. It does not reflect the actual flow of inventory in most situations, and may even yield unusual financial results that differ markedly from reality.

The Weighted Average Method

When using the weighted average method, divide the cost of goods available for sale by the number of units available for sale, which yields the weighted-average cost per unit. In this calculation, the cost of goods available for sale is the sum of beginning inventory and net purchases. This weighted-average figure is used to assign a cost to both ending inventory and the cost of goods sold.

The singular advantage of the weighted average method is the complete absence of any inventory layers, which avoids the record keeping problems that you would encounter with either the FIFO or LIFO methods that were described earlier.

EXAMPLE

Milagro Corporation elects to use the weighted-average method for the month of May. During that month, it records the following transactions:

	Quantity Change	Actual Unit Cost	Actual Total Cost
Beginning inventory	+150	$220	$33,000
Sale	-125		
Purchase	+200	270	54,000
Sale	-150		
Purchase	+100	290	29,000
Ending inventory	= 175		

The actual total cost of all purchased or beginning inventory units in the preceding table is $116,000 ($33,000 + $54,000 + $29,000). The total of all purchased or beginning inventory units is 450 (150 beginning inventory + 300 purchased). The weighted average cost per unit is therefore $257.78 ($116,000 ÷ 450 units.)

The ending inventory valuation is $45,112 (175 units × $257.78 weighted average cost), while the cost of goods sold valuation is $70,890 (275 units × $257.78 weighted average cost). The sum of these two amounts (less a rounding error) equals the $116,000 total actual cost of all purchases and beginning inventory.

In the preceding example, if Milagro used a perpetual inventory system to record its inventory transactions, it would have to recompute the weighted average after every purchase.

The following table uses the same information in the preceding example to show the recomputations:

	Units on Hand	Purchases	Cost of Sales	Inventory Total Cost	Inventory Moving Average Unit Cost
Beginning inventory	150	$--	$--	$33,000	$220.00
Sale (125 units @ $220.00)	25	--	27,500	5,500	220.00
Purchase (200 units @ $270.00)	225	54,000	--	59,500	264.44
Sale (150 units @ $264.44)	75	--	39,666	19,834	264.44
Purchase (100 units @ $290.00)	175	29,000	--	48,834	279.05
Total			$67,166		

Note that the cost of goods sold of $67,166 and the ending inventory balance of $48,834 equal $116,000, which matches the total of the costs in the original example. Thus, the totals are the same, but the moving weighted average calculation results in slight differences in the apportionment of costs between the cost of goods sold and ending inventory.

Standard Costing

The preceding methods (FIFO, LIFO, and weighted average) have all operated under the assumption that some sort of cost layering is used, even if that layering results in nothing more than a single weighted-average layer. The standard costing methodology arrives at inventory valuation from an entirely different direction, which is to set a standard cost for each item and to then value those items at the standard cost – not the actual cost at which the items were purchased.

Standard costing is clearly more efficient than any cost layering system, simply because there are no layers to keep track of. However, its primary failing is that the resulting inventory valuation may not equate to the actual cost. The difference is handled through several types of variance calculations, which may be charged to the cost of goods sold (if minor) or allocated between inventory and the cost of goods sold (if material).

At the most basic level, you can create a standard cost simply by calculating the average of the most recent actual cost for the past few months. An additional factor to consider when deriving a standard cost is whether to set it at a historical actual cost level that has been proven to be attainable, or at a rate that should be attainable, or one that can only be reached if all operations work perfectly. Here are some considerations:

- *Historical basis*. This is an average of the costs that a company has already experienced in the recent past, possibly weighted towards just the past few months. Though clearly an attainable cost, a standard based on historical results contains all of the operational inefficiencies of the existing production operation.

- *Attainable basis*. This is a cost that is more difficult to reach than a historical cost. This basis assumes some improvement in operating and purchasing efficiencies, which employees have a good chance of achieving in the short term.

- *Theoretical basis.* This is the ultimate, lowest cost that the facility can attain if it functions perfectly, with no scrap, highly efficient employees, and machines that never break down. This can be a frustrating basis to use for a standard cost, because the production facility can never attain it, and so always produces unfavorable variances.

Of the three types of standards noted here, use the attainable basis, because it gives employees a reasonable cost target to pursue. If you continually update standards on this basis, a production facility will have an incentive to continually drive down its costs over the long term.

Standard costs are stored separately from all other accounting records, usually in a bill of materials for finished goods, and in the item master file for raw materials.

At the end of a reporting period, the following steps show how to integrate standard costs into the accounting system (assuming the use of a periodic inventory system):

1. *Cost verification.* Review the standard cost database for errors and correct as necessary. Also, if it is time to do so, update the standard costs to more accurately reflect actual costs.
2. *Inventory valuation.* Multiply the number of units in ending inventory by their standard costs to derive the ending inventory valuation.
3. *Calculate the cost of goods sold.* Add purchases during the month to the beginning inventory and subtract the ending inventory to determine the cost of goods sold.
4. *Enter updated balances.* Create a journal entry that reduces the purchases account to zero and which also adjusts the inventory asset account balance to the ending total standard cost, with the offset to the cost of goods sold account.

EXAMPLE

A division of the Milagro Corporation is using a standard costing system to calculate its inventory balances and cost of goods sold. The company conducts a month-end physical inventory count that results in a reasonably accurate set of unit quantities for all inventory items. The accountant multiplies each of these unit quantities by their standard costs to derive the ending inventory valuation. This ending balance is $2,500,000.

The beginning balance in the inventory account is $2,750,000 and purchases during the month were $1,000,000, so the calculation of the cost of goods sold is:

Beginning inventory	$2,750,000
+ Purchases	1,000,000
- Ending inventory	(2,500,000)
= Cost of goods sold	$1,250,000

117

To record the correct ending inventory balance and cost of goods sold, the accountant records the following entry, which clears out the purchases asset account and adjusts the ending inventory balance to $2,500,000:

	Debit	Credit
Cost of goods sold	1,250,000	
Purchases		1,000,000
Inventory		250,000

The Retail Inventory Method

The retail inventory method is sometimes used by retailers that resell merchandise to estimate their ending inventory balances. This method is based on the relationship between the cost of merchandise and its retail price. To calculate the cost of ending inventory using the retail inventory method, follow these steps:

1. Calculate the cost-to-retail percentage, for which the formula is (Cost ÷ Retail price).
2. Calculate the cost of goods available for sale, for which the formula is (Cost of beginning inventory + Cost of purchases).
3. Calculate the cost of sales during the period, for which the formula is (Sales × Cost-to-retail percentage).
4. Calculate ending inventory, for which the formula is (Cost of goods available for sale - Cost of sales during the period).

EXAMPLE

Milagro Corporation sells home coffee roasters for an average of $200, and which cost it $140. This is a cost-to-retail percentage of 70%. Milagro's beginning inventory has a cost of $1,000,000, it paid $1,800,000 for purchases during the month, and it had sales of $2,400,000. The calculation of its ending inventory is:

Beginning inventory	$1,000,000	(at cost)
Purchases	+ 1,800,000	(at cost)
Goods available for sale	= 2,800,000	
Sales	- 1,680,000	(sales of $2,400,000 × 70%)
Ending inventory	= $1,120,000	

The retail inventory method is a quick and easy way to determine an approximate ending inventory balance. However, there are also several issues with it:

- The retail inventory method is only an estimate. Do not rely upon it too heavily to yield results that will compare with those of a physical inventory count.
- The retail inventory method only works if you have a consistent mark-up across all products sold. If not, the actual ending inventory cost may vary wildly from what you derived using this method.

- The method assumes that the historical basis for the mark-up percentage continues into the current period. If the mark-up was different (as may be caused by an after-holidays sale), then the results of the calculation will be incorrect.

The Gross Profit Method

The gross profit method can be used to estimate the amount of ending inventory. This is useful for interim periods between physical inventory counts, or when inventory was destroyed and you need to back into the ending inventory balance for the purpose of filing a claim for insurance reimbursement. Follow these steps to estimate ending inventory using the gross profit method:

1. Add together the cost of beginning inventory and the cost of purchases during the period to arrive at the cost of goods available for sale.
2. Multiply (1 - expected gross profit %) by sales during the period to arrive at the estimated cost of goods sold.
3. Subtract the estimated cost of goods sold (step #2) from the cost of goods available for sale (step #1) to arrive at the ending inventory.

The gross profit method is not an acceptable method for determining the year-end inventory balance, since it only estimates what the ending inventory balance may be. It is not sufficiently precise to be reliable for audited financial statements.

EXAMPLE

Mulligan Imports is calculating its month-end golf club inventory for March. Its beginning inventory was $175,000 and its purchases during the month were $225,000. Thus, its cost of goods available for sale is:

$175,000 beginning inventory + $225,000 purchases

= $400,000 cost of goods available for sale

Mulligan's gross margin percentage for all of the past 12 months was 35%, which is considered a reliable long-term margin. Its sales during March were $500,000. Thus, its estimated cost of goods sold is:

(1 - 35%) × $500,000 = $325,000 cost of goods sold

By subtracting the estimated cost of goods sold from the cost of goods available for sale, Mulligan arrives at an estimated ending inventory balance of $75,000.

There are several issues with the gross profit method that make it unreliable as the sole method for determining the value of inventory, which are:

- *Applicability.* The calculation is most useful in retail situations where a company is simply buying and reselling merchandise. If a company is instead manufacturing goods, then the components of inventory must also include labor and overhead, which make the gross profit method too simplistic to yield reliable results.

- *Historical basis.* The gross profit percentage is a key component of the calculation, but the percentage is based on a company's historical experience. If the current situation yields a different percentage (as may be caused by a special sale at reduced prices), then the gross profit percentage used in the calculation will be incorrect.
- *Inventory losses.* The calculation assumes that the long-term rate of losses due to theft, obsolescence, and other causes is included in the historical gross profit percentage. If not, or if these losses have not previously been recognized, then the calculation will likely result in an inaccurate estimated ending inventory (and probably one that is too high).

Overhead Allocation

The preceding section was concerned with charging the direct costs of production to inventory, but what about overhead expenses? In many businesses, the cost of overhead is substantially greater than direct costs, so you must expend considerable attention on the proper method of allocating overhead to inventory.

There are two types of overhead, which are administrative overhead and manufacturing overhead. *Administrative overhead* includes those costs not involved in the development or production of goods or services, such as the costs of front office administration and sales; this is essentially all overhead that is *not* included in manufacturing overhead. *Manufacturing overhead* is all of the costs that a factory incurs, other than direct costs.

Allocate the costs of manufacturing overhead to any inventory items that are classified as work-in-process or finished goods. Overhead is not allocated to raw materials inventory, since the operations giving rise to overhead costs only impact work-in-process and finished goods inventory.

The following items are usually included in manufacturing overhead:

Depreciation of factory equipment	Quality control and inspection
Factory administration expenses	Rent, facility and equipment
Indirect labor and production supervisory wages	Repair expenses
Indirect materials and supplies	Rework labor, scrap and spoilage
Maintenance, factory and production equipment	Taxes related to production assets
Officer salaries related to production	Uncapitalized tools and equipment
Production employees' benefits	Utilities

The typical procedure for allocating overhead is to accumulate all manufacturing overhead costs into one or more cost pools, and to then use an activity measure to apportion the overhead costs in the cost pools to inventory. Thus, the overhead allocation formula is:

$$\text{Cost pool} \div \text{Total activity measure} = \text{Overhead allocation per unit}$$

EXAMPLE

Mulligan Imports has a small production line for an in-house line of golf clubs. During April, it incurs costs for the following items:

Cost Type	Amount
Building rent	$65,000
Building utilities	12,000
Factory equipment depreciation	8,000
Production equipment maintenance	7,000
Total	$92,000

All of these items are classified as manufacturing overhead, so Mulligan creates the following journal entry to shift these costs into an overhead cost pool:

	Debit	Credit
Overhead cost pool	92,000	
Depreciation expense		8,000
Maintenance expense		7,000
Rent expense		65,000
Utilities expense		12,000

You can allocate overhead costs by any reasonable measure, as long as it is consistently applied across reporting periods. Common bases of allocation are direct labor hours charged against a product, or the amount of machine hours used during the production of a product. The amount of allocation charged per unit is known as the *overhead rate*.

The overhead rate can be expressed as a proportion, if both the numerator and denominator are in dollars. For example, Armadillo Industries has total indirect costs of $100,000 and it decides to use the cost of its direct labor as the allocation measure. Armadillo incurs $50,000 of direct labor costs, so the overhead rate is calculated as:

$$\frac{\$100{,}000 \text{ Indirect costs}}{\$50{,}000 \text{ Direct labor}}$$

The result is an overhead rate of 2.0.

Alternatively, if the denominator is not in dollars, then the overhead rate is expressed as a cost per allocation unit. For example, Armadillo decides to change its allocation measure to hours of machine time used. The company has 10,000 hours of machine time usage, so the overhead rate is now calculated as:

$$\frac{\$100{,}000 \text{ Indirect costs}}{10{,}000 \text{ Machine hours}}$$

The result is an overhead rate of $10.00 per machine hour.

EXAMPLE

Mulligan Imports has a small golf shaft production line, which manufactures a titanium shaft and an aluminum shaft. Considerable machining is required for both shafts, so Mulligan concludes that it should allocate overhead to these products based on the total hours of machine time used. In May, production of the titanium shaft requires 5,400 hours of machine time, while the aluminum shaft needs 2,600 hours. Thus, 67.5% of the overhead cost pool is allocated to the titanium shafts and 32.5% to the aluminum shafts.

In May, Mulligan accumulates $100,000 of costs in its overhead cost pool, and allocates it between the two product lines with the following journal entry:

	Debit	Credit
Finished goods – Titanium shafts	67,500	
Finished goods – Aluminum shafts	32,500	
Overhead cost pool		100,000

This entry clears out the balance in the overhead cost pool, readying it to accumulate overhead costs in the next reporting period.

If the basis of allocation does not appear correct for certain types of overhead costs, it may make more sense to split the overhead into two or more overhead cost pools, and allocate each cost pool using a different basis of allocation. For example, if warehouse costs are more appropriately allocated based on the square footage consumed by various products, then store warehouse costs in a warehouse overhead cost pool, and allocate these costs based on square footage used.

Thus far, we have assumed that only actual overhead costs incurred are allocated. However, it is also possible to set up a standard overhead rate that you continue to use for multiple reporting periods, based on long-term expectations regarding how much overhead will be incurred and how many units will be produced. If the difference between actual overhead costs incurred and overhead allocated is small, charge the difference to the cost of goods sold. If the amount is material, allocate the difference to both the cost of goods sold and inventory.

EXAMPLE

Mulligan Imports incurs overhead of $93,000, which it stores in an overhead cost pool. Mulligan uses a standard overhead rate of $20 per unit, which approximates its long-term experience with the relationship between overhead costs and production volumes. In September, it produces 4,500 golf club shafts, to which it allocates $90,000 (allocation rate of $20 × 4,500 units). This leaves a difference between overhead incurred and overhead absorbed of $3,000. Given the small size of the variance, Mulligan charges the $3,000 difference to the cost of goods sold, thereby clearing out the overhead cost pool.

A key issue is that overhead allocation is not a precisely-defined science – there is plenty of latitude in how you can go about allocating overhead. The amount of allowable diversity in practice can result in slipshod accounting, so be sure to use a standardized and well-documented method to allocate overhead using the same calculation in every reporting period. This allows for great consistency, which auditors appreciate when they validate the supporting calculations.

The Lower of Cost or Market Rule

The lower of cost or market rule is required by GAAP, and states that you record the cost of inventory at whichever cost is lower – the original cost or its current market price. This situation typically arises when inventory has deteriorated, or has become obsolete, or market prices have declined.

The "current market price" is defined as the current replacement cost of the inventory, as long as the market price does not exceed net realizable value; also, the market price shall not be less than the net realizable value, less the normal profit margin. Net realizable value is defined as the estimated selling price, minus estimated costs of completion and disposal.

EXAMPLE

Mulligan Imports resells five major brands of golf clubs, which are noted in the following table. At the end of its reporting year, Mulligan calculates the lower of its cost or net realizable value in the following table:

Product Line	Quantity on Hand	Unit Cost	Inventory at Cost	Market Per Unit	Lower of Cost or Market
Free Swing	1,000	$190	$190,000	$230	$190,000
Golf Elite	750	140	105,000	170	105,000
Hi-Flight	200	135	27,000	120	24,000
Iridescent	1,200	280	336,000	160	192,000
Titanium	800	200	160,000	215	160,000

Based on the table, the market value is lower than cost on the Hi-Flight and Iridescent product lines. Consequently, Mulligan recognizes a loss on the Hi-Flight product line of $3,000 ($27,000 - $24,000), as well as a loss of $144,000 ($336,000 - $192,000) on the Iridescent product line.

If the amount of a write-down caused by the lower of cost or market analysis is minor, charge the expense to the cost of goods sold. If the loss is material, track it in a separate account (especially if such losses are recurring), such as "Loss on LCM adjustment."

To use the information in the preceding example, the journal entry would be:

	Debit	Credit
Loss on LCM adjustment	147,000	
Finished goods inventory		147,000

Additional factors to consider when applying the lower of cost or market rule are:

- *Analysis by category.* You normally apply the lower of cost or market rule to a specific inventory item, but you can apply it to entire inventory categories. In the latter case, an LCM adjustment can be avoided if there is a balance within an inventory category of items having market prices below cost and in excess of cost.
- *Hedges.* If inventory is being hedged by a fair value hedge, add the effects of the hedge to the cost of the inventory, which frequently eliminates the need for a lower of cost or market adjustment.
- *Last in, first out layer recovery.* You can avoid a write-down to the lower of cost or market in an interim period if there is substantial evidence that inventory amounts will be restored by year end, thereby avoiding recognition of an earlier inventory layer.
- *Raw materials.* Do not write down the cost of raw materials if the finished goods in which they are used are expected to sell either at or above their costs.
- *Recovery.* You can avoid a write-down to the lower of cost or market if there is substantial evidence that market prices will increase before the inventory is sold.
- *Sales incentives.* If there are unexpired sales incentives that will result in a loss on the sale of a specific item, this is a strong indicator that there may be a lower of cost or market problem with that item.

Work in Process Accounting

Work in process (WIP) is goods in production that have not yet been completed. It typically involves the full amount of raw materials needed for a product, since that is usually included in the product at the beginning of the manufacturing process. During production, the cost of direct labor and overhead is added in proportion to the amount of work done.

In prolonged production operations, there may be a considerable amount of investment in work in process. Conversely, the production of some products occupies such a brief period of time that the accounting staff does not bother to track it at all; instead, the items in production are considered to still be in the raw materials inventory. In this latter case, inventory essentially shifts directly from the raw materials inventory to the finished goods inventory, with no separate work in process tracking.

Work in process accounting involves tracking the amount of WIP in inventory at the end of an accounting period and assigning a cost to it for inventory valuation purposes, based on the percentage of completion of the WIP items.

In situations where there are many similar products in process, it is more common to follow these steps to account for work in process inventory:

1. *Assign raw materials.* We assume that all raw materials have been assigned to work in process as soon as the work begins. This is reasonable, since many types of production involve kitting all of the materials needed to construct a product and delivering them to the manufacturing area at one time.
2. *Compile labor costs.* The production staff can track the time it works on each product, which is then assigned to the work in process. However, this is painfully time-consuming, so a better approach is to determine the stage of completion of each item in production, and assign a standard labor cost to it based on the stage of completion. This information comes from labor routings that detail the standard amount of labor needed at each stage of the production process.
3. *Assign overhead.* If overhead is assigned based on labor hours, then it is assigned based on the labor information compiled in the preceding step. If overhead is assigned based on some other allocation methodology, then the basis of allocation (such as machine hours used) must first be compiled.
4. *Record the entry.* This journal entry involves shifting raw materials from the raw materials inventory account to the work in process inventory account, shifting direct labor expense into the work in process inventory account, and shifting factory overhead from the overhead cost pool to the WIP inventory account.

It is much easier to use standard costs for work in process accounting. Actual costs are difficult to trace to individual units of production.

The general theme of WIP accounting is to always use the simplest method that the company can convince its auditors to accept, on the grounds that a complex costing methodology will require an inordinate amount of time by the accounting staff, which in turn interferes with the time required to close the books at the end of each month.

Accounting for Obsolete Inventory

A materials review board should be used to locate obsolete inventory items. This group reviews inventory usage reports or physically examines the inventory to determine which items should be disposed of. You then review the findings of this group to determine the most likely disposition price of the obsolete items, subtract this projected amount from the book value of the obsolete items, and set aside the difference as a reserve. As the company later disposes of the items, or the estimated amounts to be received from disposition change, adjust the reserve account to reflect these events.

EXAMPLE

Milagro Corporation has $100,000 of excess home coffee roasters it cannot sell. However, it believes there is a market for the roasters through a reseller in China, but only at a sale price of $20,000. Accordingly, the accountant recognizes a reserve of $80,000 with the following journal entry:

	Debit	Credit
Cost of goods sold	80,000	
Reserve for obsolete inventory		80,000

After finalizing the arrangement with the Chinese reseller, the actual sale price is only $19,000, so the accountant completes the transaction with the following entry, recognizing an additional $1,000 of expense:

	Debit	Credit
Reserve for obsolete inventory	80,000	
Cost of goods sold	1,000	
Inventory		81,000

The example makes inventory obsolescence accounting look simple enough, but it is not. The issues are:

- *Timing.* You can improperly alter a company's reported financial results by altering the timing of the actual dispositions. As an example, if a supervisor knows that he can receive a higher-than-estimated price on the disposition of obsolete inventory, then he can either accelerate or delay the sale in order to shift gains into whichever reporting period needs the extra profit.
- *Expense recognition.* Management may be reluctant to suddenly drop a large expense reserve into the financial statements, preferring instead to recognize small incremental amounts which make inventory obsolescence appear to be a minor problem. Since GAAP mandates immediate recognition of any obsolescence as soon as it is detected, you may have a struggle enforcing immediate recognition over the objections of management.
- *Timely reviews.* Inventory obsolescence is a minor issue as long as management reviews inventory on a regular basis, so that the incremental amount of obsolescence detected is small in any given period. However, if management does not conduct a review for a long time, this allows obsolete inventory to build up to quite impressive proportions, along with an equally impressive amount of expense recognition. To avoid this issue, conduct frequent obsolescence reviews, and maintain a reserve based on historical or expected obsolescence, even if the specific inventory items have not yet been identified.

EXAMPLE

Milagro Corporation sets aside an obsolescence reserve of $25,000 for obsolete roasters. However, in January the purchasing manager knows that the resale price for obsolete roasters has plummeted, so the real reserve should be closer to $35,000, which would call for the immediate recognition of an additional $10,000 of expense. However, since this would result in an overall reported loss in Milagro's financial results in January, he waits until April, when Milagro has a very profitable month, and completes the sale at that time, thereby incorrectly delaying the additional obsolescence loss until the point of sale.

Consignment Accounting

Consignment occurs when goods are sent by their owner (the consignor) to an agent (the consignee), who undertakes to sell the goods. The consignor continues to own the goods until they are sold, so the goods appear as inventory in the accounting records of the consignor, not the consignee.

When the consignor sends goods to the consignee, there is no need to create an accounting entry related to the physical movement of goods. It is usually sufficient to record the change in location within the inventory record keeping system of the consignor. In addition, the consignor should consider the following maintenance activities:

- Periodically send a statement to the consignee, stating the inventory that should be on the consignee's premises. The consignee can use this statement to conduct a periodic reconciliation of the actual amount on hand to the consignor's records.
- Request from the consignee a statement of on-hand inventory at the end of each accounting period when the consignor is conducting a physical inventory count. The consignor incorporates this information into its inventory records to arrive at a fully valued ending inventory balance.

From the consignee's perspective, there is no need to record the consigned inventory, since it is owned by the consignor. It may be useful to keep a separate record of all consigned inventory, for reconciliation and insurance purposes.

When the consignee eventually sells the consigned goods, it pays the consignor a pre-arranged sale amount. The consignor records this prearranged amount with a debit to cash and a credit to sales. It also purges the related amount of inventory from its records with a debit to cost of goods sold and a credit to inventory. A profit or loss on the sale transaction will arise from these two entries.

Depending upon the arrangement with the consignee, the consignor may pay a commission to the consignee for making the sale. If so, this is a debit to commission expense and a credit to accounts payable.

From the consignee's perspective, a sale transaction triggers a payment to the consignor for the consigned goods that were sold. There will also be a sale transaction to record the sale of goods to the third party, which is a debit to cash or accounts receivable and a credit to sales.

Goods in Transit

Goods in transit are merchandise and other types of inventory that have left the shipping dock of the seller, but not yet reached the receiving dock of the buyer. Ideally, either the seller or the buyer should record goods in transit in its accounting records. The rule for doing so is based on the shipping terms associated with the goods, which are:

- *FOB shipping point.* If the shipment is designated as freight on board (FOB) shipping point, ownership transfers to the buyer as soon as the shipment departs the seller.
- *FOB destination.* If the shipment is designated as freight on board (FOB) destination, ownership transfers to the buyer as soon as the shipment arrives at the buyer.

EXAMPLE

Armadillo Industries ships $10,000 of merchandise to Antalya Clothiers on November 28. The terms of the delivery are FOB shipping point. Since these terms mean that Antalya takes on ownership of the merchandise as soon as they leave Armadillo's shipping dock, Armadillo should record a sale transaction on November 28, and Antalya should record an inventory receipt on the same date.

Assume the same scenario, but the terms of delivery are now FOB destination, and the shipment does not arrive at Antalya's receiving dock until December 2. In this case, the same transactions occur, but on December 2 instead of November 28. Thus, under the FOB destination shipping scenario, Armadillo does not record a sale transaction until December.

From a practical perspective, the buyer may not have a procedure in place to record inventory until it arrives at the receiving dock. This causes a problem under FOB shipping point terms, because the shipping entity records the transaction at the point of shipment, and the receiving company does not record receipt until the transaction is recorded at its receiving dock - thus, no one records the inventory while it is in transit.

Inventory Disclosures

The following information should be disclosed about a company's inventory practices in its financial statements:

- *Basis.* The basis on which inventories are stated. If there is a significant change in the basis of accounting, the nature of the change and the effect on income (if material) shall be stated.
- *LCM losses.* If there are substantial and unusual losses caused by the lower of cost or market rule, disclose this amount separately in the income statement. This is not a requirement.

- *Goods above cost.* Disclose the particulars concerning any inventory items that have been stated above cost.
- *Goods at sales prices.* Disclose the particulars concerning any inventory items that have been stated at their sales prices.
- *Firm purchase commitments.* Separately state in the income statement the amounts of any net losses that have been accrued on firm purchase commitments.
- *Estimate.* Disclose any significant estimates related to inventory.

Summary

When designing systems that will properly account for inventory, the key consideration is the sheer volume of transactions that must be tracked. It can be extremely difficult to consistently record these transactions with a minimal error rate, so tailor the accounting system to reduce the record keeping work load while still producing results that are in accordance with GAAP. In particular, be watchful for any additional accounting procedures that only refine the inventory information to a small degree, and eliminate or streamline them whenever possible. In essence, this is *the* accounting area in which having a cost-effective recordkeeping system is of some importance.

Chapter 8
Accounting for Property, Plant, and Equipment

Introduction

The accounting for property, plant, and equipment is not especially difficult in most respects, but does require a number of separate accounting transactions over the life of an asset, including acquisition, depreciation, and disposal, all of which are addressed in this chapter.

> **Related Podcast Episodes:** Episodes 122 and 139 of the Accounting Best Practices Podcast discuss fixed asset disposals and a lean system for fixed assets, respectively. You can listen to them at: **accountingtools.com/podcasts** or **iTunes**

The "fixed asset" name is used in this chapter to describe the group of assets that generate economic benefits over a long period of time. The GAAP codification uses a somewhat longer name for the same assets, which is "property, plant, and equipment" (PP&E). The PP&E term is rarely used in this chapter for two reasons:
- The name describes a subset of all fixed assets, since it only implies the existence of land, buildings, and machinery.
- The PP&E name is simply too long.

Thus, we are using the more all-encompassing "fixed assets" term throughout the chapter.

Overview of Fixed Assets

The vast majority of the expenditures that a company makes are for consumables, such as office supplies, wages, or products that it sells to customers. The effects of these items pass through a company quickly – they are used or sold and converted to cash, and they are recorded as expenses immediately, or with a slight delay (if they involve inventory). Thus, the benefits they generate are short-lived.

Fixed assets are entirely different. These are items that generate economic benefits over a long period of time. Because of the long period of usefulness of a fixed asset, it is not justifiable to charge its entire cost to expense when incurred. Instead, the *matching principle* comes into play. Under the matching principle, recognize both the benefits and expenses associated with a transaction (or, in this case, an asset) at the same time. To do so, we convert an expenditure into an asset, and use depreciation to gradually charge it to expense.

By designating an expenditure as a fixed asset, we are shifting the expenditure away from the income statement, where expenditures normally go, and instead place it in the balance sheet. As we gradually reduce its recorded cost through depreciation, the expenditure slowly flows from the balance sheet to the income statement. Thus, the main difference between a normal expenditure and a fixed asset is that the fixed asset is charged to expense over a longer period of time.

The process of identifying fixed assets, recording them as assets, and depreciating them is time-consuming, so it is customary to build some limitations into the process that route most expenditures directly to expense. One such limitation is to charge an expenditure to expense immediately unless it has a useful life of at least one year. Another limitation is to only recognize an expenditure as a fixed asset if it exceeds a certain dollar amount, known as the *capitalization limit*. These limits keep the vast majority of expenditures from being classified as fixed assets, which reduces the work of the accounting department.

EXAMPLE

Armadillo Industries incurs expenditures for three items, and must decide whether it should classify them as fixed assets. Armadillo's capitalization limit is $2,500. The expenditures are:

- It buys a used mold for its plastic injection molding operation for $5,000. Armadillo expects that the mold only has two months of useful life left, after which it should be scrapped. Since the useful life is so short, the accountant elects to charge the expenditure to expense immediately.
- It buys a laptop computer for $1,500, which has a useful life of three years. This expenditure is less than the capitalization limit, so the accountant charges it to expense.
- It buys a 10-ton injection molding machine for $50,000, which has a useful life of 10 years. Since this expenditure has a useful life of longer than one year and a cost greater than the capitalization limit, the accountant records it as a fixed asset, and will depreciate it over its 10-year useful life.

An alternative treatment of the $5,000 mold in the preceding example would be to record it under the Other Assets account in the balance sheet, and charge the cost to expense over two months. This is a useful alternative for expenditures that have useful lives of greater than one accounting period, but less than one year. It is a less time-consuming alternative for the accounting staff, which does not have to create a fixed asset record or engage in any depreciation calculations.

There are several key points in the life of a fixed asset that require recognition in the accounting records; these are the initial recordation of the asset, the recognition of any asset retirement obligations, depreciation, impairment, and the eventual derecognition of the asset. We describe these general concepts below, and include a reference to the more comprehensive treatment in later sections:

- *Initial recognition.* There are a number of factors to consider when initially recording a fixed asset, such as which costs to include, and when to stop capitalizing costs. These issues are dealt with in the Initial Fixed Asset Recognition section.

- *Depreciation.* You should gradually charge the cost of a fixed asset to expense over time, using depreciation. There are a variety of depreciation methods available, which are described further in the Depreciation and Amortization section.
- *Impairment.* If the fair value of a fixed asset falls below its recorded cost at any point during its useful life, you are required to reduce its recorded cost to its fair value, and recognize a loss for the difference between the two amounts. The Fixed Asset Impairment section delves into this accounting.
- *Disposal.* When an asset comes to the end of its useful life, a company will likely sell or otherwise dispose of it. At this time, you must remove it from the accounting records, as well as record a gain or loss (if any) on the final disposal transaction. This issue is discussed in the Fixed Asset Disposal section.

Initial Fixed Asset Recognition

You should initially record a fixed asset at the historical cost of acquiring it, which includes the costs to bring it to the condition and location necessary for its intended use. If these preparatory activities will occupy a period of time, include in the cost of the asset the interest costs related to the cost of the asset during the preparation period.

The activities involved in bringing a fixed asset to the condition and location necessary for its intended purpose include the following:

- Physical construction of the asset
- Demolition of any preexisting structures
- Renovating a preexisting structure to alter it for use by the buyer
- Administrative and technical activities during preconstruction for such activities as designing the asset and obtaining permits
- Administrative and technical work after construction commences for such activities as litigation, labor disputes, and technical problems

---

EXAMPLE

Nascent Corporation constructs a solar observatory. The project costs $10 million to construct. Also, Nascent takes out a loan for the entire $10 million amount of the project and pays $250,000 in interest costs during the six-month construction period. Further, the company incurs $500,000 in architectural fees and permit costs before work begins.

All of these costs can be capitalized into the cost of the building asset, so Nascent records $1.75 million as the cost of the building asset.

Fixed Assets Acquired through a Business Combination

If a company acquires fixed assets as part of a business combination, it should recognize all identifiable assets, including such identifiable intangible assets as a patent, customer relationship, or a brand. Record these fixed assets at their fair values as of the acquisition date.

EXAMPLE

Nascent Corporation acquires Stellar Designs for $40 million. It allocates $10 million of the purchase price among current assets and liabilities at their book values, which approximate their fair values. Nascent also assigns $22 million to identifiable fixed assets and $4 million to a customer relationships intangible asset. This leaves $4 million that cannot be allocated, and which is therefore assigned to a goodwill asset.

Nonmonetary Exchanges

What if you acquire a fixed asset through an exchange of assets? Follow this sequence of decisions to decide upon the correct cost at which to record the asset received:
1. Measure the asset acquired at the fair value of the asset surrendered to the other party.
2. If the fair value of the asset received is more clearly evident than the fair value of the asset surrendered, measure the acquired asset at its own fair value.

In either case, recognize a gain or loss on the difference between the recorded cost of the asset transferred to the other party and the recorded cost of the asset that you have acquired.

If you are unable to determine the fair value of either asset, record the asset received at the cost of the asset you have relinquished in order to obtain it. Use this latter approach under any of the following circumstances:
- You cannot determine the fair value of either asset within reasonable limits;
- The transaction is intended to facilitate a sale to a customer other than the parties to the asset exchange; or
- The transaction does not have commercial substance.

EXAMPLE

Nascent Corporation exchanges a color copier with a carrying amount of $18,000 with Declining Company for a print-on-demand publishing station. The color copier had an original cost of $30,000, and had incurred $12,000 of accumulated depreciation as of the transaction date. No cash is transferred as part of the exchange, and Nascent cannot determine the fair value of the color copier. The fair value of the publishing station is $20,000.

Nascent can record a gain of $2,000 on the exchange, which is derived from the fair value of the publishing station that it acquired, less the carrying amount of the color copier that it gave up. Nascent uses the following journal entry to record the transaction:

	Debit	Credit
Publishing equipment	20,000	
Accumulated depreciation	12,000	
Copier equipment		30,000
Gain on asset exchange		2,000

EXAMPLE

Nascent Corporation and Starlight Inc. swap spectroscopes, since the two devices have different features that the two companies need. The spectroscope given up by Nascent has a carrying amount of $25,000, which is comprised of an original cost of $40,000 and accumulated depreciation of $15,000. Both spectroscopes have identical fair values of $27,000.

Nascent's accountant tests for commercial substance in the transaction. She finds that there is no difference in the fair values of the assets exchanged, and that Nascent's cash flows will not change significantly as a result of the swap. Thus, she concludes that the transaction has no commercial value, and so should account for it at book value, which means that Nascent cannot recognize a gain of $2,000 on the transaction, which is the difference between the $27,000 fair value of the spectroscope and the $25,000 carrying amount of the asset given up. Instead, she uses the following journal entry to record the transaction, which does not contain a gain or loss:

	Debit	Credit
Spectroscope (asset received)	25,000	
Accumulated depreciation	15,000	
Spectroscope (asset given up)		40,000

What if there is an exchange of cash between the two parties, in addition to a non-monetary exchange? The accounting varies if the amount of cash, or *boot*, paid as part of the asset exchange is relatively small (which is defined under GAAP as less than 25 percent of the fair value of the exchange), or if it is larger.

In the case of a small amount of boot, the recipient of the cash records a gain to the extent that the amount of cash received exceeds a proportionate share of the cost of the surrendered asset. This proportionate share is calculated as the ratio of the cash paid to the total consideration received (which is the cash received plus the fair value of the asset received); if the amount of the consideration received is not clearly evident, you can instead use the fair value of the asset surrendered to the other party. The calculation is:

$$\frac{\text{Boot}}{\text{Boot} + \text{Fair value of asset received}} \times \text{Total gain} = \text{Gain recognized}$$

What is the accounting from the perspective of the party paying cash as part of the transaction? This entity records the asset received as the sum of the cash paid to the other party plus the recorded amount of the asset surrendered. If the transaction results in a loss, record the entire amount of the loss at once. Under no circumstances are you allowed to record a gain on such a transaction.

EXAMPLE

Nascent Corporation is contemplating the exchange of one of its heliographs for a catadioptric telescope owned by Aphelion Corporation. The two companies have recorded these assets in their accounting records as follows:

	Nascent (Heliograph)	Aphelion (Catadioptric)
Cost	$82,000	$97,000
Accumulated depreciation	22,000	27,000
Net book value	$60,000	$70,000
Fair value	$55,000	$72,000

Under the terms of the proposed asset exchange, Nascent must pay cash (boot) to Aphelion of $17,000. The boot amount is 24 percent of the fair value of the exchange, which is calculated as:

$17,000 Boot ÷ ($55,000 Fair value of heliograph + $17,000 Boot) = 24%

The parties elect to go forward with the exchange. The amount of boot is less than 25 percent of the total fair value of the exchange, so Aphelion should recognize a pro rata portion of the $2,000 gain (calculated as the $72,000 total fair value of the asset received - $70,000 net book value of the asset received) on the exchange using the following calculation:

24% Portion of boot to total fair value received × $2,000 Gain = $480 Recognized gain

Nascent uses the following journal entry to record the exchange transaction:

	Debit	Credit
Telescope (asset received)	72,000	
Accumulated depreciation	22,000	
Loss on asset exchange	5,000	
Cash		17,000
Heliograph (asset given up)		82,000

Nascent's journal entry includes a $5,000 loss; the loss is essentially the difference between the book value and fair value of the heliograph on the transaction date.

Aphelion uses the following journal entry to record the exchange transaction:

	Debit	Credit
Heliograph (asset received)	53,480	
Accumulated depreciation	27,000	
Cash	17,000	
Gain on asset exchange		480
Telescope (asset given up)		97,000

Aphelion is not allowed to recognize the full value of the heliograph at the acquisition date because of the boot rule for small amounts of cash consideration; this leaves the heliograph undervalued by $1,520 (since its fair value is actually $55,000).

The accounting is different if the amount of boot is 25 percent or more of the fair value of the exchange. In this situation, both parties should record the transaction at its fair value.

EXAMPLE

Nascent Corporation exchanges a wide field CCD camera for a Schmidt-Cassegrain telescope owned by Aphelion Corporation. The two companies have recorded these assets in their accounting records as follows:

	Nascent (Camera)	Aphelion (Schmidt-Cassegrain)
Cost	$50,000	$93,000
Accumulated depreciation	(30,000)	(40,000)
Net book value	$20,000	$53,000
Fair value	$24,000	$58,000

Under the terms of the agreement, Nascent pays $34,000 cash (boot) to Aphelion. This boot amount is well in excess of the 25 percent boot level, so both parties can now treat the deal as a monetary transaction.

Nascent uses the following journal entry to record the exchange transaction, which measures the telescope acquired at the fair value of the camera and cash surrendered:

	Debit	Credit
Telescope (asset received)	58,000	
Accumulated depreciation	30,000	
Gain on asset exchange		4,000
Cash		34,000
CCD camera (asset given up)		50,000

The gain recorded by Nascent is the difference between the $24,000 fair value of the camera surrendered and its $20,000 book value.

Aphelion uses the following journal entry to record the exchange transaction, which measures the camera acquired at the fair value of the telescope surrendered less cash received:

	Debit	Credit
Camera (asset received)	24,000	
Accumulated depreciation	40,000	
Cash	34,000	
Gain on asset exchange		5,000
Telescope (asset given up)		93,000

136

The gain recorded by Aphelion is the difference between the $58,000 fair value of the telescope surrendered and its $53,000 book value.

Depreciation and Amortization

The purpose of depreciation is to charge to expense a portion of an asset that relates to the revenue generated by that asset. This is called the matching principle, where revenues and expenses both appear in the income statement in the same reporting period, which gives the best view of how well a company has performed in a given accounting period.

There are three factors to consider in the calculation of depreciation, which are:

- *Useful life.* This is the time period over which you expect that the asset will be productive, or the number of units of production expected to be generated from it. Past its useful life, it is no longer cost-effective to continue operating the asset, so you would dispose of it or stop using it. Depreciation is recognized over the useful life of an asset.

Tip: Rather than recording a different useful life for every asset, it is easier to assign each asset to an asset class, where every asset in that asset class has the same useful life. This approach may not work for very high-cost assets, where a greater degree of precision may be needed.

- *Salvage value.* When a company eventually disposes of an asset, it may be able to sell it for some reduced amount, which is the salvage value. Depreciation is calculated based on the asset cost, less any estimated salvage value. If salvage value is expected to be quite small, it is generally ignored for the purpose of calculating depreciation. Salvage value is not discounted to its present value.

Tip: If you estimate that the amount of salvage value associated with an asset is minor, it is easier from a calculation perspective to not reduce the depreciable amount of the asset by the salvage value. Instead, assume that the salvage value is zero.

EXAMPLE

Pensive Corporation buys an asset for $100,000, and estimates that its salvage value will be $10,000 in five years, when it plans to dispose of the asset. This means that Pensive will depreciate $90,000 of the asset cost over five years, leaving $10,000 of the cost remaining at the end of that time. Pensive expects to then sell the asset for $10,000, which will eliminate the asset from its accounting records.

- *Depreciation method.* Depreciation expense can be calculated using an accelerated depreciation method, or evenly over the useful life of the asset. The advantage of using an accelerated method is that you can recognize more depreciation early in the life of a fixed asset, which defers some income tax expense recognition into a later period. The advantage of using a steady depreciation rate is the ease of calculation. Examples of accelerated depreciation methods are the double declining balance and sum-of-the-years' digits methods. The primary method for steady depreciation is the straight-line method.

The *mid-month convention* states that, no matter when you purchase a fixed asset in a month, you assume that it was purchased in the middle of the month for depreciation purposes. Thus, if you bought a fixed asset on January 5th, assume that you bought it on January 15th; or, if you bought it on January 28, still assume that you bought it on January 15th. By doing so, you can more easily calculate a standard half-month of depreciation for that first month of ownership.

If you choose to use the mid-month convention, this also means that you should record a half-month of depreciation for the *last* month of the asset's useful life. By doing so, the two-half month depreciation calculations equal one full month of depreciation.

Many companies prefer to use full-month depreciation in the first month of ownership, irrespective of the actual date of purchase within the month, so that they can slightly accelerate their recognition of depreciation, which in turn reduces their taxable income in the near term.

Straight-Line Method

Under the straight-line method of depreciation, recognize depreciation expense evenly over the estimated useful life of an asset. The straight-line calculation steps are:

1. Subtract the estimated salvage value of the asset from the amount at which it is recorded on the books.
2. Determine the estimated useful life of the asset. It is easiest to use a standard useful life for each class of assets.
3. Divide the estimated useful life (in years) into 1 to arrive at the straight-line depreciation rate.
4. Multiply the depreciation rate by the asset cost (less salvage value).

EXAMPLE

Pensive Corporation purchases the Procrastinator Deluxe machine for $60,000. It has an estimated salvage value of $10,000 and a useful life of five years. Pensive calculates the annual straight-line depreciation for the machine as:

1. Purchase cost of $60,000 – estimated salvage value of $10,000 = Depreciable asset cost of $50,000
2. $1 \div 5$-year useful life = 20% depreciation rate per year

3. 20% depreciation rate × $50,000 depreciable asset cost = $10,000 annual depreciation

Sum-of-the-Years' Digits Method

The sum of the years' digits (SYD) method is more appropriate than straight-line depreciation if the asset depreciates more quickly or has greater production capacity in earlier years than it does as it ages. Use the following formula to calculate it:

$$\text{Depreciation percentage} = \frac{\text{Number of estimated years of life as of beginning of the year}}{\text{Sum of the years' digits}}$$

The following table contains examples of the sum of the years' digits noted in the denominator of the preceding formula:

Total Depreciation Period	Initial Sum of the Years' Digits	Calculation
2 years	3	1 + 2
3 years	6	1 + 2 + 3
4 years	10	1 + 2 + 3 + 4
5 years	15	1 + 2 + 3 + 4 + 5

The concept is most easily illustrated with the following example:

EXAMPLE

Pensive Corporation buys a Procrastinator Elite machine for $100,000. The machine has no estimated salvage value, and a useful life of five years.

Pensive calculates the annual sum of the years' digits depreciation for this machine as:

Year	Number of estimated years of life as of beginning of the year	SYD Calculation	Depreciation Percentage	Annual Depreciation
1	5	5/15	33.33%	$33,333
2	4	4/15	26.67%	26,667
3	3	3/15	20.00%	20,000
4	2	2/15	13.33%	13,333
5	1	1/15	6.67%	6,667
Totals	15		100.00%	$100,000

The sum of the years' digits method is clearly more complex than the straight-line method, which tends to limit its use unless software is used to automatically track the calculations for each asset.

Double-Declining Balance Method

The double declining balance (DDB) method is a form of accelerated depreciation. It may be more appropriate than the straight-line method if an asset experiences an inordinately high level of usage during the first few years of its useful life.

To calculate the double-declining balance depreciation rate, divide the number of years of useful life of an asset into 100 percent, and multiply the result by two. The formula is:

$$(100\%/\text{Years of useful life}) \times 2$$

The DDB calculation proceeds until the asset's salvage value is reached, after which depreciation ends.

EXAMPLE

Pensive Corporation purchases a machine for $50,000. It has an estimated salvage value of $5,000 and a useful life of five years. The calculation of the double declining balance depreciation rate is:

$$(100\%/\text{Years of useful life}) \times 2 = 40\%$$

By applying the 40% rate, Pensive arrives at the following table of depreciation charges per year:

Year	Book Value at Beginning of Year	Depreciation Percentage	DDB Depreciation	Book Value Net of Depreciation
1	$50,000	40%	$20,000	$30,000
2	30,000	40%	12,000	18,000
3	18,000	40%	7,200	10,800
4	10,800	40%	4,320	6,480
5	6,480	40%	1,480	5,000
Total			$45,000	

Note that the depreciation in the fifth and final year is only for $1,480, rather than the $3,240 that would be indicated by the 40% depreciation rate. The reason for the smaller depreciation charge is that Pensive stops any further depreciation once the remaining book value declines to the amount of the estimated salvage value.

An alternative form of double declining balance depreciation is 150% declining balance depreciation. It is a less aggressive form of depreciation, since it is calculated as 1.5 times the straight-line rate, rather than the 2x multiple that is used for the double declining balance method. Thus, if you were to use it, the formula would be:

$$(100\%/\text{Years of useful life}) \times 1.5$$

EXAMPLE

[Note: We are repeating the preceding example, but using 150% declining balance depreciation instead of double declining balance depreciation]

Pensive Corporation purchases a machine for $50,000. It has an estimated salvage value of $5,000 and a useful life of five years. The calculation of the 150% declining balance depreciation rate is:

$$(100\%/\text{Years of useful life}) \times 1.5 = 30\%$$

By applying the 30% rate, Pensive arrives at the following table of depreciation charges per year:

Year	Book Value at Beginning of Year	Depreciation Percentage	DDB Depreciation	Book Value Net of Depreciation
1	$50,000	30%	$15,000	$35,000
2	35,000	30%	10,500	24,500
3	24,500	30%	7,350	17,150
4	17,150	30%	5,145	12,005
5	12,005	30%	7,005	5,000
Total			$45,000	

In this case, the depreciation expense in the fifth and final year of $3,602 ($12,005 × 30%) results in a net book value that is somewhat higher than the estimated salvage value of $5,000, so Pensive instead records $7,005 of depreciation in order to arrive at a net book value that equals the estimated salvage value.

Depletion Method

Depletion is a periodic charge to expense for the use of natural resources. Thus, it is used in situations where a company has recorded an asset for such items as oil reserves, coal deposits, or gravel pits. The calculation of depletion involves these steps:

1. Compute a depletion base
2. Compute a unit depletion rate
3. Charge depletion based on units of usage

The depletion base is the asset that is to be depleted. It is comprised of the following four types of costs:

- *Acquisition costs*. The cost to either buy or lease property.
- *Exploration costs*. The cost to locate assets that may then be depleted. In most cases, these costs are charged to expense as incurred.
- *Development costs*. The cost to prepare the property for asset extraction, which includes the cost of such items as tunnels and wells.
- *Restoration costs*. The cost to restore property to its original condition after depletion activities have been concluded.

To compute a unit depletion rate, subtract the salvage value of the asset from the depletion base and divide it by the total number of measurement units that you expect to recover. The formula for the unit depletion rate is:

$$\text{Unit depletion rate} = \frac{\text{Depletion base} - \text{Salvage value}}{\text{Total units to be recovered}}$$

The depletion charge is then created based on actual units of usage. Thus, if you extract 500 barrels of oil and the unit depletion rate is $5.00 per barrel, then you charge $2,500 to depletion expense.

The estimated amount of a natural resource that can be recovered will change constantly as you gradually extract assets from a property. As you revise the estimates of the remaining amount of extractable natural resource, incorporate these estimates into the unit depletion rate for the remaining amount to be extracted. This is not a retrospective calculation.

EXAMPLE

Pensive Corporation's subsidiary Pensive Oil drills a well with the intention of extracting oil from a known reservoir. It incurs the following costs related to the acquisition of property and development of the site:

Land purchase	$280,000
Road construction	23,000
Drill pad construction	48,000
Drilling fees	192,000
Total	$543,000

In addition, Pensive Oil estimates that it will incur a site restoration cost of $57,000 once extraction is complete, so the total depletion base of the property is $600,000.

Pensive's geologists estimate that the proven oil reserves that are accessed by the well are 400,000 barrels, so the unit depletion charge will be $1.50 per barrel of oil extracted ($600,000 depletion base ÷ 400,000 barrels).

In the first year, Pensive Oil extracts 100,000 barrels of oil from the well, which results in a depletion charge of $150,000 (100,000 barrels × $1.50 unit depletion charge).

At the beginning of the second year of operations, Pensive's geologists issue a revised estimate of the remaining amount of proven reserves, with the new estimate of 280,000 barrels being 20,000 barrels lower than the original estimate (less extractions already completed). This means that the unit depletion charge will increase to $1.61 ($450,000 remaining depletion base ÷ 280,000 barrels).

During the second year, Pensive Oil extracts 80,000 barrels of oil from the well, which results in a depletion charge of $128,800 (80,000 barrels × $1.61 unit depletion charge).

At the end of the second year, there is still a depletion base of $321,200 that must be charged to expense in proportion to the amount of any remaining extractions.

Units of Production Method

Under the units of production method, the amount of depreciation charged to expense varies in direct proportion to the amount of asset usage. Thus, you charge more depreciation in periods when there is more asset usage, and less depreciation in periods when there is less asset usage. It is the most accurate method for charging depreciation, since it links closely to the wear and tear on assets. However, it also requires that you track asset usage, which means that its use is generally limited to more expensive assets. Also, you need to be able to estimate total usage over the life of the asset.

Tip: Do not use the units of production method if there is not a significant difference in asset usage from period to period. Otherwise, you will spend a great deal of time tracking asset usage, and will be rewarded with a depreciation expense that varies little from the results that you would have seen with the straight-line method (which is far easier to calculate).

Follow these steps to calculate depreciation under the units of production method:
1. Estimate the total number of hours of usage of the asset, or the total number of units to be produced by it over its useful life.
2. Subtract any estimated salvage value from the capitalized cost of the asset, and divide the total estimated usage or production from this net depreciable cost. This yields the depreciation cost per hour of usage or unit of production.
3. Multiply the number of hours of usage or units of actual production by the depreciation cost per hour or unit, which results in the total depreciation expense for the accounting period.

If the estimated number of hours of usage or units of production changes over time, incorporate these changes into the calculation of the depreciation cost per hour or unit of production. This will alter the depreciation expense on a go-forward basis.

EXAMPLE

Pensive Corporation's gravel pit operation, Pensive Dirt, builds a conveyor system to extract gravel from a gravel pit at a cost of $400,000. Pensive expects to use the conveyor to extract 1,000,000 tons of gravel, which results in a depreciation rate of $0.40 per ton (1,000,000 tons ÷ $400,000 cost). During the first quarter of activity, Pensive Dirt extracts 10,000 tons of gravel, which results in the following depreciation expense:

$$= \$0.40 \text{ depreciation cost per ton} \times 10,000 \text{ tons of gravel}$$

= $4,000 depreciation expense

Land Depreciation

Nearly all fixed assets have a useful life, after which they no longer contribute to the operations of a company or they stop generating revenue. During this useful life, they are depreciated, which reduces their cost to what they are supposed to be worth at the end of their useful lives. Land, however, has no definitive useful life, so there is no way to depreciate it.

The one exception is when some aspect of the land is actually used up, such as when a mine is emptied of its ore reserves. In this case, depreciate the natural resources in the land using the depletion method, as described earlier in this chapter.

Land Improvement Depreciation

Land improvements are enhancements to a plot of land to make it more usable. If these improvements have a useful life, depreciate them. If there is no way to estimate a useful life, do not depreciate the cost of the improvements.

If you are preparing land for its intended purpose, include these costs in the cost of the land asset. They are not depreciated. Examples of such costs are:
- Demolishing an existing building
- Clearing and leveling the land

If you are adding functionality to the land and the expenditures have a useful life, record them in a separate land improvements account. Examples of land improvements are:
- Drainage and irrigation systems
- Fencing
- Landscaping
- Parking lots and walkways

A special item is the ongoing cost of landscaping. This is a period cost, not a fixed asset, and so should be charged to expense as incurred.

EXAMPLE

Pensive Corporation buys a parcel of land for $1,000,000. Since it is a purchase of land, Pensive cannot depreciate the cost. Pensive then razes a building that was located on the property at a cost of $25,000, fills in the old foundation for $5,000, and levels the land for $50,000. All of these costs are to prepare the land for its intended purpose, so they are all added to the cost of the land. It cannot depreciate these costs.

Pensive intends to use the land as a parking lot, so it spends $400,000 to pave the land and add walkways and fences. It estimates that the parking lot has a useful life of 20 years. It should record this cost in the land improvements account, and depreciate it over 20 years.

Depreciation Accounting Entries

The basic depreciation entry is to debit the depreciation expense account (which appears in the income statement) and credit the accumulated depreciation account (which appears in the balance sheet as a contra account that reduces the amount of fixed assets). Over time, the accumulated depreciation balance will continue to increase as more depreciation is added to it, until such time as it equals the original cost of the asset. At that time, stop recording any depreciation expense, since the cost of the asset has now been reduced to zero.

The journal entry for depreciation can be a simple two-line entry designed to accommodate all types of fixed assets, or it may be subdivided into separate entries for each type of fixed asset.

EXAMPLE

Pensive Corporation calculates that it should have $25,000 of depreciation expense in the current month. The entry is:

	Debit	Credit
Depreciation expense	25,000	
Accumulated depreciation		25,000

In the following month, Pensive's accountant decides to show a higher level of precision at the expense account level, and instead elects to apportion the $25,000 of depreciation among different expense accounts, so that each class of asset has a separate depreciation charge. The entry is:

	Debit	Credit
Depreciation expense - Automobiles	4,000	
Depreciation expense – Computer equipment	8,000	
Depreciation expense – Furniture and fixtures	6,000	
Depreciation expense – Office equipment	5,000	
Depreciation expense – Software	2,000	
Accumulated depreciation		25,000

The journal entry to record the amortization of intangible assets is fundamentally the same as the entry for depreciation, except that the accounts used substitute the word "amortization" for depreciation.

EXAMPLE

Pensive Corporation calculates that it should have $4,000 of amortization expense in the current month that is related to intangible assets. The entry is:

	Debit	Credit
Amortization expense	4,000	
Accumulated amortization		4,000

When you sell or otherwise dispose of an asset, remove all related accumulated depreciation from the accounting records at the same time. Otherwise, an unusually large amount of accumulated depreciation will build up on the balance sheet.

EXAMPLE

Pensive Corporate has $1,000,000 of fixed assets, for which it has charged $380,000 of accumulated depreciation. This results in the following presentation on Pensive's balance sheet:

Fixed assets	$1,000,000
Less: Accumulated depreciation	(380,000)
Net fixed assets	$620,000

Pensive then sells a machine for $80,000 that had an original cost of $140,000, and for which it had already recorded accumulated depreciation of $50,000. It records the sale with this journal entry:

	Debit	Credit
Cash	80,000	
Accumulated depreciation	50,000	
Loss on asset sale	10,000	
Fixed assets		140,000

As a result of this entry, Pensive's balance sheet presentation of fixed assets has changed, so that fixed assets before accumulated depreciation have declined to $860,000, and accumulated depreciation has declined to $330,000. The new presentation is:

Fixed assets	$860,000
Less: Accumulated depreciation	(330,000)
Net fixed assets	$530,000

The amount of net fixed assets declined by $90,000 as a result of the asset sale, which is the sum of the $80,000 cash proceeds and the $10,000 loss resulting from the asset sale.

Fixed Asset Impairment

There are rules under GAAP for periodically testing fixed assets to see if they are still as valuable as the costs at which they were recorded in the accounting records. If not, reduce the recorded cost of these assets by recognizing a loss. Also, under no circumstances are you allowed to reverse an impairment loss under GAAP.

You should recognize an impairment loss on a fixed asset if its carrying amount is not recoverable and exceeds its fair value. This loss is recognized within income from continuing operations on the income statement.

The carrying amount of an asset is not recoverable if it exceeds the sum of the undiscounted cash flows expected to result from the use of the asset over its remaining useful life and the final disposition of the asset. These cash flow estimates should incorporate assumptions that are reasonable in relation to the assumptions the entity uses for its budgets, forecasts, and so forth. If there are a range of possible cash flow outcomes, then consider using a probability-weighted cash flow analysis.

> **Tip:** You are supposed to base impairment analysis on the cash flows to be expected over the remaining useful life of an asset. If you are measuring impairment for a group of assets (as discussed below), then the remaining useful life is based on the useful life of the primary asset in the group. You cannot skew the results by including in the group an asset with a theoretically unlimited life, such as land or an intangible asset that is not being amortized.

The amount of an impairment loss is the difference between an asset's carrying amount and its fair value. Once you recognize an impairment loss, this reduces the carrying amount of the asset, so you may need to alter the amount of periodic depreciation being charged against the asset to adjust for this lower carrying amount (otherwise, you will incur an excessively large depreciation expense over the remaining useful life of the asset).

If you have designated an asset as held for sale, then periodically test it for a possible loss on the expected disposal of the asset. You should recognize a loss in the amount by which the fair value less costs to sell of the asset is lower than its carrying amount, and state it within income from continuing operations on the income statement.

Test assets for impairment at the lowest level at which there are identifiable cash flows that are largely independent of the cash flows of other assets. In cases where there are no identifiable cash flows at all (as is common with corporate-level assets), place these assets in an asset group that encompasses the entire entity, and test for impairment at the entity level.

Only add goodwill to an asset group for impairment testing when the asset group is a reporting unit, or includes a reporting unit. Thus, do not include goodwill in any asset groups below the reporting unit level.

Only test for the recoverability of an asset whenever the circumstances indicate that its carrying amount may not be recoverable. Examples of such situations are:

- *Cash flow*. There are historical and projected operating or cash flow losses associated with the asset.
- *Costs*. There are excessive costs incurred to acquire or construct the asset.
- *Disposal*. The asset is more than 50% likely to be sold or otherwise disposed of significantly before the end of its previously estimated useful life.
- *Legal*. There is a significant adverse change in legal factors or the business climate that could affect the asset's value.
- *Market price*. There is a significant decrease in the asset's market price.
- *Usage*. There is a significant adverse change in the asset's manner of use, or in its physical condition.

If there is an impairment at the level of an asset group, allocate the impairment among the assets in the group on a pro rata basis, based on the carrying amounts of the assets in the group. However, the impairment loss cannot reduce the carrying amount of an asset below its fair value.

Tip: You only have to determine the fair value of an asset for this test if it is "determinable without undue cost and effort." Thus, if an outside appraisal would be required to determine fair value, you can likely dispense with this requirement and simply allocate the impairment loss to all of the assets in the group.

EXAMPLE

Luminescence Corporation operates a small floodlight manufacturing facility. Luminescence considers the entire facility to be a reporting unit, so it conducts an impairment test on the entire operation. The test reveals that a continuing decline in the market for floodlights (caused by the surge in LED lights in the market) has caused a $2 million impairment charge. Luminescence allocates the charge to the four assets in the facility as follows:

Asset	Carrying Amount	Proportion of Carrying Amounts	Impairment Allocation	Revised Carrying Amount
Ribbon machine	$8,000,000	67%	$1,340,000	$6,660,000
Conveyors	1,500,000	13%	260,000	1,240,000
Gas injector	2,000,000	16%	320,000	1,680,000
Filament inserter	500,000	4%	80,000	420,000
Totals	$12,000,000	100%	$2,000,000	$10,000,000

It is allowable under GAAP to recognize a gain on any increase in the fair value less costs to sell of a fixed asset that is designated as held for sale. The amount of this gain is capped at the amount of any cumulative disposal loss that you have already recognized for the asset. This gain will increase the carrying amount of the asset.

EXAMPLE

Luminescence Corporation has designated one of its fluorescent bulb factories as held for sale. The asset group comprising the factory has a carrying amount of $18 million. After six months, Luminescence determines that the fair value less costs to sell for the factory is $16 million, due to falling prices for similar factories, so it recognizes a disposal loss of $2 million. A few months later, the market for such factories rebounds, and the company finds that the factory now has a fair value less costs to sell of $19 million, which is an increase of $3 million.

Luminescence can only recognize a $2 million gain, which reverses the prior disposal loss.

Fixed Asset Disposal

An asset is derecognized upon its disposal, or when no future economic benefits can be expected from its use or disposal. Derecognition can arise from a variety of events, such as an asset's sale, scrapping, or donation.

The net effect of asset derecognition is to remove an asset and its associated accumulated depreciation from the balance sheet, as well as to recognize any related gain or loss. You cannot record a gain on derecognition as revenue. The gain or loss on derecognition is calculated as the net disposal proceeds, minus the asset's carrying amount.

Assets Held for Sale

There is a special asset classification under GAAP that is called *held-for-sale*. This classification is important for two reasons:

- All assets classified as held for sale are presented separately on the balance sheet.
- You do not depreciate or amortize assets classified as held for sale.

Under GAAP, classify a fixed asset or a disposal group as held for sale if all of the following criteria are met:

- Management commits to a plan to sell the assets.
- The asset is available for sale immediately in its present condition.
- There is an active program to sell the asset.
- It is unlikely that the plan to sell the asset will be changed or withdrawn.
- Sale of the asset is likely to occur, and should be completed within one year.
- The asset is being marketed at a price that is considered reasonable in comparison to its current fair value.

EXAMPLE

Ambivalence Corporation plans to sell its existing headquarters facility and build a new corporate headquarters building. It will remain in its existing quarters until the new facility is complete, and will transfer ownership of the building to a buyer only after it has moved out. Since the company's continuing presence in the existing building means that it cannot be available for sale immediately, the situation fails the held-for-sale criteria, and Ambivalence should not reclassify its existing headquarters building as held-for-sale. This would be the case even if Ambivalence had a firm purchase commitment to buy the building, since the actual transfer of ownership will still be delayed.

The one-year limitation noted in the preceding criteria can be circumvented in any of the following situations:

- *Expected conditions imposed.* An entity other than the buyer is likely to impose conditions that will extend the sale period beyond one year, and the seller cannot respond to those conditions until after it receives a firm purchase commitment, and it expects that commitment within one year.

EXAMPLE

Ambivalence Corporation has a geothermal electricity-generating plant on the site of its Brew Master production facility. It plans to sell the geothermal plant to a local electric utility. The sale is subject to the approval of the state regulatory commission, which will likely require more than one year to issue its opinion. Ambivalence cannot begin to obtain the commission's approval until after it has obtained a firm purchase commitment from the local utility, but expects to receive the commitment within one year. The situation meets the criteria for maintaining an asset in the held-for-sale classification for more than one year.

- *Unexpected conditions imposed.* The seller obtains a firm purchase commitment, but the buyer or others then impose conditions on the sale that are not expected, and the seller is responding to these conditions, and the seller expects a favorable resolution of the conditions.

EXAMPLE

Ambivalence Corporation enters into a firm purchase commitment to sell its potions plant, but the buyer's inspection team finds that some potions have leaked into the local water table. The buyer demands that Ambivalence mitigate this environmental damage before the sale is concluded, which will require more than one year to complete. Ambivalence initiates these activities, and expects to mitigate the damage. The situation meets the criteria for maintaining an asset in the held-for-sale classification for more than one year.

- *Unlikely circumstances.* An unlikely situation arises that delays the sale, and the seller is responding to the change in circumstances, and is continuing to market the asset at a price that is reasonable in relation to its current fair value.

EXAMPLE

Ambivalence Corporation is attempting to sell its charm bracelet manufacturing line, but market conditions deteriorate, and it is unable to sell the line at the price point that it wants. Management believes that the market will rebound, so it leaves the same price in place, even though the market price is probably 20% lower. Given that the price now exceeds the current fair value of the manufacturing line, the company is no longer marketing it at a reasonable price, and so should no longer list the asset in the held-for-sale classification.

If a company acquires an asset as part of a business combination and wants to immediately classify it as held for sale, the asset must meet these requirements:

- Sale of the asset is likely to occur, and should be completed within one year.
- If any of the other criteria noted above are not met as of the acquisition date, it is probable that they will be met shortly after the acquisition has been completed.

Tip: The GAAP codification states that three months is "usually" the amount of time allowed for the buyer to meet the held-for-sale criteria. Given the wording of this pronouncement, there is probably some leeway in the actual amount of time allowed.

If you classify assets as held-for-sale, measure them at the lower of their carrying amount or their fair value minus any cost to sell. If you must write down the carrying amount of an asset to its fair value minus any cost to sell, then recognize a loss in the amount of the write down. You may also recognize a gain on an increase in the fair value minus any cost to sell, but only up to the amount of any cumulative losses previously recognized.

When you classify an asset as held-for-sale, do not also accrue any expected future losses associated with operating it while it is so classified. Instead, recognize these costs only as incurred.

EXAMPLE

Ambivalence Corporation sells its Brew Master product line in 20X1, recognizing a gain of $100,000 prior to applicable taxes of $35,000. During the final year of operations of the Brew Master line, Ambivalence lost $50,000 on its operation of the line; it lost $80,000 during the preceding year. The applicable amount of tax reductions related to these losses were $(17,000) and $(28,000), respectively. It reports these results in the income statement as follows:

	20X0	20X1
Discontinued operations:		
Loss from operation of the Brew Master product line (net of applicable taxes of $28,000 and $17,000)	$(52,000)	$(33,000)
Gain on disposal of Brew Master product line (net of applicable taxes of $35,000)	--	$65,000

151

Part of the sale agreement requires that Ambivalence reimburse the buyer for any outstanding warranty claims. In the following year, the amount of these claims is $31,000, prior to an applicable tax reduction of $(11,000). Ambivalence reports this update to the discontinued operation in the following year with this disclosure in the income statement:

	20X0	20X1	20X2
Discontinued operations:			
Loss from operation of the Brew Master product line (net of applicable taxes of $28,000 and $17,000)	$(52,000)	$(33,000)	--
Gain on disposal of Brew Master product line (net of applicable taxes of $35,000)	--	$65,000	--
Adjust to gain on disposal of Brew Master product line (net of applicable taxes of $11,000)	--	--	$(20,000)

When you itemize the assets and liabilities of discontinued operations in the balance sheet, do not present them as a combined net figure. Instead, present them separately as assets and liabilities.

What if, despite initial expectations, an asset that has been classified as held for sale is not sold? If an asset no longer meets any one of the preceding six criteria for classification, remove it from the held-for-sale classification. At the time of reclassification, measure it at the lower of:

- The carrying amount of the asset prior to its classification as held-for-sale, minus any depreciation or amortization that would have been charged to it during the period when it was classified as held-for-sale, or
- The fair value of the asset when the decision was made not to sell it.

This measurement requirement effectively keeps a company from shifting assets into the held for sale classification in order to fraudulently avoid incurring any related depreciation expense.

Note: The GAAP codification states that an asset being reclassified *from* the held-for-sale designation should now be classified as held and used. Since there does not appear to be any distinction between the held and used classification and the normal accounting for fixed assets that are in use, we will assume that these assets are actually returned to their normal fixed asset accounting designations.

When you adjust the accounting records for this measurement, record the transaction as an expense that is included in income from continuing operations, and record the entry in the period when you make the decision not to sell the asset. Charge the expense to the income statement classification to which you would normally charge depreciation for the asset in question. Thus, the adjustment for a production machine would likely be charged to the cost of goods sold, while the adjustment for office equipment would likely be charged to general and administrative expense.

EXAMPLE

Ambivalence Corporation intends to sell its potion brewing factory, and so classifies the related assets into a disposal group and reports the group as held for sale, in the amount of $1,000,000. The journal entry is:

	Debit	Credit
Equipment held-for-sale	1,000,000	
Production machinery		1,000,000

After six months, the accountant determines that the fair value of the disposal group has declined to $950,000, and so writes down the equipment cost with this entry:

	Debit	Credit
Loss on decline of fair value of held-for-sale equipment	50,000	
Equipment held-for-sale		50,000

The carrying value of the disposal group is now $950,000. After three more months, an independent appraiser determines that the fair value of the disposal group has now increased to $1,010,000. The accountant can only record a gain up to the amount of any previously recorded losses, so he records the gain with this entry:

	Debit	Credit
Equipment held-for-sale	50,000	
Recovery of fair value of held-for-sale equipment		50,000

The carrying value of the disposal group is now $1,000,000.

After one full year has passed, management concludes that it cannot sell the disposal group, and decides to continue operating the potion brewing factory. The accountant reclassifies the disposal group out of the held-for-sale classification with this entry:

	Debit	Credit
Production machinery	1,000,000	
Equipment held-for-sale		1,000,000

During the period when Ambivalence classified the disposal group as held for sale, it would have incurred a depreciation expense on the group of $50,000. The fair value of the group has now been re-appraised at $975,000. Since the carrying amount less depreciation of $950,000 is lower than the fair value of $975,000, Ambivalence records a charge of $50,000 to reduce the carrying amount of the group to $950,000 with the following entry:

	Debit	Credit
Depreciation – Production machinery	50,000	
Accumulated depreciation – Production machinery		50,000

> **Tip:** The reclassification of assets into and out of the held-for-sale classification requires additional accounting effort to track. To minimize this effort, maintain a high capitalization limit, so that most assets are charged to expense when purchased. Also, if you expect that an asset will be sold within a very short time period, it is easier to not shift the asset into the held-for-sale classification and then almost immediately sell it; instead, depreciate the asset up until the point of sale. Clearly, some judgment is needed to follow the intent of the held-for-sale rules without engaging in an excessive amount of unnecessary accounting work.

Abandoned Assets

If a company abandons an asset, consider the asset to be disposed of, and account for it as such (even if it remains on the premises). However, if the asset is only temporarily idle, do not consider it to be abandoned, and continue to depreciate it in a normal manner.

If you have abandoned an asset, reduce its carrying amount down to any remaining salvage value on the date when the decision is made to abandon the asset.

Idle Assets

Some fixed assets will be idle from time to time. There is no specific consideration of idle assets in GAAP, so continue to depreciate them in a normal manner. However, here are additional considerations regarding what an idle asset may indicate:

- *Asset impairment.* If an asset is idle, it may be an indicator that the value of the asset has declined, which may call for an impairment review.
- *Disclosure.* Identify idle assets separately on the balance sheet, and disclose why they are idle.
- *Useful life.* If an asset is idle, this may indicate that its useful life is shorter than the amount currently used to calculate its depreciation. This may call for a re-evaluation of its useful life.

Fixed Asset Disposal Accounting

There are two scenarios under which you may dispose of a fixed asset. The first situation arises when you are eliminating a fixed asset without receiving any payment in return. This is a common situation when a fixed asset is being scrapped because it is obsolete or no longer in use, and there is no resale market for it. In this case, reverse any accumulated depreciation and reverse the original asset cost. If the asset is fully depreciated, then that is the extent of your entry.

EXAMPLE

Ambivalence Corporation buys a machine for $100,000 and recognizes $10,000 of depreciation per year over the following ten years. At that time, the machine is not only fully depreciated, but also ready for the scrap heap. Ambivalence gives away the machine for free, and records the following entry.

	Debit	Credit
Accumulated Depreciation	100,000	
Machine asset		100,000

A variation on this situation is to write off a fixed asset that has not yet been completely depreciated. In this case, write off the remaining undepreciated amount of the asset to a loss account.

EXAMPLE

To use the same example, Ambivalence Corporation gives away the machine after eight years, when it has not yet depreciated $20,000 of the asset's original $100,000 cost. In this case, Ambivalence records the following entry:

	Debit	Credit
Loss on asset disposal	20,000	
Accumulated depreciation	80,000	
Machine asset		100,000

The second scenario arises when you sell an asset, so that you receive cash (or some other asset) in exchange for the fixed asset you are selling. Depending upon the price paid and the remaining amount of depreciation that has not yet been charged to expense, this can result in either a gain or a loss on sale of the asset.

EXAMPLE

Ambivalence Corporation still disposes of its $100,000 machine, but does so after seven years, and sells it for $35,000 in cash. In this case, it has already recorded $70,000 of depreciation expense. The entry is:

	Debit	Credit
Cash	35,000	
Accumulated depreciation	70,000	
Gain on asset disposal		5,000
Machine asset		100,000

What if Ambivalence had sold the machine for $25,000 instead of $35,000? Then there would be a loss of $5,000 on the sale. The entry would be:

	Debit	Credit
Cash	25,000	
Accumulated depreciation	70,000	
Loss on asset disposal	5,000	
Machine asset		100,000

If there is a gain or loss on disposal of a fixed asset, include it in income from continuing operations before income taxes on the income statement.

Fixed Asset Disclosures

This section contains the disclosures for various aspects of fixed assets that are required under GAAP. At the end of each set of requirements is a sample disclosure containing the more common elements of the requirements.

General Fixed Asset Disclosures

The financial statements should disclose the following information about a company's fixed assets:

- *Accumulated depreciation.* The balances in each of the major classes of fixed assets as of the end of the reporting period.
- *Asset aggregation.* The balances in each of the major classes of fixed assets as of the end of the reporting period.
- *Depreciation expense.* The amount of depreciation charged to expense in the reporting period.
- *Depreciation methods.* A description of the methods used to depreciate assets in the major asset classifications.

EXAMPLE

Suture Corporation gives a general description of its fixed asset recordation and depreciation as follows:

The company states its fixed assets at cost. For all fixed assets, the company calculates depreciation utilizing the straight-line method over the estimated useful lives for owned assets or, where appropriate, over the related lease terms for leasehold improvements. Useful lives range from 1 to 7 years.

Our fixed assets include the following approximate amounts:

	December 31,	
	20X2	20X1
Computer equipment	$9,770,000	$8,410,000
Computer software	2,800,000	1,950,000
Furniture and fixtures	860,000	780,000
Intangible assets	1,750,000	4,500,000
Leasehold improvements	400,000	360,000
Less: Accumulated depreciation and amortization	(5,400,000)	(4,800,000)
Totals	$10,180,000	$11,200,000

156

Change in Estimate Disclosures

It is relatively common to have changes in estimates related to fixed assets, since there are a variety of situations in which you may conclude that it is necessary to alter an asset's useful life, salvage value, or depreciation method – all of which are considered changes in estimate. If so, disclose the effect of a change in estimate on income from continuing operations, net income, and any per-share amounts for the reporting period. This disclosure is required only if the change is material.

EXAMPLE

Suture Corporation reports the following change in estimate within the notes accompanying its financial statements:

> During 20X4, management assessed its estimates of the residual values and useful lives of the company's fixed assets. Management revised its original estimates and now estimates that the medical production equipment that it had acquired in 20X1 and initially estimated to have a useful life of 8 years and salvage value of $100,000 will instead have a useful life of 12 years and salvage value of $80,000. The effects of this change in accounting estimate on the company's 20X4 financial statements are:
>
> Increase in:
>
> | | |
> |---|---|
> | Income from continuing operations and net income | $250,000 |
> | Earnings per share | $0.03 |

Intangible Asset Impairment Disclosures

If you have recognized an impairment loss for an intangible asset, disclose the following information for each such impairment:

- *Amount*. Note the amount of the impairment loss and the method used to determine fair value.
- *Description*. Describe the asset and the circumstances causing the impairment.
- *Location*. Note the line item in the income statement in which the loss is reported.
- *Segment*. State the segment in which the impaired asset is reported.

EXAMPLE

Suture Corporation determines that the values of several acquired patents have declined, which it discloses as follows:

> The company has written down the value of its patents related to the electronic remediation of cancer, on the grounds that subsequent testing of this equipment has not resulted in the levels of cancer remission that management had anticipated. The

company employed an appraiser to derive a new value that was based on anticipated cash flows. The resulting loss of $4.5 million was charged to the cancer treatment segment of the company, and is contained within the "Other Gains and Losses" line item on the income statement. The remaining value ascribed to these intangible assets as of the balance sheet date is $1.75 million. Management does not plan to sell the patents.

Intangible Asset Disclosures

If you have acquired individual intangible assets or such assets that are part of a group, disclose the following information about them:

For Assets Subject to Amortization

- *Amortization expense.* Disclose the amortization charged to expense in the reporting period, as well as the estimated aggregate amortization expense for each of the next five fiscal years.
- *Amortization period.* Note the weighted-average amortization period, both for all intangible assets and by major intangible asset class.
- *Carrying amount.* Disclose the total amount of intangible assets, as well as the amount assigned to any major class of intangible asset. Also disclose accumulated amortization, both in total and by class of intangible asset.
- *Residual value.* If there is any significant residual value, disclose it in total and by major intangible asset class.

For Assets Not Subject to Amortization

- *Carrying amount.* Disclose the total amount of intangible assets, as well as the amount assigned to any major class of intangible asset.
- *Policy.* Describe the company's accounting policy for the treatment of any costs incurred in the renewal of an intangible asset's term.
- *Renewal costs.* If you capitalize renewal costs, disclose by major intangible asset class the total costs incurred during the reporting period to renew the term of an intangible asset.
- *Renewal period.* If these assets have renewal terms, state the weighted-average period before the next renewal for each major class of intangible asset.

EXAMPLE

Suture Corporation discloses the following information about its intangible assets:

	As of December 31, 20X1	
	Gross Carrying Amount	Accumulated Amortization
Amortized intangible assets		
Patents	$4,000,000	$1,450,000
Trademarks	1,200,000	400,000
Unpatented technology	800,000	650,000
Total	$6,000,000	$2,500,000
Unamortized intangible assets		
Distribution license	$500,000	
Trademark	450,000	
Total	$950,000	

Aggregate amortization expense:	
For the year ended 12/31/X1	$560,000
Estimated amortization expense:	
For the year ended 12/31/X2	$560,000
For the year ended 12/31/X3	$420,000
For the year ended 12/31/X4	$420,000
For the year ended 12/31/X5	$380,000
For the year ended 12/31/X6	$380,000

Summary

Even a brief perusal of this chapter will make it clear that the accounting for fixed assets is one of the more time-consuming accounting activities, simply because the related accounting records must be monitored (and possibly adjusted) for years. Accordingly, the efficient accountant will do anything possible to charge expenditures to expense at once, rather than recording them as fixed assets. The best options for reducing the number of fixed assets are to maintain a high capitalization limit, and to adopt a skeptical attitude when anyone wants to add subsequent expenditures to a fixed asset. The result should be a considerably reduced number of high-value fixed assets.

Chapter 9
Accounting for Intangibles

Introduction

A business may record goodwill as part of a business combination, to account for the difference between the fair value of all other assets and liabilities and the purchase price. The initial recognition of goodwill is addressed in the Business Combinations chapter. In this chapter, we deal with the subsequent accounting for goodwill, and also address the accounting for and disclosure of the costs of internally developed goodwill, other intangible assets, internal-use software, and website development costs.

Goodwill

Goodwill is a common byproduct of a business combination, where the purchase price paid for the acquiree is higher than the fair values of the identifiable assets acquired. After goodwill has initially been recorded as an asset, do not amortize it. Instead, test it for impairment at the reporting unit level. Impairment exists when the carrying amount of the goodwill is greater than its implied fair value.

A reporting unit is defined as an operating segment or one level below an operating segment. At a more practical level, a reporting unit is a separate business for which the parent compiles financial information, and for which management reviews the results. If several components of an operating segment have similar economic characteristics, they can be combined into a reporting unit. In a smaller business, it is entirely possible that one reporting unit could be an entire operating segment, or even the entire entity.

The examination of goodwill for the possible existence of impairment involves a multi-step process, which is:

1. *Assess qualitative factors.* Review the situation to see if it is necessary to conduct further impairment testing, which is considered to be a likelihood of more than 50% that impairment has occurred, based on an assessment of relevant events and circumstances. Examples of relevant events and circumstances that make it more likely that impairment is present are the deterioration of macroeconomic conditions, increased costs, declining cash flows, possible bankruptcy, a change in management, and a sustained decrease in share price. If impairment appears to be likely, continue with the impairment testing process. You can choose to bypass this step and proceed straight to the next step.

2. *Identify potential impairment.* Compare the fair value of the reporting unit to its carrying amount. Be sure to include goodwill in the carrying amount of the reporting unit, and also consider the presence of any significant unrec-

ognized intangible assets. If the fair value is greater than the carrying amount of the reporting unit, there is no goodwill impairment, and there is no need to proceed to the next step. If the carrying amount exceeds the fair value of the reporting unit, proceed to the next step to calculate the amount of the impairment loss.

3. *Calculate impairment loss.* Compare the implied fair value of the goodwill associated with the reporting unit to the carrying amount of that goodwill. If the carrying amount is greater than the implied fair value, recognize an impairment loss in the amount of the difference, up to a maximum of the entire carrying amount (i.e., the carrying amount of goodwill can only be reduced to zero).

These steps are illustrated in the following flowchart.

To calculate the implied fair value of goodwill, assign the fair value of the reporting unit with which it is associated to all of the assets and liabilities of that reporting unit (including research and development assets). The excess amount (if any) of the fair value of the reporting unit over the amounts assigned to its assets and liabilities is the implied fair value of the associated goodwill. The fair value of the reporting unit is assumed to be the price that the company would receive if it were to sell the unit in an orderly transaction (i.e., not a rushed sale) between market participants. Other alternatives to the quoted market price for a reporting unit may be acceptable, such as a valuation based on multiples of earnings or revenue.

The following additional issues are associated with goodwill impairment testing:

- *Asset and liability assignment.* Assign acquired assets and liabilities to a reporting unit if they relate to the operations of the unit *and* they will be considered in the determination of reporting unit fair value. If these criteria can be met, even corporate-level assets and liabilities can be assigned to a reporting unit. If some assets and liabilities could be assigned to multiple reporting units, assign them in a reasonable manner (such as an allocation based on the relative fair values of the reporting units), consistently applied.

- *Asset recognition.* It is not allowable to recognize an additional intangible asset as part of the process of evaluating goodwill impairment.

- *Goodwill assignment.* All of the goodwill acquired in a business combination must be assigned to one or several reporting units as of the acquisition date, and not shifted among the reporting units thereafter. The assignment should be in a reasonable manner, consistently applied. If goodwill is to be assigned to a reporting unit that has not been assigned any acquired assets or liabilities, the assignment could be based on the difference between the fair value of the reporting unit before and after the acquisition, which represents the improvement in value caused by goodwill.

- *Impairment estimation.* If it is probable that there is goodwill impairment and the amount can be reasonably estimated, despite the testing process not being complete when financial statements are issued, recognize the estimated amount of the impairment. The estimate should be adjusted to the final impairment amount in the following reporting period.

Goodwill Impairment Decision Steps

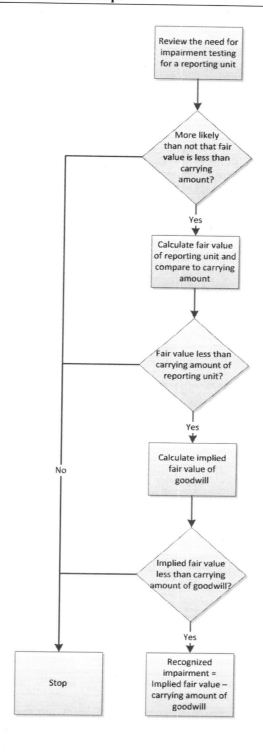

- *No reversal.* Once impairment of goodwill has been recorded, it cannot be reversed, even if the condition originally causing the impairment is no longer present.
- *Reporting structure reorganization.* If a company reorganizes its reporting units, reassign assets and liabilities to the new reporting units based on a reasonable methodology, consistently applied. Goodwill should be reassigned based on the relative fair values of the portions of the old reporting unit to be integrated into the new reporting units.
- *Reporting unit disposal.* If a reporting unit is disposed of, include the goodwill associated with that unit in determining any gain or loss on the transaction. If only a portion of a reporting unit is disposed of, you must associate some of the goodwill linked to the reporting unit to the portion being disposed of, based on the relative fair values of the portions being disposed of and retained. Then test the remaining amount of goodwill assigned to the residual portion of the reporting unit for impairment.

EXAMPLE

Armadillo Industries is selling off a portion of a reporting unit for $500,000. The remaining portion of the unit, which Armadillo is retaining, has a fair value of $1,500,000. Based on these values, 25% of the goodwill associated with the reporting unit should be included in the carrying amount of the portion being sold.

- *Reporting unit disposal, minority owner.* If a company has less than complete ownership of a reporting unit, attribute any impairment losses to the parent entity and the noncontrolling interest in the reporting unit on a rational basis. However, if the reporting unit includes goodwill that is attributable to the parent entity, then attribute the loss entirely to the parent, not the noncontrolling interest.
- *Subsidiary goodwill impairment testing.* Any goodwill recognized by a corporate subsidiary should be dealt with in the same manner described elsewhere in this section for the impairment of goodwill. If there is a goodwill impairment loss at the subsidiary level, also test the reporting unit of which that subsidiary is a part for goodwill impairment, if the triggering event is more likely than not to have also reduced the fair value of that reporting unit below its carrying amount.
- *Taxable transaction.* As part of the fair value estimation, determine whether the reporting unit could be bought or sold in a taxable or non-taxable transaction, since this affects its fair value.

> **Tip:** From a practical perspective, it is almost always easier to estimate the fair value of the reporting unit based on a multiple of its earnings or revenues, though this should only be done when there are comparable operations whose fair values and related multiples are known, and which can therefore be used as the basis for a fair value estimate of the reporting unit.

Impairment testing is to be conducted at annual intervals. You may conduct the impairment test at any time of the year, provided that the test is conducted thereafter at the same time of the year. If the company is comprised of different reporting units, there is no need to test them all at the same time.

> **Tip:** Each reporting unit is probably subject to a certain amount of seasonal activity. If so, select a period when activity levels are at their lowest to conduct impairment testing, so it does not conflict with other activities. Impairment testing should not coincide with the annual audit.

It may be necessary to conduct more frequent impairment testing if there is an event that makes it more likely than not that the fair value of a reporting unit has been reduced below its carrying amount. Examples of triggering events are a lawsuit, regulatory changes, the loss of key employees, and the expectation that a reporting unit will be sold.

The information used for an impairment test can be quite detailed. To improve the efficiency of the testing process, it is permissible to carry forward this information to the next year, as long as the following criteria have been met:

- There has been no significant change in the assets and liabilities comprising the reporting unit.
- There was a substantial excess of fair value over the carrying amount in the last impairment test.
- The likelihood of the fair value being less than the carrying amount is remote.

As an additional note for publicly-held companies that report segment information, the asset, liability, and goodwill allocations used for goodwill impairment testing do not have to be the same as the amounts stated in segment reports. However, aligning the two sets of information will make it easier to conduct both impairment testing and segment reporting.

General Intangibles Other than Goodwill

In general, recognize costs as incurred when they are related to internally developing, maintaining, or restoring intangible assets that have any of the following characteristics:

- There is no specifically identifiable asset
- The useful life is indeterminate

- The cost is inherent in the continuing operation of the business

Conversely, it is possible to recognize an acquired intangible item as an asset. If a group of assets are acquired in a transaction that is not defined as a business combination, the acquisition cost should be entirely allocated to the individual acquired assets, based on their relative fair values. In such an arrangement, goodwill is not recognized.

If a business acquires an intangible asset specifically to deny its use to others (a *defensive intangible asset*), treat the asset as a separate unit of accounting. Assign the asset a useful life that reflects the period over which the company will benefit from the denial of use of the asset to others; this period is essentially the period over which the fair value of the asset will decline.

The general accounting for an intangible asset is to record the asset as a long-term asset and amortize the asset over its useful life, along with regular impairment reviews. The accounting is essentially the same as for other types of fixed assets. The key differences between the accounting for tangible and intangible fixed assets are:

- *Amortization*. If an intangible asset has a useful life, amortize the cost of the asset over that useful life, less any residual value. Amortization is the same as depreciation, except that amortization is applied only to intangible assets. In this context, useful life refers to the time period over which an asset is expected to enhance future cash flows.
- *Asset combinations*. If several intangible assets are operated as a single asset, combine them for the purposes of impairment testing. This treatment is probably not suitable if they independently generate cash flows, would be sold separately, or are used by different asset groups.
- *Residual value*. If any residual value is expected following the useful life of an intangible asset, subtract it from the carrying amount of the asset for the purposes of calculating amortization. You should assume that the residual value will always be zero for intangible assets, unless there is a commitment from another party to acquire the asset at the end of its useful life, *and* the residual value can be determined by reference to transactions in an existing market, *and* that market is expected to be in existence when the useful life of the asset ends.

EXAMPLE

Armadillo Industries purchases a patent from a third party. The remaining life of the patent's coverage of a key piece of production technology is eight years. Armadillo obtains a written commitment from a supplier to buy the patent in two years for 75% of the $100,000 price paid by Armadillo for the patent. Armadillo intends to sell the patent to the supplier in two years.

Based on this information, Armadillo should amortize $25,000 of the purchase price over the two years that the company expects to retain ownership of the patent.

- *Useful life.* An intangible asset may have an indefinite useful life. If so, do not initially amortize it, but review the asset at regular intervals to see if a useful life can then be determined. If so, test the asset for impairment and begin amortizing it. The reverse can also occur, where an asset with a useful life is judged to now have an indefinite useful life; if so, stop amortizing the asset and test it for impairment. Examples of intangible assets that have indefinite useful lives are taxicab licenses, broadcasting rights, and trademarks.

EXAMPLE

Milford Sound acquires a license to broadcast in the Milwaukee area for five years. The license is automatically renewable every five years, unless Milford violates a number of Federal Communications Commission rules. There is no limit to the number of renewals that Milford can obtain to the license period, and Milford intends to renew the license in perpetuity. Despite the impact of music streaming over the Internet, the cash flows associated with the license are not expected to decline appreciably in the foreseeable future. Thus, the cash flows that Milford expects to realize from the license should continue indefinitely. The license can be treated as an intangible asset having an indefinite useful life.

- *Useful life revisions.* You should regularly review the duration of the remaining useful lives of all intangible assets, and adjust them if circumstances warrant the change. This will require a change in the remaining amount of amortization recognized per period.
- *Life extensions.* It is possible that the life of some intangible assets may be extended a considerable amount, usually based on contract extensions. If so, estimate the useful life of an asset based on the full duration of expected useful life extensions. These presumed extensions may result in an asset having an indefinite useful life, which avoids amortization.

EXAMPLE

Milford Sound entered into a license for noise cancelling technology three years ago, and plans to renew the license for an additional three-year period. However, management is aware of the development of a new technology that will probably render the current noise cancelling technology obsolete in two years. Milford had previously been amortizing the cost of the license over each three-year licensing period. However, given the expected change in technology, management elects to amortize the cost of the license extension over just two years.

- *Straight-line amortization.* Use the straight-line basis of amortization to reduce the carrying amount of an intangible asset, unless the pattern of benefit usage associated with the asset suggests a different form of amortization.

- *Impairment testing.* An intangible asset is subject to impairment testing in the same manner as tangible assets. In short, recognize impairment if the carrying amount of the asset is greater than its fair value, and the amount is not recoverable. Once recognized, the impairment cannot be reversed.
- *Research and development assets.* If intangible assets are acquired through a business combination for use in research and development activities, initially treat them as having indefinite useful lives, and regularly test them for impairment. Once the related research and development activities have been completed or abandoned, charge them to expense.

Tip: The usage pattern of nearly all intangible assets will suggest the use of straight-line amortization. Since this is also the simplest amortization method, use it unless the underlying usage pattern of an asset is substantially different.

Internal-Use Software

Companies routinely develop software for internal use, and want to understand how these development costs are to be accounted for. Software is considered to be for internal use when it has been acquired or developed *only* for the internal needs of a business. Examples of situations where software is considered to be developed for internal use are:

- Accounting systems
- Cash management tracking systems
- Membership tracking systems
- Production automation systems

Further, there can be no reasonably possible plan to market the software outside of the company. A market feasibility study is not considered a reasonably possible marketing plan. However, a history of selling software that had initially been developed for internal use creates a reasonable assumption that the latest internal-use product will also be marketed for sale outside of the company.

The accounting for internal-use software varies, depending upon the stage of completion of the project. The relevant accounting is:

- *Stage 1: Preliminary.* All costs incurred during the preliminary stage of a development project should be charged to expense as incurred. This stage is considered to include making decisions about the allocation of resources, determining performance requirements, conducting supplier demonstrations, evaluating technology, and supplier selection.
- *Stage 2: Application development.* Capitalize the costs incurred to develop internal-use software, which may include coding, hardware installation, and testing. Any costs related to data conversion, user training, administration, and overhead should be charged to expense as incurred. Only the following costs can be capitalized:

- ○ Materials and services consumed in the development effort, such as third party development fees, software purchase costs, and travel costs related to development work.
- ○ The payroll costs of those employees directly associated with software development.
- ○ The capitalization of interest costs incurred to fund the project.
- *Stage 3. Post-implementation.* Charge all post-implementation costs to expense as incurred. Samples of these costs are training and maintenance costs.

Any allowable capitalization of costs should begin *after* the preliminary stage has been completed, management commits to funding the project, it is probable that the project will be completed, and the software will be used for its intended function.

The capitalization of costs should end when all substantial testing has been completed. If it is no longer probable that a project will be completed, stop capitalizing the costs associated with it, and conduct impairment testing on the costs already capitalized. The cost at which the asset should then be carried is the lower of its carrying amount or fair value (less costs to sell). Unless there is evidence to the contrary, the usual assumption is that uncompleted software has no fair value.

A business may purchase software for internal use. If the purchase price of this software includes other elements, such as training and maintenance fees, only capitalize that portion of the purchase price that relates to the software itself.

In addition, any later upgrades of the software can be capitalized, but only if it is probable that extra system functionality will result from the upgrade. The costs of maintaining the system should be charged to expense as incurred. If the maintenance is provided by a third party and payment is made in advance for the services of that party, then amortize the cost of the maintenance over the service period.

Once costs have been capitalized, amortize them over the expected useful life of the software. This is typically done on a straight-line basis, unless another method more clearly reflects the expected usage pattern of the software. Amortization should begin when a software module is ready for its intended use, which is considered to be when all substantial system testing has been completed. If a software module cannot function unless other modules are also completed, do not begin amortization until the related modules are complete.

It may be necessary to regularly reassess the useful life of the software for amortization purposes, since technological obsolescence tends to shorten it.

You should routinely review the capitalized cost of internal-use software for impairment, as described in the Accounting for Property, Plant, and Equipment chapter. The following are all indicators of the possible presence of asset impairment:

- The software is not expected to be of substantive use
- The manner in which the software was originally intended to be used has now changed
- The software is to be significantly altered

- The development cost of the software significantly exceeded original expectations

Once a business has developed software for internal use, management may decide to market it for external use by third parties. If so, the proceeds from software licensing, net of selling costs, should be applied against the carrying amount of the software asset. For the purposes of this topic, selling costs are considered to include commissions, software reproduction costs, servicing obligations, warranty costs, and installation costs. The business should not recognize a profit on sales of the software until the application of net sales to the carrying amount of the software asset have reduced the carrying amount to zero. The business can recognize all further proceeds as revenue.

Website Development Costs

A company may allocate a considerable amount of funds to the development of a company website, in such areas as coding, graphics design, the addition of content, and site operation. The accounting for website development varies, depending upon the stage of completion of the project. The relevant accounting is:

- *Stage 1: Preliminary.* Charge all site planning costs to expense as incurred. This stage is considered to include project planning, the determination of site functionality, hardware identification, technology usability, alternatives analysis, supplier demonstrations, and legal considerations.
- *Stage 2: Application development and infrastructure.* The accounting matches what was just described in the last section for internal-use software. In essence, capitalize these costs. More specifically, capitalize the cost of obtaining and registering an Internet domain, as well as the procurement of software tools, code customization, web page development, related hardware, hypertext link creation, and site testing. Also, if a site upgrade provides new functions or features to the website, capitalize these costs.
- *Stage 3: Graphics development.* For the purposes of this topic, graphics are considered to be software, and so are capitalized, unless they are to be marketed externally. Graphics development includes site page design and layout.
- *Stage 4: Content development.* Charge data conversion costs to expense as incurred, as well as the costs to input content into a website.
- *Stage 5: Site operation.* The costs to operate a website are the same as any other operating costs, and so should be charged to expense as incurred. The treatment of selected operating costs associated with a website are:
  - Charge website hosting fees to expense over the period benefited by the hosting
  - Charge search engine registration fees to expense as incurred, since they are advertising costs

Intangibles Disclosures

A company that has recognized goodwill as an asset should disclose the following information in its financial statements:

- *Estimated impairment.* If a company recognizes an estimated amount of impairment in its financial statements, disclose the fact that the amount recognized is an estimate. In later periods, disclose the nature and amount of any significant adjustments made to the initial estimate.
- *Goodwill carrying amount.* Disclose a reconciliation of changes in the carrying amount of goodwill during the period, showing the beginning gross amount and accumulated impairment losses, additional goodwill recognition, adjustments for deferred tax assets, goodwill related to assets held for sale, impairment losses, other changes, and the ending gross amount and accumulated impairment losses.
- *Goodwill by segment.* If a company is reporting segment information (which is required for publicly-held companies), disclose the amount of goodwill in total, and for each reportable segment, as well as significant changes in the allocation of goodwill by segment.
- *Goodwill impairment activity.* If there has been goodwill impairment, present the related losses in a separate line item in the income statement, positioned before the subtotal of income from continuing operations. If the goodwill is associated with a discontinued operation, then present the loss, net of taxes, in a line item in the discontinued operations section of the income statement.
- *Goodwill impairment loss.* If there is a goodwill impairment loss, disclose the facts and circumstances associated with the loss, the amount of the loss, and how the fair value of the related reporting unit was determined.
- *Goodwill presentation.* State the aggregate amount of goodwill in a separate line item in the balance sheet.
- *Unallocated goodwill.* If any goodwill has not been allocated to a reporting unit, disclose the unallocated amount and the reasons why no allocation has been made.

EXAMPLE

Armadillo Industries discloses the following information about changes in the carrying amount of its goodwill for the year ended December 31, 20X4:

(000s)	Body Armor Segment	High Pressure Container Segment	Total
Balance as of January 1, 20X4			
Goodwill	$5,700	$4,200	$9,900
Accumulated impairment losses	-400	-170	-570
	5,300	4,030	9,330
Goodwill acquired during year	360	1,080	1,440
Impairment losses	-250	--	-250
Goodwill written off related to disposal of business unit	--	-200	-200
Balance as of December 31, 20X4			
Goodwill	6,060	5,080	11,140
Accumulated impairment losses	-650	-170	-820
	$5,410	$4,910	$10,320

The company tests the body armor segment in the second quarter of each year, which is the low point in the company's sales cycle. Due to an increase in lower-priced competition from Asian manufacturers, management revised its estimate of future cash flows likely to be generated by the body armor segment, and concluded that a goodwill impairment of $250,000 should be recognized. The fair value of the body armor reporting unit was derived using the expected present value of future cash flows.

A company that has recognized other intangible assets should disclose the following information in its financial statements:

- *Intangible presentation.* Aggregate all recognized intangible assets into one line in the balance sheet (though the breakdown of this information into additional lines is allowed).
- *Amortization expense.* Report amortization expense within the continuing operations section of the income statement.
- *Impairment losses.* Report intangible asset impairment losses within the continuing operations section of the income statement.
- *Acquired intangibles.* If intangible assets are acquired, disclose the following:
  - The amount assigned to the major intangible asset classes
  - The amount of any residual value (if significant) by asset class and in total
  - The weighted average amortization period by asset class
  - The total amount of intangible assets with indefinite lives, by asset class

○ The research and development asset cost acquired and written off (other than through a business combination), and the income statement line item where this information is located

○ The weighted-average period before the next terms extension, by asset class, for those assets having renewal terms

When a company presents a balance sheet as part of its financial statements, it should also disclose the following information:

- *Amortization expense.* Note the total amortization expense for the period.

- *Assets with indefinite lives.* List the total carrying amount of all intangible assets that are not subject to amortization, as well as the same information by asset class.

- *Extended assets.* For those assets whose lives have been renewed or extended in the period, state the amount of renewal costs capitalized by asset class, as well as the weighted-average period before the next renewal, by asset class.

- *Future amortization.* State the estimated amount of amortization expense in each of the next five fiscal years.

- *Impairment losses.* For each impairment loss recognized, disclose the period of recognition, the nature of the asset, the reasons for impairment, the amount of the loss, the method used to determine fair value, the income statement line item into which the loss is aggregated, and the segment in which the impaired asset is reported (only applicable to publicly-held companies).

- *Intangible asset totals.* State the gross carrying amount and related accumulated amortization for all intangible assets, and for each major asset class.

- *Life extension policy.* Describe the company policy for how it treats any costs incurred to renew the life of an intangible asset.

- *Renewal impact on cash flows.* Provide sufficient information for users to judge how cash flows will be affected by the ability of the business to renew the contractual life of an asset.

EXAMPLE

Armadillo Industries discloses the following information related to its acquisition of intangible assets:

Note X: Acquired Intangible Assets

(000s)	Gross Carrying Amount	As of December 31, 20X1 Accumulated Amortization
Amortized intangible assets		
Customer list	$2,130	-$720
Internet domain names	1,600	-870
Trademarks	420	-380
Total	$4,150	-$1,970
Unamortized intangible assets		
Trade secrets	$4,350	
Trademarks	1,880	
Total	$6,230	

Aggregate amortization expense:	
For the year ended 12/31/20X1	$395
Estimated amortization expense:	
For the year ended 12/31/20X2	580
For the year ended 12/31/20X3	520
For the year ended 12/31/20X4	490
For the year ended 12/31/20X5	370

Summary

The testing for goodwill impairment can be both time-consuming and expensive, so take full advantage of the option to avoid testing by reviewing qualitative factors to see if there is a low likelihood of impairment.

You should be aware of how the capitalization of software for internal use or for the development of a website can skew the results reported by a business. If a company is developing a massive in-house system, the amount of costs capitalized may represent a significant proportion of all expenditures, resulting in financial statements that may reveal a profit, even while the business is hemorrhaging cash to pay for the development effort. If this is the case, consider full disclosure of the situation in the company's financial statements, as well as a narrow interpretation of the accounting standards to charge as much of these expenditures as possible to expense as incurred.

Chapter 10
Accounting for Equity

Introduction

This chapter addresses a variety of topics that are related to equity. The topics covered include equity appropriations, stock dividends, stock splits, stock repurchases, equity-based payments, spinoffs, and more. These topics are only related to each other in that they have an impact on the equity classification of transactions, and can otherwise be considered something of a smorgasbord of information. In this chapter, we deal with the concepts linked to each of these equity topics.

Overview of Equity

Equity is the residual interest of owners in a business, once liabilities have been subtracted from assets. From the perspective of the accountant, key areas of concern are the issuance and repurchase of stock, though there are many lesser issues that can also impact equity.

The equity topics in this chapter are quite varied, and so cannot easily be combined into a single section. Instead, we have separated the larger topics into their own sections, and provide below only a few minor items related to equity:

- *Appropriations*. It is permissible to appropriate retained earnings for specific purposes, such as acquisitions, debt reductions, new construction, stock buybacks, and so forth. If there is an appropriation, disclose the amount in the equity section of the balance sheet. It is not permissible to charge expenses or losses against an appropriation. It is also not permissible to transfer an appropriation to income.
- *Note paid for equity*. There may be cases where an investor issues a note to a business in exchange for an equity position in the company (as opposed to the usual cash payment). If there is not clear evidence that the investor intends to pay and has the ability to do so within a short period of time, do not record the note as an asset. Instead, offset the note against the corresponding equity line item in the equity section of the balance sheet.

Stock Dividends and Stock Splits

A company may issue additional shares to its shareholders, which is called a stock dividend. This type of dividend does not involve the reduction of any company assets, nor does it increase the cash inflow to the recipient, so it can be considered a neutral event that has no impact on either party. However, the sheer volume of shares issued can have an effect on the value of the shareholdings of the recipient, which calls for different types of accounting. The two volume-based accounting treatments are:

- *Low-volume stock issuance.* If a stock issuance is for less than 20% to 25% of the number of shares outstanding prior to the issuance, account for the transaction as a stock dividend.
- *High-volume stock issuance.* If a stock issuance is for more than 20% to 25% of the number of shares outstanding prior to the issuance, account for the transaction as a stock split.

The dividing line between these two treatments is an estimate provided in GAAP, based on the assumption that a relatively small stock issuance will not appreciably alter the price of a share, which therefore creates value for the recipient of these shares. A larger share issuance is presumed to reduce the market price of shares outstanding, so that share recipients do not experience a net increase in the value of their shares.

If there are an ongoing series of stock issuances that would individually be accounted for as stock dividends, consider aggregating these issuances to see if the result would instead trigger treatment as a stock split.

Stock Dividend

When there is a stock dividend, transfer from retained earnings to the capital stock and additional paid-in capital accounts an amount equal to the fair value of the additional shares issued. The fair value of the additional shares issued is based on their market value after the dividend is declared. A stock dividend is never treated as a liability, since it does not reduce assets.

EXAMPLE

Davidson Motors declares a stock dividend to its shareholders of 10,000 shares. The fair value of the stock is $5.00, and its par value is $1.00. Davidson's accountant records the following entry:

	Debit	Credit
Retained earnings	50,000	
Common stock, $1 par value		10,000
Additional paid-in capital		40,000

Stock Split

When a stock issuance is sufficiently large to be classified as a stock split, the only accounting is to ensure that the legally-required amount of par value has been properly designated as such in the accounting records. If a company's stock has no par value, then no reallocation of funds into the par value account is required.

EXAMPLE

Davidson Motors declares a stock dividend to its shareholders of 1,000,000 shares, which represents a doubling of the prior number of shares outstanding. Davidson's stock has a par value of $1, so the accountant records the following entry to ensure that the correct amount of capital is apportioned to the par value account:

	Debit	Credit
Additional paid-in capital	1,000,000	
Common stock, $1 par value		1,000,000

Treasury Stock

A company may elect to buy back its own shares. These repurchased shares are called treasury stock. Management may intend to permanently retire these shares, or it could intend to hold them for resale or reissuance at a later date. Common reasons for the repurchase of stock include the following:

- A stock buyback program that is intended to reduce the overall number of shares and thereby increase the earnings per share
- When a company is forced to buy back shares from someone who is attempting to gain control of the business
- When a company has the right of first refusal to reacquire shares
- When management wants to take a publicly-held company private, and needs to reduce the number of shareholders in order to do so

Stock that has been repurchased does not qualify for voting purposes, nor should it be included in the earnings per share calculation.

The two aspects of accounting for treasury stock are the purchase of stock by a company, and its resale of those shares. We deal with these issues next.

Purchase of Treasury Stock

When a company buys back its stock, the circumstances of the repurchase arrangement may indicate that the amount paid incorporates a larger payment than would be justified by the current market price of the stock. Indicators of this situation are a repurchase from only a small group of shareholders, or when the price is higher than the current market price. For example, a company may buy back the shares of a suitor at a high price, in exchange for an agreement by the suitor not to acquire additional shares in the company. In these cases, separate the excess amount of the payment, and charge it to expense as incurred.

EXAMPLE

Armadillo Industries settles a lawsuit with a former employee regarding payouts under his employment contract, under which the company agrees to pay $150,000 to buy back his 10,000 shares and settle all other claims under the contract. On the date when the agreement is reached, the market price of Armadillo's stock was $9. Based on this information, the company allocates $90,000 to treasury stock and $60,000 to compensation expense.

When treasury stock is acquired by the issuing business, the most common treatment of the transaction is to record it as a contra account, where the treasury stock appears as a deduction from the other equity items in the balance sheet.

Resale of Treasury Stock

If a company elects to resell shares that it had previously purchased, do not include any aspect of the sale in the income statement, since this is not a profit-generating activity; rather, it is a means of acquiring funds.

Cost Method

The simplest and most widely-used method for accounting for the repurchase of stock is the cost method. The accounting is:

- *Repurchase.* To record a repurchase, simply record the entire amount of the purchase in the treasury stock account.
- *Resale.* If the treasury stock is resold at a later date, offset the sale price against the treasury stock account, and credit any sales exceeding the repurchase cost to the additional paid-in capital account. If the sale price is less than the repurchase cost, charge the differential to any additional paid-in capital remaining from prior treasury stock transactions, and any residual amount to retained earnings if there is no remaining balance in the additional paid-in capital account.
- *Retirement.* If management decides to permanently retire stock that it has already accounted for under the cost method, it reverses the par value and additional paid-in capital associated with the original stock sale, with any remaining amount being charged to retained earnings.

EXAMPLE

The board of directors of Armadillo Industries authorizes the repurchase of 50,000 shares of its stock, which has a $1 par value. The company originally sold the sales for $12 each, or $600,000 in total. It repurchases the shares for the same amount. The accountant records the transaction with this entry:

	Debit	Credit
Treasury stock	600,000	
Cash		600,000

Later, the company has a choice of either selling the shares to investors again, or of permanently retiring the shares. If the board were to resell the shares at a price of $13 per share, the entry would be:

	Debit	Credit
Cash	650,000	
Additional paid-in capital		50,000
Treasury stock		600,000

Alternatively, the board may elect to retire the shares. If it were to do so, the entry would be:

	Debit	Credit
Common stock, $1 par value	50,000	
Additional paid-in capital	550,000	
Treasury stock		600,000

Constructive Retirement Method

An alternative method of accounting for treasury stock is the constructive retirement method, which is used under the assumption that repurchased stock will not be reissued in the future. Under this approach, you are essentially reversing the amount of the original price at which the stock was sold. The remainder of the purchase price is debited to the retained earnings account.

EXAMPLE

The board of directors of Armadillo Industries authorizes the repurchase of 100,000 shares of its stock, which has a $1 par value. The company originally sold the shares for $12 each, or $1,200,000 in total. Armadillo pays $1,500,000 to repurchase the shares. The accountant records the transaction with this journal entry:

	Debit	Credit
Common stock, $1 par value	100,000	
Additional paid-in capital	1,100,000	
Retained earnings	300,000	
Cash		1,500,000

In the journal entry, the accountant is eliminating the $100,000 originally credited to the common stock account and associated with its par value. There is also an elimination from the additional paid-in capital account of the $1,100,000 originally paid into that account. The excess expenditure over the original proceeds is charged to the retained earnings account.

We do not show an example for the resale of treasury stock that was accounted for under the constructive retirement method, since these shares were recorded under the assumption that they would not be resold.

Equity-Based Payments to Non-Employees

An equity-based payment is one in which a business pays a provider of goods or services with its equity, such as shares or warrants. The accounting for equity-based payments depends upon the definition of the recipient, since the accounting for a payment to an employee differs from the accounting when payment is made to anyone else. In this section, we deal with the accounting for equity-based payments to non-employees. In the following sub-sections, we will deal with a number of variations on the concept of equity-based payments to non-employees.

Initial Recognition

The two main rules for equity-based payments are that you must:
- Recognize the fair value of the equity instruments issued or the fair value of the consideration received, whichever can be more reliably measured; and
- Recognize the asset or expense related to the provided goods or services at the same time.

The following additional conditions apply to more specific circumstances:
- *Fully vested equity issued.* If fully vested, nonforfeitable equity instruments are issued, the grantor should recognize the equity on the date of issuance. The offset to this recognition may be a prepaid asset, if the grantee has not yet delivered on its obligations.
- *Option expiration.* If the grantor recognizes an asset or expense based on its issuance of stock options to a grantee, and the grantee does not exercise the options, do not reverse the asset or expense.
- *Sales incentives.* If sales incentives are paid with equity instruments, measure them at the fair value of the equity instruments or the sales incentive, whichever can be more reliably measured.
- *Equity recipient.* If a business is the recipient of an equity instrument in exchange for goods or services, it should recognize revenue in the normal manner.

The grantor usually recognizes an equity-based payment as of a measurement date. The measurement date is the earlier of:
- The date when the grantee's performance is complete; or
- The date when the grantee's commitment to complete is probable, given the presence of large disincentives related to nonperformance. Note that forfeiture of the equity instrument is not considered a sufficient disincentive to trigger this clause.

It is also possible to reach the measurement date when the grantor issues fully vested, nonforfeitable equity instruments to the grantee, since the grantee does not have an obligation to perform in order to receive payment.

If the grantor issues a fully vested, nonforfeitable equity instrument that can be exercised early if a performance target is reached, the grantor measures the fair value of the instrument at the date of grant. If early exercise is granted, then measure and record the incremental change in fair value as of the date of revision to the terms of the instrument. Also, recognize the cost of the transaction in the same period as if the company had paid cash, instead of using the equity instrument as payment.

EXAMPLE

Armadillo Industries issues fully vested warrants to a grantee. The option agreement contains a provision that the exercise price will be reduced if a project on which the grantee is working is completed to the satisfaction of Armadillo management by a certain date.

In another arrangement, Armadillo issues warrants that vest in five years. The option agreement contains a provision that the vesting period will be reduced to six months if a project on which the grantee is working is accepted by an Armadillo client by a certain date.

In both cases, the company should record the fair value of the instruments when granted, and then adjust the recorded fair values when the remaining provisions of the agreements have been settled.

In rare cases, it may be necessary for the grantor to recognize the cost of an equity payment before the measurement date. If so, measure the fair value of the equity instrument at each successive interim period until the measurement date is reached. If some terms of the equity instrument have not yet been settled during these interim periods (as is the case when the amount of equity paid will vary based on market conditions or counterparty performance), then measure the instrument at its lowest aggregate fair value during each interim period, until all terms have been settled.

The grantee must also record payments made to it with equity instruments. The grantee should recognize the fair value of the equity instruments paid using the same rules applied to the grantor. If there is a performance condition, the grantee may have to alter the amount of revenue recognized, once the condition has been settled.

EXAMPLE

Gatekeeper Corporation operates a private toll road. It contracts with International Bridge Development (IBD) to build a bridge along the toll way. Gatekeeper agrees to pay IBD $10,000,000 for the work, as well as an additional 1,000,000 warrants if the bridge is completed by a certain date. IBD agrees to forfeit $2,000,000 of its fee if the bridge has not been completed by that date. The forfeiture clause is sufficiently large to classify the arrangement as a performance commitment.

Gatekeeper should measure the 1,000,000 warrants at the performance commitment date, which have a fair value of $500,000. Gatekeeper should then charge the $500,000 to expense over the normal course of the bridge construction project, based on milestone and completion payments.

EXAMPLE

Archaic Corporation hires a writer to create a series of books about ancient Greece. The terms of the deal are that Archaic will pay the writer $20,000 and 10,000 warrants per book completed. There is no penalty associated with the writer declining to continue writing books for the series. The writer completes work on the first book in the series on October 31, and then refuses to continue writing books for Archaic.

Archaic should recognize the fair value of the 10,000 warrants associated with the writer's completion of the first book when the writer completes the manuscript on October 31. On that date, the warrants have a fair value of $5,000, so Archaic should recognize a total expense of $25,000, which is comprised of the cash and warrant portions of the payment.

Spinoffs and Reverse Spinoffs

A company (the spinnor) may spin off a portion of its operations to shareholders, typically by transferring assets into a separate legal entity (the spinnee) and distributing shares in the spinnee to existing shareholders. This transaction is called a spinoff. In rare cases, the legal form of the transaction is that the spinnee is the surviving entity, in which case the event is called a reverse spinoff.

In general, the accounting for a spinoff is to record the assets of the spinnee at their carrying value. The transaction is not to be accounted for as a combination sale of the spinnee and subsequent distribution of the proceeds to shareholders.

If there is a reverse spinoff, treat the spinnee (which is the surviving entity) for accounting purposes as the spinnor. This approach bases the accounting on the substance of the transaction, not on its legal form. The proper treatment of a reverse spinoff as a spinoff for accounting purposes is based on the facts and circumstances of each individual situation. The following flags indicate that a spinoff could actually be a reverse spinoff:

- *Fair value.* The fair value of the legal spinnee is larger than the fair value of the legal spinnor.
- *Management.* The legal spinnee retains the senior management team.
- *Size.* The legal spinnee is larger than the legal spinnor, based on a comparison of assets, revenues, and earnings.
- *Time held.* The legal spinnee has been held for a longer period of time than the legal spinnor.

EXAMPLE

Armadillo Industries has a small division that produces films. Since this division is entirely unrelated to Armadillo's core business of manufacturing protective plating, senior management wants to shift the assets associated with the film division into a new entity, and distribute shares in the entity to shareholders on a pro rata basis. This is a spinoff.

Henderson Industrial is comprised of two subsidiaries, of which one produces milk cartons and the other manufactures conveyor systems. The milk carton unit is three times the size of the conveyor division. Henderson shareholders believe that the milk carton business has better prospects, and so want to dispose of the conveyor division. To do so, the company distributes shares in the milk carton subsidiary to shareholders and then sells all shares in the conveyor division to a third party. This is a reverse spinoff.

Equity Disclosures

There are a large number of disclosures related to the equity topic, so the disclosures related to each topic are addressed separately within the following sub-sections.

Rights and Privileges

Disclose a summary of the rights and privileges accorded to the holders of the various securities outstanding during the presented accounting periods. This may include the following items, or other rights and privileges:

- Conversion rights to other securities (and the associated prices and dates)
- Dividends
- Liquidation rights
- Participation rights
- Special voting rights

Preferred Stock

If there is preferred stock outstanding and those shares have a liquidation preference that significantly exceeds their par value, disclose the aggregate liquidation preference on the balance sheet. Also disclose the following information anywhere in the financial statements:

- *Arrearages*. The amount by which there are cumulative preferred dividends in arrears, both in aggregate and on a per-share basis.
- *Redemption*. The amounts of preferred stock subject to redemption, both in aggregate and on a per-share basis.

Contingently Convertible Securities

Disclose the significant conversion terms associated with contingently convertible securities. There must be sufficient information for readers to understand the contingent conversion option and what the impact of the conversion would be. The following disclosures would be helpful for gaining this understanding:

- Events that would alter the terms of the contingency
- Events that would trigger the contingency
- The conversion price
- The number of shares into which a security can be converted
- The timing of conversion rights
- The type of settlement (such as in cash or shares)

EXAMPLE

Armadillo Industries includes the following disclosure in the notes that accompany its financial statements, regarding the issuance of shares related to a recent acquisition:

The company issued 2,000,000 shares of its common stock to the shareholders of Susquehanna Plating when it acquired that entity. If the market price of Armadillo's stock declines below $10 per share before December 31, 20X4, the company will be obligated to issue an additional 500,000 shares of its common stock to those shareholders.

Also disclose the excess amount by which the aggregate fair value of the securities to be issued at conversion exceeds the proceeds received, as well as the time period over which the discount would be amortized.

Redeemable Securities

If a business issues redeemable securities, disclose the redemption requirements in each of the five years following the date of the last balance sheet presented. The disclosure can be in aggregate or separately for each issuance of these securities.

Treasury Stock

If the company repurchases its stock at a price significantly in excess of the market price, disclose how the price is allocated between other items and the repurchase of stock, and how the transaction is accounted for.

If the company is organized in a state which has stock repurchase laws that restrict the availability of retained earnings for distributions, disclose this situation.

Changes in Shareholders' Equity

If both the income statement and balance sheet are presented, also disclose the changes in the shareholders' equity accounts, as well as any changes in shares outstanding during at least the most recent fiscal year and subsequent interim periods. A sample statement, not including changes in shares outstanding, is shown in the following exhibit.

Statement of Retained Earnings

	Common Stock, $1 Par	Additional Paid-In Capital	Retained Earnings	Total Shareholders' Equity
Retained earnings at December 31, 20X2	$10,000	$40,000	$100,000	$150,000
Net income for the year ended 12/31/X3			40,000	40,000
Dividends paid to shareholders			-25,000	-25,000
Retained earnings at December 31, 20X3	$10,000	$40,000	$115,000	$165,000

The Securities and Exchange Commission also requires disclosure of adjustments to the beginning balance in this reconciliation for items that were retroactively applied to prior periods.

Equity-Based Payments to Non-Employees

There may be situations where a company issues fully vested, non-forfeitable equity instruments in exchange for goods or services. A likely outcome of this arrangement is that the goods or services have not yet been provided or performed, and so are recorded as a prepaid asset. This prepaid asset should be included within the assets section of the balance sheet, not as a deduction from equity.

An entity that has received an equity instrument should disclose the amount of gross operating revenue attributable to the instrument, since this is a nonmonetary transaction.

Summary

Many equity-related topics were addressed in this chapter. An accountant may not see most of these topics for years, or only have to deal with a few minor disclosures. However, the repurchase of shares is a relatively common event, so you should be familiar with the accounting for and presentation of treasury stock transactions. We recommend the cost method of accounting for treasury stock, since it is the easiest of the available accounting methods.

It is also relatively common to pay for goods and services with equity instruments, so be familiar with the concepts related to how these instruments are recognized. The level of judgment and accounting complexity increases when a business enters into arrangements where the issuance of equity instruments is subject to several variables. Consequently, it is best to provide advice on these arrangements before the business is contractually committed to them, in order to have commitments that require the least accounting effort and measurement uncertainty.

Chapter 11
Revenue Recognition

Introduction

Historically, the accounting standards related to the recognition of revenue have built up in a piecemeal manner, with guidance being established separately for certain industries and types of transactions. The result has been an inconsistent set of standards that, while workable, have not resulted in revenue recognition principles that could be applied consistently across many industries.

The accounting for revenue has been streamlined to a considerable extent with the release of Topic 606 in GAAP. Now, the overall intent of revenue recognition is to do so in a manner that reasonably depicts the transfer of goods or services to customers, for which consideration is paid that reflects the amount to which the seller expects to be entitled. The following sections describe the five-step process of revenue recognition, as well as a number of ancillary topics.

Topic 606, Revenue from Contracts with Customers

The most comprehensive accounting standard to date that deals with revenue recognition is Topic 606 of the Accounting Standards Codification, *Revenue from Contracts with Customers*. This standard establishes a consistent framework for how to address revenue issues, while at the same time eliminating a number of inconsistencies in prior accounting standards relating to revenue. The result should be a higher level of comparability of revenue practices across multiple industries.

Topic 606 is now the overarching revenue standard, since it applies to any entity that contractually sells goods or services to customers. This accounting standard focuses on the overall principles guiding the recognition of revenue, rather than establishing a large number of detailed rules to govern the actions of accountants. The result is a topic that emphasizes the use of judgment in following general guidelines.

Topic 606 does not completely supplant the revenue-related guidance in other accounting standards. In cases where more detailed guidance is available in the accounting standards that deal with a transaction, the more detailed guidance should be applied rather than the guidance found in Topic 606.

The following sections delve into the essentials of *Revenue from Contracts with Customers*.

The Nature of a Customer

Revenue recognition only occurs if the third party involved is a customer. A customer is an entity that has contracted to obtain goods or services from the seller's ordinary activities in exchange for payment.

In some situations, it may require a complete examination of the facts and circumstances to determine whether the other party can be classified as a customer. For example, it can be difficult to discern whether there is a customer in collaborative research and development activities between pharmaceutical entities. Another difficult area is payments between oil and gas partners to settle differences between their entitlements to the output from a producing field.

EXAMPLE

The Red Herring Fish Company contracts with Lethal Sushi to co-develop a fish farm off the coast of Iceland, where the two entities share equally in any future profits. Lethal Sushi is primarily in the restaurant business, so developing a fish farm is not one of its ordinary activities. Also, there is no clear consideration being paid to Lethal. Based on the circumstances, Red Herring is not a customer of Lethal Sushi.

Steps in Revenue Recognition

Topic 606 establishes a series of actions that an entity takes to determine the amount and timing of revenue to be recognized. The main steps are:

1. Link the contract with a specific customer.
2. Note the performance obligations required by the contract.
3. Determine the price of the underlying transaction.
4. Match this price to the performance obligations through an allocation process.
5. Recognize revenue as the various obligations are fulfilled.

We will expand upon each of these steps in the following sections.

Step One: Link Contract to Customer

The contract is used as a central aspect of revenue recognition, because revenue recognition is closely associated with it. In many instances, revenue is recognized at multiple points in time over the duration of a contract, so linking contracts with revenue recognition provides a reasonable framework for establishing the timing and amounts of revenue recognition.

A contract only exists if there is an agreement between the parties that establishes enforceable rights and obligations. It is not necessary for an agreement to be in writing for it to be considered a contract. More specifically, a contract only exists if the following conditions are present:

- *Approval.* All parties to the contract have approved the document and substantially committed to its contents (based on all relevant facts and circumstances). The parties can be considered to be committed to a contract despite occasional lapses, such as not enforcing prompt payment or sometimes shipping late. Approval can be in writing or orally.
- *Rights.* The document clearly identifies the rights of the parties.
- *Payment.* The payment terms are clearly stated. It is acceptable to recognize revenue related to unpriced change orders if the seller expects that the price will be approved and the scope of work has been approved.
- *Substance.* The agreement has commercial substance; that is, the cash flows of the seller will change as a result of the contract, either in terms of their amount, timing, or risk of receipt. Otherwise, organizations could swap goods or services to artificially boost their revenue.
- *Probability.* It is probable that the organization will collect the amount stated in the contract in exchange for the goods or services that it commits to provide to the other party. In this context, "probable" means "likely to occur." This evaluation is based on the customer's ability and intention to pay when due. The evaluation can incorporate a consideration of the past practice of the customer in question, or of the class of customers to which that customer belongs.

If these criteria are not initially met, the seller can continue to evaluate the situation to see if the criteria are met at a later date.

Note: These criteria do not *have* to be re-evaluated at a later date, unless the seller notes a significant change in the relevant facts and circumstances.

EXAMPLE

Prickly Corporation has entered into an arrangement to sell a large quantity of rose thorns to Ambivalence Corporation, which manufactures a number of potions for the amateur witch brewing market. The contract specifies monthly deliveries over the course of the next year.

Prior to the first shipment, Prickly's collections manager learns through her contacts that Ambivalence has just lost its line of credit and has conducted a large layoff. It appears that the customer's ability to pay has deteriorated significantly, which calls into question the probability of collecting the amount stated in the contract. In this case, there may no longer be a contract for the purposes of revenue recognition.

EXAMPLE

Domicilio Corporation, which develops commercial real estate, enters into a contract with Cupertino Beanery to sell a building to Cupertino to be used as a coffee shop. This is Cupertino's first foray into the coffee shop business, having previously only been a distributor of coffee beans to shops within the region. Also, there are a massive number of coffee shops already established in the area.

Domicilio receives a $100,000 deposit from Cupertino when the contract is signed. The contract also states that Cupertino will pay Domicilio an additional $900,000 for the rest of the property over the next three years, with interest. This financing arrangement is nonrecourse, meaning that Domicilio can repossess the building in the event of default, but cannot obtain further cash from Cupertino. Cupertino expects to pay Domicilio from the cash flows to be generated by the coffee shop operation.

Domicilio's management concludes that it is not probable that Cupertino will pay the remaining contractual amount, since its source of funds is a high-risk venture in which Cupertino has no experience. In addition, the loan is nonrecourse, so Cupertino can easily walk away from the arrangement. Accordingly, Domicilio accounts for the initial deposit and future payments as a deposit liability, and continues to recognize the building asset. If it later becomes probable that Cupertino will pay the full contractual amount, Domicilio can then recognize revenue and an offsetting receivable.

Whether a contract exists can depend upon standard industry practice, or vary by legal jurisdiction, or even vary by business segment.

There may be instances in which the preceding criteria are not met, and yet the customer is paying consideration to the seller. If so, revenue can be recognized only when one of the following events has occurred:

- The contract has been terminated and the consideration received by the seller is not refundable; or
- The seller has no remaining obligations to the customer, substantially all of the consideration has been received, and the payment is not refundable.

These alternatives focus on whether the contract has been concluded in all respects. If so, there is little risk that any revenue recognized will be reversed in a later period, and so is a highly conservative approach to recognizing revenue.

If the seller receives consideration from a customer and the preceding conditions do not exist, then the payment is to be recorded as a liability until such time as the sale criteria have been met.

A contract is not considered to exist when each party to the contract has a unilateral right to terminate a contract that has not been performed, and without compensating the other party. An unperformed contract is one in which no goods or services have been transferred to the customer, nor has the seller received any consideration from the customer in exchange for any promised goods or services.

In certain situations, it can make sense to combine several contracts into one for the purposes of revenue recognition. For example, if there is a portfolio of contracts that have similar characteristics, and the entity expects that treating the portfolio as a single unit will have no appreciable impact on the financial statements, it is acceptable to combine the contracts for accounting purposes. This approach may be particularly valuable in industries where there are a large number of similar contracts, and where applying the model to each individual contract could be impractical.

> **Tip:** When accounting for a portfolio of contracts, adjust the accompanying estimates and assumptions to reflect the greater size of the portfolio.

If the seller enters into two or more contracts with a customer at approximately the same time, these contracts can be accounted for as a single contract if any of the following criteria are met:

- *Basis of negotiation.* The contracts were negotiated as a package, with the goal of attaining a single commercial objective.
- *Interlinking consideration.* The consideration that will be paid under the terms of one contract is dependent upon the price or performance noted in the other contract.
- *Performance obligation.* There is essentially one performance obligation inherent in the two contracts.

EXAMPLE

Domicilio Corporation enters into three contracts with Milford Sound to construct a concert arena. These contracts involve construction of the concrete building shell, installation of seating, and the construction of a staging system. The three contracts are all needed in order to arrive at a functioning concert arena. Final payment on all three contracts shall be made once the final customer (a local municipality) approves the entire project.

Domicilio should account for these contracts as a single contract, since they are all directed toward the same commercial goal, payment is dependent on all three contracts being completed, and the performance obligation is essentially the same for all of the contracts.

Step Two: Note Performance Obligations

A performance obligation is essentially the unit of account for the goods or services contractually promised to a customer. The performance obligations in the contract must be clearly identified. This is of considerable importance in recognizing revenue, since revenue is considered to be recognizable when goods or services are transferred to the customer. Examples of goods or services are:

Item Sold	Example of the Seller
Arranging for another party to transfer goods or services	Travel agent selling airline tickets
Asset construction on behalf of a customer	Building construction company
Grant of a license	Software company issuing licenses to use its software
Grant of options to purchase additional goods or services	Airline granting frequent flier points
Manufactured goods	Manufacturer
Performance of contractually-mandated tasks	Consultant
Readiness to provide goods or services as needed	Snow plow operator, alarm system monitoring

Item Sold	Example of the Seller
Resale of merchandise	Retailer
Resale of rights to goods or services	Selling a priority for a new-model car delivery
Rights to future goods or services that can be resold	Wholesaler gives additional services to retailer buying a particular product

There may also be an implicit promise to deliver goods or services that is not stated in a contract, as implied by the customary business practices of the seller. If there is a valid expectation by the customer to receive these implicitly-promised goods or services, they should be considered a performance obligation. Otherwise, the seller might recognize the entire transaction price as revenue when in fact there are still goods or services yet to be provided.

If there is no performance obligation, then there is no revenue to be recognized. For example, a company could continually build up its inventory through ongoing production activities, but just because it has more sellable assets does not mean that it can report an incremental increase in the revenue in its income statement. If such an activity-based revenue recognition model were allowed, organizations could increase their revenues simply by increasing their rate of activity.

If there is more than one good or service to be transferred under the contract terms, only break it out as a separate performance obligation if it is a distinct obligation or there are a series of transfers to the customer of a distinct good or service. In the latter case, a separate performance obligation is assumed if there is a consistent pattern of transfer to the customer.

The "distinct" label can be applied to a good or service only if it meets both of the following criteria:

- *Capable of being distinct.* The customer can benefit from the good or service as delivered, or in combination with other resources that the customer can readily find; and
- *Distinct within the context of the contract.* The promised delivery of the good or service is separately identified within the contract.

Goods or services are more likely to be considered distinct when:

- The seller does not use the goods or services as a component of an integrated bundle of goods or services.
- The items do not significantly modify any other goods or services listed in the contract.
- The items are not highly interrelated with other goods or services listed in the contract.

The intent of these evaluative factors is to place a focus on how to determine whether goods or services are truly distinct within a contract. There is no need to assess the customer's intended use of any goods or services when making this determination.

EXAMPLE

Aphelion Corporation sells a package of goods and services to Nova Corporation. The goods include a deep field telescope, an observatory to house the telescope, and calibration services for the telescope.

The observatory building can be considered distinct from the telescope and calibration services, because Nova could have the telescope installed in an existing facility instead. However, the telescope and calibration services are linked, since the telescope will not function properly unless it has been properly calibrated. Thus, one performance obligation can be considered the observatory, while the telescope and associated calibration can be stated as a separate obligation.

EXAMPLE

Norrona Software enters into a contract with a Scandinavian clothing manufacturer to transfer a software license for its clothing design software. The contract also states that Norrona will install the software and provide technical support for a two-year period. The installation process involves adjusting the data entry screens to match the needs of the clothing designers who will use the software. The software can be used without these installation changes. The technical support assistance is intended to provide advice to users regarding advanced features, and is not considered a key requirement for software users.

Since the software is functional without the installation process or the technical support, Norrona concludes that the items are not highly interrelated. Since these goods and services are distinct, the company should identify separate performance obligations for the software license, installation work, and technical support.

In the event that a good or service is not classified as distinct, aggregate it with other goods or services promised in the contract, until such time as a cluster of goods or services have been accumulated that can be considered distinct.

Note: If a different GAAP topic describes how to separate out the elements of a contract or initially measure it, follow that guidance before the requirements of Topic 606.

The administrative tasks needed to fulfill a contract are not considered to be performance obligations, since they do not involve the transfer of goods or services to customers. For example, setting up information about a new contract in the seller's contract management software is not considered a performance obligation.

Step Three: Determine Prices

This step involves the determination of the transaction price built into the contract. The transaction price is the amount of consideration to be paid by the customer in exchange for its receipt of goods or services. The transaction price does not include any amounts collected on behalf of third parties.

EXAMPLE

The Twister Vacuum Company sells its vacuum cleaners to individuals through its chain of retail stores. In the most recent period, Twister generated $3,800,000 of receipts, of which $200,000 was sales taxes collected on behalf of local governments. Since the $200,000 was collected on behalf of third parties, it cannot be recognized as revenue.

The transaction price may be difficult to determine, since it involves consideration of the effects noted in the following subsections.

Variable Consideration

The terms of some contracts may result in a price that can vary, depending on the circumstances. For example, there may be discounts, rebates, penalties, or performance bonuses in the contract. Or, the customer may have a reasonable expectation that the seller will offer a price concession, based on the seller's customary business practices, policies, or statements. Another example is when the seller intends to accept lower prices from a new customer in order to develop a strong customer relationship. If so, set the transaction price based on either the most likely amount or the probability-weighted expected value, using whichever method yields that amount of consideration most likely to be paid. In more detail, these methods are:

- *Most likely.* The seller develops a range of possible payment amounts, and selects the amount most likely to be paid. This approach works best when there are only two possible amounts that will be paid.
- *Expected value.* The seller develops a range of possible payment amounts, and assigns a probability to each one. The sum of these probability-weighted amounts is the expected value of the variable consideration. This approach works best when there are a large number of possible payment amounts. However, the outcome may be an expected value that does not exactly align with any amount that could actually be paid.

EXAMPLE

Grissom Granaries operates grain storage facilities along the Mississippi River. Its accounting staff is reviewing a contract that has just been signed with a major farming co-operative, and concludes that the contract could have four possible outcomes, which are noted in the following expected value table:

Price Scenario	Transaction Price	Probability	Probability-Weighted Price
1	$1,500,000	20%	$300,000
2	1,700,000	35%	595,000
3	2,000,000	40%	800,000
4	2,400,000	5%	120,000
		Expected Value	$1,815,000

The expected value derived from the four possible pricing outcomes is $1,815,000, even though this amount does not match any one of the four pricing outcomes.

Whichever method is chosen, be sure to use it consistently throughout the contract, as well as for similar contracts. However, it is not necessary to use the same measurement method to measure each uncertainty contained within a contract; different methods can be applied to different uncertainties.

Also, review the circumstances of each contract at the end of each reporting period, and update the estimated transaction price to reflect any changes in the circumstances.

EXAMPLE

Cantilever Construction has entered into a contract to tear down and replace five bridges along Interstate 70. The state government (which owns and maintains this section of the highway) is extremely concerned about how the work will interfere with traffic on the highway. Accordingly, the government includes in the contract a clause that penalizes Cantilever $10,000 for every hour over the budgeted amount that each bridge demolition and construction project shuts down the interstate, and a $15,000 bonus for every hour saved from the budgeted amount.

Cantilever has extensive experience with this type of work, having torn down and replaced 42 other bridges along the interstate highway system in the past five years. Based on the company's experience with these other projects and an examination of the budgeted hours allowed for shutting down the interstate, the company concludes that the most likely outcome is $120,000 of variable consideration associated with the project. Cantilever accordingly adds this amount to the transaction price.

Possibility of Reversal

Do not include in the transaction price an estimate of variable consideration if, when the uncertainty associated with the variable amount is settled, it is probable that there will be a significant reversal of cumulative revenue recognized. The assessment of a possible reversal of revenue could include the following factors, all of which might increase the probability of a revenue reversal:

- *Beyond seller's influence.* The amount of consideration paid is strongly influenced by factors outside of the control of the seller. For example, goods sold may be subject to obsolescence (as is common in the technology industry), or weather conditions could impede the availability of goods (as is common in the production of farm products).

- *Historical practice*. The seller has a history of accepting a broad range of price concessions, or of changing the terms of similar contracts.
- *Inherent range of outcomes*. The terms of the contract contain a broad range of possible consideration amounts that might be paid.
- *Limited experience*. The seller does not have much experience with the type of contract in question. Alternatively, the seller's prior experience cannot be translated into a prediction of the amount of consideration paid.
- *Long duration*. A considerable period of time may have to pass before the uncertainty can be resolved.

Note: The probability of a significant reversal of cumulative revenue recognized places a conservative bias on the recognition of revenue, rather than a neutral bias, so there will be a tendency for recognized revenue levels to initially be too low. However, this approach is reasonable when considering that revenue information is more relevant when it is not subject to future reversals.

If management expects that a retroactive discount will be applied to sales transactions, the seller should recognize a refund liability as part of the revenue recognition when each performance obligation is satisfied. For example, if the seller is currently selling goods for $100 but expects that a 20% volume discount will be retroactively applied at the end of the year, the resulting entry should be:

	Debit	Credit
Accounts receivable	100	
Revenue		80
Refund liability		20

EXAMPLE

Medusa Medical sells a well-known snake oil therapy through a number of retail store customers. In the most recent month, Medusa sells $100,000 of its potent Copperhead Plus combination healing balm and sunscreen lotion. The therapy is most effective within one month of manufacture and then degrades rapidly, so that Medusa must accept increasingly large price concessions in order to ensure that the goods are sold. Historically, this means that the range of price concessions varies from zero (in the first month) to 80% (after four months). Of this range of outcomes, Medusa estimates that the expected value of the transactions is likely to be revenue of $65,000. However, since the risk of obsolescence is so high, Medusa cannot conclude that it is probable that there will not be a significant reversal in the amount of cumulative revenue recognized. Accordingly, management concludes that the price point at which it is probable that there will not be a significant reversal in the cumulative amount of revenue recognized is actually closer to $45,000 (representing a 55% price concession). Based on this conclusion, the controller initially recognizes $45,000 of revenue when the goods are shipped to retailers, and continues to monitor the situation at the end of each reporting period, to see if the recognized amount should be adjusted.

EXAMPLE

Iceland Cod enters into a contract with Lethal Sushi to provide Lethal with 10,000 pounds of cod per year, at $15 per pound. If Lethal purchases more than 10,000 pounds within one calendar year, then a 12% retroactive price reduction will be applied to all of Lethal's purchases for the year.

Iceland has dealt with Lethal for a number of years, and knows that Lethal has never attained the 10,000 pound level of purchases. Accordingly, through the first half of the year, Iceland records its sales to Lethal at their full price, which is $30,000 for 2,000 pounds of cod.

In July, Lethal acquires Wimpy Fish Company, along with its large chain of seafood restaurants. With a much larger need for fish to supply the additional restaurants, Lethal now places several large orders that make it quite clear that passing the 10,000 pound threshold will be no problem at all. Accordingly, Iceland's controller records a cumulative revenue reversal of $3,600 to account for Lethal's probable attainment of the volume purchase discount.

EXAMPLE

Armadillo Industries is a new company that has developed a unique type of ceramic-based body armor that is extremely light. To encourage sales, the company is offering a 90-day money back guarantee. Since the company is new to the industry and cannot predict the level of returns, there is no way of knowing if a sudden influx of returns might trigger a significant reversal in the amount of cumulative revenue recognized. Accordingly, the company must wait for the money back guarantee to expire before it can recognize any revenue.

Time Value of Money

If the transaction price is to be paid over a period of time, this implies that the seller is including a financing component in the contract. If this financing component is a significant financing benefit for the customer and provides financing for more than one year, adjust the transaction price for the time value of money. In cases where there is a financing component to a contract, the seller will earn interest income over the term of the contract.

A contract may contain a financing component, even if there is no explicit reference to it in the contract. When adjusting the transaction price for the time value of money, consider the following factors:

- *Standalone price.* The amount of revenue recognized should reflect the price that a customer would have paid if it had paid in cash.
- *Significance.* In order to be recognized, the financing component should be significant. This means evaluating the amount of the difference between the consideration to be paid and the cash selling price. Also note the combined

effect of prevailing interest rates and the time difference between when delivery is made and when the customer pays.

If it is necessary to adjust the compensation paid for the time value of money, use as a discount rate the rate that would be employed in a separate financing transaction between the parties as of the beginning date of the contract. The rate used should reflect the credit characteristics of the customer, including the presence of any collateral provided. This discount rate is not to be updated after the commencement of the contract, irrespective of any changes in the credit markets or in the credit standing of the customer.

EXAMPLE

Hammer Industries sells a large piece of construction equipment to Eskimo Construction, under generous terms that allow Eskimo to pay Hammer the full amount of the $119,990 receivable in 24 months. The cash selling price of the equipment is $105,000. The contract contains an implicit interest rate of 6.9%, which is the interest rate that discounts the purchase price of $119,990 down to the cash selling price over the two year period. The controller examines this rate and concludes that it approximates the rate that Hammer and Eskimo would use if there had been a separate financing transaction between them as of the contract inception date. Consequently, Hammer recognizes interest income during the two-year period prior to the payment due date, using the following calculation:

Year	Beginning Balance	Interest (at 6.9% Rate)	Ending Balance
1	$105,000	$7,245	$112,245
2	112,245	7,745	$119,990

As of the shipment date, Hammer records the following entry:

	Debit	Credit
Loan receivable	105,000	
Revenue		105,000

At the end of the first year, Hammer recognizes the interest associated with the transaction for the first year, using the following entry:

	Debit	Credit
Loan receivable	7,245	
Interest income		7,245

At the end of the second year, Hammer recognizes the interest associated with the transaction for the second year, using the following entry:

	Debit	Credit
Loan receivable	7,745	
Interest income		7,745

These entries increase the size of the loan receivable until it reaches the original sale price of $119,990. Eskimo then pays the full amount of the receivable, at which point Hammer records the following final entry:

	Debit	Credit
Cash	119,990	
Loan receivable		119,990

Also, note that the financing concept can be employed in reverse; that is, if a customer makes a deposit that the seller expects to retain for more than one year, the financing component of this arrangement should be recognized by the seller. Doing so properly reflects the economics of the arrangement, where the seller is using the cash of the customer to fund its purchase of materials and equipment for a project; if the seller had not provided the deposit, the seller would instead have needed to obtain financing.

There is assumed *not* to be a significant financing component to a contract in the presence of any of the following factors:

- *Advance payment.* The customer paid in advance, and the customer can specify when goods and services are to be delivered.
- *Variable component.* A large part of the consideration to be paid is variable, and payment timing will vary based on a future event that is not under the control of either party.
- *Non-financing reason.* The reason for the difference between the contractual consideration and the cash selling price exists for a reason other than financing, and the amount of the difference is proportional to the alternative reason.

EXAMPLE

Spinner Maintenance offers global technical support to the owners of rooftop solar power systems in exchange for a $400 fee. The fee pays for service that spans the first five years of the life of the power systems, and is purchased as part of the package of solar panels and initial installation work. This maintenance is intended to provide phone support to homeowners who are researching why their power systems are malfunctioning. The support does not include any replacement of solar panels for hail damage.

The support period is quite extensive, but Spinner concludes that there is no financing component to these sales, for the following reasons:

- The administrative cost of a monthly billing would be prohibitive, since the amount billed on a monthly basis would be paltry.
- Those more technologically proficient customers would be less likely to renew if they could pay on a more frequent basis, leaving Spinner with the highest-maintenance customers who require the most support.
- Customers are more likely to make use of the service if they are reminded of it by the arrival of monthly invoices.

In short, Spinner has several excellent reasons for structuring the payment plan to require an advance payment, all of which are centered on maintaining a reasonable level of profitability. The intent is not to provide financing to customers.

EXAMPLE

Glow Atomic sells a nuclear power plant to a French provincial government. The certification process for the plant is extensive, spanning a six-month test period. Accordingly, the local government builds into the contract a provision to withhold 20% of the contract price until completion of the test period. The rest of the payments are made on a milestone schedule, as the construction work progresses. Based on the circumstances and the amount of the withholding, the arrangement is considered to be non-financing, so Glow Atomic does not break out a financing component from the total consideration paid.

Noncash Consideration

If the customer will be paying with some form of noncash consideration, measure the consideration at its fair value. If it is not possible to measure the payment at its fair value, instead use the standalone selling price of the goods or services to be delivered to the customer. This approach also applies to payments made with equity instruments. In rare cases, the customer may supply the seller with goods or services that are intended to assist the seller in its fulfillment of the related contract. If the seller gains control of these assets or services, it should consider them to be noncash consideration paid by the customer.

EXAMPLE

Industrial Landscaping is hired by Pensive Corporation to mow the lawns and trim shrubbery at Pensive's corporate headquarters on a weekly basis throughout the year. Essentially the same service is provided each week. Pensive is a startup company with little excess cash, so it promises to pay Industrial with 25 shares of Pensive stock at the end of each week.

Industrial considers itself to have satisfied its performance obligation at the end of each week. Industrial should determine the transaction price as being the fair value of the shares at the end of each week, and recognizes this amount as revenue. There is no subsequent change in the amount of revenue recognized, irrespective of any changes in the fair value of the shares.

Payments to Customers

The contract may require the seller to pay consideration to the customer, perhaps in the form of credits or coupons that the customer can apply against the amounts it owes to the seller. This may also involve payments to third parties that have purchased the seller's goods or services from the original customer. If so, treat this consideration as a reduction of the transaction price. The following special situations may apply:

- *Customer supplies a good or service.* The customer may provide the seller with a distinct good or service; if so, the seller treats the payment as it would a payment to any supplier.
- *Supplier payment exceeds customer delivery.* If the customer provides a good or service to the seller, but the amount paid by the seller to the customer exceeds the fair value of the goods or services it receives in exchange, the excess of the payment is considered a reduction of the transaction price. If the fair value of the goods or services cannot be determined, then consider the entire amount paid by the seller to the customer to be a reduction of the transaction price.

If it is necessary to account for consideration paid to the customer as a reduction of the transaction price, do so when the later of the following two events have occurred:

- When the seller recognizes revenue related to its provision of goods or services to the customer; or
- When the seller either pays or promises to pay the consideration to the customer. The timing of this event could be derived from the customary business practices of the seller.

EXAMPLE

Dillinger Designs manufactures many types of hunting rifles. Dillinger enters into a one-year contract with Backwoods Survival, which has not previously engaged in rifle sales. Backwoods commits to purchase at least $240,000 of rifles from Dillinger during the contract period. Also, due to the considerable government-mandated safety requirements associated with the sale of rifles, Dillinger commits to pay $60,000 to Backwoods at the inception of the contract; these funds are intended to pay for a locking gun safe to be kept at each Backwoods store, as per firearms laws pertaining to retailers.

Dillinger determines that the $60,000 payment is to be treated as a reduction of the $240,000 sale price. Consequently, whenever Dillinger fulfills a performance obligation by shipping goods under the contract, it reduces the amount of revenue it would otherwise recognize by 25%, which reflects the proportion of the $60,000 payment related to locking gun safes of the $240,000 that Dillinger will be paid by Backwoods.

Refund Liabilities

In some situations, a seller may receive consideration from a customer, with the likelihood that the payment will be refunded. If so, the seller records a refund liability in the amount that the seller expects to refund back to the customer. The seller should review the amount of this liability at the end of each reporting period, to see if the amount should be altered.

Step Four: Allocate Prices to Obligations

Once the performance obligations and transaction prices associated with a contract have been identified, the next step is to allocate the transaction prices to the obligations. The basic rule is to allocate that price to a performance obligation that best reflects that amount of consideration to which the seller expects to be entitled when it satisfies each performance obligation. To determine this allocation, it is first necessary to estimate the standalone selling price of those distinct goods or services as of the inception date of the contract. If it is not possible to derive a standalone selling price, the seller must estimate it. This estimation should involve all relevant information that is reasonably available, such as:

- Competitive pressure on prices
- Costs incurred to manufacture or provide the item
- Item profit margins
- Pricing of other items in the same contract
- Standalone selling price of the item
- Supply and demand for the items in the market
- The seller's pricing strategy and practices
- The type of customer, distribution channel, or geographic region
- Third-party pricing

The following three approaches are acceptable ways in which to estimate a standalone selling price:

- *Adjusted market assessment.* This involves reviewing the market to estimate the price at which a customer in that market would be willing to pay for the goods and services in question. This can involve an examination of the prices of competitors for similar items and adjusting them to incorporate the seller's costs and margins.
- *Expected cost plus a margin.* This requires the seller to estimate the costs required to fulfill a performance obligation, and then add a margin to it to derive the estimated price.
- *Residual approach.* This involves subtracting all of the observable standalone selling prices from the total transaction price to arrive at the residual price remaining for allocation to any non-observable selling prices. This method can only be used if one of the following situations applies:
  - The seller sells the good or service to other customers for a wide range of prices; or
  - No price has yet been established for that item, and it has not yet been sold on a standalone basis.

The residual approach can be difficult to use when there are several goods or services with uncertain standalone selling prices. If so, it may be necessary to use a combination of methods to derive standalone selling prices, which should be used in the following order:

1. Estimate the aggregate amount of the standalone selling prices for all items having uncertain standalone selling prices, using the residual method.
2. Use another method to develop standalone selling prices for each item in this group, to allocate the aggregate amount of the standalone selling prices.

Once all standalone selling prices have been determined, allocate the transaction price amongst these distinct goods or services based on their relative standalone selling prices.

Tip: Appropriate evidence of a standalone selling price is the observable price of a good or service when the seller sells it to a similar customer under similar circumstances.

Once the seller derives an approach for estimating a standalone selling price, it should consistently apply that method to the derivation of the standalone selling prices for other goods or services with similar characteristics.

EXAMPLE

Luminescence Corporation manufactures a wide range of light bulbs, and mostly sells into the wholesaler market. The company receives an order from the federal government for two million fluorescent bulbs, as well as for 100,000 units of a new bulb that operates outdoors at very low temperatures. Luminescence has not yet sold these new bulbs to anyone. The total price of the order is $7,000,000. Luminescence assigns $6,000,000 of the total price to the fluorescent bulbs, based on its own sales of comparable orders. This leaves $1,000,000 of the total price that is allocable to the low temperature bulbs. Since Luminescence has not yet established a price for these bulbs and has not sold them on a standalone basis, it is acceptable to allocate $1,000,000 to the low temperature bulbs under the residual approach.

If there is a subsequent change in the transaction price, allocate that change amongst the distinct goods or services based on the original allocation that was used at the inception of the contract. If this subsequent allocation is to a performance obligation that has already been completed and for which revenue has already been recognized, the result can be an increase or reduction in the amount of revenue recognized. This change in recognition should occur as soon as the subsequent change in the transaction price occurs.

Allocation of Price Discounts

It is assumed that a customer has received a discount on a bundled purchase of goods or services when the sum of the standalone prices for these items is greater than the consideration to be paid under the terms of a contract. The discount can be allocated to a specific item within the bundled purchase, if there is observable evidence that the discount was intended for that item. In order to do so, all of the following criteria must apply:

1. Each distinct item in the bundle is regularly sold on a standalone basis;
2. A bundle of some of these distinct items is regularly sold at a discount to their standalone selling prices; and
3. The discount noted in the second point is essentially the same as the discount in the contract, and there is observable evidence linking the entire contract discount to that bundle of distinct items.

If this allocation system is used, the seller must employ it before using the residual approach noted earlier in this section. Doing so ensures that the discount is not applied to the other performance obligations in the contract to which prices have not yet been allocated.

In all other cases, the discount is to be allocated amongst all of the items in the bundle. In this latter situation, the allocation is to be made based on the standalone selling prices of all of the performance obligations in the contract.

EXAMPLE

The Hegemony Toy Company sells board games that re-enact famous battles. Hegemony regularly sells the following three board games:

Product	Standalone Selling Price
Hastings Battle Game	$120
Stalingrad Battle Game	100
Waterloo Battle Game	80
Total	$300

Hegemony routinely sells the Stalingrad and Waterloo products as a bundle for $120.

Hegemony enters into a contract with the War Games International website to sell War Games the set of three games for $240, which is a 20% discount from the standard price. Deliveries of these games to War Games will be at different times, so the related performance obligations will be settled on different dates.

The $60 discount would normally be apportioned among all three products based on their standalone selling prices. However, because Hegemony routinely sells the Stalingrad/Waterloo bundle for a $60 discount, it is evident that the entire discount should be allocated to these two products.

If Hegemony later delivers the Stalingrad and Waterloo games to War Games on different dates, it should allocate the $60 discount between the two products based on their standalone selling prices. Thus, $33.33 should be allocated to the Stalingrad game and $26.67 to the Waterloo game. The allocation calculation is:

Game	Allocation
Stalingrad	($100 individual game price ÷ $180 combined price) × $60 discount = $33.33
Waterloo	($80 individual game price ÷ $180 combined price) × $60 discount = $26.67

If the two games are instead delivered at the same time, there is no need to conduct the preceding allocation. Instead, the discount can be assigned to them both as part of a single performance obligation.

Allocation of Variable Consideration

There may be a variable amount of consideration associated with a contract. This consideration may apply to the contract as a whole, or to just a portion of it. For example, a bonus payment may be tied to the completion of a specific performance obligation. It is allowable to allocate variable consideration to a specific performance obligation or a distinct good or service within a contract when the variable payment terms are specifically tied to the seller's efforts to satisfy the performance obligation.

EXAMPLE

Nova Corporation contracts with the Deep Field Scanning Authority to construct two three-meter telescopes that will operate in tandem in the low-humidity Atacama Desert in Chile. The terms of the contract include a provision that can increase the allowable price charged, if the commodity cost of the titanium required to build the telescope frames increases. Based on the prices stated in forward contracts at the contract inception date, it is likely that this variable cost element will increase the transaction price by $250,000. The variable component of the price is allocated to each of the telescopes equally.

Subsequent Price Changes

There are a number of reasons why the transaction price could change after a contract has begun, such as the resolution of uncertain events that were in need of clarification at the contract inception date. When there is a price change, the amount of the change is to be allocated to the performance obligations on the same basis used for the original price allocation at the inception of the contract. This has the following ramifications:

- Do not re-allocate prices based on subsequent changes in the standalone selling prices of goods or services.
- When there is a price change and that price is allocated, the result may be the recognition of additional or reduced revenue that is to be recognized in the period when the transaction price changes.
- When there has been a contract modification prior to a price change, the price allocation is conducted in two steps. First, allocate the price change to those performance obligations identified prior to the modification if the price change is associated with variable consideration promised before mod-

ification. In all other cases, allocate the price change to those performance obligations still remaining to be settled as of the modification date.

The result should be a reported level of cumulative revenue that matches the amount of revenue an organization would have recognized if it had the most recent information at the inception date of the contract.

Step Five: Recognize Revenue

Revenue is to be recognized as goods or services are transferred to the customer. This transference is considered to occur when the customer gains control over the good or service. Indicators of this date include the following:

- When the seller has the right to receive payment.
- When the customer has legal title to the transferred asset. This can still be the case even when the seller retains title to protect it against the customer's failure to pay.
- When physical possession of the asset has been transferred by the seller. Possession can be inferred even when goods are held elsewhere on consignment, or by the seller under a bill-and-hold arrangement. Under a bill-and-hold arrangement, the seller retains goods on behalf of the customer, but still recognizes revenue.
- When the customer has taken on the significant risks and rewards of ownership related to the asset transferred by the seller. For example, the customer can now sell, pledge, or exchange the asset.
- When the customer accepts the asset.
- When the customer can prevent other entities from using or obtaining benefits from the asset.

It is possible that a performance obligation will be transferred over time, rather than as of a specific point in time. If so, revenue recognition occurs when any one of the following criteria are met:

- *Immediate use*. The customer both receives and consumes the benefit provided by the seller as performance occurs. This situation arises if another entity would not need to re-perform work completed to date if the other entity were to take over the remaining performance obligation. Routine and recurring services typically fall into this classification.

EXAMPLE

Long-Haul Freight contracts to deliver a load of goods from Los Angeles to Boston. This service should be considered a performance obligation that is transferred over time, despite the fact that the customer only benefits from the goods once they are delivered. The reason for the designation as a transference over time is that, if a different trucking firm were to take over partway through the journey, the replacement firm would not have to re-perform the freight hauling that has already been completed to date.

EXAMPLE

Maid Marian is a nationwide home cleaning service run by friars within the Franciscan Order. Its customers both receive and simultaneously consume the cleaning services provided by its staff. Consequently, the services provided by Maid Marian are considered to be performance obligations satisfied over time.

- *Immediate enhancement.* The seller creates or enhances an asset controlled by the customer as performance occurs. This asset can be tangible or intangible.
- *No alternative use.* The seller's performance does not create an asset for which there is an alternative use to the seller (such as selling it to a different customer). In addition, the contract gives the seller an enforceable right to payment for the performance that has been completed to date. A lack of alternative use happens when a contract restricts the seller from directing the asset to another use, or when there are practical limitations on doing so, such as the incurrence of significant economic losses to direct the asset elsewhere. The determination of whether an asset has an alternative use is made at the inception of the contract, and cannot be subsequently altered unless both parties to the contract approve a modification that results in a substantive change in the performance obligation.

Construction contracts are likely to be designated as being performance obligations that are transferred over time. Under this approach, they can use the percentage-of-completion method to recognize revenue, rather than the completed contract method. This means that they can recognize revenue as a construction project progresses, rather than waiting until the end of the project to recognize any revenue.

EXAMPLE

Oberlin Acoustics is contractually obligated to deliver a highly-customized version of its Rhino brand electric guitar to a diva-grade European rock star. The contract clearly states that this customized version can only be delivered to the designated customer, and it is likely that this individual would pursue legal action if Oberlin were to attempt to sell it elsewhere (such as to the lead guitarist of a rival band). Also, Oberlin might have to incur significant costs to reconfigure the guitar for sale to a different customer. In this situation, there is no alternative use.

However, if Oberlin had instead contracted to deliver one of its standard Rhino brand guitars, the company could easily transfer the asset to a different customer, since the products are essentially interchangeable. In this case, there would be a clear alternative use.

EXAMPLE

Tesla Power Company is hired by a local government to construct one of its new, compact fusion power plants in the remote hinterlands of Malawi. There is clearly no alternative use for the power plant, since Tesla would have to incur major costs to dismantle the facility and truck it out of the remote area before it could be sold to a different customer. However, the contract states that 50% of the price will be paid at the end of the contract period, and there is no enforceable right to any payment; this means that Tesla must consider its performance obligation to be satisfied as of a point in time, rather than over time.

EXAMPLE

Hassle Corporation is in talks with a potential acquirer. The acquirer insists that Hassle have soil tests conducted in the area around its main production facility, to see if there has been any leakage of pollutants. Hassle engages Wilson Environmental to conduct these tests, which is a three-month process. The contract includes a clause that Wilson will be paid for its costs plus a 20% profit if Hassle cancels the contract. The acquisition talks break off after two months, so Hassle notifies Wilson that it no longer needs the environmental report. Since Wilson cannot possibly sell the information it has collected to a different customer, there is no alternative use. Also, since Wilson has an enforceable right to payment for all work completed to date, the company can recognize revenue over time by measuring its progress toward satisfying the performance obligation.

Measurement of Progress Completion

When a performance obligation is being completed over a period of time, the seller recognizes revenue through the application of a progress completion method. The goal of this method is to determine the progress of the seller in achieving complete satisfaction of its performance obligation. This method is to be consistently applied over time, and shall be re-measured at the end of each reporting period.

> **Note:** The method used to measure progress should be applied consistently for a particular performance obligation, as well as across multiple contracts that have obligations with similar characteristics. Otherwise, reported revenue will not be comparable across different reporting periods.

Both output methods and input methods are considered acceptable for determining progress completion. The method chosen should incorporate due consideration of the nature of the goods or services being provided to the customer. The following sub-sections address the use of output and input methods.

Output Methods

An output method recognizes revenue based on a comparison of the value to the customer of goods and services transferred to date to the remaining goods and services not yet transferred. There are numerous ways to measure output, including:

- Surveys of performance to date

206

- Milestones reached
- The passage of time
- The number of units delivered
- The number of units produced

Another output method that may be acceptable is the amount of consideration that the seller has the right to invoice, such as billable hours. This approach works when the seller has a right to invoice an amount that matches the amount of performance completed to date.

The number of units delivered or produced may not be an appropriate output method in situations where there is a large amount of work-in-process, since the value associated with unfinished goods may be so substantial that revenue could be materially under-reported.

The method picked should closely adhere to the concept of matching the seller's progress toward satisfying the performance obligation. It is not always possible to use an output method, since the cost of collecting the necessary information can be prohibitive, or progress may not be directly observable.

EXAMPLE

Viking Fitness operates a regional chain of fitness clubs that are oriented toward younger, very athletic people. Members pay a $1,200 annual fee, which gives them access to all of the clubs in the chain during all operating hours. In effect, Viking's performance obligation is to keep its facilities open for use by members, irrespective of whether they actually use the facilities. Clearly, this situation calls for measurement of progress completion based on the passage of time. Accordingly, Viking recognizes revenue from its annual customer payments at the rate of $100 per member per month.

Input Methods

An input method derives the amount of revenue to be recognized based on the to-date effort required by the seller to satisfy a performance obligation relative to the total estimated amount of effort required. Examples of possible inputs are costs incurred, labor hours expended, and machine hours used. If there are situations where the effort expended does not directly relate to the transfer of goods or services to a customer, do not use that input. The following are situations where the input used could lead to incorrect revenue recognition:

- The costs incurred are higher than expected, due to seller inefficiencies. For example, the seller may have wasted a higher-than-expected amount of raw materials in the performance of its obligations under a contract.
- The costs incurred are not in proportion to the progress of the seller toward satisfying the performance obligation. For example, the seller might purchase a large amount of materials at the inception of a contract, which comprise a significant part of the total price.

> **Tip:** If the effort expended to satisfy performance obligations occur evenly through the performance period, consider recognizing revenue on the straight-line basis through the performance period.

EXAMPLE

Eskimo Construction is hired to build a weather observatory in Barrow, Alaska, which is estimated to be a six-month project. Utilities are a major concern, especially since the facility is too far away from town for a power line to be run out to it. Accordingly, a large part of the construction cost is a diesel-powered turbine generator. The total cost that Eskimo intends to incur for the project is:

Turbine cost	$1,250,000
All other costs	2,750,000
Total costs	$4,000,000

The turbine is to be delivered and paid for at the beginning of the construction project, but will not be incorporated into the facility until late summer, when the building is scheduled to be nearly complete.

Eskimo intends to use an input method to derive the amount of revenue, using costs incurred. However, this approach runs afoul of the turbine cost, since the immediate expenditure for the turbine gives the appearance of the project being 31.25% complete before work has even begun. Accordingly, Eskimo excludes the cost of the turbine from its input method calculations, only using the other costs as the basis for deriving revenue.

The situation described in the preceding example is quite common, since materials are typically procured at the inception of a contract, rather than being purchased in equal quantities over the duration of the contract. Consequently, the accountant should be particularly mindful of this issue and incorporate it into any revenue recognition calculations based on an input method.

A method based on output is preferred, since it most faithfully depicts the performance of the seller under the terms of a contract. However, an input-based method is certainly allowable if using it would be less costly for the seller, while still providing a reasonable proxy for the ongoing measurement of progress.

Change in Estimate

Whichever method is used, be sure to update it over time to reflect changes in the seller's performance to date. If there is a change in the measurement of progress, treat the change as a change in accounting estimate.

A change in accounting estimate occurs when there is an adjustment to the carrying amount of an asset or liability, or the subsequent accounting for it. Changes in accounting estimate occur relatively frequently, and so would require a considerable amount of effort to make an ongoing series of retroactive changes to prior financial statements. Instead, GAAP only requires that changes in accounting estimate be accounted for in the period of change and thereafter. Thus, no retrospective change is required or allowed.

Progress Measurement

It is only possible to recognize the revenue associated with progress completion if it is possible for the seller to measure the seller's progress. If the seller lacks reliable progress information, it will not be possible to recognize the revenue associated with a contract over time. There may be cases where the measurement of progress completion is more difficult during the early stages of a contract. If so, it is allowable for the seller to instead recognize just enough revenue to recover its costs in satisfying its performance obligations, thereby deferring the recognition of other revenue until such time as the measurement system yields more accurate results.

Right of Return

A common right granted to customers is to allow them to return goods to the seller within a certain period of time following the customer's receipt of the goods. This return may take the form of a refund of any amounts paid, a general credit that can be applied against other billings from the seller, or an exchange for a different unit. The proper accounting for this right of return involves three components, which are:

1. Recognize the net amount of revenue to which the seller expects to be entitled after all product returns have been factored into the sale.
2. A refund liability that encompasses the number of units that the seller expects to have returned to it.
3. An asset based on the right to recover products from customers who have demanded refunds. This asset represents a reduction in the cost of goods sold. The amount is initially based on the former carrying amount of the inventory, less recovery costs and expected reductions in the value of the returned products.

This accounting requires the seller to update its assessment of future product returns at the end of each reporting period, both for the refund liability and the recovery asset. This update may result in a change in the amount of revenue recognized.

> **Note:** When a customer exchanges one product for another product with the same characteristics (such as an exchange of one size shirt for another), this is not considered a return.

EXAMPLE

Ninja Cutlery sells high-end ceramic knife sets through its on-line store and through select retailers. All customers pay up-front in cash. In the most recent month, Ninja sold 5,000 knife sets, which sold for an average price of $250 each ($1,250,000 in total). The unit cost is $150. Based on the history of actual returns over the preceding 12-month period, Ninja can expect that 200 of the sets (4% of the total) will be returned under the company's returns policy. Recovery costs are immaterial, and Ninja expects to be able to repackage and sell all returned products for a profit. Based on this information, Ninja records the following transactions when the knife sets are originally delivered:

	Debit	Credit
Cash	1,250,000	
Revenue		1,200,000
Refund liability		50,000

	Debit	Credit
Cost of goods sold	720,000	
Recovery asset	30,000	
Inventory		750,000

In these entries, the refund liability is calculated as the 200 units expected to be returned, multiplied by the average price of $250 each. The recovery asset is calculated as the 200 units expected to be returned, multiplied by the unit cost of $150.

Consistency

The preceding five steps must be applied consistently to all customer contracts that have similar characteristics, and under similar circumstances. The intent is to create a system of revenue recognition that can be relied upon to yield consistent results.

Contract Modifications

A contract modification occurs when there is a scope or price change to the contract, and the change is approved by both signatories to the contract. Other terms may be used for a contract modification, such as a change order. It is possible that a contract modification exists, despite the presence of a dispute between the parties concerning scope or price. All of the relevant facts and circumstances must be considered when determining whether there is an enforceable contract modification that can impact revenue recognition.

If a change in contract scope has already been approved, but the corresponding change in price to reflect the scope change is still under discussion, the seller must estimate the change in price. This estimate is based on the criteria used to determine variable consideration.

Treatment as Separate Contract

There are circumstances under which a contract modification might be accounted for as a separate contract. For this to be the case, the following two conditions must both be present:

- *Distinct change*. The scope has increased, to encompass new goods or services that are distinct from those offered in the original contract.

210

- *Price change.* The price has increased enough to encompass the standalone prices of the additional goods and services, adjusted for the circumstances related to that specific contract.

When these circumstances are met, there is an economic difference between a modified contract for the additional goods or services and a situation where an entirely new contract has been created.

EXAMPLE

Blitz Communications is buying one million cell phone batteries from Creekside Industrial. The parties decide to alter the contract to add the purchase of 200,000 battery chargers for a price increase of $2.8 million. The associated price increase includes a 30% discount, which Creekside was already offering to Blitz under the terms of the original contract. This contract change reflects a distinct change that adds new goods to the contract, and includes an associated price change that has been adjusted for the discount terms of the contract. This contract modification can be accounted for as a separate contract.

Treatment as Continuing Contract

It may not be possible to treat a contract modification as a separate contract. If so, there are likely to be goods or services not yet transferred to the customer as of the modification date. The seller can account for these residual deliveries using one of the following methods:

- *Remainder is distinct.* If the remaining goods or services to be delivered are distinct from those already delivered under the contract, account for the modification as a cancellation of the old contract and creation of a new one. In this case, the consideration that should be allocated to the remaining performance obligations is the sum total of:
  - The original consideration promised by the customer but not yet received; and
  - The new consideration associated with the modification.

EXAMPLE

Grizzly Golf Carts, maker of sturdy golf carts for overweight golfers, contracts with a local suburban golf course to deliver two golf carts for a total price of $12,000. The carts are different models, but have the same standalone price, so Grizzly allocates $6,000 of the transaction price to each cart. One cart is delivered immediately, so Grizzly recognizes $6,000 of revenue. Before the second cart can be delivered, the golf course customer requests that a third cart be added to the contract; this is a heftier cart that has a built-in barbecue grill. The contract price is increased by $8,000, which is less than the $10,000 standalone price of this model.

Since the second and third carts are distinct from the first cart model, there is a distinct change in the contract, which necessitates treating the change as a new contract.

Accordingly, the second and third carts are treated as though they are part of a new contract, with the remaining $14,000 of the transaction price totally allocated to the new contract.

EXAMPLE

As noted in an earlier example, Nova Corporation contracted with the Deep Field Scanning Authority to construct two three-meter telescopes. The terms of the contract included a provision that could increase the allowable price charged by $250,000, with this price being apportioned equally between the two telescopes. One month into the contract period, Deep Field completely alters the configuration of the second telescope, from a reflector to a catadioptric model. The change is so significant that this telescope can now be considered a separate contract. However, since the variable price was already apportioned at the inception of the original contract, the $125,000 allocated to each telescope will continue. This is because the variable consideration was promised prior to the contract modification.

- *Remainder is not distinct.* If the remaining goods or services to be delivered are not distinct from those already delivered under the contract, account for the modification as part of the existing contract. This results in an adjustment to the recognized amount of revenue (up or down) as of the modification date. Thus, the adjustment involves calculating a change in the amount of revenue recognized on a cumulative catch-up basis.

EXAMPLE

Domicilio Corporation enters into a contract to construct the world headquarters building of the International Mushroom Farmers' Cooperative. Mushroom requires its architects to be true to the name of the organization, with the result being a design for a squat, dark building with no windows, high humidity, and a unique waste recycling system. Domicilio has not encountered such a design before, and so incorporates a cautious stance into its assumptions regarding the contract terms.

The contract terms state that Domicilio will be paid a total of $12,000,000, broken into a number of milestone payments. There is also a $100,000 on-time completion bonus. At the inception of the contract, Domicilio expects the following financial results:

Transaction price	$12,000,000
Expected costs	9,000,000
Expected profit (25%)	$3,000,000

The project manager anticipates trouble with several parts of the construction project, and advises strongly against including any part of the completion bonus in the transaction price.

At the end of seven months, the project manager is surprised to find that Domicilio is on target to complete the work on time. Also, the company has completed 65% of its performance obligation, based on the $5,850,000 of costs incurred to date relative to the total amount of expected costs. Through this point, the company has recognized the following revenues and costs:

Revenue	$7,800,000
Costs	5,850,000
Gross profit	$1,950,000

The project manager is still uncomfortable with recognizing any part of the completion bonus.

With one month to go on the project, the project manager finally allows that Domicilio will likely complete the project one week early, though he has completely lost all interest in eating mushrooms. At this point, the company has completed 92.5% of its performance obligation (based on costs incurred), so the controller recognizes an additional $92,500 for that portion of the $100,000 on-time completion bonus that has already been earned.

- *Mix of elements.* If the remaining goods or services to be delivered are comprised of a mix of distinct and not-distinct elements, separately identify the different elements and account for them as per the dictates of the preceding two methods.

Entitlement to Payment

At all points over the duration of a contract, the seller should have the right to payment for the performance completed to date, if the customer were to cancel the contract for reasons other than the seller's failure to perform. The amount of this payment should approximate the selling price of the goods or services transferred to the customer to date; this means that costs are recovered, plus a reasonable profit margin. This reasonable profit margin should be one of the following:

- A reasonable proportion of the expected profit margin, based on the extent of the total performance completed prior to contract termination; or
- A reasonable return on the cost of capital that the seller has experienced on its cost of capital for similar contracts, if the margin on this particular contract is higher than the return the seller typically generates from this type of contract.

An entitlement to payment depends on contractual factors, such as only being paid when certain milestones are reached or when the customer is completely satisfied with a deliverable. There may not be an entitlement to payment if one of these contractual factors is present. Further, there may be legal precedents or legislation that may interfere with or bolster an entitlement to payment. For example:

- There may be a legal precedent that gives the seller the right to payment for all performance to date, even though this right is not clarified within the contract terms.
- Legal precedent may reveal that other sellers having similar rights to payment in their contracts have not succeeded in obtaining payment.
- The seller may not have attempted to enforce its right to payment in the past, which may have rendered its rights legally unenforceable.

Conversely, the terms of a contract may not legally allow a customer to terminate a contract. If so, and the customer still attempts to terminate the contract, the seller may be entitled to continue to provide goods or services to the customer, and require the customer to pay the amounts stated in the contract. In this type of situation, the seller has an enforceable right to payment.

An enforceable right to payment may not match the payment schedule stated in a contract. The payment schedule does not necessarily sync with the seller's right to payment for performance. For example, the customer could have insisted upon delayed payment dates in the payment schedule in order to more closely match its ability to make payments to the seller.

EXAMPLE

A customer of Hodgson Industrial Design pays a $50,000 nonrefundable upfront payment to Hodgson at the inception of a contract to overhaul the design of the customer's main product. The customer does not like Hodgson's initial set of design prototypes, and cancels the contract. On the cancellation date, Hodgson's billable hours on the project sum to $65,000. Hodgson has an enforceable right to retain the $50,000 it has already been paid. The right to be paid for the remaining $15,000 depends on the contract terms and legal precedents.

Bill-and-Hold Arrangements

There is a bill-and-hold arrangement between a seller and customer when the seller bills the customer, but initially retains physical possession of the goods that were sold; the goods are transferred to the customer at a later date. This situation may arise if a customer does not initially have the storage space available for the goods it has ordered.

In a bill-and-hold arrangement, the seller must determine when the customer gains control of the goods, since this point in time indicates when the seller can recognize revenue. Customer control can be difficult to discern when the goods are still located on the premises of the seller. The following are indicators of customer control:

- The customer can direct the use of the goods, no matter where they are located
- The customer can obtain substantially all of the remaining benefits of the goods

Further, the following conditions must all be present for the seller to recognize revenue under a bill-and-hold arrangement:

- *Adequate reason.* There must be a substantive reason why the seller is continuing to store the goods, such as at the direct request of the customer.
- *Alternate use.* The seller must not be able to redirect the goods, either to other customers or for internal use.

- *Complete.* The product must be complete in all respects and ready for transfer to the customer.
- *Identification.* The goods must have been identified specifically as belonging to the customer.

Under a bill-and-hold arrangement, the seller may have a performance obligation to act as the custodian for the goods being held at its facility. If so, the seller may need to allocate a portion of the transaction price to the custodial function, and recognize this revenue over the course of the custodial period.

EXAMPLE

Micron Metallic operates stamping machines that produce parts for washing machines. Micron's general manager has recently decided to implement the just-in-time philosophy throughout the company, which includes sourcing goods with suppliers who are located as close to Micron as possible. One of these suppliers is Horton Corporation, which designs and builds stamping machines for Micron. In a recent contract, Micron buys a customized stamping machine and a set of spare parts intended for that machine. Since Micron is implementing just-in-time concepts, it does not want to store the spare parts on its premises, and instead asks Horton to store the parts in its facility, which is just down the street from the Micron factory.

Micron's receiving staff travels to the Horton facility to inspect the parts and formally accepts them. Horton also sets them aside in a separate storage area, and flags them as belonging to Micron. Since the parts are customized, they cannot be used to fulfill any other customer orders. Under the just-in-time system, Horton commits to having the parts ready for delivery to Micron within ten minutes of receiving a shipping order.

The arrangement can clearly be defined as a bill-and-hold situation. Consequently, Horton should apportion the transaction price between the stamping machine, the spare parts, and the custodial service involved in storing the parts on behalf of Micron. The revenue associated with the machine and parts can be recognized at once, while the revenue associated with the custodial service can be recognized with the passage of time.

Consideration Received from a Supplier

A supplier may pay consideration to its customer, which may be in the form of cash, credits, coupons, and so forth. The customer can then apply this consideration to payments that it owes to the supplier, thereby reducing its net accounts payable.

The proper accounting for this type of consideration is to reduce the purchase price of the goods or services that the customer is acquiring from the supplier in the amount of the consideration received. If the consideration received relates to the customer attaining a certain amount of purchasing volume with the supplier (i.e., a volume discount), recognize the consideration as a reduction of the purchase price of the underlying transactions. This recognition can be made if attainment of the consideration is both probable and can be reasonably estimated. If these criteria cannot be met, then wait for the triggering milestones, and recognize them as the milestones are reached. Factors that can make it more difficult to determine whether this type of consideration is probable or reasonably estimated include:

- *Duration*. The relationship between the consideration to be received and purchase amounts spans a long period of time.
- *Experience*. The customer has no historical experience with similar products, or cannot apply its experience to changing circumstances.
- *External factors*. External factors can influence the underlying activity, such as changes in demand.
- *Prior adjustments*. It has been necessary to make significant adjustments to similar types of expected consideration in the past.

EXAMPLE

Puller Corporation manufactures plastic door knobs. Its primary raw material is polymer resin, which it purchases in pellet form from a regional chemical facility. Puller will receive a 2% volume discount if it purchases at least $500,000 of pellets from the supplier by the end of the calendar year. Puller has a long-term relationship with this supplier, has routinely earned the discount for the last five years, and plans to place orders in this year that will comfortably exceed the $500,000 mark. Accordingly, Puller accrues the 2% discount as a reduction of the purchase price of its pellet purchases throughout the year.

EXAMPLE

Puller has just entered into a new relationship with another supplier that will deliver black dye to the factory for inclusion in all of the company's black door knob products. This supplier offers a 5% discount if purchases exceed $50,000 for the calendar year. Puller has not sold this color of door knob before and so has no idea of what customer demand may be. Given the high level of uncertainty regarding the probability of being awarded the discount, Puller elects to record all purchases at their full price, and will re-evaluate the probability of attaining the discount as the year progresses.

The only exceptions to this accounting are:

- When the customer specifically transfers an asset to the supplier in exchange. If so, the customer treats the transaction as it would any sale to one of its customers in the normal course of business. If the amount paid by the supplier is higher than the standalone selling price of the item transferred to the supplier, the customer should account for the excess amount as a reduction of the purchase price of any goods or services received from the supplier.
- The supplier is reimbursing the customer for selling costs that the customer incurred to sell the supplier's products to third parties. If so, the amount of cash received is used to reduce the indicated selling costs. If the amount paid by the supplier is greater than the amount for which the customer ap-

plied for reimbursement, record the excess as a reduction of the cost of sales.

- The consideration is related to sales incentives offered by manufacturers who are selling through a reseller. When the reseller is receiving compensation in exchange for honoring incentives related to the manufacturer's products, the reseller records the amount received as a reduction of its cost of sales. This situation only arises when all of the following conditions apply:
  - The customer can tender the incentive to any reseller as part of its payment for the product;
  - The reseller receives reimbursement from the manufacturer based on the face amount of the incentive;
  - The reimbursement terms to the reseller are only determined from the incentive terms offered to consumers; they are not negotiated between the manufacturer and reseller; and
  - The reseller is an agent of the manufacturer in regard to the sales incentive transaction.

If only a few or none of these criteria are met for a sales incentive offered by a manufacturer, account for the transaction as a reduction of the purchase price of the goods or services that the reseller acquired from the manufacturer. If all of the criteria *are* met, consider the transaction to be a revenue-generating activity for the reseller.

Customer Acceptance

A customer may include an acceptance clause in a contract with a seller. An acceptance clause states that the customer has the right to inspect goods and reject them or demand proper remedial efforts before formal acceptance. Normally, customer control over goods occurs as soon as this acceptance step has been completed.

There are situations in which the seller can determine that control has passed to a customer, even if a formal acceptance review has not yet taken place. This typically occurs when customer acceptance is based upon a delivery meeting very specific qualifications, such as certain dimension or weight requirements. If the seller can determine in advance that these criteria have been met, it can recognize revenue prior to formal customer acceptance. If the seller cannot determine in advance that a customer will accept the delivered goods, it must wait for formal acceptance before it can confirm that the customer had taken control of the delivery, which then triggers revenue recognition.

EXAMPLE

Stout Tanks, Inc. manufactures scuba tanks, which it sells in bulk to a large customer in Bonaire, Drive-Thru Scuba. Drive-Thru insists upon a complete hydrostatic test of each tank before accepting delivery, since an exploding air tank is a decidedly terminal experience for a diver wearing the tank. Stout decides to conducts its own hydrostatic test of every tank leaving its factory. Since Stout is conducting the same test as Drive-Thru, Stout can reasonably establish that customer acceptance has occurred as soon as the scuba tanks leave its factory. As such, Stout can recognize revenue on the delivery date, and not wait for Drive-Thru to conduct its test.

Even if a customer recognizes revenue in advance of formal customer acceptance, it may still be necessary to determine whether there are any remaining performance obligations to which a portion of the transaction price should be allocated. For example, a seller may have an obligation to not only manufacture production equipment, but also to install it at the customer site. This later step could be considered a separate performance obligation.

A variation on the customer acceptance concept is when a seller delivers goods to a customer for evaluation purposes. In this case, the customer has no obligation to accept or pay for the goods until the end of a trial period, so control cannot be said to have passed to the customer until such time as the customer accepts the goods or the trial period ends.

Customer Options for Additional Purchases

A seller may offer customers a number of ways in which to obtain additional goods or services at reduced rates or even for free. For example, the seller may offer a discount on a contract renewal, award points to frequent buyers, host periodic sales events, and so on.

When a contract grants a customer the right to acquire additional goods or services at a discount, this can be considered a performance obligation if the amount is material and the customer is essentially paying in advance for future goods or services. In this case, the seller recognizes revenue associated with the customer option when:

- The option expires; or
- The future goods or services are transferred to the customer.

If revenue is to be recognized for such an option, allocate the transaction price to the option based on the relative standalone price of the option. In the likely event that the standalone selling price of the option is not directly observable, use an estimate of its price. The derivation of this estimate should include the discount that the customer would obtain by exercising the option, adjusted for the following two items:

- Reduced by the amount of any discount that the customer could have received without the option, such as a standard ongoing discount offered to all customers; and
- The probability that the customer will not exercise the option.

A material right to additional purchases of goods or services is not considered to have been passed to a customer if the option is at a price that reflects the standalone selling price of a good or service. In this case, there is no particular advantage being granted to the customer, since it could just as easily purchase the goods or services at the same price, even in the absence of the option.

EXAMPLE

Twister Vacuum Company sells its top-of-the-line F5 vacuum cleaner to 50 customers for $800 each. As part of each sale, Twister gives each customer a discount code that, if used, gives the customer a 50% discount on the purchase of Twister's F1 hand-held vacuum cleaner, which normally sells for $100. The discount expires in 60 days.

In order to determine the standalone selling price of the discount code, Twister estimates (based on past experience) that 30% of all customers will use the code to purchase the F1 model. This means that the standalone selling price of the discount code is $15, which is calculated as follows:

$$\$100 \text{ F1 standalone price} \times 50\% \text{ discount} \times 30\% \text{ probability of code usage} = \$15$$

The combined standalone selling prices of the F5 vacuum and the discount code sum to $815. Twister uses this information to allocate the $800 transaction price between the product and the discount code, using the following calculation:

Performance Obligation	Allocated Price	Calculation
F5 vacuum cleaner	$785.28	($800 ÷ $815) × $800
Discount code	14.72	($15 ÷ $815) × $800
Total	$800.00	

This allocation means that Twister can recognize $785.28 of revenue whenever it completes a performance obligation related to the sale of the F5 units to the 50 customers. Twister also allocates $14.72 to the discount code and recognizes the revenue associated with this item either when it is redeemed by a customer in the purchase of an F1 vacuum cleaner, or when the code expires.

EXAMPLE

Sojourn Hotel has a customer loyalty program that grants customers one loyalty point for each night that they stay in a Sojourn-affiliated hotel. Each loyalty point can be redeemed to reduce another stay at a Sojourn hotel by $5. If not used, the points expire after 24 months. During the most recent reporting period, customers earn 60,000 loyalty points on $2,000,000 of customer purchases. Based on past experience, Sojourn expects 60% of the points to be redeemed. Based on the likelihood of redemption, each point is worth $3 (calculated as $5 redemption value × 60% probability of redemption), so all of the points awarded are worth $180,000 (calculated as $3/ point × 60,000 points issued).

The loyalty points program gives a material right to customers that they would not otherwise have had if they had not stayed at a Sojourn hotel (i.e., entered into a contract with Sojourn). Thus, Sojourn concludes that the issued points constitute a performance obligation. Sojourn then allocates the $2,000,000 of customer purchases for hotel rooms to the hotel room product and the points awarded based on their standalone selling prices, based on the following calculations:

Performance Obligation	Allocated Price	Calculation
Hotel rooms	$1,834,862	($2,000,000 ÷ $2,180,000) × $2,000,000
Loyalty points	165,138	($180,000 ÷ $2,180,000) × $2,000,000
Total	$2,000,000	

The $165,138 allocated to loyalty points is initially recorded as a contract liability. The $1,834,862 allocated to hotel rooms is recognized as revenue, since Sojourn has completed its performance obligation related to these overnight stays.

As of the end of the next quarterly period, Sojourn finds that 8,000 of the loyalty points have been redeemed, so it recognizes revenue related to the loyalty points of $22,018 (calculated as 8,000 points ÷ 60,000 points × $165,138).

Licensing

A seller may offer a license to use intellectual property owned by the seller. Examples of licensing arrangements are:
- Licensing to use software
- Licensing to listen to music
- Licensing to view a movie
- Franchising the name and processes of a restaurant
- Licensing of a book copyright to republish the book
- Licensing to use a patent within a product

If a contract contains both a licensing agreement and a provision to provide goods or services to the customer, the seller must identify each performance obligation within the contract and allocate the transaction price to each one.

If the licensing agreement can be separated from the other elements of a contract, the seller must decide whether the license is being transferred to the customer over a period of time, or as of a point in time. A key point in making this determination is whether the license is intended to give the customer access to the intellectual property of the seller only as of the point in time when the license is granted, or over the duration of the license period. The first case would indicate that the revenue associated with the license is recognized as of a point in time, while the second case would indicate that the revenue is recognized over a period of time.

A license is more likely to have been granted as of a point in time when a customer can direct the use of a license and obtain substantially all of the remaining benefits from the license on the date when the license is granted to it. This will not be the case if the intellectual property to which the customer has rights continues to change throughout the license period, which occurs when the seller continues to engage in activities that significantly affect its intellectual property.

The intent of the seller of a license is to provide the customer with the right to access its intellectual property when the seller commits to update the property, the customer will be exposed to the effects of those updates, and the updates do not result in the transfer of a good or service to the customer. These conditions may not be stated in a contract, but could be inferred from the seller's customary business practices. For example, if the customer pays the seller a royalty based on its sales of products derived from intellectual property provided by the seller, this implies that the seller will be updating the underlying intellectual property. If these conditions are present, the associated revenue should be recognized over time, rather than as of a point in time.

If the facts and circumstances of a contract indicate that the revenue associated with a contract should be recognized as of a point in time, this does not mean that the revenue can be recognized prior to the point in time when the customer can use and benefit from the license. This date may be later than the commencement date of the underlying contract. For example, the license to use intellectual property may be granted, but the actual property may not yet have been delivered to the customer or activated.

If it is not possible to separate the licensing agreement from the other components of a contract, account for them as a single performance obligation. An example of when this situation arises is when a license is integrated into a tangible product to such an extent that the product cannot be used without the license.

> **Note:** A guarantee by the seller that it will defend a patent from unauthorized use is not considered a performance obligation.

A contract under which there is a right to use a license may include the payment of a royalty to the seller. This arrangement may occur, for example, when the customer is acting as a distributor to re-sell the licensed intellectual property to other parties. In this situation, the seller may only recognize the royalty as revenue as of the later of these two events:

- The subsequent sale to or usage by the third party has occurred; or
- The underlying performance obligation associated with the royalty has been satisfied.

EXAMPLE

Territorial Lease Corporation (TLC) has spent years accumulating a massive database of oil and gas leases throughout the United States and Canada. It sells this information to oil and gas exploration companies, which use it to derive the prices at which they are willing to bid for oil and gas leases. TLC sells the information in three ways, which are:

- It sells a CD that contains lease information that is current as of the ship date. TLC does not issue any further updates to customers. Since TLC does not update the intellectual property, the associated revenue recognition can be considered to occur as of a point in time, which is the delivery date of the CD.

- The company also sells subscriptions to an on-line database of lease information, which it updates every day. Since TLC is continually upgrading the database, the recognition of revenue is considered to take place over time. Accordingly, TLC recognizes revenue over the term of the subscriptions it sells.
- TLC sells its lease information to another company, Enviro Consultants, which repurposes the information for the environmental remediation industry. The information is billed to the customers of Enviro, and Enviro pays TLC a 50% royalty once Enviro receives payment from its customers. Since the subsequent sale of the information has occurred by the time TLC receives royalty payments, it can recognize the payments as revenue upon receipt.

Nonrefundable Upfront Fees

In some types of contracts, it is customary for the seller to charge a customer a nonrefundable upfront fee. Examples of these fees are:
- Health club member ship fee
- Phone service activation fee
- Long-term contract setup fee

There may be a performance obligation associated with these fees. In some cases, it could actually relate to an activity that the seller completes at the beginning of a contract. However, this activity rarely relates to the fulfillment of a performance obligation by the seller, and simply represents an expenditure. Consequently, the most appropriate treatment of this fee is to recognize it as revenue when the goods or services stated in the contract are provided to the customer. Several additional issues to consider are:

- *Recognition period.* If the seller grants the customer a material option to renew the contract, the revenue recognition period associated with the upfront fee is extended over the additional contract term.
- *Setup costs.* It is possible that the costs incurred to set up a contract are an asset, which should be charged to expense over the course of the contract.

EXAMPLE

Providence Alarm Systems offers its customers a home monitoring system that includes a $200 setup fee and a monthly $35 charge to monitor their homes through an alarm system, for a minimum one-year period. Providence does not charge the setup fee again if a customer chooses to renew.

The setup activities that Providence engages in do not transfer a good or service to customers, and so do not create a performance obligation. Thus, the upfront fee can be considered an advance payment relating to the company's monthly monitoring activities. Providence should recognize the $200 fee over the initial one-year monitoring period, as services are provided.

Principal versus Agent

There are situations where the party providing goods or services to a customer is actually arranging to have another party provide the goods and services. In this case, the party is an agent, not the principal party acting as seller. Use the following rules to differentiate between the two concepts of principal and agent:

Criterion	Principal	Agent
Controls the good or service before transfer to customer	Yes	No
Obtains legal title just prior to transfer to seller	Either	Either
Hires a subcontractor to fulfill some performance obligations	Yes	No
Arranges for the provision of goods or services by another party	No	Yes
Does not have inventory risk before or after the customer orders goods, including the absence of risk related to product returns	No	Yes
Does not have discretion in establishing prices	No	Yes
The consideration paid to the selling entity is in the form of a commission	No	Yes
There is no exposure to credit risk that the customer will not pay	No	Yes

The differentiation between principal and agent is of some importance, for a principal recognizes the gross amount of a sale, while an agent only recognizes the fee or commission it earns in exchange for its participation in the transaction. This fee or commission may be the net amount remaining after the agent has paid the principal the amount billed for its goods or services provided to the customer.

In a situation where the seller is initially the principal in a transaction but then hands off the performance obligation to a third party, the seller should not recognize the revenue associated with the performance obligation. Instead, the seller may have assumed the role of an agent.

EXAMPLE

High Country Vacations operates a website that puts prospective vacationers in touch with resorts located in ski towns around the world. When a vacationer purchases a hotel room on the website, High Country takes a 15% commission from the resort where the hotel room is located. The resort sets the prices for hotel rooms. High Country is not responsible for the actual provision of hotel rooms to vacationers.

Since High Country does not control the hotel rooms being provided, is arranging for the provision of services by a third party, does not maintain an inventory of rooms, cannot establish prices, and is paid a commission, the company is clearly an agent in these transactions. Consequently, High Country should only recognize revenue in the amount of the commissions paid to it, not the amount paid by vacationers for their hotel rooms.

EXAMPLE

Dirt Cheap Tickets sells discounted tickets for cruises with several prominent cruise lines. The company purchases tickets in bulk from cruise lines and must pay for them, irrespective of its ability to re-sell the tickets to the public. Dirt Cheap can alter the prices of the tickets that it purchases, which typically means that the company gradually lowers prices as cruise dates approach, in order to ensure that its excess inventory of tickets is sold. There is no credit risk, since tickets are paid for at the point of purchase. If customers have issues with the cruise lines, Dirt Cheap will intercede on their behalf, but generally encourages them to go directly to the cruise lines with their complaints.

Based on its business model, Dirt Cheap is acting as the principal. It controls the goods being sold, has inventory risk, and actively alters prices. Consequently, Dirt Cheap can recognize revenue in the gross amount of the tickets sold.

Repurchase Agreements

A repurchase agreement is a contract in which the seller agrees to sell an asset and either promises or has the option to repurchase the asset. The asset that the seller repurchases can be the original asset sold, a substantially similar asset, or an asset of which the original unit is a part. There are three variations on the repurchase agreement:

- *Forward.* The seller has an obligation to repurchase the asset.
- *Call option.* The seller has the right to repurchase the asset.
- *Put option.* The seller has an obligation to repurchase the asset if required to by the customer.

If the contract is essentially a forward or call option, the customer never gains control of the asset, since the seller can or will take it back. Given the circumstances, revenue recognition can vary as follows:

- *Reduced repurchase price.* If the seller either can or must repurchase the asset for an amount less than the original selling price (considering the time value of money), the seller accounts for the transaction as a lease.
- *Same or higher repurchase price.* If the seller either can or must repurchase the asset for an amount equal to or greater than the original selling price (considering the time value of money), the seller accounts for the transaction as a financing arrangement.
- *Sale-leaseback.* If the transaction is a sale-leaseback arrangement, the seller accounts for the transaction as a financing arrangement.

When a customer has a put option, the proper accounting depends upon the market price of the asset and the existence of a sale-leaseback arrangement. The alternatives are:

- *Incentive to exercise option.* If the customer has a significant economic incentive to exercise the option, the seller accounts for the transaction as a lease. Such an incentive would exist, for example, when the repurchase price exceeds the expected market value of an asset through the period when the put option can be exercised (considering the time value of money).

- *No incentive to exercise option.* If the customer does not have an economic incentive to exercise a put option, the seller accounts for the agreement as a sale of a product with a right of return.
- *Sale-leaseback.* Even if the seller has a significant economic incentive, as noted in the last bullet point, if the arrangement is a sale-leaseback arrangement, the seller accounts for it as a financing arrangement.
- *Higher repurchase price.* If the repurchase price is equal to or higher than the selling price and is more than the asset's expected market value (considering the time value of money), the seller accounts for it as a financing arrangement.
- *Higher repurchase price with no incentive.* In the rare case where the repurchase price is equal to or higher than the original purchase price, but is less than or equal to the expected market value of the asset (considering the time value of money), this indicates that the customer has no economic incentive to exercise the option. In this case, the seller accounts for the transaction as a sale of a product with a right of return.

When the seller accounts for a transaction as a financing arrangement, the seller continues to recognize the asset, as well as a liability for any consideration it has received from the customer. The difference between the amount of consideration paid by and due to the customer is to be recognized as interest and processing (or related) costs.

If a call option or put option expires without being exercised, the seller can derecognize the repurchase liability and recognize revenue instead.

EXAMPLE

Domicilio Corporation sells a commercial property to Mole Industries for $3,000,000 on March 1, but retains the right to repurchase the property for $3,050,000 on or before December 31 of the same year. This transaction is a call option.

Control over the property does not pass to Mole Industries until after the December 31 termination date of the call option, since Domicilio can repurchase the asset. In the meantime, Domicilio accounts for the arrangement as a financing transaction, since the exercise price exceeds the amount of Mole's purchase price. This means that Domicilio retains the asset in its accounting records, records the $3,000,000 of cash received as a liability, and recognizes interest expense of $50,000 over the intervening months, which gradually increases the amount of the liability to $3,050,000.

On December 31, Domicilio lets the call option lapse; it can now derecognize the liability and recognize $3,050,000 of revenue.

EXAMPLE

Assume the same transaction, except that the option is a requirement for Domicilio to repurchase the property for $2,900,000 at the behest of the customer, Mole Industries. This is a put option. The market value by the end of the year is expected to be lower than $2,900,000.

At the inception of the contract, it is apparent that Mole will have an economic incentive to exercise the put option, since it can earn more from exercising the option than from retaining the property. This means that control over the property does not really pass to Mole. In essence, then, the transaction is to be considered a lease.

Unexercised Rights of Customers

A customer may prepay for goods or services to be delivered at a later date, which the seller initially records as a liability, and later as revenue when the goods or services are delivered. However, what if the customer does not exercise all of its rights to have goods or services delivered? The unexercised amount of this prepayment may be referred to as *breakage*.

The amount of breakage associated with a customer prepayment should be recognized as revenue. The question is, when should the recognition occur? There are two possible scenarios:

- *Existing pattern.* If there is a historical pattern of how a customer exercises the rights associated with its prepayments, the seller can estimate the amount of breakage likely to occur, and recognize it in proportion to the pattern of rights exercised by the customer.
- *No expectation.* If there is no expectation that the seller will be entitled to any breakage, the seller recognizes revenue associated with breakage only when there is a remote likelihood that the customer will exercise any remaining rights.

No revenue related to breakage should be recognized if it is probable that such recognition will result in a significant revenue reversal at a later date.

In a situation where there are unclaimed property laws, the seller is legally required to remit breakage to the applicable government entity. In this case, the breakage is recorded as a liability (rather than revenue), which is cleared from the seller's books when the funds are remitted to the government.

EXAMPLE

Clyde Shotguns receives a $10,000 deposit from a customer, to be used for the construction of a custom-made shotgun. Clyde completes the weapon and delivers it to the customer, recognizing $9,800 of revenue based on the number of billable hours expended. Clyde notifies the customer of the residual deposit amount, but the customer does not respond, despite repeated attempts at communication. Under the escheatment laws of the local state government, Clyde is required to remit these residual funds to the state if they have not been claimed within three years. Accordingly, Clyde initially records the $200 as an escheatment liability, and pays over the funds to the government once three years have passed.

Warranties

A warranty is a guarantee related to the performance of delivered goods or services. If related to a product, the seller typically guarantees the replacement or repair of the delivered goods. If related to a service, the warranty may involve replacement services, or a full or partial refund.

If a customer has the option to separately purchase a warranty, this is to be considered a distinct service to be provided by the seller. As such, the warranty is to be considered a separate performance obligation, with a portion of the transaction price allocated to it. If there is no option for the customer to separately purchase a warranty, the warranty is instead considered an obligation of the seller, in which case the following accounting applies:

- Accrue a reserve for product warranty claims based on the prior experience of the business. In the absence of such experience, the company can instead rely upon the experience of other entities in the same industry. If there is considerable uncertainty in regard to the amount of projected product warranties, it may not be possible to record a product sale until the warranty period has expired or more experience has been gained with customer claims.
- Adjust the reserve over time to reflect changes in prior and expected experience with warranty claims. This can involve a credit to earnings if the amount of the reserve is too large, and should be reduced.
- If there is a history of minimal warranty expenditures, there is no need to accrue a reserve for product warranty claims.

A warranty may provide a customer with a service, as well as a guarantee that provided goods or services will function as claimed. Consider the following items when determining whether a service exists:

- *Duration*. The time period needed to discover whether goods or services are faulty is relatively short, so a long warranty period is indicative of an additional service being offered.
- *Legal requirement*. There is a legal requirement to provide a warranty, in which case the seller is more likely to just be offering the mandated warranty without an additional service.
- *Tasks*. If the warranty requires the seller to perform specific tasks that are identifiable with the remediation of faulty goods or services, there is unlikely to be any additional identifiable service being offered.

If an additional service is being offered through a warranty, consider this service to be a performance obligation, and allocate a portion of the transaction price to that service. If the seller cannot reasonably account for this service separately, instead account for both the assurance and service aspects of the warranty as a bundled performance obligation.

There may be a legal obligation for the seller to compensate its customers if its goods or services cause harm. If so, this is not considered a performance obligation. Instead, this legal obligation is considered a loss contingency. A loss contingency arises when there is a situation for which the outcome is uncertain, and which should be resolved in the future, possibly creating a loss. For example, there may be injuries caused by a company's products when it is discovered that lead-based paint has been used on toys sold by the business.

When deciding whether to account for a loss contingency, the basic concept is that you should only record a loss that is probable, and for which the amount of the loss can be reasonably estimated. If the best estimate of the amount of the loss is within a range, accrue whichever amount appears to be a better estimate than the other estimates in the range. If there is no "better estimate" in the range, accrue a loss for the minimum amount in the range.

If it is not possible to arrive at a reasonable estimate of the loss associated with an event, only disclose the existence of the contingency in the notes accompanying the financial statements. Or, if it is not probable that a loss will be incurred, even if it is possible to estimate the amount of a loss, only disclose the circumstances of the contingency without accruing a loss.

If the conditions for recording a loss contingency are initially not met, but then *are* met during a later accounting period, the loss should be accrued in the later period. Do not make a retroactive adjustment to an earlier period to record a loss contingency.

Contract-Related Costs

Thus far, the discussion has centered on the recognition of revenue – but what about the costs that an organization incurs to fulfill a contract? In this section, we separately address the accounting for the costs incurred to initially obtain a contract, costs incurred during a contract, and how these costs are to be charged to expense.

Costs to Obtain a Contract

An organization may incur certain costs to obtain a contract. If so, it is allowable to record these costs as an asset, and amortize them over the life of the contract. The following conditions apply:

- The costs must be incremental; that is, they would not have been incurred if the organization had not obtained the contract.
- If the amortization period will be one year or some lesser period, it is allowable to simply charge these costs to expense as incurred.
- There is an expectation that the costs will be recovered.

An example of a contract-related cost that could be recorded as an asset and amortized is the sales commission associated with a sale, though as a practical expedient it is usually charged to expense as incurred.

EXAMPLE

A water engineering firm bids on a contract to investigate the level of silt accumulation in the Oswego Canal in New York, and wins the bid. The firm incurs the following costs as part of its bidding process.

Staff time to prepare proposal	$18,000
Printing fees	2,500
Travel costs	5,000
Commissions paid to sales staff	15,000
	$40,500

The firm must charge the staff time, printing fees, and travel costs to expense as incurred, since it would have incurred these expenses even if the bid had failed. Only the commissions paid to the sales staff can be considered a contract asset, since that cost should be recovered through its future billings for consulting services.

Costs to Fulfill a Contract

In general, any costs required to fulfill a contract should be recognized as assets, as long as they meet all of these criteria:
- The costs are tied to a specific contract;
- The costs will be used to satisfy future performance obligations; and
- There is an expectation that the costs will be recovered.

Costs that are considered to relate directly to a contract include the following:
- *Direct labor*. Includes the wages of those employees directly engaged in providing services to the customer.
- *Direct materials*. Includes the supplies consumed in the provision of services to the customer.
- *Cost allocations*. Includes those costs that relate directly to the contract, such as the cost of managing the contract, project supervision, and depreciation of the equipment used to fulfill the contract.
- *Chargeable costs*. Includes those costs that the contract explicitly states can be charged to the customer.
- *Other costs*. Includes costs that would only be incurred because the seller entered into the contract, such as payments to subcontractors providing services to the customer.

Other costs are to be charged to expense as incurred, rather than being classified as contract assets. These costs include:
- *Administration*. General and administrative costs, unless the contract terms explicitly state that they can be charged to the contract.
- *Indistinguishable*. Costs for which it is not possible to determine whether they relate to unsatisfied or satisfied performance obligations. In this case,

the default assumption is that they relate to satisfied performance obligations.

- *Past performance costs.* Any costs incurred that relate to performance obligations that have already been fulfilled.
- *Waste.* The costs of resources wasted in the contract fulfillment process, which were not included in the contract price.

EXAMPLE

Tele-Service International enters into a contract to take over the phone customer service function of Artisan's Delight, a manufacturer of hand-woven wool shopping bags. Tele-Service incurs a cost of $50,000 to construct an interface between the inventory and customer service systems of Artisan's Delight and its own call database. This cost relates to activities needed to fulfill the requirements of the contract, but does not result in the provision of any services to Artisan's Delight. This cost should be amortized over the term of the contract.

Tele-Service assigns four of its employees on a full-time basis to handle incoming customer calls from Artisan's customers. Though this group is providing services to the customer, it is not generating or enhancing the resources of Tele-Service, and so its cost cannot be recognized as an asset. Instead, the cost of these employees is charged to expense as incurred.

Amortization of Costs

When contract-related costs have been recognized as assets, they should be amortized on a systematic basis that reflects the timing of the transfer of related goods and services to the customer. If there is a change in the anticipated timing of the transfer of goods and services to the customer, update the amortization to reflect this change. This is considered a change in accounting estimate.

Impairment of Costs

The seller should recognize an impairment loss in the current period when the carrying amount of an asset associated with a contract is greater than the remaining payments to be received from the customer. The calculation is:

Remaining consideration to be received − Costs not yet recognized as expenses
= Impairment amount (if result is a negative figure)

Note: When calculating possible impairment, adjust the amount of the remaining consideration to be received for the effects of the customer's credit risk.

It is not allowable to reverse an impairment loss on contract assets that has already been recognized.

Exclusions

The revenue recognition rules contained within Topic 606 do not apply to the following areas, for which more specific recognition standards apply:

- Lease contracts
- Insurance contracts
- Financial instruments involving receivables, investments, liabilities, debt, derivatives, hedging, or transfers and servicing
- Guarantees, not including product or service warranties
- Nonmonetary exchanges between entities in the same line of business, where the intent is to facilitate sales transactions to existing or potential customers

EXAMPLE

Two distributors of heating oil swap stocks of different grades of heating oil, so that they can better meet the forecasted demand of their customers. No revenue recognition occurs in this situation, since the two parties are in the same line of business and the intent of the transaction is to facilitate sales to potential customers.

Since Topic 606 only applies to contracts with customers, there are a number of transactions that do not incorporate these elements, and so are not covered by the provisions of this Topic. Consequently, the following transactions and events are not covered:

- Dividends received
- Non-exchange transactions, such as donations received
- Changes in regulatory assets and liabilities caused by alternative revenue programs for rate-regulated entities

Revenue Disclosures

There are a number of disclosures related to revenue. As a general overview, the intent of the disclosures is to reveal enough information so that readers will understand the nature of the revenue, the amount being recognized, the timing associated with its recognition, and the uncertainty of the related cash flows. More specifically, disclosures are required in the following three areas for both annual and interim financial statements:

- *Contracts.* Disclose the amount of revenue recognized, any revenue impairments, the disaggregation of revenue, performance obligations, contract balances, and the amount of the transaction price allocated to the remaining performance obligations. Contract balances should include beginning and ending balances of receivables, contract assets, and contract liabilities. In particular:

- ○ *Revenue.* Separately disclose the revenue recognized from contracts with customers.
- ○ *Impairment losses.* Separately disclose any impairment losses on receivables or contract assets that arose from contracts with customers. These disclosures must be separated from the disclosure of losses from other types of contracts.
- ○ *Disaggregation.* Disaggregate the reported amount of revenue recognized into categories that reflect the nature, amount, timing, and uncertainty of cash flows and revenue. Examples are:
  - By contract type (such as by cost-plus versus fixed-price contract)
  - By country or region
  - By customer type (such as by retail versus government customer)
  - By duration of contract
  - By major product line
  - By market
  - By sales channels (such as by Internet store, retail chain, or wholesaler)
  - By transfer timing (such as sales as of a point in time versus over time)

The nature of this disaggregation may be derived from how the organization discloses information about revenue in other venues, such as within annual reports, in presentations to investors, or when being evaluated for financial performance or resource allocation judgments. If the entity is publicly-held and therefore reports segment information, consider how the reporting of disaggregated revenue information might relate to the revenue information reported for segments of the business. It is also allowable for certain non-public entities to *not* disaggregate revenue information, but only if this disclosure is replaced by the disclosure of revenue by the timing of transfers to customers, and with a discussion of how economic factors (such as contract types or customer types) impact the nature, amount, timing, and uncertainty of cash flows and revenue.

EXAMPLE

Lowry Locomotion operates a number of business segments generally related to different types of trains. It compiles the following information for its disaggregation disclosure:

(000s) Segments	Freight Trains	Passenger Trains	Railbus	Total
Primary Geographical Markets				
Europe	$53,000	$41,000	$14,000	$108,000
North America	91,000	190,000	---	281,000
	$144,000	$231,000	$14,000	$389,000
Major Product Lines				
Diesel	$106,000	$---	$---	$106,000
Electric	38,000	190,000	14,000	242,000
Trolleys	---	41,000	---	41,000
	$144,000	$231,000	$14,000	$389,000
Timing of Revenue Recognition				
Goods transferred at a point in time	$129,000	$189,000	$11,000	$329,000
Services transferred over time	15,000	42,000	3,000	60,000
	$144,000	$231,000	$14,000	$389,000

- o *Contract-related.* The disclosure of contract balances for all entities shall include the opening and closing balances of receivables, contract assets, and contract liabilities. Publicly-held and certain other entities must provide considerably more information. This includes:
  - Revenue recognized in the period that was included in the contract liability at the beginning of the period, and revenue recognized in the period from performance obligations at least partially satisfied in previous periods (such as from changes in transaction prices).
  - How the timing of the completion of performance obligations relates to the timing of payments from customers and the impact this has on the balances of contract assets and contract liabilities.
  - Explain significant changes in the balances of contract assets and contract liabilities in the period. Possible causes to discuss might include changes caused by business combinations, impairments, or cumulative catch-up adjustments.
- o *Performance obligations.* Describe the performance obligations related to contracts with customers, which should include the timing of when these obligations are typically satisfied (such as upon delivery), significant payment terms, the presence of any significant financing components, whether consideration is variable, and whether the consideration may be constrained. Also note the nature

of the goods or services being transferred, and describe any obligations to have a third party transfer goods or services to customers (as is the case in an agent relationship). Finally, describe any obligations related to returns, refunds, and warranties.

○ *Price allocations.* If there are remaining performance obligations to which transaction prices are to be allocated, disclose the aggregate transaction price allocated to those unsatisfied obligations. Also note when this remaining revenue is likely to be recognized, either in a qualitative discussion or by breaking down the amounts to be recognized by time band. None of these disclosures are needed if the original expected duration of a contract's performance obligation is for less than one year. Also, certain non-public entities can elect to not disclose any of this information.

EXAMPLE

Franklin Oilfield Support provides gas field maintenance to gas exploration companies in North America. Franklin discloses the following information related to the allocation of transaction prices to remaining performance obligations:

Franklin provides gas field maintenance services to several of the larger gas exploration firms in the Bakken field in North Dakota. The company typically enters into two-year maintenance service agreements. Currently, the remaining performance obligations are for $77,485,000, which are expected to be satisfied within the next 24 months. These obligations are noted in the following table, which also states the year in which revenue recognition is expected:

(000s)	20X1	20X2	Totals
Revenue expected to be recognized:			
Gates contract	$14,250	$7,090	$21,340
Hollander contract	23,825	17,900	41,725
Ives contract	9,070	5,350	14,420
Totals	$47,145	$30,340	$77,485

- *Judgments.* Note the timing associated with when performance obligations are satisfied, as well as how the transaction price was determined and how it was allocated to the various performance obligations. In particular:
  - ○ *Recognition methods.* When performance obligations are to be satisfied over time, describe the methods used to recognize revenue, and explain why these methods constitute a faithful depiction of the transfer of goods or services to customers.
  - ○ *Transfer of control.* When performance obligations are satisfied as of a point in time, disclose the judgments made to determine when a customer gains control of the goods or services promised under contracts.

- *Methods, inputs and assumptions.* Disclose sufficient information about the methods, inputs, and assumptions used to determine transaction prices, the constraints on any variable consideration, allocation of transaction prices, and measurement of obligations for returns, refunds, and so forth. The discussion of transaction prices should include how variable consideration is estimated, how non-cash consideration is measured, and how the time value of money is used to adjust prices.
- *Disclosure avoidance.* Certain non-public entities can elect not to disclose information about the following items pertaining to judgments:
  - Why revenue recognition methods constitute a faithful depiction of the transfer of goods or services to customers.
  - The judgments made to determine when a customer gains control of the goods or services promised under contracts.
  - All methods, inputs, and assumptions used, though this information must still be supplied in regard to the determination of whether variable consideration is constrained.

- *Asset recognition.* Note the recognized assets associated with obtaining or completing the terms of the contract. This shall include the closing balances of contract-related assets by main category of asset, such as for setup costs and the costs to obtain contracts. The disclosure should also include the amount of amortization expenses and impairment losses recognized in the period. Also describe:
  - *Judgments.* The judgments involved in determining the amount of costs incurred to obtain or fulfill a customer contract.
  - *Amortization.* The amortization method used to charge contract-related costs to expense in each reporting period.

A non-public entity can elect not to make the disclosures just noted for asset recognition.

It may be necessary to aggregate or disaggregate these disclosures to clarify the information presented. In particular, do not obscure information by adding large amounts of insignificant detail, or by combining items whose characteristics are substantially different.

There may be a change in estimate related to the measurement of progress toward completion of a performance obligation. If the change in estimate will affect several future periods, disclose the effect on income from continuing operations, net income, and any related per-share amounts (if the entity is publicly held). This disclosure is only required if the change is material. If there is not an immediate material effect, but a material effect is expected in later periods, provide a description of the change in estimate.

Summary

A key benefit of Topic 606 is that the recognition of revenue from contracts with customers will now be quite consistent across a number of contract types and industries. Previously, industry-specific standards did not always treat essentially the same types of transactions in a similar manner. This may mean that some industries, such as software, may experience significant recognition changes, since they were previously governed by highly specific recognition rules. Some entities, irrespective of their industry, may find that their recognition accounting will also change to a considerable extent if they had previously been using an interpretation of the existing standards that is no longer valid. For many industries, however, especially those involving retail transactions, the net effect of this standard is minimal.

Chapter 12
Accounting for Payroll

Introduction

The payroll system may be entirely separate from a company's primary system of recording accounting transactions. This is especially true if it has outsourced the payroll function entirely. Thus, you need a process for transferring the information accumulated in the payroll system to the accounting system. The chief tool for doing so is the journal entry, which is used to transfer a variety of types of expense-related information at a summary level into the accounting system. This chapter describes where payroll information is stored in an accounting system, and the journal entries used to record payroll information in that system.

The Chart of Accounts

The chart of accounts is a listing of all the accounts in the general ledger. The following chart of accounts shows only those accounts most likely to be used for payroll-related transactions (the account numbers used are examples only – your account numbers will likely differ):

Payroll-Related Accounts in the Chart of Accounts

Number	Description	Usage
Assets		
1000	Cash	Source of payments to employees
1100	Payroll advances	Tracks advances that have not yet been paid back to the company
Liabilities		
2100	Federal unemployment taxes payable	Tracks federal unemployment taxes owed but not yet paid
2110	Federal withholding taxes payable	Tracks federal income taxes withheld from employee pay but not yet remitted to the government
2120	Garnishments payable	Tracks garnishments withheld from employee pay but not yet remitted to the garnishing authority
2130	Medicare taxes payable	Tracks Medicare taxes withheld and matched, but not yet remitted to the government
2140	Social security taxes payable	Tracks social security taxes withheld and matched, but not yet remitted to the government
2150	State unemployment taxes payable	Tracks state unemployment taxes owed but not yet paid
2160	Accrued benefits liability	Tracks benefits expenses incurred but not yet paid
2170	Accrued bonus liability	Tracks bonus expense incurred but not yet paid
2180	Accrued commissions	Tracks commission expense incurred but not yet paid

Number	Description	Usage
2190	Accrued payroll taxes	Tracks payroll taxes associated with accrued wages that have not yet been paid
2200	Accrued salaries and wages	Tracks salaries and wages that have been earned by employees but not yet paid
Expenses		
3100	Direct labor expense	Tracks the incurred labor expense associated with the cost of goods sold
4200	Bonus expense	Tracks the incurred cost of bonuses paid or payable to employees
4210	Commission expense	Tracks the incurred cost of commissions paid or payable to employees
4220	Wage expense	Tracks the incurred labor expense associated with administrative and selling activities
4230	Payroll taxes expense	Tracks the incurred cost of payroll taxes paid or payable to the government
4240	Medical insurance expense	Tracks the incurred cost of medical insurance paid or payable to suppliers
4250	Dental insurance expense	Tracks the incurred cost of dental insurance paid or payable to suppliers
4260	Disability insurance expense	Tracks the incurred cost of disability insurance paid or payable to suppliers
4270	Life insurance expense	Tracks the cost of life insurance paid or payable to suppliers

Tip: When constructing a chart of accounts, always leave gaps in the numbering between accounts, so that you can more easily add accounts later, as the business expands and its information storage needs grow.

Types of Payroll Journal Entries

There are several types of journal entries that involve the recordation of compensation. The primary entry is for the initial recordation of a payroll. This entry records the gross wages earned by employees, as well as all withholdings from their pay, and any additional taxes owed by the company. There may also be an accrued wages entry that is recorded at the end of each accounting period, and which is intended to record the amount of wages owed to employees but not yet paid. Under some circumstances, it may also be prudent to accrue a portion of the bonus that an employee may be paid at the end of a period if he or she meets certain performance criteria. A more common entry is for the accrual of commissions earned by the sales staff, but which have not yet been paid. Each of these types of compensation is based on different source documents and requires separate calculations and journal entries.

There are also a number of other payroll-related journal entries that a payroll staff must deal with on a regular basis. They include:
- Benefit payments
- Accrued benefits
- Stock subscriptions

- Manual paychecks
- Employee advances
- Accrued vacation pay
- Tax deposits

All of these journal entries are described in the following sections.

Primary Payroll Journal Entry

The primary journal entry for payroll is the summary-level entry that is compiled from the payroll register, and which is recorded in either the payroll journal or the general ledger. This entry usually includes debits for the direct labor expense, wages, and the company's portion of payroll taxes. There will also be credits to a number of other accounts, each one detailing the liability for payroll taxes that have not been paid, as well as for the amount of cash already paid to employees for their net pay. The basic entry (assuming no further breakdown of debits by individual department) is:

	Debit	Credit
Direct labor expense	xxx	
Wages expense	xxx	
Payroll taxes expense	xxx	
Cash		xxx
Federal withholding taxes payable		xxx
Social security taxes payable		xxx
Medicare taxes payable		xxx
Federal unemployment taxes payable		xxx
State unemployment taxes payable		xxx
Garnishments payable		xxx

Note: The reason for the payroll taxes expense line item in this journal entry is that the company incurs the cost of matching the social security and Medicare amounts paid by employees, and directly incurs the cost of unemployment insurance. The employee-paid portions of the social security and Medicare taxes are not recorded as expenses; instead, they are liabilities for which the company has an obligation to remit cash to the taxing government entity.

A key point with this journal entry is that the direct labor expense and salaries expense contain employee gross pay, while the amount actually paid to employees through the cash account is their net pay. The difference between the two figures (which can be substantial) is the amount of deductions from their pay, such as payroll taxes and withholdings to pay for benefits.

There may be a number of additional employee deductions to include in this journal entry. For example, there may be deductions for 401(k) pension plans, health insurance, life insurance, vision insurance, and for the repayment of advances.

When you later pay the withheld taxes and company portion of payroll taxes, use the following entry to reduce the balance in the cash account, and eliminate the balances in the liability accounts:

	Debit	Credit
Federal withholding taxes payable	xxx	
Social security taxes payable	xxx	
Medicare taxes payable	xxx	
Federal unemployment taxes payable	xxx	
State withholding taxes payable	xxx	
State unemployment taxes payable	xxx	
Garnishments payable	xxx	
Cash		xxx

Thus, when a company initially deducts taxes and other items from an employee's pay, the company incurs a liability to pay the taxes to a third party. This liability only disappears from the company's accounting records when it pays the related funds to the entity to which they are owed.

> **Note:** If your payroll system is tightly integrated into the accounting system, it is not necessary to create the entries just described. Instead, the software will automatically transfer detailed payroll information into the payroll journal, which will eventually be transferred to the general ledger.

Accrued Wages

It is quite common to have some amount of unpaid wages at the end of an accounting period, so accrue this expense (if it is material). The accrual entry, as shown next, is simpler than the comprehensive payroll entry already shown, because you typically clump all payroll taxes into a single expense account and offsetting liability account. After recording this entry, reverse it at the beginning of the following accounting period, and then record the actual payroll expense whenever it occurs.

	Debit	Credit
Direct labor expense	xxx	
Wages expense	xxx	
Accrued salaries and wages		xxx
Accrued payroll taxes		xxx

Companies with predominantly salaried staffs frequently avoid making the accrued wages entry, on the grounds that the wages due to a small number of hourly personnel at the end of the reporting period have a minimal impact on reported financial results.

The information for the wage accrual entry is most easily derived from a spreadsheet that itemizes all employees to whom the calculation applies, the amount of unpaid time, and the standard pay rate for each person. It is not necessary to also calculate the cost of overtime hours earned during an accrual period if the amount of such hours is relatively small. A sample spreadsheet for calculating accrued wages is:

Hourly Employees	Unpaid Days	Hourly Rate	Pay Accrual
Anthem, Jill	4	$20.00	$640
Bingley, Adam	4	18.25	584
Chesterton, Elvis	4	17.50	560
Davis, Ethel	4	23.00	736
Ellings, Humphrey	4	21.50	688
Fogarty, Miriam	4	16.00	512
		Total	$3,720

Accrued Bonuses

Accrue a bonus expense whenever there is an expectation that the financial or operational performance of a company at least equals the performance levels required in any active bonus plans.

The decision to accrue a bonus calls for considerable judgment, for the entire period of performance may encompass many future months, during which time a person may *not* continue to achieve his bonus plan objectives, in which case any prior bonus accrual should be reversed. Here are some alternative ways to treat a bonus accrual during the earlier stages of a bonus period:

- Accrue no expense at all until there is a reasonable probability that the bonus will be achieved.
- Accrue a smaller expense early in a performance period to reflect the higher risk of performance failure, and accrue a larger expense later if the probability of success improves.

One thing you should *not* do is accrue a significant bonus expense in a situation where the probability that the bonus will be awarded is low; such an accrual is essentially earnings management, since it creates a false expense that is later reversed when the performance period is complete.

EXAMPLE

The management team of High Noon Armaments will earn a year-end group bonus of $240,000 if profits exceed 12 percent of revenues. There is a reasonable probability that the team will earn this bonus, so the accountant records the following accrual in each month of the performance year:

	Debit	Credit
Bonus expense	20,000	
Accrued bonus liability		20,000

The management team does not quite meet the profit criteria required under the bonus plan, so the group instead receives a $150,000 bonus. This results in the following entry to eliminate the liability and pay out the bonus:

	Debit	Credit
Accrued bonus liability	240,000	
Bonus expense		90,000
Cash		150,000

The actual payout of $150,000 would be reduced by any social security and Medicare taxes applicable to each person in the management group being paid.

Tip: Employee performance plans are usually maintained by the human resources department. The payroll manager should summarize these plans into a format that the payroll staff can consult when calculating its estimates of bonus accruals.

Accrued Commissions

Accrue an expense for a commission in the same period as you record the sale generated by the salesperson, *and* when you can calculate the amount of the commission. This is a debit to the commission expense account and a credit to a commission liability account. You can classify the commission expense as part of the cost of goods sold, since it directly relates to the sale of goods or services. It is also acceptable to classify it as part of the expenses of the sales department.

EXAMPLE

Wes Smith sells a $1,000 item for High Noon Armaments. Under the terms of his commission agreement, he receives a 5% commission on the revenue generated by the transaction, and will be paid on the 15th day of the following month. At the end of the accounting period in which Mr. Smith generates the sale, High Noon creates the following entry to record its liability for the commission:

	Debit	Credit
Commission expense	50	
Accrued commissions (liability)		50

High Noon then reverses the entry at the beginning of the following accounting period, because it is going to record the actual payment on the 15th of the month. Thus, the reversing entry is:

	Debit	Credit
Accrued commissions (liability)	50	
Commission expense		50

On the 15th of the month, High Noon pays Mr. Smith his commission and records this entry:

	Debit	Credit
Commission expense	50	
Cash		50

Benefit Payments

Benefits are paid through the accounts payable system, while the employee-paid portion of benefits is deducted from their pay through the payroll system. Thus, two different systems are required to process benefits, on the assumption that employees are paying for a portion or all of the benefits.

A company enrolls an employee in a benefit plan with a supplier, and is usually billed in advance for benefits, with payment due to the supplier by the beginning of the month in which the benefits are to be incurred. This early payment means that the proper recordation of such a benefit is as a prepaid expense, which is classified as a current asset. The entry is:

	Debit	Credit
Prepaid expenses (asset)	xxx	
Accounts payable		xxx

At the beginning of the next month, which is the month to which the benefits apply, shift the amount in the prepaid expenses account to the applicable benefits expense account. A sample entry for medical benefits would be:

	Debit	Credit
Medical benefits expense	xxx	
Prepaid expenses (asset)		xxx

Any deductions taken from employee pay are then recorded as credits to the applicable benefits expense account, thereby reducing the amount of the expense borne by the company.

EXAMPLE

Giro Cabinetry pays $20,000 for its employee medical insurance per month. The company requires all participating employees to pay 20% of the total cost of the insurance, which is $4,000. The company pays its employees twice a month.

The entries into its medical benefits expense account in May are:

Date	Description	Source	Debit	Credit	Balance
	Beginning balance				$63,900
5/1	Payment to First Medical	AP	20,000		83,900
5/15	Payroll deductions	PJ		2,000	81,900
5/31	Payroll deductions	PJ		2,000	79,900
	Ending balance				$79,900

The transaction detail reveals that Giro records the medical insurance expense at the beginning of the month, with the source document being the accounts payable journal. The payroll deductions come from the mid-month and end-of-month payrolls, and the source document in both cases is the payroll journal.

Tip: When there is a change in the cost of a benefit charged by a supplier, some portion of this cost increase is usually paid by employees through an increased pay deduction. However, there may be a disconnect between a change in a benefit cost and the related deduction, resulting in deductions being too low, and the company paying all of the cost increase. To avoid this problem, schedule a periodic internal audit of employee deductions, where the auditors are specifically verifying that deduction amounts are correct.

Accrued Benefits

The proper way to account for the accrual of employee benefits is to use a journal entry template to record the amount of any benefits that have been consumed by employees, and for which a supplier billing has not yet arrived.

Certain types of insurance may be billed after the fact, when the insurer has sufficient information about employees to create an invoice. For example, an employer might send employee information to its insurer at the end of each month, so that the insurer can devise an accurate billing that is issued in the next month, but which applies to the preceding month. In this case, the company accrues the estimated cost of the insurance in the current month, and sets the entry to automatically reverse in the next month, when the insurer's invoice arrives.

A sample of this transaction is:

	Debit	Credit
Medical insurance expense	xxx	
Dental insurance expense	xxx	
Disability insurance expense	xxx	
Life insurance expense	xxx	
Accrued benefits liability		xxx

Most benefit providers issue billings in advance of a reporting period, so there may be few benefit accruals to record. Also, if a proposed accrual is a small one, it may make little sense to record it, on the grounds that it has no material impact on the financial statements, requires accounting labor, and introduces the risk of incorrectly recording or reversing the transaction.

Stock Subscriptions

A publicly-held company can create a stock subscription arrangement, where employees pay for shares in the company by having a standard amount deducted from their pay. Under this arrangement, a receivable is set up for the full amount expected from employees, with an offset to a common stock account and the additional paid-in capital account (for the par value of the subscribed shares). When the cash is collected and the stock is issued, the funds are deducted from these accounts and shifted to the common stock account.

EXAMPLE

High Noon Armaments sets up a stock subscription system for its employees. They choose to purchase 10,000 shares of common stock with a par value of $1 for a total of $52,000. Employees are paying $1,000 per week through payroll deductions. The company has a weekly payroll. The initial entry is:

	Debit	Credit
Stock subscriptions receivable	52,000	
Common stock subscribed		42,000
Additional paid-in capital		10,000

When High Noon receives a cash payment, it offsets the stock subscriptions receivable account and shifts funds stored in the common stock subscribed account to the common stock account. The following entry shows the processing of a typical $1,000 payment arising from the deductions in one of the weekly payrolls:

	Debit	Credit
Cash	1,000	
Stock subscriptions receivable		1,000
Common stock subscribed	1,000	
Common stock		1,000

Manual Paycheck Entry

It is all too common to create a manual paycheck, either because an employee was short-paid in a prior payroll, or because the company is laying off or firing an employee, and so is obligated to pay that person before the next regularly scheduled payroll. This check may be paid through the corporate accounts payable bank account, rather than its payroll account, so you may need to make this entry through the accounts payable system. If you are recording it directly into the general ledger or the payroll journal, then use the same line items already noted for the primary payroll journal entry.

EXAMPLE

High Noon Armaments lays off Mr. Jones. High Noon owes Mr. Jones $5,000 of wages at the time of the layoff. The payroll staff calculates that it must withhold $382.50 from Mr. Jones' pay to cover the employee-paid portions of social security and Medicare taxes. Mr. Jones has claimed a large enough number of withholding allowances that there is no income tax withholding. Thus, the company pays Mr. Jones $4,617.50. The journal entry it uses is:

	Debit	Credit
Wage expense	5,000	
Social security taxes payable		310.00
Medicare taxes payable		72.50
Cash		4,617.50

At the next regularly-scheduled payroll, the payroll staff records this payment as a notation in the payroll system, so that it will properly compile the correct amount of wages for Mr. Jones for his year-end Form W-2. In addition, the payroll system calculates that High Noon must pay a matching amount of social security and Medicare taxes (though no unemployment taxes, since Mr. Jones already exceeded his wage cap for these taxes). Accordingly, an additional liability of $382.50 is recorded in the payroll journal entry for that payroll. High Noon pays these matching amounts as part of its normal tax remittances associated with the payroll.

Employee Advances

When an employee asks for an advance, this is recorded as a current asset in the company's balance sheet. There may not be a separate account in which to store advances, especially if employee advances are infrequent; possible asset accounts you can use are:

- Employee advances (for high-volume situations)
- Other assets (probably sufficient for smaller companies that record few assets other than trade receivables, inventory, and fixed assets)
- Other receivables (useful if you are tracking a number of different types of assets, and want to segregate receivables in one account)

EXAMPLE

High Noon Armaments issues a $1,000 advance to employee Wes Smith. High Noon issues advances regularly, and so uses a separate account in which to record advances.

It records the transaction as:

	Debit	Credit
Other assets	1,000	
Cash		1,000

One week later, Mr. Smith pays back half the amount of the advance, which is recorded with this entry:

	Debit	Credit
Cash	500	
Other assets		500

No matter what method is later used to repay the company – a check from the employee, or payroll deductions – the entry will be a credit to whichever asset account was used, until such time as the balance in the account has been paid off.

Employee advances require considerable vigilance by the accounting staff, because employees who have limited financial resources will tend to use the company as their personal banks, and so will be reluctant to pay back advances unless pressed repeatedly. Thus, it is essential to continually monitor the remaining amount of advances outstanding for every employee.

Accrued Vacation Pay

Accrued vacation pay is the amount of vacation time that an employee has earned as per a company's employee benefit manual, but which he has not yet used. The calculation of accrued vacation pay for each employee is:

1. Calculate the amount of vacation time earned through the beginning of the accounting period. This should be a roll-forward balance from the preceding period.
2. Add the number of hours earned in the current accounting period.
3. Subtract the number of vacation hours used in the current period.
4. Multiply the ending number of accrued vacation hours by the employee's hourly wage to arrive at the correct accrual that should be on the company's books.
5. If the amount already accrued for the employee from the preceding period is lower than the correct accrual, record the difference as an addition to the accrued liability. If the amount already accrued from the preceding period is higher than the correct accrual, record the difference as a reduction of the accrued liability.

A sample spreadsheet follows that uses the preceding steps, and which can be used to compile accrued vacation pay:

Name	Vacation Roll-Forward Balance	+ New Hours Earned	- Hours Used	= Net Balance	× Hourly Pay	= Accrued Vacation $
Hilton, David	24.0	10	34.0	0.0	$25.00	$0.00
Idle, John	13.5	10	0.0	23.5	17.50	411.25
Jakes, Jill	120.0	10	80.0	50.0	23.50	1,175.00
Kilo, Steve	114.5	10	14.0	110.5	40.00	4,420.00
Linder, Alice	12.0	10	0.0	22.0	15.75	346.50
Mills, Jeffery	83.5	10	65.00	28.5	19.75	562.88
					Total	$6,915.63

It is not necessary to reverse the vacation pay accrual in each period if you choose to instead record just incremental changes in the accrual from month to month.

EXAMPLE

There is already an existing accrued balance of 40 hours of unused vacation time for Wes Smith on the books of High Noon Armaments. In the most recent month that has just ended, Mr. Smith accrued an additional five hours of vacation time (since he is entitled to 60 hours of accrued vacation time per year, and 60 ÷ 12 = five hours per month). He also used three hours of vacation time during the month. This means that, as of the end of the month, High Noon should have accrued a total of 42 hours of vacation time for him (calculated as 40 hours existing balance + 5 hours additional accrual − 3 hours used).

Mr. Smith is paid $30 per hour, so his total vacation accrual should be $1,260 (42 hours × $30/hour), so High Noon accrues an additional $60 of vacation liability.

What if a company has a "use it or lose it" policy? This means that employees must use their vacation time by a certain date (such as the end of the year), and can only carry forward a small number of hours (if any) into the next year. One issue is that this policy may be illegal, since vacation is an earned benefit that cannot be taken away (which depends on state law). If this policy is considered to be legal, then it is acceptable to reduce the accrual as of the date when employees are supposed to have used their accrued vacation, thereby reflecting the reduced liability to the company as represented by the number of vacation hours that employees have lost.

What if an employee receives a pay raise? Then you need to increase the amount of his entire vacation accrual by the incremental amount of the pay raise. This is because, if the employee were to leave the company and be paid all of his unused vacation pay, he would be paid at his most recent rate of pay.

Tax Deposits

When an employer withholds taxes from employee pay, it must deposit these funds with the government at stated intervals. The journal entry for doing so is a debit to the tax liability account being paid and a credit to the cash account, which reduces the cash balance. For example, if a company were to pay a state government for unemployment taxes, the entry would be:

	Debit	Credit
State unemployment taxes payable	xxx	
Cash		xxx

Payroll Information in the Financial Statements - Wages

When a company pays wages, the effect is a reduction in the cash balance on the balance sheet and an increase in the wages expense line item in the income statement. In addition, if there is a wage, commission, or bonus accrual to reflect an unpaid wage amount, this appears in the balance sheet as an increase in the accrued wages, commissions, or bonuses liability, and in the income statement as an increase in one of the compensation expense line items.

If expenses are categorized by line item in the income statement, the various compensation expenses may be charged to specific departments. It is particularly common to shift the cost of direct labor into the cost of goods sold line item in the income statement.

Payroll Information in the Financial Statements – Payroll Taxes

When a company incurs an obligation to pay payroll taxes to the government, a portion of it appears on the income statement, and a portion on the balance sheet.

You would record an expense on the income statement for the employer matching portion of any social security and Medicare taxes, as well as the entire amount of any federal and state unemployment taxes (since they are paid by the company and not the employees). In some locations, there may be additional taxes owed by the company, such as a head tax for every person employed within the boundaries of a city. All of these payroll taxes are valid expenses of the company, and so will appear on its income statement.

These taxes should be charged to expense in the period incurred. They may be charged to a single payroll taxes account, or to a payroll taxes account within each department. If the latter is the case, some part of the taxes will likely be charged to the production department, in which case you have the option of including them in an overhead cost pool, from which you can allocate them to the cost of goods sold and ending inventory; this can defer the recognition of a portion of the payroll taxes until such time as the inventory is sold.

A company also incurs a liability for payroll taxes, which appears as a short-term liability on its balance sheet. This liability is comprised of all the taxes just noted (until they are paid), plus the amount of any social security and Medicare taxes that are withheld from the pay of employees. In the later situation, the company is essentially an agent for the government, and is responsible for transferring the funds to the government. Thus, the employee portion of social security and Medicare taxes are not an expense of the company, but they are a liability.

Summary

This chapter has shown a broad array of journal entries that can be used to record payroll-related transactions. Given the large number of journal entries, it is common for errors to arise in the accounting for payroll. Here are several ways to reduce payroll accounting errors:

- *Journal entry templates.* Use a standard format for each type of journal entry, so that you always consistently use the same account numbers. This can be a simple form if you have a manual payroll system, or a template function within an accounting software package.
- *Automated reversing entries.* If it is necessary to reverse a journal entry in the next accounting period and you are using an accounting software package, use the automated reversing feature in the software, so that the reversal occurs without any further actions from you.
- *Integrated payroll module.* If you process payroll in-house, do so through the payroll module provided by the supplier of your accounting software (if there is such a module). This module usually generates all journal entries related to payroll processing, and posts them to the accounting system.
- *Horizontal analysis.* Even if your payroll entries are properly filled out, you could have entered an incorrect wage amount, or charged it to the wrong department. A good way to spot these problems is to run a preliminary set of financial statements that show the results of each department over several consecutive periods. An incorrect payroll entry will likely result in a spike or drop in a payroll line item in comparison to the rest of the preceding periods.

The accrual journal entries recommended in this chapter are based on the assumption that you are using the accrual basis of accounting. If you are instead using the cash basis of accounting, where transactions are only recorded when there is a cash receipt or expenditure, none of the accrual entries are needed.

Chapter 13
Accounting for Stock-Based Compensation

Introduction

A company may issue shares to its employees that are intended to be compensation for past or future services rendered. These payments can take many forms, such as stock grants, stock options, and discounted employee stock purchase plans. In this chapter, we address how to account for each of these types of stock compensation, as well as similar arrangements.

Overview of Stock Compensation

A company may issue payments to its employees in the form of shares in the business. When these payments are made, the essential accounting is to recognize the cost of the related services as they are received by the company, at their fair value. The offset to this expense recognition is either an increase in an equity or liability account, depending on the nature of the transaction. In rare cases, the cost of the services received by the company may be capitalized into a fixed asset, if the services are related to the acquisition or construction of the asset.

The following issues relate to the measurement and recognition of stock-based compensation:

- *Employee designation.* The accounting for stock compensation noted in this chapter only applies to employees. It also applies to the board of directors, as long as they were elected by company shareholders. However, the accounting only applies to stock grants issued in compensation for their services as directors, not for other services provided.
- *Employee payments.* If an employee pays the issuer an amount in connection with an award, the fair value attributable to employee service is net of the amount paid. For example, if a stock option has a fair value on the grant date of $100, and the recipient pays $20 for the option, the award amount attributable to employee service is $80.

EXAMPLE

Armadillo Industries issues 1,000 shares of common stock to Mr. Jones, the vice president of sales, at a large discount from the market price. On the grant date, the fair value of these shares is $20,000. Mr. Jones pays $1,000 to the company for these shares. Thus, the amount that can be attributed to Mr. Jones' services to the company is $19,000 (calculated as $20,000 fair value - $1,000 payment).

- *Expense accrual.* When the service component related to a stock issuance spans several reporting periods, accrue the related service expense based on the probable outcome of the performance condition. Thus, always accrue the expense when it is probable that the condition will be achieved. Also, accrue the expense over the initial best estimate of the employee service period, which is usually the service period required in the arrangement related to the stock issuance.

EXAMPLE

The board of directors of Armadillo Industries grants stock options to its president that have a fair value of $80,000, which will vest in the earlier of four years or when the company achieves a 20% market share in a new market that the company wants to enter. Since there is not sufficient historical information about the company's ability to succeed in the new market, the accountant elects to set the service period at four years, and accordingly accrues $20,000 of compensation in each of the next four years.

If both performance conditions had been required before the stock options would be awarded, and there was no way of determining the probability of achieving the 20% market share condition, the accountant would only begin to accrue any compensation expense after it became probable that the market share condition could be achieved. In this latter case, compensation expense would be recognized at once for all of the earlier periods during which no compensation expense had been accrued.

- *Expired stock options.* If stock option grants expire unused, do not reverse the related amount of compensation expense.
- *Fair value determination.* Stock-based compensation is measured at the fair value of the instruments issued as of the grant date, even though the stock may not be issued until a much later date. Fair value is based on the share price at the grant date, though this information is not typically available for the shares of a privately-held company. The fair value of a stock option is estimated with a valuation method, such as an option-pricing model.
- *Fair value of nonvested shares.* The fair value of a nonvested share is based on its value as though it were vested on the grant date.
- *Fair value of restricted shares.* The fair value of a restricted share is based on its value as a restricted share, which is likely to be less than the fair value of an unrestricted share.
- *Fair value restrictions.* If a restriction is imposed on awarded equity instruments that continue after the required service period, such as being unable to sell shares for a period of time, this restriction is considered in determining the fair value of the stock award.
- *Grant date.* The date on which a stock-based award is granted is assumed to be the date when the award is approved under the corporate governance requirements. The grant date can also be considered the date on which an employee initially begins to benefit from or be affected by subsequent

changes in the price of a company's stock, as long as subsequent approval of the grant is considered perfunctory.

- *Non-compete agreement.* If a share-based award contains a non-compete agreement, the facts and circumstances of the situation may indicate that the non-compete is a significant service condition. If so, accrue the related amount of compensation expense over the period covered by the non-compete agreement.

EXAMPLE

Armadillo Industries grants 200,000 restricted stock units to its chief high-pressure module design engineer, which are vested on the grant date. The fair value of the grant is $500,000, which is triple his compensation for the past year. Under the terms of the arrangement, the RSUs will only be transferred to the engineer ratably over the next five years if he complies with the terms of the non-compete agreement.

Since the RSUs are essentially linked to the non-compete agreement, and the amount of the future payouts are quite large, it is evident that the arrangement is really intended to be compensation for future services yet to be rendered to the company. Consequently, the appropriate accounting treatment is not to recognize the expense at once, but rather to recognize it ratably over the remaining term of the non-compete agreement.

- *Payroll taxes.* Accrue an expense for the payroll taxes associated with stock-based compensation at the same time as the related compensation expense.
- *Reload valuation.* A compensation instrument may have a reload feature, which automatically grants additional options to an employee once that person exercises existing options that use company shares to pay the exercise price. Do not include the value of the reload feature in the fair value of an award. Instead, measure reload options as separate awards when they are granted.
- *Service not rendered.* If an employee does not render the service required for an award, you may then reverse any related amount of compensation expense that had previously been recognized.

EXAMPLE

Uncanny Corporation grants 5,000 restricted stock units (RSUs) to its vice president of sales, with a three-year cliff vesting provision. The fair value of the RSUs on the grant date is $60,000, so the company accrues $20,000 of compensation expense per year for three years.

One week prior to the cliff vesting date, the vice president of sales unexpectedly resigns. Since the award has not yet vested, the company reverses all of the accrued compensation expense.

- *Service period.* The service period associated with a stock-based award is considered to be the vesting period, but the facts and circumstances of the arrangement can result in a different service period for the purpose of determining the number of periods over which to accrue compensation expense. This is called the *implicit service period.*

EXPENSE

Mrs. Smith is granted 10,000 stock options by the board of directors of Uncanny Corporation, which vest over 24 months. There is no service specified under the arrangement, so the service period is assumed to be the 24-month vesting period. Thus, the fair value of the award should be recognized ratably over the vesting period.

- *Service rendered prior to grant date.* If some or all of the requisite service associated with stock-based compensation occurs prior to the grant date, accrue the compensation expense during these earlier reporting periods, based on the fair value of the award at each reporting date. When the grant date is reached, adjust the compensation accrued to date based on the per-unit fair value assigned on the grant date. Thus, the initial recordation is a best guess of what the eventual fair value will be.
- *Subsequent changes.* If the circumstances later indicate that the number of instruments to be granted has changed, recognize the change in compensation cost in the period in which the change in estimate occurs. Also, if the initial estimate of the service period turns out to be incorrect, adjust the expense accrual to match the updated estimate.

EXAMPLE

The board of directors of Armadillo Industries initially grants 5,000 stock options to the engineering manager, with a vesting period of four years. The shares are worth $100,000 at the grant date, so the accountant plans to recognize $25,000 of compensation expense in each of the next four years. After two years, the board is so pleased with the performance of the engineering manager that they accelerate the vesting schedule to the current date. The accountant must therefore accelerate the remaining $50,000 of compensation expense that had not yet been recognized to the current date.

If the offsetting increase to stock-based compensation is equity, it should be to the paid-in capital account, as noted in the following example.

EXAMPLE

Armadillo Industries issues stock options with 10-year terms to its employees. All of these options vest at the end of four years (known as *cliff vesting*). The company uses a lattice-based valuation model to arrive at an option fair value of $15.00. The company grants

100,000 stock options. On the grant date, it assumes that 10% of the options will be forfeited. The exercise price of the options is $25.

Given this information, Armadillo charges $28,125 to expense in each month. The calculation of this compensation expense accrual is:

($15 Option fair value × 100,000 Options × 90% Exercise probability) ÷ 48 Months
= $28,125

The monthly journal entry to recognize the compensation expense is:

	Debit	Credit
Compensation expense	28,125	
Additional paid-in capital		28,125

Armadillo is subject to a 35% income tax rate, and expects to have sufficient future taxable income to offset the deferred tax benefits of the share-based compensation arrangements. Accordingly, the company records the following monthly entry to recognize the deferred tax benefit:

	Debit	Credit
Deferred tax asset	9,844	
Deferred tax benefit		9,844

Thus, the net after-tax effect of the monthly compensation expense recognition is $18,281 (calculated as $28,125 compensation expense - $9,844 deferred tax benefit).

At the end of the vesting period, the actual number of forfeitures matches the originally estimated amount, leaving 90,000 options. All of the 90,000 options are exercised once they have vested, which results in the following entry to record the conversion of options to shares:

	Debit	Credit
Cash (90,000 shares × $25/share)	2,250,000	
Additional paid-in capital	1,350,000	
Common stock		3,600,000

The Volatility Concept

A key component of the value of a company's stock is its volatility, which is the range over which the price varies over time, or is expected to vary. Since an employee holding a stock option can wait for the highest possible stock price before exercising the option, that person will presumably wait for the stock price to peak before exercising the option. Therefore, a stock that has a history or expectation of high volatility is worth more from the perspective of an option holder than one that has little volatility. The result is that a company with high stock price volatility will likely charge more employee compensation to expense for a given number of shares than a company whose stock experiences low volatility.

> **Tip:** It is useful for a publicly-held company to engage in a high level of investor relations activity in order to manage stock price expectations and thereby reduce the volatility of the stock price. Doing so reduces the cost of stock-based compensation, which is based on the level of price volatility.

Stock price volatility is partially driven by the amount of leverage that a company employs in its financing. Thus, if a business uses a large amount of debt to fund its operations, its profit will fluctuate in a wider range than a business that uses less debt, since the extra debt can be used to generate more sales, but the associated interest expense will reduce net profits if revenues decline.

Fair Value Calculation Alternatives

When a publicly-held company issues stock compensation, it can derive fair value from the current market price of its stock, which is readily available. This information is not available to a privately-held organization, for which there is no ready market for its stock. The alternative is to estimate share value based on the historical volatility of a related industry sector index, which is comprised of companies that are similar to the entity conducting the measurement in terms of size, leverage, industry, and so forth. This latter approach is called the *calculated value method*. If a nonpublic company operates in several markets, it is permissible to model its stock price volatility on a weighted average of several related industry sector indexes that approximately mirror the structure of the company, or simply rely upon that industry sector that is most representative of its operations. Broad-based market indexes are not acceptable, since they are not sufficiently closely-related to a specific industry.

EXAMPLE

Abbreviated Corporation is a privately-held company that produces short versions of famous literature. The company grants 60,000 stock options to its editorial staff. The company accountant elects to use the calculated value method to derive a valuation for the stock options. She locates an industry stock price index for publicly-held publishing companies, from which she derives historical stock price volatility of 27%. She plugs this information and other factors into the Black-Scholes-Merton formula to derive a fair value of $3.18 per share. When multiplied by the 60,000 options granted, the result is total compensation expense of $190,800. Forfeitures are expected to be 20%, so the net compensation expense is $152,640. Since the vesting period of the options is three years, the accountant recognizes the net expense at the rate of $50,880 per year, through the vesting period.

When it is not possible to estimate the fair value of an equity instrument, it is permissible to use an alternative valuation technique, as long as it is applied consistently, reflects the key characteristics of the instrument, and is based on accepted standards of financial economic theory. Models that are commonly used to derive fair value are the Black-Scholes-Merton formula and the lattice model. Key characteristics of these models are:

- *Black-Scholes-Merton formula*. Assumes that options are exercised at the end of the arrangement period, and that price volatility, dividends, and interest rates are constant through the term of the option being measured.
- *Lattice model*. Can incorporate ongoing changes in price volatility and dividends over successive time periods in the term of an option. The model assumes that at least two price movements are possible in each measured time period.

EXAMPLE

Armadillo Industries grants an option on $25 stock that will expire in 12 months. The exercise price of the option matches the $25 stock price. Management believes there is a 40% chance that the stock price will increase by 25% during the upcoming year, a 40% chance that the price will decline by 10%, and a 20% chance that the price will decline by 50%. The risk-free interest rate is 5%. The steps required to develop a fair value for the stock option using the lattice model are:

1. Chart the estimated stock price variations.
2. Convert the price variations into the future value of options.
3. Discount the options to their present values.

The following lattice model shows the range and probability of stock prices for the upcoming year:

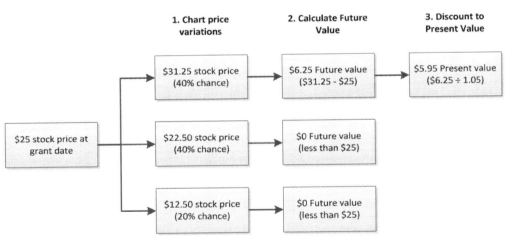

In short, the option will expire unexercised unless the stock price increases. Since there is only a 40% chance of the stock price increasing, the present value of the stock option associated with that scenario can be assigned the following expected present value for purposes of assigning a fair value to the option at the grant date:

$5.95 Option present value × 40% Probability = $2.38 Option value at grant date

It is acceptable to employ a different valuation model to develop the fair value of different equity instruments. It is also permissible to switch valuation methods if the replacement method can yield a better estimate of fair value.

Whatever valuation method is used, it must take into account the exercise price and expected term of the option being measured, the risk-free interest rate over the expected term of the option, and the expected dividends and volatility of the underlying shares. Accounting notes related to these inclusions are:

- *Interest-free rate*. Use the implied yield on U.S. Treasury zero-coupon issuances over the term of the option.
- *Expected term*. The expected term of an option is generally shorter than its contractual term, and can be based on historical experience. Another choice is to estimate the term based upon expected future price points of the under-lying stock.
- *Volatility*. A reasonable way to estimate volatility is the historical pattern of changes in the price of a company's stock, adjusted for anticipated future issues that may impact volatility.
- *Dividends*. Include the historical pattern of changes in dividend payments in the estimation of future dividends.

When developing estimates for these inputs to the valuation model, select the amount that is the most likely; if no value appears to be the most likely, then use an average of the range of possible outcomes.

> **Tip:** From an accounting efficiency perspective, it is useful to aggregate individual awards into homogeneous groups for valuation purposes.

Awards Classified as Equity

In this section, we address a number of variations on how to account for awards that are classified as equity arrangements (that is, the offset to compensation expense is an increase in equity). The bulk of these issues relate to subsequent modifications of existing stock-based awards.

Award Measurement Problems

When it is not possible to reasonably estimate the fair value of a stock-based award at its grant date, continue to remeasure the award at each successive reporting date until the award has been settled. Once the award has been settled, adjust the compensation-to-date associated with the award to the intrinsic value of the award. Intrinsic value is the excess amount of the fair value of a share over the exercise price of an underlying stock option.

Contingent Features

If there is a contingent feature in a stock-based award that allows the recipient to return equity instruments earned or to pay for equity instruments at less than their fair value when sold, account for the feature only if it is actually used.

Award Modifications

If a stock-based award is modified, treat the modification as an exchange of the original award for an entirely new award. Thus, the company is assumed to buy back the original award and exchange it for an award of equal or greater value. The accounting for a modified award includes the following points:

- *Fair value basis.* If there is an incremental change in value between the "old" and "new" awards, this is treated as additional compensation expense. The amount of expense is calculated by determining the fair value of the "old" award immediately prior to the terms modification, and subtracting it from the fair value of the modified award.

- *Intrinsic value basis.* If intrinsic value is being used instead of fair value to calculate the associated cost of compensation, measure the incremental change in value by comparing the intrinsic value of the award just prior to modification with the intrinsic value of the modified award.

- *Short-term inducements.* If the company offers short-term inducements to convince employees to accept an alteration of their stock-based compensation plans, only treat these inducements as modifications if they are accepted by employees.

- *Equity restructuring.* If there is an equity restructuring and awards are replaced with new ones that have the same fair values, do not alter the existing accounting. However, if the fair values have changed, treat the effects of the equity restructuring as a modification.

- *Repurchase of award.* If the company repurchases an award, it should charge the amount of the payment to equity, up to the amount of the fair value of the instruments repurchased. If the amount paid exceeds the fair value of the instruments repurchased, charge the difference to compensation expense.

- *Cancellation and replacement.* If the company cancels a stock-based award and concurrently grants a replacement award or other form of payment, treat these two events as the modification of terms of the original award.

- *Award cancellation.* If the company cancels an award outright, without any offer to replace the award, then accelerate the recognition of any remaining unrecognized compensation expense to the cancellation date.

EXAMPLE

Armadillo Industries issues 10,000 stock options to various employees in 20X1. The designated exercise price of the options is $25, and the vesting period is four years. The total fair value of these options is $20,000, which the company charges to expense ratably over four years, which is $5,000 per year.

One year later, the market price of the stock has declined to $15, so the board of directors decides to modify the options to have an exercise price of $15.

Armadillo incurs additional compensation expense of $30,000 for the amount by which the fair value of the modified options exceeds the fair value of the original options as of the date of the modification. The accounting department adds this additional expense to the remaining $15,000 of compensation expense associated with the original stock options, which is a total unrecognized compensation expense of $45,000. The company recognizes this amount ratably over the remaining three years of vesting, which is $15,000 per year.

Income Tax Effects

If there is a compensation cost associated with the issuance of equity instruments that would normally result in a tax deduction at a future date, it is considered a deductible temporary difference for income tax purposes. If some portion of this compensation cost is capitalized into the cost of an asset (such as inventory or a fixed asset), the capitalized cost is considered part of the tax basis of the asset.

If there is a compensation cost that does not result in a tax deduction, do not treat it as a deductible temporary difference. If a future event will change the treatment of such an item to a tax deduction, wait until the future event occurs before treating the item as a tax deduction.

Awards Classified as Liabilities

A key element of stock-based compensation arrangements is whether these arrangements result in an offsetting increase in equity or liabilities. The following situations indicate the presence of a liability:

- *Cash settlement.* An employee can require the issuing company to settle an option by paying in cash or other assets, rather than stock.
- *Indexing.* An award is indexed to some additional factor, such as the market price of a commodity.
- *Puttable shares.* An employee has the right to require the issuing company to repurchase shares at their fair value, where the put feature essentially allows the employee to avoid the risks associated with owning stock.
- *Share classification.* Certain types of share-based payments, such as mandatorily-redeemable shares, are themselves classified as liabilities.

If an award is classified as a liability, the offsetting expense should be remeasured at its fair value as of the end of each reporting period, until the related service has been completed. Any change in value is to be recognized in the measurement period, adjusted for the percentage of required service rendered through the reporting period. Thus, the measurement date for a liability is the settlement date, not the grant date.

If a company is privately-held, management should make a policy decision to either measure the liabilities incurred under share-based payment arrangements at their fair value or their intrinsic value. Further, if the company is unable to estimate the volatility of its share price, the policy decision is to measure the liabilities based on either the calculated value or intrinsic value of the arrangements.

If an award is modified, treat it as the exchange of the "old" award for a "new" award. However, since the accounting for awards classified as liabilities already provides for the ongoing remeasurement of a liability, there is no need for any additional accounting for a modified award.

EXAMPLE

Uncanny Corporation grants 20,000 stock appreciation rights (SARs) to its chief executive officer (CEO). Each SAR entitles the CEO to receive a cash payment that equates to the increase in value of one share of company stock above a baseline value of $25. The award cliff vests after two years. The fair value of each SAR is calculated to be $11.50 as of the grant date. The entry to record the associated amount of compensation expense for the first year, along with the company's deferred tax asset at its 35% income tax rate, is:

	Debit	Credit
Compensation expense	115,000	
Share-based compensation liability		115,000
Deferred tax asset	40,250	
Deferred tax benefit		40,250

At the end of the first year of vesting, the fair value of each SAR has increased to $12.75, so an additional entry is needed to adjust the vested amount of compensation expense and deferred tax asset for the $12,500 incremental increase in the value of the award over the first year (calculated as $01.25 increase in SAR fair value × 20,000 SARs × 0.5 service period).

At end of the vesting period, the fair value of each SAR has increased again, to $13.00, which increases the total two-year vested compensation expense for the CEO to $260,000. Since $127,500 of compensation expense has already been recognized at the end of the first year, the company must recognize an additional $132,500 of compensation expense, along with the related amount of deferred tax asset. When the cash payment is made to the CEO, the entry is:

	Debit	Credit
Share-based compensation liability	260,000	
Cash		260,000

Employee Share Purchase Plans

A company may offer its employees the opportunity to directly purchase shares in the business through an employee share purchase plan (ESPP). These plans frequently offer sales without any brokerage charge, and possibly also at a price somewhat below the market rate.

From an accounting perspective, the main issue with an ESPP is whether it represents a form of compensation to employees. An ESPP is not considered compensatory if it meets all of the following criteria:

- *Employee qualification.* Essentially all employees meeting a limited set of employment qualifications can participate in the plan.
- *Favorable terms.* The terms offered under the plan are no more favorable than those available to investors at large, or does not offer a purchase discount of greater than five percent (which is considered the per-share cost that would otherwise be required to raise funds through a public offering). It is possible to justify a percentage greater than five percent, but you must reassess the justification on an annual basis.
- *Option features.* The plan only allows a maximum 31-day notice period to enroll in the plan after the share price has been fixed, the share price is based only on the market price on the purchase date, and employees can cancel their participation before the purchase date.

Under the following circumstances, an ESPP is considered to be compensatory, which means that the company must record the difference between the market price of the stock and the lower price at which employees purchase the shares as compensation expense:

- The purchase discount offered under the plan is greater than five percent.
- The purchase price is the lesser of the market price on the grant date or the market price on the purchase date.

EXAMPLE

Armadillo Industries has an employee stock purchase plan, under which employees can purchase shares for a 10% discount from the market price of the company's stock. In the most recent quarter, employees authorized the deduction of $90,000 from their pay, which was used to purchase $100,000 of company stock. Since the discount exceeds the 5% threshold, Armadillo must record the $10,000 discount as compensation expense.

Stock-Based Compensation Disclosures

A company that issues stock-based compensation should disclose sufficient information to ensure that users of its financial statements are aware of the nature of these arrangements, the effect of the resulting compensation cost on the income statement, how the fair value of the services received or instruments granted is derived, and the cash flow effects of these arrangements. Disclosure at this level of detail is not required for interim financial statements.

The following disclosures are considered to be the minimum level of information required to meet the preceding disclosure requirements:

- *General description.* The general terms of the arrangements, including service periods, the maximum term of stock options, and the number of shares authorized for awards.
- *Cash payments.* The cash paid by the company to settle equity instruments that were granted under share-based compensation arrangements.
- *Cash receipts.* The cash paid to the company for the exercise of stock options, and the tax benefit realized from the exercised stock options.
- *Compensation cost not recognized.* As of the latest balance sheet date, the total cost of compensation related to unvested awards not yet recognized, and the weighted-average period over which this cost will be recognized.
- *Compensation cost.* For each year in which an income statement is presented, the aggregate compensation cost recognized that was related to share-based payment arrangements, net of taxes, as well as any amount capitalized. Also, the terms of any modifications and the related change in cost, and the number of employees affected by the modifications.
- *Fair value assumptions.* For each year for which an income statement is presented, the method used to estimate fair value, and the assumptions incorporated into these estimations, including expected option terms (which includes expected employee behavior), expected volatility and how it is estimated, expected dividends, the risk-free rate, and the discount for post-vesting restrictions. A privately-held company should also disclose the industry sector index and how it calculates volatility from that index.
- *Fair values.* For the most recent year, the number and weighted-average grant-date fair values of those stock options nonvested at the beginning and end of the year, and for those granted, vested, and forfeited during the year.
- *Measurement.* The method used to measure compensation cost from these stock-based payment arrangements.
- *Multi-year information.* For each year for which an income statement is presented, the weighted-average grant date fair values of stock options granted, the intrinsic value of options exercised, share-based liabilities paid, and the aggregate fair value of shares vested.
- *Option information.* For the most recent year, the number and weighted-average exercise prices of those stock options at the beginning and end of the year, as well as for those exercisable at year-end, and for those granted, exercised, forfeited, and expired during the year.
- *Policy.* The company policy for issuing shares related to exercised stock options, including the source of the shares (such as treasury stock). If this policy will result in the repurchase of shares in a later period, state the range or estimated amount of shares that will be repurchased.
- *Vested information.* For stock options that have vested or are expected to vest by the balance sheet date, the number of options outstanding, as well as their weighted-average exercise price, aggregate intrinsic value, and weighted-average remaining option term, stated both for options outstanding and options currently exercisable.

EXAMPLE

Armadillo Industries discloses the following information about its stock options as part of its year-end financial statements:

The company's 20X2 employee stock option plan permits the granting of stock options to its employees for up to 2,000,000 shares of common stock. All option awards are granted with an exercise price equal to the market price of Armadillo's stock on the grant date. Option awards vest after four years of service and have 10-year terms. All awards issued thus far vest on an accelerated basis if there is a change in control of the company.

The fair value of all option awards are estimated using a lattice-based model that uses as inputs the assumptions noted in the following table:

	20X2	20X1
Expected dividends	2%	0%
Expected term (years)	4.8 – 7.7	4.3 – 7.2
Expected volatility	30% - 55%	35% - 60%
Weighted-average volatility	45%	47%
Risk-free rate	2.3% - 3.0%	2.5% - 3.2%

The expected term of options granted is based on historical experience; expected volatility ranges are based on the implied volatilities of an industry index of stocks; the risk-free rate is based on the U.S. Treasury yield curve on the grant dates.

Option activity under the Armadillo stock option plan as of December 31, 20X2, and changes during that year are noted in the following table:

Options	Shares (000s)	Weighted-Average Exercise Price	Weighted-Average Remaining Contractual Term	Aggregate Intrinsic Value ($000s)
Outstanding at 1/1/X2	985	$18		
Granted	420	25		
Exercised	-570	17		
Expired or forfeited	-120	23		
Outstanding at 12/31/X2	715	20	5.3	$2,860
Exercisable at 12/31/X2	405	18	4.9	$1,620

The weighted-average grant-date fair value of stock options granted during the years 20X2 and 20X1 were $10.15 and $9.68, respectively. The total intrinsic value of options exercised during the years ended 20X2 and 20X1 were $953,000 and $802,000, respectively.

Nonvested share activity as of December 31, 20X2 and changes during that year are noted in the following table:

Nonvested Shares	Shares (000s)	Weighted-Average Grant-Date Fair Value
Nonvested at 1/1/X1	500	$19.80
Granted	75	24.17
Vested	-120	18.25
Forfeited	-20	23.50
Nonvested at 12/31/X2	435	20.52

As of December 31, 20X2, $8,900,000 of compensation cost related to nonvested share-based compensation arrangements had not yet been recognized. We estimate that this cost will be recognized over a weighted-average period of 4.2 years. The total fair value of shares vested in 20X2 and 20X1 was $2,190,000 and $1,990,000, respectively.

Summary

The measurement of stock-based compensation can be complex, but is not inordinately so, as long as the accounting staff develops a standard procedure for dealing with these arrangements, and follows it consistently. It is also useful to gain the cooperation of the human resources department in formulating compensation arrangements that consistently include the same terms, so that the pre-existing accounting procedures can be readily applied to them. The worst-case scenario is when stock-based compensation plans are issued with substantially different terms, which forces the accounting department to adopt unique and detailed accounting plans to deal with each one. In short, a consistently-applied pay system greatly reduces the effort of accounting for stock-based compensation.

Chapter 14
Accounting for Income Taxes

Introduction

If a company generates a profit, it will probably be necessary to record income tax expense that is a percentage of the profit. However, the calculation of income tax is not so simple, since it may be based on a number of adjustments to net income that are allowed by the taxing authorities. The result can be remarkably complex tax measurements. In this chapter, we describe the general concepts of income tax accounting, as well as the calculation of the appropriate tax rate, the evaluation of tax positions, how to treat deferred taxes, the taxation of undistributed earnings, how to record taxes in interim periods, and other related topics.

Overview of Income Taxes

Before delving into the income taxes topic, we must clarify several concepts that are specific to the income taxes topic, and which are essential to understanding the related accounting. The concepts are:

- *Temporary differences*. A company may record an asset or liability at one value for financial reporting purposes, while maintaining a separate record of a different value for tax purposes. The difference is caused by the tax recognition policies of taxing authorities, who may require the deferral or acceleration of certain items for tax reporting purposes. These differences are temporary, since the assets will eventually be recovered and the liabilities settled, at which point the differences will be terminated. A difference that results in a taxable amount in a later period is called a *taxable temporary difference*, while a difference that results in a deductible amount in a later period is called a *deductible temporary difference*. Examples of temporary differences are:
    - Revenues or gains that are taxable either prior to or after they are recognized in the financial statements. For example, an allowance for doubtful accounts may not be immediately tax deductible, but instead must be deferred until specific receivables are declared bad debts.
    - Expenses or losses that are tax deductible either prior to or after they are recognized in the financial statements. For example, some fixed assets are tax deductible at once, but can only be recognized through long-term depreciation in the financial statements.
    - Assets whose tax basis is reduced by investment tax credits.

EXAMPLE

In its most recent year of operations, Table Furniture earns $250,000. Table also has $30,000 of taxable temporary differences and $80,000 of deductible temporary differences. Based on this information, Table's taxable income in the current year is calculated as:

$250,000 Profit - $30,000 Taxable temporary differences
+ $80,000 Deductible temporary differences
= $300,000 Taxable profit

- *Carrybacks and carryforwards.* A company may find that it has more tax deductions or tax credits (from an operating loss) than it can use in the current year's tax return. If so, it has the option of offsetting these amounts against the taxable income or tax liabilities (respectively) of the tax returns in earlier periods, or in future periods. Carrying these amounts back to the tax returns of prior periods is always more valuable, since the company can apply for a tax refund at once. Thus, these excess tax deductions or tax credits are carried back first, with any remaining amounts being reserved for use in future periods. Carryforwards eventually expire, if not used within a certain number of years. A company should recognize a receivable for the amount of taxes paid in prior years that are refundable due to a carryback. A deferred tax asset can be realized for a carryforward, but possibly with an offsetting valuation allowance that is based on the probability that some portion of the carryforward will not be realized.

EXAMPLE

Spastic Corporation has created $100,000 of deferred tax assets through the diligent generation of losses for the past five years. Based on the company's poor competitive stance, management believes it is more likely than not that there will be inadequate profits (if any) against which the deferred tax assets can be offset. Accordingly, Spastic recognizes a valuation allowance in the amount of $100,000 that fully offsets the deferred tax assets.

- *Deferred tax liabilities and assets.* When there are temporary differences, the result can be deferred tax assets and deferred tax liabilities, which represent the change in taxes payable or refundable in future periods.

EXAMPLE

Armadillo Industries elects to account for a government contract on the percentage of completion method for financial reporting purposes, and on the completed contract method for tax reporting purposes. By doing so, the company recognizes income in its financial statements throughout the term of the contract, but does not do so for tax reporting purposes until the end of the contract.

EXAMPLE

Uncanny Corporation has recorded the following carrying amount and tax basis information for certain of its assets and liabilities:

(000s)	Carrying Amount	Tax Basis	Temporary Difference
Accounts receivable	12,000	12,250	-$250
Prepaid expenses	350	350	0
Inventory	8,000	8,400	-400
Fixed assets	17,300	14,900	2,400
Accounts payable	3,700	3,700	0
Totals	$41,350	$39,600	$1,750

In the table, Uncanny has included a reserve for bad debts in its accounts receivable figure and for obsolete inventory in its inventory number, neither of which are allowed for tax purposes. Also, the company applied an accelerated form of depreciation to its fixed assets for tax purposes and straight-line depreciation for its financial reporting. These three items account for the total temporary difference between the carrying amount and tax basis of the items shown in the table.

All of these factors can result in complex calculations to arrive at the appropriate income tax information to recognize and report in the financial statements.

Accounting for Income Taxes

Despite the complexity inherent in income taxes, the essential accounting in this area is derived from the need to recognize two items, which are:

- *Current year.* The recognition of a tax liability or tax asset, based on the estimated amount of income taxes payable or refundable for the current year.
- *Future years.* The recognition of a deferred tax liability or tax asset, based on the estimated effects in future years of carryforwards and temporary differences.

Based on the preceding points, the general accounting for income taxes is:

+/-	Create a tax liability for estimated taxes payable, and/or create a tax asset for tax refunds, that relate to the current or prior years
+/-	Create a deferred tax liability for estimated future taxes payable, and/or create a deferred tax asset for estimated future tax refunds, that can be attributed to temporary differences and carryforwards
=	Total income tax expense in the period

Tax Positions

A tax position is a stance taken by a company in its tax return that measures tax assets and liabilities, and which results in the permanent reduction or temporary deferral of income taxes. When constructing the proper accounting for a tax position, the accountant follows these steps:

1. Evaluate whether the tax position taken has merit, based on the tax regulations.
2. If the tax position has merit, measure the amount that can be recognized in the financial statements.
3. Determine the probability and amount of settlement with the taxing authorities. Recognition should only be made when it is more likely than not (i.e., more than 50% probability) that the company's tax position will be sustained once it has been examined by the governing tax authorities.
4. Recognize the tax position, if warranted.

Tip: Given the considerable financial impact of some tax positions, it makes sense to obtain an outside opinion of a proposed position by a tax expert, and document the results of that review thoroughly. This is helpful not only if the position is reviewed by the taxing authorities, but also when it is reviewed by the company's outside auditors.

EXAMPLE

Armadillo Industries takes a tax position on an issue and determines that the position qualifies for recognition, and so should be recognized. The following table shows the estimated possible outcomes of the tax position, along with their associated probabilities:

Possible Outcome	Probability of Occurrence	Cumulative Probability
$250,000	5%	5%
200,000	20%	25%
150,000	40%	65%
100,000	20%	85%
50,000	10%	95%
0	5%	100%

Since the benefit amount just beyond the 50% threshold level is $150,000, Armadillo should recognize a tax benefit of $150,000.

If a company initially concludes that the probability of a tax position being sustained is less than 50%, it should not initially recognize the tax position. However, it can recognize the position at a later date if the probability increases to be in excess of 50%, or if the tax position is settled through interaction with the taxing authorities, or the statute of limitations keeps the taxing authorities from challenging the tax position. If a company subsequently concludes that it will change a tax position previously taken, it should recognize the effect of the change in the period in which it alters its tax position. An entity can also derecognize a tax position that it had previously recognized if the probability of the tax position being sustained drops below 50%.

EXAMPLE

Armadillo Industries takes a tax position under which it accelerates the depreciation of certain production equipment well beyond the normally-allowed taxable rate, resulting in a deferred tax liability after three years of $120,000.

After three years, a tax court ruling convinces Armadillo management that its tax position is untenable. Consequently, the company recognizes a tax liability for the $120,000 temporary difference. At the company's current 35% tax rate, this results in increased taxes of $42,000 and the elimination of the temporary difference.

If there is a change in the tax laws or tax rates, a business cannot recognize alterations in its income tax liability in advance of the enactment of these laws and rates. Instead, the company must wait until enactment has been completed, and can then recognize the changes on the enactment date.

Deferred Tax Expense

Deferred tax expense is the net change in the deferred tax liabilities and assets of a business during a period of time. The amount of deferred taxes should be compiled for each tax-paying component of a business that provides a consolidated tax return. Doing so requires that the business complete the following steps:

1. Identify the existing temporary differences and carryforwards.
2. Determine the deferred tax liability amount for those temporary differences that are taxable, using the applicable tax rate.
3. Determine the deferred tax asset amount for those temporary differences that are deductible, as well as any operating loss carryforwards, using the applicable tax rate.
4. Determine the deferred tax asset amount for any carryforwards involving tax credits.
5. Create a valuation allowance for the deferred tax assets if there is a more than 50% probability that the company will not realize some portion of these assets. Any changes to this allowance are to be recorded within income from continuing operations on the income statement. The need for a valuation allowance is especially likely if a business has a history of letting various carryforwards expire unused, or it expects to incur losses in the next few years.

Applicable Tax Rate

In general, when measuring a deferred tax liability or asset, a business should use the tax rate that it expects to apply to the taxable income that results from the realization of deferred tax assets or settlement of deferred tax liabilities. Also consider the following issues:

- *Alternative minimum tax.* The alternative minimum tax may increase the effective tax rate used. It may be necessary to reduce the deferred tax asset for the alternative minimum tax credit carryforward with a valuation allowance, if it is more than 50% probable that the asset will not be realized.
- *Discounting.* Deferred taxes are not to be discounted to their present value when they are recognized.
- *Graduated tax rates.* If the applicable tax law has graduated tax rates, and the graduated rates significantly affect the average tax rate paid, use the average tax rate that applies to the estimated annual taxable income in those periods when deferred tax liabilities are settled or deferred tax assets are realized. If a company earns such a large amount of income that the graduated rate is not significantly different from the top-tier tax rate, use the top-tier rate for the estimation of annual taxable income.
- *New tax laws or rates.* A company should adjust the amount of its deferred tax liabilities and assets for the effect of any changes in tax laws or tax rates, which shall be recorded within income from continuing operations. Doing so may also call for an adjustment to the related valuation allowance.

Interest and Penalties

When there is a requirement in the tax law that interest be paid when income taxes are not fully paid, a company should begin recognizing the amount of this interest expense as soon as the expense would be scheduled to begin accruing under the tax law.

If a company takes a tax position that will incur penalties, it should recognize the related penalty expense as soon as the company takes the position in a tax return. Whether penalties should be recognized may depend on management's judgment of whether a tax position exceeds the minimum statutory threshold required to avoid the payment of a penalty.

If a tax position is eventually sustained, reverse in the current period any related interest and penalties that had been accrued in previous periods under the expectation that the position would not be sustained.

Intraperiod Tax Allocation

Intraperiod tax allocation is the allocation of income taxes to different parts of the results appearing in the income statement of a business, so that some items are stated net of tax. Income taxes are allocated among the following items:

- Continuing operations
- Discontinued operations

- Extraordinary items
- Other comprehensive income
- Items assigned directly to shareholders' equity

The intraperiod tax allocation concept is used to reveal the "true" results of certain transactions net of all effects, rather than disaggregating them from income taxes. For example, a company records an extraordinary gain of $1 million. Its tax rate is 35%, so the company reports the extraordinary gain net of taxes, at $650,000.

When allocating income taxes among the various income statement items just noted, allocate the taxes using either of the following methodologies:

- *One allocation target*. First assign income taxes to continuing operations, and then assign all remaining income taxes to the remaining allocation target.
- *Multiple allocation targets*. First assign income taxes to continuing operations, and then assign the remaining income taxes to the other items in proportion to their individual impact on the amount of remaining income taxes.

Note that, though the income tax included in these net calculations is usually an expense, it may also be a credit, so that any of the preceding items presented net of tax would include the tax credit.

Most elements of the income statement are not presented net of the intraperiod tax allocation. For example, revenue, the cost of goods sold, and administrative expenses are not presented net of income taxes.

EXAMPLE

Uncanny Corporation earns $500,000 of income from continuing operations, and experiences a loss of $150,000 from a discontinued operation. At the beginning of the year, Uncanny had a $600,000 tax loss carryforward. Uncanny applies the tax loss carryforward against the $500,000 income from continuing operations. Since the offset eliminates the $500,000 of income from operations, no income tax is applied to it. The company then applies the remaining $100,000 of tax loss carryforward against the loss from a discontinued operation, leaving $50,000 of taxable loss to be reported for the discontinued operation.

Taxes Related to Undistributed Earnings

There are a few instances where a business is not required to engage in the standard accounting and disclosure of deferred income taxes for temporary differences. These exceptions relate to investments in subsidiaries and corporate joint ventures, and whether they remit earnings to the corporate parent or investors, respectively.

A corporate subsidiary typically remits earnings to the parent entity only after a number of issues have been considered, such as the need for cash by the subsidiary and parent, tax issues, and creditor and government restrictions. Funds may be remitted from a corporate joint venture based on the payout clauses in the original joint venture agreement, or with the agreement of the investing parties. In many situations, no funds are remitted, or only a small portion of the full amount of earnings.

Generally, the accounting for these undistributed earnings is to include them in the earnings of the parent entity, which results in a temporary difference, unless there is a means by which an investment in a domestic subsidiary can be recovered, free of tax. The same accounting approach applies to the pretax income of corporate joint ventures that are unlikely to be remitted to investors, and where the investors account for their investments in the joint ventures with the equity method.

A corporate joint venture may have a limited life span that will likely trigger the release of undistributed earnings to investors at the end of that lifespan. If so, investors should record deferred taxes when the profits or losses of the venture are recorded in its financial statements.

An investor entity should record a deferred tax liability when there is an excess of the reported taxable temporary difference over the tax basis:

- Of an investment in a domestic subsidiary
- In an investee that is ≤ 50% owned

A temporary difference is not considered a taxable temporary difference when there is a method permitted under the tax law for recovering the amount of an investment tax-free, *and* the investing entity expects to use that method. For example, it is possible to do so under certain types of acquisition structures, such as when a subsidiary is merged into the parent company, with noncontrolling shareholders receiving the stock of the parent company in exchange for their shares in the subsidiary.

When there is an excess of tax basis for an investment in a subsidiary or joint venture over the amount recorded in the financial statements, and the temporary difference will reverse in the foreseeable future, the corporate parent or investor should recognize a deferred tax asset in the amount of the difference. For example, the decision to sell a subsidiary would make it likely that a temporary difference will reverse in the near future.

The tax benefit associated with a deferred tax asset should be recognized when it is more than 50% probable that the temporary difference will reverse in the foreseeable future. Similarly, a tax expense should be recognized when it is more than 50% probable that a deferred tax liability will reverse in the foreseeable future.

It may be necessary to create a valuation allowance that will offset a deferred tax asset. The amount of this allowance (if any) shall be based on a periodic assessment of the allowance.

The parent entity should *not* accrue income taxes for unremitted earnings only in those situations where a subsidiary will permanently retain its earnings (which requires a reinvestment plan), or where the remittance will involve a tax-free liquidation. If circumstances change, and it appears that some portion of a subsidiary's undistributed earnings will be remitted, the parent should accrue income taxes related to the amount that will be remitted. If the reverse situation arises, where it no longer appears likely that earnings will be remitted, reduce the amount of income tax expense that had been previously recognized.

Interim Reporting

If a business reports its financial results during interim reporting periods (such as monthly or quarterly financial statements), it must report income taxes in those interim reports. In general, the proper accounting is to report income taxes using an estimated effective tax rate in all of the interim periods. However, the application of this general principle varies somewhat as noted below:

- *Ordinary income.* Calculate the income tax on ordinary income at the estimated annual effective tax rate.
- *Other items.* Calculate and recognize the income tax on all items other than ordinary income at the rates that are applicable when the items occur. This means that the related tax effect is recognized in the period in which the underlying items occur.

The following factors apply to the determination of the estimated annual effective tax rate:

- The tax benefit associated with any applicable operating loss carryforward
- The tax effect of any valuation allowance used to offset the deferred tax asset
- Anticipated investment tax credits (for the amount expected to be used within the year)
- Foreign tax rates
- Capital gains rates
- The effects of new tax legislation, though only after it has been passed
- Other applicable factors

EXAMPLE

In the current fiscal year, Armadillo Industries anticipates $1,000,000 of ordinary income, to which will be applied the statutory tax rate of 40%, which will result in an income tax expense of $400,000. Armadillo also expects to take advantage of a $100,000 investment tax credit. Thus, the effective tax rate for the year is expected to be 30%, which is calculated as $300,000 of net taxes, divided by $1,000,000 of ordinary income.

Do not include in the determination of the estimated annual effective tax rate the effect of taxes related to unusual or extraordinary items or discontinued operations that are expected to be reported separately in the financial statements.

The estimated tax rate is to be reviewed at the end of each interim period and adjusted as necessary, based on the latest estimates of taxable income to be reported for the full year. If it is not possible to derive an estimated tax rate, it may be necessary to instead use the actual effective tax rate for the year to date.

If the estimated tax rate is revised in an interim period from the rate used in a prior period, use the new estimate to derive the year-to-date tax on ordinary income for all interim periods to date.

The tax benefit associated with a loss recorded in an earlier interim period may not be recognized, on the grounds that it is less than 50% probable that the benefit will be realized. If so, do not recognize any income tax for ordinary income reported in subsequent periods until the unrecognized tax benefit associated with the original loss has been offset with income.

EXAMPLE

Through its first two quarters, Uncanny Corporation has experienced losses of $400,000 and $600,000. Management concludes that it is more likely than not that the tax benefit associated with these losses will not be realized. The company then earns profits in the third and fourth quarters, resulting in the following application of taxes at the statutory 40% corporate rate:

(000s)	Ordinary Income Current Period	Ordinary Income Cumulative	Cumulative Tax (40%)	Less Previous Amount	Tax Provision
Quarter 1	-$400	-$400	--	---	--
Quarter 2	-600	-1,000	--	---	--
Quarter 3	1,100	100	$40	---	$40
Quarter 4	300	400	160	$40	120
Totals	$400				$160

If a company records a loss during an interim period, the company should only recognize the tax effects of the loss (i.e., a corresponding reduction in taxes) when there is an expectation that the tax reduction will be realized later in the year, or will be recognized as a deferred tax asset by year-end. This recognition may occur later in the year, if it later becomes more likely than not that the tax effects of the loss can be realized.

EXAMPLE

Uncanny Corporation has a history of recording losses in its first and second quarters, after which sales increase during the summer and winter holiday seasons. In the first half of the current year, Uncanny records a $1,000,000 loss, but expects a $2,000,000 profit in the final half of the year. Based on the company's history of seasonal sales, realization of the tax loss appears to be more likely than not, so Uncanny records the tax effect of the loss in the first half of the year.

If a business is subject to a variety of tax rates because of its operations in multiple tax jurisdictions, the estimated tax rate shall be based on a single tax rate for the entire company. When developing the single company-wide tax rate, exclude the effects of ordinary losses within jurisdictions, and develop a separate estimated tax rate for those jurisdictions. Also, if it is impossible to estimate a tax rate or ordinary income in a foreign jurisdiction, exclude that jurisdiction from the computation of the company-wide tax rate.

A company may decide to record a change in accounting principle. If so, the amount of the change included in retained earnings at the beginning of the fiscal year shall include the effect of the applicable amount of tax expense or benefit, employing the tax rate used for the full fiscal year. If the change in principle is made in an interim period other than the first interim period of a fiscal year, retrospectively apply the change to the preceding interim periods in the same year; when doing so, apply the estimated tax rate that originally applied to those periods, modified for the effects of the change in principle.

Income Taxes Presentation

The following income tax issues can affect the presentation of tax information in the financial statements:

- *Deferred tax accounts*. Separately classify deferred tax assets and deferred tax liabilities as current and noncurrent amounts.
- *Interest and penalties*. Any recognized interest expense related to tax positions can be classified within either the interest expense or income taxes line items. Any penalties expense related to tax positions can be classified within either the income taxes or some other expense line items.
- *Intraperiod tax allocation*. If income taxes are being allocated among income statement line items in an interim period, allocate taxes based on the estimated amount of annual ordinary income, plus other items that have occurred during the year to date.
- *Netting*. Within a tax jurisdiction for a single entity, it is permissible to net the current deferred tax assets and current deferred tax liabilities; you can also net the noncurrent deferred tax assets and the noncurrent deferred tax liabilities. Do not net those deferred tax assets and deferred tax liabilities that are attributed to unrelated tax jurisdictions or components of the business.
- *Tax status*. If there is a change in the tax status of an entity, record the change within the income from continuing operations section of the income statement.
- *Undistributed earnings*. All changes in the income tax accruals related to undistributed earnings from subsidiaries and joint ventures should be recorded in the income tax expense line item, not as extraordinary items.
- *Valuation allowance*. Allocate on a pro rata basis the valuation allowance (if any) between current and noncurrent deferred tax assets.

Income Taxes Disclosure

A business should disclose the following information in its financial statements that relates to income taxes, broken down by where the information should be disclosed.

Balance Sheet

The following information about income taxes should be disclosed within the balance sheet or the accompany notes:

- *Carryforwards.* The amounts of all operating loss carryforwards and tax credit carryforwards, as well as their related expiration dates.
- *Deferrals.* The total of all deferred tax liabilities, the total of all deferred tax assets, and the total valuation allowance associated with the deferred tax assets. Also disclose the net change in the valuation allowance during the year.
- *Tax status.* A change in tax status, if the change occurred after the end of the reporting year but before the related financial statements have been issued or are available to be issued.
- *Temporary differences and carryforwards.* The types of significant temporary differences and carryforwards, if the company is not publicly-held. If the entity is publicly-held, it must also disclose the tax effect of each temporary difference and carryforward that causes a significant part of the reported deferred tax assets and liabilities.
- *Valuation allowance.* That portion of the valuation allowance (if any) related to deferred tax assets for which recognized tax benefits are to be credited to contributed capital (such as a deductible expenditure that reduces the proceeds from a stock issuance).

EXAMPLE

Armadillo Industries discloses the following information about the realizability of its deferred tax assets:

The company has recorded a $10 million deferred tax asset, which reflects the $25 million benefit to be derived from loss carryforwards. These carryforwards expire during the period 20X5 to 20X9. The realization of this tax asset is dependent upon the company generating a sufficient amount of taxable income before the loss carryforwards expire. Management believes it is more likely than not that all $10 million of the deferred tax asset will be realized.

Income Statement

The following information about income taxes should be disclosed within the income statement or the accompanying notes:

- *Comparison to statutory rate.* The nature of significant reasons why the reported income tax differs from the statutory tax rate, for a privately-held company. Also, expand the discussion to a numerical reconciliation, if the entity is publicly-held.
- *Interest and penalties.* The amount of interest and penalties recognized in the period.

- *Tax allocations.* The income tax amount allocated to continuing operations and to other items.
- *Tax components.* The components of income taxes attributable to continuing operations, including the current tax expense, deferred tax expense, investment tax credits, government grants, benefits related to operating loss carryforwards, the tax expense resulting from the allocation of tax benefits to contributed capital, adjustments related to enacted tax laws or rates, adjustments from a change in tax status, and adjustments to the beginning valuation allowance.

EXAMPLE

Armadillo Industries discloses the following information about its income taxes in the notes accompanying its financial statements:

(000s)	
Current tax expense	$810
Deferred tax expense	1,240
Tax expense from continuing operations	$2,050
Tax expense at statutory rate	$2,250
Benefit of investment tax credits	-80
Benefit of operating loss carryforwards	-120
Tax expense from continuing operations	$2,050

Other

The following disclosures are not associated with a particular financial statement. They must be disclosed as part of the general set of financial statements.

- *Examination years.* The tax years remaining that are subject to examination by taxing authorities.
- *Impact on tax rate.* If the entity is publicly-held, the amount of unrecognized tax benefits that would impact the effective tax rate if they were recognized.
- *Interim period tax variations.* If the application of accounting standards for income taxes in interim periods results in a significant variation from the usual income tax percentage, state the reasons for the variation.
- *Policies.* The policy for the classification of interest and penalty expenses. Also, the policy for the methods used to account for investment tax credits.
- *Tax holiday.* If the entity is publicly-held, the aggregate and per-share effect of a tax holiday, a description of the circumstances, and when the tax holiday will end.
- *Undistributed earnings.* Whenever a deferred tax liability is not recognized, disclose the following:
  - Description of the underlying temporary differences, and what would cause them to be taxable

- o The cumulative amount of each temporary difference
- o The amount related to permanent investments in foreign subsidiaries and foreign joint ventures, or a statement that the amount cannot be determined
- o The amount related to permanent investment in domestic subsidiaries and domestic joint ventures
- *Unrecognized tax benefits reconciliation.* If the entity is publicly-held, a tabular reconciliation of unrecognized tax changes during the period, including changes caused by tax positions taken in the current period and separately for the prior period, decreases based on settlements concluded, and any decreases caused by a lapse in the statute of limitations.

EXAMPLE

Uncanny Corporation discloses the following reconciliation of its unrecognized tax benefits:

(000s)	20X4	20X3
Balance at January 1	$5,170	$4,080
Additions based on tax positions related to the current year	880	1,530
Additions for tax positions of prior years	240	930
Reductions for tax positions of prior years	-390	-570
Settlements	-2,810	-800
Balance at December 31	$3,090	$5,170

- *Unrecognized tax benefits.* If unrecognized tax benefits are expected to change significantly within the next 12 months, the reason for the change, the type of event that will cause the change, and the estimated range of the change (or a statement that the range cannot be estimated).

Summary

Many accountants consider income tax accounting to be an area best left to a tax specialist, who churns through the information provided and creates a set of tax-related journal entries. While this approach should result in accurate tax accounting, it does not give management a good view of how its actions are affecting the taxes the company is paying – instead, the tax accounting function is treated as a black box whose contents are unknown to all, save the tax specialist who guards it.

A better approach is to engage the management team in tax planning by instructing them on the essential tax issues that can be impacted by strategic and tactical decisions. Even if management does not become conversant at a detailed level in how their actions impact income taxes, they will at least know when to call in a tax expert to advise them. Thus, a certain amount of transparency in the tax area can improve the results of a business.

Chapter 15
Accounting for Business Combinations

Introduction

The business combination, or acquisition, is a relatively uncommon event that entails a considerable amount of detailed accounting. At its least-complex level, the accounting involves the allocation of the purchase price to the acquiree's assets and liabilities, with any overage assigned to a goodwill asset. However, there are a multitude of additional issues that may apply, such as noncontrolling interests, reverse acquisitions, asset purchases, pushdown accounting, income taxes, and more. This chapter deals with the accounting required for all of these issues.

Overview of Business Combinations

A business combination has occurred when a group of assets acquired and liabilities assumed constitute a business. A business exists when processes are applied to inputs to create outputs. Examples of inputs are fixed assets, intellectual property, inventory, and employees. An output is considered to have the ability to generate a return to investors.

A business combination must be accounted for using the *acquisition method.* This method requires the following steps:

1. *Identify the acquirer.* The entity that gains control of the acquiree is the acquirer. This is typically the entity that pays assets or incurs liabilities as a result of a transaction, or whose owners receive the largest portion of the voting rights in the combined entity. If a variable interest entity is acquired, the main beneficiary of that entity is the acquirer. One of the combining entities must be the acquirer.
2. *Determine the acquisition date.* The acquisition date is when the acquirer gains control of the acquiree, which is typically the closing date.
3. *Recognize and measure all assets acquired and liabilities assumed.* These measurements should be at the fair values of the acquired assets and liabilities as of the acquisition date.
4. *Recognize any noncontrolling interest in the acquiree.* The amount recognized should be the fair value of the noncontrolling interest.
5. *Recognize and measure any goodwill or gain from a bargain purchase.* See the Goodwill or Gain from Bargain Purchase section for a discussion of goodwill and bargain purchases.

There are two types of business combinations that can result in some modification of the preceding accounting treatment. These types are:

- *Step acquisition.* A business may already own a minority interest in another entity, and then acquires an additional equity interest at a later date that results in an acquisition event. In this situation, the acquirer measures the fair value of its existing equity interest in the acquiree at the acquisition date, and recognizes a gain or loss in earnings at that time. If some of this gain or loss had previously been recognized in other comprehensive income, reclassify it into earnings.
- *No transfer of consideration.* There are rare cases where no consideration is paid while gaining control of an acquiree, such as when the acquiree repurchases enough of its own shares to raise an existing investor into a majority ownership position. In this situation, recognize and measure the noncontrolling interest(s) in the acquiree.

There are a number of additional issues that can affect the accounting for a business combination, as outlined below:

- *Contingent consideration.* Some portion of the consideration paid to the owners of the acquiree may be contingent upon future events or circumstances. If an event occurs after the acquisition date that alters the amount of consideration paid, such as meeting a profit or cash flow target, the accounting varies depending on the type of underlying consideration paid, as noted next:
  - *Asset or liability consideration.* If the consideration paid is with assets or liabilities, remeasure these items at their fair values until such time as the related consideration has been fully resolved, and recognize the related gains or losses in earnings.
  - *Equity consideration.* If the consideration paid is in equity, do not remeasure the amount of equity paid.
- *Provisional accounting.* If the accounting for a business combination is incomplete at the end of a reporting period, report provisional amounts, and later adjust these amounts to reflect information that existed as of the acquisition date.
- *New information.* If new information becomes available about issues that existed at the acquisition date concerning the acquiree, adjust the recordation of assets and liabilities, as appropriate.

EXAMPLE

Armadillo Industries acquires Cleveland Container on December 31, 20X3. Armadillo hires an independent appraiser to value Cleveland, but does not expect a valuation report for three months. In the meantime, Armadillo issues its December 31 financial statements with a provisional fair value of $4,500,000 for the acquisition. Three months later, the appraiser reports a valuation of $4,750,000 as of the acquisition date, based on an unexpectedly high valuation for a number of fixed assets.

In Armadillo's March 31 financial statements, it retrospectively adjusts the prior-year information to increase the carrying amount of fixed assets by $250,000, as well as to reduce the amount of goodwill by the same amount.

Any changes to the initial accounting for an acquisition must be offset against the recorded amount of goodwill. These changes to the initial provisional amounts should be recorded retrospectively, as though all accounting for the acquisition had been finalized at the acquisition date.

The measurement period during which the recordation of an acquisition may be adjusted ends as soon as the acquirer receives all remaining information concerning issues existing as of the acquisition date, not to exceed one year from the acquisition date.

The acquirer will probably incur a number of costs related to an acquisition, such as fees for valuations, legal advice, accounting services, and finder's fees. These costs are to be charged to expense as incurred.

Identifiable Assets and Liabilities, and Noncontrolling Interests

When the acquirer recognizes an acquisition transaction, it should recognize identifiable assets and liabilities separately from goodwill, and at their fair values as of the acquisition date. The following special situations also apply:

- No asset or liability is recognized in relation to an acquired operating lease in which the acquiree is the lessee, except to the extent of any favorable or unfavorable lease feature relative to market terms, or the willingness of third parties to acquire a lease even at market rates.
- Do not include any costs that the acquirer expects to incur in the future, but is not obligated to incur in relation to the acquiree, such as possible employee relocation costs.

It is entirely possible that the acquirer will recognize assets and liabilities that the acquiree had never recorded in its own accounting records. In particular, the acquirer will likely assign value to a variety of intangible assets that the acquiree may have developed internally, and so was constrained by GAAP from recognizing as assets. Examples of intangible assets are:

Broadcast rights	Internet domain names	Noncompetition agreements
Computer software	Lease agreements	Order backlog
Customer lists	Licensing agreements	Patented technology
Customer relationships	Literary works	Pictures
Employment contracts	Motion pictures	Service contracts
Franchise agreements	Musical works	Trademarks

A key intangible asset for which GAAP does not allow separate recognition is the concept of the assembled workforce, which is the collected knowledge and experience of company employees. This intangible must be included in the goodwill asset.

The accounting treatment for special cases related to the recognition of assets and liabilities is as follows:

- *Contingency fair value not determinable.* It is quite common for a contingent asset or liability to not be measurable on the acquisition date, since these items have not yet been resolved. If so, only recognize them if the amount can be reasonably estimated, and events during the measurement period confirm that an asset or liability existed at the acquisition date.
- *Defined benefit pension plan.* If the acquiree sponsored a defined benefit pension plan, the acquirer should recognize an asset or liability that reflects the funding status of that plan.
- *Indemnification clause.* The seller of the acquiree may agree to an indemnification clause in the acquisition agreement, whereby it will indemnify the acquirer for changes in the value of certain assets or liabilities, such as for unusual bad debt losses from receivables in existence at the acquisition date. In these cases, the seller recognizes an indemnification asset when it recognizes a loss on an item to be indemnified; this should be retrospectively applied as of the acquisition date.

Tip: Realistically, if you are still attempting to establish a valuation for assets and liabilities more than a few months after an acquisition, they probably had no value at the acquisition date, and so should not be recognized as part of the acquisition.

Acquired assets and liabilities are supposed to be measured at their fair values as of the acquisition date. Fair value measurement can be quite difficult, and may call for different valuation approaches, as noted below:

- *Alternative use assets.* Even if the acquirer does not intend to apply an asset to its best use (or use the asset at all), the fair value of the asset should still be derived as though it were being applied to its best use. This guidance also applies to situations where an asset is acquired simply to prevent it from being used by competitors.
- *Assets where acquiree is the lessor.* If the acquiree owns assets that it leases to a third party (such as a building lease), derive fair values for these assets in the normal manner, irrespective of the existence of the lease.
- *Fair value exceptions.* There are exceptions to the general rule of recognizing acquired assets and liabilities at their fair values. The GAAP related to the recognition of income taxes, employee benefits, indemnification assets, reacquired rights, share-based awards, assets held for sale, and certain contingency situations overrides the use of fair value.
- *Noncontrolling interest.* The best way to measure the fair value of a noncontrolling interest is based on the market price of the acquiree's stock. However, this information is not available for privately-held companies, so alternative valuation methods are allowed. This valuation may differ from

the valuation assigned to the acquirer, since the acquirer also benefits from gaining control over the entity, which results in a control premium.

- *Valuation allowances.* Some assets, such as receivables and inventory, are normally paired with a valuation allowance. The valuation allowance is not used when deriving fair values for these assets, since the fair value should already incorporate a valuation allowance.

A few assets and liabilities that are initially measured as part of an acquisition require special accounting during subsequent periods. These items are:

- *Contingencies.* If an asset or liability was originally recognized as part of an acquisition, derive a systematic and consistently-applied approach to measuring it in future periods.
- *Indemnifications.* Reassess all indemnification assets and the loss items with which they are paired in each subsequent reporting period, and adjust the recorded amounts as necessary until the indemnifications are resolved.
- *Reacquired rights.* An acquirer may regain control over a legal right that it had extended to the acquiree prior to the acquisition date. If these reacquired rights were initially recognized as an intangible asset as part of the acquisition accounting, amortize the asset over the remaining period of the contract that the acquiree had with the acquirer.
- *Leasehold improvements.* If the acquirer acquires leasehold improvement assets as part of an acquisition, amortize them over the lesser of the useful life of the assets or the remaining reasonably assured lease periods and renewals.

Tip: The amortization period for leasehold improvements may be a significant issue for the acquirer, if it intends to shut down acquiree leases as soon as practicable. Doing so may accelerate the recognition of leasehold improvement assets.

The Securities and Exchange Commission (SEC) does not allow use of the residual method in deriving the value of intangible assets. The residual method is the two-step process of first assigning the purchase price to all identifiable assets, and then allocating the remaining residual amount to other intangible assets. This SEC guidance only applies to publicly-held companies.

Goodwill or Gain from Bargain Purchase

This section addresses the almost inevitable calculation of goodwill that is associated with most acquisitions. It also addresses the considerably less common recognition of a bargain purchase.

Goodwill Calculation

Goodwill is an intangible asset that represents the future benefits arising from assets acquired in a business combination that are not otherwise identified. Goodwill is a common element in most acquisition transactions, since the owners of acquirees generally do not part with their companies unless they are paid a premium.

The acquirer must recognize goodwill as an asset as of the acquisition date. The goodwill calculation is as follows:

$$\text{Goodwill} = (\text{Consideration paid} + \text{Fair value of noncontrolling interest}) \\ - (\text{Assets acquired} - \text{Liabilities assumed})$$

If no consideration is transferred in an acquisition transaction, use a valuation method to determine the fair value of the acquirer's interest in the acquiree as a replacement value.

When calculating the total amount of consideration paid as part of the derivation of goodwill, consider the following additional factors:

- *Fair value of assets paid.* When the acquirer transfers its assets to the owners of the acquiree as payment for the acquiree, measure this consideration at its fair value. If there is a difference between the fair value and carrying amount of these assets as of the acquisition date, record a gain or loss in earnings to reflect the difference. However, if these assets are simply being transferred to the acquiree entity (which the acquirer now controls), do not restate these assets to their fair value; this means there is no recognition of a gain or loss.
- *Share-based payment awards.* The acquirer may agree to swap the share-based payment awards granted to employees of the acquiree for payment awards based on the shares of the acquirer. If the acquirer must replace awards made by the acquiree, include the fair value of these awards in the consideration paid by the acquirer, where the portion attributable to pre-acquisition employee service is considered consideration paid for the acquiree. If the acquirer is not obligated to replace these awards but does so anyways, record the cost of the replacement awards as compensation expense.

Bargain Purchase

When an acquirer gains control of an acquiree whose fair value is greater than the consideration paid for it, the acquirer is said to have completed a bargain purchase. A bargain purchase transaction most commonly arises when a business must be sold due to a liquidity crisis, where the short-term nature of the sale tends to result in a less-than-optimum sale price from the perspective of the owners of the acquiree. To account for a bargain purchase, follow these steps:

1. Record all assets and liabilities at their fair values.
2. Reassess whether all assets and liabilities have been recorded.
3. Determine and record the fair value of any contingent consideration to be paid to the owners of the acquiree.
4. Record any remaining difference between these fair values and the consideration paid as a gain in earnings. Record this gain as of the acquisition date.

EXAMPLE

The owners of Failsafe Containment have to rush the sale of the business in order to obtain funds for estate taxes, and so agree to a below-market sale to Armadillo Industries for $5,000,000 in cash of a 75% interest in Failsafe. Armadillo hires a valuation firm to analyze the assets and liabilities of Failsafe, and concludes that the fair value of its net assets is $7,000,000 (of which $8,000,000 is assets and $1,000,000 is liabilities), and the fair value of the 25% of Failsafe still retained by its original owners has a fair value of $1,500,000.

Since the fair value of the net assets of Failsafe exceeds the consideration paid and the fair value of the noncontrolling interest in the company, Armadillo must recognize a gain in earnings, which is calculated as follows:

$7,000,000 Net assets - $5,000,000 Consideration - $1,500,000 Noncontrolling interest
= $500,000 Gain on bargain purchase

Armadillo records the transaction with the following entry:

	Debit	Credit
Assets acquired	8,000,000	
Cash		5,000,000
Liabilities assumed		1,000,000
Gain on bargain purchase		500,000
Equity – noncontrolling interest in Failsafe		1,500,000

Reverse Acquisitions

A reverse acquisition occurs when the legal acquirer is actually the acquiree for accounting purposes. The reverse acquisition concept is most commonly used when a privately-held business buys a public shell company for the purposes of rolling itself into the shell and thereby becoming a publicly-held company. This approach is used to avoid the expense of engaging in an initial public offering.

To conduct a reverse acquisition, the legal acquirer issues its shares to the owners of the legal acquiree (which is the accounting acquirer). The fair value of this consideration is derived from the fair value amount of equity the legal acquiree would have had to issue to the legal acquirer to give the owners of the legal acquirer an equivalent percentage ownership in the combined entity.

When a reverse acquisition occurs, the legal acquiree may have owners who do not choose to exchange their shares in the legal acquiree for shares in the legal acquirer. These owners are considered a noncontrolling interest in the consolidated financial statements of the legal acquirer. The carrying amount of this noncontrolling interest is based on the proportionate interest of the noncontrolling shareholders in the net asset carrying amounts of the legal acquiree prior to the business combination.

EXAMPLE

The management of High Noon Armaments wants to take their company public through a reverse acquisition transaction with a public shell company, Peaceful Pottery. The transaction is completed on January 1, 20X4. The balance sheets of the two entities on the acquisition date are as follows:

	Peaceful (Legal Acquirer, Accounting Acquiree)	High Noon (Legal Subsidiary, Accounting Acquirer)
Total assets	$100	$8,000
Total liabilities	$0	$4,500
Shareholders' equity		
Retained earnings	10	3,000
Common stock		
100 shares	90	
1,000 shares		500
Total shareholders' equity	100	3,500
Total liabilities and shareholders' equity	$100	$8,000

On January 1, Peaceful issues 0.5 shares in exchange for each share of High Noon. All of High Noon's shareholders exchange their holdings in High Noon for the new Peaceful shares. Thus, Peaceful issues 500 shares in exchange for all of the outstanding shares in High Noon.

The quoted market price of Peaceful shares on January 1 is $10, while the fair value of each common share of High Noon shares is $20. The fair values of Peaceful's few assets and liabilities on January 1 are the same as their carrying amounts.

As a result of the stock issuance to High Noon investors, those investors now own 5/6ths of Peaceful shares, or 83.3% of the total number of shares. To arrive at the same ratio, High Noon would have had to issue 200 shares to the shareholders of Peaceful. Thus, the fair value of the consideration transferred is $4,000 (calculated as 200 shares × $20 fair value per share).

Goodwill for the acquisition is the excess of the consideration transferred over the amount of Peaceful's assets and liabilities, which is $3,900 (calculated as $4,000 consideration - $100 of Peaceful net assets).

Based on the preceding information, the consolidated balance sheet of the two companies immediately following the acquisition transaction is:

	Peaceful	High Noon	Adjustments	Consolidated
Total assets	$100	$8,000	$3,900	$12,000
Total liabilities	$0	$4,500	--	$4,500
Shareholders' equity				
Retained earnings	10	3,000	-10	3,000
Common stock				
100 shares	90		-90	--
1,000 shares		500		500
600 shares			4,000	4,000
Total shareholders' equity	100	3,500	3,900	7,500
Total liabilities and shareholders' equity	$100	$8,000	$3,900	$12,000

Related Issues

This section addresses several issues that are similar to business combinations, but which are not treated in the same manner as business combinations.

Acquisition of Assets

A common form of acquisition is to acquire only selected assets and liabilities of an acquiree. This approach is used to avoid any undocumented liabilities that may be associated with the acquiree. See the author's *Mergers & Acquisitions* book for more information about why this type of acquisition is used. The accounting for asset acquisitions encompasses the following situations.

- *Cash consideration paid.* When cash is paid for assets, recognize the assets at the amount of cash paid for them.
- *Noncash assets paid.* Measure assets acquired at the fair value of the consideration paid or the fair value of the assets acquired, whichever is more reliably measurable. Do not recognize a gain or loss on an asset acquisition, unless the fair value of any noncash assets used by the acquirer to pay for the assets differs from the carrying amounts of these assets.
- *Cost allocation.* If assets and liabilities are acquired in a group, allocate the cost of the entire group to the individual components of that group based on their relative fair values.

EXAMPLE

Armadillo Industries acquires the sheet metal stamping facility of a competitor, which includes production equipment, a manufacturing facility, and the real estate on which the facility is located. The total purchase price of this group of assets was $800,000.

Armadillo allocates the purchase price to the individual assets in the following manner:

Asset	Fair Value	Percent of Total Fair Value		Purchase Price		Cost Allocation
Production equipment	$325,000	35%	×	$800,000	=	$280,000
Manufacturing facility	400,000	43%	×	800,000	=	344,000
Real estate	200,000	22%	×	800,000	=	176,000
	$925,000	100%				$800,000

Transactions between Entities under Control of Same Parent

When two or more entities are owned by a common parent, it is relatively common for them to enter into a variety of business transactions with each other, such as the transfer of assets or the sale of goods or services. Other examples of these transactions are shifting assets to a new entity, shifting assets into the parent, and the parent shifting its ownership interest in partially-owned subsidiaries into a new subsidiary.

When transferring assets or exchanging shares between entities under common control, the entity receiving the assets or equity interests should recognize the transferred items at their carrying amounts as stated in the records of the transferring entity on the transfer date. If these carrying amounts have been altered due to pushdown accounting (see next), then the entity receiving the assets or equity interests should instead recognize the transferred items at the historical cost of the parent entity.

If the sending and receiving entities use different accounting methods to account for similar types of assets and liabilities, it is permissible to adjust the carrying amounts of transferred items to the accounting method used by the recipient, if doing so represents a preferable treatment. If there is a change in accounting method, it must be applied retrospectively to the transferred items for all prior periods for which financial statements are presented, unless it is impracticable to do so.

Pushdown Accounting

Pushdown accounting involves requiring the acquiree to adopt a new basis of accounting for its assets and liabilities. This approach is used when a master limited partnership is formed from the assets of existing businesses (though usage is restricted), as well as when there is a step-up in the tax basis of a subsidiary. The SEC has stated that it believes pushdown accounting should be used in purchase transactions where the acquiree becomes substantially wholly owned. Pushdown accounting is not required if a business is not publicly-held.

Income Taxes

The nature of an acquisition transaction represents a balance of the taxation goals of the acquirer and the owners of the acquiree, as is described further in the author's

Mergers & Acquisitions book. The likely result of the acquisition structure is that some deferred tax liabilities and deferred tax assets should be recognized. Specifically, the following tax-related accounting may be required:

- *Goodwill.* The amortization of goodwill is allowed as a tax deduction in some tax jurisdictions, but not in others. The result may be a difference in the book and tax basis for goodwill in future years, for which a deferred tax asset or liability should be recorded.

- *Replacement awards.* If the acquirer issues replacement awards to the employees of the acquiree, and those awards are classified as equity and eligible to be tax deductions, recognize a deferred tax asset for the deductible temporary difference relating to that portion of the award relating to the precombination service of the awardee. The deduction may exceed the fair value of the award; if so, record the excess as additional paid-in capital.

- *Tax allocation to acquired entity.* If the acquirer retains the historical basis for the financial reporting of an acquiree in conjunction with a step-up in the tax basis of acquired assets, it is allowable to use any of the following methods to allocate the consolidated tax provision:
  - Allocate taxes to the acquiree on a preacquisition tax basis
  - When realized, credit the tax benefit caused by the step-up in tax basis to the additional paid-in capital account of the acquiree
  - When realized, credit the tax benefit caused by the step-up in tax basis to the income of the acquiree

- *Temporary differences.* If there are temporary differences related to deferred tax liabilities or assets related to a business combination, recognize them at the acquisition date.

- *Valuation allowance or tax position change.* If there is a change in the valuation allowance or tax position of an acquiree that occurs during the post-acquisition measurement period, and which results from new information about issues in existence at the acquisition date, record the offset to the change as an adjustment to goodwill. If goodwill has been reduced to zero, the offset is then recorded as a bargain purchase. All other changes in the acquiree's allowance or tax position are recognized as a change in income tax expense.

- *Valuation allowance.* Assess the need for a valuation allowance that offsets any deferred tax asset for which there is uncertainty about the recoverability of the asset. If the acquirer has already established a valuation allowance, it may be necessary to alter the allowance based on tax laws that may restrict the future use of deductible temporary differences or carryforwards of either the acquirer or the acquiree.

Business Combination Disclosures

Business combinations are one of the areas in which GAAP requires unusually thorough disclosures. Disclosure topics are addressed under the following headers that describe different aspects of business combinations.

General Disclosures

If an acquirer enters into a business combination during the current reporting period or after the reporting date but before the financial statements are issued or available to be issued, disclose the following information:

- The name of the acquiree and its description
- The acquisition date
- The acquired percentage of voting equity interest in the acquiree
- The reason(s) for the combination
- How the acquirer gained control of the acquiree

In addition, there may be other transactions with an acquiree that are recognized separately from the acquisition transaction. If so, disclose the following information:

- The transaction and how it was accounted for
- The amounts recognized for each transaction, and the line item(s) in the financial statements where these amounts are located
- If the result is settlement of a preexisting relationship, describe how the settlement was determined
- The amount of costs related to the acquisition, the amount of these costs recognized as expense, any issuance costs not charged to expense, and how these costs were recognized

If a business combination was achieved in stages, disclose the following information:

- The fair value of the acquirer's equity interest in the acquiree just prior to the acquisition date
- Any gain or loss resulting from the remeasurement of the existing equity interest to fair value, and where that gain or loss is recorded in the income statement
- The valuation technique used to measure the fair value of the existing equity interest
- Additional information that assists users to assess the development of this fair value measurement

If the acquirer is a publicly-held company, disclose the following information:

- The amount of revenue and earnings attributable to the acquiree since the acquisition date and included in the results of the reporting period
- A pro forma statement of the revenue and earnings of the combined entity, as though the acquisition had been completed at the beginning of the year
- If there are comparative financial statements, a pro forma statement of the revenue and earnings of the combined entity, as though the acquisition had been completed at the beginning of all the periods presented
- The nature and amount of any nonrecurring pro forma adjustments attributable to a business combination that are material

- If it is impracticable to report any of the preceding items required for a publicly-held company, disclose why the reporting is impracticable

If the acquirer recognized adjustments in the current reporting period that relate to prior periods, disclose the following information:

- The reason(s) why the initial accounting for a business combination is incomplete
- The specific items for which the accounting is incomplete, including assets, liabilities, equity interests, and/or payments
- The amount and type of any adjustments recognized during the period

It is allowable to aggregate the preceding disclosure information if there are several business combinations in a period that are individually immaterial, but material when reported as a group.

The preceding disclosures are still required if a business combination occurs after the reporting date of the financial statements, but before the statements are issued or available to be issued. The only exception is when the initial accounting for the combination is incomplete, in which case you should describe which disclosures were not made, and why they were not made.

EXAMPLE

Armadillo Industries discloses the following information pertaining to its acquisition of High Pressure Designs:

On June 30, 20X1, Armadillo acquired 20% of the outstanding common stock of High Pressure Designs ("High Pressure"). On March 31, 20X3, Armadillo acquired 45% of the outstanding common stock of High Pressure. High Pressure designs the containment walls for deep-sea submersible devices, and typically sells its services to oceanographic and military customers. As a result of the acquisition, Armadillo expects to solidify its leading market position in the submersible construction market.

The fair value of Armadillo's equity holdings in High Pressure was $3,500,000 at the acquisition date, which represented a $200,000 gain. The valuation technique to derive the fair value was the discounted cash flows method, which incorporated an 8% discount rate. The gain is recorded in other income in the company's income statement for the quarter ended March 31, 20X3.

Armadillo paid $8,750,000 for its March 31 purchase of 45% of High Pressure's common stock. This payment was made with 437,500 shares of the company's common stock, which had a closing market price of $20 on the acquisition date.

Identifiable Assets and Liabilities, and any Noncontrolling Interest

If an acquirer completes a business combination, it should disclose the following information in the period in which the combination was completed:

- *Indemnification assets.* If there are indemnification assets, describe the arrangement, and state the amount recognized as of the acquisition date and the basis for determining it. Also estimate the range of undiscounted outcomes, the reasons why a range cannot be estimated, or if the maximum amount is unlimited.
- *Acquired receivables.* By major class of receivables, state the gross amount and fair value of the receivables, and estimate the contractual cash flow you do not expect to collect.
- *Major asset and liability classes.* State the amount recognized for each major class of assets and liabilities.
- *Contingencies.* State the nature and amount of each asset or liability recognized in relation to a contingency, and how they were measured. You may aggregate disclosures for similar assets and liabilities.
- *Noncontrolling interests.* If you hold less than 100% ownership of the acquiree, state the fair value of the noncontrolling interest and the valuation method used to arrive at that figure.

If there were several acquisitions in the period that were individually immaterial but material when aggregated, disclose the preceding items in aggregate for the group of acquisitions.

If acquisitions are completed after the balance sheet date but before the financial statements have been issued or are available to be issued, you should still disclose all of the preceding information. However, if the initial accounting for the acquisitions is incomplete, describe the disclosures you were unable to report, and why they could not be made.

Goodwill or Gain from Bargain Purchase

If the acquirer recognizes goodwill as part of an acquisition transaction, disclose the following information for each business combination completed in a reporting period:

- *Bargain purchase.* If the acquisition is a bargain purchase, disclose the resulting gain and the line item in which it is located in the income statement, as well as the reasons why the acquisition generated a gain.
- *Consideration paid.* State the fair value of all consideration paid, as well as by class of asset, liability, and equity item.
- *Contingent assets and liabilities.* In later periods, continue to report any changes in the fair values of unsettled contingent assets and liabilities, as well as changes in (and the reasons for) the range of possible outcomes.
- *Contingent consideration.* If there is consideration contingent upon future events or circumstances, state the amount of this consideration already recognized on the acquisition date, describe the arrangement, estimate the

range of undiscounted outcomes or reasons why a range cannot be presented, and whether the maximum payment can be unlimited.

- *Goodwill content.* Describe the factors that comprise goodwill, such as expected synergies from combining the companies.
- *Reconciliation.* Present a reconciliation of the carrying amount of goodwill at the beginning and end of the reporting period.
- *Segment reporting.* If the acquirer is publicly-held, disclose the amount of goodwill assigned to each reportable segment. If this assignment has not yet been completed, disclose this point.
- *Tax deductibility.* Note the amount of resulting goodwill expected to be tax deductible.

If there were several acquisitions in the period that were individually immaterial but material when aggregated, disclose the preceding items in aggregate for the group of acquisitions.

If acquisitions are completed after the balance sheet date but before the financial statements have been issued or are available to be issued, you should still disclose all of the preceding information. However, if the initial accounting for the acquisitions is incomplete, describe the disclosures you were unable to report, and why they could not be made.

Reverse Acquisitions

When there is a reverse acquisition, consolidated financial statements are issued under the name of the legal acquirer (which is the accounting acquiree). The accompanying notes should clarify that the financial statements are actually a continuation of the financial statements formerly issued by the legal acquiree, with a retroactive adjustment to reflect the legal capital of the legal acquirer. If comparative information is presented for prior periods, this means that the presented amount of legal capital should also be adjusted in the prior periods. The following additional points apply to the presentation of the consolidated financial statements of the two entities:

- *Carrying amounts.* Assets and liabilities are stated at their precombination carrying amounts – there is no fair value restatement.
- *Equity structure.* The equity structure in the statements reflects the equity structure of the legal acquirer, which includes any equity changes resulting from the combination.
- *Earnings per share.* Assuming that the reverse acquisition was completed in order to take the legal acquiree public, it must now report earnings per share. The earnings per share calculation requires the formulation of the weighted-average number of shares outstanding during each reporting period. To calculate the number of shares for the period in which the acquisition occurs, use the following guidance:
  - o *Shares outstanding from beginning of period to acquisition date.* This is the weighted-average number of shares of the legal acquiree

outstanding in the period, multiplied by the exchange ratio used to replace them with shares of the legal acquirer.

o *Shares outstanding from acquisition date to end of period*. This is the actual weighted-average number of shares of the legal acquirer outstanding.

To calculate the basic earnings per share information for any comparative periods presented for periods prior to the date of a reverse acquisition, use the following formula:

$$\frac{\text{Income of legal acquiree attributable to common shareholders}}{(\text{Legal acquiree's weighted-average common shares outstanding} \times \text{Exchange ratio})}$$

Transactions between Entities under Control of Same Parent

When there is an exchange of assets or equity interests between entities under common control, the receiving entity records these transactions as though they occurred at the beginning of the reporting period. In addition, retrospectively adjust all comparative financial statements presented for previous reporting periods to reflect the amounts of these transactions. This prior-period adjustment is only required for those periods during which the entities had a common parent.

When there is a transfer of assets and/or liabilities, or an exchange of equity interests, disclose the following information:

- *Description*. State the name and description of the entity being included in the reporting entity.
- *Method of accounting*. Describe the method of accounting for the indicated transaction.

Income Taxes

If there is a change in the valuation allowance of the deferred tax assets of an acquirer that is caused by a business combination, disclose the adjustments to the beginning balance of the valuation.

Summary

The accountant may deal with acquisitions on only rare occasions, and so may be unfamiliar with the proper accounting to be used to recognize these transactions. While texts such as this one can certainly provide guidelines for how to structure these transactions, there is still a strong likelihood of incorrectly accounting for an acquisition. Given the high level of accounting complexity in this area, it is best to engage the services of an acquisition accounting expert, for whom a recommendation may be obtained from the company's certified public accountants. Either this person's work can be thoroughly documented and copied for use in later acquisitions, or the company can continue to engage his or her services whenever an acquisition is completed. The latter approach is recommended, since it reduces the risk of a reporting error.

Chapter 16
Foreign Currency Matters

Introduction

A large number of businesses routinely engage in foreign currency transactions with their business partners, in which case they will probably deal with foreign currencies. Others have subsidiaries located in foreign countries, and need to convert the financial statements of these entities into the currency used by the parent for consolidation purposes. We deal with the accounting for and disclosure of these two situations in the following sections.

Foreign Currency Transactions

A business may enter into a transaction where it is scheduled to receive a payment from a customer that is denominated in a foreign currency, or to make a payment to a supplier in a foreign currency. On the date of recognition of each such transaction, record it in the functional currency of the reporting entity, based on the exchange rate in effect on that date. If it is not possible to determine the market exchange rate on the date of recognition of a transaction, use the next available exchange rate.

If there is a change in the expected exchange rate between the functional currency of the entity and the currency in which a transaction is denominated, record a gain or loss in earnings in the period when the exchange rate changes. This can result in the recognition of a series of gains or losses over a number of accounting periods, if the settlement date of a transaction is sufficiently far in the future. This also means that the stated balances of the related receivables and payables will reflect the current exchange rate as of each subsequent balance sheet date.

The two situations in which you should not recognize a gain or loss on a foreign currency transaction are:

- When a foreign currency transaction is designed to be an economic hedge of a net investment in a foreign entity, and is effective as such; or
- When there is no expectation of settling a transaction between entities that are to be consolidated.

EXAMPLE

Armadillo Industries sells goods to a company in the United Kingdom, to be paid in pounds having a value at the booking date of $100,000. Armadillo records this transaction with the following entry:

	Debit	Credit
Accounts receivable	100,000	
Sales		100,000

Later, when the customer pays Armadillo, the exchange rate has changed, resulting in a payment in pounds that translates to a $95,000 sale. Thus, the foreign exchange rate change related to the transaction has created a $5,000 loss for Armadillo, which it records with the following entry:

	Debit	Credit
Cash	95,000	
Foreign currency exchange loss	5,000	
Accounts receivable		100,000

The following table shows the impact of transaction exposure on different scenarios.

Risk When Transactions Denominated in Foreign Currency

	Import Goods	Export Goods
Home currency weakens	Loss	Gain
Home currency strengthens	Gain	Loss

Financial Statement Translation

A company may have subsidiaries located in other countries, and creates financial statements for those subsidiaries that are denominated in the local currency. If so, the parent company will need to translate the results of these subsidiaries into the currency used by the parent company when it creates consolidated financial statements for the entire entity (called the *reporting currency*). The steps in this process are as follows:

1. Determine the functional currency of the foreign entity.
2. Remeasure the financial statements of the foreign entity into the reporting currency of the parent company.
3. Record gains and losses on the translation of currencies.

Determination of Functional Currency

The financial results and financial position of a company should be measured using its functional currency, which is the currency that the company uses in the majority of its business transactions.

If a foreign business entity operates primarily within one country and is not dependent upon the parent company, its functional currency is the currency of the country in which its operations are located. However, there are other foreign operations that are more closely tied to the operations of the parent company, and whose financing is mostly supplied by the parent or other sources that use the dollar. In this latter case, the functional currency of the foreign operation is probably the dollar. These two examples anchor the ends of a continuum on which you will find foreign operations. Unless an operation is clearly associated with one of the two examples provided, it is likely that you must make a determination of functional currency based on the unique circumstances pertaining to each entity. For example, the functional currency may be difficult to determine if a business conducts an equal amount of business in two different countries. An examination of the following factors can assist in determining a functional currency:

Indicators	Indicates Use of Foreign Currency as Functional Currency	Indicates use of Reporting Currency as Functional Currency
Cash flow	The cash flows relating to an entity's assets and liabilities are primarily in the foreign currency, and have no direct impact on the cash flows of the parent	The cash flows relating to an entity's assets and liabilities directly affect the cash flows of the parent and are available for remittance to it
Expenses	The labor, material, and other costs of the entity are primarily obtained locally	The labor, material, and other costs of the entity are primarily obtained from the parent's country
Financing	Any financing obtained is primarily denominated in a foreign currency, and locally-generated funds should be able to service the entity's existing and expected debts	Financing is obtained from the parent or is in dollar-denominated obligations, or locally-generated funds are not sufficient for the servicing of existing and expected debts without a cash infusion
Intra-entity transactions	There are few intra-entity transactions, and operations are not tightly integrated with those of the parent	There are many intra-entity transactions, and operations are more likely to be tightly integrated with those of the parent
Sales market	There is an active local market for the products of the entity	The primary market for the entity's products is the country of the parent, or sales are denominated in the currency of the parent's country
Sales price	Sales prices are mostly based on local competition and regulations, rather than on exchange rate changes	Sales prices are mostly based on exchange rate changes, which can be driven by international price competition

The functional currency in which a business reports its financial results should rarely change. A shift to a different functional currency should be used only when there is a significant change in the economic facts and circumstances. If there is a change in functional currency, do not restate previously-issued financial statements into the new currency.

If there is a change in functional currency from the reporting currency of an entity (i.e., the functional currency of the parent company) to a foreign currency, report the adjustment associated with the current-rate translation of any nonmonetary assets in other comprehensive income. Conversely, if the functional currency changes from a foreign currency to the reporting currency, the translated amounts previously stated for nonmonetary assets as of the prior period become the cost basis for these assets going forward; also, do not remove any prior period translation adjustments from equity.

EXAMPLE

Armadillo Industries has a subsidiary in Australia, to which it ships its body armor products for sale to local police forces. The Australian subsidiary sells these products and then remits payments back to corporate headquarters. Armadillo should consider U.S. dollars to be the functional currency of this subsidiary.

Armadillo also owns a subsidiary in Russia, which manufactures its own body armor for local consumption, accumulates cash reserves, and borrows funds locally. This subsidiary rarely remits funds back to the parent company. In this case, the functional currency should be the Russian ruble.

Translation of Financial Statements

When translating the financial statements of an entity for consolidation purposes into the reporting currency of a business, translate the financial statements using the following rules:

- *Assets and liabilities*. Translate using the current exchange rate at the balance sheet date for assets and liabilities.
- *Income statement items*. Translate revenues, expenses, gains, and losses using the exchange rate as of the dates when those items were originally recognized.
- *Allocations*. Translate all cost and revenue allocations using the exchange rates in effect when those allocations are recorded. Examples of allocations are depreciation and the amortization of deferred revenues.
- *Different balance sheet date*. If the foreign entity being consolidated has a different balance sheet date than that of the reporting entity, use the exchange rate in effect as of the foreign entity's balance sheet date.
- *Profit eliminations*. If there are intra-entity profits to be eliminated as part of the consolidation, apply the exchange rate in effect on the dates when the underlying transactions took place.
- *Statement of cash flows*. In the statement of cash flows, state all foreign currency cash flows at their reporting currency equivalent using the exchange rates in effect when the cash flows occurred. A weighted average exchange rate may be used for this calculation.

If there are translation adjustments resulting from the implementation of these rules, record the adjustments in the equity section of the parent company's consolidated balance sheet.

EXAMPLE

Armadillo Industries has a subsidiary located in England, which has its net assets denominated in pounds. The functional currency of Armadillo is U.S. dollars. At year-end, when the parent company consolidates the financial statements of its subsidiaries, the U.S.

dollar has depreciated in comparison to the pound, resulting in a decline in the value of the subsidiary's net assets.

The following table shows the impact of translation exposure on different scenarios.

Risk When Net Assets Denominated in Foreign Currency

	Assets	Liabilities
Reporting currency weakens	Gain	Loss
Reporting currency strengthens	Loss	Gain

If the process of converting the financial statements of a foreign entity into the reporting currency of the parent company results in a translation adjustment, report the related profit or loss in other comprehensive income.

EXAMPLE

A subsidiary of Armadillo Industries is located in Argentina, and its functional currency is the Argentine peso. The relevant peso exchange rates are:
- 0.20 to the dollar at the beginning of the year
- 0.24 to the dollar at the end of the year
- 0.22 to the dollar for the full-year weighted average rate

The subsidiary had no retained earnings at the beginning of the year. Based on this information, the financial statement conversion is as follows:

(000s)	Argentine Pesos	Exchange Rate	U.S. Dollars
Assets			
Cash	89,000	0.24	21,360
Accounts receivable	267,000	0.24	64,080
Inventory	412,000	0.24	98,880
Fixed assets, net	608,000	0.24	145,920
Total assets	1,376,000		330,240
Liabilities and Equity			
Accounts payable	320,000	0.24	76,800
Notes payable	500,000	0.24	120,000
Common stock	10,000	0.20	2,400
Additional paid-in capital	545,000	0.20	130,800
Retained earnings	1,000	(*)	220
Translation adjustments	0	--	20
Total liabilities and equity	1,376,000		330,240

* Reference from the following income statement

(000s)	Argentine Pesos	Exchange Rate	U.S. Dollars
Revenue	1,500,000	0.22	330,000
Expenses	1,499,000	0.22	329,780
Net income	1,000		220
Beginning retained earnings	0		0
Add: Net income	1,000	0.22	220
Ending retained earnings	1,000		220

Use of Average Exchange Rates

We have noted that the remeasurement of financial statements may require the use of historical exchange rate information. It can be burdensome to keep track of these exchange rates and the dates on which the rates are to be applied. To reduce the work involved, GAAP allows the use of an average exchange rate, or other labor-saving methods that reasonably approximate the exchange rates that were more frequently applied. If you use an average exchange rate, derive a weighted average based on the volume of currency transactions in the period. For example, a reasonably accurate result might be achieved by developing an average rate for each month of the year, to be applied to those transactions occurring within each month.

Hyperinflationary Effects

An entity may find itself operating in an environment that has cumulative inflation of 100% or more. If this level of inflation continues over a three-year period, a country is considered to have a highly inflationary economy. When this is the case, remeasure the financial statements of the entity operating in that environment as though the functional currency were the reporting currency.

If the economy is no longer considered to be hyperinflationary, restate the financial statements of the relevant entity so that the local currency is now the functional currency. This means translating the reporting currency amounts into the local currency amounts at the current exchange rate on the date of change; these translated amounts then become the new functional currency for the nonmonetary assets and liabilities of the entity.

EXAMPLE

A subsidiary of Armadillo Industries is operating in a highly inflationary economy. On March 31 of 20X3, it bought a machine for 50,000 units of the local currency. The exchange rate at that time was 5 units of the local currency to one U.S. dollar, so the equivalent cost of the machine in U.S. dollars was $10,000. Five years later, on March 31, 20X8, the machine's net book value on the subsidiary's books has declined to 25,000 units of the local currency, due to ongoing depreciation. On March 31 of 20X8, hyperinflation has altered the exchange rate to 25 to one U.S. dollar. During this time, the parent company has been using the historical exchange rate to account for the machine, so the recorded amount has declined to $5,000, based on the depreciation incurred during the intervening years.

On April 1 of 20X8, Armadillo's management no longer considers the local economy of the subsidiary to be highly inflationary, so it establishes a new cost basis for the equipment by translating the current $5,000 cost of the machine back into the local currency at the current exchange rate of 25:1. This means the functional accounting basis for the machine on April 1 of 20X8 would be 125,000 units of the local currency.

Derecognition of a Foreign Entity Investment

When a company sells or liquidates its investment in a foreign entity, complete the following steps to account for the situation:
- Remove the translation adjustment recorded in equity for the investment
- Report a gain or loss in the period in which the sale or liquidation occurs

If a company only sells a portion of its investment in a foreign entity, recognize only a pro rata portion of the accumulated translation adjustment recorded in equity.

Foreign Currency Disclosures

Disclose the following information related to transactions denominated in foreign currencies:
- *Gains and losses*. If there are transaction-based gains or losses during the period that are caused by changes in foreign exchange rates, disclose the aggregate amount in the financial statements or in the accompanying notes.
- *Subsequent rate changes*. If there is a foreign currency rate change after the date of the financial statements that has a significant effect on unsettled balances, disclose the impact of the rate on unsettled transactions between the date of the financial statements and the date of the rate change.
- *Rate change effects*. GAAP encourages you to discuss the effects of rate changes on the reported results of operations, but does not require it.

If translation adjustments have been reported in equity, disclose an analysis of the changes during the period in the financial statements. This information can be integrated into the statement of changes in equity. The analysis should state the following:

	Beginning balance of cumulative translation adjustments
+/-	The aggregate adjustment caused by translation adjustments, as well as from the gains and losses caused by certain hedges and intra-entity balances
+/-	The amount of income taxes allocated to translation adjustments
+/-	Transfers from cumulative translation adjustments as a result of the sale or liquidation of an investment in a foreign entity
=	Ending balance of cumulative translation adjustments

If there are income taxes associated with translation adjustments, report them in other comprehensive income.

Report in the statement of cash flows the effect of any changes in exchange rates on cash balances held in foreign currencies. This information should be stated in separate line items within the reconciliation of the change in cash and cash equivalents during the period.

Summary

The key factor to consider when translating financial statements into the reporting currency is the use of average exchange rates. Consider creating a standard procedure for calculating the weighted average exchange rate for each relevant currency for each reporting period, and then retain the calculation, to justify the exchange rate(s) for audit purposes. Using a weighted average is much more efficient from an accounting perspective than translating specific transactions at the associated exchange rate on a daily basis.

Chapter 17
Accounting for Leases

Introduction

The lease financing of assets is governed by a strict set of rules that require a lessee to either treat a leasing arrangement as a series of rental payments or as the purchase of an asset. The accounting by the lessor is more complicated, with four possible alternative methods of accounting for a leased asset. Given the number of alternative methods and the significantly different results that a business may report under each one, it is of considerable importance to understand the circumstances under which each set of rules applies. In this chapter, we cover the accounting for operating leases, capital leases, leasehold improvements, sale-leaseback transactions, and similar issues related to leases.

Overview of Leases

A lease is a transaction in which an entity allows another entity the use of an asset in exchange for some form of consideration. The *lessor* owns the asset, and the *lessee* uses the asset. Arrangements in which a lease does *not* exist include the following:
- The lessee does not have the right to use the asset, or the arrangement can be fulfilled without using a specific designated asset
- Licensing agreements
- Workforce leasing

While the leasing concept appears simple enough, there are many variations on it, resulting in a multitude of different accounting scenarios.

Capital Lease Criteria

The main concept driving the formulation of accounting rules for leases is that a lease transferring substantially all of the benefits and risks associated with the ownership of a property should be accounted for as ownership of the asset by the lessee, and sale of the asset by the lessor. This type of lease is called a *capital lease*. All other transactions are to be accounted for as *operating leases*. If a lease agreement contains either of the following two elements, it is to be accounted for as a capital lease:
- *Ownership change.* By the end of the lease term, ownership of the leased property has shifted from the lessor to the lessee.
- *Bargain purchase option.* There is an option in the lease agreement that allows the lessee to buy the leased asset for a below-market price.

If the term of the lease does not fall within just the final 25% of the estimated economic life of the asset, then either of the following two elements can also be used to judge whether a lease is to be designated as a capital lease:

- *Long lease term*. The term of the lease covers at least 75% of the estimated economic life of the leased asset.
- *Present value of payments*. The present value of the minimum lease payments required under a lease arrangement, not including executory costs, is at least 90% of the fair value of the leased property. The fair value should be that amount above any investment tax credit to be realized by the lessor in connection with the leased asset.

The following factors can impact the classification of a lease as either an operating or capital lease:

- *Acquired lease*. When an acquirer buys an acquiree, the acquirer should continue to classify the acquiree's leases in the same manner in which they were originally classified, unless lease terms have been modified.
- *Combined property*. If the lease contains both land and buildings and the ownership change and bargain purchase criteria are not met, apply the following guidance:
  - *Land value < 25%*. If the land fair value is under 25% of the fair value of all the property in the lease, combine all the property in the lease when applying the lease term and minimum payments criteria.
  - *Land value ≥ 25%*. If the land fair value is 25% or more of the fair value of all the property in the lease, split the land from the buildings when applying the lease term and minimum payments criteria.
- *Contingent rentals*. If a lease payment is dependent upon the future use of an asset (such as hours of flight time for a leased airplane), consider these payments contingent, and therefore not applicable to the calculation of the present value of minimum lease payments just referred to as a possible criterion for the classification of a lease as a capital lease.
- *Facilities owned by government*. When the lessee is leasing space within a permanent structure from a government authority (such as within an airport terminal) where there is no transfer of ownership to the lessee, classify the lease as an operating lease.
- *Fiscal funding clause*. A fiscal funding clause allows the lessee to cancel a lease if a funding authority does not provide sufficient funding to make scheduled lease payments (this clause is usually only demanded by government entities). If a lease contains such a clause and there is a non-remote chance of the clause being exercised, the lease must be classified as an operating lease.
- *Land lease*. If the lease only involves land, only use the bargain purchase option or the ownership change criteria to determine if the lease should be classified as a capital lease.

- *Lease for part of building.* If a lease is for only part of a building and the fair value of the leased portion of the property is not objectively determinable, only apply the lease-term criterion when determining whether the lease is a capital lease. If the fair value can be determined, then you can also apply the minimum lease payments criterion.
- *Property appraisal.* If it appears likely that a lease will be classified as a capital lease, and the resulting effects would have a significant impact on the lessee's financial statements, it is strongly recommended (but not required) that the lessee obtain an appraisal of a lease when the lease involves only part of a building.
- *Residual value guarantee.* If the lessee of a combined building and land lease provides a residual value guarantee, and the fair value of the land portion of the lease is at least one-quarter of the total fair value of the lease, multiply the fair value of the land by the lessee's incremental borrowing rate to determine the lease rates applicable to the land. The remainder of the lease payments are attributable to the building. This information is needed to see if the present value of minimum lease payments will qualify either portion of the lease as a capital lease.
- *Sub lessee treatment.* The lessee in a sublease arrangement should use the same four criteria noted above to determine whether a lease can be classified as a capital lease. If the sub lease terms release the original lessee from obligations under the lease, the original lessee can consider the original lease agreement to be terminated.

EXAMPLE

Armadillo Industries enters into an automobile lease on behalf of the CEO of the company. The fair value of the leased vehicle is $120,000, and its estimated economic life is seven years. The lease term is fixed at 60 months. A lease payment of $2,400 is due at the beginning of each month. Armadillo's incremental borrowing rate is 8%. The company evaluates the arrangement to see if it meets any of the criteria for a capital lease. The evaluation results are:

- There is no ownership change by the end of the lease term.
- There is no bargain purchase option.
- The lease term covers 71% of the estimated economic life of the asset, so it is not considered a long-term lease.
- The present value of the minimum lease payments is $118,366, which is 99% of the fair value of the asset.

Thus, the present value of payment criterion qualifies the lease for treatment by Armadillo as a capital lease.

Lease Classification by Lessor

The lessor also uses the four lease classification criteria to determine the status of a lease. However, the calculation of these criteria varies somewhat from those used by the lessee, as noted below:

- *Minimum lease payments criterion.* When calculating the present value of minimum lease payments, use the interest rate implicit in the lease as the discount rate.
- *Additional criteria.* The lease must qualify as a capital lease under one of the four criteria already stated; in addition, the collectability of the minimum lease payments must be reasonably predictable, and there are no material uncertainties remaining about the costs for which the lessor will not be reimbursed under the lease.

If a lease qualifies under one of the original four lease criteria used by a lessee to establish treatment as a capital lease, as well as both of the "additional criteria" just noted, the lessor then has the choice of classifying the lease as one of the following lease types:

- *Sales-type lease.* This classification applies when the fair value of the leased property at the start of a lease varies from its carrying amount, it involves real estate, and there is a transfer of ownership to the lessee by the end of the lease term. The additional criteria need not apply. Alternatively, a qualifying lease may not involve real estate, meets both additional criteria, and any one of the original four criteria. This classification is typically used when a manufacturer or a dealer uses a lease as a tool for marketing what they sell.
- *Direct financing lease.* This classification applies when a lease cannot be classified as a leveraged lease (see next), the fair value of the leased property matches its carrying amount, and the arrangement meets any of the original four criteria plus both of the additional criteria. This classification is typically used when the business of the lessor is primarily financing.
- *Leveraged lease.* This classification applies when a lease qualifies as a direct financing lease, includes a long-term creditor who provides nonrecourse financing, the lessor has substantial leverage in relation to the lease, and the lessor's investment in the lease initially declines and later increases.
- *Operating lease.* This classification applies when a lease does not meet any of the original four criteria for a capital lease.

Lease Reassessment

You should reassess whether an arrangement contains a lease if there has been a change in the terms of the arrangement, it has been extended, it is no longer dependent on specific fixed assets, or there has been a physical change in the fixed assets. Exercise of a renewal option does not trigger a lease reassessment.

If reassessment results in treatment of an arrangement as a different classification of lease, consider the revised lease to be a new lease for accounting purposes.

EXAMPLE

Armadillo Industries enters into a facility lease that contains an eight-year term. The agreement also contains a five-year lease extension clause that imposes a $500,000 penalty on Armadillo if it chooses not to renew the lease. Given the size of the non-renewal penalty, it is considered reasonably assured that Armadillo will take the renewal option. Given the facts, the eventual exercise of the renewal option would not trigger a reassessment of the lease.

Accounting for Leasehold Improvements

Leasehold improvements are defined as the enhancements paid for by a tenant to leased space. Examples of leasehold improvements are:

- Interior walls and ceilings
- Electrical and plumbing additions
- Built-in cabinetry
- Carpeting and tiles

Leasehold improvements generally revert to the ownership of the landlord upon termination of a lease, unless the tenant can remove them without damaging the leased property.

The lessee should capitalize leasehold improvements, and then depreciate them over the shorter of their useful life or the remaining term of the lease. The remaining lease term for depreciation purposes can be extended into additional lease renewal periods if the renewal is reasonably assured (such as when there is a bargain renewal option). If the lessor subsequently purchases the property, the improvements can then be depreciated over the estimated remaining useful life of the building.

EXAMPLE

Armadillo Industries has a five-year lease on an office building, as well as an option to renew the lease for an additional five years at the then-prevailing market rate. Armadillo pays $150,000 to build offices in the building immediately after it leases the space. The useful life of these offices is 20 years. Since there is no bargain purchase option to renew the lease, it is not reasonably assured that Armadillo will renew the lease. Consequently, the company should depreciate the $150,000 over the five years of the existing lease, which is the shorter of the useful life of the improvements or the lease term. The annual entry to recognize the depreciation is:

	Debit	Credit
Depreciation expense	30,000	
Accumulated depreciation		30,000

Special Lease Terms

There are several special lease terms that may require variations from the normal lease accounting. These terms are:

- *Default for non-performance.* There may be clauses in the lease agreement that require the lessee to pay the lessor a certain amount, or buy the leased property from the lessor, if the lessee defaults on certain provisions of the lease agreement.
- *Environmental indemnities.* There is a risk that a lessee could cause environmental contamination, in which case the lessor may require the lessee to make an indemnity payment, or even require the lessee to buy the leased property from the lessor.
- *Maintenance deposits.* If leased property requires ongoing maintenance, the lessee may be required to deposit funds with the lessor to protect the lessor against inadequate maintenance by the lessee. At the end of the lease term, the lessor may be contractually obligated to return some of these funds to the lessee, or may be allowed to retain the funds. The lessee should regularly evaluate whether the deposit will probably be returned; if return is not probable, recognize the deposit as an expense.
- *Manufacturer guarantees.* If a manufacturer guarantees the resale value of the equipment it is selling to the buyer, it must account for the transaction as a lease, rather than a sale.
- *Multiple-element arrangements.* If there are multiple elements in a transaction, such as the leasing of equipment, installation, training, and site remediation, separate the consideration related to the arrangement between that part related to the lease, and the other elements on a relative fair value basis.

Operating Leases

An operating lease is the most common type of lease, where the lessor continues to own the leased asset, and the lessee uses the asset over a fixed period of time, with the intent of eventually returning the asset to the lessor. The accounting treatment of an operating lease by the lessee and lessor is described in this section.

Operating Lease Treatment by Lessee

If the lessee is subject to a leasing arrangement that is classified as an operating lease, classify each lease payment as an expense when it becomes payable. If an operating lease includes scheduled rent increases over the term of the lease, there are two ways to account for the altered payments:

- *Scheduled increases.* Recognize scheduled rent increases on a straight-line basis over the term of the lease, unless some other recognition system better represents the usage of the underlying assets.
- *Contingent rentals.* If there may be changes in lease payments that are based on such future events as inflation or the amount of property taxes incurred, charge these items to expense as they become accruable.

If an incentive is included in a lease (such as several months of free or reduced rent), the lessee recognizes the lease incentive on a straight-line basis over the term of the lease. Thus, most lease incentives are deferred and recognized over time, rather than being recognized in full as incurred.

If the lessee has agreed to a residual value guarantee, it should measure the guarantee at its fair value at the inception of the lease, even if a deficiency in the residual value is unlikely. If the deficiency becomes probable, the lessee should accrue the expected amount of the deficiency for which it is responsible over the remainder of the lease term, using the straight-line method.

Operating Lease Treatment by Lessor

If the lessor classifies a lease as an operating lease, it should account for the lease in the following manner:

- Depreciate the leased property over its useful life.
- Defer the initial employee-related direct costs of the lease. These are costs that would not have been incurred if there had been no leasing transaction, and which involve evaluating the lessee, negotiating the lease, preparing lease documents, or closing the transaction. These costs should then be recognized over the lease term, in proportion to the amount of rental income recognized.
- If there is a lease of real estate where the lessor classifies the arrangement as a sales-type lease, except there is no transfer of ownership, the lessor must recognize at lease inception a loss if the fair value of the property is less than its carrying amount.

If the lessor sells property that is being leased under an operating lease, but retains substantial risks of ownership in the property, it should not record the transaction as a sale. Instead, account for it as a collateralized borrowing arrangement.

Capital Leases

Under a capital lease, the leased asset is accounted for as though asset ownership has transferred to the lessee (even if that is not actually the case). This section outlines the relevant accounting for the lessee and lessor.

Capital Lease Treatment by Lessee

In general, the lessee recognizes the underlying asset in a capital lease, as well as the related obligation to pay the lessor. The key items to account for are:

1. *Asset.* Measure the asset being leased at the present value of the minimum lease payments, not including executory costs included in these payments, and record this amount as a fixed asset. To determine present value, use the lessee's incremental borrowing rate as the discount rate. However, use the lessor's implicit rate as the discount rate if it is practicable to learn the rate, and the rate is lower than the lessee's incremental borrowing rate. If the

amount of included executory costs is not clearly determinable, estimate the amount. The offset to the asset entry is to a capital lease liability account. For example, if the present value of all lease payments for a production machine is $100,000, record it as a debit of $100,000 to the machinery account and a credit of $100,000 to the capital lease liability account.

2. *Depreciation.* Depreciate the asset (except for land) in accordance with the company's depreciation policy, but only if the lease qualified under the capital lease criteria as indicating an ownership change or a bargain purchase option. If the lease had instead qualified as a capital lease under another criterion than ownership change or the bargain purchase option, only depreciate the asset over the lease term. In the latter case, depreciation should not include the ending expected value of the asset (such as a lessee-guaranteed residual value). For example, if an asset has a cost of $100,000, no expected salvage value, and a 10-year useful life, the annual depreciation entry for it is a debit of $10,000 to the depreciation expense account and a credit of $10,000 to the accumulated depreciation account.

3. *Lease payments.* Split all subsequent lease payments into their principal and interest components, and offset the principal component of each payment against the capital lease liability account, so that the liability is reduced to zero by the end of the lease term. For example, if a lease payment were for a total of $1,000 and $120 of that amount were for interest expense, the entry would be a debit of $880 to the capital lease liability account, a debit of $120 to the interest expense account, and a credit of $1,000 to the accounts payable account.

If there is a residual value guarantee or non-renewal penalty at the end of the lease term, incorporate this liability into the preceding accounting, so that the liability remains at the end of the lease term.

If the lessee renews a lease and classifies the renewed lease as an operating lease, it should continue to account for the original lease as a capital lease, and then account for the renewed lease as an operating lease.

If the lessee terminates a capital lease prior to the expiration date of the lease, remove the asset and offsetting capital lease obligation from the lessee's accounting records, and record a gain or loss on settlement of the transaction.

Capital Lease Treatment of Sublease by Lessee

If the party designated as the lessee in an original capital lease arrangement creates a sublease with a third party, the accounting for the sublease falls into one of the following two scenarios:

- *Original lessee released from obligation.* In the rare case where the original lessor relieves the original lessee from obligations under the lease, the original lessee can consider the lease agreement to be terminated.

- *Original lessee not released from obligation.* When the original lessor continues to require the original lessee to be the primary obligor on the lease, the lessee continues its accounting uninterrupted.

If the lease originally qualified as a capital lease under the ownership change or bargain purchase option criteria, the original lessee should account for the sublease as either a sales-type or direct financing lease; if the sublease does not qualify as a sales-type or direct financing lease, the original lessee should account for it as an operating lease.

Capital Lease Treatment by Lessor (Sales-Type Lease)

If the lessor has classified a lease as a sales-type lease and the asset being leased is real estate, account for the transaction as though the lessor is selling the property.

If the transaction is classified as a sales-type lease and it does not involve real estate, the lessor should account for the transaction by recognizing the following:

> Sale price
> - Gross amount of investment in the lease
> - Initial direct costs
> + Present value of unguaranteed residual value benefiting the lessor
> = Unearned income

Where,
- The sale price is calculated as the present value of minimum lease payments, net of executory costs, discounted using the interest rate implicit in the lease.
- The gross amount of the investment in the lease is calculated as:

> Sum of minimum lease payments, less executory cost component
> + Unguaranteed residual value benefiting lessor

Unearned income should be recognized in earnings over the term of the lease. Use the interest method to recognize that amount of unearned income that produces a constant rate of return over the lease term. If the lessor will benefit from a residual value guarantee or penalty from a failure to renew the lease, the interest method should be calculated to leave the amount of the guarantee or penalty outstanding at the end of the lease term.

At least once a year, review the estimated residual value of the leased property. If the residual value has declined and the decline is other than temporary, account for the decline as a loss in the current period. If the residual value has increased, do not recognize a gain.

If a lease originally classified as a sales-type lease is renewed and the renewed lease is classified as an operating lease, the lessor should continue to account for the original lease as a sales-type lease, and then account for the renewed lease as an operating lease.

If the remaining minimum lease payments of a sales-type lease are subsequently altered, change the minimum lease payments receivable, with the offset charged to unearned income. If the change constitutes a new lease, terminate the accounting for the old lease and account for the post-change lease as a new lease.

Capital Lease Treatment by Lessor (Direct Financing Lease)

If the lessor has classified a lease as a direct financing lease, it recognizes the gross investment in the lease and the related amount of unearned income. The gross investment in the lease is calculated as:

Sum of minimum lease payments, less executory cost component
+ Unguaranteed residual value benefiting lessor

The amount of unearned income is the difference between the gross investment in the lease and its carrying amount.

Unearned income should be recognized in earnings over the term of the lease. Use the interest method to recognize that amount of unearned income that produces a constant rate of return over the lease term.

At least once a year, review the estimated residual value of the leased property. If the residual value has declined and the decline is other than temporary, account for the decline as a loss in the current period. If the residual value has increased, do not recognize a gain.

If a lease originally classified as a direct financing lease is renewed and the renewed lease is classified as an operating lease, the lessor should continue to account for the original lease as a direct financing lease, and then account for the renewed lease as an operating lease.

If the remaining minimum lease payments of a direct financing lease are subsequently altered, change the minimum lease payments receivable, with the offset charged to unearned income. If the change constitutes a new lease, terminate the accounting for the old lease and account for the post-change lease as a new lease.

EXAMPLE

Currency Bank leases an automobile to Armadillo Industries. Currency's cost of the automobile is $120,000, which is also the fair value of the vehicle as of the lease inception date. The estimated economic life of the automobile is seven years.

The noncancelable term of the lease is five years, and requires a payment of $2,400 from the lessee at the beginning of each month. Armadillo also guarantees the residual value of the vehicle at the end of the lease period in the amount of $10,000.

The minimum lease payments associated with the lease are calculated as:

($2,400 × 60 months) + $10,000 Residual value guarantee
= $154,000 Minimum lease payments

The interest rate implicit in the lease that discounts the minimum lease payments and residual guarantee to the initial automobile fair value of $120,000 is 9.8%. The breakdown of the present value of minimum lease payments at the 9.8% rate to equate to the $120,000 fair value is:

Present value of lease payments	$113,481
Present value of residual guarantee	6,519
Total present value	$120,000

Based on this information, the present value of minimum lease payments exceeds 90% of the fair value of the asset, so it is classified as a capital lease by the lessee. Currency Bank classifies the lease as a direct finance lease.

In the first month of the lease, Currency creates the following entries:

	Debit	Credit
Minimum lease payments receivable	154,000	
Automobile		120,000
Unearned income		34,000
[To record investment of lessor in direct financing lease]		

	Debit	Credit
Cash	2,400	
Minimum lease payments receivable		2,400
[To record receipt of first month's lease payment]		

	Debit	Credit
Unearned income	960	
Earned income		960
[To recognize that portion of unearned income earned during the month]		

The calculation of unearned income that can be recognized in the first month is:

Gross investment – less monthly lease payment	=	$154,000 - $2,400 = $151,600
Less: Unearned income	=	-$34,000
Subtotal	=	= $117,600
÷ Implicit monthly rate (9.8% ÷ 12)	=	× 0.8167%
Earned income	=	= $960

Capital Lease Treatment by Lessor (Leveraged Lease)

If the lessor has classified a lease as a leveraged lease, it records its investment in the underlying asset, and then records its continuing investment in receivables for rent and investment tax credits, as well as for the estimated residual value of the underlying asset and any unearned and deferred income. The lessor's investment in a leveraged lease is as follows:

+	Rents receivable, net of the portion attributable to principal and interest on the related nonrecourse debt
+	Receivable related to an investment tax credit
+	Estimated asset residual value
+	Unearned and deferred income (estimated pretax lease income and investment tax credit to be allocated over the lease term)
=	Investment in leveraged lease

To calculate the amount of income to recognize, the lessor computes the rate of return from all projected cash receipts and disbursements and the lessor's net investment in the lease for those years in which the return is positive. The lessor then applies this interest rate to the net investment to derive net income in those periods when the return is positive. In each year, apply the difference between the net cash flows and the recognized income to the net investment balance.

The lessor should split the amount of recognized net income into three parts, which are as follows:

- Pretax lease income or loss
- Investment tax credit
- Tax effect of pretax lease income or loss

If application of this method will result in the deferral of a loss to future periods, recognize the loss in the current period instead.

If the lessor estimates at the inception of the lease that the future net cash receipts from the lease will be less than its initial investment in the leased asset, it should recognize a loss at once in the amount of the differential.

A lessor using leveraged leases should examine all of its leasing assumptions at least once a year. If there is an other-than-temporary reduction in the estimated residual value of a leased asset, or if a change in assumption alters the estimated net income, or the timing of tax-related cash flows changes, then recalculate the rate of return and the allocation of income by year. This will likely result in a change in the net investment balance; if so, recognize the change in the investment balance as a gain or loss in the period in which the assumptions were altered. No upward adjustment of the estimated residual value is allowed.

Capital Lease Treatment by Lessor (Broadly Applicable)

The following accounting applies to the lessor for any lease classified as a sales-type, direct financing, or leveraged lease:

- *Lease modification.* If the provisions of a capital lease are changed sufficiently to reclassify it as a new agreement that is classified as an operating lease, remove the remaining net investment from the accounts of the lessor, record the leased asset at the lower of its cost or fair value, and charge the adjustment to income.
- *Lease termination.* If a lease is terminated, remove the remaining net investment from the accounts of the lessor, record the leased asset at the lower of its cost or fair value, and charge the adjustment to income.

Sale-Leaseback Transactions

A sale-leaseback transaction is one in which the owner of a property sells it to a third party and then leases it back from the buyer. The situation can also arise when the lessee has all of the construction period risks for a property that it will lease from a third party when the property is complete. Evidence of construction risk retention can include such factors as guaranteeing the construction debt or funding cost overruns. The accounting from the perspectives of the lease participants follows.

Sale-Leaseback Treatment by Lessee

If a sale-leaseback transaction qualifies as a capital lease under the criteria noted in the Overview of Leases section, the lessee classifies the lease as a capital lease. Otherwise, classify it as an operating lease.

The lessee should defer its recognition of a profit or loss on the sale portion of the transaction, except when one of the following conditions is present:

- *Rights relinquished.* The seller leases back only a minor portion of the property sold, in which case the sale and the lease elements are to be accounted for separately.
- *Partial rights retention.* The seller leases back less than the entire amount of the property sold, but more than a minor amount, and realizes a profit greater than either the present value of the minimum lease payments (if classified as an operating lease) or the recorded amount of the leased asset (if classified as a capital lease).
- *Fair value less than cost.* If the fair value of the property on the transaction date is less than its undepreciated cost, recognize a loss at once.

For the purposes of these exceptions, "minor" is when the present value of a rental is not more than 10% of the fair value of the asset sold.

If the recognition of profit on the sale part of the transaction is allowed, measure it by subtracting either the present value of minimum lease payments or the recorded amount of the asset from the sale price. Do not include executory costs in the derivation of profit.

If the recognition of profit on the sale part of the transaction is to be deferred, use the following rules to amortize the profit over time:

- *Land only.* If the leased property is strictly land, recognize the profit over the lease term on a straight-line basis.
- *Other (capital lease).* If the leased property encompasses additional types of property and qualifies as a capital lease, recognize the profit in proportion to the depreciation of the underlying leased asset.
- *Other (operating lease).* If the leased property encompasses additional types of property and qualifies as an operating lease, recognize the profit in proportion to the rent charged to expense over the term of the lease.

If the lessee has instead retained all of the benefits and risks of ownership of the property it has ostensibly sold, the transaction is to be considered a financing. In this case, the lessee cannot recognize a profit on sale of the property if the lease transaction qualifies as a capital lease. If the arrangement involves real estate, evidence of retaining an ownership interest includes the lessee having the option or obligation to repurchase the property, the lessee guaranteeing the lessor's return on investment, or the lessee sharing in any subsequent appreciation of the property.

If the fair value of the asset sold by the lessee is greater than its carrying amount, the difference is treated as a rent prepayment. This means the lessee should defer recognition of the indicated loss, and instead recognize it over the lease term as rent expense.

EXAMPLE

Armadillo Industries sells its headquarters building to a buyer for $2,000,000 and agrees to lease back the building for the next six years for a monthly rental charge of $10,000 for the first three years and $12,000 for the next three years. The building has an estimated remaining life of 20 years. The carrying amount of the property is $1,800,000. The lease is classified as an operating lease.

The total gain on sale of the building is $200,000. Since the arrangement is classified as an operating lease, Armadillo can recognize the profit in proportion to the rent charged to expense over the lease term. The total amount of rent to be paid is $792,000 over the six years of the lease. In each of the first 36 months of the lease, the percentage of the total rent paid is 1.26%, and the percentage is 1.52% in the final 36 months of the lease. Thus, Armadillo can recognize $2,520 of profit in each of the first 36 months of the lease, and $3,040 in each of the final 36 months of the lease (the result is slightly high, due to rounding of the percentages).

Sale-Leaseback Treatment by Lessor

If a sale-leaseback transaction meets the criteria listed earlier in the Overview of Leases section for a capital lease, the lessor should record the property sale as a purchase and an associated direct financing lease. Otherwise, the lessor still records the property sale as a purchase, but accounts for the associated lease as an operating lease.

Lease Disclosures

This section separately addresses the lease-related disclosures required for a lessee and lessor.

Lessee Disclosures

If the lessee has entered into a lease arrangement, disclose the following information in the financial statements:

- *Description*. How contingent rental payments are determined, any renewal, purchase, or escalation clauses, and any restrictions imposed by leasing arrangements.
- *Related parties*. The nature of any leasing transactions with related parties.
- *Sale-leaseback*. The terms of any sale-leaseback transaction, as well as any future obligations or commitments that may require the continuing involvement of the lessee.
- *Rent expense*. Include the rent expense related to operating leases in income from continuing operations. Also disclose the rent expense for every period presented, which should be broken down by minimum, contingent, and sublease rentals.
- *Future payments*. For those operating leases having minimum lease terms of at least one year, disclose the minimum rental payments for each of the next five years, as well as in aggregate, as well as the total amount of minimum sublease rentals to be received in the future.

A lessee recording capital leases should present or disclose the following information pertaining to these arrangements:

- *Assets*. The gross amounts of assets associated with capital leases, by major class. This information can be aggregated with the asset class information for other fixed assets.
- *Capital lease depreciation*. Separately disclose the amount of depreciation related to capital leases in the financial statements or accompanying notes.
- *Capital lease obligations*. Separately identify capital lease obligations in the balance sheet.
- *Contingent rentals*. The amount of contingent rentals incurred during the period.
- *Minimum lease payments*. The minimum lease payments for each of the next five years, and in aggregate, with deductions for any executory costs and the imputed interest used to reduce the payments to their present value.
- *Sublease rentals*. The total amount to be received in the future from noncancelable subleases.

EXAMPLE

Armadillo Industries provides the following disclosures related to leases in the notes accompanying its financial statements:

The company leases the facilities used for most of its production and distribution activities. It currently leases six production facilities and four regional warehouses. The production facility leases are all classified as capital leases, while the warehouse leases are classified as operating leases, all of which expire within the next eight years. The operating leases contain lease renewal options which will be priced at the market rates then in existence if the options are exercised.

Approximately half of the space in one warehouse has been sublet under a short-term lease that expires within two years. The company expects to take over the sublet space once this sublease expires.

The capital lease agreement for one production facility prohibits the company from releasing substances that may enter the water table.

The following is an analysis of the leased production facilities that are classified as capital leases for the past two years:

(000s)	Asset Balances at December 31,	
Property Class	20X1	20X0
Production facilities	$23,700	$18,400
Less: Accumulated amortization	-7,100	-3,900
	$16,600	$14,500

The following schedule shows the future minimum lease payments scheduled for the capital leases, as well as the present value of those payments:

Year ending December 31:	(000s)
20X2	4,000
20X3	4,000
20X4	4,000
20X5	3,000
20X6	2,000
Later years	1,000
Total minimum lease payments	$18,000
Less: Amount representing interest	-1,500
Present value of net minimum lease payments	$16,500

The following schedule shows the future minimum rental payments scheduled for those operating leases with remaining lease terms of greater than one year as of December 31, 20X1:

Year ending December 31:	(000s)
20X2	2,500
20X3	2,650
20X4	3,350
20X5	3,500
20X6	3,600
Later years	6,210
Total minimum payments required	$21,810

Lessor Disclosures

If the lessor has entered into lease arrangements, disclose the following information in the financial statements:

- *Description.* The company's leasing arrangements, if leasing is a significant part of its business. This includes the carrying amount of property designated for leasing by function and the related amount of accumulated depreciation. Also disclose the minimum future rentals related to noncancelable leases for each of the next five years and in aggregate.
- *Contingent rental income.* The policy for how the lessor records contingent rental income. Note any impact on rental income if the lessor were to defer such income until a triggering event occurs. Also disclose the total amount of contingent rentals included in income for each period presented.
- *Leveraged leases.* Present the amount of deferred taxes related to leveraged leases separately from the net investment in the balance sheet. Also, separately present leveraged lease pretax income, the tax effect of pretax income, and the recognized amount of investment tax credit in the income statement. If a change in tax rates yields a significant difference in the usual relationship between income tax expense and pretax income, state the reason for the difference.
- *Related parties.* The nature of any leasing transactions with related parties.
- *Sales-type and direct financing leases.* If the lessor has a significant amount of sales-type or direct financing leases, disclose the following:
  - Total contingent rentals recognized in income
  - The future minimum lease payments to be received in each of the next five years
  - The net investment in these lease types, subdivided by future minimum lease payments not yet received (with deductions for executory costs and the uncollectible payments allowance), unguaranteed residual values benefiting the lessor, and unearned income. Also state initial direct costs for direct financing leases.

EXAMPLE

Currency Leasing discloses the following information in its financial statements related to its leasing operations:

The company's leasing operations are restricted to the leasing of office equipment and production machinery. All of the company's leases are classified as direct financing leases. All office equipment leases expire over the next three years, and the production machinery leases expire over the next ten years.

The following table itemizes the components of Currency's net investment in direct financing leases as of December 31:

(000s)	20X1	20X0
Total minimum lease payments receivable	$42,600	$39,800
Less: Estimated executory costs included in lease payments	-700	-650
Minimum lease payments receivable	41,900	39,150
Less: Allowance for doubtful accounts	-420	-380
Net minimum lease payments receivable	41,480	38,770
Add: Estimated residual values of leased property	8,040	7,900
Less: Unearned income	-1,500	-1,400
Net investment in direct financing leases	$48,020	$45,270

The balance sheet presentation of leased property by the lessor should be within or near the property, plant, and equipment line items. Accumulated depreciation should be deducted from these reported assets.

Summary

Organizations tend to use the same types of financing solutions for certain types of assets over long periods of time, perhaps because they use the same leasing companies for many transactions. A common result is that certain asset classes are always financed with operating leases, while other asset classes are always financed with capital leases. For example, photocopiers are more likely to be financed with operating leases, while production equipment tends to be financed with capital leases. The result can be a simplified accounting environment where the accounting staff develops a procedure for how to account for each type of lease, and then applies it to entire asset classes that have been financed in the same manner.

Conversely, the most difficult leasing environment is when a jumble of leases are obtained from different leasing firms, with each lease using a different set of leasing criteria that makes it much less efficient for the accounting staff to identify lease types and apply the appropriate accounting to each leased asset.

Clearly, a consistent approach to lease financing can be very efficient from an accounting perspective.

Chapter 18
Accounting Changes and Error Corrections

Introduction

From time to time, a company will find that it must change its accounting to reflect a change in accounting principle or estimate, or it may locate an accounting error that must be corrected. In this chapter, we address the rules for both situations and how to disclose them, as well as for several related situations.

Changes in Accounting Principle

There is an assumption in GAAP that, once an accounting principle has been adopted by a business, the principle shall be consistently applied in recording transactions and events from that point forward. Consistent application is a cornerstone of accounting, since it allows the readers of financial statements to compare the results of multiple accounting periods. Given how important it is to maintain consistency in the application of accounting principles, a business should only change an accounting principle in one of the two following situations:
- The change is required by an update to GAAP
- The use of an alternative principle is preferable

Tip: Thoroughly document the reason for any change in accounting principle, since it will likely be reviewed by the company's auditors.

Whenever there is a change in accounting principle, retrospective application of the new principle to prior accounting periods is required, unless it is impracticable to do so. If it is impracticable to retroactively apply changes to prior interim periods of the current fiscal year, then the change in accounting principle can only be made as of the start of a subsequent fiscal year.

Tip: Where possible, companies are encouraged to adopt changes in accounting principle as of the first interim period of a fiscal year.

The activities required for retrospective application are:
1. Alter the carrying amounts of assets and liabilities for the cumulative effect of the change in principle as of the beginning of the first accounting period presented.
2. Adjust the beginning balance of retained earnings to offset the change noted in the first step.

3. Adjust the financial statements for each prior period presented to reflect the impact of the new accounting principle.

If it is impracticable to make these changes, then do so as of the earliest reported periods for which it is practicable to do so. It is considered impracticable to make a retrospective change when any of the following conditions apply:

- *Assumptions*. Making a retrospective application calls for assumptions about what management intended to do in prior periods, and those assumptions cannot be independently substantiated.
- *Efforts made*. The company has made every reasonable effort to do so.
- *Estimates*. Estimates are required, which are impossible to provide due to the lack of information about the circumstances in the earlier periods.

When making prior period adjustments due to a change in accounting principle, do so only for the direct effects of the change. A direct effect is one that is *required* to switch accounting principles.

EXAMPLE

Armadillo Industries changes from the last in, first out method of inventory accounting to the first in, first out method. Doing so calls for an increase in the ending inventory in the preceding period, which in turn increases net profits for that period. Altering the inventory balance is a direct effect of the change in principle.

An indirect effect of the change in principle would be a change in the corporate accrual for profit sharing in the prior period. Since it is an indirect effect, Armadillo does not record the change.

Changes in Accounting Estimate

A change in accounting estimate occurs when there is an adjustment to the carrying amount of an asset or liability, or the subsequent accounting for it. Examples of changes in accounting estimate are changes in:

- The allowance for doubtful accounts
- The reserve for obsolete inventory
- Changes in the useful life of depreciable assets
- Changes in the salvage values of depreciable assets
- Changes in the amount of expected warranty obligations

Changes in accounting estimate occur relatively frequently, and so would require a considerable amount of effort to make an ongoing series of retroactive changes to prior financial statements. Instead, GAAP only requires that changes in accounting estimate be accounted for in the period of change and thereafter. Thus, no retrospective change is required or allowed.

Changes in Reporting Entity

There are situations where a change in the entities included in consolidated financial statements effectively means that there is a change in reporting entity. If so, apply the change retrospectively to all of the periods being reported. The result should be the consistent presentation of financial information for the same reporting entity for all periods, including interim periods.

Correction of an Error in Previously Issued Financial Statements

From time to time, financial statements will be inadvertently issued that contain one or more errors. When such an error is discovered, the prior period financial statements to which the error applies must be restated. Restatement requires the following steps:

1. Alter the carrying amounts of assets and liabilities for the cumulative effect of the error as of the beginning of the first accounting period presented.
2. Adjust the beginning balance of retained earnings to offset the change noted in the first step.
3. Adjust the financial statements for each prior period presented to reflect the impact of the error.

Corrections Related to Prior Interim Periods

GAAP specifies several situations in which the financial statements of prior interim periods of the current fiscal year should be adjusted. These adjustments are for the following:

- Adjustment or settlement of litigation
- Income taxes
- Renegotiation proceedings
- Utility revenue under rate-making processes

Adjustments for these items are only necessary if all of the following criteria apply:

- The effect of the change is material to income from continuing operations, or its trend
- The adjustments are directly related to the prior interim periods
- The adjustment amount could not be reasonably estimated prior to the current interim period, but can now be estimated

If an adjustment occurs in any interim period other than the first period, use the following steps to account for it:

1. Include any portion of the adjustment that relates to current business activities in the current interim period.
2. Restate prior interim periods of the current fiscal year to include that portion of the item that relates to the business activities in those periods.

3. Restate the first interim period of the current fiscal year to include that portion of the item that relates to the business activities in prior fiscal years.

The Materiality of an Error

When an accounting error is discovered, determine whether it is material enough to report. To do so, compare its effect to the full-year estimated income or the full-year earnings trend. If it is not material, there is no need to disclose it. However, it the error is material in relation to the estimated income or earnings trend for an interim period, disclose the error in the financial statements for that interim period.

Accounting Changes and Error Corrections Disclosures

There are a number of variations on the disclosures required for the various types of accounting changes and error corrections, so we address each one within the following sub-sections.

Change in Accounting Principle

When there is a change in accounting principle, disclose all of the following items in the period in which the change takes place:

- *Nature of the change.* The nature of the change and why the new principle is preferable.
- *Application method.* State the method used to apply the change, including:
  - The information being adjusted
  - The effect of the change on income from continuing operations, net income, any other affected financial statement line items, and any affected per-share amounts
  - The cumulative effect of the change on retained earnings in the balance sheet as of the beginning of the earliest period presented
  - The reasons why retrospective application is impracticable (if this is the case), and the alternative method used to report the change
- *Indirect effects.* If you have elected to recognize the indirect effects of a change in principle, disclose the effects, the amounts recognized in the current period, and any applicable per-share amounts, and the same information for all prior periods presented (unless impracticable to do so).

These disclosures are required for all interim and annual financial statements that are reported.

When you adopt a new accounting principle, disclose the effect of the change on income from continuing operations, net income, and any related per-share amounts for all remaining interim periods in the current fiscal year.

Change in Accounting Estimate

If there is a change in estimate that will affect several future periods, disclose the effect on income from continuing operations, net income, and any related per-share amounts. This disclosure is not needed for ongoing changes in estimate that arise in the ordinary course of business, such as changes in reserves. In effect, this disclosure is only required if the change is material. If there is not an immediate material effect, but a material effect is expected in later periods, provide a description of the change in estimate.

Change in Reporting Entity

In those rare cases where there has been a change in reporting entity, disclose the nature of and reason for the change. In addition, report the effect of the change on income before extraordinary items, net income, other comprehensive income, and any related per-share amounts for all periods presented. If there is not an immediate material effect, but a material effect is expected in later periods, state the nature of and reason for the change in the period in which the change occurred.

Error Corrections

When you restate financial statements to correct an error, disclose the following information:
- A statement that the previously issued financial statements have been restated, and describe the error
- The effect of the error correction on financial statement line items and per-share amounts for each period presented
- The cumulative effect of the error correction on retained earnings as of the beginning of the earliest period presented
- The before-tax and after-tax effect on net income for each prior period reported. If the results of only one period are reported, indicate the effect on net income for the immediately preceding period

If there is an error correction related to prior interim periods of the current fiscal year, disclose the effect on income from continuing operations, net income, and related per-share amounts for all of the prior interim periods of the current fiscal year, as well as the restated results for these line items.

Historical Summaries

If a business issues historical summaries of its results for a number of prior years, be sure to adjust these summaries for any errors found in affected years, and disclose the changes alongside the summaries.

EXAMPLE

Armadillo Industries provides the following disclosure regarding a change in its method of accounting for the valuation of its inventory:

On January 1, 20X1, Armadillo changed its method for valuing inventory to the weighted-average method. The company had previously used the LIFO method to value its inventory. The new method was adopted because management felt that having very old inventory layers misrepresented the value of the company's reported inventory. The company's comparative financial statements for previous years have been adjusted to apply the new method retrospectively.

The following financial statement line items for fiscal years 20X1 and 20X0 were affected by this change in accounting principle:

20X1 Income Statement

	As Computed under LIFO	As Reported under Weighted Average	Effect of Change
Sales	$1,000,000	$1,000,000	$0
Cost of goods sold	600,000	580,000	20,000
Selling, general and administrative expenses	375,000	375,000	0
Income before taxes	25,000	45,000	20,000
Income taxes	9,000	16,000	-7,000
Net income	$16,000	$29,000	$13,000

20X0 Income Statement

	As Originally Reported	As Adjusted	Effect of Change
Sales	$900,000	$900,000	$0
Cost of goods sold	540,000	525,000	15,000
Selling, general and administrative expenses	350,000	350,000	0
Income before taxes	10,000	25,000	15,000
Income taxes	3,000	9,000	-6,000
Net income	$7,000	$16,000	$9,000

20X1 Balance Sheet

	As Computed under LIFO	As Reported under Weighted Average	Effect of Change
Cash	$100,000	$100,000	$0
Accounts receivable	350,000	350,000	0
Inventory	400,000	420,000	20,000
Total assets	$850,000	$870,000	$20,000
Accounts payable	$125,000	$125,000	$0
Income tax liability	9,000	16,000	7,000
Paid-in capital	500,000	500,000	0
Retained earnings	216,000	229,000	13,000
Total liabilities and stockholders' equity	$850,000	$870,000	$20,000

20X0 Balance Sheet

	As Originally Reported	As Adjusted	Effect of Change
Cash	$80,000	$80,000	$0
Accounts receivable	320,000	320,000	0
Inventory	360,000	375,000	15,000
Total assets	$760,000	$775,000	$15,000
Accounts payable	$100,000	$100,000	$0
Income tax liability	3,000	9,000	6,000
Paid-in capital	500,000	500,000	0
Retained earnings	157,000	166,000	9,000
Total liabilities and stockholders' equity	$760,000	$775,000	$15,000

Summary

Retrospective changes can require a considerable amount of detective accounting work, judgment, and thorough documentation of the changes made. Given the amount of labor involved, it is cost-effective to find justifiable reasons for not making retrospective changes. Two valid methods for doing so are to question the materiality of the necessary changes, or to find reasons to instead treat issues as changes in accounting estimate.

If retrospective application is completely unavoidable, it may make sense to have the company's auditors review proposed retrospective changes in advance. Doing so minimizes the risk that an issue will be discovered by the auditors during the annual audit, which will require additional retrospective changes.

Chapter 19
Closing the Books

Introduction

A great many steps are required to close the books and issue financial statements. In this chapter, we give an overview of the most prevalent closing activities that you are likely to need.

The closing process does not begin after a reporting period has been completed. Instead, you should be preparing for it well in advance. By doing so, you can complete a number of activities in a leisurely manner before the end of the month, leaving fewer items for the busier period immediately following the end of the period. Accordingly, we have grouped closing steps into the following categories:

1. *Prior steps.* These are steps needed to complete the processing of the financial statements, and which can usually be completed before the end of the reporting period.
2. *Core steps.* These are the steps that are required for the creation of financial statements, and which cannot be completed prior to the end of the reporting period.
3. *Delayed steps.* These are the activities that can be safely delayed until after the issuance of the financial statements, but which are still part of the closing process.

The sections in this chapter do not necessarily represent the exact sequence of activities to follow when closing the books; you may want to alter the sequence based on the processes of your company, and the availability of employees to work on them.

> **Related Podcast Episodes:** Episodes 17 through 25, 77, and 160 of the Accounting Best Practices Podcast discuss the fast close and the soft close, respectively. You can listen to them at: **accountingtools.com/podcasts** or **iTunes**

Prior Steps: Update Reserves

Under the accrual basis of accounting, create a reserve in the expectation that expenses will be incurred in the future that are related to revenues generated now. This concept is called the matching principle. Under the matching principle, you record the cause and effect of a business transaction at the same time. Thus, when you record revenue, you should also record within the same accounting period any expenses directly related to that revenue.

The most common of all reserves is the allowance for doubtful accounts. It is used to charge to expense the amount of bad debts that you expect from a certain amount of sales, before you know precisely which invoices will not be paid. This allowance is updated as part of the closing process.

Review the balance in the allowance for doubtful accounts as part of the month-end closing process, to ensure that the balance is reasonable in comparison to the latest bad debt forecast. For companies having minimal bad debt activity, a quarterly update may be sufficient. The following example demonstrates how the allowance is handled.

EXAMPLE

Milagro Corporation records $10,000,000 of sales to several hundred customers, and projects (based on historical experience) that it will incur 1% of this amount as bad debts, though it does not know exactly which customers will default. It records the 1% of projected bad debts as a $100,000 debit to the bad debt expense account and a credit to the allowance for doubtful accounts. The bad debt expense is charged to expense right away, and the allowance for doubtful accounts becomes a reserve account that offsets the accounts receivable of $10,000,000 (for a net receivable on the balance sheet of $9,900,000). The entry is:

	Debit	Credit
Bad debt expense	100,000	
Allowance for doubtful accounts		100,000

Later, several customers default on payments totaling $40,000. Accordingly, the company credits the accounts receivable account by $40,000 to reduce the amount of outstanding accounts receivable, and debits the allowance for doubtful accounts by $40,000. This entry reduces the balance in the allowance account to $60,000. The entry does not impact earnings in the current period. The entry is:

	Debit	Credit
Allowance for doubtful accounts	40,000	
Accounts receivable		40,000

A few months later, a collection agency succeeds in collecting $15,000 of the funds that Milagro had already written off. The company can now reverse part of the previous entry, thereby increasing the balances of both the accounts receivable and the allowance for doubtful accounts. The entry is:

	Debit	Credit
Accounts receivable	15,000	
Allowance for doubtful accounts		15,000

There are a number of other reserves to consider, such as:

- *Inventory obsolescence reserve.* If there is an expectation that there are some higher-cost items in inventory that will be rendered obsolete and disposed of, even if you are not sure which items they are, create an obsolescence reserve, and charge any losses against the reserve as you locate and dispose of these items.

- *Reserve for product returns.* If there is a history of significant product returns from customers, estimate the percentage of these returns based on prior history, and create a reserve using that percentage whenever you record related sales.
- *Reserve for warranty claims.* If the company has experienced a material amount of warranty claims in the past, and it can reasonably estimate the amount of these claims in the future, create a reserve in that amount whenever you record related sales.

The reserves just noted are among the more common ones. You may find a need for more unique types of reserves that are specific to your company's industry or business model.

There is no need to create a reserve if the balance in the account is going to be immaterial. Instead, many businesses can generate perfectly adequate financial statements that only have a few reserves, while charging all other expenditures to expense as incurred.

Core Steps: Issue Customer Invoices

Part of the closing process nearly always includes the issuance of month-end invoices to customers, especially in situations (such as consulting) where billable hours are compiled throughout the month and then billed at one time, or where a company has a practice of shipping most of its products near the end of the month. In other cases, invoices may have been issued throughout the month, leaving only a residual number to be issued as part of the closing process.

Irrespective of the number of invoices to be issued, invoices are always an important part of the closing process, because they are the primary method for recognizing revenue. Consequently, you normally spend a significant part of the closing process verifying that all possible invoices have, in fact, been created. This verification process may include a comparison of the shipping log to the invoice register, or a comparison of the shipping log to the timekeeping system where billable hours are stored or to a listing of open contracts.

If some revenues are considered to not yet be billable, but to have been fully earned by the company, you can accrue the revenue with a journal entry. If you use this approach, be sure to address the following issues:

- *Auditor documentation.* Auditors do not like accrued revenue, since there are a number of restrictions placed on its use under GAAP. Consequently, you should fully document the reasons for accruing revenue, with complete backup of the revenue calculations. The auditors will review this information. However, if you are only accruing revenue partway through a year, it may not be necessary to document the transactions in detail, since they should no longer be present on the balance sheet by the end of the fiscal year.
- *Reversing entry.* When you accrue revenue, the assumption is that you are likely to issue an invoice soon thereafter, probably in the next month. Con-

sequently, set up every revenue accrual journal entry to automatically reverse in the next month. This clears the revenue accrual from the books, leaving room to record the revenue on the invoice. The following example illustrates the technique.

EXAMPLE

Milagro Corporation has fulfilled all of the terms of a contract with a customer to deliver a coffee bean roasting facility, but is unable to issue an invoice until July, which is the following month. Accordingly, the accountant creates a revenue accrual with the following entry in June:

	Debit	Credit
Accrued revenue receivable (asset)	6,500,000	
Accrued revenue (revenue)		6,500,000

The accountant sets the journal entry to automatically reverse in the next month, so the accounting software creates the following entry at the beginning of July:

	Debit	Credit
Accrued revenue (revenue)	6,500,000	
Accrued revenue receivable (asset)		6,500,000

In July, Milagro is now able to issue the invoice to the customer. When the invoice is created, the billing module of the accounting software creates the following entry in July:

	Debit	Credit
Accounts receivable	6,500,000	
Revenue		6,500,000

Thus, the net impact of these transactions is:

June:	Accrued revenue =	$6,500,000
July:	Accrued revenue reversal =	-$6,500,000
	Invoice generated =	+6,500,000
	Net effect in July =	$0

Core Steps: Value Inventory

Potentially the most time-consuming activity in the closing process is valuing ending inventory. This involves the following steps:

1. *Physical count.* Either conduct an ending inventory count or have an adequate perpetual inventory system in place that yields a verifiable ending inventory.

2. *Determine the cost of the ending inventory.* There are several methods available for assigning a cost to the ending inventory, such as the first in first out method, the last in first out method, and standard costing.

3. *Allocate overhead.* Allocate the costs of manufacturing overhead to any inventory items that are classified as work-in-process or finished goods. Overhead is not allocated to raw materials inventory, since the operations giving rise to overhead costs only impact work-in-process and finished goods inventory. The following items are usually included in manufacturing overhead:

Depreciation of factory equipment	Quality control and inspection
Factory administration expenses	Rent, facility and equipment
Indirect labor and production supervisory wages	Repair expenses
Indirect materials and supplies	Rework labor, scrap and spoilage
Maintenance, factory and production equipment	Taxes related to production assets
Officer salaries related to production	Uncapitalized tools and equipment
Production employees' benefits	Utilities

The typical procedure for allocating overhead is to accumulate all manufacturing overhead costs into one or more cost pools, and to then use an activity measure to apportion the overhead costs in the cost pools to inventory. Thus, the overhead allocation formula is:

Cost pool ÷ Total activity measure = Overhead allocation per unit

4. *Adjust the valuation.* It may be necessary to reduce the amount of ending inventory due to the lower of cost or market rule, or for the presence of obsolete inventory. The lower of cost or market rule is required by GAAP, and requires that you record the cost of inventory at whichever cost is lower – the original cost or its current market price. This situation typically arises when inventory has deteriorated, or has become obsolete, or market prices have declined. The "current market price" is defined as the current replacement cost of the inventory, as long as the market price does not exceed net realizable value; also, the market price shall not be less than the net realizable value, less the normal profit margin. Net realizable value is defined as the estimated selling price, minus estimated costs of completion and disposal.

EXAMPLE

Milagro Corporation has a small production line for toy coffee roasters. During April, it incurs costs for the following items:

Cost Type	Amount
Building rent	$65,000
Building utilities	12,000
Factory equipment depreciation	8,000
Production equipment maintenance	7,000
Total	$92,000

All of these items are classified as manufacturing overhead, so Milagro creates the following journal entry to shift these costs into an overhead cost pool for later allocation:

	Debit	Credit
Overhead cost pool	92,000	
Depreciation expense		8,000
Maintenance expense		7,000
Rent expense		65,000
Utilities expense		12,000

EXAMPLE

Milagro Corporation resells five major brands of coffee, which are noted in the following table. At the end of its reporting year, Milagro calculates the lower of its cost or net realizable value in the following table:

Product Line	Quantity on Hand	Unit Cost	Inventory at Cost	Market per Unit	Lower of Cost or Market
Arbuthnot	1,000	$190	$190,000	$230	$190,000
Bagley	750	140	105,000	170	105,000
Chowdry	200	135	27,000	120	24,000
Dingle	1,200	280	336,000	160	192,000
Ephraim	800	200	160,000	215	160,000

Based on the table, the market value is lower than cost on the Chowdry and Dingle coffee lines. Consequently, Milagro recognizes a loss on the Chowdry line of $3,000 ($27,000 - $24,000), as well as a loss of $144,000 ($336,000 - $192,000) on the Dingle line.

There are many steps because of the complexity of inventory valuation, but also because the investment in inventory may be so large that you simply cannot afford to arrive at an incorrect valuation – an error here could require a considerable adjustment to the financial statements in a later period.

If there is a relatively small investment in inventory, it may not be so necessary to invest a large amount of time in closing inventory, since the size of potential errors is substantially reduced.

Core Steps: Calculate Depreciation

Once all fixed assets have been recorded in the accounting records for the month, calculate the amount of depreciation (for tangible assets) and amortization (for intangible assets). This is a significant issue for companies with a large investment in fixed assets, but may be so insignificant in other situations that it is sufficient to only record depreciation at the end of the year.

The basic depreciation entry is to debit the depreciation expense account (which appears in the income statement) and credit the accumulated depreciation account (which appears in the balance sheet as a contra account that reduces the amount of fixed assets). Over time, the accumulated depreciation balance will continue to increase as more depreciation is added to it, until such time as it equals the original cost of the asset. At that time, stop recording any depreciation expense, since the cost of the asset has now been reduced to zero.

The journal entry for depreciation can be a simple two-line entry designed to accommodate all types of fixed assets, or it may be subdivided into separate entries for each type of fixed asset.

EXAMPLE

Milagro Corporation calculates that it should have $25,000 of depreciation expense in the current month. The entry is:

	Debit	Credit
Depreciation expense	25,000	
Accumulated depreciation		25,000

In the following month, Milagro's accountant decides to show a higher level of precision at the expense account level, and instead elects to apportion the $25,000 of depreciation among different expense accounts, so that each class of asset has a separate depreciation charge. The entry is:

	Debit	Credit
Depreciation expense – Automobiles	4,000	
Depreciation expense – Computer equipment	8,000	
Depreciation expense – Furniture and fixtures	6,000	
Depreciation expense – Office equipment	5,000	
Depreciation expense – Software	2,000	
Accumulated depreciation		25,000

An intangible asset is a non-physical asset having a useful life greater than one year. Examples of intangible assets are trademarks, patents, and non-competition agreements. The journal entry to record the amortization of intangible assets is fundamentally the same as the entry for depreciation, except that the accounts used substitute the word "amortization" for depreciation.

EXAMPLE

Milagro Corporation calculates that it should have $4,000 of amortization expense in the current month that is related to intangible assets. The entry is:

	Debit	Credit
Amortization expense	4,000	
Accumulated amortization		4,000

If you are constructing fixed assets (as would be the case for a factory or company headquarters) and have incurred debt to do so, it may be necessary to capitalize some interest expense into the cost of the fixed assets. Interest capitalization is the inclusion of any interest expense directly related to the construction of a fixed asset in the cost of that fixed asset.

Follow these steps to calculate the amount of interest to be capitalized for a specific project:

1. Construct a table itemizing the amounts of expenditures made and the dates on which the expenditures were made.
2. Determine the date on which interest capitalization ends.
3. Calculate the capitalization period for each expenditure, which is the number of days between the specific expenditure and the end of the interest capitalization period.
4. Divide each capitalization period by the total number of days elapsed between the date of the first expenditure and the end of the interest capitalization period to arrive at the capitalization multiplier for each line item.
5. Multiply each expenditure amount by its capitalization multiplier to arrive at the average expenditure for each line item over the capitalization measurement period.
6. Add up the average expenditures at the line item level to arrive at a grand total average expenditure.
7. If there is project-specific debt, multiply the grand total of the average expenditures by the interest rate on that debt to arrive at the capitalized interest related to that debt.
8. If the grand total of the average expenditures exceeds the amount of the project-specific debt, multiply the excess expenditure amount by the weighted average of the company's other outstanding debt to arrive at the remaining amount of interest to be capitalized.
9. Add together both capitalized interest calculations. If the combined total is more than the total interest cost incurred by the company during the calculation period, reduce the amount of interest to be capitalized to the total interest cost incurred by the company during the calculation period.

10. Record the interest capitalization with a debit to the project's fixed asset account and a credit to the interest expense account.

EXAMPLE

Milagro Corporation is building a company headquarters building. Milagro makes payments related to the project of $10,000,000 and $14,000,000 to a contractor on January 1 and July 1, respectively. The building is completed on December 31.

For the 12-month period of construction, Milagro can capitalize all of the interest on the $10,000,000 payment, since it was outstanding during the full period of construction. Milagro can capitalize the interest on the $14,000,000 payment for half of the construction period, since it was outstanding during only the second half of the construction period. The average expenditure for which the interest cost can be capitalized is calculated in the following table:

Date of Payment	Expenditure Amount	Capitalization Period*	Capitalization Multiplier	Average Expenditure
January 1	$10,000,000	12 months	12 ÷ 12 months = 100%	$10,000,000
July 1	14,000,000	6 months	6 ÷ 12 months = 50%	7,000,000
				$17,000,000

* In the table, the capitalization period is defined as the number of months that elapse between the expenditure payment date and the end of the interest capitalization period.

The only debt that Milagro has outstanding during this period is a line of credit, on which the interest rate is 8%. The maximum amount of interest that Milagro can capitalize into the cost of the building project is $1,360,000, which is calculated as:

8% Interest rate × $17,000,000 Average expenditure = $1,360,000

Milagro records the following journal entry:

	Debit	Credit
Buildings (asset)	1,360,000	
Interest expense		1,360,000

Tip: There may be an inordinate number of expenditures related to a larger project, which could result in a large and unwieldy calculation of average expenditures. To reduce the workload, consider aggregating these expenses by month, and then assume that each expenditure was made in the middle of the month, thereby reducing all of the expenditures for each month to a single line item.

You cannot capitalize more interest cost in an accounting period than the total amount of interest cost incurred by the business in that period. If there is a corporate parent, this rule means that the amount capitalized cannot exceed the total amount of interest cost incurred by the business on a consolidated basis.

Core Steps: Create Accruals

An accrual allows you to record expenses and revenues for which you expect to expend cash or receive cash, respectively, in a future reporting period. The offset to an accrued expense is an accrued liability account, which appears in the balance sheet. The offset to accrued revenue is an accrued asset account (such as unbilled consulting fees), which also appears in the balance sheet. Examples of accruals are:

- *Revenue accrual.* A consulting company works billable hours on a project that it will eventually invoice to a client for $5,000. It can record an accrual in the current period so that its current income statement shows $5,000 of revenue, even though it has not yet billed the client.
- *Expense accrual – general.* A supplier provides $10,000 of services before month-end, but does not issue an invoice to the company by the time it closes its books. Accordingly, the company accrues a $10,000 expense to reflect the receipt of services.
- *Expense accrual – interest.* A company has a loan with the local bank for $1 million, and pays interest on the loan at a variable rate of interest. The invoice from the bank for $3,000 in interest expense does not arrive until the following month, so the company accrues the expense in order to show the amount on its income statement in the proper month.
- *Expense accrual – wages.* A company pays its employees at the end of each month for their hours worked through the 25th day of the month. To fully record the wage expense for the entire month, it also accrues $32,000 in additional wages, which represents the cost of wages for the remaining days of the month.

Most accruals are initially created as reversing entries, so that the accounting software automatically creates a reverse version of them in the following month. This happens when you are expecting revenue to actually be billed, or supplier invoices to actually arrive, in the next month.

Core Steps: Consolidate Division Results

If there are company divisions that forward their financial results to the parent company, the largest issue from the perspective of the close is simply obtaining the information in a timely manner. This information may be provided in the format of a trial balance report. You should then input the summary totals for all accounts provided into the general ledger of the parent company. This process is repeated for all of the divisions.

If the company uses the same accounting software throughout the business, then it may be quite simple to consolidate the division results, but only if the software is networked together. Otherwise, it will be necessary to create a separate journal entry to record the results of each division.

> **Tip:** If you record division results with a journal entry, the transaction likely involves a large number of line items. To reduce the risk of recording this information incorrectly, create a journal entry template in the accounting software that includes only the relevant accounts. If the entries for the various divisions are substantially different, consider creating a separate template for each one.

Core Steps: Eliminate Intercompany Transactions

If there are several divisions within a company for which accounting transactions are recorded separately, it is possible that they do business with each other. For example, if a company is vertically integrated, some subsidiaries may sell their output to other subsidiaries, which in turn sell their output to other subsidiaries. If this is the case, they are generating intercompany transactions to record the sales. Intercompany transactions must be eliminated from the consolidated financial statements of the business, since not doing so would artificially inflate the revenue of the company as a whole. This elimination requires you to reverse the sale and offsetting account receivable for each such transaction.

Intercompany transactions can be difficult to spot, especially in businesses where such transactions are rare, and therefore not closely monitored. In a larger business, it is relatively easy to flag these transactions as being intercompany when they are created, so that the system automatically reverses them when the financial statements are consolidated. However, this feature is usually only available in the more expensive accounting software packages.

Core Steps: Review Journal Entries

It is entirely possible that some journal entries were made incorrectly, in duplicate, or not at all. You should print the list of standard journal entries and compare it to the actual entries made in the general ledger, just to ensure that they were entered in the general ledger correctly. Another test is to have someone review the detailed calculations supporting each journal entry, and trace them through to the actual entries in the general ledger. This second approach takes more time, but is quite useful for ensuring that all necessary journal entries have been made correctly.

If you are interested in closing the books quickly, the latter approach could interfere with the speed of the close; if so, authorize this detailed review at a later date, when someone can conduct the review under less time pressure. However, any errors found can only be corrected in the *following* accounting period, since the financial statements will already have been issued.

Core Steps: Reconcile Accounts

It is very important to examine the contents of the balance sheet accounts to verify that the recorded assets and liabilities are supposed to be there. It is quite possible that some items are still listed in an account that should have been flushed out of the balance sheet a long time ago, which can be quite embarrassing if they are still on record when the auditors review the company's books at the end of the year. Here are several situations that a proper account reconciliation would have caught:

- *Prepaid assets.* A company issues a $10,000 bid bond to a local government. The company loses the bid, but is not repaid. The asset lingers on the books until year-end, when the auditors inquire about it, and the company then recovers the funds from the local government.

- *Accrued revenue.* A company accrues revenue of $50,000 for a services contract, but forgets to reverse the entry in the following month, when it invoices the full $50,000 to the customer. This results in the double recordation of revenue, which is not spotted until year-end. The accountant then reverses the accrual, thereby unexpectedly reducing revenues for the full year by $50,000.

- *Depreciation.* A company calculates the depreciation on several hundred assets with an electronic spreadsheet, which unfortunately does not track when to stop depreciating assets. A year-end review finds that the company charged $40,000 of excess depreciation to expense.

- *Accumulated depreciation.* A company has been disposing of its assets for years, but has never bothered to eliminate the associated accumulated depreciation from its balance sheet. Doing so reduces both the fixed asset and accumulated depreciation accounts by 50%.

- *Accounts payable.* A company does not compare its accounts payable detail report to the general ledger account balance, which is $8,000 lower than the detail. The auditors spot the error and require a correcting entry at year-end, so that the account balance matches the detail report.

These issues and many more are common problems encountered at year-end. To prevent the extensive embarrassment and error corrections caused by these problems, conduct account reconciliations every month for the larger accounts, and occasionally review the detail for the smaller accounts, too. The following are some of the account reconciliations to conduct, as well as the specific issues to look for:

Sample Account Reconciliation List

Account	Reconciliation Discussion
Cash	There can be a number of unrecorded checks, deposits, and bank fees that you will only spot with a bank reconciliation. It is permissible to do a partial bank reconciliation a day or two before the close, but completely ignoring it is not a good idea.
Accounts receivable, trade	The accounts receivable detail report should match the account balance. If not, you probably created a journal entry that should be eliminated from this account.
Accounts receivable, other	This account usually includes a large proportion of accounts receivable from employees, which are probably being deducted from their paychecks over time. This is a prime source of errors, since payroll deductions may not have been properly reflected in this account.

Account	Reconciliation Discussion
Accrued revenue	It is good practice to reverse all accrued revenue out of this account at the beginning of every period, so that you are forced to create new accruals every month. Thus, if there is a residual balance in the account, it probably should not be there.
Prepaid assets	This account may contain a variety of assets that will be charged to expense in the short term, so it may require frequent reviews to ensure that items have been flushed out in a timely manner.
Inventory	If you are using a periodic inventory system, you must match the inventory account to the ending inventory balance, which calls for a monthly reconciliation. However, if you are using a perpetual inventory system, inadequate cycle counting can lead to incorrect inventory balances. Thus, the level of reconciliation work depends upon the quality of the supporting inventory tracking system.
Fixed assets	It is quite likely that fixed assets will initially be recorded in the wrong fixed asset account, or that they are disposed of incorrectly. You should reconcile the account to the fixed asset detail report at least once a quarter to spot and correct these issues.
Accumulated depreciation	The balance in this account may not match the fixed asset detail if you have not removed the accumulated depreciation from the account upon the sale or disposal of an asset. This is not a critical issue, but still warrants occasional review.
Accounts payable, trade	The accounts payable detail report should match the account balance. If not, you probably included the account in a journal entry, and should reverse that entry.
Accrued expenses	This account can include a large number of accruals for such expenses as wages, vacations, and benefits. It is good practice to reverse all of these expenses in the month following recordation. Thus, if there is a residual balance, there may be an excess accrual still on the books.
Sales taxes payable	If state and local governments mandate the forwarding of collected sales taxes every month, this means that beginning account balances should have been paid out during the subsequent month. Consequently, there should not be any residual balances from the preceding month, unless payment intervals are longer than one month.
Income taxes payable	The amount of income taxes paid on a quarterly basis does not have to match the accrued liability, so there can be a residual balance in the account. However, you should still examine the account, if only to verify that scheduled payments have been made.
Notes payable	The balance in this account should exactly match the account balance of the lender, barring any exceptions for in-transit payments to the lender.
Equity	In an active equity environment where there are frequent stock issuances or treasury stock purchases, these accounts may require considerable review to ensure that the account balances can be verified. However, if there is only sporadic account activity, it may be acceptable to reconcile at much longer intervals.

The number of accounts that can be reconciled makes it clear that this is one of the larger steps involved in closing the books. You can skip selected reconciliations from time to time, but doing so presents the risk of an error creeping into the financial statements and not being spotted for quite a few months. Consequently, there is a significant risk of issuing inaccurate financial statements if you continually avoid some reconciliations.

Core Steps: Close Subsidiary Ledgers

Depending on the type of accounting software you are using, it may be necessary to resolve any open issues in subsidiary ledgers, create a transaction to shift the totals in these balances to the general ledger (called *posting*), and then close the accounting periods within the subsidiary ledgers and open the next accounting period. This may involve ledgers for inventory, accounts receivable, and accounts payable.

Other accounting software systems (typically those developed more recently) do not have subsidiary ledgers, or at least use ones that do not require posting, and so are essentially invisible from the perspective of closing the books. Posting is the process of copying either summary-level or detailed entries in an accounting journal into the general ledger. Posting is needed in order to have a complete record of all accounting transactions in the general ledger.

Core Steps: Create Financial Statements

When you have completed all of the preceding steps, print the financial statements, which include the following items:

- Income statement
- Balance sheet
- Statement of cash flows
- Statement of retained earnings
- Disclosures

If the financial statements are only to be distributed internally, it may be acceptable to only issue the income statement and balance sheet, and dispense with the other items just noted. Reporting to people outside of the company generally calls for issuance of the complete set of financial statements.

Core Steps: Review Financial Statements

Once you have completed all of the preceding steps, review the financial statements for errors. There are several ways to do so, including:

- *Horizontal analysis*. Print reports that show the income statement, balance sheet, and statement of cash flows for the past twelve months on a rolling basis. Track across each line item to see if there are any unusual declines or spikes in comparison to the results of prior periods, and investigate those items. This is the best review technique.
- *Budget versus actual*. Print an income statement that shows budgeted versus actual results, and investigate any larger variances. This is a less effective review technique, because it assumes that the budget is realistic, and also because a budget is not usually available for the balance sheet or statement of cash flows.

There will almost always be problems with the first iteration of the financial statements. Expect to investigate and correct several items before issuing a satisfactory set of financials. To reduce the amount of time needed to review financial statement errors during the core closing period, consider doing so a few days prior to month-end; this may uncover a few errors, leaving a smaller number to investigate later on.

Core Steps: Accrue Tax Liabilities

Once you have created the financial statements and have finalized the information in it, there may be a need to accrue an income tax liability based on the amount of net profit or loss. There are several issues to consider when creating this accrual:

- *Income tax rate.* In most countries that impose an income tax, the tax rate begins at a low level and then gradually moves up to a higher tax rate that corresponds to higher levels of income. When accruing income taxes, use the average income tax rate that you expect to experience for the full year. Otherwise, the first quarter of the year will have a lower tax rate than later months, which is caused by the tax rate schedule, rather than any changes in company operational results.
- *Losses.* If the company has earned a profit in a prior period of the year, and has now generated a loss, accrue for a tax rebate, which will offset the tax expense that you recorded earlier. Doing so creates the correct amount of tax liability when you look at year-to-date results. If there was no prior profit and no reasonable prospect of one, do not accrue for a tax rebate, since it is more likely than not that the company will not receive the rebate.
- *Net operating loss carryforwards.* A net operating loss (NOL) carryforward is a loss experienced in an earlier period that could not be completely offset against prior-period profits. If the company has a net operating loss carryforward on its books, you may be able to use it to offset any income taxes in the current period. If so, there is no need to accrue for an income tax expense.

Once you have accrued the income tax liability, print the complete set of financial statements.

Core Steps: Close the Month

Once all accounting transactions have been entered in the accounting system, you should close the month in the accounting software. This means prohibiting any further transactions in the general ledger in the old accounting period, as well as allowing the next accounting period to accept transactions. These steps are important, so that you do not inadvertently enter transactions into the wrong accounting periods.

> **Tip:** There is a risk that an accounting person might access the accounting software to re-open an accounting period to fraudulently adjust the results from a prior period. To avoid this, password-protect the relevant data entry screens in the software.

Core Steps: Add Disclosures

If you are issuing financial statements to readers other than the management team, consider adding disclosures to the basic set of financial statements. There are many disclosures required under GAAP and International Financial Reporting Standards. It is especially important to include a complete set of disclosures if the financial statements are being audited. If so, your auditors will offer advice regarding which disclosures to include. Allocate a large amount of time to the proper construction and error-checking of disclosures, for they contain a number of references to the financial statements and subsets of financial information extracted from the statements, and this information could be wrong. Thus, every time you create a new iteration of the financial statements, update the accompanying disclosures.

If you are issuing financial statements solely for the management team, do not include any disclosures. By avoiding them, you can cut a significant amount of time from the closing process. Further, the management team is already well aware of how the business is run, and so presumably does not need the disclosures. If there are disclosure items that are unusual (such as violating the covenants on a loan), then attach just those items to the financial statements, or note them in the cover letter that accompanies the financials (see the next section).

Core Steps: Write Cover Letter

When you issue financial statements, readers are receiving several pieces of information that they may not have the time, interest, or knowledge to properly interpret. Accordingly, create a cover letter that itemizes the key aspects of the financial results and position of the business during the reporting period. This should not be an exhaustive analysis. Instead, point out the *key* changes in the business that might be of interest to the readers. Conversely, if changes were expected but did not occur, point that out. Further, discuss events that will occur in the near future, and their financial impact. Finally, use a standard format for the cover letter that lists all major topic areas, just so that you can refer to each topic as you write the contents of the letter. Doing so ensures that you will not miss any areas. A sample cover letter follows:

Sample Cover Letter

To:	Milagro Management Team
Fr:	Accountant
Re:	April Financial Statements

Income statement: The profit for the past month was $100,000 below budget, because we did not ship the ABC widget order on time. This was caused by a quality problem that was not spotted until the final quality review at the shipping dock. The order could have shipped on time if the quality review had been positioned after the widget trimming machine.

We also paid $20,000 more than expected for rent, because we leased 12 storage trailers to accommodate a work-in-process overflow that did not fit into the warehouse. This was caused by the failure of the widget stamping machine. A replacement machine will arrive next week, and we expect it to require two months to eliminate the backlog of stored items. Thus, we will incur most of these leasing costs again through the next two months.

Balance Sheet: Accounts receivable were lower than expected by $180,000, primarily because of the ABC widget order just noted. This means that incoming cash flows will be reduced by that amount in one month. In anticipation of this cash shortfall, we have finalized an increase in the company's line of credit of $200,000.

Future Events: We expect to hear from the Marine Corps regarding the Combat Coffee order in late May. That order could increase the backlog by $1,000,000. Also, the office rent agreement expires on June 1. Market rates have increased, so we expect the replacement lease to cost at least $8,000 more per month.

Note that the sample cover letter addressed three key areas: the income statement, the balance sheet, and future events. These general categories are used to remind you to review each area for discussion topics. If there are areas of particular ongoing concern, such as cash or debt, then it is acceptable to list these items as separate categories.

Tip: When writing the cover letter, always round up the numbers in the report to the nearest thousand (if not higher). Managers will not change their decision if you report a variance as $82,000 or as $81,729.32, and the report will be much easier to read.

Whenever possible, state the causes of issues in the cover letter, so that recipients do not have to spend time conducting their own investigations. In essence, the ideal cover letter should highlight key points, discuss why they happened, and perhaps even point out how to correct them in the future.

Core Steps: Issue Financial Statements

The final core step in closing the books is to issue the financial statements. There are several ways to do this. If you are interested in reducing the total time required for someone to receive the financial statements, then convert the entire package to PDF documents and e-mail them to the recipients. Doing so eliminates the mail float that would otherwise be required. If you are incorporating a number of reports into the financial statement package, this may require the purchase of a document scanner.

When you issue financial statements, always print a copy for yourself and store it in a binder. This gives you ready access to the report during the next few days, when managers from around the company are most likely to contact you with questions about it.

Delayed Steps: Issue Customer Invoices

From the perspective of closing the books, it is more important to formulate all customer invoices than it is to issue those invoices to customers.

Taking this delaying step can delay a company's cash flow. The problem is that a customer is supposed to pay an invoice based on pre-arranged terms that may also be stated on the invoice, so a delayed receipt of the invoice delays the corresponding payment. However, this is not necessarily the case. The terms you set with customers should state that they must pay the company following a certain number of days from the invoice date, not the date when they receive the invoices. Thus, if you print invoices that are dated as of the last day of the month being closed, and then mail them a few days later, you should still be paid on the usual date.

From a practical perspective, this can still be a problem, because the accounting staff of the customer typically uses the current date as the default date when it enters supplier invoices into its accounting system. If they do so, you will likely be paid late. You can follow up with any customers that appear to being paying late for this reason, but this will likely be a continuing problem.

Delayed Steps: Closing Metrics

If you have an interest in closing the books more quickly, consider tracking a small set of metrics related to the close. The objective of having these metrics is not necessarily to attain a world-class closing speed, but rather to spot the bottleneck areas of the close that are preventing a more rapid issuance of the financial statements. Thus, you need to have a set of metrics that delve sufficiently far into the workings of the closing process to spot the bottlenecks. An example of such metrics follows. Note that the total time required to close the books and issue financial statements is six days, but that the closing time for most of the steps needed to close the books is substantially shorter. Only the valuation of inventory and the bank reconciliation metrics reveal long closing intervals. Thus, this type of metric measurement and presentation allows you to quickly spot where there are opportunities to compress the closing process.

Sample Metrics Report for Closing the Books

	Day 1	Day 2	Day 3	Day 4	Day 5	Day 6
Issue financials	xxx	xxx	xxx	xxx	xxx	**Done**
Supplier invoices	xxx	**Done**				
Customer invoices	xxx	xxx	**Done**			
Accrued expenses	xxx	xxx	**Done**			
Inventory valuation	xxx	xxx	xxx	xxx	**Done**	
Bank reconciliation	xxx	xxx	xxx	**Done**		
Fixed assets	xxx	**Done**				
Payroll	**Done**					

Delayed Steps: Document Future Closing Changes

After reviewing the closing metrics in the preceding step, you will likely want to make some improvements to the closing process. Incorporate these changes into a schedule of activities for the next close, and review any resulting changes in responsibility with the accounting staff. Do this as soon after the close as possible, since this is the time when any problems with the close will be fresh in your mind, and you will be most interested in fixing them during the next close.

Even if you are satisfied with the timing of closing activities, it is possible that one or more employees in the accounting department will be on vacation during the next close, so you will need to incorporate their absence into the plan. Further, if you have inexperienced people in the department, consider including them in peripheral closing activities, and then gradually shifting them into positions of greater responsibility within the process. Thus, from the perspective of improvements, employee absences, and training, it is important to document any changes to the next closing process.

Delayed Steps: Update Closing Procedures

When you first implement a rigorous set of closing procedures, you will find that they do not yield the results that you expect. Some steps may be concluded too late to feed into another step, or some activities may be assigned to the wrong employee. As you gradually sort through these issues, update the closing procedures and schedule of events. This process will require a number of iterations, after which the closing procedures will yield more satisfactory results. Further, every time the company changes its operations, you will need to update the procedures again.

Examples of situations that may require a change in the closing procedures are:

Situation	Impact on Closing Procedure
New accounting software	Every accounting package has a different built-in methodology for closing the books, which you must incorporate into the closing procedures.
New business transaction procedures	If other parts of the business alter their approaches to processing purchasing, inventory counts, and shipping, and so forth, you will need to adjust the closing procedures for them.
Acquisition or sale of a subsidiary	Add procedures to encompass new lines of business, while shutting down closing activities for those segments that have been disposed of.
Change in bank accounts	Different banks have different systems for providing on-line access to bank account information, which may alter the bank reconciliation procedure.
Change in credit policy	This may require a different method for compiling the allowance for doubtful accounts.
Change in inventory management system	If a business changes to just-in-time inventory management, it may flush out many older LIFO inventory layers, or uncover more obsolete inventory. These changes may also require different inventory costing methods, new overhead allocation methodologies, or altered obsolescence reserves.

The preceding list is by no means all-encompassing. It merely illustrates the fact that you should consider the impact of almost *any* change in the business on the closing procedures. It is quite likely that at least minor tweaking will be needed every few months for even the most finely-tuned closing procedures. In particular, be wary of closing steps that are no longer needed, or whose impact on the financial statements have become so minor that their impact is immaterial; such steps clutter up the closing process and can significantly delay the issuance of financial statements.

Summary

This chapter has outlined a large number of steps that are needed to close the books. You may feel that the level of organization required to close the books in this manner is overkill. However, consider that the primary work product of the accounting department as a whole is the financial statements. If a reputation can be established for consistently issuing high-quality financial statements within a reasonable period of time, this will likely be the basis for the company's view of the entire department.

You may find that additional closing steps are needed beyond the extensive list noted in this chapter. This is particularly common when a business has an unusual operating model, or operates in an industry with unique accounting rules. If so, you should certainly incorporate the additional closing steps into the list described in this chapter.

If you would like to peruse a more in-depth analysis of closing the books, see the author's *Closing the Books*, which is available at accountingtools.com. This book provides more detail about all aspects of the closing process, as well as instructions regarding how to close the books within a very short period of time.

Chapter 20
The Financial Statements

Introduction

The financial records of a business are summarized into a set of financial statements at the end of each reporting period. These statements reveal the results, financial position, cash flows, and retained earnings of the organization. In this chapter, we describe the nature of each of the financial statements, different presentation formats, and how to construct each statement.

The Income Statement

In most organizations, the income statement is considered the most important of the financial statements, and may even be the only one of the financial statements that is produced (though we do not recommend doing so). Given its importance, we spend extra time in this section addressing different income statement formats, and then walk through the steps needed to create an income statement.

Income Statement Overview

The income statement is an integral part of an entity's financial statements, and contains the results of its operations during an accounting period, showing revenues and expenses, and the resulting profit or loss.

There are two ways to present the income statement. One method is to present all items of revenue and expense for the reporting period in a statement of comprehensive income. Alternatively, you can split this information into an income statement and a statement of other comprehensive income. Other comprehensive income contains all changes that are not permitted in the main part of the income statement. These items include unrealized gains and losses on available-for-sale securities, cash flow hedge gains and losses, foreign currency translation adjustments, and pension plan gains or losses. Smaller companies tend to ignore the distinction and simply aggregate the information into a document that they call the income statement; this is sufficient for internal reporting, but auditors will require the expanded version before they will certify the financial statements.

There are no specific requirements for the line items to include in the income statement, but the following line items are typically used, based on general practice:
- Revenue
- Tax expense
- Post-tax profit or loss for discontinued operations and their disposal
- Profit or loss
- Extraordinary gains or losses

- Other comprehensive income, subdivided into each component thereof
- Total comprehensive income

A key additional item is to present an analysis of the expenses in profit or loss, using a classification based on their nature or functional area; the goal is to maximize the relevance and reliability of the presented information. If you elect to present expenses by their nature, the format looks similar to the following:

Sample Presentation by Nature of Items

Revenue		$xxx
Expenses		
Direct materials	$xxx	
Direct labor	xxx	
Salaries expense	xxx	
Payroll taxes	xxx	
Employee benefits	xxx	
Depreciation expense	xxx	
Telephone expense	xxx	
Other expenses	xxx	
Total expenses		$xxx
Profit before tax		$xxx

Alternatively, if you present expenses by their functional area, the format looks similar to the following, where most expenses are aggregated at the department level:

Sample Presentation by Function of Items

Revenue	$xxx
Cost of goods sold	xxx
Gross profit	xxx
Administrative expenses	$xxx
Distribution expenses	xxx
Research and development expenses	xxx
Sales and marketing expenses	xxx
Other expenses	xxx
Total expenses	$xxx
Profit before tax	$xxx

Of the two methods, presenting expenses by their nature is easier, since it requires no allocation of expenses between functional areas. Conversely, the functional area presentation may be more relevant to users of the information, who can more easily see where resources are being consumed.

You should add additional headings, subtotals, and line items to the items noted above if doing so will increase the user's understanding of the entity's financial performance.

An example follows of an income statement that presents expenses by their nature, rather than by their function.

EXAMPLE

Milagro Corporation presents its results in two separate statements by their nature, resulting in the following format, beginning with the income statement:

Milagro Corporation
Income Statement
For the years ended December 31

(000s)	20x2	20x1
Revenue	$900,000	$850,000
Expenses		
Direct materials	$270,000	$255,000
Direct labor	90,000	85,000
Salaries	300,000	275,000
Payroll taxes	27,000	25,000
Depreciation expense	45,000	41,000
Telephone expense	30,000	20,000
Other expenses	23,000	22,000
Finance costs	29,000	23,000
Other income	-25,000	-20,000
Profit before tax	$111,000	$124,000
Income tax expense	38,000	43,000
Profit from continuing operations	$73,000	$81,000
Loss from discontinued operations	42,000	0
Profit	$31,000	$81,000

Milagro Corporation then continues with the following statement of comprehensive income:

Milagro Corporation
Statement of Comprehensive Income
For the years ended December 31

(000s)	20x2	20x1
Profit	$31,000	$81,000
Other comprehensive income		
Exchange differences on translating foreign operations	$5,000	$9,000
Available-for-sale financial assets	10,000	-2,000
Actuarial losses on defined benefit pension plan	-2,000	-12,000
Other comprehensive income, net of tax	$13,000	-$5,000
Total comprehensive income	$18,000	$76,000

The Single-Step Income Statement

The simplest format in which you can construct an income statement is the single-step income statement. In this format, you present a single subtotal for all revenue line items, and a single subtotal for all expense line items, with a net gain or loss appearing at the bottom of the report. A sample single-step income statement follows:

Sample Single-Step Income Statement

Revenues	$1,000,000
Expenses:	
Cost of goods sold	350,000
Advertising	30,000
Depreciation	20,000
Rent	40,000
Payroll taxes	28,000
Salaries and wages	400,000
Supplies	32,000
Travel and entertainment	50,000
Total expenses	950,000
Net income	$50,000

The single-step format is not heavily used, because it forces the reader of an income statement to separately summarize information for subsets of information within the income statement. For a more readable format, try the following multi-step approach.

The Multi-Step Income Statement

The multi-step income statement involves the use of multiple sub-totals within the income statement, which makes it easier for readers to aggregate selected types of information within the report. The usual subtotals are for the gross margin, operating expenses, and other income, which allow readers to determine how much the company earns just from its manufacturing activities (the gross margin), what it spends on supporting operations (the operating expense total) and which components of its results do not relate to its core activities (the other income total). A sample format for a multi-step income statement follows:

Sample Multi-Step Income Statement

Revenues	$1,000,000
Cost of goods sold	350,000
Gross margin	$650,000
Operating expenses	
Advertising	30,000
Depreciation	20,000
Rent	40,000
Payroll taxes	28,000
Salaries and wages	380,000
Supplies	32,000
Travel and entertainment	50,000
Total operating expenses	$580,000
Other income	
Interest income	-5,000
Interest expense	25,000
Total other income	$20,000
Net income	$50,000

The Condensed Income Statement

A condensed income statement is simply an income statement with many of the usual line items condensed down into a few lines. Typically, this means that all revenue line items are aggregated into a single line item, while the cost of goods sold appears as one line item, and all operating expenses appear in another line item. A typical format for a condensed income statement is:

Sample Condensed Income Statement

Revenues	$1,000,000
Cost of goods sold	350,000
Sales, general, and administrative expenses	580,000
Financing income and expenses	20,000
Net income	$50,000

A condensed income statement is typically issued to those external parties who are less interested in the precise sources of a company's revenues or what expenses it incurs, and more concerned with its overall performance. Thus, bankers and investors may be interested in receiving a condensed income statement.

The Contribution Margin Income Statement

A contribution margin income statement is an income statement in which all variable expenses are deducted from sales to arrive at a contribution margin, from which all fixed expenses are then subtracted to arrive at the net profit or loss for the period. This income statement format is a superior form of presentation, because the contribution margin clearly shows the amount available to cover fixed costs and generate a profit (or loss).

In essence, if there are no sales, a contribution margin income statement will have a zero contribution margin, with fixed costs clustered beneath the contribution margin line item. As sales increase, the contribution margin will increase in conjunction with sales, while fixed costs remain approximately the same.

A contribution margin income statement varies from a normal income statement in the following three ways:

- Fixed production costs are aggregated lower in the income statement, after the contribution margin;
- Variable selling and administrative expenses are grouped with variable production costs, so that they are a part of the calculation of the contribution margin; and
- The gross margin is replaced in the statement by the contribution margin.

Thus, the format of a contribution margin income statement is:

Sample Contribution Margin Income Statement

+	Revenues
-	Variable production expenses (such as materials, supplies, and variable overhead)
-	Variable selling and administrative expenses
=	Contribution margin
-	Fixed production expenses (including most overhead)
-	Fixed selling and administrative expenses
=	Net profit or loss

In many cases, direct labor is categorized as a fixed expense in the contribution margin income statement format, rather than a variable expense, because this cost does not always change in direct proportion to the amount of revenue generated. Instead, management needs to keep a certain minimum staffing in the production area, which does not vary even if there are lower production volumes.

The key difference between gross margin and contribution margin is that fixed production costs are included in the cost of goods sold to calculate the gross margin, whereas they are not included in the same calculation for the contribution margin. This means that the contribution margin income statement is sorted based on the variability of the underlying cost information, rather than by the functional areas or expense categories found in a normal income statement.

It is useful to create an income statement in the contribution margin format when you want to determine that proportion of expenses that truly varies directly with revenues. In many businesses, the contribution margin will be substantially higher than the gross margin, because such a large proportion of production costs are fixed and few of its selling and administrative expenses are variable.

The Multi-Period Income Statement

A variation on any of the preceding income statement formats is to present them over multiple periods, preferably over a trailing 12-month period. By doing so, readers of the income statement can see trends in the information, as well as spot changes in the trends that may require investigation. This is an excellent way to present the income statement, and is highly recommended. The following sample shows the layout of a multi-period income statement over a four-quarter time span.

Sample Multi-Period Income Statement

	Quarter 1	Quarter 2	Quarter 3	Quarter 4
Revenues	$1,000,000	$1,100,000	$1,050,000	$1,200,000
Cost of goods sold	350,000	385,000	368,000	**480,000**
Gross margin	$650,000	$715,000	$682,000	$720,000
Operating expenses				
Advertising	30,000	**0**	**60,000**	30,000
Depreciation	20,000	21,000	22,000	24,000
Rent	40,000	40,000	**50,000**	50,000
Payroll taxes	28,000	28,000	28,000	26,000
Salaries and wages	380,000	385,000	385,000	370,000
Supplies	32,000	30,000	31,000	33,000
Travel and entertainment	50,000	45,000	40,000	60,000
Total operating expenses	$580,000	$549,000	$616,000	$593,000
Other income				
Interest income	-5,000	-5,000	-3,000	-1,000
Interest expense	25,000	25,000	30,000	**39,000**
Total other income	$20,000	$20,000	$27,000	$38,000
Net income	$50,000	$146,000	$39,000	$89,000

The report shown in the sample reveals several issues that might not have been visible if the report had only spanned a single period. These issues are:

- *Cost of goods sold.* This cost is consistently 35% of sales until Quarter 4, when it jumps to 40%.

- *Advertising.* There was no advertising cost in Quarter 2 and double the amount of the normal $30,000 quarterly expense in Quarter 3. The cause could be a missing supplier invoice in Quarter 2 that was received and recorded in Quarter 3.
- *Rent.* The rent increased by $10,000 in Quarter 3, which may indicate a scheduled increase in the rent agreement.
- *Interest expense.* The interest expense jumps in Quarter 3 and does so again in Quarter 4, while interest income declined over the same periods. This indicates a large increase in debt.

In short, the multi-period income statement is an excellent tool for spotting anomalies in the presented information from period to period.

How to Construct the Income Statement

If you use an accounting software package, it is quite easy to construct an income statement. Just access the report writing module, select the time period for which you want to print the income statement, and print it.

Tip: If you have used a report writer to create an income statement in the accounting software, there is a good chance that the first draft of the report will be wrong, due to some accounts being missed or duplicated. To ensure that your income statement is correct, compare it to the default income statement report that is usually provided with the accounting software, or compare the net profit or loss on your report to the current year earnings figure listed in the equity section of the balance sheet. If there is a discrepancy, you have an incorrect income statement report.

The situation is more complex if you choose to create the income statement by hand. This involves the following steps:
1. Create the trial balance report (available through the accounting software as a standard report).
2. List each account pertaining to the income statement in a separate column of the trial balance.
3. Aggregate these lines into those you want to report in the income statement on a separate line.
4. Shift the result into the format of the income statement that you prefer.

The following example illustrates the construction of an income statement.

EXAMPLE

The accounting software for Milagro Corporation breaks down at the end of July, and the accountant has to create the financial statements by hand. He has a copy of Milagro's trial balance, which is shown below. He transfers this information to an electronic spreadsheet, creates separate columns for accounts to include in the income statement, and copies those balances into these columns. This leaves a number of accounts related to the balance sheet, which he can ignore for the purposes of creating the income statement.

Milagro Corporation Extended Trial Balance

	Adjusted Trial Balance		Income Statement		Aggregation	
	Debit	Credit	Debit	Credit	Debit	Credit
Cash	$60,000					
Accounts receivable	230,000					
Inventory	300,000					
Fixed assets (net)	210,000					
Accounts payable		$90,000				
Accrued liabilities		75,000				
Notes payable		420,000				
Equity		350,000				
Revenue		450,000		$450,000		$450,000
Cost of goods sold	290,000		$290,000		$290,000	
Salaries expense	225,000		225,000		245,000	
Payroll tax expense	20,000		20,000			
Rent expense	35,000		35,000			
Other expenses	15,000		15,000		50,000	
Totals	$1,385,000	$1,385,000	$585,000	$450,000	$585,000	$450,000

In the "Aggregation" columns of the extended trial balance, the accountant has aggregated the expenses for salaries and payroll taxes into the salaries expense line, and aggregated the rent expense and other expenses into the other expenses line. He then transfers this information into the following condensed income statement:

Milagro Corporation
Income Statement
For the month ended July 31, 20X1

Revenue	$450,000
Cost of goods sold	290,000
Salaries expenses	245,000
Other expenses	50,000
Net loss	-$135,000

The Balance Sheet

In most organizations, the balance sheet is considered the second most important of the financial statements, after the income statement. A common financial reporting package is to issue the income statement and balance sheet, along with supporting materials. This does not comprise a complete set of financial statements, but it is considered sufficient for internal reporting purposes in many organizations.

In this section, we explore several possible formats for the balance sheet, and also describe how to create it.

Overview of the Balance Sheet

A balance sheet (also known as a statement of financial position) presents information about an entity's assets, liabilities, and shareholders' equity, where the compiled result must match this formula:

Total assets = Total liabilities + Equity

The balance sheet reports the aggregate effect of transactions as of a specific date. The balance sheet is used to assess an entity's liquidity and ability to pay its debts.

There is no specific requirement for the line items to be included in the balance sheet. The following line items, at a minimum, are normally included in it:

Current Assets:

- Cash and cash equivalents
- Trade and other receivables
- Investments
- Inventories
- Assets held for sale

Non-Current Assets:

- Property, plant, and equipment
- Intangible assets
- Goodwill

Current Liabilities:

- Trade and other payables
- Accrued expenses
- Current tax liabilities
- Current portion of loans payable
- Other financial liabilities
- Liabilities held for sale

Non-Current Liabilities:

- Loans payable
- Deferred tax liabilities
- Other non-current liabilities

Equity:

- Capital stock
- Additional paid-in capital
- Retained earnings

Here is an example of a balance sheet which presents information as of the end of two fiscal years:

Milagro Corporation
Balance Sheet
As of December 31, 20X2 and 20X1

(000s)	12/31/20X2	12/31/20x1
ASSETS		
Current assets		
Cash and cash equivalents	$270,000	$215,000
Trade receivables	147,000	139,000
Inventories	139,000	128,000
Other current assets	15,000	27,000
Total current assets	$571,000	$509,000
Non-current assets		
Property, plant, and equipment	551,000	529,000
Goodwill	82,000	82,000
Other intangible assets	143,000	143,000
Total non-current assets	$776,000	$754,000
Total assets	$1,347,000	$1,263,000
LIABILITIES AND EQUITY		
Current liabilities		
Trade and other payables	$217,000	$198,000
Short-term borrowings	133,000	202,000
Current portion of long-term borrowings	5,000	5,000
Current tax payable	26,000	23,000
Accrued expenses	9,000	13,000
Total current liabilities	$390,000	$441,000
Non-current liabilities		
Long-term debt	85,000	65,000
Deferred taxes	19,000	17,000
Total non-current liabilities	$104,000	$82,000
Total liabilities	$494,000	$523,000
Shareholders' equity		
Capital	100,000	100,000
Additional paid-in capital	15,000	15,000
Retained earnings	738,000	625,000
Total equity	$853,000	$740,000
Total liabilities and equity	$1,347,000	$1,263,000

Classify an asset on the balance sheet as current when an entity expects to sell or consume it during its normal operating cycle or within 12 months after the reporting period. If the operating cycle is longer than 12 months, use the longer period to judge whether an asset can be classified as current. Classify all other assets as non-current.

Classify all of the following as current assets:

- *Cash.* This is cash available for current operations, as well as any short-term, highly liquid investments that are readily convertible to known amounts of cash and which are so near their maturities that they present an insignificant risk of value changes. Do not include cash whose withdrawal is restricted, to be used for other than current operations, or segregated for the liquidation of long-term debts; such items should be classified as longer-term.
- *Accounts receivable.* This includes trade accounts, notes, and acceptances that are receivable. Also, include receivables from officers, employees, affiliates, and others if they are collectible within a year. Do not include any receivable that you do not expect to collect within 12 months; such items should be classified as longer-term.
- *Marketable securities.* This includes those securities representing the investment of cash available for current operations, including trading securities.
- *Inventory.* This includes merchandise, raw materials, work-in-process, finished goods, operating supplies, and maintenance parts.
- *Prepaid expenses.* This includes prepayments for insurance, interest, rent, taxes, unused royalties, advertising services, and operating supplies.

Classify a liability as current when the entity expects to settle it during its normal operating cycle or within 12 months after the reporting period, or if it is scheduled for settlement within 12 months. Classify all other liabilities as non-current.

Classify all of the following as current liabilities:

- *Payables.* This is all accounts payable incurred in the acquisition of materials and supplies that are used to produce goods or services.
- *Prepayments.* This is amounts collected in advance of the delivery of goods or services by the entity to the customer. Do not include a long-term prepayment in this category.
- *Accruals.* This is accrued expenses for items directly related to the operating cycle, such as accruals for compensation, rentals, royalties, and various taxes.
- *Short-term debts.* This is debts maturing within the next 12 months.

Current liabilities include accruals for amounts that can only be determined approximately, such as bonuses, and where the payee to whom payment will be made cannot initially be designated, such as a warranty accrual.

The Common Size Balance Sheet

A common size balance sheet presents not only the standard information contained in a balance sheet, but also a column that notes the same information as a percentage of the total assets (for asset line items) or as a percentage of total liabilities and shareholders' equity (for liability or shareholders' equity line items).

It is extremely useful to construct a common size balance sheet that itemizes the results as of the end of multiple time periods, so that you can construct trend lines to ascertain changes over longer time periods. The common size balance sheet is also useful for comparing the proportions of assets, liabilities, and equity between different companies, particularly as part of an industry or acquisition analysis.

For example, if you were comparing the common size balance sheet of your company to that of a potential acquiree, and the acquiree had 40% of its assets invested in accounts receivable versus 20% by your company, this may indicate that aggressive collection activities might reduce the acquiree's receivables if your company were to acquire it.

The common size balance sheet is not required under the GAAP or IFRS accounting frameworks. However, being a useful document for analysis purposes, it is commonly distributed within a company for review by management.

There is no mandatory format for a common size balance sheet, though percentages are nearly always placed to the right of the normal numerical results. If you are reporting balance sheet results as of the end of many periods, you may even dispense with numerical results entirely, in favor of just presenting the common size percentages.

EXAMPLE

Milagro Corporation creates a common size balance sheet that contains the balance sheet as of the end of its fiscal year for each of the past two years, with common size percentages to the right:

Milagro Corporation
Common Size Balance Sheet
As of 12/31/20x02 and 12/31/20x1

	($) 12/31/20x2	($) 12/31/20x1	(%) 12/31/20x2	(%) 12/31/20x1
Current assets				
Cash	$1,200	$900	7.6%	7.1%
Accounts receivable	4,800	3,600	30.4%	28.3%
Inventory	3,600	2,700	22.8%	21.3%
Total current assets	$9,600	$7,200	60.8%	56.7%
Total fixed assets	6,200	5,500	39.2%	43.3%
Total assets	$15,800	$12,700	100.0%	100.0%
Current liabilities				
Accounts payable	$2,400	$41,800	15.2%	14.2%
Accrued expenses	480	360	3.0%	2.8%

363

	($) 12/31/20x2	($) 12/31/20x1	(%) 12/31/20x2	(%) 12/31/20x1
Short-term debt	800	600	5.1%	4.7%
Total current liabilities	$3,680	$2,760	23.3%	21.7%
Long-term debt	9,020	7,740	57.1%	60.9%
Total liabilities	$12,700	$10,500	80.4%	82.7%
Shareholders' equity	3,100	2,200	19.6%	17.3%
Total liabilities and equity	$15,800	$12,700	100.0%	100.0%

The Comparative Balance Sheet

A comparative balance sheet presents side-by-side information about an entity's assets, liabilities, and shareholders' equity as of multiple points in time. For example, a comparative balance sheet could present the balance sheet as of the end of each year for the past three years. Another variation is to present the balance sheet as of the end of each month for the past 12 months on a rolling basis. In both cases, the intent is to provide the reader with a series of snapshots of a company's financial condition over a period of time, which is useful for developing trend line analyses.

The comparative balance sheet is not required under the GAAP accounting framework for a privately-held company, but the Securities and Exchange Commission (SEC) does require it in numerous circumstances for the reports issued by publicly-held companies, particularly the annual Form 10-K and the quarterly Form 10-Q. The usual SEC requirement is to report a comparative balance sheet for the past two years, with additional requirements for quarterly reporting.

There is no standard format for a comparative balance sheet. It is somewhat more common to report the balance sheet as of the least recent period furthest to the right, though the reverse is the case when you are reporting balance sheets in a trailing twelve months format.

The following is a sample of a comparative balance sheet that contains the balance sheet as of the end of a company's fiscal year for each of the past three years:

Sample Comparative Balance Sheet

	as of 12/31/20X3	as of 12/31/20X2	as of 12/31/20X1
Current assets			
Cash	$1,200,000	$900,000	$750,000
Accounts receivable	4,800,000	3,600,000	3,000,000
Inventory	3,600,000	2,700,000	2,300,000
Total current assets	$9,600,000	$7,200,000	$6,050,000
Total fixed assets	6,200,000	5,500,000	5,000,000
Total assets	$15,800,000	$12,700,000	$11,050,000
Current liabilities			
Accounts payable	$2,400,000	$1,800,000	$1,500,000

	as of 12/31/20X3	as of 12/31/20X2	as of 12/31/20X1
Accrued expenses	480,000	360,000	300,000
Short-term debt	800,000	600,000	400,000
Total current liabilities	$3,680,000	$2,760,000	$2,200,000
Long-term debt	9,020,000	7,740,000	7,350,000
Total liabilities	$12,700,000	$10,500,000	$9,550,000
Shareholders' equity	3,100,000	2,200,000	1,500,000
Total liabilities and equity	$15,800,000	$12,700,000	$11,050,000

The sample comparative balance sheet reveals that the company has increased the size of its current assets over the past few years, but has also recently invested in a large amount of additional fixed assets that have likely been the cause of a significant boost in its long-term debt.

How to Construct the Balance Sheet

If you use an accounting software package, it is quite easy to construct the balance sheet. Just access the report writing module, select the time period for which you want to print the balance sheet, and print it.

Tip: It is generally not necessary to create your own version of the balance sheet in the accounting software package, since the default version is usually sufficient. If you choose to do so, test it by verifying that the total of all asset line items equals the total of all liability and equity line items. An error is usually caused by some accounts not being included in the report, or added to it multiple times.

If you choose to construct the balance sheet manually, follow these steps:
1. Create the trial balance report (usually available through the accounting software as a standard report).
2. List each account pertaining to the balance sheet in a separate column of the trial balance.
3. Add the difference between the revenue and expense line items on the trial balance to a separate line item in the equity section of the balance sheet.
4. Aggregate these line items into those you want to report in the balance sheet as a separate line item.
5. Shift the result into the format of the balance sheet that you prefer.

The following example illustrates the construction of a balance sheet.

EXAMPLE

The accounting software for Milagro Corporation breaks down at the end of July, and the accountant has to create the financial statements by hand. He has a copy of Milagro's trial balance, which is shown below. He transfers this information to an electronic spreadsheet, creates separate columns for accounts to include in the balance sheet, and copies those balances into these columns. This leaves a number of accounts related to the income statement, which he can ignore for the purposes of creating the balance sheet. However, he *does* include the net loss for the period in the "Current year profit" row, which is included in the equity section of the balance sheet.

Milagro Corporation Extended Trial Balance

	Adjusted Trial Balance		Balance Sheet		Aggregation	
	Debit	Credit	Debit	Credit	Debit	Credit
Cash	$60,000		$60,000		$60,000	
Accounts receivable	230,000		230,000		230,000	
Inventory	300,000		300,000		300,000	
Fixed assets (net)	210,000		210,000		210,000	
Accounts payable		$90,000		$90,000		$165,000
Accrued liabilities		75,000		75,000		
Notes payable		420,000		420,000		420,000
Equity		350,000		350,000		215,000
Current year profit			135,000			
Revenue		450,000				
Cost of goods sold	290,000					
Salaries expense	225,000					
Payroll tax expense	20,000					
Rent expense	35,000					
Other expenses	15,000					
Totals	$1,385,000	$1,385,000	$935,000	$935,000	$800,000	$800,000

In the "Aggregation" columns of the extended trial balance, the accountant has aggregated the liabilities for accounts payable and accrued liabilities in the accounts payable line, and aggregated equity and current year profit into the equity line. He then transfers this information into the following condensed balance sheet:

Milagro Corporation
Balance Sheet
For the month ended July 31, 20X1

Assets	
Cash	$60,000
Accounts receivable	230,000
Inventory	300,000
Fixed Assets	210,000
Total assets	$800,000
Liabilities	
Accounts payable	$165,000
Notes payable	420,000
Total liabilities	$585,000
Equity	$215,000
Total liabilities and equity	$800,000

The Statement of Cash Flows

The statement of cash flows is the least used of the primary financial statements, and may not be issued at all for internal financial reporting purposes. The recipients of financial statements seem to be mostly concerned with the profit information on the income statement, and to a lesser degree with the financial position information on the balance sheet. Nonetheless, the cash flows on the statement of cash flows can provide valuable information, especially when combined with the other elements of the financial statements. At a minimum, be prepared to construct a statement of cash flows for the annual financial statements, which will presumably be issued outside of the company.

This section addresses the two formats used for the statement of cash flows, as well as how to assemble the information needed for the statement.

Overview of the Statement of Cash Flows

The statement of cash flows contains information about the flows of cash into and out of a company; in particular, it shows the extent of those company activities that generate and use cash. The primary activities are:

- *Operating activities.* These are an entity's primary revenue-producing activities. Examples of operating activities are cash receipts from the sale of goods, as well as from royalties and commissions, amounts received or paid to settle lawsuits, fines, payments to employees and suppliers, cash payments to lenders for interest, contributions to charity, and the settlement of asset retirement obligations.

- *Investing activities.* These involve the acquisition and disposal of long-term assets. Examples of investing activities are cash receipts from the sale of property, the sale of the debt or equity instruments of other entities, the repayment of loans made to other entities, and proceeds from insurance settlements related to damaged fixed assets. Examples of cash payments that are investment activities include the acquisition of fixed assets, as well as the purchase of the debt or equity of other entities.
- *Financing activities.* These are the activities resulting in alterations to the amount of contributed equity and the entity's borrowings. Examples of financing activities include cash receipts from the sale of the entity's own equity instruments or from issuing debt, proceeds from derivative instruments, and cash payments to buy back shares, pay dividends, and pay off outstanding debt.

The statement of cash flows also incorporates the concept of cash and cash equivalents. A cash equivalent is a short-term, very liquid investment that is easily convertible into a known amount of cash, and which is so near its maturity that it presents an insignificant risk of a change in value because of changes in interest rates.

You can use the *direct method* or the *indirect method* to present the statement of cash flows. These methods are described below.

The Direct Method

The direct method of presenting the statement of cash flows presents the specific cash flows associated with items that affect cash flow. Items that typically do so include:

- Cash collected from customers
- Interest and dividends received
- Cash paid to employees
- Cash paid to suppliers
- Interest paid
- Income taxes paid

The format of the direct method appears in the following example.

EXAMPLE

Milagro Corporation constructs the following statement of cash flows using the direct method:

Milagro Corporation
Statement of Cash Flows
For the year ended 12/31/20X1

Cash flows from operating activities		
Cash receipts from customers	$45,800,000	
Cash paid to suppliers	-29,800,000	
Cash paid to employees	-11,200,000	
Cash generated from operations	4,800,000	
Interest paid	-310,000	
Income taxes paid	-1,700,000	
Net cash from operating activities		$2,790,000
Cash flows from investing activities		
Purchase of fixed assets	-580,000	
Proceeds from sale of equipment	110,000	
Net cash used in investing activities		-470,000
Cash flows from financing activities		
Proceeds from issuance of common stock	1,000,000	
Proceeds from issuance of long-term debt	500,000	
Principal payments under capital lease obligation	-10,000	
Dividends paid	-450,000	
Net cash used in financing activities		1,040,000
Net increase in cash and cash equivalents		3,360,000
Cash and cash equivalents at beginning of period		1,640,000
Cash and cash equivalents at end of period		$5,000,000

Reconciliation of net income to net cash provided by operating activities:

Net income		$2,665,000
Adjustments to reconcile net income to net cash provided by operating activities:		
Depreciation and amortization	$125,000	
Provision for losses on accounts receivable	15,000	
Gain on sale of equipment	-155,000	
Increase in interest and income taxes payable	32,000	
Increase in deferred taxes	90,000	
Increase in other liabilities	18,000	
Total adjustments		125,000
Net cash provided by operating activities		$2,790,000

The standard-setting bodies encourage the use of the direct method, but it is rarely used, for the excellent reason that the information in it is difficult to assemble; companies simply do not collect and store information in the manner required for this format. Instead, they use the indirect method, which is described next.

The Indirect Method

Under the indirect method of presenting the statement of cash flows, the presentation begins with net income or loss, with subsequent additions to or deductions from that amount for non-cash revenue and expense items, resulting in net income provided by operating activities. The format of the indirect method appears in the following example.

EXAMPLE

Milagro Corporation constructs the following statement of cash flows using the indirect method:

Milagro Corporation
Statement of Cash Flows
For the year ended 12/31/20X1

Cash flows from operating activities		
Net income		$3,000,000
Adjustments for:		
Depreciation and amortization	$125,000	
Provision for losses on accounts receivable	20,000	
Gain on sale of facility	-65,000	
		80,000
Increase in trade receivables	-250,000	
Decrease in inventories	325,000	
Decrease in trade payables	-50,000	
		25,000
Cash generated from operations		3,105,000
Cash flows from investing activities		
Purchase of fixed assets	-500,000	
Proceeds from sale of equipment	35,000	
Net cash used in investing activities		-465,000
Cash flows from financing activities		
Proceeds from issuance of common stock	150,000	
Proceeds from issuance of long-term debt	175,000	
Dividends paid	-45,000	
Net cash used in financing activities		280,000
Net increase in cash and cash equivalents		2,920,000
Cash and cash equivalents at beginning of period		2,080,000
Cash and cash equivalents at end of period		$5,000,000

The indirect method is very popular, because the information required for it is relatively easily assembled from the accounts that a business normally maintains.

How to Prepare the Statement of Cash Flows

The most commonly used format for the statement of cash flows is the indirect method (as described earlier in this chapter). The general layout of an *indirect method* statement of cash flows is shown below, along with an explanation of the source of the information in the statement.

Company Name
Statement of Cash Flows
For the year ended 12/31/20X1

Line Item	Derivation
Cash flows from operating activities	
Net income	From the net income line on the income statement
Adjustment for:	
Depreciation and amortization	From the corresponding line items in the income statement
Provision for losses on accounts receivable	From the change in the allowance for doubtful accounts in the period
Gain/loss on sale of facility	From the gain/loss accounts in the income statement
Increase/decrease in trade receivables	Change in trade receivables during the period, from the balance sheet
Increase/decrease in inventories	Change in inventories during the period, from the balance sheet
Increase/decrease in trade payables	Change in trade payables during the period, from the balance sheet
Cash generated from operations	Summary of the preceding items in this section
Cash flows from investing activities	
Purchase of fixed assets	Itemized in the fixed asset accounts during the period
Proceeds from sale of fixed assets	Itemized in the fixed asset accounts during the period
Net cash used in investing activities	Summary of the preceding items in this section
Cash flows from financing activities	
Proceeds from issuance of common stock	Net increase in the common stock and additional paid-in capital accounts during the period
Proceeds from issuance of long-term debt	Itemized in the long-term debt account during the period
Dividends paid	Itemized in the retained earnings account during the period
Net cash used in financing activities	Summary of the preceding items in this section
Net change in cash and cash equivalents	Summary of all preceding subtotals

A less commonly-used format for the statement of cash flows is the *direct method*. The general layout of this version is shown below, along with an explanation of the source of the information in the statement.

Company Name
Statement of Cash Flows
For the year ended 12/31/20X1

Line Item	Derivation
Cash flows from operating activities	
Cash receipts from customers	Summary of the cash receipts journal for the period
Cash paid to suppliers	Summary of the cash disbursements journal for the period (less the financing and income tax payments noted below)
Cash paid to employees	Summary of the payroll journal for the period
Cash generated from operations	Summary of the preceding items in this section
Interest paid	Itemized in the cash disbursements journal
Income taxes paid	Itemized in the cash disbursements journal
Net cash from operating activities	Summary of the preceding items in this section
Cash flows from investing activities	
Purchase of fixed assets	Itemized in the fixed asset accounts during the period
Proceeds from sale of fixed assets	Itemized in the fixed asset accounts during the period
Net cash used in investing activities	Summary of the preceding items in this section
Cash flows from financing activities	
Proceeds from issuance of common stock	Net increase in the common stock and additional paid-in capital accounts during the period
Proceeds from issuance of long-term debt	Itemized in the long-term debt account during the period
Principal payment under capital leases	Itemized in the capital leases liability account during the period
Dividends paid	Itemized in the retained earnings account during the period
Net cash used in financing activities	Summary of the preceding items in this section
Net change in cash and cash equivalents	Summary of all preceding subtotals

As you can see from the explanations for either the indirect or direct methods, the statement of cash flows is much more difficult to create than the income statement and balance sheet. In fact, a complete statement may require a substantial supporting spreadsheet that shows the details for each line item in the statement.

If your accounting software contains a template for the statement of cash flows, use it! The information may not be aggregated quite correctly, and it may not contain all of the line items required for the statement, but it *will* produce most of the information you need, and is much easier to modify than the alternative of creating the statement entirely by hand.

The Statement of Retained Earnings

The statement of retained earnings, also known as the statement of shareholders' equity, is essentially a reconciliation of the beginning and ending balances in a company's equity during an accounting period. It is not considered an essential part of the monthly financial statements, and so is the least likely of all the financial statements to be issued. However, it is a common part of the annual financial statements. This section discusses the format of the statement and how to create it.

Overview of the Statement of Retained Earnings

The statement of retained earnings reconciles changes in the retained earnings account during an accounting period. The statement starts with the beginning balance in the retained earnings account, and then adds or subtracts such items as profits and dividend payments to arrive at the ending retained earnings balance. The general calculation structure of the statement is:

Beginning retained earnings + Net income – Dividends +/- Other changes = Ending retained earnings

The statement of retained earnings is most commonly presented as a separate statement, but can also be added to another financial statement. The following example shows a simplified format for the statement.

EXAMPLE

Milagro Corporation's accountant assembles the following statement of retained earnings to accompany his issuance of the financial statements of the company:

Milagro Corporation
Statement of Retained Earnings
For the year ended 12/31/20X1

Retained earnings at December 31, 20X0	$150,000
Net income for the year ended December 31, 20X1	40,000
Dividends paid to shareholders	-25,000
Retained earnings at December 31, 20X1	$165,000

It is also possible to provide a greatly expanded version of the statement of retained earnings that discloses the various elements of retained earnings. For example, it could separately identify the par value of common stock, additional paid-in capital, retained earnings, and treasury stock, with all of these elements then rolling up into the total just noted in the last example. The following example shows what the format could look like.

EXAMPLE

Milagro Corporation's accountant creates an expanded version of the statement of retained earnings in order to provide more visibility into activities involving equity. The statement follows:

Milagro Corporation
Statement of Retained Earnings
For the year ended 12/31/20X1

	Common Stock, $1 par	Additional Paid-in Capital	Retained Earnings	Total Shareholders' Equity
Retained earnings at December 31, 20X0	$10,000	$40,000	$100,000	$150,000
Net income for the year ended December 31, 20X1			40,000	40,000
Dividends paid to shareholders			-25,000	-25,000
Retained earnings at December 31, 20X1	$10,000	$40,000	$115,000	$165,000

How to Prepare the Statement of Retained Earnings

A simplified version of the statement of retained earnings was shown in the first of the examples in this section. This format works well if there are few equity transactions during the year. However, a more active environment calls for a considerable amount of detail in the statement. In the latter case, consider following these steps:

1. Create separate accounts in the general ledger for each type of equity. Thus, there should be different accounts for the par value of stock, additional paid-in capital, and retained earnings. Each of these accounts is represented by a separate column in the statement.

2. Transfer every transaction within each equity account to a spreadsheet, and identify it in the spreadsheet.

3. Aggregate the transactions within the spreadsheet into similar types, and transfer them to separate line items in the statement of retained earnings.

4. Complete the statement, and verify that the beginning and ending balances in it match the general ledger, and that the aggregated line items within it add up to the ending balances for all columns.

If you do not use the spreadsheet recommended in the preceding steps, you may find it difficult to compile the aggregated line items in the statement, resulting in incorrect subtotals and totals within the statement.

Summary

This chapter has discussed each of the financial statements, and revealed a number of possible layouts for them. When in doubt, issue the minimal number of financial statements, and use the standard template versions of these statements that are provided with the company's accounting software. There are several reasons for doing so:

- *No value.* The statement of retained earnings is rarely read by internal recipients, with the statement of cash flows taking a close second. If no one reads these statements, why issue them? They only take additional time to prepare and review, so a simplified set of financial statements might be an economical alternative.

- *Errors*. It is entirely possible that if you create customized versions of the financial statements, they will contain errors. Consequently, if the template versions look acceptable, use them instead.

The financial statements are generally considered to be the primary work product of the accountant, so only the highest-quality statements should be issued. Consult the author's *Closing the Books* book for more information on this important topic. It is available at the accountingtools.com website.

Chapter 21
Public Company Financial Reporting

Introduction

If a company is publicly-held, there are several more reporting requirements than the standard set of financial statements. In addition, there are issues related to quarterly interim reports, segment reporting that is added to the financial statement disclosures, and earnings per share to calculate and report. This information is then included in the quarterly Form 10-Q and annual Form 10-K. All of these financial reporting topics are addressed in the following sections.

Interim Reporting

If a company is publicly-held, the Securities and Exchange Commission requires that it file a variety of quarterly information on the Form 10-Q. This information is a reduced set of the requirements for the more comprehensive annual Form 10-K. The requirement to issue these additional financial statements may appear to be simple enough, but you must consider whether to report information assuming that quarterly results are stand-alone documents, or part of the full-year results of the business. This section discusses the disparities that these different viewpoints can cause in the financial statements, as well as interim reporting issues related to inventory.

The Integral View

Under the integral view of producing interim reports, you assume that the results reported in interim financial statements are an integral part of the full-year financial results (hence the name of this concept). This viewpoint produces the following accounting issues:

- *Accrue expenses not arising in the period.* If you know that an expense will be paid later in the year that is incurred at least partially in the reporting period, accrue some portion of the expense in the reporting period. Here are several examples:
  - *Advertising.* If you pay in advance for advertising that is scheduled to occur over multiple time periods, recognize the expense over the entire range of time periods.
  - *Bonuses.* If there are bonus plans that may result in bonus payments later in the year, accrue the expense in all accounting periods. Only accrue this expense if you can reasonably estimate the amount of the bonus, which may not always be possible during the earlier months covered by a performance contract.

- Contingencies. If there are contingent liabilities that will be resolved later in the year, and which are both probable and reasonably estimated, then accrue the related expense.
- Profit sharing. If employees are paid a percentage of company profits at year-end, and the amount can be reasonably estimated, then accrue the expense throughout the year as a proportion of the profits recognized in each period.
- Property taxes. A local government entity issues an invoice to the company at some point during the year for property taxes. These taxes are intended to cover the entire year, so you would accrue a portion of the expense in each reporting period.
- Tax rate. A company is usually subject to a graduated income tax rate that incrementally escalates through the year as the business generates more profit. Under the integral view, use the expected tax rate for the entire year in every reporting period, rather than the incremental tax rate that applies only to the profits earned for the year to date.

EXAMPLE

The board of directors of Milagro Corporation approves a senior management bonus plan for the upcoming year that could potentially pay the senior management team a maximum of $240,000. It initially seems probable that the full amount will be paid, but by the third quarter it appears more likely that the maximum amount to be paid will be $180,000. In addition, the company pays $60,000 in advance for a full year of advertising in *Coffee Times* magazine. Milagro recognizes these expenses as follows:

	Quarter 1	Quarter 2	Quarter 3	Quarter 4	Full Year
Bonus expense	$60,000	$60,000	$30,000	$30,000	$180,000
Advertising	15,000	15,000	15,000	15,000	60,000

The accounting staff spreads the recognition of the full amount of the projected bonus over the year, but then reduces its recognition of the remaining expense starting in the third quarter, to adjust for the lowered bonus payout expectation.

The accounting staff initially records the $60,000 advertising expense as a prepaid expense, and recognizes it ratably over all four quarters of the year, which matches the time period over which the related advertisements are run by *Coffee Times*.

One problem with the integral view is that it tends to result in a significant number of expense accruals. Since these accruals are usually based on estimates, it is entirely possible that adjustments should be made to the accruals later in the year, as the company obtains more precise information about the expenses that are being accrued. Some of these adjustments could be substantial, and may materially affect the reported results in later periods.

The Discrete View

Under the discrete view of producing interim reports, you assume that the results reported for a specific interim period are *not* associated with the revenues and expenses arising during other reporting periods. Under this view, you would record the entire impact of a transaction within the reporting period, rather than ratably over the entire year. The following are examples of the situations that can arise under the discrete method:

- *Reduced accruals.* A substantially smaller number of accruals are likely under the discrete method, since the assumption is that you should not anticipate the recordation of transactions that have not yet arisen.
- *Extraordinary items.* An extraordinary item is considered a one-time event, so you should record it entirely within the period in which it occurs.
- *Gains and losses.* Do not spread the recognition of a gain or loss across multiple periods. If you were to do so, it would allow a company to spread a loss over multiple periods, thereby making the loss look smaller on a per-period basis than it really is.

Comparison of the Integral and Discrete Views

The integral view is clearly the better method from a theoretical perspective, since the causes of some transactions can span an entire year. For example, a manager may be awarded a bonus at the end of December, but he probably had to achieve specific results throughout the year to earn it. Otherwise, if you were to adopt the discrete view, interim reporting would yield exceedingly varied results, with some periods revealing inordinately high or low profitability.

However, you should adopt the integral view from the perspective of accounting *efficiency*; that is, it is very time-consuming to maintain a mass of revenue and expense accruals, their ongoing adjustments, and documentation of the reasons for them throughout a year. Instead, use the integral view only for the more material transactions that are anticipated, and use the discrete view for smaller transactions. Thus, you could accrue the expense for property taxes throughout the year if the amount were significant, or simply record it in the month when the invoice is received, if the amount is small.

Interim Reporting Issues

When you are reporting interim results, there are several issues involving the recordation of inventory that vary from the normal handling of inventory for the year-end financial statements.

One issue is the method you are allowed to use for calculating the cost of goods sold. Normally, you would be required to use a periodic or perpetual inventory tracking system to derive the on-hand quantities of inventory. However, this can be too burdensome for interim reporting, so you are allowed to estimate it instead. A good method for doing so is the gross profit method, under which you estimate the cost of goods sold based on the expected gross profit.

Another issue concerns the use of the last in, first out (LIFO) method for calculating the cost of inventory. A key issue when using LIFO is that you cannot recover an inventory layer that was liquidated as of year-end. However, you *can* recover such a layer if it is liquidated during an interim period and you expect to replace the layer by year-end. If that is the case, add the expected inventory replacement cost to the cost of sales for the interim period.

Yet another issue is the recognition of any losses that may have been caused by the lower of cost or market (LCM) rule (see the Accounting for Inventory chapter). If you recognized LCM losses during an interim period, you are allowed to offset the full amount of these losses with any gains in subsequent periods within the same year on the same inventory items. Further, you can simply avoid recognizing these losses in an interim period if there are seasonal price fluctuations that you expect to result in an offsetting increase in market prices by the end of the year.

Segment Reporting

A publicly-held company must report segment information, which is part of the disclosures attached to the financial statements. This information is supposedly needed to give the readers of the financial statements more insights into the operations and prospects of a business. In this section, we describe how to determine which business segments to report separately, and how to report that information.

Primary Segment Reporting Issues

A segment is a distinct component of a business that produces revenue, and for which the business produces separate financial information that is regularly reviewed internally by a chief operation decision maker. A chief operation decision maker is a person who is responsible for making decisions about resource allocations to the segments of a business, and for evaluating those segments. The primary issue with segment reporting is determining which business segments to report. The rules for this selection process are quite specific.

You should only report segment information if a business segment passes any one of the following three tests:

1. *Revenue*. The revenue of the segment is at least 10% of the consolidated revenue of the entire business; or
2. *Profit or loss*. The absolute amount of the profit or loss of the segment is at least 10% of the greater of the combined profits of all the operating segments reporting a profit, or of the combined losses of all operating segments reporting a loss (see the following example for a demonstration of this concept); or
3. *Assets*. The assets of the segment are at least 10% of the combined assets of all the operating segments of the business.

Some parts of a business are not considered to be reportable business segments under the following circumstances:

- *Corporate overhead.* The corporate group does not usually earn outside revenues, and so is not considered a segment.
- *Post-retirement benefit plans.* A benefit plan can earn income from investments, but it has no operating activities, and so is not considered a segment.
- *One-time events.* If an otherwise-insignificant segment has a one-time event that boosts it into the ranks of reportable segments, do not report it, since there is no long-term expectation for it to remain a reportable segment.

If you run the preceding tests and arrive at a group of reportable segments whose combined revenues are not at least 75% of the consolidated revenue of the entire business, add more segments until the 75% threshold is surpassed.

If you have a business segment that used to qualify as a reportable segment and does not currently qualify, but which you expect to qualify in the future, then continue to treat it as a reportable segment.

If you have several smaller segments that would normally be considered too small to be reported separately, combine them for reporting purposes if they have similar regulatory environments, types of customers, production processes, products, distribution methods, *and* economic characteristics. The number of restrictions on this type of reporting makes it unlikely that you would be able to aggregate smaller segments.

Tip: The variety of methods available for segment testing makes it possible that you will have quite a large number of reportable segments. If so, it can be burdensome to create a report for so many segments, and it may be confusing for the readers of the company's financial statements. Consequently, consider limiting the number of reportable segments to ten; you can aggregate the information for additional segments for reporting purposes.

EXAMPLE

Milagro Corporation has six business segments whose results it reports internally. Milagro's accountant needs to test the various segments to see which ones qualify as being reportable. He collects the following information:

Segment	(000s) Revenue	(000s) Profit	(000s) Loss	(000s) Assets
Commercial roasters	$120,000	$10,000	$--	$320,000
Home roasters	85,000	8,000	--	180,000
Coffee brokerage	29,000	--	-21,000	90,000
Coffee sales	200,000	32,000		500,000
Coffee storage	15,000	--	-4,000	4,000
International	62,000	--	-11,000	55,000
	$511,000	$50,000	-$36,000	$1,149,000

In the table, the total profit exceeds the total loss, so the accountant uses the total profit for the 10% profit test. The accountant then lists the same table again, but now with the losses column removed and with test thresholds at the top of the table that are used to determine which segments are reported. An "X" mark below a test threshold indicates that a segment is reportable. In addition, the accountant adds a new column on the right side of the table, which is used to calculate the total revenue for the reportable segments.

Segment	(000s) Revenue	(000s) Profit	(000s) Assets	75% Revenue Test
Reportable threshold (10%)	$51,100	$5,000	$114,900	
Commercial roasters	X	X	X	$120,000
Home roasters	X	X	X	85,000
Coffee brokerage				
Coffee sales	X	X	X	200,000
Coffee storage				
International	X			62,000
			Total	$467,000

This analysis shows that the commercial roasters, home roasters, coffee sales, and international segments are reportable, and that the combined revenue of these reportable segments easily exceeds the 75% reporting threshold. Consequently, the company does not need to separately report information for any additional segments.

The Segment Report

The key requirement of segment reporting is that the revenue, profit or loss, and assets of each segment be separately reported. In addition, reconcile this segment information back to the company's consolidated results, which requires the inclusion of any adjusting items. Also disclose the methods by which you determined which segments to report. The essential information to include in a segment report includes:

- The types of products and services sold by each segment
- The basis of organization (such as by geographic region or product line)
- Revenues
- Interest expense
- Depreciation and amortization
- Material expense items
- Equity method interests in other entities
- Income tax expense or income
- Extraordinary items
- Other material non-cash items
- Profit or loss

EXAMPLE

Milagro Corporation's accountant produces the following segment report for the segments identified in the preceding example:

(000s)	Commercial Roasters	Home Roasters	Coffee Sales	International	Other	Consolidated
Revenues	$120,000	$85,000	$200,000	$62,000	$44,000	$511,000
Interest income	11,000	8,000	28,000	8,000	2,000	57,000
Interest expense	--	--	--	11,000	39,000	50,000
Depreciation	32,000	18,000	50,000	6,000	10,000	116,000
Income taxes	4,000	3,000	10,000	-3,000	-7,000	7,000
Profit	10,000	8,000	32,000	-11,000	-25,000	14,000
Assets	320,000	180,000	500,000	55,000	94,000	1,149,000

Earnings per Share

Earnings per share is a company's net income divided by the weighted-average number of shares outstanding. If your company is publicly-held, you are required to report two types of earnings per share information within the financial statements. These can be complex calculations, and so may slow down the closing process. In this section, we describe how to calculate both basic and diluted earnings per share, as well as how to present this information within the financial statements.

Basic Earnings per Share

Basic earnings per share is the amount of a company's profit or loss for a reporting period that is available to the shares of its common stock that are outstanding during a reporting period. If a business only has common stock in its capital structure, it presents only its basic earnings per share for income from continuing operations and net income. This information is reported on its income statement.

The formula for basic earnings per share is:

$$\frac{\text{Profit or loss attributable to common equity holders of the parent business}}{\text{Weighted average number of common shares outstanding during the period}}$$

In addition, subdivide this calculation into:

- The profit or loss from continuing operations attributable to the parent company
- The total profit or loss attributable to the parent company

When calculating basic earnings per share, you should incorporate in the numerator an adjustment for dividends. You should deduct from the profit or loss the after-tax amount of any dividends declared on non-cumulative preferred stock, as well as the after-tax amount of any preferred stock dividends, even if the dividends are not declared; this does not include any dividends paid or declared during the current period that relate to previous periods.

Also, add the following adjustments into the denominator of the basic earnings per share calculation:

- *Contingent stock.* If there is contingently issuable stock, treat it as though it were outstanding as of the date when there are no circumstances under which the shares would *not* be issued.
- *Issuance date.* Include shares under any of the following circumstances:
  - A liability is settled in exchange for shares
  - An acquisition paid for with shares is recognized
  - Any shares related to a mandatorily convertible instrument as of the contract date
  - Cash is receivable for sold shares
  - Dividends are reinvested
  - Interest stops accruing on convertible debt instruments on which shares can be issued
  - Services are paid for with shares
- *Weighted-average shares.* Use the weighted-average number of shares during the period in the denominator. This is done by adjusting the number of shares outstanding at the beginning of the reporting period for common shares repurchased or issued in the period. This adjustment is based on the proportion of the days in the reporting period that the shares are outstanding.

EXAMPLE

Milagro Corporation earns a profit of $1,000,000 net of taxes in Year 1. In addition, Milagro owes $200,000 in dividends to the holders of its cumulative preferred stock. Milagro calculates the numerator of its basic earnings per share as follows:

$$\$1,000,000 \text{ Profit} - \$200,000 \text{ Dividends} = \underline{\$800,000}$$

Milagro had 4,000,000 common shares outstanding at the beginning of Year 1. In addition, it sold 200,000 shares on April 1 and 400,000 shares on October 1. It also issued 500,000 shares on July 1 to the owners of a newly-acquired subsidiary. Finally, it bought back 60,000 shares on December 1. Milagro calculates the weighted-average number of common shares outstanding as follows:

Date	Shares	Weighting (Months)	Weighted Average
January 1	4,000,000	12/12	4,000,000
April 1	200,000	9/12	150,000
July 1	500,000	6/12	250,000
October 1	400,000	3/12	100,000
December 1	-60,000	1/12	-5,000
			4,495,000

Milagro's basic earnings per share is:

$800,000 adjusted profits ÷ 4,495,000 weighted-average shares = <u>$0.18</u> per share

---

Diluted Earnings per Share

Diluted earnings per share is the profit for a reporting period per share of common stock outstanding during that period; it includes the number of shares that would have been outstanding during the period if the company had issued common shares for all potential dilutive common stock outstanding during the period.

If a company has more types of stock than common stock in its capital structure, it must present both basic earnings per share and diluted earnings per share information; this presentation must be for both income from continuing operations and net income. This information is reported on the company's income statement.

To calculate diluted earnings per share, include the effects of all dilutive potential common shares. This means that you increase the number of shares outstanding by the weighted average number of additional common shares that would have been outstanding if the company had converted all dilutive potential common stock to common stock. This dilution may affect the profit or loss in the numerator of the dilutive earnings per share calculation. The formula is:

(Profit or loss attributable to common equity holders of parent company
<u>+ After-tax interest on convertible debt + Convertible preferred dividends)</u>
(Weighted average number of common shares outstanding during the period
+ All dilutive potential common stock)

You may need to make two adjustments to the numerator of this calculation. They are:

- *Interest expense*. Eliminate any interest expense associated with dilutive potential common stock, since you assume that these shares are converted to common stock. The conversion would eliminate the company's liability for the interest expense.
- *Dividends*. Adjust for the after-tax impact of dividends or other types of dilutive potential common shares.

You may need to make several adjustments to the denominator of this calculation. They are:

- *Contingent shares dependency*. If there is a contingent share issuance that is dependent upon the future market price of the company's common stock, include the shares in the diluted earnings per share calculation, based on the market price at the end of the reporting period; however, only include the issuance if the effect is dilutive. If the shares have a contingency feature, do not include them in the calculation until the contingency has been met.
- *Contingent shares in general*. Treat common stock that is contingently issuable as though it was outstanding as of the beginning of the reporting

period, but only if the conditions have been met that would require the company to issue the shares.

- *Anti-dilutive shares.* If there are any contingent stock issuances that would have an anti-dilutive impact on earnings per share, do not include them in the calculation. This situation arises when a business experiences a loss, because including the dilutive shares in the calculation would reduce the loss per share.

In addition to these three adjustments to the denominator, you should also apply all of the adjustments to the denominator already noted for basic earnings per share.

> **Tip:** The rules related to diluted earnings per share appear complex, but they are founded upon one principle – that you are trying to establish the absolute worst-case scenario to arrive at the smallest possible amount of earnings per share. If you are faced with an unusual situation involving the calculation of diluted earnings per share and are not sure what to do, that rule will likely apply.

If there is a share issuance that is contingent upon certain conditions being satisfied, and those conditions were met by the end of the reporting period, then include them in the calculation as of the beginning of the period. However, if the conditions were not met by the end of the period, then include in the calculation, as of the beginning of the period, any shares that would be issuable if:

- The end of the reporting period were the end of the contingency period; and
- The result would be dilutive.

If the number of contingent shares issued is based on a certain amount of earnings, and the company achieved those earnings during the reporting period, then include the contingent shares in the calculation; but only if the effect is dilutive.

In addition to the issues just noted, here are a number of additional situations that could impact the calculation of diluted earnings per share:

- *Most advantageous exercise price.* When you calculate the number of potential shares that could be issued, do so using the most advantageous conversion rate from the perspective of the person or entity holding the security to be converted.
- *Settlement assumption.* If there is an open contract that could be settled in common stock or cash, assume that it will be settled in common stock, but only if the effect is dilutive.
- *Effects of convertible instruments.* If there are convertible instruments outstanding, include their dilutive effect if they dilute earnings per share. Consider convertible preferred stock to be anti-dilutive when the dividend on any converted shares is greater than basic earnings per share. Similarly, convertible debt is considered anti-dilutive when the interest expense on any converted shares exceeds basic earnings per share. The following example illustrates the concept.

EXAMPLE

Milagro Corporation earns a net profit of $2 million, and it has 5 million common shares outstanding. In addition, there is a $1 million convertible loan that has an eight percent interest rate. The loan may potentially convert into 500,000 of Milagro's common shares. Milagro's incremental tax rate is 35 percent.

Milagro's basic earnings per share is $2,000,000 ÷ 5,000,000 shares, or $0.40/share. The following calculation shows the compilation of Milagro's diluted earnings per share:

Net profit	$2,000,000
+ Interest saved on $1,000,000 loan at 8%	80,000
- Reduced tax savings on foregone interest expense	-28,000
= Adjusted net earnings	$2,052,000
Common shares outstanding	5,000,000
+ Potential converted shares	500,000
= Adjusted shares outstanding	5,500,000
Diluted earnings per share ($2,052,000 ÷ 5,500,000)	**$0.37/share**

- *Option exercise.* If there are any dilutive options and warrants, assume that they are exercised at their exercise price. Then, convert the proceeds into the total number of shares that the holders would have purchased, using the average market price during the reporting period. Then use in the diluted earnings per share calculation the difference between the number of shares assumed to have been issued and the number of shares assumed to have been purchased. The following example illustrates the concept.

EXAMPLE

Milagro Corporation earns a net profit of $200,000, and it has 5,000,000 common shares outstanding that sell on the open market for an average of $12 per share. In addition, there are 300,000 options outstanding that can be converted to Milagro's common stock at $10 each.

Milagro's basic earnings per share is $200,000 ÷ 5,000,000 common shares, or $0.04 per share.

Milagro's accountant wants to calculate the amount of diluted earnings per share. To do so, he follows these steps:
1. *Calculate the number of shares would have been issued at the market price.* Thus, he multiplies the 300,000 options by the average exercise price of $10 to arrive at a total of $3,000,000 paid to exercise the options by their holders.
2. *Divide the amount paid to exercise the options by the market price to determine the number of shares that could be purchased.* Thus, he divides the $3,000,000 paid to

exercise the options by the $12 average market price to arrive at 250,000 shares that could have been purchased with the proceeds from the options.

3. *Subtract the number of shares that could have been purchased from the number of options exercised.* Thus, he subtracts the 250,000 shares potentially purchased from the 300,000 options to arrive at a difference of 50,000 shares.

4. *Add the incremental number of shares to the shares already outstanding.* Thus, he adds the 50,000 incremental shares to the existing 5,000,000 to arrive at 5,050,000 diluted shares.

Based on this information, the accountant arrives at diluted earnings per share of $0.0396, for which the calculation is:

$200,000 net profit ÷ 5,050,000 common shares

- *Put options.* If there are purchased put options, only include them in the diluted earnings per share calculation if the exercise price is higher than the average market price during the reporting period.
- *Call options.* If there are purchased call options, only include them in the diluted earnings per share calculation if the exercise price is lower than the market price.

Tip: There is only a dilutive effect on the diluted earnings per share calculation when the average market price is greater than the exercise prices of any options or warrants.

- *Compensation in shares.* If company employees are awarded shares that have not vested or stock options as forms of compensation, then treat these grants as options when calculating diluted earnings per share. Consider these grants to be outstanding on the grant date, rather than any later vesting date.
- *Repurchase agreements.* If there is a contract that requires a business to reacquire its own shares, *and* the repurchase price is higher than the average market price during the past period, *and* there is a dilutive effect, include them in the calculation of diluted earnings per share. To do so, assume that a sufficient number of shares were issued at the beginning of the reporting period to raise the funds needed to repurchase the shares. You should then include the difference between the number of shares issued to raise funds and the number of shares retired in the calculation of diluted earnings per share.
- *Dilutive shares.* If there is potential dilutive common stock, add all of it to the denominator of the diluted earnings per share calculation. Unless there is more specific information available, assume that these shares are issued at the beginning of the reporting period.

Always calculate the number of potential dilutive common shares independently for each reporting period presented in the financial statements.

Presentation of Earnings per Share

The basic and diluted earnings per share information is normally listed at the bottom of the income statement, and should be listed there for every period included in the income statement. Also, if you report diluted earnings per share in *any* of the periods included in the company's income statement, you must report it for *all* of the periods included in the statement. The following sample illustrates the concept.

Sample Presentation of Earnings per Share

Earnings per Share	20x3	20x2	20x1
From continuing operations			
Basic earnings per share	$1.05	$0.95	$0.85
Diluted earnings per share	1.00	0.90	0.80
From discontinued operations			
Basic earnings per share	$0.20	$0.17	$0.14
Diluted earnings per share	0.15	0.08	0.07
From total operations			
Basic earnings per share	$1.25	$1.12	$0.99
Diluted earnings per share	1.15	0.98	0.87

The Public Company Closing Process

A publicly-held company is required by the SEC to file a large report concerning its financial condition at the end of each quarter. These are the Form 10-Q (for quarterly filings) and Form 10-K (for annual filings). The contents of both reports are discussed in the following sections.

The additional steps needed to close the books for a publicly held company include all of the following:

1. *Auditor investigation.* The company's outside auditors must conduct a review of the company's financial statements and disclosures for its quarterly results, and a full audit of its annual results. This is the most time-consuming of the public company requirements. The company can reduce the amount of time required for a review or audit by providing full staff support to the audit team, as well as by having all requested information available as of the beginning of the audit or review work.

2. *Legal review.* It would be extremely unwise to issue the financial statement package without first having legal counsel review the statements and (especially) the disclosures to ensure that all required disclosures have been made, and to verify that all statements made are correct and fully supportable. This review is usually completed near or after the end of the work done by the auditors, but can be scheduled slightly sooner if you believe the disclosures to be substantially complete at that time.

3. *Officer certification.* Depending upon what type of Form is being issued, different company officers are required to certify that the information in the

financial statements presents fairly the financial condition and results of operations of the business. Since there are substantial penalties and jail time involved if an officer were to make a false certification, it should be no surprise that the signing officers will want to spend time reviewing the complete set of financial statements and disclosures. This review can be done before the auditors have completed their work, so officer certification does not usually increase the duration of the closing process.

4. *Audit committee and board approvals.* The audit committee must approve every Form 10-Q, and the board of directors must approve every Form 10-K. Given the number of people involved, you should schedule review and approval meetings well in advance, to be conducted a few days prior to the required filing date of the applicable Form. Scheduling the review slightly early gives you time to make adjustments, in case anyone expresses concerns during the review, and wants changes to be made prior to filing.

Issue the complete set of financial statements and disclosures to the audit committee or board members at least one full day in advance of a review and approval meeting, so that they have sufficient time to examine the material.

5. *EDGARize and file.* Once the Form 10-Q or Form 10-K is complete and fully approved, file it with the SEC. The filing is done using the Electronic Data Gathering, Analysis, and Retrieval (EDGAR) system that is operated by the SEC. You can submit this information in various formats, but you will almost certainly have to convert it from the format in which the documents were originally prepared. This means hiring someone to convert the reports to the applicable format, which is a process known as *EDGARizing.* Not only is the conversion specialist responsible for converting the financial statements, but this person also files the statements with the SEC on behalf of the company. The conversion process usually takes one or two days, but you should factor in additional time for the auditors to review the converted format – the auditors must give their approval before it is filed with the SEC.

The closing process described here is very slow, so be sure to have the financial statements prepared as soon as possible after the end of the applicable reporting period. Doing so should leave enough time to prepare the statements for filing by the designated due date.

The Form 10-Q

A publicly held company is required to issue the Form 10-Q to report the results of its first, second, and third fiscal quarters. The Form 10-Q includes not just the financial statements, but also a number of disclosures. The following table itemizes the more common disclosures:

Selection of Form 10-Q Disclosures

Item Header	Description
Item 1A. Risk factors	This is a thorough listing of all risks that the company may experience. It warns investors of what could reduce the value of their investments in the company.
Item 3. Legal proceedings	Describe any legal proceedings currently involving the company, and its estimate of the likely outcome of those proceedings.
Item 4. Submission of matters to a vote of security holders	Describe matters submitted to the shareholders for a vote during the most recent quarter of the fiscal year.
Item 7. Management's discussion and analysis (MD&A)	Describe opportunities, challenges, risks, trends, future plans, and key performance indicators, as well as changes in revenues, the cost of goods sold, other expenses, assets, and liabilities.
Item 7A. Quantitative and qualitative disclosures about market risk	Quantify the market risk at the end of the last fiscal year for the company's market risk-sensitive instruments.
Item 8. Financial statements and supplementary data	Make all disclosures required by GAAP, including descriptions of: • Accrued liabilities • Acquisitions • Discontinued operations • Fixed assets • Income taxes • Related party transactions • Segment information • Stock options
Item 9A. Controls and procedures	Generally describe the system of internal controls, testing of controls, changes in controls, and management's conclusions regarding the effectiveness of those controls.
Item 15. Exhibits and financial statement schedules	Item 601 of Regulation S-K requires that a business attach a number of exhibits to the Form 10-K, including (but not limited to): • Code of ethics • Material contracts • Articles of incorporation • Bylaws • Acquisition purchase agreements

Before filing, the Form 10-Q must be signed by an authorized officer, as well as the principal financial or chief accounting officer.

The Form 10-Q must be filed within 40 days of the end of the fiscal quarter if the company is either a large accelerated filer or an accelerated filer. If that is not the case, file it within 45 days of the end of the fiscal quarter. A large accelerated filer is a company having an aggregate market value owned by investors who are not affiliated with the company of a minimum of $700 million. This measurement is as of the last business day of the most recent second fiscal quarter. An accelerated filer is a company having an aggregate market value owned by investors who are not affiliated with the company of less than $700 million, but more than $75 million. This measurement is as of the last business day of the most recent second fiscal quarter.

The Form 10-K

A publicly held company is required to issue the Form 10-K to report the results of its fiscal year. The Form 10-K includes not just the financial statements, but also a number of additional disclosures. The following table itemizes the more common disclosures:

Selection of Form 10-K Disclosures

Item Header	Description
Item 1. Business	Provide a description of the company's purpose, history, operating segments, customers, suppliers, sales and marketing operations, customer support, intellectual property, competition, and employees. It should tell readers what the company does and describe its business environment.
Item 1A. Risk factors	This is a thorough listing of all risks that the company may experience. It warns investors of what could reduce the value of their investments in the company.
Item 1B. Unresolved staff comments	Disclose all unresolved comments received from the SEC if they are material. (only applies to written comments from the SEC received at least 180 days before the fiscal year-end by an accelerated or large accelerated filer)
Item 2. Properties	Describe the leased or owned facilities of the business, including square footage, lease termination dates, and lease amounts paid per month.
Item 3. Legal proceedings	Describe any legal proceedings currently involving the company, and its estimate of the likely outcome of those proceedings.
Item 4. Submission of matters to a vote of security holders	Describe matters submitted to the shareholders for a vote during the fourth quarter of the fiscal year.
Item 5. Market for company stock	Describe where the company's stock trades and the number of holders of record, as well as the high and low closing prices per share, by quarter.
Item 6. Selected financial data	For the last five years, state selected information from the company's income statement and balance sheet (should be in tabular comparative format).

Item Header	Description
Item 7. Management's discussion and analysis (MD&A)	Describe opportunities, challenges, risks, trends, future plans, and key performance indicators, as well as changes in revenues, the cost of goods sold, other expenses, assets, and liabilities.
Item 7A. Quantitative and qualitative disclosures about market risk	Quantify the market risk at the end of the last fiscal year for the company's market risk-sensitive instruments.
Item 8. Financial statements and supplementary data	Make all disclosures required by GAAP, including descriptions of: • Accrued liabilities • Acquisitions • Discontinued operations • Fixed assets • Income taxes • Related party transactions • Segment information • Stock options
Item 9. Changes in and disagreements with accountants on accounting and financial disclosure	Describe any disagreements with the auditors when management elects to account for or disclose transactions in a manner different from what the auditors want.
Item 9A. Controls and procedures	Generally describe the system of internal controls, testing of controls, changes in controls, and management's conclusions regarding the effectiveness of those controls.
Item 10. Directors, executive officers and corporate governance	Identify the executive officers, directors, promoters, and individuals classified as control persons.
Item 11. Executive compensation	Itemize the types of compensation paid to company executives.
Item 12. Security ownership of certain beneficial owners and management and related stockholder matters	State the number of shares of all types owned or controlled by certain individuals classified as beneficial owners and/or members of management.
Item 13. Certain relationships and related transactions, and director independence	If there were transactions with related parties during the past fiscal year, and the amounts involved exceeded $120,000, describe the transactions.

Item Header	Description
Item 14. Principal accountant fees and services	State the aggregate amount of any fees billed in each of the last two fiscal years for professional services rendered by the company's auditors for: • Reviews and audits; • Audit-related activities; • Taxation work; and • All other fees.
Item 15. Exhibits and financial statement schedules	Item 601 of Regulation S-K requires that a business attach a number of exhibits to the Form 10-K, including (but not limited to): • Code of ethics • Material contracts • Articles of incorporation • Bylaws • Acquisition purchase agreements

Before filing, the Form 10-K must be signed by *all* of the following:
- Principal executive officer
- Principal financial officer
- Controller
- A majority of the board of directors

The Form 10-K must be filed within 60 days of the end of the fiscal year if the company is a large accelerated filer or an accelerated filer, or within 75 days of the end of the fiscal year if the company is an accelerated filer. If the company does not have either designation, then it must be filed within 90 days of the end of the fiscal year.

Summary

For the accountant of a publicly-held company, it may sometimes appear as though the *only* responsibility involves the filing of the Forms 10-Q and 10-K, because they take so much time to prepare. Never underestimate the workload associated with public company financial reporting – it is downright oppressive. We recommend that you conduct a thorough review of the time required to prepare the necessary filings, including a discussion of any concerns the auditors may have about the timeliness of work completion and errors found, and present these findings to senior management along with a request for additional resources. Otherwise, you may find that you do not have sufficient time to engage in all of the other responsibilities of the accountant position.

Chapter 22
Management Reports

Introduction

The accountant may be responsible for the issuance of a startling number of management reports that address not only financial issues, but also possibly operational ones. In this chapter, we address not only the types of reports that you may want to issue, but also their contents and ongoing maintenance. Ideally, the result should be a small core group of reports that are continually adjusted to match the needs of the business.

Related Podcast Episode: Episode 148 of the Accounting Best Practices Podcast discusses best practices for accounting reports. You can listen to it at: **accounting-tools.com/podcasts** or **iTunes**

The Duration of a Report

Before you delve into the array of management reports that are available, first consider the effort required to create and distribute each one, as well as the extent to which the reports will be used. What you will likely find is that only a few line items on a report are truly useful to the recipients, and also that the level of report usefulness declines over time.

These issues mean that you should examine every report issued by the accounting department on a regular basis to see if they should be modified or possibly discontinued entirely. It should be a rare report that continues unchanged for more than a year.

By continually examining the usage level of reports and adjusting the reports accordingly, you may reduce the workload of the accounting staff. Also, this should increase the cost-benefit of the reports – that is, the effort that goes into a report is paid for by being highly applicable to the recipient.

Responsibility Reporting

Responsibility reporting is the concept that every revenue item and cost in a business can be traced to one person within the organization, so that person should receive reports about the specific items for which he or she is responsible. Here are several examples of responsibility reporting:
- *Raw materials cost*. Report it to the purchasing manager.
- *Rent expense*. Report it to the person who negotiated and signed the building lease.
- *Wages*. Report it to the person supervising the employee earning the wages.

- *Warranty expense*. Report it to the engineering manager.

Further, responsibility reporting requires different levels of information aggregation, depending on the position of the recipient within the business. Thus, the president receives the income statement for the entire business, while the production manager only sees the cost incurred by the production department, and a machine operator may be limited to seeing the excess scrap produced by his machine.

This concept is terrific from the perspective of the company president, since it means that everyone in the company is aware of the revenues and expenses for which they are responsible. The accountant may have a somewhat less enthusiastic viewpoint, since this calls for a virtual blizzard of reports. To avoid becoming overwhelmed by reports, the accounting staff should create a customized report template for each report recipient, and then set up the templates to automatically run at fixed intervals throughout the month. This approach completely automates report creation, though it also means that the reports will probably not be tweaked at regular intervals to meet the needs of recipients, since there are so many reports.

The Flash Report

The single most crucial report that the accountant issues is the flash report. This is the ultimate in short-term information, for it is designed to inform management of issues that are occurring either right now or in the immediate past. The intent of the flash report is to warn management of problems in areas necessary for the short-term survival of the company. Thus, the report should not contain any information on which managers are unlikely to take action. Examples of items that might appear in a flash report are:

Related to Cash

- *Cash balance*. This is a perennial favorite for the flash report, since an impending cash shortage can shut down any business.
- *Debt remaining*. It is more important to know how much untapped debt is remaining on the company's line of credit than the amount of debt that the company already has, because the latter information is already available on the balance sheet. This line item is closely associated with the cash balance, since it reveals the company's available liquidity.
- *Receivables 90+ days*. This is the amount of accounts receivable more than 90 days old, and shows the amount of cash that is most at risk of not being collected. It may be necessary to provide an accompanying detail of who is not paying, and the amount unpaid by each customer.
- *Obsolete inventory*. This is the disposal value of any inventory designated as obsolete. You do not need to report the original cost of this inventory, since the intent of this line item is to state the amount of cash that can be gleaned from selling the inventory. A large balance could trigger fast action by management to convert the designated inventory to cash.

Related to Sales

- *Backlog.* This is the order backlog that has not yet been shipped. You might consider listing this item first on the flash report, since it is the key indicator for the generation of sales to support the business.
- *Contribution margin.* The size of the backlog is not sufficient information for management if the sales staff is buying sales by offering low prices. Hence the need for this line item, which is revenues minus the direct costs of selling products. This information may only be available on a monthly basis, so include the latest information when available. This information is not listed on the income statement, since that document is organized to report the gross margin, which also includes a number of fixed costs.

Related to Bottlenecks

- *Bottleneck utilization.* This is the percentage of theoretically available time during which the bottleneck operation ran during the reporting period. The company needs to maximize this percentage in order to earn a profit.

Related to Customer Service

- *Percent order line items shipped on time.* Customers respond well to receiving goods on time, so track the percentage shipped by the promise date.

Tip: Do not include too many line items in the flash report, since managers do not want to wade through too much information. Instead, present just the top ten metrics that really matter to company operations.

A sample flash report is shown below. Note that the information is listed on a trend line, so that managers can see where there may be a potential problem in comparison to the results of prior periods.

EXAMPLE

After much discussion with management, Milagro Corporation's accountant unveils the following flash report:

	This Week	Last Week	2 Weeks Ago	3 Weeks Ago
Cash Issues				
Cash balance	$150,000	$180,000	$190,000	$200,000
Debt remaining	310,000	325,000	350,000	400,000
Receivables 90+ days	89,000	62,000	35,000	15,000
Obsolete inventory	5,000	6,000	8,000	10,000
Sales Issues				
Backlog	520,000	590,000	620,000	650,000
Contribution margin	42%	41%	55%	58%
Bottleneck Issues				
Bottleneck utilization	86%	88%	91%	93%
Customer Service Issues				
Percent orders shipped on time	82%	85%	90%	96%

The accountant includes a commentary with the flash report, pointing out a variety of problems. The company is losing its order backlog, has a growing amount of unpaid accounts receivable, and is rapidly losing contribution margin on its sales. Further, the company is suffering from a rapid decline in its percentage of order line items shipped on time. In short, this flash report reveals a company in significant disarray.

Tip: Note the complete absence of ratios in the flash report. Ratios are useful for investigating the long-term performance of a business, but the flash report is all about short-term performance that management can act upon – and ratios are not useful for that purpose.

You will likely need to evaluate the flash report at regular intervals and alter its contents to match the changing circumstances of the business. For example, if the company enters a new market, there may be a need for metrics related to that market. Or, if the bottleneck operation has shifted, discontinue reporting on the old bottleneck and switch to the new one.

Expense Reporting

The accounting department is continually being asked to provide reports concerning expenses incurred in various parts of the business. When you issue this information, do not simply state the expense incurred in the previous period (which is the usual request), since it provides little useful information. You could provide the information in comparison to the budgeted expense for the period, but the budgeted amount could be exceedingly unrealistic, so the comparison is less than useful. A better approach is to present the information alongside the same expenses incurred in previous periods. Doing so provides a solid basis of comparison, and reveals whether the most recent expenses are in accordance with historical trends. The following sample report shows the concept:

Sample Expense Report Format

	September	October	November	December
Wages	$45,000	$46,500	$47,250	$53,000
Payroll taxes	3,150	3,250	3,300	3,700
Rent	3,500	3,500	3,750	3,750
Office expenses	1,200	1,350	1,400	1,650
Travel and entertainment	800	950	800	4,000
Utilities	620	600	700	750
Other expenses	450	425	470	510
Totals	$54,720	$56,575	$57,670	$67,360

The sample shows the expenses incurred by a typical department. Compensation expenses are listed near the top of the report, since this expense is frequently the largest one incurred by many departments, with other expenses listed in declining order by the amounts usually incurred. Thus, the reader's attention is drawn to the top of the report, where most of the expenses are located. Also, the presentation of side-by-side results by month makes it easy for the report recipient to skim through the report and make note of anything that rises above or falls below the long-term average.

Expenses are similar to Newton's first law of motion. That first law states:

> The velocity of a body remains constant unless the body is acted upon by an external force.

You can change a few words to arrive at Bragg's first law of accounting, which is:

> Expense levels remain constant unless the business is acted upon by a supplier or manager.

Suppliers tend to raise prices, while managers take steps to reduce expenses. These opposing forces appear in the expense reports as changes in expense levels. A good accountant can take advantage of Bragg's first law by reporting expenses only by exception. Thus, the preceding sample expense report might trigger a statement that the change in office rent in November was triggered by a new lease, while the surge in the travel and entertainment expense in December was caused by the company Christmas party. This additional level of reporting centers the attention of management on the key expense exceptions, while ignoring all of the other expenses that are not changing.

An exceptional accountant will go one step further and make recommendations regarding how to make changes to expenses. Here are examples of accountant-provided commentary:

- "The rent expense is 20% above the rents for similar buildings within one mile of the company facility; recommend negotiating with the landlord to drop the lease rate in exchange for extending the term of the lease."
- "Telephone expenses can be reduced by 15% if the company adopts a single cell phone carrier for all employees."
- "Travel expenses can be reduced by 5% if the company adopts a common travel agent for all company travel."

However, the level of accountant-provided commentary noted here is extremely time-consuming, so even the best accountant will probably only be able to make an occasional recommendation that includes a sufficient level of detail to convince management to act upon it.

> **Tip:** Proactive accountant commentary should be welcome for office and administration expenses, since this is the key area in which the accounting staff should have some expertise. However, the accountant's advice may not be so welcome in other areas; consequently, be more circumspect in making recommendations regarding the cost of materials, product designs, marketing campaigns, and so forth.

Margin Reporting

Management will likely make inquiries about the earnings that the company is achieving in such areas as customers, products, product lines, stores, and operating units. If the chart of accounts has been constructed to accumulate information for any of these categories, the accounting department should be able to provide the requested information. However, here are several issues to consider regarding the construction of margin reports:

- *Information sources.* For many margin analyses, such as margins by customer, it requires a considerable amount of manual analysis to obtain the required information. If so, push back if the requesting person wants this information on a continuing basis, since it will take up too much staff time to create.
- *Cost allocations.* It is rarely advisable to allocate overhead costs in a margin report. By doing so, you are artificially reducing the reported margin on every line item in the report, which may lead to management shutting down products, product lines, stores, or divisions that actually have adequate profit margins.
- *Automation.* If a margin report proves to be valuable, take all possible steps to automate it. For example, if management wants to see a margin report by product, create standard costs for the direct costs associated with each product, include those standard costs in the margin report, and set up a process for routinely reviewing how closely the standard costs match actual costs.

Perhaps the most common of all margin reports is one that details the margin for individual products during a particular time period. When creating this report, only include those costs that vary directly with changes in unit volume; this usually means that only the cost of materials is included in the report, since manufacturing overhead and direct labor costs do not vary at the unit level. A sample product margin report is shown below.

Sample Product Margin Report

	Revenue	Units Sold	×	Standard Cost of Materials	=	Total Cost of Materials	Margin $
French press	$180,000	900		$90.00		$81,000	$99,000
Moka pot	62,000	380		73.25		27,835	34,165
Percolator pro	220,000	1,500		66.00		99,000	121,000
Roaster home edition	470,000	3,760		56.50		212,440	257,560
Roaster junior	100,000	1,100		40.90		44,990	55,010
Roaster pro	250,000	800		140.00		112,000	138,000
Vacuum coffee maker	123,000	300		184.50		55,350	67,650
Totals	$1,405,000	8,740				$632,615	$772,385

Another possible addition to the product margin report is the cost of commissions (if any), since they usually vary directly with unit sales.

If a company has a number of similar products that are aggregated into a product line, there may be a request to determine the margin associated with the entire product line. When constructing this report, you can include more expenses than just the cost of materials, since other expense types may be directly associated with the product line. The following expenses might be included:

- *Advertising.* This is the cost of any advertising or other marketing expenses related to the product line in question.
- *Engineering.* There may be a dedicated team of engineers involved with the design of only those products included in the product line. Only include those engineering compensation and other costs that would disappear if the product line were to be cancelled.
- *Manufacturing overhead.* There may be a considerable amount of overhead cost associated with a product line, such as a production manager, equipment maintenance, and utilities. Only include those costs that would disappear if the product line were to be cancelled.
- *Selling expenses.* There may be a dedicated sales force that only sells the product line. Their compensation, payroll taxes, and travel and entertainment expenses should be included.

A sample product line margin report that includes the preceding expense elements is shown below.

Sample Product Line Margin Report

Product Line	Revenue	Direct Materials	Engineering	Overhead	Sales and Marketing	Margin
Home products	$800,000	$320,000	$65,000	$165,000	$130,000	$120,000
Restaurant products	390,000	156,000	82,000	80,000	40,000	32,000
School products	640,000	320,000	39,000	128,000	90,000	63,000
Totals	$1,830,000	$796,000	$186,000	$373,000	$260,000	$215,000

The same format just shown for a product line works well for a margin report constructed for a retail location, though you should replace the engineering, overhead, and sales and marketing costs with expenses that would terminate if the store were closed, such as:

- *Wages and payroll taxes.* This is the compensation and related payroll taxes that would disappear if the store were closed. Thus, you would not include an apportionment of the cost of a regional store manager.
- *Advertising.* There may be advertising expenses related to a specific location. Do not include advertising if the expenditures are for a group of stores.
- *Rent.* This is the rent that would be eliminated if the store were closed. Do not include it if the company must still pay the rent even if the store closes.
- *Utilities.* There are usually some electrical and heating costs that would be eliminated as a result of a store closure.

A sample store margin report that includes the preceding expense elements is shown below.

Sample Store Margin Report

Store Location	Revenue	Direct Materials	Wages	Advertising	Other Expenses	Margin
Evanston	$900,000	$360,000	$270,000	$25,000	$200,000	$45,000
Freeport	1,050,000	420,000	270,000	25,000	230,000	105,000
Muncie	820,000	328,000	270,000	20,000	190,000	12,000
Totals	$2,770,000	$1,108,000	$810,000	$70,000	$620,000	$162,000

If you are asked to create a margin report for customers, be extremely careful about adding any expenses to the report. The reason is that most expenses related to the servicing of customers are incurred for *many* customers, not just one. For example, it would be unwise to include in a margin report the labor cost associated with the customer service or field service calls related to a specific customer, because those costs are likely to still exist even if the customer were to be terminated. However, it is acceptable to include other costs in a customer margin analysis, such as:

- *Commissions.* Salesperson commissions are almost certainly related to specific sales, so you can include them in the analysis.

- *Deductions.* Some customers claim an inordinate number of deductions when paying their invoices, which should certainly be included in the analysis.

A sample customer margin report that includes the preceding expense elements is shown below:

Sample Customer Margin Report

Customer Name	Revenue	Direct Materials	Commissions	Deductions	Margin
Gadzooks Coffee	$95,000	$48,000	$4,000	$13,000	$30,000
Kona Distributors	130,000	70,000	5,000	32,000	23,000
Marlowe Coffee	247,000	136,000	10,000	20,000	81,000
Peaberry Coffee	86,000	41,000	3,000	1,000	41,000
Totals	$558,000	$295,000	$22,000	$66,000	$175,000

The preceding customer margin report reveals a common issue that triggers the request to develop the report – there are substantial differences in the amount of payment deductions taken by customers. In the sample, the second-largest customer, Kona Distributors, takes such large deductions that it is the least profitable of the customers listed in the report.

As you can see from the various sample margin reports presented here, you should be careful to *only* include those expenses in the analysis that would be eliminated if the subject of the report were to be terminated. All other expenses are irrelevant, and so should not be included.

Variance Reporting

If you have a standard costing system, consider setting up a variance reporting system. A variance is the difference between the actual cost incurred and the standard cost against which it is measured. A variance can also be used to measure the difference between actual and expected sales. Thus, variance analysis can be used to review the performance of both revenue and expenses.

There are two basic types of variances from a standard that can arise, which are the rate variance and the volume variance. Here is more information about both types of variances:

- *Rate variance.* A rate variance (which is also known as a *price* variance) is the difference between the actual price paid for something and the expected price, multiplied by the actual quantity purchased. The "rate" variance designation is most commonly applied to the labor rate variance, which involves the actual cost of direct labor in comparison to the standard cost of direct labor. The rate variance uses a different designation when applied to the purchase of materials, and may be called the *purchase price variance* or the *material price variance*.
- *Volume variance.* A volume variance is the difference between the actual quantity sold or consumed and the budgeted amount, multiplied by the

standard price or cost per unit. If the variance relates to the sale of goods, it is called the *sales volume variance*. If it relates to the use of direct materials, it is called the *material yield variance*. If the variance relates to the use of direct labor, it is called the *labor efficiency variance*. Finally, if the variance relates to the application of overhead, it is called the *overhead efficiency variance*.

Thus, variances are based on either changes in cost from the expected amount, or changes in the quantity from the expected amount. The most common variances that an accountant elects to report on are subdivided within the rate and volume variance categories for direct materials, direct labor, and overhead. It is also possible to report these variances for revenue.

Thus, the primary variances are:

	Rate Variance	Volume Variance
Materials	Purchase price variance	Material yield variance
Direct labor	Labor rate variance	Labor efficiency variance
Fixed overhead	Fixed overhead spending variance	Not applicable
Variable overhead	Variable overhead spending variance	Variable overhead efficiency variance
Revenue	Selling price variance	Sales volume variance

All of the variances noted in the preceding table are explained below, including examples to demonstrate how they are applied.

The Purchase Price Variance

The purchase price variance is the difference between the actual price paid to buy an item and its standard price, multiplied by the actual number of units purchased. The formula is:

(Actual price - Standard price) × Actual quantity = Purchase price variance

A positive variance means that actual costs have increased, and a negative variance means that actual costs have declined.

The standard price is the price that your engineers believe the company should pay for an item, given a certain quality level, purchasing quantity, and speed of delivery. Thus, the variance is really based on a standard price that was the collective opinion of several employees based on a number of assumptions that may no longer match a company's current purchasing situation.

EXAMPLE

During the development of its annual budget, the engineers and purchasing staff of Milagro Corporation decide that the standard cost of a green widget should be set at $5.00, which is based on a purchasing volume of 10,000 for the upcoming year. During the subsequent year, Milagro only buys 8,000 units, and so cannot take advantage of purchasing discounts, and ends up paying $5.50 per widget. This creates a purchase price variance of $0.50 per widget, and a variance of $4,000 for all of the 8,000 widgets that Milagro purchased.

There are a number of possible causes of a purchase price variance. For example:

- *Layering issue*. The actual cost may have been taken from an inventory layering system, such as a first-in first-out system, where the actual cost varies from the current market price by a substantial margin.
- *Materials shortage*. There is an industry shortage of a commodity item, which is driving up the cost.
- *New supplier*. The company has changed suppliers for any number of reasons, resulting in a new cost structure that is not yet reflected in the standard.
- *Rush basis*. The company incurred excessive shipping charges to obtain materials on short notice from suppliers.
- *Volume assumption*. The standard cost of an item was derived based on a different purchasing volume than the amount at which the company now buys.

Material Yield Variance

The material yield variance is the difference between the actual amount of material used and the standard amount expected to be used, multiplied by the standard cost of the materials. The formula is:

$$\text{(Actual unit usage - Standard unit usage)} \times \text{Standard cost per unit} = \text{Material yield variance}$$

An unfavorable variance means that the unit usage was greater than anticipated.

The standard unit usage is developed by the engineering staff, and is based on expected scrap rates in a production process, the quality of raw materials, losses during equipment setup, and related factors.

EXAMPLE

The engineering staff of Milagro Corporation estimates that 8 ounces of rubber will be required to produce a green widget. During the most recent month, the production process used 315,000 ounces of rubber to create 35,000 green widgets, which is 9 ounces per product. Each ounce of rubber has a standard cost of $0.50. Its material yield variance for the month is:

$$\text{(315,000 Actual unit usage - 280,000 Standard unit usage)} \times \$0.50 \text{ Standard cost/unit} = \$17,500 \text{ Material yield variance}$$

There are a number of possible causes of a material yield variance. For example:

- *Scrap*. Unusual amounts of scrap may be generated by changes in machine setups, or because changes in acceptable tolerance levels are altering the amount of scrap produced. A change in the pattern of quality inspections can also alter the amount of scrap.
- *Material quality*. If the material quality level changes, this can alter the amount of quality rejections. If an entirely different material is substituted, this can also alter the amount of rejections.
- *Spoilage*. The amount of spoilage may change in concert with alterations in inventory handling and storage.

Labor Rate Variance

The labor rate variance is the difference between the actual labor rate paid and the standard rate, multiplied by the number of actual hours worked. The formula is:

$$(\text{Actual rate - Standard rate}) \times \text{Actual hours worked} = \text{Labor rate variance}$$

An unfavorable variance means that the cost of labor was more expensive than anticipated.

The standard labor rate is developed by the human resources and engineering employees, and is based on such factors as the expected mix of pay levels among the production staff, the amount of overtime likely to be incurred, the amount of new hiring at different pay rates, the number of promotions into higher pay levels, and the outcome of contract negotiations with any unions representing the production staff.

EXAMPLE

The human resources manager of Milagro Corporation estimates that the average labor rate for the coming year for Milagro's production staff will be $25/hour. This estimate is based on a standard mix of personnel at different pay rates, as well as a reasonable proportion of overtime hours worked.

During the first month of the new year, Milagro has difficulty hiring a sufficient number of new employees, and so must have its higher-paid existing staff work overtime to complete a number of jobs. The result is an actual labor rate of $30/hour. Milagro's production staff worked 10,000 hours during the month. Its labor rate variance for the month is:

$$(\$30/\text{hour Actual rate} - \$25/\text{hour Standard rate}) \times 10,000 \text{ hours}$$
$$= \$50,000 \text{ Labor rate variance}$$

There are a number of possible causes of a labor rate variance. For example:

- *Incorrect standards*. The labor standard may not reflect recent changes in the rates paid to employees (which tend to occur in bulk for all staff).

- *Pay premiums*. The actual amounts paid may include extra payments for shift differentials or overtime.
- *Staffing variances*. A labor standard may assume that a certain job classification will perform a designated task, when in fact a different position with a different pay rate may be performing the work.

Labor Efficiency Variance

The labor efficiency variance is the difference between the actual labor hours used to produce an item and the standard amount that should have been used, multiplied by the standard labor rate. The formula is:

(Actual hours - Standard hours) × Standard rate = Labor efficiency variance

An unfavorable variance means that labor efficiency has worsened, and a favorable variance means that labor efficiency has increased.

The standard number of hours represents the best estimate of the industrial engineers regarding the optimal speed at which the production staff can manufacture goods. This figure can vary considerably, based on assumptions regarding the setup time of a production run, the availability of materials and machine capacity, employee skill levels, the duration of a production run, and other factors. Thus, the multitude of variables involved makes it especially difficult to create a standard that you can meaningfully compare to actual results.

EXAMPLE

During the development of its annual budget, the industrial engineers of Milagro Corporation decide that the standard amount of time required to produce a green widget should be 30 minutes, which is based on certain assumptions about the efficiency of Milagro's production staff, the availability of materials, capacity availability, and so forth. During the month, widget materials were in short supply, so Milagro had to pay production staff even when there was no material to work on, resulting in an average production time per unit of 45 minutes. The company produced 1,000 widgets during the month. The standard cost per labor hour is $20, so the calculation of its labor efficiency variance is:

(750 Actual hours - 500 Standard hours) × $20 Standard rate
= $5,000 Labor efficiency variance

There are a number of possible causes of a labor efficiency variance. For example:
- *Instructions*. The employees may not have received written work instructions.
- *Mix*. The standard assumes a certain mix of employees involving different skill levels, which does not match the actual staffing.
- *Training*. The standard may be based on an assumption of a minimum amount of training that employees have not received.

- *Work station configuration.* A work center may have been reconfigured since the standard was created, so the standard is now incorrect.

Variable Overhead Spending Variance

The variable overhead spending variance is the difference between the actual and budgeted rates of spending on variable overhead. The formula is:

Actual hours worked × (Actual overhead rate - standard overhead rate)
= Variable overhead spending variance

A favorable variance means that the actual variable overhead expenses incurred per labor hour were less than expected.

The variable overhead spending variance is a compilation of production expense information submitted by the production department, and the projected labor hours to be worked, as estimated by the industrial engineering and production scheduling staffs, based on historical and projected efficiency and equipment capacity levels.

EXAMPLE

The Milagro Corporation's accountant calculates, based on historical and projected cost patterns, that the company should experience a variable overhead rate of $20 per labor hour worked, and builds this figure into the budget. In April, the actual variable overhead rate turns out to be $22 per labor hour. During that month, production employees work 18,000 hours. The variable overhead spending variance is:

18,000 Actual hours worked × ($22 Actual variable overhead rate
- $20 Standard overhead rate)
= $36,000 Variable overhead spending variance

There are a number of possible causes of a variable overhead spending variance. For example:
- *Account misclassification.* The variable overhead category includes a number of accounts, some of which may have been incorrectly classified and so do not appear as part of variable overhead (or vice versa).
- *Outsourcing.* Some activities that had been sourced in-house have now been shifted to a supplier, or vice versa.
- *Supplier pricing.* Suppliers have changed their prices, which have not yet been reflected in updated standards.

Variable Overhead Efficiency Variance

The variable overhead efficiency variance is the difference between the actual and budgeted hours worked, which are then applied to the standard variable overhead rate per hour. The formula is:

$$\text{Standard overhead rate} \times (\text{Actual hours - standard hours})$$
$$= \text{Variable overhead efficiency variance}$$

A favorable variance means that the actual hours worked were less than the budgeted hours, resulting in the application of the standard overhead rate across fewer hours, so that less expense is incurred.

The variable overhead efficiency variance is a compilation of production expense information submitted by the production department, and the projected labor hours to be worked, as estimated by the industrial engineering and production scheduling staffs, based on historical and projected efficiency and equipment capacity levels.

EXAMPLE

The accountant of Milagro Corporation calculates, based on historical and projected labor patterns, that the company's production staff should work 20,000 hours per month and incur $400,000 of variable overhead costs per month, so it establishes a variable overhead rate of $20 per hour. In May, Milagro installs a new materials handling system that significantly improves production efficiency and drops the hours worked during the month to 19,000. The variable overhead efficiency variance is:

$$\$20 \text{ Standard overhead rate/hour} \times (19,000 \text{ hours worked - 20,000 standard hours})$$
$$= \$20,000 \text{ Variable overhead efficiency variance}$$

Fixed Overhead Spending Variance

The fixed overhead spending variance is the difference between the actual fixed overhead expense incurred and the budgeted fixed overhead expense. An unfavorable variance means that actual overhead expenditures were greater than planned. The formula is:

Actual fixed overhead - Budgeted fixed overhead = Fixed overhead spending variance

The amount of expense related to fixed overhead should (as the name implies) be relatively fixed, and so the fixed overhead spending variance should not theoretically vary much from the budget. However, if the manufacturing process reaches a step cost trigger point where a whole new expense must be incurred, this can cause a significant unfavorable variance. Also, there may be some seasonality in fixed overhead expenditures, which may cause both favorable and unfavorable variances in individual months of a year, but which cancel each other out over the full year.

EXAMPLE

The production manager of Milagro Corporation estimates that the fixed overhead should be $700,000 during the upcoming year. However, since a production manager left the company and was not replaced for several months, actual expenses were lower than expected, at $672,000. This created the following favorable fixed overhead spending variance:

($672,000 Actual fixed overhead - $700,000 Budgeted fixed overhead)
= $(28,000) Fixed overhead spending variance

There are a number of possible causes of a fixed overhead spending variance. For example:

- *Account misclassification.* The fixed overhead category includes a number of accounts, some of which may have been incorrectly classified and so do not appear as part of fixed overhead (or vice versa).
- *Outsourcing.* Some activities that had been sourced in-house have now been shifted to a supplier, or vice versa.
- *Supplier pricing.* Suppliers have changed their prices, which have not yet been reflected in updated standards.

Selling Price Variance

The selling price variance is the difference between the actual and expected revenue that is caused by a change in the price of a product or service. The formula is:

(Actual price - Budgeted price) × Actual unit sales = Selling price variance

An unfavorable variance means that the actual price was lower than the budgeted price.

The budgeted price for each unit of product or sales is developed by the sales and marketing managers, and is based on their estimation of future demand for these products and services, which in turn is affected by general economic conditions and the actions of competitors. If the actual price is lower than the budgeted price, the result may actually be favorable to the company, as long as the price decline spurs demand to such an extent that the company generates an incremental profit as a result of the price decline.

EXAMPLE

The marketing manager of Milagro Corporation estimates that the company can sell a green widget for $80 per unit during the upcoming year. This estimate is based on the historical demand for green widgets.

During the first half of the new year, the price of the green widget comes under extreme pressure as a new supplier in Ireland floods the market with a lower-priced green widget. Milagro must drop its price to $70 in order to compete, and sells 20,000 units during that period. Its selling price variance during the first half of the year is:

($70 Actual price - $80 Budgeted price) × 20,000 units = $(200,000) Selling price variance

There are a number of possible causes of a selling price variance. For example:

- *Discounts*. The company has granted various discounts to customers to induce them to buy products.
- *Marketing allowances*. The company is allowing customers to deduct marketing allowances from their payments to reimburse them for marketing activities involving the company's products.
- *Price points*. The price points at which the company is selling are different from the price points stated in its standards.
- *Product options*. Customers are buying different product options than expected, resulting in an average price that differs from the price points stated in the company's standards.

Sales Volume Variance

The sales volume variance is the difference between the actual and expected number of units sold, multiplied by the budgeted price per unit. The formula is:

$$(\text{Actual units sold - Budgeted units sold}) \times \text{Budgeted price per unit}$$
$$= \text{Sales volume variance}$$

An unfavorable variance means that the actual number of units sold was lower than the budgeted number sold.

The budgeted number of units sold is derived by the sales and marketing managers, and is based on their estimation of how the company's product market share, features, price points, expected marketing activities, distribution channels, and sales in new regions will impact future sales. If the product's selling price is lower than the budgeted amount, this may spur sales to such an extent that the sales volume variance is favorable, even though the selling price variance is unfavorable.

EXAMPLE

The marketing manager of Milagro Corporation estimates that the company can sell 25,000 blue widgets for $65 per unit during the upcoming year. This estimate is based on the historical demand for blue widgets, as supported by new advertising campaigns in the first and third quarters of the year.

During the new year, Milagro does not have a first quarter advertising campaign, since it is changing advertising agencies at that time. This results in sales of just 21,000 blue widgets during the year. Its sales volume variance is:

$$(21,000 \text{ Units sold - 25,000 Budgeted units}) \times \$65 \text{ Budgeted price per unit}$$
$$= \$260,000 \text{ Unfavorable sales volume variance}$$

There are a number of possible causes of a sales volume variance. For example:

- *Cannibalization.* The company may have released another product that competes with the product in question. Thus, sales of one product cannibalize sales of the other product.
- *Competition.* Competitors may have released new products that are more attractive to customers.
- *Price.* The company may have altered the product price, which in turn drives a change in unit sales volume.
- *Trade restrictions.* A foreign country may have altered its barriers to competition.

Problems with Variance Analysis

There are several problems with the variances just described in this chapter, which are:

- *The use of standards.* A central issue is the use of standards as the basis for calculating variances. What is the motivation for creating a standard? Standard creation can be a political process where the amount agreed upon is designed to make a department look good, rather than setting a target that will improve the company. If standards are politically created, variance analysis becomes useless from the perspective of controlling the company.
- *Feedback loop.* The accounting department does not calculate variances until after it has closed the books and created financial statements, so there is a gap of potentially an entire month from when a variance arises and when it is reported to management. A faster feedback loop would be to eliminate variance reporting and instead create a reporting process that provides for feedback within moments of the occurrence of a triggering event.
- *Information drill down.* Many of the issues that cause variances are not stored within the accounting database. For example, the reason for excessive material usage may be a machine setup error, while excessive labor usage may be caused by the use of an excessive amount of employee overtime. In neither case will the accounting staff discover these issues by examining their transactional data. Thus, a variance report only highlights the general areas within which problems occurred, but does not necessarily tell anyone the nature of the underlying problems.

The preceding issues do not always keep accountants from calculating complete sets of variances for management consumption, but they do bring the question of whether the work required to calculate variances is a good use of the accounting staff's time.

Which Variances to Report

Many variances have been described in this section. Do you really need to report them all to management? Not necessarily. If management agrees with a reduced reporting structure, report on just those variances over which management has some ability to reduce costs, and which contain sufficiently large variances to be worth reporting on. The following table provides commentary on the characteristics of the variances:

Name of Variance	Commentary
Materials	
Purchase price variance	Material costs are controllable to some extent, and comprise a large part of the cost of goods sold; possibly the most important variance
Material yield variance	Can contain large potential cost reductions driven by quality issues, production layouts, and process flow; a good opportunity for cost reductions
Labor	
Labor rate variance	Labor rates are difficult to change; do not track unless you can shift work into lower pay grades
Labor efficiency variance	Can drive contrary behavior in favor of long production runs, when less labor efficiency in a just-in-time environment results in greater overall cost reductions; not recommended
Overhead	
Variable overhead spending variance	Caused by changes in the actual costs in the overhead cost pool, and so should be reviewed
Variable overhead efficiency variance	Caused by a change in the basis of allocation, which has no real impact on underlying costs; not recommended
Fixed overhead spending variance	Since fixed overhead costs should not vary much, a variance here is worth careful review; however, most components of fixed overhead are long-term costs that cannot be easily changed in the short term
Revenue	
Selling price variance	Caused by a change in the product price, which is under management control, and therefore should be brought to their attention
Sales volume variance	Caused by a change in the unit volume sold, which is not under direct management control, though this can be impacted by altering the product price

The preceding table shows that the variances most worthy of management's attention are the purchase price variance, variable overhead spending variance, fixed overhead spending variance, and selling price variance. Reducing the number of reported variances is well worth the accountant's time, since reporting the entire suite of variances calls for a great deal of investigative time to track down variance causes and then configure the information into a report suitable for management consumption.

How to Report Variances

A variance is a simple number, such as an unfavorable purchase price variance of $15,000. It tells management very little, since there is not enough information on which to base any corrective action. Consequently, the accountant needs to dig down into the underlying data to determine the actual causes of each variance, and then report the causes. Doing so is one of the most important value-added activities of the accounting department, since it leads directly to specific cost reductions. The following table is an example of the level of variance detail to report to management:

Variance Item	Amount*	Variance Cause
Purchase Price		
Order quantity	$500	Bought wrappers at half usual volume, and lost purchase discount
Substitute material	1,500	Used more expensive PVC piping; out of stock on regular item
Variable Overhead		
Rush order	300	Overnight charge to bring in grease for bearings
Utility surcharge	2,400	Charged extra for power usage during peak hours
Fixed Overhead		
Property taxes	3,000	Tax levy increased by 8%
Rent override	8,000	Landlord charge for proportional share of full-year expenses
Selling Price		
Marketing discounts	4,000	Customers took discounts for advertising pass-through
Sales returns	11,000	450 units returned with broken spring assembly

* Note: All amounts are unfavorable variances

The preceding table can be expanded to include the names of the managers responsible for correcting each item noted.

Summary

The accountant is probably responsible for the issuance of more management reports than everyone else in a business, combined. This means that there is a considerable responsibility to not issue erroneous or misleading information that might lead to serious missteps by management. Thus, you should withhold the distribution of any reports that initially appear to contain unusual results, to verify that the information is correct (or not). Also, do not issue reports that may be misleading. This is a particular concern when issuing margin reports, since allocated expenses can artificially create a low margin that might incorrectly lead management to terminate a product, product line, or store, or drop a customer. Finally, do not overwhelm the company with reports. As noted in the Variance Reporting section, just because there is a variance does not mean that you must report it. Instead, only issue reports containing meaningful information that management should act upon. All other reports are simply wasting their time, and make it more difficult to find the relevant information that they need to run the business.

Chapter 23
Cash Receipts Management

Introduction

Cash management begins with the inflow of cash from the sale of goods and services. The process for receiving cash is by no means simple, and is laced with inefficiencies and added costs. In this chapter, we explore the processing of received cash, checks, and credit cards, and discuss how to improve all three processes. The result should be more rapid access to cash for operational and investment purposes, as well as a net reduction in costs.

> **Related Podcast Episodes:** Episodes 38, 41 and 137 of the Accounting Best Practices Podcast discuss automatic cash application, remote deposit capture, and a lean system for cash receipts, respectively. You can listen to them at: **accounting-tools.com/podcasts** or **iTunes**

Check Receipts

The primary form of payment to many businesses remains the check. The basic process flow for the handling of received checks involves the receipt, recordation, and depositing of checks by different people, where there are controls in place to monitor the checks at each transfer from one person to the next. This process is designed to mitigate the risk of loss, but does so at the price of being extremely inefficient.

The processing of check receipts involves the transfer of incoming payments from the mailroom to the cashier, then to a bank courier, and finally to a person who reconciles received to deposited cash. The following steps show the basic transaction flow.

1. *Record incoming checks.* The mailroom staff opens incoming mail, records all checks received, and stamps checks "for deposit only," before forwarding payments to the cashier. This step is a control point, designed to keep a second record of check receipts in case the cashier attempts to abscond with any funds.
2. *Transfer checks.* The mailroom uses a locked pouch to transfer checks to the cashier, along with a copy of their record of checks received.
3. *Apply checks.* The cashier records the received checks, either directly to sales or as reductions of specific accounts receivable. The amount of the checks recorded by the cashier should match the amount of the checks recorded by the mailroom staff.

4. *Deposit checks.* The cashier creates a deposit slip for the checks. A courier takes the deposit to the bank, where a bank teller tallies the deposit and issues a receipt.
5. *Match to bank receipt.* The cashier matches the company's record of checks transferred to the bank to the bank's record of the amount received. This step is a control point that can detect checks removed from the deposit by the courier, or a recordation difference between the cashier and the bank teller.
6. *Conduct bank reconciliation.* At month-end, reconcile the bank's record of check and cash transactions to the company's record. This is not part of the daily check receipts process flow, but is closely related to it.

There are two key bottlenecks in check receipts processing. The first resides in the mailroom, where the mail may not arrive until late in the day, and the mailroom staff may not assign much priority to tabulating check receipts. The cashier is another bottleneck, since this person may have difficulty ascertaining how some payments are to be applied. Further, the company has no control over bank teller availability, which can extend the time period required to deposit funds. The net result is a possible overnight delay before payments can be forwarded to the bank and accepted for deposit. In some businesses where payment processing is given a low priority, multiple days may pass before checks are finally sent to the bank.

> **Tip:** A simple way to ensure that cash application is not delaying the daily bank deposit is to have the accounting staff record all unapplied payments in a suspense account, and keep copies of the related payments. The originals can then be deposited at once.

The check receipts process is laced with controls, since a business wants to ensure that no payments are lost or stolen. This means that payments are recorded at each step of the process and reconciled to the information recorded in the preceding step, which slows down the entire transaction. Errors are most likely to arise because check totals were incorrectly recorded during one processing step, requiring reconciliation at the next processing step. Thus, the system of controls is itself causing errors that must be reviewed and corrected.

In addition to the delays caused by in-house processing, the bank also imposes a delay on the usage of cash. When a bank receives a check, it cannot immediately post the payment to the payee's account, since the bank has not yet received the cash from the bank on which the check was drawn. Instead, the deposit bank assigns a *value date* to the check, which is the date on which the funds will be made available to the payee. The value date may be just one day in the future, or several days longer. Some banks assign value dates that are further in the future than necessary, so that they have a short interval in which to use the cash before giving it to the payees who actually own the cash.

> **Tip:** Consider negotiating with the bank for a value date of shorter duration, in order to gain faster access to funds.

Check Receipt Improvements

There are several excellent techniques available that can truncate most or a portion of the check receipts process, or introduce automation that improves processing speed. These techniques are noted in the remainder of this section.

The Bank Lockbox

The cash receipts process and related controls can be vastly reduced by having customers send their payments to a bank lockbox. Under this approach, the bank manages the mailbox address to which payments are sent, so that the company is taken out of the business of handling checks. Instead, the bank deposits all checks received, and posts scanned images of all receipts on its website. The cashier then accesses the check images on this secure site, which are then used to record the payments. This approach has the added advantage of posting cash to the company's bank account somewhat sooner, so that the company can take advantage of additional interest income on its invested funds. The cash receipts process flow when a lockbox is used is compressed to the following steps:

1. The bank processes receipts that arrive at the lockbox. This involves depositing payments into the company's bank account, as well as storing digital images of checks and remittances on-line.
2. The cashier accesses the bank's website each day to view the images of scanned payments from the preceding day. The cashier uses this information to apply the payments to open accounts receivable.
3. The cashier reconciles the applied amount of cash to the amount reported by the bank.

It is possible to expand upon the lockbox concept by opening a *lockbox network*. The larger banks offer lockboxes throughout the country that are linked to a single bank account, so that customers can be instructed to send payments to the lockbox located closest to them, thereby reducing the amount of mail float. The lockbox network is especially useful for those companies that cater to many customers throughout a large geographic region. Conversely, a company with a regional presence may find that a single lockbox is sufficient for its needs.

EXAMPLE

Suture Corporation is exploring the need for a lockbox in the company's new southwest sales region. The following information is collected about sales in the region:

Average payment size	$1,740
Average number of daily payments	210
Rate of interest per day	0.015%
Average mail time saved	1.0 days
Processing time saved	0.7 days

The collected balance at a new lockbox should therefore be:

210 items per day × $1,740 each × (1.0 + 0.7) days saved = $621,180 collected balance

The daily interest income that can be generated from this collected balance is calculated as:

0.00015 × $621,180 = $93 daily interest income

The fee charged by the bank for each check processed is $0.20, so the offsetting daily processing cost is:

210 checks × $0.20 processing fee = $42 daily processing fee

Therefore, the net profit per business day from having a lockbox is $51 (calculated as $93 of daily interest income, less the $42 daily processing fee), which is $13,260 when calculated for a year containing 260 business days.

The bank also charges $150 per month as a fixed fee for operating the lockbox, which reduces the $13,260 annual profit by $1,800. Thus, the net profit from operating the proposed lockbox is expected to be $11,460.

Tip: The bank offering lockbox network services should periodically include a free analysis of the most cost-effective locations in which to position lockboxes.

The downside of the bank lockbox is a combination of fixed monthly fees and per-receipt fees charged by the bank, which makes this alternative cost-effective only for medium to larger-size companies that receive large numbers of checks. If this method does not appear to be cost-effective, consider the later discussion of remote deposit capture, which may be available for free, and which can accelerate the speed with which cash becomes available to earn interest.

It can be quite a chore to convince customers to route their payments to a lockbox. You should schedule several reminder messages to customers, as well as a number of follow-up phone calls, and even then will still probably have a few intransigent customers who persist in mailing their payments to the company. If so, have the mailroom staff immediately mail these payments to the lockbox. Doing so eliminates the need for in-house cash controls.

> **Tip:** Include in customer billings a return envelope that is stamped with the lockbox address. Also, make sure that all billing documents sent to customers only include the lockbox address; there should be no reference to the company's normal mailing address.

If the company does not want to use a lockbox, an alternative that can speed the collection of cash is to rent a post office box in or near the primary mail processing facility for the local area, and then have an employee or courier pick up the mail as soon as it is made available at the post office box. The primary mail processing facility should receive cash several hours prior to the local branch offices, so this approach can shave hours from the time required to process payments and deposit them at the local bank. Also, if the bank has a local operations center that is not located too far from the company, take deposits there, rather than to the local bank branch office. The operations center probably has a delayed deposit cutoff time that can be useful when the deposit is not ready by the normal cutoff time.

The use of a lockbox is the key enhancement of the cash receipts process, since the only person directly involved in check receipts is now the cashier; the bottlenecks related to the mailroom staff, courier, and bank teller are eliminated. If a lockbox is implemented, there is no need for any of the other improvements noted through the remainder of this section, with the exception of automatic cash application.

Automatic Cash Application

When a company receives a large number of customer payments every day, it can be quite difficult for the cashier to apply the receipts against open accounts receivable in a timely manner. If so, deposits may be delayed. The cash application process can be substantially compressed through the use of automatic cash application.

Automatic cash application requires that the lockbox operator use a data feed to forward to the company the magnetic ink character recognition (MICR) information from each check received at the lockbox, as well as the total payment amount. The cash application software uses a decision table to decide how to apply these payments to open accounts receivable. The automated decision process generally follows these steps:

1. Match the bank account number shown in each check's MICR information to the correct customer. This accesses the correct customer record of open accounts receivable.
2. Only match payments to invoices where the payment amount exactly matches the invoice amount.
3. Of the remaining payments, only match cash to invoices where the cash amount matches the exact amount of several invoices that have just come due for payment.

4. Kick out all remaining payments for manual review.

The decision table can contain more sophisticated rules, such as applying cash if payment amounts do not include the freight and/or sales tax elements of an invoice. As a company examines the payments kicked out by the system, it can gradually adjust the decision table to increase the number of automatic cash applications. However, the variety of deductions taken makes it unlikely that it will ever be possible to completely automate the cash application process. Nonetheless, automatic cash application can greatly improve the speed with which cash is applied.

Mailstop Number

A potential delay in cash processing is when the mailroom sorts through all of the day's mail, opens those items containing cash or checks, and forwards them to the accounting department as part of its general distribution of mail. A faster approach is to have all customers incorporate a mailstop number into the address to which they mail funds. When the mailroom employees see these addresses, they immediately forward them to the accounting department without opening the envelopes. To encourage the use of a mailstop number, include it in all invoices, and also consider sending a separate mailing to customers that announces the change.

A potential problem is that payments will no longer be recorded by the mail-room staff, which reduces the level of control over cash. There are two ways to deal with this concern:

- Have someone in the accounting department who is not involved with cash receipts record all incoming checks to replace the work done in the mail-room.
- Instead of making a separate list of incoming checks against which receipts are later reconciled, have the accounting person handling the incoming checks make two complete photocopies of all payments made, and then immediately prepare the original checks for deposit. One of the photocopies goes to the cash application staff, to be used as the source document for cash applications, while the other copy is used as a control document that can be reconciled to the register of cash receipts.

Remote Deposit Capture

A remote deposit capture system involves the use of a check scanner and bank-provided scanning software that creates an electronic image of each check to be deposited. The accounting staff then sends the scanned check information in an electronic message to the bank, rather than making a physical deposit. The bank accepts the deposit information directly into its database, posts the related funds to the company's account, and assigns funds availability based on a predetermined schedule.

Remote deposit capture requires slightly more time by the accounting staff to prepare a deposit (by scanning checks) than by the traditional approach of preparing a deposit slip. However, it completely eliminates the time required to make a physical deposit at the bank, as well as the control point of matching the bank's receipt to the deposit slip.

> **Tip:** Remote deposit capture has the side benefit of allowing a company to do business with a bank that is not located nearby. Thus, a business can search among a larger group of banks for the best pricing deal.

> **Tip:** Some banks require a monthly scanner rental fee. Consider shifting to a bank that offers the scanning equipment for free, or attempt to negotiate a lower rental charge.

Remote deposit capture will require the inclusion of new steps in the check processing work flow, which are:

1. Derive the batch total for all checks to be scanned.
2. Scan all checks in the batch.
3. Match the scanned total to the batch total and adjust as necessary.
4. Transmit the batch to the bank.
5. Print and retain a deposit slip.

There may also need to be an additional step to retain the scanned checks for a short time to ensure that they have been accepted by the bank, after which they should be shredded or perforated with a "deposited" stamp. The check destruction or mutilation is required to ensure that they are not inadvertently deposited again.

Cash Receipts

Cash is the most fungible of all assets, and therefore the one most likely to be stolen. Because of the high risk of theft, the receipt and subsequent handling of cash is choked with controls. The following steps show only the most basic cash receipts processing steps, but should convey the point that cash receipts is *not* an efficient process.

1. *Accept and record cash.* If a customer pays in cash, record the payment in a cash register. If there is no cash register (as may be the case in a low-volume sales environment), the sales clerk instead fills out a two-part sales receipt, gives a copy to the customer, and retains the other copy.
2. *Match receipts to cash.* Compare the amount of cash received to either the cash register receipt total or the total of all sales receipt copies, and investigate any differences. Complete a reconciliation form for any differences found.
3. *Aggregate and post receipt information.* Summarize the information in the cash register and post this information to the general ledger as a sale and cash receipt. If the cash register is linked to the company's accounting system and is tracking individual sales, then sales are being recorded automatically, as is the reduction of goods in the inventory records. If sales clerks are manually completing sales receipts, summarize the information in the sales

receipts and record the sales and any related inventory reductions in the general ledger.

4. *Deposit cash.* Prepare a bank deposit slip, retain a copy, and enclose the original slip along with all cash in a locked container for transport to the bank. After counting the cash, the bank issues a receipt stating the amount it has received.

5. *Match to deposit slip.* Compare the copy of the deposit slip to the bank receipt, and investigate any differences. A variation is to compare the cash receipts journal to the bank receipt.

There are two bottlenecks in cash receipts processing. The first is the sales clerk, who piles up cash receipts in batch mode until someone counts and removes the cash. This delay is not the fault of the sales clerk – the nature of the process mandates that cash will be transferred to accounting in batches. The second bottleneck is the cashier, since the relatively paltry volume of cash (in most businesses) will tend to push cash recordation down in the cashier's list of work activities, below processing checks and credit card receipts.

As was the case with handling check payments, errors are most likely to arise when cash is counted before being passed to the next person in the process flow. Again, this means that the control system itself is causing errors.

Cash Receipts Improvements

The accounting for cash is slow and inefficient. The only redeeming feature, and one which suggests a solution, is that cash comprises quite a small part of sales in many businesses (other than retail operations and casinos). If a business only deals with cash on an incidental basis, the primary solution is to completely eliminate the use of cash. There are two alternatives available:

- *Offer discounts for credit card purchases.* This alternative may seem counter-intuitive, since every business is charged a fee by its credit card processor when a payment is made by credit card. However, the complete elimination of cash payments may reduce paperwork to such an extent that the extra credit card fee still represents a cost-effective solution. Also, the discount can be more precisely targeted at the holders of debit cards, since purchases made with debit cards involve smaller processing fees for a business.

- *Offer discounts on company credit card.* As has been the case for many years, larger businesses offer their own name-brand credit card to customers, usually with an up-front cash savings. This approach immediately changes an impending cash payment to a credit card payment, while also placing the customer on the company's mailing list for future marketing activities.

In addition, and if cash deposits are large enough to warrant its use, consider hiring a money transport service to move cash from company locations to the local bank branch. This service involves handing off a locked container to a transport employee who transfers it to the bank, which then unlocks the container and processes its contents. This service provides transport on a regular schedule, so a company does not have to concern itself with finding a staff person who can personally transport the cash. The result is both more secure transport and deposits that are more likely to reach the bank on time.

In short, our primary suggestion is the complete elimination of cash from a company's list of accepted payments – there are no improvements that make a noticeable dent in this overwhelmingly inefficient procedure.

Credit Card Receipts

Credit card receipts are an important source of cash in many businesses, especially in the retail sector. There are several ways to process these receipts. In order to show the most complete process flow, we are assuming that the most complex version of credit card payments is in use, where card information is written down and then manually entered into an on-line form. The steps are:

1. *Collect information.* Record not only the information needed for the credit card payment, but also the contact information for the customer, in case it is necessary to verify or replace credit card information.
2. *Enter card information.* Access the credit card processing site on the Internet and enter the credit card information through an on-line form. When the information is accepted, print a receipt and staple it to the sales receipt. If the payment is not accepted, contact the customer to verify or replace the card information.
3. *Record the sale.* Enter the sales receipt into the accounting system as a sale. Then stamp the sales receipt as having been recorded.
4. *Issue receipt to customer.* If customers pay by phone or e-mail, send them a receipt, which they may need when they reconcile their company credit card statements at the end of the month.
5. *Verify the transaction.* Before filing sales receipts for credit card transactions, verify that the cash related to them has been posted to the company's bank account, and that they were posted to the accounting system.
6. *File documents.* File the company's copy of the sales receipt, as well as the attached credit card processing receipt, in the accounting records by customer name. If an invoice was printed as part of the sale, then file all three documents together.

The time required to record credit card information, enter it into an on-line form, and then send a receipt back to the customer is so time-consuming that the clerk handling these transactions could become a bottleneck.

When credit card information is being manually entered, the error rate is extremely high. The problem is caused by a combination of taking down credit card information incorrectly, and/or incorrectly inputting the information into the on-line form. The error rate is much lower when a credit card is swiped to obtain card information.

Credit Card Receipt Improvements

Though credit card processing involves a well-established procedure, the approach involving the manual entry of card information can be enhanced with either of the following improvements.

Enter Information in On-line Form Immediately

The largest flaw in the preceding description of credit card transactions is that the order taker is separating the collection of credit card information from the entry of this information in the on-line form provided by the company's credit card processor. This separation of tasks requires that information be written down and *then* entered, possibly also requiring a call back to the customer if the information was incorrect or the credit card was not accepted.

The lean approach is to call up the on-line form while still in contact with the customer, and enter the information immediately. Doing so eliminates the need to write down the customer's information, since it is going straight into the on-line form. Also, there is no need for a time-consuming feedback loop to obtain additional information from the customer, since the customer is still on the phone with the order taker if any problems arise.

This approach requires that the on-line form be available when customers call with orders, which may be a problem if the form is configured to automatically close after a certain amount of time has passed. However, it is still fairly efficient to log back into the form for every customer order, since logging in is much less time-consuming than the full process described earlier.

On-line Payment Apps

The full process flow described for the on-line entry of credit card information can be reduced with any of the on-line apps now available for smart phones and tablet computers. These apps allow you to create a sale transaction on a portable computing device by typing in or swiping credit card information, processing payment with an integrated on-line form, and sending an e-mail receipt to the customer.

This combination of a fully integrated payment processing and receipt issuance platform allows for the elimination of many steps in the traditional credit card processing transaction. In essence, payment information is both collected and confirmed in one step, leaving only a final step to record the sale transaction.

The main problem with these apps is that they do not also relieve inventory when a sale is made, so this approach works best when a company is not using a perpetual inventory system.

Debit Cards

From a cash management perspective, credit cards are both good and bad for a business. They accelerate cash flows well beyond what might be expected from customers paying with checks, which is a huge benefit if a company is strapped for cash. However, the credit card providers all charge high transaction fees that are at least 2%, and frequently much more. These fees are debilitating in a low-margin business, where it may appear that a large part of all profits are being handed off to a third party.

The search for an ideal combination of rapid cash flow and reduced transaction fees leads to the use of debit cards, for which the transaction fee is sharply lower. A business can encourage the use of debit cards by having credit card swipe equipment present a debit card payment as the primary option, or by instructing sales clerks to ask customers if they would like to pay with a debit card. Ultimately, a customer does not have to pay with a debit card, but the selling process should be structured to encourage its use.

Summary

In this chapter, we have described the basic process flows for different types of cash receipts, as well as several techniques for improving them. Most of these processes are inherently inefficient or expensive, so proper cash management should focus on significantly restructuring how cash receipts are handled. Of particular importance is the use of a lockbox to receive check payments, since it eliminates a number of processing steps and controls within a company. Cash payments are to be avoided in favor of other payment methods where possible, while debit cards represent a significant cost improvement over the use of credit cards.

Chapter 24
Collection Tactics

Introduction

When a customer is having cash flow problems, the easiest loan it can obtain is from its suppliers, by not paying them. This is not acceptable to the seller, who has only agreed to a small loan in the amount of the credit it is granting to the customer, and only for the number of days stated in the payment terms. There may be other cases where a customer's procedures or the lack of information are preventing the release of a payment. These scenarios are the primary reasons for delayed payments.

In this chapter, we describe a number of techniques for accelerating payments that are being delayed for either of these reasons, as well as discussions of how a collection call should be conducted and whether on-site collection visits may be warranted.

> **Related Podcast Episode:** Episode 55 of the Accounting Best Practices Podcast discusses targeted collections. You can listen to it at: **accountingtools.com/podcasts** or **iTunes**

Overview of Collection Tactics

There is no tried-and-true collection methodology that works for all overdue invoices, all of the time. Instead, the collection staff must choose from an array of collection tactics, depending on such issues as the amount of the invoice, the intransigence of the customer, and common collection practice in the industry. Accordingly, we do not present a collection methodology in this chapter, but rather a series of possible collection options. These options are listed in order from the most innocuous to the most severe. The following table shows the tactics, along with a brief statement of when they should be used.

Collection Tactic	When to be Used
Courtesy calls	For larger invoices where the customer historically has payment issues
Grace period reduction	For customers who always pay late
Dunning letters	For all sizes of invoices, to be issued shortly after due dates have passed
Check payment by e-mail	For customers who repeatedly delay payment
Pay undisputed line items	For customers who are using disputed invoice line items to delay payment
Confirm payment date	For customers who have committed to pay as of a certain date
Take back merchandise	For sales of goods where customer cannot pay

Collection Tactic	When to be Used
Hold orders	When there are orders from a customer that have not yet shipped
ACH debits	For customers with little cash on hand
Split payments	For customers able to pay in small increments
Postdated checks	For customers able to pay as of a specific future date or dates
Interest and penalties	For customers who deliberately delay payment
Promissory note	For customers without sufficient cash to pay in the short term
Salesperson assistance	When a salesperson is assigned to the customer
COD roll	For customers with unpaid balances who now pay on COD terms
Barter	For customers who are completely unable to pay by other means
Arbitration	When customers may have legitimate claims relating to a sale
Attorney letters	For somewhat larger invoices, where dunning letters have not triggered payment
Final demand letter	When all other normal collection efforts have been attempted
Small claims court complaint	When on the verge of filing a lawsuit

The collection manager (or the accountant, in a smaller firm) is responsible for training the collections staff in the use of the various collection tactics, as well as setting expectations for how collectors should spend their time. For example, the primary goal of the collections manager is obviously to collect cash as soon as possible. Since the amount of staff time and other resources available to the collections manager is limited, the manager will likely have to communicate to the staff the need to stratify accounts receivable, so that larger invoices receive a considerable amount of hands-on attention, while smaller amounts are targeted by more cost-effective methods, such as automated dunning letters. The manager then monitors actual collector activity to see if they are achieving the stated goal, and adjusts their activities as needed to maximize the amount of cash collected.

Collection Tactics

In this section, we list a number of collection tactics, sorted in order from the most innocuous to the most aggressive. The items early in this list are intended for those customers who will likely continue to be granted credit by the seller, while the more "scorched earth" items near the end of the list are intended for those customers with whom the seller has no intention of doing business again. The sales manager should be consulted before embarking on the more aggressive tactics, since they will certainly have a deadening impact on customer relations.

Courtesy Calls

Many customers do not pay their suppliers because of administrative issues, rather than a focused intent not to pay on time. For example, any of the following issues could be delaying payment:

- Invoice not received
- Invoice out for approval
- Error on invoice being investigated

- Cannot locate receiving documentation
- Cannot locate authorizing purchase order

Many of these issues can be resolved by the seller, since it has nearly the same packet of information pertaining to the sale transaction as the information being collected by the customer's accounts payable department.

A reasonable approach to collecting the larger invoices is to make a courtesy call some days before the invoices are due for payment, just to see if they are scheduled for timely payment. If not, the caller can offer to assist by providing any needed information, such as clarification of the invoiced amount, documentation of delivery, and a copy of the customer's authorizing purchase order.

These courtesy calls can be assigned to someone other than the normal collection staff, since the intent of the calls is to provide information, rather than demand payment. Given that the mindset of a courtesy call is completely different from a collection call, it makes sense to separate the two types of calls among different staff. By doing so, those assigned to courtesy calls can be trained in an entirely different method of customer contact that focuses on servicing the needs of the customers.

Tip: If someone makes a courtesy call to a customer and then suspects that payment of an invoice will be deliberately delayed, contact the regular collections staff at once, so that they can begin collection activities sooner than would normally be the case.

The use of courtesy calls is only cost-effective for the larger accounts or those accounts that have a history of being flummoxed by payables paperwork. If a customer has a proven history of reliably paying on time, there may be no point in annoying them with courtesy calls.

Grace Period Reduction

It is customary for a collections department to not begin collection activities until a number of days have passed in addition to the payment terms stated on an invoice. By doing so, collectors do not waste time contacting customers whose payments are already in transit. This is a simple cost-benefit calculation for the collections manager, who can roughly estimate the amount of time that must pass before it is reasonable to assume that there are problems with all remaining invoices that have not yet been paid.

The trouble with the grace period is that some customers abuse it. They know that no collector will contact them for a certain number of days past normal terms, so they always delay their payments through the grace period. If so, the pattern of late payments will be recurring, and so can be easily identified. The collections staff should make note of these customers in the customer master file, so that they can begin calling these customers as soon as payment dates are exceeded. In short, the grace period is ignored for certain customers who do not deserve the privilege of having a grace period.

Dunning Letters

A dunning letter is a notification sent to a customer, stating that the customer is overdue in paying an account receivable to the sender. Dunning letters typically follow a progression from polite reminders to more strident demands for payment, if the customer continues to be non-responsive in paying. The first few letters that are sent should be polite, on the theory that the customer has simply overlooked payment, and the company wants to retain its goodwill for future business.

However, as more time passes, the company begins to change its assumption of doing further business with the customer, and so tends to downplay the amount of customer goodwill that it wants to retain in favor of being paid now. Irrespective of the tone of the letter, it always states the amount due, the date of the unpaid invoice, the number of the invoice, and any late payment fines or interest penalties.

> **Tip:** If there has been no response to the first few dunning letters, send a copy of the next letter to someone more senior in the organization, such as the CFO or president, and note that this has been done on the copy going to the accounts payable department.

At some point following the normal payment date, the effectiveness of issuing dunning letters will decline, so that a company discontinues their use and relies upon personal contacts, attorneys, and collection agencies instead.

A dunning letter can take a variety of physical forms. It was originally a letter that might be sent by regular mail, registered mail, or overnight delivery in order to convey the increasing urgency of the request, as well as to create a record of receipt (in the case of registered mail or overnight delivery). However, a dunning letter can also be sent as an e-mail or text message. These electronic delivery methods can go astray, and may not be as effective as the more traditional paper-based method.

> **Tip:** The final dunning letter sent should be by overnight delivery or certified mail, to reinforce the point that the seller is about to shift to a more aggressive form of collection.

Dunning letters are frequently generated by a computer, with no human input at all. The system is configured to use a particular text if payment has not been made within a certain number of days, and to then use a different text for letters generated after a longer time period has passed without payment.

The collections staff may periodically change the timing or content of these automatically-generated letters, if they feel that some variation will improve the rate of collection. This can be accomplished with *A-B testing*, where two versions of a dunning letter are issued, and the effectiveness of each one monitored; if one version results in more customer payments, that version becomes the new default letter format to be used.

There are rules governing the level of threat that can be included in a dunning letter, depending upon the government jurisdiction in which a customer resides, so avoid excessively strident letters.

A dunning letter is not the same as a month-end statement. A statement is sent to all customers having unpaid invoices at the end of the month. The statement includes all invoices that have not yet been paid, even if they are not yet due for payment. The statement is not considered to be harassment, but rather a simple statement of account as of a point in time. However, it is still considered a collection tool, since it may result in customer inquiries about invoices that they do not have in their records, and which they therefore would not have paid.

Tip: A simple variation on the dunning letter is to mail customers a copy of overdue invoices, with a collection sticker on each invoice. The wording on the collection stickers can vary, depending on how long invoices have been overdue.

Tip: If the party issuing dunning letters is a government entity, an interesting technique is to appeal to the sense of civic duty of customers, pointing out that the cash is needed to provide services to them.

Check Payment by Fax or E-mail

It can be extremely difficult to extract a check payment from a customer, especially if you want an immediate delivery that will cost the customer an overnight delivery charge. An alternative is to have the customer fax or e-mail a scanned image of a completed and signed check to the seller, and then follow these steps:

1. Obtain check printing software, which is available from many companies (search for "check by fax software" on an Internet search engine).
2. Enter the information from the check into the software.
3. Print the check using check security paper, which can be obtained from a local office supply store. Use standard printer ink, not the special magnetic ink character recognition (MICR) ink used by banks. The check printing software will include the following text in place of the signature line:

> SIGNATURE NOT REQUIRED
> Payee to hold you harmless for
> payment of this document
> Absence of endorsement is guaranteed
> by payee's bank

4. Deposit the check at the company's bank. This may require manual processing by a bank teller, since the bank's check scanners will not detect any MICR encoding on the check.

5. Retain a copy of the faxed or e-mailed check, as proof that the customer authorized payment.

An alternative is to obtain the required information for a check payment over the phone, but doing so provides no evidence that the customer agreed to make the payment. Also, it is easier to make a mistake when writing down information obtained over the phone. Consequently, this approach is not recommended.

Yet another option is to send the customer a form to fill out that includes all of the information normally found on a check, as well as an authorizing signature line. This should be accompanied by a voided check, so the seller can reference a check number.

The end result of this process is the complete elimination of the mail float from the collections process. This approach is time-consuming, but is at no cost to the customer, who may find it an appealing alternative compared to paying for an overnight delivery.

Pay Undisputed Line Items

When a customer has a reasonable issue with a small number of line items on an invoice, the most efficient practice for them is to not pay the entire invoice until those line items have been resolved, since a single payment will then settle the entire invoice. The reasoning is different for a customer that actively wants to delay payment; they simply pick a line item on an invoice and actively dispute it, thereby delaying payment of the entire invoice. The latter tactic is most evident when a customer only questions line items on larger-value invoices.

It might initially seem obvious to always have collectors demand that all undisputed line items be paid at once. This approach should certainly be used when a customer has a history of using disputes to delay payment. However, the demand should not be made in the first case, where a customer really does have an issue, and may resent having to make an additional payment – one for all other line items right now, and one at a later date for the disputed item. This is an inconvenience for the customer, so if the seller wants to maintain good relations, it may not want to demand immediate payment of undisputed line items.

Confirm Payment Date

A common part of a collection call is when the collector asks for a date by which payment can be expected, and the customer's accounts payable person states a certain date. It is customary for the collector to write down this date and contact the customer again if payment was not received by that date. The trouble is that the payables clerk accords much less importance to this date than the collector, may not write it down, and so may not pay by the designated date.

The collector needs to give the payables clerk a strong sense of just how important the payment date is, so the collector should document the conversation with the payables clerk and send it in a letter to the clerk. Depending on the level of urgency, this letter can be in the form of an e-mail, a regular letter, certified mail, or overnight delivery.

Tip: Always keep a copy of all confirming letters sent, so there is evidence of the original conversation if the payables clerk later claims that either no letter was sent or that its contents are incorrect.

The confirmation letter approach is particularly valuable if a customer has agreed to a series of payments, since the receipt of an additional letter just prior to each scheduled payment date tells the customer that the seller is closely watching the timing of all promised payments.

Take Back Merchandise

If a company is selling goods, the buyer usually finds a use for or resells the goods in short order, leaving no asset that the company can take back in the event of nonpayment. This is particularly likely when the terms of payment are relatively long, giving the buyer more time in which to disposition the goods. However, if this is not the case and the customer still retains the goods in unused condition, a reasonable option is to take back the goods if the customer is unable to pay.

Taking back merchandise is a better option when the goods have long-term value and can be readily resold at roughly the same as the original price. If the goods decline rapidly in value, as is the case with fashion goods and some consumer electronics, the decision to cancel a receivable in exchange for taking back merchandise may be a more difficult one.

Hold Orders

A similar concept to taking back merchandise from a customer is blocking any additional shipments to the customer. To do so, the collections staff must have access to the customer orders database, and the authority to halt shipment of a pending customer order. This can be a highly effective way to dislodge a payment, especially if the seller is in the enviable position of selling goods that no other suppliers offer for sale. The company's computer system can even be set to trigger a warning message to the collections staff when a forthcoming customer order will cause a customer's actual receivable amount outstanding to exceed the amount of its credit limit.

While the order holding concept may initially sound ideal, here are two cautionary items to consider:

- When the goods on order can be commonly found elsewhere, a customer may simply cancel the order as soon as it receives an order hold notification, and take its business elsewhere.
- Holding an order may not be possible if the order is already in the production process, since doing so would throw the production schedule into disarray. If this is the case, the goods will have to be produced, and then a hold is

placed on the shipment. This can be a problem when goods are customized, since the company may have no other way to dispose of the goods.

> **Tip:** If an order hold is imposed, be sure to contact the responsible salesperson at the same time. Otherwise, the salesperson will first hear about it from an irate customer.

ACH Debits

A customer may prove to be completely unreliable in making payments, possibly because it is working with an extremely small amount of on-hand cash. If so, an option is to have the customer agree to small but very frequent ACH debits from its bank account. Under this approach, the seller sets up a recurring ACH debit transaction that withdraws the same amount of cash directly from the customer's bank account. The frequency of the withdrawals could be once a week, or even every business day. By keeping the amount of each individual debit low, the customer is less likely to resist this payment method.

For example, there may be a $1,000 invoice outstanding, which the customer is completely incapable of paying. However, if the payment method is presented as a $50 daily ACH debit for 20 business days (one calendar month), the seller will still be paid relatively soon, and the reduction in cash is less noticeable to the customer.

The only issue with the ACH debit is that the seller incurs a small fee for each transaction, so a large number of debits will cumulatively represent a fairly large bank fee.

Split Payments

If a customer claims that it cannot pay an invoice right now, offer to split the invoice into several payments over the short term. Better yet, ask for part of these split payments immediately over the phone, using a credit card. By doing so, a pattern of payment is immediately established, which the collector can follow up on at regular intervals. This may result in a series of credit card payments over the phone, but at least results in payments.

The split payments approach varies from the following promissory note concept in that split payments are intended to cover a relatively short period of time, and do not have an associated guarantee or assets used as collateral. There may or may not be an interest charge associated with split payments.

Postdated Checks

It may be possible to obtain from a customer one or more postdated checks, which the collector promises not to cash until the date listed on each check. If so, the collector notes on a calendar when each check is to be cashed, and does so on the specified date. If a postdated check is from a commercial customer, no further notifications to the customer need to be made. If a check is from an individual, the collector must send a written notification to the customer within three to ten business days of the date when the check will be cashed.

Interest and Penalties

Add interest charges and/or late fees to a customer's account once unpaid invoices exceed a predetermined threshold number of days late, and notify the customer that this is happening. The key point is to educate the customer that there are consequences to delaying payments.

If this tactic is to be used, be sure to state the seller's policy for imposing interest and penalties on unpaid invoices at the time when credit is granted to a customer. Also, verify that these fees are in accordance with any state laws regarding the amount of interest that can be charged.

> **Tip:** Customers frequently ignore interest and penalty charges. To make it clear that the company intends to collect these amounts, impose a hold on any customer orders until all interest and penalties have been paid.

Promissory Note

There will be times when a customer does not have sufficient cash to pay for an overdue invoice, but is willing to work with the seller to pay off the amount over a longer time period. If so, an option may be to convert the invoice into a promissory note that contains a series of specific payment dates, an interest component, and a guarantee or collateral. The key element of this note is that the company is either given a guarantee of payment by a third party, or collateral that can be accessed if the customer defaults on payments. This approach improves the ability of the seller to obtain some form of payment, even if it may take some time to do so.

> **Tip:** The key element in a promissory note is a guarantee or collateral; to obtain it, consider such inducements as a low interest rate, a slight reduction in principal, or allowing a restricted amount of credit for continuing purchases from the seller.

It is much easier to win a lawsuit over nonpayment of a promissory note than over nonpayment of an account receivable, since the customer has signed the note, and therefore has agreed to its specific terms.

Be sure to assign the promissory note to a collector, so that payments are regularly monitored along with other accounts receivable. In addition, send out a statement to the customer at regular intervals, showing the original amount due, the amounts and dates of prior payments, and the next amount due, with a tear-away remittance advice they can use to remit the next payment. There is a certain amount of work required to formulate and issue these statements, but they are useful not only for reminding customers, but also for formalizing the system of payment.

> **Tip:** To make a customer more inclined to agree to a promissory note, keep its language as simple as possible, and keep the interest rate reasonable. Otherwise, the customer will be more likely to bring in an attorney to examine and negotiate the terms of the note.

If the seller proposes reasonable terms for a promissory note and the customer still persists in rejecting the offer, this is a clear signal that the customer has no intention of paying, in which case a more aggressive legal solution may be required.

Salesperson Assistance

The salesperson who originally made the sale that is now unpaid can be of considerable use in obtaining payment. Salespeople have developed a completely different set of contacts at the customer, and so can work through entirely different channels to obtain payment. Thus, with the collector working through the accounts payable staff and the salesperson working through the buyer, resistance to payment may crumble. Also, an effective salesperson can sometimes be seen as a relatively neutral party between the seller and the buyer, and so can adopt the role of mediator between the two parties.

Salesperson assistance can be remarkably effective, but we caution against overuse of this approach. The primary role of the salesperson is to sell, which requires all of their attention. If they are constantly being diverted by collection issues, revenues will suffer. Accordingly, the best approach is to make all reasonable attempts to collect without the sales staff, and then request their assistance only when other approaches have failed.

The only way that salespeople will be willing to assist the collections staff is by building relations with them. This can be accomplished by pairing up collectors with salespeople, running joint meetings, solving billing problems brought to the attention of the salespeople by customers, and so forth.

COD Roll

The typical approach that a seller uses to deny credit to its customers is to switch them to cash on delivery (COD) terms once they consistently fail to pay in a timely manner. However, taking this approach means that the seller no longer has any leverage over its COD customers in regard to their old outstanding invoices, which will continue to age and will probably be written off as bad debts.

A way to ensure that the oldest invoices are eventually paid is to require COD payment on new customer orders, but the seller applies the resulting payments to the oldest invoices outstanding, rather than the invoice that was actually paid. By doing so, the oldest invoices are gradually cleared from the seller's books. This approach means that only newer invoices remain in the seller's accounts receivable aging report, which can be used as collateral for short-term loans. An advantage to the buyer is that payments are being made against old invoices for which late payment penalties would otherwise be accrued, so the payments are also reducing the amount of finance charges that they may eventually have to pay.

There can be some confusion between the seller and its COD customers regarding how many invoices are still overdue, since the buyer will apply payments against new invoices, while the seller applies payments against old invoices. Also, the COD roll concept only works as long as COD customers continue to buy from the seller. If they stop, there will still be a significant number of unpaid invoices outstanding.

> **Tip:** An alternative to the COD roll is to add the entire overdue amount to a COD payment, which must be paid before an item will be delivered. This approach usually only works when a unique item is to be delivered that the customer cannot obtain anywhere else.

Barter

Some customers own assets or can provide services that may be of value to the seller. If so, a possible consideration is to accept these assets or services in exchange for an unpaid receivable. Doing so is not recommended unless all other collection alternatives have been attempted, for two reasons:

- If accepting assets, the seller now has the burden of converting the assets into cash.
- If accepting services, the seller must now badger the customer to provide the services (which may take as long as the collection efforts!)

Barter is a more common alternative for a small business where customers are located nearby, since proximity is required to obtain the assets or services.

Arbitration

There may be cases where the customer feels that it has a legitimate complaint against the seller. For example, the customer may believe that it ordered goods with certain specifications, and received goods that did not meet the specifications. If the seller is not willing to negotiate the issue, then consider shifting the claim to arbitration. Under arbitration, the parties select a presumably impartial third party to review the claims of both sides, who then issues a judgment that the parties agree to respect. The arbitration process tends to be fairly short, but it does require time to prepare a presentation to the arbitrator, and the arbitrator's fee must be paid. Also, the resulting decision may go against the seller.

Attorney Letters

It is entirely possible that a series of dunning letters will not convince a customer to make an overdue payment, possibly because a mere letter from the seller is not sufficient to provoke real action. A possible option at this point is to have an attorney send a letter, written on the attorney's letterhead and structured as a final reminder before legal action commences.

The fact that the matter has now been turned over to an attorney is a good way of telling a customer that the seller is now extremely serious about the unpaid receivable, and is not willing to tolerate any further delays. Consequently, the probability of payment is higher following an attorney letter than it is following a dunning letter. However, sending such a letter alters the relationship between the parties, since the seller is now making the assumption that it may not want to do business with the customer on an extended basis, and simply wants the account paid off now.

The least cost-effective way to issue an attorney letter is to refer each such matter individually to an attorney, who then crafts a unique letter for each customer. Doing so can be quite expensive, and so makes little sense for lower-value receivables. A better approach involves the following actions:

- *Pre-write letters.* Have an arrangement with the attorney, where the attorney and the collections staff mutually create a set of boilerplate letters to be issued. Thereafter, when an attorney letter must be issued, the attorney simply selects one of these pre-written letters, changes the names to the applicable parties, and issues it to the customer. This approach avoids a great deal of writing time.
- *Respond to company.* State in the letter that responses are to be made to the company, not the attorney. By doing so, the time of the collections staff will be used, rather than the attorney. This can greatly reduce legal bills.

An attorney is more likely to agree to this arrangement if the seller refers some proportion of its legal work to the attorney that relates to actual legal action against the more intransigent customers.

Final Demand Letter

At some point, the collections staff will have collectively exhausted every possibility in attempting to collect overdue funds. At this point, there are three remaining options:

- *Write off the receivable.* The most common option, especially if the amount is small or the customer does not appear to have sufficient assets to pursue a legal judgment.
- *Shift to a collection agency.* The second likeliest option, when the collection manager is not willing to pursue litigation, but is willing to shift the collection burden to a third party.
- *Litigation.* Reserved for large overdue amounts where the company has a strong case, and the customer has sufficient assets to pay any resulting judgment.

In the first case, the customer is not informed that the invoice has been written off. In the other two cases, however, it may make sense to issue a final demand letter, in which the collector states that the overdue amount must be paid by a specific date, or else the issue will be escalated to a collection agency or attorney. Doing so informs the customer that life is about to become more unpleasant, which can sometimes dislodge a payment.

Issue Small Claims Court Complaint

After all manner of threats have been exhausted, one last option that may result in payment from an intransigent customer is to fill out a small claims court complaint form and send a copy of it to the customer, with a note stating that you will file the complaint form at a specific date and time, unless payment is received before then. Doing so makes it extremely clear that a judgment against the customer is likely to be made in the extremely near future, and that the seller is willing to proceed down this path.

This option has the additional advantage of being inexpensive, since there are no attorney fees involved, nor any court costs. The only downside is that the seller clearly signals no further interest in an ongoing business relationship with the customer.

The Collection Reputation

Thus far, we have described a series of steps to be followed for collecting from customers. Unfortunately, customers are also aware of these steps, and can anticipate every move that a collector may take. If the customer is a hard-core nonpayer, this can mean that nothing a company attempts will work, and the customer can roughly estimate the time period over which collection contacts must be endured before the company ceases its efforts and goes away. Further, some companies develop a reputation for being unusually easy to deal with, offering long payment terms or writing off receivables after token recovery efforts. The end result is more difficulty for the collections staff, since everyone knows that the company is a pushover.

An alternative is to develop a reputation for pursuing debtors to the ends of the earth (figuratively speaking). This means engaging in ongoing pursuit, including litigation, to collect an overdue amount, and rarely negotiating down an outstanding balance. Doing so is not cost-effective from the perspective of an individual receivable, but can create a fearsome collection reputation that the company is not to be trifled with. Taking this path depends on the commitment of the entire company to create such a reputation, which includes a discussion of what this will do to ongoing relations with customers.

Credit Repayments

Occasionally, customers will overpay for an invoice or pay twice, possibly due to systemic problems in their accounts payable systems. Or, the seller may grant a credit on an invoice that has already been paid. In both cases, this results in a credit balance on a customer's account. While this may initially appear to be "free money" from the perspective of the seller, these credit balances must eventually be remitted to the state government as unclaimed property.

Rather than remitting the funds to the statement government, consider having the collections staff periodically review the accounts receivable aging for unused credits and credit balances, and contact customers about these items. Doing so can create considerable customer goodwill, might trigger additional sales, and will at least return the funds to their rightful owners.

Contacting customers about credit balances can be conducted at fairly long intervals, since it takes time for a significant amount of these items to build up. Consequently, conducting a review at quarterly or annual intervals should be sufficient.

The Collection Call

The core of many collection efforts is the telephone call by a collector. These calls can be highly effective if properly prepared for, scheduled, and conducted by properly trained professionals. The following sub-sections describe a variety of concepts that can result in more effective collection calls.

Preparation

The primary tool of the collector is the collection call. However, before making a call, consider a number of preparatory steps that will make the call more effective. Otherwise, the collector may find that the customer simply requests information that is not immediately at hand, which will require another call after the collector has found the information. Accordingly, consider collecting the following information in advance:

- *Billing packet.* The customer's authorizing purchase order, the resulting sales order (if any), any related shipping document(s), and the issued invoice.
- *Notes.* The complete set of notes from any prior conversations with the customer.
- *Proof of delivery.* A confirmation of receipt from the delivery company, preferably including the name of the person who signed for the delivered goods.
- *Statement of completion.* If the sale involved the provision of services, locate the customer approval document, including the name of the person who signed it.

In addition, have on hand a list of other contacts at the customer. If the primary contact is not answering his or her phone, consider immediately escalating to the next person on the list.

The amount of paperwork required to prepare for a collection call may appear considerable. To reduce the work load, consider using administrative staff to collect the paperwork, or use computerized collection software to automatically assemble much of this information from other databases around the company.

Scheduling

There is an optimum time at which customers are most likely to be available to answer a call. This is partially based on the time zone in which they are located, which can be included in any autodialing software that the collection staff may use. In addition, it may become apparent over time that a customer's accounts payable person is much more likely to answer the phone at a certain time of the day. If so, make note of this time, and try to call at or near the same time for all future calls.

> **Tip:** Schedule a large block of time at that point in the day when customers are most likely to be available, and conduct *all* collection calls, in continuous sequence, at that time. Doing so gets collectors in the flow of making collection calls, and so improves call efficiency.

Phone Skills

There are several skills to be employed as a collector that will result in enhanced collection success. Here are a number of improvements to consider:

- *Scripting*. The content of a collection call should be approximately the same for every call made. It helps to practice with a prepared script in which you identify yourself and your company, and request payment. The actual conversation may vary somewhat from the script, but just be sure that the essentials are covered in every call.
- *Build a relationship*. Collection calls are not fun for the collector or the customer, and may even be considered repugnant by both parties. If you can spend a few moments of each call building even the smallest hint of a relationship, this will separate the seller from the pack of other collection calls that a payables clerk receives, and makes the clerk much more inclined to pay the company ahead of all the other sellers demanding payment.
- *Enunciate*. Do not speak so fast that the customer does not understand what you are saying. Slow down and make sure that each word is clearly stated.
- *Wait for answer*. After asking when the customer will pay, wait for an answer – which may be a long time in coming. This can become a waiting game between the caller and the customer.
- *No waffling*. Have a confident and direct manner when stating the situation and asking for payment. Any waffling in the basic approach will result in delayed or no payments.
- *Empathy*. Keeping the preceding point in mind about not waffling, this must also be combined with a certain amount of empathy, to see the situation from the customer's perspective. If the collector does not at least attempt to empathize, the customer will perceive a rigid, unyielding caller and will be less inclined to pay.
- *Negotiate*. It may initially appear that the customer simply cannot pay, but if you work through a series of options, some form of payment may be forthcoming. This can include offering to split payments, delay payments, take back merchandise, and so forth.

If a collector's phone skills have been properly honed, the result should be a much higher incidence of calls where the result is a documented commitment to pay a specific amount by a specific date.

Escalation

It is quite likely that someone higher in the customer's organization has decided to conserve cash by delaying payments to suppliers. If so, badgering the customer's accounts payable staff will not help. Instead, escalate subsequent calls higher in the organization until you reach a position that can impose payment instructions on the accounts payable staff. This may be the controller, CFO, president, or some other position. Engage in escalation as soon as it is evident that the person you are currently calling cannot authorize payment.

Documentation

Writing down the results of a discussion with a customer is critically important, since these notes are the basis for future contacts. The task is easier with an on-line note-taking function that stores notes by customer, and links to a calendar of activities for future calls.

Collect in Person

The assumption in most of this chapter has been that the collector does collections work at a distance, since doing so is more cost-effective than on-site visits. However, there are times when the overdue amount is so large, and the customer so intractable that an on-site visit is warranted. In this situation, there are three goals to be achieved through a visit:

- Establish relations with the accounts payable staff of the customer, which can be of immense use in future dealings
- Decide whether the customer is one with which the company should continue to do business
- Collect the overdue funds

Each of the preceding goals requires different tasks. Establishing relations calls for protracted (and preferably informal) discussions with the customer, while an on-site tour is useful for deciding whether the customer is a viable business. Collection of overdue funds calls for more detailed discussions about specific invoices. Given the different tasks involved, it may be necessary for several people to visit the customer, and for the visit to cover a full day. The following people could participate in the visit:

- *Collector.* The collector responsible for this account should attend, in order to establish relations with the accounts payable staff, as per the first goal.
- *Credit manager.* The credit manager should evaluate the business to see if it is worthy of the continuing grant of a credit limit, or whether the company should do business with this customer at all, as per the second goal.

- *Collection manager*. The senior collections person should attend, in order to authorize any payment deals reached as per the third goal. Alternatively, this authority can be given to the collector.
- *Salesman*. The salesperson responsible for the customer may also want to be present, to be fully briefed on any decisions reached.

Summary

When deciding upon the most appropriate set of collection tactics to use with a customer, the key issue is whether the seller wants to have an ongoing relationship with the customer. If so, then a number of the more aggressive collection tactics are probably not feasible, and should be avoided in order to keep from damaging the relationship. On the other hand, if the decision is made to terminate the relationship, the only remaining issue is how quickly the unpaid items can be collected; this decision may trigger a batch of considerably more aggressive collection techniques that would not normally be contemplated.

In general, the collector-to-customer relationship is somewhat similar to that of a parent to a child, where the collector has to be understanding, yet firm. This means working with the customer to resolve issues, while still following through to ensure that the customer does what it agrees to. Much as is the case with a child, if the collector does not follow through with any threatened actions, such as sending an invoice to a collection agency, the customer will be more difficult to deal with in the future. Consequently, consistent follow-through is perhaps the overriding principle of collection tactics.

Chapter 25
Payroll Management

Introduction

In a traditional payroll department that is indifferently managed, the payroll staff spends most of its time on payroll data entry for the next scheduled payroll, and cleaning up errors and mistakes from the last payroll. The nature of this work has two ramifications:

- The payroll staff works on nothing but data entry-level tasks; and
- The department is so inundated with the high volume of transactions that it never has any time to spare for systemic improvements.

This chapter describes a fundamental change in the responsibilities and work flow of the payroll department, which ultimately transforms it into a smaller group of well-trained employees who monitor transactions being entered into the payroll system by people outside of the department, and who are process specialists who are committed to continually enhancing the efficiency and effectiveness of the department.

Related podcast episodes: Episodes 126 through 129 of the Accounting Best Practices Podcast discuss the streamlining of payroll. You can listen to them at: **www.accountingtools.com/podcasts** or **iTunes**

Payroll Cycle Duration

One of the more important payroll management decisions is how long to set the payroll cycle. Each payroll requires a great deal of effort by the payroll staff to collect information about time worked, locate and correct errors, process wage rate and deduction changes, calculate pay, and issue payments. Consequently, it makes a great deal of sense to extend the duration of payroll cycles.

If payrolls are spaced at short intervals, such as weekly, then the payroll staff has to prepare 52 payrolls per year. Conversely, paying employees once a month reduces the payroll staff's payroll preparation activities by approximately three-quarters. Since paying employees just once a month can be a burden on the employees, companies frequently adopt a half-way measure, paying employees either twice a month (the *semimonthly* payroll) or once every two weeks (the *biweekly* payroll). The semimonthly payroll cycle results in processing 24 payrolls per year, while the biweekly payroll cycle requires you to process 26 payrolls per year.

An example of a weekly payroll cycle is shown below, where employees are paid every Tuesday for the hours they worked in the preceding week.

Weekly Payroll Cycle

January						
S	M	T	W	T	F	S
	1	2	3	4	5	6
7	8	9	10	11	12	13
14	15	16	17	18	19	20
21	22	23	24	25	26	27
28	29	30	31			

An example of a biweekly payroll cycle is shown below, where employees are paid every other Tuesday for the hours worked in the preceding two weeks:

Biweekly Payroll Cycle

January						
S	M	T	W	T	F	S
	1	2	3	4	5	6
7	8	9	10	11	12	13
14	15	16	17	18	19	20
21	22	23	24	25	26	27
28	29	30	31			

An example of a semimonthly payroll cycle is shown below, where employees are paid on the 15th and last days of the month.

Semimonthly Payroll Cycle

January						
S	M	T	W	T	F	S
	1	2	3	4	5	6
7	8	9	10	11	12	13
14	15	16	17	18	19	20
21	22	23	24	25	26	27
28	29	30	31			

An example of a monthly payroll cycle is shown below, where employees are paid on the last day of the month.

Monthly Payroll Cycle

January						
S	M	T	W	T	F	S
	1	2	3	4	5	6
7	8	9	10	11	12	13
14	15	16	17	18	19	20
21	22	23	24	25	26	27
28	29	30	31			

An argument in favor of the biweekly payroll is that employees become accustomed to receiving two paychecks per month, plus two "free" paychecks during the year, which has a somewhat more positive impact on employee morale. Nonetheless, the semimonthly payroll represents a slight improvement over the biweekly payroll from the perspective of payroll department efficiency, and is therefore recommended.

If employees are accustomed to a weekly payroll cycle and you switch them to one of a longer duration, expect to have some employees complain about not having enough cash to see them through the initial increased payroll cycle. You can mitigate this problem by extending pay advances to employees during the initial conversion to the longer payroll cycle. Once employees receive their larger paychecks under the new payroll cycle, they should be able to support themselves and will no longer need an advance.

A further issue is when a company operates a different payroll cycle for different groups of employees. For example, hourly employees may be paid on a weekly cycle and salaried employees on a semimonthly cycle. To complicate matters further, a company may have acquired other businesses and retained the payroll cycles used for their employees. Retaining all of these payroll cycles places the payroll staff in the position of perpetually preparing payrolls, so that it never has time for other activities. To avoid this problem, convert all of the different payroll cycles to a single one that applies to all employees. This may take a considerable amount of effort, but is mandatory if you wish to unburden the payroll staff from base-level data entry activities.

In short, paying employees at roughly half-month intervals and not allowing any additional payroll cycles can greatly reduce the work load of the payroll department. Once achieved, the staff will have more time available to address the improvement possibilities described in the following sections.

Streamlined Timekeeping

It is entirely common for the payroll department to be mired in the accumulation of timekeeping information; this encompasses the error-laden steps of coaxing timesheets from employees, correcting their submissions, and cajoling supervisors to approve the timesheets – followed by manually entering the information into the payroll software.

You must address several issues in order to break free of the timekeeping data entry trap. These issues are:

1. *Who submits information.* There is no need to collect hours-worked information from salaried employees, so they should not submit timesheets for payroll purposes. Further, if those employees who are paid on an hourly basis nearly always work a standard 40-hour work week, then they should only be reporting on an exception basis, when their hours worked vary from this baseline amount.

2. *How much information to collect.* The main protest against the last point is that employees must submit information irrespective of their salary or wage status, because the company is also tracking hours billed to customers or hours worked on specific jobs. This brings up two sub-issues:

   - *Is the information needed at all?* In many cases, the information collected through the payroll system was originally needed for a specific project or report. The data collection continues, though the project has long since been completed or the report is no longer used. Thus, you should periodically question the need for any information being collected through the payroll system.

   - *Can the information be separated from the payroll system?* In those cases where the information *must* be collected (such as hours worked that will be billed to customers), does the payroll staff need to collect it? For example, if a company has a large number of salaried consultants whose hours are billed to customers, the payroll staff can pay them without any timekeeping data collection at all – the collection of billed hours is more appropriately a function of the billing staff.

3. *How to automate timekeeping.* The automation of timekeeping involves two sub-issues, which are:

   - *How to automate data collection.* There are a number of solutions available that allow employees to directly enter their hours worked and a selection of additional data into a timekeeping database, thereby eliminating the traditional timesheet or time card and the need for the payroll staff to manually collect and enter this information. Technologies to choose from include the online timekeeping system, computerized time clocks, and timekeeping by smart phone.

   - *How to create an interface to the payroll system.* The automation of data collection only means that the information is stored in a computer database – you still need to shift it into the correct fields within the payroll system, so that payroll can be processed. This calls for a custom interface that automatically shifts the data, with no manual intervention.

Note that the automation of timekeeping is presented as the *last* action to take when streamlining timekeeping. That is because you should explore the *need* for timekeeping first, so that you can whittle down the timekeeping requirement to the bare minimum before investing any funds in an automated timekeeping solution.

The impact of streamlined timekeeping on the payroll department can be extraordinary - there may be no data entry work for the payroll staff at all. Instead, the department is more concerned with operating the timekeeping systems and monitoring entered information for discrepancies, missing fields, and errors. Ultimately, this means that the type of knowledge required of the payroll staff will shift away from data entry skills and toward data analysis and computer systems.

Note: The cost of the equipment, software, and training related to an automated timekeeping solution may appear excessive for a company with a small number of employees, since the cost of manually collecting timekeeping information is not large for them. If you are in this position, consider outsourcing payroll to a supplier that also provides an online timekeeping service. This solution is not expensive, and still gives you the benefit of shifting timekeeping data entry away from the payroll staff.

Electronic Payments

After timekeeping, the next largest use of payroll staff time is paying employees. There are a number of controls and processing steps associated with payments using paychecks, and an even greater number if you pay employees with cash. You can greatly reduce this labor by shifting employees to either direct deposit or pay cards. In both cases, funds are shifted electronically to employees, so there is no paycheck distribution.

Some state governments do not allow employers to switch to electronic payments without the consent of their employees. You can work through this problem by requiring new employees to opt out of electronic payments, by issuing reminders to those still receiving paychecks, and by having educational meetings to show the benefits of electronic payments. While the target should be 100% electronic payments, even a smaller percentage results in less work for the payroll staff.

To fully implement electronic payments, send remittance advices to employees by e-mail, or send them an e-mail notification of where they can access this information in a secure online data repository. Similarly, issue the annual Form W-2 to employees by storing the forms in an online data repository that employees can access.

By using online systems to pay employees and issue reports, the payroll department can completely avoid the time-consuming steps of printing checks, having them approved, and handing them out to employees.

Employee Self-Service

Employees sometimes need to change the information used to compile their net pay, such as benefits that require pay deductions, or their marriage status, or withholding allowances. Traditionally, employees fill out a form in which they authorize these changes to their payroll records, and the payroll staff enters the information into the payroll system. This is not a large chore in a smaller company, but can involve full-time staff in a larger company where the sheer volume of employees results in a great many changes.

You can eliminate this data entry task by having employees enter the information directly into the payroll system themselves, using an online portal. The types of information they can enter include the items just noted, as well as changes to their addresses and bank account information. The self-service portal is a common feature if you outsource payroll processing to a major payroll supplier, though there is usually an extra fee charged to use it.

The payroll staff should still monitor the information being entered by employees for errors. This can be done by reviewing a change log or by creating custom reports that only report changes that exceed predetermined "normal" entries (such as entering a withholding allowance that is inordinately high).

Manager Self-Service

Department managers are the source of a different set of payroll information. They submit changes to employee pay rates, department codes, and shift differentials, as well as start and termination dates. As was the case with employee self-service, it is possible to construct an online portal through which managers can make these changes themselves. And as was the case for employee self-service, the payroll staff should monitor these changes.

It is critical for the payroll staff to monitor changes made by managers, since these alterations will impact the company's compensation and payroll tax expenses. Monitoring may include comparing pay changes to the authorized pay change percentages assigned to each manager, and verifying pay rates with senior management if the rates exceed authorized levels.

Manager self-service is not as easy a feature to find in many payroll systems, since it is considered to have a smaller cost-benefit than employee self-service. Nonetheless, if you have completed the improvement steps noted in the preceding sections, this is the next logical step to pursue.

Transaction Error Analysis

It requires far more time to track down a payroll error and correct it than it does to initially enter the transaction correctly. Further, you typically assign the more experienced (and expensive) staff to investigate and correct errors. Thus, the cost of transaction errors is high, and is worthy of considerable analysis to find the causes of errors and prevent them from occurring again.

Transaction error analysis begins with the summarization of all payroll errors into a single document, so that you can classify and prioritize the errors. This may call for an informal system where the payroll staff forwards any complaints received regarding pay problems, and this information is translated into a standard format. You then select a single error type to pursue, and investigate it with the goal of isolating the specific issue that caused the error to occur. Then fix the issue, and monitor it to see if the error has now been eliminated. Examples of errors and their causes and possible corrections are shown in the following table:

Sample Payroll Errors and Corrections

Error	Source of Error	Error Correction
Timesheet not recorded	Employee did not submit timesheet	Send automated e-mail notification
Incorrect timesheet total	Clerk incorrectly added hours	Switch to computerized time clock
Overtime not approved	Supervisor did not sign card	Switch to computerized time clock
No benefits deduction	Clerk did not add deduction	Use standard deductions checklist
Allowance not updated	Clerk did not enter allowance change	Install employee self-service
Paycheck not signed	Checks stuck together	Use signature stamp
Paycheck issued for terminated employee	Clerk did not update pay status to terminated	Install manager self-service

Tip: Do not turn transaction error analysis into a witch hunt, where you assign blame for an error to a specific person. If you take this approach, the payroll staff will not inform you of any errors. Instead, make it clear that you are pursuing changes to the underlying systems that will keep errors from arising again.

Staff Training Program

An employee in the payroll department needs a considerable skill set in order to work at an optimal level of efficiency. These skills become more broad-ranging over time, as the department moves away from data entry tasks and into data analysis and system installations. Also, the legal requirements associated with payroll are considerable, and are increasing in complexity every year. Further, as the department rolls out a variety of payroll tools for employees to use throughout the company, the payroll staff must enter into a training role, where they show employees how to use these tools. Clearly, there is a need for a comprehensive and ongoing training program for the entire payroll staff.

In a modern, thoroughly computerized payroll department, the staff should receive training in the following areas:

- *Payroll software.* Every payroll software package has a different set of commands, modules, files structures, and so forth, and employees must be fully aware of how to handle transactions through the software. This usually involves a separate training class for each module of the software. Even if you outsource payroll, you must still access the supplier's online software, so training in its software is still required.

- *Payroll processes*. There is a particular flow to payroll processes that is driven by the level of automation, the type of software, and payroll regulations. Employees must be thoroughly familiar with these processes.
- *Regulatory changes*. There are regulatory changes every year that impact the payroll department. While the payroll manager could simply send everyone to a conference to learn about the most recent changes, a more cost-effective approach is to have a consultant monitor the changes and create a custom in-house training class to convey these changes to the staff. The latter approach requires a significant consulting fee, but keeps the staff in-house for the training, thereby avoiding travel and conference fees. It also results in a seminar that is expressly designed for the needs of the company and the locations where it has employees.
- *Data analysis*. As the department shifts away from data entry, there is a greater need for the payroll staff to review data entered by others, to verify that it is correct. This calls for training in report writing software, so that they can create a set of standard analysis reports that highlight possible data entry issues.
- *Training skills*. When the payroll department pushes software and hardware out from the department for use by other employees to enter information, it must also take on the task of training employees in their use. Consequently, several members of the department should be taught how to train others.

It is difficult to standardize payroll training for everyone in the payroll department, since some people are specialized on specific tasks, and their skill sets do not need to extend beyond those areas. Also, some people have more experience than others. Consequently, ascertain the skill set required by each person, and the specific areas in which extra training is needed to bring them up to the standard that you require. Then create a training plan for everyone in the department, and go over it with them on a regular basis to review their progress in meeting their training goals.

The Payroll Calendar

The payroll department's activities are driven by a large number of deadlines – for paying employees, depositing taxes, issuing reports, and so forth. Without a proper amount of documentation, it would be impossible to go through a year without missing some deadlines, and likely incurring both the wrath of employees and government-imposed penalties.

The solution to these problems is the departmental payroll calendar. This is a full-year schedule, on which you record all due dates and who is responsible for them. The payroll manager retains this full schedule, and may issue a subset of the calendar to his employees, so that each one has a calendar containing only those activities for which he or she is responsible. An example of a master department payroll calendar for a single month is shown below.

Sample Payroll Calendar

January				
Monday	Tuesday	Wednesday	Thursday	Friday
1 Issue metrics Process payroll Fund bank acct Journal entry	2 State deposit	3 Forward garnishments	4	5 Timesheets EFTPS deposit
8 Process payroll Fund bank acct Journal entry	9 Issue checks State deposit	10 Forward garnishments Form 4070	11	12 Timesheets EFTPS deposit
15 Process payroll Fund bank acct Journal entry Jones vacation	16 Issue checks State deposit Jones vacation	17 Forward garnishments Jones vacation	18 Jones vacation	19 Timesheets EFTPS deposit Jones vacation
22 Process payroll Fund bank acct Journal entry	23 Issue checks State deposit	24 Forward garnishments	25	26 Timesheets EFTPS deposit
29 Process payroll Fund bank acct Journal entry	30 Issue checks State deposit	31 Forms W-2 Forms 1099 Form 940 Form 941 Form 945 FUTA deposit		

Note that the calendar also includes a scheduled week of vacation for one employee. This information provides the staff with notice of a capacity reduction during that week, which it will need to plan around.

The payroll calendar is particularly important if there are new employees in the department who do not yet have experience with those deadlines pertaining to the operations of the department – it is a useful reminder for these individuals.

Ideally, the payroll manager should consult the payroll calendar for the following day, and verify that the staff is aware of the deadlines for that day, and how any issues will be addressed. If a specific date is likely to require a larger amount of work than usual (such as the final day of January in the preceding example), the manager can use the calendar to plan well in advance for how to handle the work load.

Information Confidentiality

A major issue for any payroll department is to ensure that a large part of the information it processes remains confidential. Most employees would consider it disastrous if information about their wages, pension plans, garnishments, social security numbers, and so forth were to be made public. This information is located in the payroll register and employee files, and may be scattered among other payroll reports, as well. The following are recommended methods for improving the confidentiality of payroll information:

- *Locked storage*. Clearly, the best single action you can take to enhance confidentiality is to keep payroll documents in a locked storage area. This can be a locked storage cabinet, or locked room with a door that automatically closes and locks.
- *Password protection*. Anyone using the payroll software must input a password to access the system. Further, set the software to require a new password at frequent intervals.
- *Limit authorization*. Even within the payroll department, it is not necessary for every employee to have full access to payroll information. For example, if there is a clerk who only handles employee timesheets, do not give that person access to other types of payroll information.
- *Shred documents*. Once the company is no longer required to continue archiving old payroll files, do not just throw them in the trash; instead, shred them. There are shredding services in most major cities that can handle this task.
- *Dissemination policy*. Have a department policy that no one ever gives out confidential information without specific authorization. In all cases, this should involve the approval of the payroll manager.

Summary

This chapter has addressed a number of general management concepts that are designed to improve the efficiency and effectiveness of the payroll department. Ultimately, this can result in a department that has shifted almost entirely away from data entry activities, and instead spends most of its time monitoring payroll transactions, installing new systems, and issuing reports related to payroll expenses. This sweeping change will also result in a department whose employees have a much higher knowledge of payroll regulations, controls, and systems.

The sections presented near the beginning of this chapter were sorted in order by the importance of their impact on the payroll department. Thus, consider implementing changes in the following order:

1. *Reduce and consolidate the number of payrolls*. This can substantially reduce the work load of the department, giving it more time to implement additional changes.
2. *Streamline timekeeping*. The time savings from eliminating data entry tasks is potentially enormous.

3. *Shift to electronic payments.* The payroll staff can avoid printing and distributing paychecks if it can persuade employees to switch to direct deposit or pay cards.
4. *Install employee self-service.* Employees can enter information directly into the payroll system related to their withholding allowances, benefits, bank accounts, mailing information, and so forth.
5. *Install manager self-service.* Managers can enter information directly into the payroll system related to employee pay rates, department codes, shift differentials, and so forth.

You will need to implement a comprehensive staff training program as you gradually work through the preceding steps, because the nature of the employees' work will diverge more and more from their original data entry-oriented tasks and into areas that require more knowledge. They will also need training skills, since they must show employees throughout the company how to use the new timekeeping and self-service systems to enter information into the payroll system. Thus, the training program may begin as a relatively small effort, and gradually change into a major undertaking that involves all of the payroll staff on an ongoing basis.

Chapter 26
Budgeting

Introduction

Only in the smallest company can a budget be contained within a single page or spreadsheet. In most cases, the level of complexity of the business demands a much more segmented approach, so that key elements of the budget are modularized and then aggregated into a master budget. In this chapter, we show the complete system of budgets, describe how to create each element of the budget, and show how they are linked together to form a complete budget.

> **Related Podcast Episodes:** Episodes 71, 76, 130, and 131 of the Accounting Best Practices Podcast discuss budget model improvement, budgeting controls, the problems with budgets, and operating without a budget, respectively. You can listen to them at: **accountingtools.com/podcasts** or **iTunes**

The System of Budgets

The key driver of any budget is the amount of revenue that is expected during the budget period. Revenue is usually compiled in a separate revenue budget. The information in this budget is derived from estimates of which products or services will sell, and the prices at which they can be sold. Forecasted revenue for this budget cannot be derived just from the sales staff, since this would limit the information to the extrapolation of historical sales figures into the future. The chief executive officer provides additional strategic information, while the marketing manager addresses new-product introductions and the purchasing staff provides input on the availability of raw materials that may restrict sales. Thus, a group effort from many parts of a company is needed to create the revenue budget.

Once the revenue budget is in place, a number of additional budgets are derived from it that relate to the production capabilities of the company. The following components are included in this cluster of budgets:

- *Ending inventory budget.* As its name implies, this budget sets the inventory level as of the end of each accounting period listed in the budget. Management uses this budget to force changes in the inventory level, which is usually driven by a policy to have more or less finished goods inventory on hand. Having more inventory presumably improves the speed with which a company can ship goods to customers, at the cost of an increased investment in working capital. A forced reduction in inventory may delay some shipments to customers due to stockout conditions, but requires less working capital to maintain. The ending inventory budget is used as an input to the production budget.

- *Production budget.* This budget shows expected production at an aggregated level. The production budget is based primarily on the sales estimates in the revenue budget, but it must also take into consideration existing inventory levels and the desired amount of ending inventory as stated in the ending inventory budget. If management wants to increase inventory levels in order to provide more rapid shipments to customers, the required increase in production may trigger a need for more production equipment and direct labor staff. The production budget is needed in order to derive the direct labor budget, manufacturing overhead budget, and direct materials budget.
- *Direct labor budget.* This budget calculates the amount of direct labor staffing expected during the budget period, based on the production levels itemized in the production budget. This information can only be generally estimated, given the vagaries of short-term changes in actual production scheduling. However, direct labor usually involves specific staffing levels to crew production lines, so the estimated amount of direct labor should not vary excessively over time, within certain production volume parameters. This budget should incorporate any planned changes in the cost of labor, which may be easy to do if there is a union contract that specifies pay increases as of specific dates. It provides rough estimates of the number of employees needed, and is of particular interest to the human resources staff in developing hiring plans. It is a key source document for the cost of goods sold budget.
- *Manufacturing overhead budget.* This budget includes all of the overhead costs expected to be incurred in the manufacturing area during the budget period. It is usually based on historical cost information, but can be adjusted for step cost situations, where a change in the structure or capacity level of a production facility strips away or adds large amounts of expenses at one time. Even if there are no changes in structure or capacity, the manufacturing overhead budget may change somewhat in the maintenance cost area if management plans to alter these expenditures as machines age or are replaced. This budget is a source document for the cost of goods sold budget.
- *Direct materials budget.* This budget is derived from a combination of the manufacturing unit totals in the production budget and the bills of material for those units, and is used in the cost of goods sold budget. If a company produces a large variety of products, this can become an excessively detailed and burdensome budget to create and maintain. Consequently, it is customary to estimate material costs in aggregate, such as at the product line level.
- *Cost of goods sold budget.* This budget contains a summarization of the expenses detailed in the direct material budget, manufacturing overhead budget, and direct materials budget. This budget usually contains such additional information as line items for revenue, the gross margin, and key production statistics. It is heavily used during budget iterations, since management can consult it to view the impact of various assumptions on gross margins and other aspects of the production process.

Once the revenue and production-related budgets have been completed, there are still several other budgets to assemble that relate to other functions of the company. They are:

- *Sales and marketing budget.* This budget is comprised of the compensation of the sales and marketing staff, sales travel costs, and expenditures related to various marketing programs. It is closely linked to the revenue budget, since the number of sales staff (in some industries) is the prime determinant of additional sales. Further, marketing campaigns can impact the timing of the sales shown in the revenue budget.
- *Administration budget.* This budget includes the expenses of the executive, accounting, treasury, human resources, and other administrative staff. These expenses are primarily comprised of compensation, followed by office expenses. A large proportion of these expenses are fixed, with some headcount changes driven by total revenues or other types of activity elsewhere in the company.

A budget that is not directly impacted by the revenue budget is the research and development budget. This budget is authorized by senior management, and is set at an amount that is deemed appropriate, given the projected level of new product introductions that management wants to achieve, and the company's competitive posture within the industry. The size of this budget is also influenced by the amount of available funding and an estimate of how many potentially profitable projects can be pursued.

Once these budgets have been completed, it is possible to determine the capital budgeting requirements of the company, as well as its financing needs. These two topics are addressed in the capital budget and the financing budget:

- *Capital budget.* This budget shows the cash flows associated with the acquisition of fixed assets during the budget period. Larger fixed assets are noted individually, while smaller purchases are noted in aggregate. The information in this budget is used to develop the budgeted balance sheet, depreciation expense, and the cash requirements needed for the financing budget. The capital budget is addressed separately in the Capital Budgeting chapter.
- *Financing budget.* This budget is the last of the component budgets developed, because it needs the cash inflow and outflow information from the other budgets. With this information in hand, the financing budget addresses how funds will be invested (if there are excess cash inflows) or obtained through debt or equity financing (if there is a need for additional cash). This budget also incorporates any additional cash usage information that is typically addressed by the board of directors, including dividends, stock repurchases, and repositioning of the company's debt to equity ratio. The interest expense or interest income resulting from this budget is incorporated into the budgeted income statement.

Once the capital budget and financing budget have been created, the information in all of the budgets is summarized into a master budget. This master budget is essentially an income statement. A more complex budget also includes a balance sheet that itemizes the major categories of assets, liabilities, and equity. There may also be a statement of cash flows that itemizes the sources and uses of funds.

The complete system of budgets is shown in the following exhibit.

Exhibit: The System of Budgets

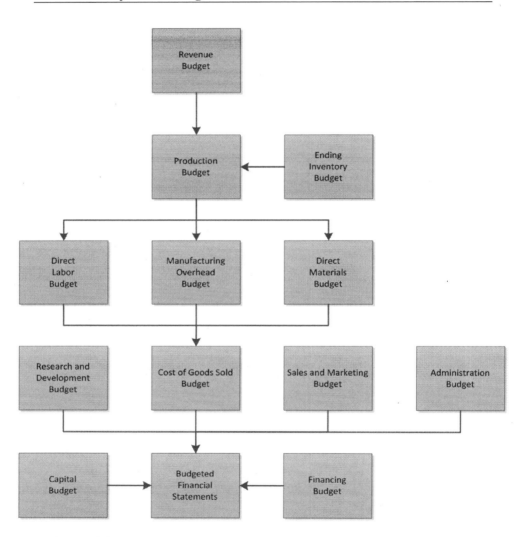

It may be useful to append a ratios page to the budget. These ratios are most useful when compared to historical trends, to see if the results generated by the budget model appear reasonable. Typical ratios to consider for this page are revenue per person, inventory turnover, accounts receivable turnover, and working capital as a percentage of sales.

In summary, the system of budgets ultimately depends upon the revenue budget and the amount of planned ending inventory. These two budgets directly or indirectly influence the amounts budgeted in many other parts of the corporate budget.

The Reasons for Budget Iterations

There are several very good reasons why the first version of a corporate budget is sent back for additional work. These issues are:

- *Constraints*. If there are bottlenecks within the company that interfere with its ability to generate additional sales, then does the budget provide sufficient funding to impact these bottlenecks? If not, the company can budget whatever results it wants, but it has virtually no chance of achieving them. For example, a machine in the production area may be a bottleneck that keeps a company from producing any more products – if you do not deal with the bottleneck, sales will not increase, irrespective of improvements anywhere else in the company.

- *Pacing*. If a company intends to expand operations in new geographical areas, or to open new distribution channels, or to offer entirely new products, it should build into the budget an adequate amount of time to ramp up each operation. This issue of pacing should include consideration of the sales cycle of customers, which may be extremely long. For example, expanding the customer base to include municipal governments may be an excellent idea, but may require a sales cycle of greater than a year, given the advance notice needed by governments to budget for purchases.

- *Financing*. If a company has a hard cap on the amount of funding that it will have available during the budget period, then the requirements of the budget must not exceed that funding limitation. This is one of the more common reasons for budget iterations, especially in small companies, where it may be difficult to obtain new funding.

- *Historical metrics*. If a company has been unable to achieve certain performance benchmarks in the past, what has changed to allow it to do so now? The chances are good that the company will still have trouble improving beyond its historical ability to do so, which means that the budget should be adjusted to meet its historical metrics. For example, if a business has historically been unable to generate more than $1 million of sales per salesperson, the preliminary budget should continue to support a similar proportion of sales to salespeople. Similarly, a historical tendency for accounts receivable to be an average of 45 days old prior to payment should probably be reflected in the preliminary budget, rather than a more aggressive collection assumption.

This section has highlighted the need to conduct a close examination of preliminary versions of a budget to see if it meets a number of reasonableness criteria. This usually calls for a number of adjustments to the budget, which typically begins with excessively optimistic assumptions, followed by a certain amount of retrenching.

We now turn to an examination of the various components of the corporate budget.

Overview of the Revenue Budget

The basic revenue budget contains an itemization of a company's sales expectations for the budget period, which may be in both units and dollars. If a company has a large number of products, it usually aggregates its expected sales into a smaller number of product categories; otherwise, the revenue budget becomes too unwieldy.

The projected unit sales information in the sales budget feeds directly into the production budget, from which the direct materials and direct labor budgets are created. The revenue budget is also used to give managers a general sense of the scale of operations, for when they create the manufacturing overhead budget, the sales and marketing budget, and the administration budget. The total net sales dollars listed in the revenue budget are carried forward into the revenue line item in the master budget.

Most companies sell a considerable number of products and services, and must find a way to aggregate them into a revenue budget that strikes a balance between revealing a reasonable level of detail and not overwhelming the reader with a massive list of line-item projections. There are several ways to aggregate information to meet this goal.

One approach is to summarize revenue information by sales territory, as shown below. This approach is most useful when the primary source of information for the revenue budget is the sales managers of the various territories, and is particularly important if the company is planning to close down or open up new sales territories; changes at the territory level may be the primary drivers of changes in sales. In the example, the Central Plains sales territory is expected to be launched midway through the budget year and to contribute modestly to total sales volume by year end.

Sample Revenue Budget by Territory

Territory	Quarter 1	Quarter 2	Quarter 3	Quarter 4	Total
Northeast	$135,000	$141,000	$145,000	$132,000	$553,000
Mid-Atlantic	200,000	210,000	208,000	195,000	813,000
Southeast	400,000	425,000	425,000	395,000	$1,645,000
Central Plains	0	0	100,000	175,000	275,000
Rocky mountain	225,000	235,000	242,000	230,000	932,000
West coast	500,000	560,000	585,000	525,000	2,170,000
Totals	$1,460,000	$1,571,000	$1,705,000	$1,652,000	$6,388,000

If you aggregate revenue information by sales territory, then the various territory managers are expected to maintain additional detail regarding sales in their territories, which is kept separate from the formal budget document.

Another approach is to summarize revenue information by contract, as shown below. This is realistically the only viable way to structure the revenue budget in situations where a company is heavily dependent upon a set of contracts that have definite ending dates. In this situation, you can divide the budget into existing and projected contracts, with subtotals for each type of contract, in order to separately show firm revenues and less-likely revenues. This type of revenue budget is commonly used when a company is engaged in services or government work.

Sample Revenue Budget by Contract

Contract	Quarter 1	Quarter 2	Quarter 3	Quarter 4	Total
Existing Contracts:					
Air Force #01327	$175,000	$175,000	$25,000	$--	$375,000
Coast Guard #AC124	460,000	460,000	460,000	25,000	1,405,000
Marines #BG0047	260,000	280,000	280,000	260,000	1,080,000
Subtotal	$895,000	$915,000	$765,000	$285,000	$2,860,000
Projected Contracts:					
Air Force resupply	$--	$--	$150,000	$300,000	$450,000
Army training	--	210,000	600,000	550,000	1,360,000
Marines software	10,000	80,000	80,000	100,000	270,000
Subtotal	$10,000	$290,000	$830,000	$950,000	$2,080,000
Totals	$905,000	$1,205,000	$1,595,000	$1,235,000	$4,940,000

Yet another approach for a company having a large number of products is to aggregate them into product lines, and then create a summary-level budget at the product line level. This approach is shown below. However, if you create a revenue budget for product lines, consider creating a supporting schedule of projected sales for each of the products within that product line, in order to properly account for the timing and revenue volumes associated with the ongoing introduction of new products and cancellation of old ones. An example of such a supporting schedule is also shown below, itemizing the "Alpha" line item in the product line revenue budget. Note that this schedule provides detail about the launch of a new product (the Alpha Windmill) and the termination of another product (the Alpha Methane Converter) that are crucial to the formulation of the total revenue figure for the product line.

Sample Revenue Budget by Product Line

Product Line	Quarter 1	Quarter 2	Quarter 3	Quarter 4	Total
Product line alpha	$450,000	$500,000	$625,000	$525,000	$2,100,000
Product line beta	100,000	110,000	150,000	125,000	485,000
Product line charlie	250,000	250,000	300,000	300,000	1,100,000
Product line delta	80,000	60,000	40,000	20,000	200,000
Totals	$880,000	$920,000	$1,115,000	$970,000	$3,885,000

Sample Supporting Schedule for the Revenue Budget by Product Line

	Quarter 1	Quarter 2	Quarter 3	Quarter 4	Total
Alpha product line detail:					
Alpha Flywheel	$25,000	$35,000	$40,000	$20,000	$120,000
Alpha Generator	175,000	225,000	210,000	180,000	790,000
Alpha Windmill	--	--	200,000	250,000	450,000
Alpha Methane Converter	150,000	140,000	25,000	--	315,000
Alpha Nuclear Converter	100,000	100,000	150,000	75,000	425,000
Totals	$450,000	$500,000	$625,000	$525,000	$2,100,000

A danger in constructing a supporting schedule for a product line revenue budget is that you delve too deeply into all of the various manifestations of a product, resulting in an inordinately large and detailed schedule. This situation might arise when a product comes in many colors or options. In such cases, engage in as much aggregation at the individual product level as necessary to yield a schedule that is not *excessively* detailed. Also, it is nearly impossible to forecast sales at the level of the color or specific option mix associated with a product, so it makes little sense to create a schedule at that level of detail.

In summary, the layout of the revenue budget is highly dependent upon the type of revenue that a company generates. We have described different formats for companies that are structured around products, contract-based services, and sales territories. If a company engages in more than one of these activities, you should still create the revenue-specific formats shown in this section in order to provide insights into the sources of revenues, and then carry forward the totals of those schedules to a master revenue budget that lists the totals in separate line items. Users of this master revenue budget can then drill down to the underlying revenue budget schedules to obtain additional information. An example of a master revenue budget that is derived from the last two example revenue budgets is shown below.

Sample Master Revenue Budget

	Quarter 1	Quarter 2	Quarter 3	Quarter 4	Total
Contract revenue	$905,000	$1,205,000	$1,595,000	$1,235,000	$4,940,000
Product revenue	880,000	920,000	1,115,000	970,000	3,885,000
Totals	$1,785,000	$2,125,000	$2,710,000	$2,205,000	$8,825,000

The Ending Finished Goods Inventory Budget

The ending finished goods inventory budget states the number of units of finished goods inventory at the end of each budget period. It also calculates the cost of finished goods inventory. The amount of this inventory tends to be similar from period to period, assuming that the production department manufactures to meet demand levels in each budget period. However, there are a variety of reasons why you may want to alter the amount of ending finished goods inventory, such as:

- *Customer service*. If management wants to improve customer service, one way to do so is to increase the amount of ending inventory, which allows the company to fulfill customer orders more quickly and avoid backorder situations.
- *Inventory record accuracy*. If your inventory record keeping system is inaccurate, it is necessary to maintain additional amounts of inventory on hand, both of raw materials and finished goods, to ensure that customer orders are fulfilled on time.
- *Manufacturing planning*. If you are using a manufacturing resources planning (MRP) system, then you are producing in accordance with a sales and production plan, which requires a certain amount of both raw materials and finished goods inventory. If you change to the just-in-time (JIT) manufacturing planning system, then you are only producing as required by customers, which tends to reduce the need for inventory.
- *Product life cycles*. If there are certain products or even entire product lines that a company is planning to terminate, factor the related inventory reductions into the amount of planned ending inventory.
- *Product versions*. If the sales and marketing staff want to offer a product in a number of versions, you may need to keep a certain amount of each type of inventory in stock. Thus, an increase in the number of product versions equates to an increase in ending inventory.
- *Supply chain duration*. If you are planning to switch to a supplier located far away from the company, be aware that this calls for having a larger safety stock of finished goods on hand, so that deliveries to customers will not be impacted if there is a problem in receiving goods on time from the supplier.
- *Working capital reduction*. If you want to increase the amount of inventory turnover, this reduces the amount of cash invested in working capital, but also has the offsetting effect of leaving less inventory in reserve to cover sudden surges in customer orders.

If you do plan to alter the ending amount of inventory, it is useful to create separate layers of ending inventory in the budget that reflect each of the decisions made, so that readers of the budget can see the numerical impact of operational decisions.

In the following example, we assume that changes made in the immediately preceding budget period will continue to have the same impact on inventory in the *next* budget period, so that the adjusted ending inventory in the last period will be the starting point for our adjustments in the next period. We can then make the following adjustments to the unadjusted ending inventory level to arrive at an adjusted ending inventory:

- *Internal systems changes.* Shows the impact of altering the manufacturing system, such as changing from an MRP to a JIT system.
- *Financing changes.* Shows the impact of altering inventory levels in order to influence the amount of working capital used.
- *Product changes.* Shows the impact of product withdrawals and product introductions.
- *Seasonal changes.* Shows the impact of building inventory for seasonal sales, followed by a decline after the selling season has concluded.
- *Service changes.* Shows the impact of changing inventory levels in order to alter order fulfillment rates.

If management is attempting to reduce the company's investment in inventory, it may mandate such a large drop in ending inventory that the company will not realistically be able to operate without significant production and shipping interruptions. You can spot these situations by including the budgeted inventory turnover level in each budget period, as well as the actual amount of turnover in the corresponding period in the preceding year. This is shown in the following example as the historical actual days of inventory, followed by the planned days of inventory for the budget period. Comparing the two measurements may reveal large period-to-period changes, which management should examine to see if it is really possible to reduce inventory levels to such an extent.

EXAMPLE

Milagro Corporation has a division that sells portable coffee machines for campers. Milagro wants to incorporate the following changes into its calculation of the ending finished goods inventory:

1. Switch from the MRP to the JIT manufacturing system in the second quarter, which will decrease inventory by 250 units.
2. Reduce inventory by 500 units in the first quarter to reduce working capital requirements.
3. Add 500 units to inventory in the third quarter as part of the rollout of a new product.
4. Build inventory in the first three quarters by 100 units per quarter in anticipation of seasonal sales in the fourth quarter.
5. Increase on-hand inventory by 400 units in the second quarter to improve the speed of customer order fulfillment for a specific product.

The ending finished goods inventory unit and cost calculation follows:

(units)	Quarter 1	Quarter 2	Quarter 3	Quarter 4
Unadjusted ending inventory level	2,000	1,600	1,850	2,450
+/- Internal system changes	0	-250	0	0
+/- Financing changes	-500	0	0	0
+/- Product changes	0	0	500	0
+/- Seasonal changes	100	100	100	-300
+/- Service changes	0	400	0	0
Adjusted ending inventory	1,600	1,850	2,450	2,150
× Standard cost per unit	$45	$45	$45	$45
Total ending inventory cost	$72,000	$83,250	$110,250	$96,750
Historical actual days of inventory	100	108	135	127
Planned days of inventory	92	106	130	114

The days of inventory calculation at the bottom of the table shows few differences from actual experience in the second and third quarters, but the differences are greater in the first and fourth quarters. Management should review its ability to achieve the indicated inventory reductions in those quarters.

The ending finished goods inventory budget shown in the preceding example is quite simplistic, for it assumes that you want to apply the same inventory policies and systems to a company's *entire* inventory. For example, this means that you want to increase inventory levels for all types of inventory in order to increase customer order fulfillment speeds, when in fact you may only want to do so for a relatively small part of the inventory.

If you want to adjust inventory levels at a finer level of detail, consider creating a budget that sets inventory levels by business unit or product line. It is generally too time-consuming to set inventory levels at the individual product level, especially if demand at this level is difficult to predict.

The Production Budget

The production budget calculates the number of units of products that must be manufactured, and is derived from a combination of the sales forecast and the planned amount of finished goods inventory to have on hand. The production budget is typically presented in either a monthly or quarterly format. The basic calculation used by the production budget is:

> \+ Forecasted unit sales
> \+ Planned finished goods ending inventory balance
> = Total production required
>
> \- Beginning finished goods inventory
> = Units to be manufactured

It can be very difficult to create a comprehensive production budget that incorporates a forecast for every variation on a product that a company sells, so it is customary to aggregate the forecast information into broad categories of products that have similar characteristics. The calculation of the production budget is illustrated in the following example.

EXAMPLE

Milagro Corporation plans to produce an array of plastic coffee cups for the upcoming budget year. Its production needs are as follows:

	Quarter 1	Quarter 2	Quarter 3	Quarter 4
Forecast unit sales	5,500	6,000	7,000	8,000
+ Planned ending inventory units	500	500	500	500
= Total production required	6,000	6,500	7,500	8,500
- Beginning finished goods inventory	-1,000	-500	-500	-500
= Units to be manufactured	5,000	6,000	7,000	8,000

The planned ending finished goods inventory at the end of each quarter declines from an initial 1,000 units to 500 units, since the materials manager believes that the company is maintaining too much finished goods inventory. Consequently, the plan calls for a decline from 1,000 units of ending finished goods inventory at the end of the first quarter to 500 units by the end of the second quarter, despite a projection for rising sales. This may be a risky forecast, since the amount of safety stock on hand is being cut while production volume increases by over 30 percent. Given the size of the projected inventory decline, there is a fair chance that Milagro will be forced to increase the amount of ending finished goods inventory later in the year.

The production budget deals entirely with unit volumes; it does not translate its production requirements into dollars. Instead, the unit requirements of the budget are shifted into other parts of the budget, such as the direct labor budget and the direct materials budget, which are then translated into dollars.

When formulating the production budget, it is useful to consider the impact of proposed production on the capacity of any bottleneck operations in the production area. It is entirely possible that some production requirements will not be possible given the production constraints, so you will either have to scale back on production requirements, invest in more fixed assets, or outsource the work. The following example illustrates the issue.

EXAMPLE

Milagro Corporation revises the production budget described in the preceding example to incorporate the usage of a bottleneck machine in its manufacturing area. The revised format follows, beginning with the last row of information from the preceding example:

	Quarter 1	Quarter 2	Quarter 3	Quarter 4
Units to be manufactured	5,000	6,000	7,000	8,000
× Minutes of bottleneck time/unit	15	15	15	15
= Planned bottleneck usage (minutes)	75,000	90,000	105,000	120,000
- Available bottleneck time (minutes)*	110,160	110,160	110,160	110,160
= Remaining available time (minutes)	35,160	20,160	5,160	-9,840

* Calculated as 90 days × 24 hours × 60 minutes × 85% up time = 110,160 minutes

The table reveals that there is not enough bottleneck time available to meet the planned production level in the fourth quarter. However, Milagro can increase production in earlier quarters to make up the shortfall, since there is adequate capacity available at the bottleneck in the earlier periods.

Note in the preceding example that the amount of available bottleneck time was set at 85 percent of the maximum possible amount of time available. We make such assumptions because of the inevitable amount of downtime associated with equipment maintenance, unavailable raw materials, scrapped production, and so forth. The 85 percent figure is only an example – the real amount may be somewhat higher or substantially lower.

Another issue impacting the production budget is the need to incur step costs when production exceeds a certain volume level. For example, a company may need to open a new production facility, production line, or work shift to accommodate any additional increase in production past a certain amount of volume. It may be possible to adjust the production schedule to accelerate production in slow periods in order to stockpile inventory and avoid such step costs in later periods.

Production Budgeting for Multiple Products

The production budget shown thus far has centered on the manufacture of a single product. How do you create a production budget if you have multiple products? The worst solution is to attempt to re-create in the budget a variation on the production schedule for the entire budget period – the level of detail required to do so would be inordinately high. Instead, consider one of the following alternatives:

- *Bottleneck focus.* Rather than focusing on the production of a variety of products, only budget for the amount of time that they require at the bottleneck operation. For example, rather than focusing on the need to manufacture every aspect of 20 different products, focus on the time that each product needs at a single production operation. If there are multiple production lines or facilities, only budget for usage of the bottleneck at each location.
- *Product line focus.* In many cases, there are only modest differences in the production activities needed to create any product within a product line. If there are such production commonalities, consider treating the entire production line as a single product with common production requirements.
- *80/20 rule.* It is likely that only a small number of products comprise most of a company's production volume. If this is the case, consider detailed

budgeting for the production of the 20 percent of all products that typically comprise 80 percent of all sales, and a vastly reduced (and aggregated) amount of budgeting for the remaining products.

- *MRP II planning.* If a company uses a manufacturing requirements planning (MRP II) system, the software may contain a planning module that allows you to input estimates of production requirements, and generate detailed requirements for machine usage, direct labor, and direct materials. If so, you can input the totals from this module into the budget without also copying in all of the supporting details.

The Direct Materials Budget (Roll up Method)

The direct materials budget calculates the materials that must be purchased, by time period, in order to fulfill the requirements of the production budget. The basic calculation for the roll up method is to multiply the estimated amount of sales (in units) in each reporting period by the standard cost of each item to arrive at the standard amount of direct materials cost expected for each product. Standard costs are derived from the bill of materials for each product. A bill of materials is the record of the materials used to construct a product. A sample calculation is:

Sample Calculation of the Cost of Direct Materials

	Quarter 1	Quarter 2	Quarter 3	Quarter 4
Product A				
Units	100	120	110	90
Standard cost/each	$14.25	$14.25	$14.25	$14.25
Total cost	$1,425	$1,710	$1,568	$1,283
Product B				
Units	300	350	375	360
Standard cost/each	$8.40	$8.40	$8.40	$8.40
Total cost	$2,520	$2,940	$3,150	$3,024
Grand total cost	$3,945	$4,650	$4,718	$4,307

Note that the preceding example only addressed the direct materials *expense* during the budget period. It did not address the amount of materials that should be purchased during the period; doing so requires that you also factor in the planned amounts of beginning and ending inventory. The calculation used for direct material purchases is:

+ Raw materials required for production
+ Planned ending inventory balance
= Total raw materials required

- Beginning raw materials inventory
= Raw materials to be purchased

The presence or absence of a beginning inventory can have a major impact on the amount of direct materials needed during a budget period – in some cases, there may be so much inventory already on hand that a company does not need to purchase *any* additional direct materials. In other cases, and especially where management wants to build the amount of ending inventory (as arises when a company is preparing for a seasonal sales surge), it may be necessary to purchase far more direct materials than are indicated by sales requirements in just a single budget period. The following example illustrates how beginning and ending inventory levels can alter direct material requirements.

EXAMPLE

Milagro Corporation plans to produce a variety of large-capacity coffee dispensers for camping, and 98% of the raw materials required for this production involve plastic resin. Thus, there is only one key commodity to be concerned with. The production needs of Milagro for the resin commodity are shown in the following direct materials budget:

	Quarter 1	Quarter 2	Quarter 3	Quarter 4
Product A (units to produce)	5,000	6,000	7,000	8,000
× Resin/unit (lbs)	2	2	2	2
= Total resin needed (lbs)	10,000	12,000	14,000	16,000
+ Planned ending inventory	2,000	2,400	2,800	3,200
= Total resin required	12,000	14,400	16,800	19,200
- Beginning inventory	1,600	2,000	2,400	2,800
= Resin to be purchased	10,400	12,400	14,400	16,400
Resin cost per pound	$0.50	$0.50	$0.55	$0.55
Total resin cost to purchase	$5,200	$6,200	$7,920	$9,020

The planned ending inventory at the end of each quarter is planned to be 20% of the amount of resin used during that month, so the ending inventory varies over time, gradually increasing as production requirements increase. The reason for the planned increase is that Milagro has some difficulty receiving resin in a timely manner from its supplier, so it maintains a safety stock of inventory on hand.

The purchasing department expects that global demand will drive up the price of resin, so it incorporates a slight price increase into the third quarter, which carries forward into the fourth quarter.

If you use the roll up method, you are basing the unit volume of materials on the quantities listed in the bill of materials for each item. It is essential that the information in bills of material be as accurate as possible, since the materials management department relies on this information to purchase materials and schedule production. However, what if the bill of materials information is incorrect, even if only by a small amount? Then, under the roll up method, that incorrect amount will be multiplied by the number of units to be produced in the budget period, which can result in quite a large error in the amount of materials used in the budget.

The Direct Materials Budget (Historical Method)

In a typical business environment, there may be a multitude of factors that impact the amount of direct materials as a percentage of sales, including scrap, spoilage, rework, purchasing quantities, and volatility in commodity prices. Many companies are unable to accurately capture these factors in their bills of material, which makes it nearly impossible for them to create a reliable direct materials budget using the roll up method that was just described.

In such cases, an alternative budget calculation is the historical method, under which you assume that the historical amount of direct materials, as a percentage of revenues, will continue to be the case during the budget period. This approach means that you copy forward the historical percentage of direct material costs, with additional line items to account for any budgeted changes in key assumptions.

Under the historical method, adjust the projected amount of sales for any increase or decrease in production that is required for planned changes in the amount of ending inventory, and express the result as adjusted revenue. You can then multiply the adjusted revenue figure by the historical percentage of direct materials to arrive at the total direct materials cost required to achieve the production budget. Despite the need for these adjustments, it is much easier to create a direct materials budget using the historical method than by using the roll up method.

EXAMPLE

Milagro Corporation finds that its last direct materials budget, which was created using the roll up method, did not come anywhere near actual results. This year, Milagro wants to use the historical method instead, using the historical direct materials rate of 32% of revenues as the basis for the budget. To avoid having the company become complacent and not work toward lower direct material costs, the budget also includes several adjustment factors that are expected from several improvement projects. There is also an adjustment factor that addresses a likely change in the mix of products to be sold during the budget period. The budget model is:

	Quarter 1	Quarter 2	Quarter 3	Quarter 4
Projected revenue	$4,200,000	$5,000,000	$5,750,000	$8,000,000
+/- planned ending inventory change	-400,000	+100,000	+250,000	-350,000
Adjusted revenue	$3,800,000	$5,100,000	$6,000,000	$7,650,000
Historical direct materials percentage	27.1%	27.1%	27.1%	27.1%
+ / - Adjustment for product mix	+3.4%	+4.0%	+1.8%	-0.9%
- Adjustment for scrap reduction	0.0%	0.0%	-0.2%	-0.2%
- Adjustment for rework reduction	0.0%	-0.1%	-0.1%	-0.1%
= Adjusted direct materials percentage	30.5%	31.0%	28.6%	25.9%
Total direct materials cost	$1,159,000	$1,581,000	$1,716,000	$1,981,350

The problem with the historical method is that it is based on a certain mix of products that were sold in the past, each possibly with a different proportion of direct materials to sales. It is unlikely that the same mix of products will continue to be sold through the budget period; thus, applying an historical percentage to a future period may yield an incorrect direct materials cost. You can mitigate this issue by including an adjustment factor in the budget (as was shown in the preceding example), which modifies the historical percentage for what is expected to be the future mix of product sales.

The Direct Labor Budget

The cost of direct labor is rarely variable. Instead, the production manager must retain experienced employees, which calls for paying them irrespective of the vagaries of the production schedule. Also, a production operation usually calls for a certain minimum number of employees in order to crew the production lines or work cells – it is not possible to operate the equipment with fewer people. Because of this crewing requirement, a company must spend a certain minimum amount for direct labor personnel, irrespective of the actual quantity of items manufactured. The resulting direct labor budget, known as the *crewing method*, is quite simple. Just budget for the number of people needed to staff the production area, which tends to remain fixed within a certain range of production volumes. The following example illustrates the concept.

EXAMPLE

Milagro Corporation determines the fixed labor cost needed to crew an entire production line, and then makes adjustments to the budget for those periods in which they expect production volumes to require the use of staff overtime. It uses this method with its titanium coffee grinder production line. This production line is staffed by eight people, and can produce 1,000 grinders per quarter with no overtime. The company expects to require additional production during the second quarter that will require the addition of two temporary workers to the production line. There are also plans for a 6% pay raise at the beginning of the fourth quarter. The direct labor budget for this production line is:

	Quarter 1	Quarter 2	Quarter 3	Quarter 4
Coffee grinder line:				
Staffing headcount	8	10	8	8
× Quarterly pay per person	$10,400	$10,400	$10,400	$11,024
= Total direct labor cost	$83,200	$104,000	$83,200	$88,192

The Manufacturing Overhead Budget

The manufacturing overhead budget contains all manufacturing costs other than the costs of direct materials and direct labor. Expenses normally considered part of manufacturing overhead include:
- Depreciation

- Facilities maintenance
- Factory rent
- Factory utilities
- Indirect materials, such as supplies
- Insurance on the factory and inventory
- Materials management staff compensation
- Personal property taxes on manufacturing equipment
- Production employee fringe benefits
- Production employee payroll taxes
- Production supervisor compensation
- Quality assurance staff compensation

The information in the manufacturing overhead budget becomes part of the cost of goods sold line item in the master budget.

EXAMPLE

Milagro Corporation owns a division that produces coffee beanery equipment for third world countries. Milagro budgets all raw materials and direct labor in the direct materials budget and direct labor budget, respectively. Its manufacturing overhead costs are stated in the manufacturing overhead budget as follows:

	Quarter 1	Quarter 2	Quarter 3	Quarter 4
Production management salaries	$142,000	$143,000	$144,000	$145,000
Management payroll taxes	10,000	10,000	11,000	11,000
Depreciation	27,000	27,000	29,000	29,000
Facility maintenance	8,000	7,000	10,000	9,000
Rent	32,000	32,000	32,000	34,000
Personal property taxes	6,000	5,000	7,000	6,000
Quality assurance expenses	3,000	3,000	3,000	3,000
Utilities	10,000	10,000	10,000	12,000
Total manufacturing overhead	$238,000	$237,000	$236,000	$237,000

The production management salaries line item contains the wages paid to the manufacturing supervisors, the purchasing staff, and production planning staff, and gradually increases over time to reflect changes in pay rates. The depreciation expense is relatively fixed, though there is an increase in the third quarter that reflects the purchase of new equipment. Both the freight and supplies expenses are closely linked to actual production volume, and so their amounts fluctuate in conjunction with planned production levels. The rent expense is a fixed cost, but does increase in the fourth quarter to reflect a scheduled rent increase.

A step cost is a cost that does not change steadily, but rather at discrete points. Thus, it is a fixed cost within certain boundaries, outside of which it will change. Several of the larger expense line items in the manufacturing overhead budget are step costs, so they tend to be incurred when a certain production volume is reached, and then stay approximately the same until production volumes change to a significant extent.

This means that some line items can be safely copied from the actual expenditures in the preceding year with only minor changes. For example, if the current production level requires a second shift, and a production supervisor for that shift, then the manufacturing overhead budget for the next year should include the salary of that supervisor as long as there is going to be a second shift. Examples of situations giving rise to step costs are:

- *Additional production line*. If an entire production line is added, expect to incur step costs for all supporting staff, including materials management, supervision, and quality assurance personnel. There will also likely be an increase in the cost of utilities.
- *Additional shift*. If the facility is to be kept open for a second or third shift, expect to incur step costs for additional supervisors, as well as increased utility costs to power the facility during the extra time period.

Other expenses in this budget will require more analysis than the step costs just described. In particular, expenditures for the maintenance of machines and buildings can vary over time, depending upon the age of the assets being maintained and the need for large maintenance overhauls from time to time. For example, the expenditure for machinery maintenance may have been $100,000 in the preceding year, but can now be dropped to $50,000 in the new budget period because the company has replaced much of the equipment that had been requiring the bulk of the maintenance.

It is very difficult to run a facility at close to 100% of capacity. In this situation, equipment tends to break down more frequently, so a high utilization level requires additional overhead expenditures for parts, supplies, and maintenance labor.

The Sales and Marketing Budget

Selling expenses are those costs incurred to demonstrate products to customers and obtain orders from them, while marketing expenses involve the positioning, placement, and advertising of a company's products and services. More specifically, the following expenses fall within the general category of sales and marketing expenses:

- *Sales compensation*. This is the cost of paying base salaries, wages, bonuses, and commissions to the sales staff.
- *Other compensation*. This is the cost of the salaries and wages paid primarily to the marketing staff.
- *Order entry compensation*. This is the wages paid to the order entry staff and its management.
- *Advertising and promotions*. This is the set of activities managed by the marketing staff, and may include print advertising, Internet advertising, radio and television advertisements, billboards, coupons, catalogs, direct mail solicitations, one-time promotions, samples, and so forth.
- *Research*. This covers the expenses incurred by the marketing department to discover the optimal ways to promote products and services.

- *Office expenses.* These are the usual expenses incurred to run an office, including rent, utilities, and supplies.

Depending on the size of the department, it may be necessary to further subdivide the preceding expenses by functional area within the department. Specifically, consider separately tracking the performance of the following areas:
- Direct selling to customers
- Sales promotions
- Market research
- Customer service
- Customer warranties
- Selling activities by region

The most common type of sales and marketing budget is one that itemizes expenses by type. This is a simple design that shows budgeted compensation, promotions, travel, office expenses, and so forth. An example of this budget format follows:

Sales and Marketing Budget by Expense Type

Expense Type	Quarter 1	Quarter 2	Quarter 3	Quarter 4	Total
Salaries and wages	$270,000	$275,000	$320,000	$380,000	$1,245,000
Commissions	10,000	70,000	120,000	140,000	340,000
Payroll taxes	22,000	27,000	35,000	41,000	125,000
Promotions	0	50,000	85,000	42,000	177,000
Advertising	20,000	22,000	22,000	28,000	92,000
Research	0	0	35,000	0	35,000
Travel and entertainment	40,000	20,000	80,000	70,000	210,000
Office expenses	15,000	15,000	21,000	21,000	72,000
Other	5,000	5,000	5,000	5,000	20,000
Totals	$382,000	$484,000	$723,000	$727,000	$2,316,000

Though the budget format by expense type is the most common, it also tends to hide what may be very important information at the sales region and customer level. Ideally, your primary sales and marketing budget should be by expense type, with additional budgeting at the territory and customer levels if you feel that the additional amount of budgeting investigation creates valuable information.

If a company is organized by sales territory, recast the sales and marketing budget to determine the projected level of expenditures by territory. This is particularly important if most of the sales staff is assigned to specific territories, since this means that most of the cost structure of the company is oriented toward the territory format. You can then match territory gross margins with territory sales and marketing costs to determine earnings by territory. A typical format for such a budget is:

Sales and Marketing Budget by Territory

Sales Territory	Quarter 1	Quarter 2	Quarter 3	Quarter 4	Total
Department overhead	$250,000	$255,000	$255,000	$260,000	$1,020,000
Northeast region					
Compensation	400,000	410,000	430,000	450,000	1,690,000
Promotions	65,000	0	75,000	0	140,000
Travel	23,000	23,000	25,000	25,000	96,000
Other	18,000	19,000	19,000	19,000	75,000
Subtotal	$506,000	$452,000	$549,000	$494,000	$2,001,000
North central region					
Compensation	450,000	600,000	620,000	630,000	2,300,000
Promotions	75,000	0	80,000	0	155,000
Travel	31,000	33,000	35,000	39,000	138,000
Other	20,000	24,000	26,000	26,000	96,000
Subtotal	$576,000	$657,000	$761,000	$695,000	$2,689,000
Totals	$1,332,000	$1,364,000	$1,565,000	$1,449,000	$5,710,000

Diminishing Returns Analysis

A company will find that, after it achieves a certain amount of sales volume, the cost of generating additional sales goes up. This is caused by a variety of factors, such as having to offer more product features, ship products into more distant sales regions, increase warranty coverage, and so forth. Thus, the cost of obtaining each incremental sale will eventually reach the point where there is no further profit to be gained.

The concept of diminishing returns analysis is a useful one for the sales manager, since he or she should realize that it requires a gradual proportional increase in the sales and marketing budget over time in order to continue to increase sales. You cannot simply assume that the costs incurred in the preceding year to generate a certain sales volume can be applied to the next tranche of projected sales growth.

The concept of diminishing returns is difficult to calculate precisely, since it can appear in varying degrees throughout the budget. Here are some areas to be aware of:

- *Incremental sales staff.* If you add a sales person to an existing sales territory, it is likely that the existing sales staff is already handling the easiest sales, which means that the new hire will have to work harder to gain a smaller amount of sales than the average salesperson. You can estimate this reduced amount and build it into the budget.
- *Incremental advertising.* If you launch a new advertising campaign designed to bring in new customers, does the campaign target a smaller group than had been the case with previous campaigns, or is the targeted group one with less income to spend? Has research shown that increasing amounts of advertising result in incrementally fewer sales? If so, is there an optimal

474

advertising expenditure level beyond which the return on funds expended declines?

- *Incremental region.* When you add a new geographic area, consider how the new region varies from the company's existing sales territories. If it has a less dense population, it may be more expensive to contact them regarding a sale. If there is entrenched competition, expect a lower market share than normal. If products must be converted for use in a different language, how does the cost of doing so alter the product profit?
- *Incremental product.* If you add a product to an existing product line, will the new addition cannibalize the sales of other products in the product line?
- *Incremental sales channel.* When you add a new sales channel, does it cannibalize the sales of an existing channel? What is the cost of the infra- structure required to maintain the new channel? Will the new channel dam- age the company's relations with distributors or retailers?

This discussion does not mean that the sales manager should not push for continual sales growth, only that a detailed analysis is needed to clarify the diminishing returns that will be generated from the increased sales, and to ensure that those returns are noted in the budget.

The Research and Development Budget

The amount of funds to allocate to the research and development (R&D) budget can be an extraordinarily difficult discussion, for there is no correct answer – a small amount carefully invested can have an enormous payback, while a large investment can be frittered away among a variety of ho-hum projects. Still, there are several ways to generate a general estimate of how much funding to assign to R&D. They are:

- *Historical.* If a certain funding level has worked for the company in the past, then consider using it again – adjusted for inflation.
- *Industry benchmark.* If the industry as a whole spends a certain proportion of sales on R&D, this at least gives an indication of the level of spending required to compete over the long term. Better yet, isolate the same metric for just the top-performing competitors, since their level of R&D spending is more likely to be your target.
- *Best in class benchmark.* Look outside of the industry for companies that do a very good job on their R&D, and match their spending level as a propor- tion of sales. This is a particularly important approach when your company is in a moribund industry where R&D spending is minimal, and you want to take a different approach.
- *Percent of cash flow.* Management may be willing to spend a certain proportion of its available cash on R&D on an ongoing basis, irrespective of what competitors are spending. This is a much better approach than appor- tioning a percentage of net income to R&D, since net income does not nec-

essarily equate to cash flow, and a commitment to spend a certain proportion of net income could lead to a cash shortage.

No matter what method is used to derive the appropriate funding level, senior management should settle upon the *minimum* R&D funding level that must be maintained over the long term in order to remain competitive in the industry, and be sure never to drop below that figure.

The R&D budget is typically comprised of the following expense categories:

- *Compensation and benefits*. Compensation tends to be the largest R&D expenditure.
- *Contract services*. It is common to shift some research work to independent laboratories that specialize in particular types of work. In some cases, virtually all R&D work may be contracted out, in which case this becomes the largest R&D expenditure category.
- *Consumable supplies*. In some types of R&D, the staff may use (or destroy) a significant amount of supplies as part of its work. Depending on the situation, this can be a major expense.
- *Office expenses*. These are the standard operational costs of running a department, such as utilities and office rent.
- *Depreciation on equipment*. There will be recurring depreciation charges for any fixed assets used by the R&D staff.
- *Amortization of acquired intangible assets*. If a company has acquired a patent or other intangible asset from another entity, it will likely have to amortize the asset over its useful life.

There are three general formats you can use to construct an R&D budget. They are:

- *Integrated into engineering department*. If the amount of funds expended on R&D is minor, you do not have to budget for it separately. Instead, include it within the budget for the engineering department, either aggregated into a single line item or spread among the various expense line items attributable to that department.
- *Treated as a separate department*. If the expenditures associated with specific projects are relatively minor, and the R&D staff is occupied with several projects at the same time, it may be sufficient to simply aggregate all expenses into a department-level budget for R&D, and not attempt to further assign expenses to specific projects.
- *Treated as projects within a department*. If there are significant expenditures that can be traced to individual projects, consider creating an R&D budget that clearly shows which projects are expected to consume funds.

The following two examples show the budget reporting format for treating R&D as a separate department with no further subdivision by project, and for revealing projects within the department.

Sample R&D Budget at the Department Level

	Quarter 1	Quarter 2	Quarter 3	Quarter 4	Total
Compensation	$150,000	$150,000	$160,000	$165,000	$625,000
Contract services	320,000	180,000	450,000	250,000	1,200,000
Consumable supplies	25,000	25,000	25,000	25,000	100,000
Office expenses	8,000	8,000	9,000	9,000	34,000
Depreciation	10,000	10,000	10,000	10,000	40,000
Amortization	15,000	15,000	15,000	15,000	60,000
Totals	$528,000	$388,000	$669,000	$474,000	$2,059,000

Sample R&D Budget at the Project Level

	Quarter 1	Quarter 2	Quarter 3	Quarter 4	Total
Department overhead	$23,000	$24,000	$24,000	$26,000	$97,000
Project Alpha					
Compensation	82,000	82,000	84,000	84,000	332,000
Contract services	65,000	65,000	75,000	70,000	275,000
Other	15,000	18,000	18,000	20,000	71,000
Project subtotal	162,000	165,000	177,000	174,000	678,000
Project Beta					
Compensation	40,000	60,000	60,000	60,000	220,000
Contract services	35,000	30,000	30,000	30,000	125,000
Other	5,000	7,000	7,000	10,000	29,000
Project subtotal	80,000	97,000	97,000	100,000	374,000
Totals	$265,000	$286,000	$298,000	$300,000	$1,149,000

Note in the second example that not all expenses could be assigned to a specific project, so they were instead listed separately from the projects under the "department overhead" designation.

The Administration Budget

The administration budget contains all of the expenses that are not directly involved in the provision of products or services to customers, or their sale to customers. This usually means that the following departments are included in the administration budget:

Accounting	Human resources	Public relations
Corporate	Information technology	Risk management (insurance)
Facilities	Internal auditing	Treasury
	Legal	

In a larger company, there may be individual budgets for each of these departments, rather than an administration department.

The expense line items included in the administration budget generally include the following:

Audit fees	Director fees	Payroll taxes
Bank fees	Dues and subscriptions	Property taxes
Charitable contributions	Employee benefits	Rent
Compensation	Insurance	Supplies
Consulting fees	Legal fees	Travel and entertainment
Depreciation		Utilities

The information in the administration budget is not directly derived from any other budgets. Instead, managers use the general level of corporate activity to determine the appropriate amount of expenditure. When creating this budget, consider the following issues:

- *Compensation.* The largest item in this budget is usually employee compensation, so pay particular attention to the formulation of this amount and test it for reasonableness.
- *Historical basis.* The amounts in this budget are frequently carried forward from actual results in the preceding year. This may be reasonable, but some costs may disappear due to the termination of a contract, or increase due to contractually scheduled price increases.
- *Step costs.* Determine when any step costs may be incurred, such as additional staff to support reporting requirements when a company goes public, and incorporate them into the budget.
- *Zero base analysis.* It may be useful to occasionally re-create the administration budget from the ground up, justifying the need for each expense. This is a time-consuming process, but may uncover a few expense items that can be eliminated.

The following example illustrates the basic layout of an administration budget.

EXAMPLE

Milagro Corporation compiles the following administration budget, which is organized by expense line item:

	Quarter 1	Quarter 2	Quarter 3	Quarter 4
Audit fees	$35,000	$0	$0	$0
Bank fees	500	500	500	500
Insurance	5,000	5,500	6,000	6,000
Payroll taxes	10,000	10,500	10,500	11,000
Property taxes	0	25,000	0	0
Rent	11,000	11,000	11,000	14,000
Salaries	140,000	142,000	144,000	146,000
Supplies	2,000	2,000	2,000	2,000
Travel and entertainment	4,500	8,000	4,000	4,000
Utilities	2,500	3,000	3,000	4,000
Other expenses	1,500	1,500	1,500	2,000
Total expenses	$212,000	$209,000	$182,500	$189,500

The CEO of Milagro likes to restate the administration budget by department, so that he can assign responsibility for expenditures to the managers of those departments. This results in the following variation on the same budget:

	Quarter 1	Quarter 2	Quarter 3	Quarter 4
Accounting department	$130,500	$102,500	$102,000	$108,000
Corporate department	30,000	30,000	30,000	30,000
Human resources department	19,500	19,500	18,000	19,000
IT department	25,000	25,000	25,000	25,000
Treasury department	7,000	7,000	7,500	7,500
Unassigned expenses	0	25,000	0	0
Total expenses	$212,000	$209,000	$182,500	$189,500

The reconfigured administration budget contains an "unassigned expenses" line item for property taxes, since management does not believe that expense is specifically controllable by any of the administrative departments.

The preceding example reveals a common characteristic of most line items in the administration budget, which is that most costs are fixed over the short term, and so only vary slightly from period to period. The exceptions are pay increases and scheduled events, such as audits. Otherwise, the main reason for a sudden change in an administrative expense is a step cost, such as increasing the headcount.

The Compensation Budget

The key goals of a compensation budget are to itemize the pay rates of all employees, the dates on which you expect to alter their pay, and all associated payroll taxes. This budget is usually contained within the various departmental budgets. We describe it separately here, because it involves several unique budgeting issues.

The compensation budget in the following example separates the calculation of compensation, social security taxes, Medicare taxes, and federal unemployment taxes. The separate calculation of these items is the only way to achieve a reasonable level of accuracy in the calculation of payroll taxes, since there are different tax rates and wage caps associated with each of the taxes. The pertinent information related to each of the indicated payroll taxes is:

Tax Type	Tax Rate	2014 Wage Cap
Social security	6.20%	$117,000
Medicare	1.45%	No cap
Federal unemployment	0.80%	$7,000

In a lower-wage environment, there may be few employees whose pay exceeds the social security wage cap, which makes the social security tax budget quite simple to calculate. However, in situations where compensation levels are quite high, expect to meet social security wage caps within the first two or three quarters of the year.

Given the size of the social security match paid by employers, it is especially important to budget for the correct amount of tax; otherwise, the compensation budget could be inaccurate by a significant amount.

The simplest of the tax calculations is for the Medicare tax, since there is no wage cap for it. We have presented its calculation in the example as a table in which we calculate it for each individual employee. However, given the lack of a wage cap, you can more easily create a budget for it with a single line item that multiplies total compensation in every budget period by the Medicare tax rate.

Given the size of the social security and Medicare expenses, the paltry amount of the federal unemployment tax may seem like an afterthought. However, since it is based on a very low wage cap, nearly all of the expense is incurred in the first calendar quarter of each year, where it represents a modest expense bump. Some companies create a separate budget schedule for this expense, just to ensure that the correct amount is included in the first quarter of each year. Others find the cost to be so insignificant that they do not track it.

These concepts are noted in the following example, where we present separate budgets for base pay, social security, Medicare, and federal unemployment taxes, and then aggregate them into a master compensation budget.

EXAMPLE

Milagro Corporation is starting up a small group that will deal with research concerning the flavor of Kenyan and Ethiopian coffee beans. The company decides to create a separate compensation budget for the group, which includes five employees. The compensation budget is as follows, with quarters in which pay raises are scheduled being highlighted. Note that the annual salary is stated in each calendar quarter.

Base Pay Budget

	Quarter 1	Quarter 2	Quarter 3	Quarter 4
Erskin, Donald	$75,000	$75,000	$79,500	$79,500
Fells, Arnold	45,000	46,250	46,250	46,250
Gainsborough, Amy	88,000	88,000	88,000	91,500
Harmon, Debra	68,500	68,500	70,000	70,000
Illescu, Adriana	125,000	125,000	125,000	125,000
Annual compensation	$401,500	$402,750	$408,750	$412,250
Quarterly compensation	$100,375	$100,688	$102,188	$103,063

Social Security Budget (6.2% tax, $117,000 wage cap)

	Quarter 1	Quarter 2	Quarter 3	Quarter 4
Erskin, Donald	$1,163	$1,163	$1,232	$1,232
Fells, Arnold	698	717	717	717
Gaisborough, Amy	1,364	1,364	1,364	1,418
Harmon, Debra	1,062	1,062	1,085	1,085
Illescu, Adriana	1,938	1,938	1,938	1,440
Totals	$6,225	$6,244	$6,336	$5,892

Medicare Budget (1.45% tax, no wage cap)

	Quarter 1	Quarter 2	Quarter 3	Quarter 4
Erskin, Donald	$272	$272	$288	$288
Fells, Arnold	163	168	168	168
Gaisborough, Amy	319	319	319	332
Harmon, Debra	248	248	254	254
Illescu, Adriana	453	453	453	453
Totals	$1,455	$1,460	$1,482	$1,495

Federal Unemployment Tax Budget (0.8% tax, $7,000 wage cap)

	Quarter 1	Quarter 2	Quarter 3	Quarter 4
Erskin, Donald	$56	$0	$0	$0
Fells, Arnold	56	0	0	0
Gaisborough, Amy	56	0	0	0
Harmon, Debra	56	0	0	0
Illescu, Adriana	56	0	0	0
Totals	$280	$0	$0	$0

Milagro then shifts the summary totals from each of the preceding tables into a master compensation budget, as follows:

Master Compensation Budget

	Quarter 1	Quarter 2	Quarter 3	Quarter 4
Total base pay	$100,375	$100,688	$102,188	$103,063
Total social security	6,225	6,244	6,336	5,892
Total Medicare	1,455	1,460	1,482	1,495
Total unemployment	280	0	0	0
Grand totals	$108,335	$108,392	$110,006	$110,450

In the preceding example, compensation is shown in each quarter on an annualized basis, since it is easier to review the budget for errors when the information is presented in this manner. The information is then stepped down to a quarterly basis, which is used to calculate payroll taxes.

Overtime is difficult to predict at the level of an individual employee, but can be estimated at a more aggregated level. It is easiest to use the historical proportion of overtime hours, adjusted for expectations in the budget period. This means that you can multiply an overtime percentage by the aggregate amount of employee compensation to derive the amount of budgeted overtime pay. The following example illustrates the concept.

EXAMPLE

Milagro Corporation operates a production line for which the sales season is November through January. Milagro prefers to deactivate the production line for the first half of the calendar year and then run it with substantial employee overtime during the third quarter and a portion of the fourth quarter of the year. This results in the following overtime budget, which also assumes that a production crew is still working during the first half of the year – they just happen to be working on other production lines.

	Quarter 1	Quarter 2	Quarter 3	Quarter 4
Total wage expense	$250,000	$255,000	$270,000	$240,000
Overtime percentage	0%	2%	28%	12%
Overtime pay	$0	$5,100	$75,600	$28,800
Social security for overtime pay	$0	$316	$4,687	$1,786
Medicare for overtime pay	0	$74	$1,096	$418
Total overtime compensation	$0	$390	$5,783	$2,204

There is no calculation of the federal unemployment tax in the overtime budget, since that amount has such a low wage cap that the maximum amount would already have been included in the compensation budget.

The trouble with the overtime calculation format just presented is that it does not account for the social security wage cap, which is calculated at the level of the individual employee. It is easiest to simply assume that the wage cap is never reached, which may result in some excess amount of social security tax being budgeted. Realistically, few employees who are paid on an hourly basis will exceed the wage cap, so this should be a minor issue for most companies.

The Budgeted Income Statement

The core of the master budget is the budgeted income statement. It is derived from nearly all of the budgets that we have already discussed, and looks quite a bit like a standard income statement. This is a sufficient summarization of the budget for many companies, because they are primarily concerned with *financial performance*. However, some companies may still have an interest in their projected *financial position* (especially cash), which is contained in the balance sheet. Since the balance sheet is more difficult to derive than the income statement, they may be content to use a rough calculation of ending cash position whose components are mostly derived from information already in the budget. The following sample income statement contains this rough estimation of the ending cash balance in each period:

Sample Budgeted Income Statement

	Quarter 1	Quarter 2	Quarter 3	Quarter 4
Revenue	$2,200,000	$2,425,000	$2,500,000	$2,545,000
Cost of goods sold:				
Direct labor expense	220,000	253,000	253,000	253,000
Direct materials expense	767,000	838,000	831,000	840,000
Manufacturing overhead	293,000	293,000	309,000	310,000
Total cost of goods sold	1,280,000	1,384,000	1,393,000	1,403,000
Gross margin	$920,000	$1,041,000	$1,107,000	$1,142,000
Sales and marketing	315,000	351,000	374,000	339,000
Administration	453,500	452,500	435,000	447,000
Research and development	50,000	52,000	54,000	55,500
Profits before taxes	$101,500	$185,500	$244,000	$300,500
Income taxes	35,500	65,000	85,500	105,000
Profits after taxes	$66,000	$120,500	$158,500	$195,500
Cash flow:				
Beginning cash	$50,000	-$52,500	$77,500	$7,000
+ Net profit	66,000	120,500	158,500	195,500
+ Depreciation	19,500	17,500	18,000	18,000
- Capital purchases	-38,000	-8,000	-47,000	-28,000
- Dividends	-150,000	0	-200,000	0
Ending cash	-$52,500	$77,500	$7,000	$192,500

The calculation of ending cash is appended to the budgeted income statement because it is partly derived from the net income figure located directly above it in the budget. Also, if a company does not intend to create a balance sheet, it is practical to include a cash calculation on the same page as the income statement.

The trouble with the ending cash measurement presented in the sample is that it is not complete. It does not incorporate any timing delays for when cash may be received or issued, and it also does not factor in the impact of changes in working capital. Thus, it can present inaccurate estimates of cash flow. For a more detailed derivation of ending cash, we need a balance sheet. The compilation of that document is discussed in the next section.

The Budgeted Balance Sheet

The balance sheet is difficult to derive as part of the budgeting process, because little of the information derived through the budgeting process is designed for it. Instead, you need to make a variety of estimates to approximate the amounts of various asset and liability line items as of the end of each budgeted reporting period. The key elements of the balance sheet that require estimation are accounts receivable, inventory, fixed assets, and accounts payable. We will address the derivation of these items below.

Accounts Receivable

Accounts receivable is the amount of sales made on credit that have not yet been paid by customers. It is closely correlated with sales, with a delay measured using days sales outstanding (DSO). DSO is calculated as:

$$\frac{\text{Accounts receivable}}{\text{Annual sales} \div 365 \text{ days}}$$

You then apply the DSO figure to projected credit sales during the budget period to determine the amount of accounts receivable outstanding at any given time.

EXAMPLE

Milagro Corporation has a division whose annual sales are $10 million. Its accounts receivable balance at the end of the most recent month was $1,400,000. Its DSO is calculated as:

$$\frac{\$1,400,000 \text{ accounts receivable}}{\$10,000,000 \text{ annual sales} \div 365 \text{ days}}$$

$$= 51 \text{ days sales outstanding}$$

Thus, it takes an average of 51 days for Milagro to collect an account receivable. In its balance sheet budget, Milagro would record as accounts receivable the current month's sales plus 21/30ths of the sales budgeted in the immediately preceding month. Thus, Milagro's budgeted receivables would be calculated as follows for a four-month sample period:

	December*	January	February	March
Credit sales	$790,000	$810,000	$815,000	$840,000
Receivables for month	--	810,000	815,000	840,000
Receivables from prior month	--	553,000	567,000	571,000
Total receivables in balance sheet	--	$1,363,000	$1,382,000	$1,411,000

* Prior year

An alternative approach for calculating the amount of accounts receivable is to calculate the percentage of credit sales that are collected within the month of sales and then within each of the next 30-day time buckets, and apply these layers of collections to a calculation of the ending accounts receivable in each budget period. The following example illustrates the concept.

EXAMPLE

Milagro Corporation's accountant decides to use an alternative method for deriving the ending accounts receivable balance for the division described in the preceding example. The accountant finds that, historically, the following percentages of credit sales are paid within the stated time periods:

	Percent Paid	Percent Unpaid
In month of sale	10%	90%
In following month	65%	25%
In 2nd month	18%	7%
In 3rd month	5%	2%
In 4th month	2%	0%
Total	100%	

The accountant then uses the following table to derive the ending accounts receivable balance for the month of January, which is part of the budget period. The information from the preceding three months is needed to derive the ending accounts receivable balance in January.

	October (prior year)	November (prior year)	December (prior year)	January
Credit sales	$815,000	$820,000	$790,000	$810,000
90% of January sales				729,000
25% of December sales				198,000
7% of November sales				57,000
2% of October sales				16,000
Total ending accounts receivable				$1,000,000

A truly detailed model would assume an even longer collection period for some receivables, which may extend for twice the number of months shown in the model. If you choose to use this method, the increased accuracy from adding more months to the model does not appreciably improve the accuracy of the ending accounts receivable figure. Thus, restrict the accounts receivable layering to no more than three or four months.

The receivables layering method is clearly more labor intensive than the DSO method, though it may result in slightly more accurate results. In the interests of modeling efficiency, we prefer the DSO method. It requires much less space in the budget model, is easy to understand, and produces reasonably accurate results.

Inventory

There should be a relatively constant relationship between the level of sales and the amount of inventory on hand. Thus, if you can calculate the historical number of days of inventory on hand and then match it against the budgeted amount of cost of goods sold through the budget period, you can estimate the amount of inventory that should be on hand at the end of each budget period. The calculation of the days of inventory on hand is:

Budgeting

Inventory
Annual cost of goods sold ÷ 365 days

The estimation concept is shown in the following example.

EXAMPLE

Milagro Corporation has a division that manufactures industrial-grade coffee bean roasters. It maintains a substantial amount of raw materials and finished goods. The company calculates the days of inventory on hand for the preceding quarter as follows:

$1,000,000 ending inventory
$1,875,000 quarterly cost of goods sold ÷ 91 days

= 49 days of inventory on hand

Milagro expects that the division will continue to have roughly the same proportion of inventory to sales throughout the budget period, so it uses the same days of inventory on hand calculation to derive the ending inventory for each budget period as follows:

	Quarter 1	Quarter 2	Quarter 3	Quarter 4
Cost of goods sold (quarterly)	$1,875,000	$2,000,000	$2,100,000	$1,900,000
Cost of goods sold (monthly)	625,000	667,000	700,000	633,000
Days of inventory assumption	49 days	49 days	49 days	49 days
Ending inventory*	$1,021,000	$1,089,000	$1,143,000	$1,034,000

* Calculated as monthly cost of goods sold × (49 days ÷ 30 days)

The calculation reduces the quarterly cost of goods sold to a monthly figure, so that it can more easily be compared to the days of inventory on hand.

Fixed Assets

The amount and timing of expenditures for fixed assets come from the capital budgeting process (see the Capital Budgeting chapter), and are easily transferred into a fixed asset table that can be used as a source document for the budgeted balance sheet. Further, it may be useful to include in the schedule a standard amount of capital expenditures for each new employee hired; this typically includes the cost of office furniture and computer equipment. Finally, there will always be unforeseen asset purchases, so be sure to reserve some funds for them.

In addition, you can add to the table a calculation of the depreciation associated with newly-acquired assets. Also include an estimate of the depreciation associated with *existing* assets, which you can easily derive either from your fixed asset tracking spreadsheet or software. This information is used in the budgeted income statement.

The following example illustrates the concepts of scheduling fixed assets and depreciation.

EXAMPLE

Milagro Corporation plans to hire 10 administrative staff into one of its divisions during the budget year, and also plans to buy a variety of fixed assets. The following schedule itemizes the major types of fixed assets and the timing of their acquisition. It also includes a summary of the depreciation for both the existing and to-be-acquired assets.

	Quarter 1	Quarter 2	Quarter 3	Quarter 4
Fixed asset purchases:				
Furniture and fixtures	$28,000	$0	$0	$32,000
Office equipment	0	40,000	0	0
Production equipment	100,000	25,000	80,000	0
Vehicles	32,000	0	32,000	0
Unspecified purchases	15,000	15,000	15,000	15,000
Subtotal	$175,000	$80,000	$127,000	$47,000
Purchases for new hires:				
Headcount additions	3	2	1	4
$6,000 × New hires	$18,000	$12,000	$6,000	$24,000
Total fixed asset purchases	$193,000	$92,000	$133,000	$71,000
Depreciation on new purchases:				
Furniture and fixtures (7 year)	$1,000	$1,000	$1,000	$2,142
Office equipment (5 year)	0	2,000	2,000	2,000
Production equipment (10 year)	2,500	3,125	5,125	5,125
Vehicles (5 year)	1,600	1,600	3,200	3,200
Unspecified purchases (5 year)	750	1,500	2,250	3,000
Subtotal	$5,850	$9,225	$13,575	$15,467
Depreciation on existing assets	108,000	107,500	105,000	99,500
Total depreciation	$113,850	$116,725	$118,575	$114,967

Accounts Payable

You can estimate accounts payable with a reasonable amount of precision, because there is usually a constant relationship between the level of credit purchases from suppliers and the amount of unpaid accounts payable. Thus, if you can calculate the days of accounts payable that are usually on hand, then you can relate it to the estimated amount of credit purchases per accounting period and derive the ending accounts payable balance. The formula for accounts payable days is:

$$\frac{\text{Accounts payable}}{\text{Annual credit purchases} \div 365}$$

The estimation concept is illustrated in the following example.

EXAMPLE

Milagro Corporation has a division whose annual purchases on credit in the past year were $4,250,000. Its average accounts payable balance during that period was $410,000. The calculation of its accounts payable days is:

$$\frac{\$410,000 \text{ accounts payable}}{\$4,250,000 \text{ annual credit purchases} \div 365}$$

$$= 35 \text{ accounts payable days}$$

Milagro expects that the division will continue to have roughly the same proportion of credit terms with its suppliers through the budget period, so it uses the same accounts payable days amount to derive the ending accounts payable for each budget period as follows:

	Quarter 1	Quarter 2	Quarter 3	Quarter 4
Purchases on credit (monthly)	$350,000	$380,000	$390,000	$400,000
Accounts payable days assumption	35 days	35 days	35 days	35 days
Ending accounts payable*	$408,000	$443,000	$455,000	$467,000

* Calculated as monthly purchases on credit × (35 days ÷ 30 days)

The problem with the calculation of accounts payable is where to find the information about credit purchases. To calculate the amount of credit purchases, start with the total expenses for the measurement period and subtract from it all payroll and payroll tax expenses, as well as depreciation and amortization. There are other adjusting factors, such as expense accruals and payments made in cash, but this simple calculation should approximate the amount of purchases on credit.

Additional Estimation Elements

There are a few other line items in the balance sheet that require estimation for the budget period. These items are usually adjusted manually, rather than through the use of any formulas. They are:

- *Prepaid expenses.* This line item includes expenses that were paid in advance, and which therefore may be charged to expense at some point during or after the budget period. Examples of prepaid expenses are prepaid rent and insurance. These items may not change in proportion to the level of general corporate activity, so it is best to track them on a separate spreadsheet and manually determine when there will be additions to and deletions from the account.
- *Other assets.* There are likely to be a smorgasbord of stray assets on a company's books that are aggregated into this account. Examples of other assets are rent deposits, payroll advances, and accounts receivable from company officers. As was the case with prepaid expenses, these items may

not change in proportion to the level of corporate activity, so track them separately and manually adjust the budget for any changes in them.

- *Income taxes payable.* If a company is earning a taxable profit, then it must make estimated tax payments on the 15th days of April, June, September, and December. You can either schedule these payments to equal the tax paid in the previous year, or a proportion of the actual tax liability in the budget year. Budgeting for this liability based on the tax paid in the previous year is quite simple. If you choose to instead budget for a liability equal to a proportion of the actual tax liability in the budget year, then use the effective tax rate expected for the entire year.

  If you are budgeting for this liability based on the net income in the budget year, it can be difficult to estimate. You may be using accelerated depreciation for the calculation of taxable income, as well as other deferred tax recognition strategies that cause a difference between taxable and actual net income. If such is the case, track these differences in a supporting budget schedule.

- *Accrued liabilities.* There may be a variety of accrued liabilities, such as unpaid vacation time, unpaid wages, and unpaid property taxes. In some cases, such as property taxes, the liability is unlikely to vary unless the company alters its property ownership, and so can be safely extended through the budget period with no alterations. In other cases, such as unpaid vacation time and unpaid wages, there is a direct correlation between the general level of corporate activity (such as headcount) and the amount of the liability. In these cases, use a formula to adjust the liability based on the appropriate underlying measure of activity.

- *Notes payable.* This can encompass loans and leases. Most of these items are on fixed repayment schedules, so a simple repayment table is usually sufficient for tracking the gradual reduction of notes payable. Also, the amount of each periodic debt repayment should be deducted from the amount of cash on hand. Additions to the notes payable line are addressed in the financing budget.

- *Equity.* The equity section of the balance sheet is composed of a beginning balance that is rolled forward from the previous period, a retained earnings balance into which you incorporate any gains and losses as the budget period progresses over time, and various equity-related financing issues that are addressed in the financing budget.

The Cash Line Item

After filling in all other parts of the balance sheet, the cash line item becomes the "plug" entry to make the statement balance. Just because you enter an amount in the cash line item does not mean that the company will necessarily generate that amount of cash. An early iteration of a budgeted balance sheet has a strange way of revealing an astonishing surplus of cash! Instead, once you have created the initial version of the balance sheet, test it to see if all of the line items are reasonable. Use the following techniques to do so:

- *Growth impact.* If the company is planning on substantial growth, this means that the investment in accounts receivable and inventory should grow significantly, which will consume cash. Conversely, if the company plans to shrink, it should be converting these same items into cash. Thus, if the proposed balance sheet appears to be retaining a consistent amount of working capital through the budget period, irrespective of the sales level, you probably need to revise the working capital line items.
- *Historical comparison.* Compare all line items in the proposed balance sheet to the same line items in the balance sheet for various periods in the preceding year. Are the numbers about the same, or are they approximately in the same proportions to each other? If not, investigate why there are differences.
- *Turnover analysis.* Compare the amount of accounts receivable, inventory, and accounts payable turnover in the proposed budget to the actual turnover ratios for these items in the preceding year. Unless you are making significant structural changes in the business, it is likely that the same turnover ratios should apply to the budget period.

If you are satisfied that the budgeted balance sheet appears reasonable after these tests, then the cash line item may also be considered achievable.

The Financing Budget

Once a first draft of the budget has been prepared and a preliminary balance sheet constructed, you will have an idea of the cash requirements of the business, and can then construct a financing budget.

This budget addresses the need of a business for *more* cash. You can construct a financing budget that addresses this need in two ways:

- *Obtain a loan.* At a minimum, it is usually possible to obtain an asset-based loan (i.e., one that is backed by a company's accounts receivable and inventory). However, these loans are also limited to a proportion of those assets, and so may not be overly large. Other loans that are not tied to assets usually carry a substantially higher interest rate.
- *Sell stock.* If the existing shareholders are amenable, consider selling stock in the company to current or new investors. Unlike a loan, there is no obligation to pay the money back, so this addition to equity reduces the financial risk of the company. However, investors expect a high return on their investment through an increase in the value of the company or increased dividends.

In addition to these financing solutions, also consider going back into the main budget and making one or more of the following changes, thereby altering the amount of cash needed by the business:

- *Cost reduction*. There may be some parts of the business where expenses can be pruned in order to fund more activities elsewhere. Across-the-board reductions are usually a bad idea, since some parts of the business may already be running at a minimal expenditure level, and further reductions would cut into their performance.
- *Discretionary items*. If there are discretionary expenditures in the budget whose absence will not have an immediate impact on the business, consider reducing or eliminating them or changing the date on which you purchase them.
- *Dividends*. If there are dividends planned that have not yet been authorized by the board of directors, consider either reducing them or delaying the payment date.
- *Sales growth*. If the budgeted level of sales is creating a significant requirement for more working capital and capital expenditures, consider reducing the amount of planned growth to meet the amount of financing that you have available.
- *Sell assets*. If there is a strong need for cash that is driven by an excellent business opportunity, it may be time to sell off assets in lower-performing parts of the business and invest the funds in the new opportunity.

Once you have made all of the preceding adjustments, construct the financing budget. It should contain an itemization of the cash position as stated in the budgeted balance sheet, after which you itemize the various types of financing needed to ensure that the company maintains a positive cash balance at all times. In addition, there should be a section that derives from the balance sheet the total amount that the company can potentially borrow against its assets; this establishes an upper limit on the amount of borrowing. The following example illustrates the concept of the financing budget.

EXAMPLE

Milagro Corporation has completed a first draft of its budget, and finds that there are several cash shortfalls during the budget period. The accountant constructs the following financing budget to address the problem.

	Quarter 1	Quarter 2	Quarter 3	Quarter 4
Available asset base:				
Ending inventory	$1,200,000	$1,280,000	$1,310,000	$1,350,000
Ending trade receivables	1,800,000	1,850,000	1,920,000	1,980,000
Allowable inventory (60%)	720,000	768,000	786,000	810,000
Allowable receivables (80%)	1,440,000	1,480,000	1,536,000	1,584,000
Total borrowing base	$2,160,000	$2,248,000	$2,322,000	$2,394,000
Preliminary ending cash balance	-$320,000	-$480,000	-$600,000	-$680,000

Debt Funding:				
Beginning loan balance	$2,000,000			
Available debt*	160,000	88,000	74,000	72,000
Adjusted ending cash balance	-$160,000	-$232,000	-$278,000	-$286,000
Equity Funding:				
Stock issuance	400,000	0	0	0
Final ending cash balance	$240,000	$168,000	$122,000	$114,000

* Calculated as the total borrowing base minus existing debt

The financing budget reveals that Milagro has already used most of the debt available under its loan agreement, and is only able to incrementally borrow in each quarter as the amount of underlying assets gradually increases. To fund the remaining cash shortfall, Milagro plans to sell $400,000 of stock to investors in the first quarter. This not only provides enough cash to cover the projected shortfall, but also leaves a small residual cash buffer.

If the financing budget includes a provision for more debt, include a line item in the budgeted income statement to address the associated incremental increase in interest expense. This means that there is a feedback loop between the financing budget and the balance sheet from which it draws its beginning cash balance; your financing solutions may impact the beginning cash balance upon which the financing budget is based, which in turn may impact the amount of financing needed.

The Compiled Balance Sheet

The budgeted balance sheet is derived from the all of the preceding discussions in this section about the components of the balance sheet. The balance sheet should be compiled in two parts: a detailed compilation that contains a variety of calculations, and a summary-level version that is indistinguishable from a normal balance sheet. The following sample of a detailed balance sheet compilation includes a discussion of each line item. The numbers in the sample are irrelevant – we are only showing how the balance sheet is constructed.

Sample Detailed Balance Sheet Compilation

Line Item	Source	Amount
Assets		
Cash	The amount needed to equalize both sides of the balance sheet	$225,000
Accounts receivable	Based on sales by period and days receivables outstanding	450,000
Inventory	Based on cost of goods sold by period and days of inventory on hand	520,000
Prepaid expenses	Based on beginning balance and adjusted for specific changes	55,000
Fixed assets	Based on beginning balance and changes in the capital budget	1,490,000
Accumulated depreciation	Based on beginning balance and changes in the capital budget	-230,000

Line Item	Source	Amount
Other assets	Based on beginning balance and adjusted for specific changes	38,000
Total assets		$2,548,000
Liabilities		
Accounts payable	Based on credit purchases and days of accounts payable	$182,000
Accrued liabilities	Based on schedule of specific liabilities or based on corporate activity	99,000
Income taxes payable	Based on either the tax paid in the previous year or a proportion of the actual tax liability in the current year	75,000
Notes payable	Based on the beginning balance	720,000
- Debt repayments	Based on a schedule of required repayments	-120,000
+ New debt	From the financing budget	90,000
Total liabilities		$1,046,000
Equity		
Retained earnings	Based on the beginning balance	802,000
- Dividends	As per management instructions	-75,000
- Treasury stock purchases	As per management instructions	-50,000
+ Profit/loss	From the budgeted income statement	475,000
+ Stock sales	From the financing budget	350,000
Total equity		$1,502,000
Total liabilities and equity		$2,548,000

Summary

This chapter has addressed how to compile an annual budget, using a variety of supporting schedules to create a budgeted income statement and balance sheet. When creating this budget, be careful to examine how well the various elements of the budget support each other, and whether the budgeted outcome is a reasonable extension of how well the company has performed in the past. If not, recommend another iteration of the budget to correct these potential problem areas. If senior management instead elects to operate under the current budget version, it is likely that actual results will soon depart from budgeted expectations.

Despite the length of this chapter, it is actually a relatively brief treatment of the budgeting concept. For a more comprehensive view of budgeting, and also a discussion of how to operate without a budget, see the author's *Budgeting* book, which is available on the accountingtools.com website.

Chapter 27
Capital Budgeting

Introduction

Capital budgeting is a series of analysis steps used to evaluate whether a fixed asset should be purchased, usually including an analysis of the costs, related benefits, and impact on capacity levels of the prospective purchase. In this chapter, we will address a broad array of issues that you should consider when deciding whether to recommend the purchase of a fixed asset, as well as the lease versus buy decision, and post-acquisition auditing.

> **Related Podcast Episodes:** Episodes 45, 144, 145, and 147 of the Accounting Best Practices Podcast discuss throughput capital budgeting, evaluating capital budgeting proposals, capital budgeting with minimal cash, and net present value analysis, respectively. You can listen to them at: **accountingtools.com/podcasts** or **iTunes**

Overview of Capital Budgeting

The normal capital budgeting process is for the management team to request proposals to acquire fixed assets from all parts of the company. Managers respond by filling out a standard request form, outlining what they want to buy and how it will benefit the company. The financial analyst or accountant then assists in reviewing these proposals to determine which are worthy of an investment. Any proposals that are accepted are included in the annual budget, and will be purchased during the next budget year. Fixed assets purchased in this manner also require a certain number of approvals, with more approvals required by increasingly senior levels of management if the sums involved are substantial.

These proposals come from all over the company, and so are likely not related to each other in any way. Also, the number of proposals usually far exceeds the amount of funding available. Consequently, management needs a method for ranking the priority of projects, with the possible result that some proposals are not accepted at all. The traditional method for doing so is net present value (NPV) analysis, which focuses on picking proposals with the largest amount of discounted cash flows.

The trouble with NPV analysis is that it does not account for how an investment might impact the profit generated by the entire system of production; instead, it tends to favor the optimization of specific work centers, which may have no particular impact on overall profitability. Also, the results of NPV are based on future projections of cash flows, which may be wildly inaccurate. Managers may even tweak their cash flow estimates upward in order to gain project approval, when they know that actual cash flows are likely to be lower. Given these issues, we favor constraint analysis over NPV, though NPV is also discussed in this chapter.

A better method for judging capital budget proposals is constraint analysis, which focuses on how to maximize use of the bottleneck operation. The bottleneck operation is the most constricted operation in a company; if you want to improve the overall profitability of the company, concentrate all attention on management of that bottleneck. This has a profound impact on capital budgeting, since a proposal should have some favorable impact on that operation in order to be approved.

There are two scenarios under which certain project proposals may avoid any kind of bottleneck or cash flow analysis. The first is a legal requirement to install an item. The prime example is environmental equipment, such as smokestack scrubbers, that are mandated by the government. In such cases, there may be some analysis to see if costs can be lowered, but the proposal *must* be accepted, so it will sidestep the normal analysis process.

The second scenario is when a company wants to mitigate a high-risk situation that could imperil the company. In this case, the emphasis is not on profitability at all, but rather on the avoidance of a situation. If so, the mandate likely comes from top management, so there is little additional need for analysis, other than a review to ensure that the lowest-cost alternative is selected.

A final scenario is when there is a sudden need for a fixed asset, perhaps due to the catastrophic failure of existing equipment or a strategic shift. These purchases can happen at any time, and so usually fall outside of the capital budget's annual planning cycle. It is generally best to require more than the normal number of approvals for these items, so that management is made fully aware of the situation. Also, if there is time to do so, they are worthy of an unusually intense analysis, to see if they really must be purchased at once, or if they can be delayed until the next capital budgeting approval period arrives.

Once all items are properly approved and inserted into the annual budget, this does not end the capital budgeting process. There is a final review just prior to actually making each purchase, with appropriate approval, to ensure that the company still needs each fixed asset.

The last step in the capital budgeting process is to conduct a post-implementation review, in which you summarize the actual costs and benefits of each fixed asset, and compare these results to the initial projections included in the original application. If the results are worse than expected, this may result in a more in-depth review, with particular attention being paid to avoiding any faulty aspects of the original proposal in future proposals.

Bottleneck Analysis

Under constraint analysis, the key concept is that an entire company acts as a single system, which generates a profit. Under this concept, capital budgeting revolves around the following logic:

1. Nearly all of the costs of the production system do not vary with individual sales; that is, nearly every cost is an operating expense; therefore,
2. You need to maximize the throughput (revenues minus totally variable costs) of the *entire* system in order to pay for the operating expense; and

3. The only way to increase throughput is to maximize the throughput passing through the bottleneck operation.

Consequently, give primary consideration to those capital budgeting proposals that favorably impact the throughput passing through the bottleneck operation.

This does not mean that all other capital budgeting proposals will be rejected, since there are a multitude of possible investments that can reduce costs elsewhere in a company, and which are therefore worthy of consideration. However, throughput is more important than cost reduction, since throughput has no theoretical upper limit, whereas costs can only be reduced to zero. Given the greater ultimate impact on profits of throughput over cost reduction, any non-bottleneck proposal is simply not as important.

Net Present Value Analysis

Any capital investment involves an initial cash outflow to pay for it, followed by a mix of cash inflows in the form of revenue, or a decline in existing cash flows that are caused by expense reductions. We can lay out this information in a spreadsheet to show all expected cash flows over the useful life of an investment, and then apply a discount rate that reduces the cash flows to what they would be worth at the present date. A discount rate is the interest rate used to discount a stream of future cash flows to their present value. Depending upon the application, typical rates used as the discount rate are a firm's cost of capital or the current market rate. This cash flows calculation is known as *net present value*.

Net present value is the traditional approach to evaluating capital proposals, since it is based on a single factor – cash flows – that can be used to judge any proposal arriving from anywhere in a company. However, the net present value method can be a poor evaluation method if you suspect that the cash flows used to derive an analysis are incorrect.

EXAMPLE

Milagro Corporation is planning to acquire an asset that it expects will yield positive cash flows for the next five years. Its cost of capital is 10%, which it uses as the discount rate to construct the net present value of the project. The following table shows the calculation:

Year	Cash Flow	10% Discount Factor	Present Value
0	-$500,000	1.0000	-$500,000
1	+130,000	0.9091	+118,183
2	+130,000	0.8265	+107,445
3	+130,000	0.7513	+97,669
4	+130,000	0.6830	+88,790
5	+130,000	0.6209	+80,717
		Net Present Value	-$7,196

The net present value of the proposed project is negative at the 10% discount rate, so Milagro should not invest in the project.

In the "10% Discount Factor" column, the factor becomes smaller for periods further in the future, because the discounted value of cash flows is reduced as they progress further from the present day. The discount factor is widely available in textbooks, or can be derived from the following formula:

$$\text{Present value of a future cash flow} = \frac{\text{Future cash flow}}{(1 + \text{Discount rate})^{\text{squared by the number of periods of discounting}}}$$

To use the formula for an example, if we forecast the receipt of $100,000 in one year, and are using a discount rate of 10 percent, then the calculation is:

$$\text{Present value} = \frac{\$100,000}{(1+.10)^1}$$

Present value = $90,909

A net present value calculation that truly reflects the reality of cash flows will likely be more complex than the one shown in the preceding example. It is best to break down the analysis into a number of sub-categories, so that you can see exactly when cash flows are occurring and with what activities they are associated. Here are the more common contents of a net present value analysis:

- *Asset purchases*. All of the expenditures associated with the purchase, delivery, installation, and testing of the asset being purchased.
- *Asset-linked expenses*. Any ongoing expenses, such as warranty agreements, property taxes, and maintenance, that are associated with the asset.
- *Contribution margin*. Any incremental cash flows resulting from sales that can be attributed to the project.
- *Depreciation effect*. The asset will be depreciated, and this depreciation shelters a portion of any net income from income taxes, so note the income tax reduction caused by depreciation.
- *Expense reductions*. Any incremental expense reductions caused by the project, such as automation that eliminates direct labor hours.
- *Tax credits*. If an asset purchase triggers a tax credit (such as for a purchase of energy-reduction equipment), note the amount of the credit.
- *Taxes*. Any income tax payments associated with net income expected to be derived from the asset.
- *Working capital changes*. Any net changes in inventory, accounts receivable, or accounts payable associated with the asset. Also, when the asset is

eventually sold off, this may trigger a reversal of the initial working capital changes.

By itemizing the preceding factors in a net present value analysis, you can more easily review and revise individual line items.

We have given priority to bottleneck analysis over net present value as the preferred method for analyzing capital proposals, because bottleneck analysis focuses on throughput. The key improvement factor is throughput, since there is no upper limit on the amount of throughput that can be generated, whereas there are only so many operating expenses that can be reduced. This does not mean that net present value should be eliminated as a management tool. It is still quite useful for operating expense reduction analysis where throughput issues are not involved.

The Payback Method

The most discerning method for evaluating a capital budgeting proposal is its impact on the bottleneck operation, while net present value analysis yields a detailed review of cash flows. The simplest and least accurate evaluation technique is the payback method. This approach is still heavily used, because it provides a very fast "back of the envelope" calculation of how soon a company will earn back its investment. This means that it provides a rough measure of how long a company will have its investment at risk before earning back the original amount expended. There are two ways to calculate the payback period, which are:

1. *Simplified*. Divide the total amount of an investment by the average resulting cash flow. This approach can yield an incorrect assessment, because a proposal with cash flows skewed far into the future can yield a payback period that differs substantially from when actual payback occurs.

2. *Manual calculation*. Manually deduct the forecasted positive cash flows from the initial investment amount from Year 1 forward, until the investment is paid back. This method is slower, but ensures a higher degree of accuracy.

EXAMPLE

Milagro Corporation has received a proposal from a manager, asking to spend $1,500,000 on equipment that will result in cash inflows in accordance with the following table:

Year	Cash Flow
1	+$150,000
2	+150,000
3	+200,000
4	+600,000
5	+900,000

The total cash flows over the five-year period are projected to be $2,000,000, which is an average of $400,000 per year. When divided into the $1,500,000 original investment, this results in a payback period of 3.75 years. However, the briefest perusal of the projected cash flows reveals that the flows are heavily weighted toward the far end of the time period, so the results of this calculation cannot be correct.

Instead, the accountant runs the calculation year by year, deducting the cash flows in each successive year from the remaining investment. The results of this calculation are:

Year	Cash Flow	Net Invested Cash
0		-$1,500,000
1	+$150,000	-1,350,000
2	+150,000	-1,200,000
3	+200,000	-1,000,000
4	+600,000	-400,000
5	+900,000	0

The table indicates that the real payback period is located somewhere between Year 4 and Year 5. There is $400,000 of investment yet to be paid back at the end of Year 4, and there is $900,000 of cash flow projected for Year 5. The accountant assumes the same monthly amount of cash flow in Year 5, which means that he can estimate final payback as being just short of 4.5 years.

The payback method is not overly accurate, does not provide any estimate of how profitable a project may be, and does not take account of the time value of money. Nonetheless, its extreme simplicity makes it a perennial favorite in many companies.

Capital Budget Proposal Analysis

Reviewing a capital budget proposal does not necessarily mean passing judgment on it exactly as presented. You can attach a variety of suggestions to your analysis of the proposal, which management may incorporate into a revised proposal. Here are some examples:

- *Asset capacity.* Does the asset have more capacity than is actually needed under the circumstances? Is there a history of usage spikes that call for extra capacity? Depending on the answers to these questions, consider using smaller assets with less capacity. If the asset is powered, this may also lead to reductions in utility costs, installation costs, and floor space requirements.
- *Asset commoditization.* Wherever possible, avoid custom-designed machinery in favor of standard models that are readily available. By doing so, it is easier to obtain repair parts, and there may even be an aftermarket for disposing of the asset when the company no longer needs it.
- *Asset features.* Managers have a habit of wanting to buy new assets with all of the latest features. Are all of these features really needed? If an asset is being replaced, it is useful to compare the characteristics of the old and new assets, and examine any differences between the two to see if they are required. If the asset is the only model offered by the supplier, would the supplier be willing to strip away some features and offer it at a lower price?

- *Asset standardization.* If a company needs a particular asset in large quantities, adopt a policy of always buying from the same manufacturer, and preferably only buying the same asset every time. By doing so, the maintenance staff becomes extremely familiar with the maintenance requirements of several identical machines, and only has to stock replacement parts for one model.
- *Bottleneck analysis.* As noted earlier in this chapter, assets that improve the amount of throughput in a production operation are usually well worth the investment, while those not impacting the bottleneck require substantially more justification, usually in the direction of reducing operating expenses.
- *Extended useful life.* A manager may be applying for an asset replacement simply because the original asset has reached the end of its recommended useful life. But is it really necessary to replace the asset? Consider conducting a formal review of these assets to see if they can still be used for some additional period of time. There may be additional maintenance costs involved, but this will almost certainly be lower than the cost of replacing the asset.
- *Facility analysis.* If a capital proposal involves the acquisition of additional facility space, consider reviewing any existing space to see if it can be compressed, thereby eliminating the need for more space. For example, shift storage items to less expensive warehouse space, shift from offices to more space-efficient cubicles, and encourage employees to work from home or on a later shift. If none of these ideas work, at least consider acquiring new facilities through a sublease, which tends to require shorter lease terms than a lease arranged with the primary landlord.
- *Monument elimination.* A company may have a large fixed asset around which the rest of the production area is configured; this is called a monument. If there is a monument, consider adopting a policy of using a larger number of lower-capacity assets. By doing so, you avoid the risk of having a single monument asset go out of service and stopping all production, in favor of having multiple units among which work can be shifted if one unit fails.

The sponsors of capital proposals frequently do *not* appreciate this additional review of their proposals, since it implies that they did not consider these issues themselves. Nonetheless, the savings can be substantial, and so are well worth the aggravation of dealing with annoyed managers.

If the additional review indicates some promising alternatives that may substantially reduce the cost of a proposal, if not eliminate it entirely, then it may be politically wise to route the proposed changes through the controller or chief financial officer, who may have the clout to force a serious review of the alternatives by the project sponsor.

The Outsourcing Decision

It may be possible to avoid a capital purchase entirely by outsourcing the work to which it is related. By doing so, the company may be able to eliminate all assets related to the area (rather than acquiring more assets), while the burden of maintaining a sufficient asset base now shifts to the supplier. The supplier may even buy the company's assets related to the area being outsourced. This situation is a well-established alternative for high technology manufacturing, as well as for information technology services, but is likely not viable outside of these areas.

If you are in a situation where outsourcing is a possibility, the likely cash flows resulting from doing so will be highly favorable for the first few years, as capital expenditures vanish. However, the supplier must also earn a profit and pay for its own infrastructure, so the cost over the long term will probably not vary dramatically from what a company would have experienced if it had kept a functional area in-house. There are three exceptions that can bring about a long-term cost reduction. They are:

- *Excess capacity.* A supplier may have such a large amount of excess capacity already that it does not need to invest further for some time, thereby potentially depressing the costs that it would otherwise pass through to its customers. However, this excess capacity pool will eventually dry up, so it tends to be a shorter-term anomaly.
- *High volume.* There are some outsourcing situations where the supplier is handling such a massive volume of activity from multiple customers that its costs on a per-unit basis decline below the costs that a company could ever achieve on its own. This situation can yield long-term savings to a company.
- *Low costs.* A supplier may locate its facility and work force in low-cost countries or regions within countries. This can yield significant cost reductions in the short term, but as many suppliers use the same technique, it is driving up costs in all parts of the world. Thus, this cost disparity is useful for a period of time, but is gradually declining as a long-term option.

There are risks involved in shifting functions to suppliers. First, a supplier may go out of business, leaving the company scrambling to shift work to a new supplier. Second, a supplier may gradually ramp up prices to the point where the company is substantially worse off than if it had kept the function in-house. Third, the company may have so completely purged the outsourced function from its own operations that it is now completely dependent on the supplier, and has no ability to take the work back in-house. Fourth, the supplier's service level may decline to the point where it is impairing the ability of the company to operate. And finally, the company may have entered into a multi-year deal, and cannot escape from the contract if the business arrangement does not work out. These are significant issues, and must be weighed as part of the outsourcing decision.

The cautions noted here about outsourcing do not mean that it should be avoided as an option. On the contrary, a rapidly growing company that has minimal access to funds may cheerfully hand off multiple operations to suppliers in order to avoid the up-front costs associated with those operations. Outsourcing is less attractive to stable, well-established companies that have better access to capital.

In summary, outsourcing is an attractive option for rapidly growing companies that do not have sufficient cash to pay for capital expenditures, but also carries with it a variety of risks involving shifting key functions to a supplier over which a company may not have a great deal of control.

The Capital Budgeting Application Form

Most companies require managers to fill out a standardized form for all capital budgeting proposals. The type of information included in the form will vary, depending on whether you are basing the approval decision on bottleneck considerations or the results of a net present value analysis. However, the header section of the form will likely be the same in all circumstances. It identifies the project, its sponsor, the date on which it was submitted, and a unique product identification number that is filled in by the recipient. A sample header is:

Sample Application Header

Project name:	*50 ton coffee roaster*		
Project sponsor:	*J. R. Valdez*		
Submission date:	*May 28*	Project number:	*2014-14*

If a proposal is for a legal requirement or a risk mitigation issue, then it is absolved from most analysis, and will likely move to the top of the approved project list. Consequently, the form should contain a separate section for these types of projects, and involve a different set of approvers. The corporate attorney may be involved, as well as anyone involved in risk management. A sample block in the application form for legal and risk mitigation issues is:

Sample Legal and Risk Mitigation Block

		Required Approvals	
Initial cash flow:	*-$250,000*	All proposals	*Susan Lafferty*
Year 1 cash flow:	*-10,000*		Attorney
Year 2 cash flow:	*-10,000*		
Year 3 cash flow:	*-10,000*	< $100,000	*George Mason*
			Risk Officer
Describe legal or risk mitigation issue:			
Construction of coffee grounds firing facility, per		$100,000+	*Fred Scurry*
new zoning requirements			President

If you elect to focus on bottleneck considerations for capital budgeting approvals, then include the following block of text in the application form. This block focuses on the changes in cash flow that are associated with a capital expenditure. The block requests an itemization of the cash flows involved in the purchase (primarily for finance planning considerations), followed by requests for information about how the investment will help the company – via an improvement in throughput, a reduction in operating costs, or an increase in the return on investment. In the example, note that the primary improvement used as the basis for the proposal is the improvement in throughput. This also leads to an enhancement of the return on investment. There is an increase in the total net operating cost, which represents a reduction in the positive effect of the throughput, and which is caused by the annual $8,000 maintenance cost associated with the investment.

The approvals for a bottleneck-related investment change from the ones shown previously for a legal or risk mitigation investment. In this case, a process analyst should verify the information include in the block, to ensure that the applicant's claims are correct. The supervisor in whose area of responsibility the investment falls should also sign off, thereby accepting responsibility for the outcome of the investment. A higher-level manager, or even the board of directors, should approve any really large investment proposals.

Sample Bottleneck Approval Block

		Required Approvals	
Initial cash flow:	-$125,000	All proposals	*Monica Byers*
Year 1 cash flow:	-8,000		Process Analyst
Year 2 cash flow:	-8,000		
Year 3 cash flow:	-8,000	< $100,000	*Al Rogers*
			Responsible
			Supervisor
Net throughput change:*	+$180,000		
		$100,000+	*Fred Scurry*
Net operating cost change:*	+$8,000		President
Change in ROI:*	+0.08%		

* On an annual basis

If you do not choose to use a bottleneck-oriented application, then the following block may be useful instead. It is based on the more traditional analysis of net present value. Also consider using this block as a supplement to the bottleneck block just noted, in case some managers prefer to work with both sets of information.

Sample Net Present Value Approval Block

Year	Cash Out (payments)	Cash In (Revenue)	Incremental Tax Effect	Totals
0	-$1,000,000			-$1,000,000
1	-25,000	+$200,000	+$8,750	+183,750
2	-25,000	+400,000	-61,250	+313,750
3	-25,000	+400,000	-61,250	+313,750
4	-25,000	+400,000	-61,250	+313,750
5	-25,000	+400,000	-61,250	+313,750
Totals	-$1,125,000	+$1,800,000	-$236,250	+$438,750
			Tax Rate:	35%
			Hurdle Rate:	12%
			Net Present Value:	+$13,328

The net present value block requires the presentation of cash flows over a five-year period, as well as the net tax effect resulting from this specific transaction. The tax effect is based on $25,000 of maintenance expenses in every year shown, as well as $200,000 of annual depreciation, and a 35% incremental tax rate. Thus, in Year 2, there is $400,000 of revenue, less $225,000 of depreciation and maintenance expenses, multiplied by 35%, resulting in an incremental tax effect of $61,250.

The block then goes on to state the corporate hurdle rate, which is 12% in the example. We then discount the stream of cash flows from the project at the hurdle rate of 12%, which results in a positive net present value of $13,328. Based on just the net present value analysis, this appears to be an acceptable project.

The text blocks shown here contain much of the key information that management should see before it decides whether to approve a capital investment. In addition, there should be a considerable amount of supporting information that precisely describes the nature of the proposed investment, as well as backup information that supports each number included in the form.

The Post Installation Review

It is important to conduct a post installation review of any capital expenditure project, to see if the initial expectations for it were realized. If not, then the results of this review can be used to modify the capital budgeting process to include better information.

Another reason for having a post installation review is that it provides a control over those managers who fill out the initial capital budgeting proposals. If they know there is no post installation review, they can wildly overstate the projected results of their projects with impunity, just to have them approved. Of course, this control is only useful if it is conducted relatively soon after a project is completed. Otherwise, the responsible manager may have moved on in his career, and can no longer be tied back to the results of his work.

It is even better to begin a post installation review while a project is still being implemented, and especially when the implementation period is expected to be long. This initial review gives senior management a good idea of whether the cost of a project is staying close to its initial expectations. If not, management may need to authorize more vigorous management of the project, scale it back, or even cancel it outright.

If the post implementation review results in the suspicion that a project proposal was unduly optimistic, this brings up the question of how to deal with the responsible manager. At a minimum, the proposal reviews can flag any future proposals by this reviewer as suspect, and worthy of especially close attention.

EXAMPLE

Milagro Corporation has just completed a one-year project to increase the amount of production capacity at its primary coffee roasting facility. The original capital budgeting proposal was for an initial expenditure of $290,000, resulting in additional annual throughput of $100,000 per year. The actual result is somewhat different. The accountant's report includes the following text:

> **Findings:** The proposal only contained the purchase price of the equipment. However, since the machinery was delivered from Columbia, Milagro also incurred $22,000 of freight charges and $3,000 in customs fees. Further, the project required the installation of a new concrete pad, a breaker box, and electrical wiring that cost an additional $10,000. Finally, the equipment proved to be difficult to configure, and required $20,000 of consulting fees from the manufacturer, as well as $5,000 for the raw materials scrapped during testing. Thus, the actual cost of the project was $350,000.

> Subsequent operation of the equipment reveals that it cannot operate without an average of 20% downtime for maintenance, as opposed to the 5% downtime that was advertised by the manufacturer. This reduces throughput by 15%, which equates to a drop of $15,000 in throughput per year, to $85,000.

> **Recommendations:** To incorporate a more comprehensive set of instructions into the capital budgeting proposal process to account for transportation, setup, and testing costs. Also, given the wide difference between the performance claims of the manufacturer and actual results, to hire a consultant to see if the problem is caused by our installation of the equipment; if not, we recommend not buying from this supplier in the future.

The Lease versus Buy Decision

Once the asset acquisition decision has been made, management still needs to decide if it should buy the asset outright or lease it. In a leasing situation, a lessor buys the asset and then allows the lessee to use it in exchange for a monthly fee. Depending on the terms of the lease, it may be treated in one of two ways:

- *Capital lease*. The lessee records the leased asset on its books as a fixed asset and depreciates it, while recording interest expense separately.
- *Operating lease*. The lessor records the leased asset on its books as a fixed asset and depreciates it, while the lessee simply records a lease payment.

The decision to use a lease may be based on management's unwillingness to use its line of credit or other available sources of financing to buy an asset. Leases can be easier to obtain than a line of credit, since the lease agreement always designates the asset as collateral. Collateral is an asset that a borrower has pledged as security for a loan. The lender has the legal right to seize and sell the asset if the borrower is unable to pay back the loan by an agreed date.

There are a multitude of factors that a lessor includes in the formulation of the monthly rate that it charges, such as the down payment, the residual value of the asset at the end of the lease, and the interest rate, which makes it difficult to break out and examine each element of the lease. Instead, it is much easier to create separate net present value tables for the lease and buy alternatives, and then compare the results of the two tables to see which is the better alternative.

EXAMPLE

Milagro Corporation is contemplating the purchase of an asset for $500,000. It can buy the asset outright, or do so with a lease. Its cost of capital is 8%, and its incremental income tax rate is 35%. The following two tables show the net present values of both options.

Buy Option

Year	Depreciation	Income Tax Savings (35%)	Discount Factor (8%)	Net Present Value
0				-$500,000
1	$100,000	$35,000	0.9259	32,407
2	100,000	35,000	0.8573	30,006
3	100,000	35,000	0.7938	27,783
4	100,000	35,000	0.7350	25,725
5	100,000	35,000	0.6806	23,821
Totals	$500,000	$175,000		$360,258

Lease Option

Year	Pretax Lease Payments	Income Tax Savings (35%)	After-Tax Lease Cost	Discount Factor (8%)	Net Present Value
1	$135,000	47,250	$87,750	0.9259	$81,248
2	135,000	47,250	87,750	0.8573	75,228
3	135,000	47,250	87,750	0.7938	69,656
4	135,000	47,250	87,750	0.7350	64,496
5	135,000	47,250	87,750	0.6806	59,723
Totals	$675,000	$236,250	$438,750		$350,351

Thus, the net purchase cost of the buy option is $360,258, while the net purchase cost of the lease option is $350,351. The lease option involves the lowest cash outflow for Milagro, and so is the better option.

Summary

This chapter addressed a variety of issues you should consider when deciding whether to recommend the purchase of a fixed asset. We put less emphasis on net present value analysis, which has been the primary capital budgeting tool in industry for years, because it does not take into consideration the impact on throughput of a company's bottleneck operation. The best capital budgeting analysis process is to give top priority to project proposals that have a strong favorable impact on throughput, and then use net present value to evaluate the impact of any remaining projects on cost reduction.

Chapter 28
Business Ratios

Introduction

The accountant is usually expected to provide some analysis alongside the financial statements, as well as of other financial aspects of the business. The starting point of this analysis is typically a standard set of ratios. When a ratio indicates a problem, the accountant then investigates the underlying reasons in more detail, and reports any actionable findings back to management. In this chapter, we describe a selection of the more useful ratios that can form the foundation of an accountant's analysis responsibilities. We address ratios and calculations for sales and earnings performance, expenses, liquidity, return on equity, the size of various asset groups, and the performance of the sales department.

> **Related Podcast Episodes:** Episodes 26, 27, 28, 29, 30, 31, and 35 of the Accounting Best Practices Podcast discuss ratios for payroll, inventory, liquidity, cash flow, asset utilization, operating performance, and the accounting department, respectively. You can listen to them at: **accountingtools.com/podcasts** or **iTunes**

What to Measure

When setting up a measurement system, a key concern is what to measure. Employees have a strong tendency to improve whatever is being measured, so focusing their attention on the wrong measurement can lead to results that are injurious to a business. Here are several examples of the issue:

- *Sales growth.* A common focus of attention is period-over-period increases in sales. Typically, a business starts with a small number of products and customer accounts that are sufficiently profitable to pay for additional rounds of sales growth. However, these additional rounds of growth may come at the expense of profitability, which gradually declines. In particular, there is a danger of specifically targeting customers only to obtain more sales volume, with no regard to how they will contribute to profits.
- *Expense growth.* Management may closely monitor expenses in order to keep expense growth in check. However, doing so may lead to the reduction of several key discretionary expenses, such as research and development, that are needed to fund future growth.
- *Days sales outstanding.* A commonly-followed metric is days sales outstanding, which compares the amount of receivables to sales. The number of days sales outstanding should generally be kept as low as possible, thereby reducing the investment in accounts receivable. However, an undue focus on

this measurement could lead to the restriction of credit to customers, which will in turn result in reduced sales.

- *Square feet per person.* One of the larger expenses in most organizations is the cost of facilities, which means that the number of square feet per person may be closely monitored. A typical outcome of this focus is the installation of large numbers of cubicles. However, some employees, such as engineers, require minimal noise in order to concentrate on their work, and so must have a certain amount of square feet of office space in order to function effectively.

Consequently, the selection of the most appropriate measurements is crucial. Management should consider the negative impact of using a particular measurement before rolling it out, and should also monitor the results of its use. In some cases, it may be necessary to terminate a measurement at once, to keep contrary behavior from occurring.

There is no ideal set of measurements to follow. Instead, measurements must be tailored to the circumstances in which a business finds itself. For example, a company whose investors are willing to plow money into the business in order to obtain significant market share may be willing to focus solely on sales growth, even at the expense of profits. Conversely, a company in a monopoly position in a low-growth industry may have a greater interest in maximizing cash flow. Or, if a market demands a constant flow of new products, the emphasis may instead be on the time required to generate new products.

The focus of a business may change over time, necessitating a change in measurements. Most commonly, a business will shift from an initial growth phase to a low-growth situation, and so alters its measurements to focus less on sales and more on profitability. The same issue arises when a business enters a new market. It is entirely possible that different rules apply to each market, which requires the use of different measurements. For example, a business may sell its goods through a chain of retail stores, as well as through an Internet-based direct sales channel. The measurements for the retail stores may include a same-store sales growth trend line, while the Internet store may require a measurement for the number of page views converted into sales. In short, a completely different set of measurements may be required for each market in which a company competes; there may be no common measurements that are applicable to *all* of the markets.

Measurement Consistency

When a measurement is being presented for multiple periods, the calculation should be identical for all periods presented. For example, the inclusion of sales in a return on sales figure should always be net sales, not gross sales in one period and net sales in others. Otherwise, results will be so unreliable that managers will learn not to rely upon the presented information. There are several steps that can be taken to ensure a high degree of measurement consistency. Consider the following:

- *Audits*. Have the company's internal auditors occasionally review the measurements to ensure that they are being consistently calculated, and report to a senior manager if this is not the case.
- *Standards sheet*. Create a report on which are listed the calculations for all measurements. This standards sheet can be distributed to all recipients of measurement reports, as well as anyone whose performance is being monitored through the measurements. By doing so, everyone is aware of exactly how measurements are being developed.
- *Measurement locks*. Ideally, measurements should be included in the financial statements report writer, and then locked down with password access. By doing so, it is very difficult for anyone to adjust the calculations without proper authorization.

An issue with the use of a standards sheet is that the person responsible for reporting measurements will be pressured by those employees whose performance is being monitored through the measurements. This pressure will take the form of requests to use alternative calculations that cast the employees' performance in a better light. To counteract this pressure, require the accountant to seek the approval of a senior manager (such as the president) before any measurement calculation changes are allowed.

Measurement Timing

The timing of measurements can have an impact on the extent to which the information is acted upon. Of particular concern is avoiding situations where measurements are being spewed out so frequently that recipients feel inundated with information, and so take no action. Conversely, a measurement that is only issued at long intervals can result in the passage of too much time before corrective action is taken.

To avoid either situation, discuss the appropriate timing of measurement reports with recipients. In rare cases where constant monitoring is required, a few measurements may be issued on a daily or continual basis. In most other cases, the default reporting interval is likely to be monthly or quarterly. If daily or continual measurements are needed, a different reporting system will probably be needed, such as an automated system that transmits information to desktop dashboards, or which is manually posted on whiteboards.

Deflated Sales Growth

In an inflationary environment, it is relatively easy for a company to report continually increasing sales, for it can routinely ratchet up its prices. It is possible to factor out this inflationary increase by deflating the reported sales level by the amount of the consumer price index, or some similar measure of inflation. To calculate deflated sales growth, follow these steps:

1. Determine which inflation index to use for the deflation calculation. The consumer price index is most commonly used.
2. Divide the price index for the preceding year by the price index for this year, and multiply the result by the net sales of the business for the current year. This yields the deflated sales for the current year.
3. Subtract the net sales for the preceding year from the deflated sales for the current year, and divide by the net sales for the preceding year.

The main issue with the measurement of deflated sales growth is to apply the same type of inflation index to the measurement from year to year, so that ongoing measurements are comparable.

EXAMPLE

Viking Fitness has opened a chain of health clubs in a country that is experiencing a high rate of inflation. In the preceding year, the country had a consumer price index of 132. In the current year, the index increased to 158. In the preceding year, Viking reported sales of 58,000,000 pesos. In the current year, the company reported sales of 73,000,000 pesos, with no additional health clubs having been opened. Based on this information, Viking's deflated sales growth is:

$$\frac{(73{,}000{,}000 \text{ Pesos} \times (132 \text{ CPI} \div 158 \text{ CPI})) - 58{,}000{,}000 \text{ Pesos}}{58{,}000{,}000 \text{ Pesos}}$$

$$= 5.2\% \text{ Deflated sales growth}$$

Thus, despite the high inflation rate, the company did indeed succeed in increasing its same-location sales by 5.2% during the current year.

Sales per Person

In some industries, there is a direct relationship between the efficiency and effectiveness of a company's employees and its resulting sales. This relationship is particularly true in industries where employees bill customers for their time. In such industries, the sales per person measurement is closely watched.

To calculate sales per person, divide the total sales for the preceding 12 months by the average number of full-time equivalents during that period. The calculation is:

$$\frac{\text{Revenues (trailing 12 months)}}{(\text{Beginning FTEs} + \text{Ending FTEs}) / 2}$$

EXAMPLE

Pulsed Laser Drilling Corporation (PLD) manufactures lasers that use a pulsed laser beam to drill through rock. Its products are used in such applications as drilling for oil and gas, water wells, and laying subsurface fiber optic cables. The company only employs full-time technicians who assemble and field service its complex laser products. Headcount tends to closely follow sales levels, since a great deal of the manufacturing process is by hand. During the past year, PLD had revenues of $18 million and 90 full-time equivalents. The calculation of its sales per person is:

$$\frac{\$18,000,000 \text{ Sales}}{90 \text{ Full-time equivalents}} = \$200,000 \text{ Sales per employee}$$

The sales per person measurement is not useful, and may even be misleading, in the following situations:

- *Product based.* If a company derives its sales from standardized manufactured goods, there may not be a causal relationship between sales and headcount, especially when production activities are highly automated.
- *Step headcount.* It is possible that a company may be able to use a fixed number of employees to generate an increasing amount of sales, until it reaches a "step" point where the company must hire a number of additional employees to support the next incremental block of sales. This situation arises when sales are supported by a single facility that requires a certain minimum amount of staffing.

The sales per person measurement is a popular one, but it only focuses on top-line sales. A company may have an astoundingly high sales per person measurement, and still lose money. A more focused measurement is the profit per person measurement, which is covered later in this chapter.

Deflated Profit Growth

When a business operates in a highly inflationary environment, a decline in the value of its home currency can cause the business to report unusually high profits in comparison to prior periods. To gain a better understanding of the underlying profit growth of the business, it is necessary to deflate the profits for the current period and then compare them to the profits reported for the prior period. To calculate deflated profit growth, follow these steps:

1. Divide the price index for the prior reporting period by the price index for the current reporting period.
2. Multiply the result by the net profit figure reported for the current reporting period.
3. Subtract the net profits for the prior reporting period from the result.
4. Divide the result by the net profit figure for the prior reporting period.

The formula is:

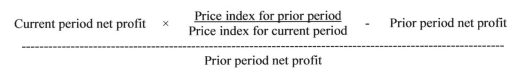

The use of price indexes only approximates the true impact of inflation on a business. A price index is based on the changes in prices for a mix of common goods and services, which a company may not use in the same proportions built into the index. For example, a price index may have increased primarily because of a jump on the price of oil, but a company may have minimal expenditures for oil. Consequently, there can be differences between the deflated profit growth calculation and the actual impact of inflation on a business.

EXAMPLE

Aphelion Corporation operates telescopes in the Atacama Desert in northern Chile, and uses the Chilean peso as its home currency. The company reported profits of 5,000,000 pesos in the most recent year, and 4,500,000 pesos in the immediately preceding year. The price index for the current year was 127, as opposed to 106 for the preceding year. Based on this information, the deflated profit growth of the company is:

$$\frac{5{,}000{,}000 \text{ pesos current period profit} \times \frac{106 \text{ Prior period index}}{127 \text{ Current period index}} - 4{,}500{,}000 \text{ pesos prior period profit}}{4{,}500{,}000 \text{ Prior period net profit}}$$

$$= \frac{4{,}173{,}228 \text{ Deflated pesos} - 4{,}500{,}000 \text{ Profit prior period}}{4{,}500{,}000 \text{ Profit prior period}} = -7.3\%$$

Thus, when adjusted for inflation, the profits of Aphelion declined by 7.3% in the current reporting period.

Profit per Person

In a service-intensive industry, there is a direct relationship between employees and the amount of profits generated. This is particularly true in such service areas as equipment field servicing, management consulting, and auditing. In these situations, it makes considerable sense to track profits per employee, not only for the company as a whole, but also for those individual employees who are billable.

To calculate profit per employee, divide the company's operating profit by the average number of full-time equivalent employees. Do *not* use net after-tax profits for this measurement, since doing so would include such financing line items as interest expense and interest income, which have nothing to do with employee performance. Also, do not include the impact of income taxes, since this expense can be altered by tax strategy that has nothing to do with the operational efficiency of employees. The calculation is:

$$\frac{\text{Operating profit}}{(\text{Beginning FTEs} + \text{Ending FTEs}) / 2}$$

EXAMPLE

Maid Marian is a nationwide maid service that is run by friars within the Franciscan Order. The friars want to introduce a bonus system that encourages part-time maids to work additional hours, and needs to determine the existing profit per employee, so that it can determine how large a bonus pool to create.

During the past 12-month period, employees of Maid Marian worked a total of 832,000 hours, which is an FTE equivalent of 400 employees. This equivalent is calculated as 832,000 hours divided by the 2,080 hours worked by a full-employee in one year (52 weeks × 40 hours/week). During that period, the service generated an operating profit of $3 million, which is a profit per employee of:

$$\frac{\$3,000,000 \text{ Operating profit}}{400 \text{ Full-time equivalents}} = \$7,500 \text{ Profit per employee}$$

The friars want to create a bonus pool that is 20% of operating profits, which is a $600,000 pool. Based on the 400 FTEs in Maid Marian, this works out to a potential bonus per FTE per year of $1,500.

There are three caveats to the use of the profit per employee measurement, which are:

- *Industry-specific.* The profit per employee measurement is least useful in industries where there is a large investment in fixed assets and a proportionally smaller number of employees, such as heavy industry. In these situations, there is not such a direct linkage between profits and the quality or quantity of employees, which makes the profit per employee measurement less relevant.
- *Minimal profits.* There is no point in measuring profit per employee when the operating profit is near zero, since it divulges no relevant information.
- *Manipulation.* The measurement is subject to manipulation by shifting work to suppliers. Doing so reduces headcount, which drives up the profit per employee.

Despite the caveats just noted, profit per person is an excellent measurement in many services industries.

Core Earnings Ratio

There are many ways in which the net profit ratio of a business can be skewed by events that have little to do with the core operating capabilities of a business. To get to the root of the issue and concentrate on only the essential operations of a business, Standard & Poor's has promulgated the concept of core earnings, which strips away all non-operational transactions from a company's reported results.

There are a multitude of unrelated transactions that can be eliminated from net profits, some of which are so specific to certain industries that Standard & Poor's probably never thought of them. The most common of these unrelated transactions are:

- Asset impairment charges
- Costs related to merger activities
- Costs related to the issuance of bonds and other forms of financing
- Gains or losses on hedging activities that have not yet been realized
- Gains or losses on the sale of assets
- Gains or losses related to the outcome of litigation
- Profits or losses from pension income
- Recognized cost of stock options issued to employees
- Recognized cost of warrants issued to third parties
- The accrued cost of restructuring operations that have not yet occurred

Many of these special adjustments only occur at long intervals, so a company may find that its core earnings ratio is quite close to its net profit ratio in one year, and substantially different in the next year. The difference tends to be much larger when a company adds complexity to the nature of its operations, so that more factors can impact net profits.

The calculation of the core earnings ratio is to adjust reported net income for as many of the preceding items as are present, and divide by net sales. The formula is:

$$\frac{\text{Net profits} - \text{Core earnings adjustments}}{\text{Net sales}}$$

EXAMPLE

Subterranean Access, maker of drilling equipment, has reported a fabulous year, with profits of $10,000,000 on sales of $50,000,000. A credit analyst that rates the company's bonds is suspicious of this good fortune, and digs through the company's annual report to derive the core earnings ratio of the business. She uncovers the following items:

Profit from favorable settlement of a lawsuit	$8,000,000
Profit on earnings from pension fund	500,000
Gain on sale of a subsidiary	3,500,000
Impairment charge on acquired intangible assets	-1,000,000
Total	$11,000,000

When these adjustments are factored out of the company's net profits, it turns out that the core earnings figure is actually a $1,000,000 loss, which results in a core earnings ratio of -2%. Based on this information, the analyst issues a downgrade on the company's debt, on the assumption that the multitude of favorable adjustments will not continue.

Breakeven Point

The breakeven point is the sales volume at which a business earns exactly no money. It is mostly used for internal analysis purposes, but it is also useful for a credit analyst, who can use it to determine the amount of losses that could be sustained if a credit applicant were to suffer a sales downturn.

To calculate the breakeven point, divide total fixed expenses by the contribution margin. Contribution margin is sales minus all variable expenses, divided by sales. The formula is:

$$\frac{\text{Total fixed expenses}}{\text{Contribution margin percentage}}$$

A more refined approach is to eliminate all non-cash expenses (such as depreciation) from the numerator, so that the calculation focuses on the breakeven cash flow level.

EXAMPLE

A credit analyst is reviewing the financial statements of a customer that has a large amount of fixed costs. The industry is highly cyclical, so the analyst wants to know what a large downturn in sales will do to the customer. The customer has total fixed expenses of $3,000,000, sales of $8,000,000, and variable expenses of $4,000,000. Based on this information, the customer's contribution margin is 50%. The breakeven calculation is:

$$\frac{\$3,000,000 \text{ Total fixed costs}}{50\% \text{ Contribution margin}}$$

$$= \$6,000,000 \text{ Breakeven sales level}$$

Thus, the customer's sales can decline by $2,000,000 from their current level before the customer will begin to lose money.

Margin of Safety

The margin of safety is the reduction in sales that can occur before the breakeven point of a business is reached. The amount of this buffer is expressed as a percentage. The concept is especially useful when a significant proportion of sales are at risk of decline or elimination, as may be the case when a sales contract is coming to an end. By knowing the amount of the margin of safety, management can gain a better understanding of the risk of loss to which a business is subjected by changes in sales. The opposite situation may also arise, where the margin is so large that a business is well-protected from sales variations.

The margin of safety concept does not work well when sales are strongly seasonal, since some months will yield catastrophically low results. In such cases, annualize the information in order to integrate all seasonal fluctuations into the outcome.

To calculate the margin of safety, subtract the current breakeven point from sales, and divide by sales. The formula is:

$$\frac{\text{Current sales level} - \text{Breakeven point}}{\text{Current sales level}}$$

Here are two alternative versions of the margin of safety:

1. *Budget based*. A company may want to project its margin of safety under a budget for a future period. If so, replace the current sales level in the formula with the budgeted sales level.
2. *Unit based*. If you want to translate the margin of safety into the number of units sold, then use the following formula instead (though note that this version works best if a company only sells one product):

$$\frac{\text{Current sales level} - \text{Breakeven point}}{\text{Selling price per unit}}$$

EXAMPLE

Lowry Locomotion is considering the purchase of new equipment to expand the production capacity of its toy tractor product line. The addition will increase Lowry's operating costs by $100,000 per year, though sales will also be increased. Relevant information is noted in the following table:

	Before Machinery Purchase	After Machinery Purchase
Sales	$4,000,000	$4,200,000
Gross margin percentage	48%	48%
Fixed expenses	$1,800,000	$1,900,000
Breakeven point	$3,750,000	$3,958,000
Profits	$120,000	$116,000
Margin of safety	6.3%	5.8%

The table reveals that both the margin of safety and profits worsen slightly as a result of the equipment purchase, so expanding production capacity is probably not a good idea.

Current Ratio

One of the first ratios that a lender or supplier reviews when examining a company is its current ratio. The current ratio measures the short-term liquidity of a business;

that is, it gives an indication of the ability of a business to pay its bills. A ratio of 2:1 is preferred, with a lower proportion indicating a reduced ability to pay in a timely manner. Since the ratio is current assets divided by current liabilities, the ratio essentially implies that current assets can be liquidated to pay for current liabilities.

To calculate the current ratio, divide the total of all current assets by the total of all current liabilities. The formula is:

$$\frac{\text{Current assets}}{\text{Current liabilities}}$$

The current ratio can yield misleading results under the following circumstances:

- *Inventory component.* When the current assets figure includes a large proportion of inventory assets, since these assets can be difficult to liquidate. This can be a particular problem if management is using aggressive accounting techniques to apply an unusually large amount of overhead costs to inventory, which further inflates the recorded amount of inventory.
- *Paying from debt.* When a company is drawing upon its line of credit to pay bills as they come due, which means that the cash balance is near zero. In this case, the current ratio could be fairly low, and yet the presence of a line of credit still allows a business to pay in a timely manner.

EXAMPLE

A supplier wants to learn about the financial condition of Lowry Locomotion. The supplier calculates the current ratio of Lowry for the past three years:

	Year 1	Year 2	Year 3
Current assets	$8,000,000	$16,400,000	$23,400,000
Current liabilities	$4,000,000	$9,650,000	$18,000,000
Current ratio	2:1	1.7:1	1.3:1

The sudden rise in current assets over the past two years indicates that Lowry has undergone a rapid expansion of its operations. Of particular concern is the increase in accounts payable in Year 3, which indicates a rapidly deteriorating ability to pay suppliers. Based on this information, the supplier elects to restrict the extension of credit to Lowry.

Quick Ratio

The quick ratio formula matches the most easily liquidated portions of current assets with current liabilities. The intent of this ratio is to see if a business has sufficient assets that are immediately convertible to cash to pay its bills. The key elements of current assets that are included in the quick ratio are cash, marketable securities, and accounts receivable. Inventory is not included in the quick ratio, since it can be quite difficult to sell off in the short term. Because of the exclusion of inventory from the formula, the quick ratio is a better indicator than the current ratio of the ability of a company to pay its obligations.

To calculate the quick ratio, summarize cash, marketable securities and trade receivables, and divide by current liabilities. Do not include in the numerator any excessively old receivables that are unlikely to be paid. The formula is:

$$\frac{\text{Cash} + \text{Marketable securities} + \text{Accounts receivable}}{\text{Current liabilities}}$$

Despite the absence of inventory from the calculation, the quick ratio may still not yield a good view of immediate liquidity, if current liabilities are payable right now, while receipts from receivables are not expected for several more weeks.

EXAMPLE

Rapunzel Hair Products appears to have a respectable current ratio of 4:1. The breakdown of the ratio components is:

Item	Amount
Cash	$100,000
Marketable securities	50,000
Accounts receivable	420,000
Inventory	3,430,000
Current liabilities	1,000,000
Current ratio	4:1
Quick ratio	0.57:1

The component breakdown reveals that nearly all of Rapunzel's current assets are in the inventory area, where short-term liquidity is questionable. This issue is only visible when the quick ratio is substituted for the current ratio.

Tip: It may be necessary to determine the ability of a business to pay off its most essential liabilities in the short term. If so, strip away from the quick ratio all liabilities that can be safely delayed, and use the remaining liabilities in the denominator.

Working Capital Productivity

The working capital productivity measurement compares sales to working capital. The intent is to measure whether a business has invested in a sufficient amount of working capital to support its sales. From a financing perspective, management wants to maintain low working capital levels in order to keep from having to raise more cash to operate the business. This can be achieved by such techniques as issuing less credit to customers, implementing just-in-time systems to avoid investing in inventory, and lengthening payment terms to suppliers.

Conversely, if the ratio indicates that a business has a large amount of receivables and inventory, this means that the organization is investing too much capital in return for the amount of sales that it is generating.

To decide whether the working capital productivity ratio is reasonable, compare a company's results to those of competitors or benchmark businesses.

To derive working capital productivity, divide annual revenues by the total amount of working capital. The formula is:

$$\frac{\text{Annual revenues}}{\text{Total working capital}}$$

When using this measurement, consider including the annualized quarterly sales in order to gain a better short-term understanding of the relationship between working capital and sales. Also, the measurement can be misleading if calculated during a seasonal spike in sales, since the formula will match high sales with a depleted inventory level to produce an unusually high ratio.

EXAMPLE

A lender is concerned that Pianoforte International does not have sufficient financing to support its sales. The lender obtains Pianoforte's financial statements, which contain the following information:

Annual revenues	$7,800,000
Cash	200,000
Accounts receivable	800,000
Inventory	2,000,000
Accounts payable	400,000

With this information, the lender derives the working capital productivity measurement as follows:

$$\frac{\$7,800,000 \text{ Annual revenues}}{\$200,000 \text{ Cash} + \$800,000 \text{ Receivables} + \$2,000,000 \text{ Inventory} - \$400,000 \text{ Payables}}$$
$$= 3:1 \text{ Working capital productivity}$$

This ratio is lower than the industry average of 4:1, which indicates poor management of the company's receivables and inventory. The lender should investigate further to see if the receivable and inventory figures may contain large amounts of overdue or obsolete items, respectively.

Debt to Equity Ratio

The debt to equity ratio of a business is closely monitored by the lenders and creditors of the company, since it can provide early warning that an organization is so overwhelmed by debt that it is unable to meet its payment obligations. This may also be triggered by a funding issue. For example, the owners of a business may not want to contribute any more cash to the company, so they acquire more debt to address the cash shortfall. Or, a company may use debt to buy back shares, thereby increasing the return on investment to the remaining shareholders.

Whatever the reason for debt usage, the outcome can be catastrophic, if corporate cash flows are not sufficient to make ongoing debt payments. This is a concern to lenders, whose loans may not be paid back. Suppliers are also concerned about the ratio for the same reason. A lender can protect its interests by imposing collateral requirements or restrictive covenants; suppliers usually offer credit with less restrictive terms, and so can suffer more if a company is unable to meet its payment obligations to them.

To calculate the debt to equity ratio, simply divide total debt by total equity. In this calculation, the debt figure should also include all lease obligations. The formula is:

$$\frac{\text{Long-term debt} + \text{Short-term debt} + \text{Leases}}{\text{Equity}}$$

EXAMPLE

An analyst is reviewing the credit application of New Centurion Corporation. The company reports a $500,000 line of credit, $1,700,000 in long-term debt, and a $200,000 operating lease. The company has $800,000 of equity. Based on this information, New Centurion's debt to equity ratio is:

$$\frac{\$500,000 \text{ Line of credit} + \$1,700,000 \text{ Debt} + \$200,000 \text{ Lease}}{\$800,000 \text{ Equity}}$$

$$= 3:1 \text{ debt to equity ratio}$$

The debt to equity ratio exceeds the 2:1 ratio threshold above which the analyst is not allowed to grant credit. Consequently, New Centurion is kept on cash in advance payment terms.

Interest Coverage Ratio

The interest coverage ratio measures the ability of a company to pay the interest on its outstanding debt. A high interest coverage ratio indicates that a business can pay for its interest expense several times over, while a low ratio is a strong indicator that an organization may default on its loan payments.

It is useful to track the interest coverage ratio on a trend line, in order to spot situations where a company's results or debt burden are yielding a downward trend in the ratio. An investor would want to sell the equity holdings in a company showing such a downward trend, especially if the ratio drops below 1.5:1, since this indicates a likely problem with meeting debt obligations.

To calculate the interest coverage ratio, divide earnings before interest and taxes (EBIT) by the interest expense for the measurement period. The formula is:

$$\frac{\text{Earnings before interest and taxes}}{\text{Interest expense}}$$

EXAMPLE

Carpenter Holdings generates $5,000,000 of earnings before interest and taxes in its most recent reporting period. Its interest expense in that period is $2,500,000. Therefore, the company's interest coverage ratio is calculated as:

$$\frac{\$5,000,000 \text{ EBIT}}{\$2,500,000 \text{ Interest expense}}$$

$$= 2:1 \text{ Interest coverage ratio}$$

The ratio indicates that Carpenter's earnings should be sufficient to enable it to pay the interest expense.

A company may be accruing an interest expense that is not actually due for payment yet, so the ratio can indicate a debt default that will not really occur, or at least until such time as the interest is due for payment.

Cost per Square Foot

An excellent way to measure the cost of any facility is to aggregate all rent, maintenance, and utility costs for it and then divide by the square footage of the facility to derive the cost per square foot. This information can be used to compare the cost of the facility to alternative forms of housing elsewhere in the area. The result may be a switch to a facility with a lower aggregate cost per square foot.

This measurement does not track the usage level of a facility, only its total cost. Thus, even an inexpensive facility could be shut down if its usage level is minimal.

EXAMPLE

Kelvin Corporation's CFO is reviewing information regarding the possible lease of replacement office space for the company. The company's current facility contains 20,000 square feet, and the company pays its share of utility and maintenance costs, as well as for the rental of parking spaces for employees. The proposed replacement facility contains

25,000 square feet and has the same cost sharing arrangement, except that parking is free. The relevant information is noted in the following table:

	Current Facility	Proposed Facility
Square footage	20,000	25,000
Total rent	$340,000	$400,000
Utilities and maintenance cost	52,000	60,000
Parking fees	28,000	0
Total cost	$420,000	$460,000
Cost per square foot	$21.00	$18.40

Based on the total cost of these facilities, it initially appears that the company should retain the current facility. However, the lower cost per square foot of the larger facility could make it more attractive if the company expects to add staff during the lease term, or can sublease the excess space.

This measurement does not factor in the duration of a lease agreement, which could be a critical issue. For example, if there is a choice between a long-term lease at a very low rate per square foot and a short-term lease at a much higher rate, it may still make sense to enter into the short-term lease, to give the company the option in the near term to shift its operations elsewhere.

Occupancy Cost Ratio

The cost of company facilities is one of the higher expenditures made, usually in third place after the cost of goods sold and compensation costs. Given its considerable size, it makes sense to track occupancy cost as a percentage of net sales, and see if this percentage is reasonable in comparison to the same measurement for competitors and nearby companies.

To calculate occupancy cost, aggregate all costs of a facility, such as rent (or depreciation, if the business owns a facility), maintenance, insurance, real estate taxes, and utilities, and divide by net sales. The formula is:

$$\frac{\text{Rent expense} + \text{Depreciation} + \text{Utilities} + \text{Maintenance} + \text{Insurance} + \text{Real estate taxes}}{\text{Net sales}}$$

There is no ideal occupancy cost ratio. A company may have an inordinately high ratio, but chooses to incur this expense because its target pool of employees is located within a major metropolitan area, or because the facility must be located next to a key customer. Conversely, a company's strategic vision might require that the occupancy cost be as low as possible, irrespective of whether qualified employees live nearby, and so a facility is located in a rural area.

EXAMPLE

Big Data Corporation builds and leases out enormous server farms. The key cost of these farms is the availability of cheap electricity, so all of the company's locations are situated near hydroelectric or geothermal generating stations, usually deep in the countryside. In this case, utilities are the key element of the occupancy cost ratio.

Big Apple Produce sells its organic food products to restaurants in the New York City area. Because of high property taxes, Big Apple's facilities are always located just outside of the property lines of the incorporated areas near New York.

The Twister Vacuum Company elects to move to Arizona from its current location near Oklahoma City. The reason is the insurance component of the company's occupancy cost. The weather damage insurance associated with being located in Tornado Alley in Oklahoma is too much for the company, so moving to the more benign environment in Arizona allows the company to reduce its occupancy cost.

Return on Equity

The return on equity (ROE) ratio reveals the amount of return earned by investors on their investments in a business. It is one of the metrics most closely watched by investors. Given the intense focus on ROE, it is frequently used as the basis for bonus compensation for senior managers.

ROE is essentially net income divided by shareholders' equity. ROE performance can be enhanced by focusing on improvements to three underlying measurements, all of which roll up into ROE. These sub-level measurements are:

- *Profit margin*. Calculated as net income divided by sales. Can be improved by trimming expenses, increasing prices, or altering the mix of products or services sold.
- *Asset turnover*. Calculated as sales divided by assets. Can be improved by reducing receivable balances, inventory levels, and/or the investment in fixed assets, as well as by lengthening payables payment terms.
- *Financial leverage*. Calculated as assets divided by shareholders' equity. Can be improved by buying back shares, paying dividends, or using more debt to fund operations.

Or, stated as a formula, the return on equity is as follows:

$$\text{Return on Equity} = \frac{\text{Net income}}{\text{Sales}} \times \frac{\text{Sales}}{\text{Assets}} \times \frac{\text{Assets}}{\text{Shareholders' equity}}$$

EXAMPLE

Hammer Industries manufactures construction equipment. The company's return on equity has declined from a high of 25% five years ago to a current level of 10%. The CFO wants to know what is causing the problem, and assigns the task to an accountant, Wendy. She reviews the components of ROE for both periods, and derives the following information:

	ROE		Profit Margin		Asset Turnover		Financial Leverage
Five Years Ago	25%	=	12%	×	1.2x	×	1.75x
Today	10%	=	10%	×	0.6x	×	1.70x

The information in the table reveals that the primary culprit causing the decline is a sharp reduction in the company's asset turnover. This has been caused by a large buildup in the company's inventory levels, which have been caused by management's insistence on stocking larger amounts of finished goods in order to increase the speed of order fulfillment.

The multiple components of the ROE calculation present an opportunity for a business to generate a high ROE in several ways. For example, a grocery store has low profits on a per-unit basis, but turns over its assets at a rapid rate, so that it earns a profit on many sale transactions over the course of a year. Conversely, a manufacturer of custom goods realizes large profits on each sale, but also maintains a significant amount of component parts that reduce asset turnover. The following illustration shows how both entities can earn an identical ROE, despite having such a different emphasis on profits and asset turnover. In the illustration, we ignore the effects of financial leverage.

Comparison of Returns on Equity

	ROE		Profit Margin		Asset Turnover
Grocery Store	20%	=	2%	×	10x
Custom manufacturer	20%	=	40%	×	0.5x

Usually, a successful business is able to focus on either a robust profit margin *or* a high rate of asset turnover. If it were able to generate both, its return on equity would be so high that the company would likely attract competitors who want to emulate the underlying business model. If so, the increased level of competition usually drives down the overall return on equity in the market to a more reasonable level.

A high level of financial leverage can increase the return on equity, because it means a business is using the minimum possible amount of equity, instead relying on debt to fund its operations. By doing so, the amount of equity in the denominator of the return on equity equation is minimized. If any profits are generated by funding activities with debt, these changes are added to the numerator in the equation, thereby increasing the return on equity.

The trouble with employing financial leverage is that it imposes a new fixed expense in the form of interest payments. If sales decline, this added cost of debt could trigger a steep decline in profits that could end in bankruptcy. Thus, a business that relies too much on debt to enhance its shareholder returns may find itself in significant financial trouble. A more prudent path is to employ a modest amount of additional debt that a company can comfortably handle even through a business downturn.

EXAMPLE

The president of Finchley Fireworks has been granted a bonus plan that is triggered by an increase in the return on equity. Finchley has $2,000,000 of equity, of which the president plans to buy back $600,000 with the proceeds of a loan that has a 6% after-tax interest rate. The following table models this plan:

	Before Buyback	After Buyback
Sales	$10,000,000	$10,000,000
Expenses	9,700,000	9,700,000
Debt interest expense	---	36,000
Profits	300,000	264,000
Equity	2,000,000	1,400,000
Return on equity	15%	19%

The model indicates that this strategy will work. Expenses will be increased by the new amount of interest expense, but the offset is a steep decline in equity, which increases the return on equity. An additional issue to be investigated is whether the company's cash flows are stable enough to support this extra level of debt.

A business that has a significant asset base (and therefore a low asset turnover rate) is more likely to engage in a larger amount of financial leverage. This situation arises because the large asset base can be used as collateral for loans. Conversely, if a company has high asset turnover, the amount of assets on hand at any point in time is relatively low, giving a lender few assets to designate as collateral for a loan.

> **Tip:** A highly successful company that spins off large amounts of cash may generate a low return on equity, because it chooses to retain a large part of the cash. Cash retention increases assets and so results in a low asset turnover rate, which in turn drives down the return on equity. Actual ROE can be derived by stripping the excess amount of cash from the ROE equation.

Return on equity is one of the primary tools used to measure the performance of a business, particularly in regard to how well management is enhancing shareholder value. As noted in this section, there are multiple ways to enhance ROE. However, we must warn against the excessive use of financial leverage to improve ROE, since the use of debt can turn into a considerable burden if cash flows decline.

A case can be made that ROE should be ignored, since an excessive focus on it may drive management to pare back on a number of discretionary expenses that are needed to build the long-term value of a company. For example, the senior management team may cut back on expenditures for research and development, training, and marketing in order to boost profits in the short term and elevate ROE.

However, doing so impairs the ability of the business to build its brand and compete effectively over the long term. Some management teams will even buy their companies back from investors, so that they are not faced with the ongoing pressure to enhance ROE. In a buyback situation, managers see that a lower ROE combined with a proper level of reinvestment in the business is a better path to long-term value.

Days Sales Outstanding

When evaluating the amount of accounts receivable outstanding, it is best to compare the receivables to the sales activity of the business, in order to see the proportion of receivables to sales. This proportion can be expressed as the average number of days over which receivables are outstanding before they are paid, which is called days sales outstanding, or DSO. DSO is the most popular of all collection measurements.

Days sales outstanding is most useful when compared to the standard number of days that customers are allowed before payment is due. Thus, a DSO figure of 40 days might initially appear excellent, until you realize that the standard payment terms are only five days. A combination of prudent credit granting and robust collections activity is the likely cause when the DSO figure is only a few days longer than the standard payment terms. From a management perspective, it is easiest to spot collection problems at a gross level by tracking DSO on a trend line, and watching for a sudden spike in the measurement in comparison to what was reported in prior periods.

To calculate DSO, divide 365 days into the amount of annual credit sales to arrive at credit sales per day, and then divide this figure into the average accounts receivable for the measurement period. Thus, the formula is:

$$\frac{\text{Average accounts receivable}}{\text{Annual sales} \div 365 \text{ days}}$$

EXAMPLE

The accountant of Oberlin Acoustics, maker of the famous Rhino brand of electric guitars, wants to derive the days sales outstanding for the company for the April reporting period. In April, the beginning and ending accounts receivable balances were $420,000 and $540,000 respectively. The total credit sales for the 12 months ended April 30 were $4,000,000. The accountant derives the following DSO calculation from this information:

$$\frac{(\$420{,}000 \text{ Beginning receivables} + \$540{,}000 \text{ Ending receivables}) \div 2}{\$4{,}000{,}000 \text{ Credit sales} \div 365 \text{ Days}}$$

$$=$$

$$\frac{\$480{,}000 \text{ Average accounts receivable}}{\$10{,}959 \text{ Credit sales per day}}$$

$$= 43.8 \text{ Days}$$

The correlation between the annual sales figure used in the calculation and the average accounts receivable figure may not be close, resulting in a misleading DSO number. For example, if a company has seasonal sales, the average receivable figure may be unusually high or low on the measurement date, depending on where the company is in its seasonal billings. Thus, if receivables are unusually low when the measurement is taken, the DSO days will appear unusually low, and vice versa if the receivables are unusually high. There are two ways to eliminate this problem:

- *Annualize receivables*. Generate an average accounts receivable figure that spans the entire, full-year measurement period.
- *Measure a shorter period*. Adopt a rolling quarterly DSO calculation, so that sales for the past three months are compared to average receivables for the past three months. This approach is most useful when sales are highly variable throughout the year.

Whatever measurement methodology is adopted for DSO, be sure to use it consistently from period to period, so that the results will be comparable on a trend line.

> **Tip:** If DSO is increasing, the problem may be that the processing of credit memos has been delayed. If there is a processing backlog, at least have the largest ones processed first, which may reduce the amount of receivables outstanding by a noticeable amount.

Best Possible DSO

After running the DSO calculation, it may be useful to establish a benchmark against which to compare the DSO. This benchmark is the best possible DSO, which is the best collection performance that you can expect, given the existing payment terms given to customers. The calculation is:

$$\frac{\text{Current receivables}}{\text{Annual credit sales}} \times 365$$

The key element in this formula is the *current* receivables. The calculation is essentially designed to show the best possible level of receivables, based on the assumption that DSO is only based on current receivables (i.e., there are no delinquent invoices present in the calculation).

EXAMPLE

The collections manager of the Red Herring Fish Company has established that the company's DSO is 22 days. Since the company requires short payment terms on its short-lived products, the question arises – is 22 days good or bad? At the end of the current period, Red Herring's current receivables were $30,000, and its trailing 12-month credit sales were $1,000,000. Based on this information, the best possible DSO is:

$$\frac{\$30,000 \text{ Current receivables}}{\$1,000,000 \text{ Credit sales}} \times 365$$

$$= 11 \text{ Days}$$

In short, actual DSO is running at a rate double that of the company's best possible DSO, and so should be considered an opportunity for improvement.

Collection Effectiveness Index

The days sales outstanding measurement operates at a relatively high level, and only gives a general indication of the state of receivables in comparison to sales over a fairly long period of time. An alternative that yields a somewhat higher level of precision is the collection effectiveness index (CEI). This measurement compares the amount that was collected in a given time period to the amount of receivables that were available for collection in that time period. A result near 100% indicates that a collection department has been very effective in collecting from customers.

The formula for the CEI is to combine the beginning receivables for the measurement period with the credit sales for that period, less the amount of ending receivables, and then divide this number by the sum of the beginning receivables for the measurement period and the credit sales for that period, less the amount of ending *current* receivables. Then multiply the result by 100 to arrive at a CEI percentage. Thus, the formula is stated as:

$$\frac{\text{Beginning receivables} + \text{Credit sales for the period} - \text{Ending total receivables}}{\text{Beginning receivables} + \text{Credit sales for the period} - \text{Ending current receivables}} \times 100$$

A collections manager can attain a high CEI number by focusing on the collection of the largest receivables. This means that a favorable CEI can be generated, even if there are a number of smaller receivables that are very overdue.

The CEI figure can be calculated for a period of any duration, such as a single month. Conversely, the DSO calculation tends to be less accurate for very short periods of time, since it includes receivables from prior periods that do not directly relate to the credit sales figure in that calculation.

EXAMPLE

Milagro Corporation, maker of espresso coffee machines, has been relying on DSO to measure its collection effectiveness, but wants to supplement it with a measurement designed for a shorter period of time. The collection effectiveness index is selected as that measure. For the most recent month, the company had $400,000 of beginning receivables, $350,000 of credit sales, $425,000 of ending total receivables, and $300,000 of ending current receivables. The calculation of its CEI reveals the following information:

$$\frac{\$400,000 \text{ Beginning receivables} + \$350,000 \text{ Credit sales for the period} - \$425,00 \text{ Ending total receivables}}{\$400,000 \text{ Beginning receivables} + \$350,000 \text{ Credit sales for the period} - \$300,000 \text{ Ending current receivables}} \times 100$$

$$= 72\% \text{ Collection effectiveness index}$$

Thus, Milagro was able to collect 72% of the receivables that were available for collection in that month.

Inventory Turnover

The turnover of inventory is the rate at which inventory is used over a measurement period. This is an important measurement, for many businesses are burdened by an excessively large investment in inventory, which can consume the bulk of available cash. When there is a low rate of inventory turnover, this implies that a business may have a flawed purchasing system that bought too many goods, or that stocks were increased in anticipation of sales that did not occur. In both cases, there is a high risk of inventory aging, in which case it becomes obsolete and has reduced resale value.

When there is a high rate of inventory turnover, this implies that the purchasing function is tightly managed. However, it may also mean that a business does not have the cash reserves to maintain normal inventory levels, and so is turning away prospective sales. The latter scenario is most likely when the amount of debt is high and there are minimal cash reserves.

To calculate inventory turnover, divide the ending inventory figure into the annualized cost of sales. If the ending inventory figure is not a representative number, use an average figure instead. The formula is:

$$\frac{\text{Annual cost of goods sold}}{\text{Inventory}}$$

You can also divide the result of this calculation into 365 days to arrive at days of inventory on hand. Thus, a turnover rate of 4.0 becomes 91 days of inventory.

EXAMPLE

An analyst is reviewing the inventory situation of the Hegemony Toy Company. The business incurred $8,150,000 of cost of goods sold in the past year, and has ending inventory of $1,630,000. Total inventory turnover is calculated as:

$$\frac{\$8,150,000 \text{ Cost of goods sold}}{\$1,630,000 \text{ Inventory}}$$

= 5 Turns per year

The five turns figure is then divided into 365 days to arrive at 73 days of inventory on hand.

Sales Productivity

Sales productivity is the ability of the sales staff to generate profitable sales. A profitable sale is considered to be one that has a high throughput, where throughput is sales minus all totally variable expenses. We do not measure the sales generated by the sales staff, since there may be little throughput associated with those sales.

To calculate sales productivity, divide the total estimated throughput booked by the sales staff by the total sales department expense incurred. The formula is:

$$\frac{\text{Total sales booked} - \text{All variable expenses associated with sales booked}}{\text{Total sales department expenses}}$$

EXAMPLE

The president of Armadillo Security Armor is concerned that the sales department is not being overly productive in booking new sales. He has the company accountant accumulate the following information:

	January	February	March
Bookings	$4,200,000	$4,315,000	$4,520,000
Related variable expenses	$1,470,000	$1,726,000	$2,034,000
Throughput percentage	65%	60%	55%
Sales expenses	$250,000	$260,000	$265,000
Sales productivity	10.9x	10.0x	9.4x

The analysis reveals that the sales staff is increasing sales, but giving away margin in order to do so. The result is an ongoing decline in the department's sales productivity. It would be better to book fewer sales at higher margins, thereby generating more profit for the company.

Sales productivity should be judged over multiple periods, since some sales can take several reporting periods to finalize, and so might yield a measurement that spikes and slumps from month to month. Also, the measurement correlates with the experience level of the sales staff, so expect it to decline immediately after new sales employees are hired.

Sales Backlog Ratio

The sales backlog ratio provides an indicator of the ability of a business to maintain its current level of sales. When noted on a trend line, the measurement clearly indicates changes that will likely translate into future variations in sales volume. For example, if the ratio exhibits an ongoing trend of declines, this is a strong indicator

531

that a business is rapidly working through its backlog, and may soon begin to report sales reductions. The opposite trend of an increasing sales backlog does not necessarily translate into improved future sales, if a company has a bottleneck that prevents it from accelerating the rate at which it converts customer orders into sales.

To calculate the sales backlog ratio, divide the total dollar value of booked customer orders by the net sales figure for the past quarter. Only quarterly sales are used, rather than sales for the past year, in order to more properly reflect a company's short-term revenue-generating capability. The formula is:

$$\frac{\text{Total order backlog}}{\text{Quarterly sales}}$$

A different way of deriving the same information is to calculate for the number of days sales that can be derived from the existing order backlog. This figure is derived by dividing the average sales per day into the total backlog. The formula is:

$$\frac{\text{Total order backlog}}{\text{Quarterly sales} \div 90 \text{ days}}$$

The customer order information needed for this ratio cannot be entirely derived from a company's financial statements. Instead, it must be derived from internal reports that aggregate customer order information.

The ratio is of less use in the following situations:

- A retail environment, where there is no backlog
- A seasonal business, where the intent of the business model is to build order volume until the prime selling season, and then fulfill all orders
- A just-in-time "pull" model, where the intent is to fulfill orders as soon after receipt as possible

EXAMPLE

Henderson Mills reports the following sales and backlog information:

	April	May	June
Rolling 3-month sales	$9,000,000	$9,500,000	$9,600,000
Month-end backlog	5,000,000	4,000,000	3,500,000
Sales backlog ratio	0.55:1	0.42:1	0.36:1

The table indicates that Henderson is increasing its sales by chewing through its order backlog, which the company has been unable to replace. The result is likely to be the complete elimination of the order backlog in the near future, after which sales can be expected to plummet, unless steps are taken to book more customer orders.

Customer Turnover

It is usually much less expensive to retain existing customers than to acquire new ones, so companies typically go to considerable lengths to retain existing customers. However, this logic is not entirely correct, for some customers order in such low volume or require so much maintenance that a business should be indifferent to their departure. Only the core group of customers that buy in volume or yield significant profits should be encouraged to remain. For this select group, a company should track the customer turnover rate.

To calculate the customer turnover rate, divide the number of customers not having placed orders within a set time period by the total number of customers. The set time period should be an interval judged sufficiently long that a customer is likely not planning to place an order if they have not done so within this time period. The formula is:

$$\frac{\text{Number of core customers} - \text{Number of these customers placing orders}}{\text{Number of core customers}}$$

There are two elements of this measurement that are subject to interpretation. The first issue is which customers to include in the core group being tracked. One possible threshold for this group is to use the 20% of customers that comprise 80% of the company's profits (i.e., pareto analysis). The second issue is the time period within which orders must be placed in order to be considered a current customer. This latter issue could be defined by individual customer, based on their ordering history, or as an average ordering interval with an additional buffer period added.

EXAMPLE

The owners of Ambivalence Corporation sell various potions and brews to self-styled witches around the world. An in-depth customer analysis finds that the company receives 90% of its sales from just 10% of its customers. To ensure that the company retains these customers, the president decides that customer turnover for this key group will be the number one metric followed by the measurement team. Over the past three quarters, the turnover rate has been as follows:

	Quarter 1	Quarter 2	Quarter 3
Customers not ordering	6	9	37
Total core customers	320	314	305
	2%	3%	12%

Further investigation of the sudden decline in the third quarter reveals that all of the lost customers are based in Jamaica, where a new competitor has opened a warehouse and is offering same-day delivery. The management team decides to do the same, and notifies its former customers of an impending plan to deliver within two hours of order placement.

Summary

Ratio analysis is a simple way to review the financial results and position of a business, especially when the information is tracked on a trend line. However, do not confine ratio analysis to the contents of the financial statements. Ratios can also provide insights into the operations of *every* department. For example, the accountant could create an expanded analysis that is used to review such issues as the proportion of customer warranty claims, the amount of time required to fulfill customer orders, the effectiveness of marketing campaigns, and the rate at which customers are turning over. These additional areas of analysis can provide early warning about problems that might not appear in the financial statements for many months to come. For more information about the full range of available ratios, see the author's *Business Ratios Guidebook*.

Chapter 29
Cost Object Analysis

Introduction

A cost object is any item for which costs are separately measured. It may be necessary to track a cost object in order to derive pricing from a baseline cost, or to see if costs are reasonable, or to derive the full cost of a relationship with another entity. Here are several types of cost objects:

- *Output*. The most common cost objects are a company's products and services, since it wants to know the cost of its output for profitability analysis and price setting.
- *Operational*. A cost object can be within a company, such as a department, machining operation, or process. Examples are the design of a new product, a customer service call, or the reworking of a returned product.
- *Business relationship*. A cost object could be a business partner, such as a supplier or customer.

In this chapter, we address which costs to assign to a cost object that are relevant to decisions concerning that cost object. A sample group of the more common cost objects are described.

Factors in Cost Object Analysis

From a cost management perspective, why review cost objects? The main point is that there are vast differences in the amount of cost accumulated by each cost object, and your intent is to spotlight those cost objects that are soaking up more costs than their counterparts. The intent is not to spotlight slight differences in the costs of cost objects, since these could just as easily be caused by measurement problems as by actual differences in costs. Instead, the focus is on major spikes in cost that are causing significant profitability issues.

When reviewing cost objects, any of the following factors can be causing unusually high costs:

- *High complexity*. Any extremely complex cost object attracts more costs. This can include a higher initial investment, as well as more maintenance and training costs. For example, a large piece of automated equipment will attract more costs than a simpler device that can be manually operated.
- *High investment*. A high initial investment immediately applies a significant cost to a cost object, even if no additional costs accrue over time.
- *High support levels*. This concept applies specifically to customers, and refers to the greatly increased level of customer support that some customers

require. This concept can also involve the cost of bad debts, product returns, and warranties.

- *Low volume*. A cost object may attract a large amount of costs because there are so few units of it. Any costs incurred cannot be allocated across a large number of units, so the cost per cost object tends to be quite high.
- *Small lot size*. This concept mostly applies to production lines. When a significant amount of time is required to retool a production line, a small lot size will accumulate more setup costs on a per-unit basis than a larger lot size.

An unusually high cost in a cost object is not necessarily to be avoided, as long as a sufficient amount of profit can still be derived from the object. A business may intentionally invest in extremely expensive cost objects, with the intent of charging premium prices on products relating to these objects. For example:

- *Employees*. A company hires only the best programmers and rewards them with high-end compensation and a rich benefits package. The company then charges premium prices to customers for their services.
- *Machinery*. A company invests in a massively expensive automated factory that allows it to alter the production schedule on a moment's notice. The company then charges far more than the usual price for its products, based on its ability to customize orders and ship to customers on the same day.
- *Products*. A watchmaker manufactures very short production runs of premium watches and sells them to collectors at inordinately high prices.

However, all of these examples highlight the fact that only a premium pricing strategy can be used when cost objects collect unusually large costs. If a business pursues any other type of strategy, it must pay close attention to its cost objects.

The Assignability of Costs

The bulk of this chapter is concerned with the accumulation of costs for specific cost objects. When doing so, a key issue is which costs to include or exclude. The concept is not a minor one, for the resulting report may trigger a management decision to eliminate the cost object – which may be, for example, an employee, a store, a product, or a customer. Consequently, assigning the correct costs is crucial.

When assigning costs to cost objects, the rule is to do so if the elimination of the cost object in question would also eliminate the cost. Thus, the termination of employment for a single individual will certainly eliminate that person's compensation, but will not affect the additional costs of the payroll or human resources departments. However, the situation changes considerably when the scope of the cost object expands. Thus, if an entire production facility is considered a cost object, it is entirely likely that the payroll and human resources departments of that facility should be included in the cost, since those departments would be eliminated if the facility were to be eliminated.

Overhead costs should never be allocated to cost objects. The reason is that the most common management decision related to a cost object is whether to retain or eliminate it, so only costs that will verifiably be eliminated should be attached to a cost object. Since overhead is, by its nature, not associated with a cost object, it should not be assigned to a cost object.

EXAMPLE

The president of Grubstake Brothers is concerned that the cost reports for the company's new Trench Demon digger machine indicate that it is losing money. A close examination of the cost report reveals that one cost assigned to this cost object is not actually closely related to the product, and so should be stripped away. The revised report is noted in the following table:

	Assignable Cost or Revenue	Costs not Assignable	Notes
Revenue	$1,000,000		
Direct materials	350,000		
Direct labor	120,000		All direct labor staff work on this product, and so should be included
Corporate overhead		$150,000	No corporate costs would be terminated if the product were cancelled
Facility overhead	450,000		The facility would be shut down if the product were cancelled, and so should be included
Warranty costs	35,000		
Net profit/loss	$45,000	-$150,000	

Because the production facility would be shut down if the product were terminated, it is acceptable to assign all costs of the facility to the product. This is not the case for the corporate overhead costs, which should therefore not be allocated to the product. In short, once the corporate overhead cost has been excluded from the cost object, there is a discernible profit.

In summary, the assignability of cost will vary, depending on the nature of the cost object, and should always be restricted to the variable costs incurred by a cost object.

The Customer Cost Object

A major cost object is the customer, since the primary purpose of a business is to expend funds specifically to serve its customers. Unfortunately, the cost accounting system is not designed to track costs for individual customers, so new systems will be needed to track the customer service time devoted to each customer, salesperson time by customer, and the cost of returned goods. Consider the assignable costs in the following table:

Costs to Assign to a Customer

+/-	Assignable Cost	Commentary
+	Customer service	Only include the cost of customer service if there would be a reduction in this cost if a customer were to be terminated
+	Salesperson	Only include the cost of the sales staff if salespeople would be terminated along with a customer
+	Returned goods	Include the out-of-pocket cost to handle returned goods, which may include freight, repackaging, and the profit lost from reselling these goods at a reduced price
+	Credits	Include the cost of all credits claimed by a customer, which may include volume discounts, damaged goods claims, and so forth
+	Early payment discounts	All early payment discounts taken by a customer are a cost of doing business with that specific customer, and so should be included

When a customer demands a great deal of attention, management is most likely to hear complaints from all over the company regarding how much staff time this customer requires. However, the issue is irrelevant unless the termination of the customer would directly trigger a reduction in company support staff. If not, and despite all the complaining, there is no incremental staff cost associated with a demanding customer.

EXAMPLE

Dude Skis sells to Stuffy Skis, which is a high-end retailer of the most expensive all-mountain skis, as well as Warehouse Sports, which retails the lowest-cost skis through many outlets to beginner skiers. The skis that Dude sells to Stuffy have the highest margins, and Stuffy requires little administrative support. Warehouse buys in massive volume, but only buys low-margin items, and returns 20% of its purchases under various pretexts in order to clear out its inventory at the end of the season. Dude's management wants to know how much it earns from each customer, and whether it should drop either one. Dude's financial analyst constructs the following table:

	Stuffy Customer	Warehouse Customer
Revenue	$520,000	$2,780,000
Direct costs		
Materials	210,000	1,390,000
Direct labor	100,000	550,000
Customer service cost	0	130,000
Sales returns cost	0	600,000
Total direct costs	310,000	2,670,000
Contribution margin ($)	$210,000	$110,000
Contribution margin (%)	40%	4%

In the table, there is no customer service cost at all for Stuffy Skis, since no customer service positions would be eliminated if Dude were to drop Stuffy as a customer. On the other hand,

538

there are four customer service employees assigned to the Warehouse Sports account who would be laid off if Dude were to drop that account.

The analysis reveals that Stuffy Skis produces far more contribution margin than Warehouse Sports, despite much lower revenues. However, this does not mean that Dude should eliminate Warehouse as a customer, since it still produces $110,000 of contribution margin. If Dude has a considerable amount of overhead to cover, it may be quite necessary to continue dealing with Warehouse Sports in order to retain the associated amount of contribution margin.

Customer Acquisition Costs

Thus far, we have only addressed the cost of *maintaining* a relationship with a customer. In addition, there is the cost of *acquiring* a customer, which can be extraordinarily high. There may be a marketing campaign that triggers a few expressions of interest from potential customers, followed by salesperson visits that further reduce the pool of prospects, followed by product demonstrations that finally yield a small number of actual customers. If the total cost of this acquisition process were to be spread across the few resulting customers, it would be apparent that an existing customer relationship is extremely valuable. Knowledge of this acquisition cost might trigger additional actions, such as:

- *More analysis of acquisition methods.* The profits garnered from newly-acquired customers may not justify the cost of their acquisition, resulting in the testing of alternative acquisition methods.
- *More initial analysis of customers.* Management is likely to spend more time reviewing the incremental cost of acquiring a new customer. It may pay to be picky about acquiring new customers in order to avoid those that will soak up an excessive amount of company resources.
- *More customer service.* Since it is less expensive to maintain an existing relationship than to acquire a new relationship, management could commit to spend more money on existing customers in order to improve the relationship, such as faster customer service response times or paying for faster shipping to customers.

Customer Lifetime Value

The typical analysis of the value represented by an individual customer is based on the identifiable profits generated from sales to a customer within a measurement period, typically a month, quarter, or year. This measurement approach does not result in a complete view of a customer relationship, however, for it fails to consider the initial investment in acquiring the customer. This could be a substantial amount, which may call for a long-term relationship before a notable return on that investment is achieved.

When valuing a customer based on its lifetime value to the company (or CLV), it may not be possible to simply extrapolate current buying patterns into the future.

A customer's buying needs may change over time, resulting in different types of sales or changes in the level of effort required to complete a sale. For example:

- Since the relationship is already established, additional sales can be made with less selling effort, such as not being forced to engage in a bidding process.
- The customer may be amenable to the company's effort to cross-sell other types of products and services to it.
- A change in the size of the customer over time may require it to ask for alternative products from the company that are different in size, complexity, or features.

If so, these changes in buying patterns may be predictable, and can be incorporated into an analysis of lifetime value. The following example illustrates the concept:

EXAMPLE

AirLife Turbines competes in the wind turbine market, where it sells turbines to power generation companies. The industry is fiercely competitive, with initial sales margins of only 3% being the average on turbine sales. However, once a sales relationship is established, Airlife can reliably achieve after-market servicing margins of 25% per customer over the remaining 30-year life of a turbine.

A new financial analyst is hired, examines the company's margins for new sales, and promptly recommends an immediate 10% increase in turbine prices to increase the margins on initial sales. However, the vastly more experienced CFO points out that, when a full customer lifetime value analysis is made, the actual profitability of every customer is really quite high. In effect, the low initial product prices are needed to lock customers into long-term service agreements.

A likely outcome of CLV analysis is an enhanced emphasis on customer turnover rates. If there is a high rate of customer turnover, then the initial cost of customer acquisition must be correspondingly low, so that the CLV remains profitable. Conversely, if the turnover rate is extremely low, it makes more sense to spend what might otherwise be considered an inordinate amount of money to acquire new customers, since these customers are more likely to generate profits over a long period of time.

A company can also take a variety of steps to keep customer turnover from occurring, thereby expanding the average customer lifetime. Ways to reduce customer turnover include:

- *Enhanced product quality*. Create a feedback loop from the customer service department to the engineering staff, to ensure that all customer complaints regarding products result in product design changes or materials upgrades.
- *Enhanced customer experience*. Improve the response time for customer calls, and increase the speed with which field service calls are made.

- *Enhanced customer relations*. Assign customer relations officers to the most profitable customers, and ask customers to serve on customer advisory boards.

The Employee Cost Object

One of the most commonly-reviewed cost objects is the employee, particularly in regard to those administrative positions that can be more easily culled in the event of a downturn in business. However, the typical analysis only includes base-level compensation and the related payroll taxes, which does not yield a complete picture of the situation. Instead, a more comprehensive view should be assembled. Consider the assignable costs in the following table:

Costs to Assign to an Employee

+/-	Assignable Cost	Commentary
+	Base compensation	Base compensation is always included in the cost of an employee
+	Historical overtime	If a person has a history of incurring overtime, then include the average amount of this overtime, plus applicable payroll taxes
+	Bonuses	Only include the amount of bonuses that are likely to be earned, plus applicable payroll taxes
-	Increased compensation elsewhere	If an employee is to be let go, consider the cost of increased overtime for those employees remaining, as well as the payroll taxes associated with that overtime
+	Payroll taxes	This includes the social security, Medicare, and federal unemployment taxes paid by the employer
+	Benefits	This is the net cost of benefits paid by the company, after employee payroll deductions are subtracted
+	Travel and entertainment	This includes the historical average cost of travel and entertainment incurred by the employee

Several costs should not be included in an employee cost analysis, since they would still remain if an employee were to be let go. Consider the following costs:

- *Cell phones*. If a cell phone is considered common property that is simply passed along to a different person when one individual leaves the company, then its cost should not be assigned to a specific individual.
- *Commissions*. In many cases, a customer will be assigned to a different salesperson if the original salesperson is let go, so the company continues to incur a commission. However, if each sale is unique and there is no transfer of customers to a replacement salesperson, then the cost of commissions could be assigned to an employee.
- *Depreciation*. The depreciation on computer equipment and furniture used by an employee will remain if the position is eliminated, so do not assign the cost to an employee.

- *Profit sharing*. If an employee were to be laid off, profits would simply be shared with someone else who remains on the staff.
- *Square footage allocation*. The department to which an employee is assigned may be charged for the square footage occupied by the employee. Since this cost would remain even if an employee were not on staff, it should not be considered an employee-specific cost.

A particularly large point that is frequently missed is to assign the *actual* net cost of benefits to employees, rather than the *average* net cost per employee. For example, it is entirely likely that an employee taking family medical insurance is much more expensive than one taking single coverage, since there is such a large disparity in the costs of these two variations on medical insurance.

The Product Cost Object

A common analysis is to accumulate costs for a product, and use this as the basis for a decision to cancel the product. In this case, the analysis should be entirely based on the variable cost of the product, and nothing else. Since most costs in the production area are fixed, this means that comparatively few costs should be assigned to a product. Consider the assignable costs in the following table:

Costs to Assign to a Product

+/-	Assignable Cost	Commentary
+	Direct materials	Always assigned as a product cost
+	Packaging costs	Always assigned as a product cost
+	Commissions	Only assigned to a product if the commission specifically relates to the sale of that product
+	Piece rate pay	Add the cost of labor and related payroll taxes when employees are being paid for the incremental production of each individual unit, as occurs under a piece rate pay plan
+	Outside processing charges	If a third party is being paid for some or all of the processing work on a product, include this cost
+	Licensing fees	When the company is paying a third party a licensing fee for each unit sold, include this cost

Several costs should not be included in a product cost analysis, since they would still remain if the product were to be eliminated. Consider the following costs:

- *Non-product commissions*. Do not assign to a product any commissions paid for other reasons than a product sale, such as a quarterly override or a bonus for managing a new sales region.
- *Direct labor*. Most direct labor is incurred to provide minimum staffing for a product line, rather than to produce an individual unit. Theoretically, direct labor costs could be incurred even if there is *no* production. Thus, this cost should be considered part of factory overhead.

The cost of many purchased components varies considerably, based on the quantities in which you purchase them. For example, if you buy a widget in a standard supplier's economy pack of 100 units, the supplier charges $5.00 per unit. However, if you need a smaller quantity, which requires the supplier to break its normal packaging and ship the widget in a custom-sized shipping container, the price increases to $15.00. Further, if you need to buy in massive quantities, such as a truckload, the supplier can reduce the price further, to $3.50 per unit. Thus, the cost of a purchased component can vary substantially, depending upon the quantities in which it is purchased. It may be necessary to include this concept in the derivation of costs for a product.

EXAMPLE

Blitz Communications is considering developing a new desktop phone. The marketing department estimates that there is a 25% chance that the phone will sell 20,000 units or less, a 60% chance that it will sell between 20,000 and 50,000 units, and a 15% chance that it will sell more than 50,000 units. The phone is to be constructed almost entirely from purchased parts, with final assembly at the Blitz factory. The cost analysis is:

Component	(25% Probability) 20,000 Units or Less	(60% Probability) 20,001 – 50,000 Units	(15% Probability) 50,000+ Units
Price/Unit	$25.00	$25.00	$25.00
Base	3.00	2.50	2.00
Keypad	0.54	0.45	0.36
Microphone	0.78	0.65	0.52
Cord	0.96	0.80	0.64
Shell	4.50	3.75	3.00
Speaker	1.38	1.15	0.92
Direct labor	3.75	3.75	3.75
Overhead	8.00	4.20	2.00
Cost Total	$22.91	$17.25	$13.19
Profit	$2.09	$7.75	$11.81
Profit %	8%	31%	47%

The analysis uses the 20,001 to 50,000 unit range as the baseline. If product sales fall below the 20,001 unit level, the analysis shows that purchased component costs will increase by 20%, and that costs will decrease by 20% if the product sells more than 50,000 units. Further, the amount of fixed overhead costs must be spread over fewer units if the product sells 20,000 units or less, with the reverse effect if it sells more than 50,000 units.

The preceding example reveals the problem that management faces when evaluating product costs that could change with purchasing volumes; there is a possibility that profits could severely underperform. When this situation arises, management needs to decide if it should take the risk of releasing a product into the market, or of setting a lower price to attract more sales, or of reengineering the product to reduce its cost.

The Product Line Cost Object

It may be necessary to reach a decision regarding the termination of an entire product line. If so, the number of costs to include in the decision skyrockets, as compared to the meager cost listing for a single product. There may also be issues in the reverse direction, when costs must be added in order to expand a product line.

An entire facility may be used to create all of the products in a product family. If so, all of the costs of that facility are now considered variable when deciding whether to retain the product line. Consider the assignable costs in the following table, which are in addition to those listed in the last section for a product:

Additional Costs to Assign to a Product Line

+/-	Assignable Cost	Commentary
+	Direct labor	Direct labor is a fixed cost of the production line, and would be eliminated if the product line is terminated
+	Factory overhead	If the entire factory only produced that production line, then all of factory overhead is associated with the production line
+	Marketing costs	There is usually a separate budget for marketing the product line, which therefore varies with the product line
+	Sales costs	If the sales staff only sells the product line, they are a variable cost of the line. If they sell other items as well, then do not include their cost.
+	Factory administration costs	All of the administrative costs associated with running the factory are associated with the product line, if the factory only produces the product line

A sample product line margin report follows.

Sample Product Line Margin Report

Product Line	Revenue	Direct Materials	Engineering	Overhead	Sales and Marketing	Margin
Home products	$800,000	$320,000	$65,000	$165,000	$130,000	$120,000
Restaurant products	390,000	156,000	82,000	80,000	40,000	32,000
School products	640,000	320,000	39,000	128,000	90,000	63,000
Totals	$1,830,000	$796,000	$186,000	$373,000	$260,000	$215,000

It is quite likely that the only cost *not* assigned to a product line will be the allocation of corporate overhead to the facility that produces these goods, since that would not necessarily be impacted by the termination of the product line.

Costs related to a product line can vary whenever they reach a step cost boundary. For example, a production manager finds that his facility can produce a maximum of 3,000 widgets per week if he uses one shift, but that he needs to start a second shift in order to meet any additional demand. When he adds the shift, the company will have to incur certain additional fixed costs, such as the salary of a supervisor for that shift.

When a company exceeds a step cost boundary and incurs a new step cost, how does this impact the cost of an individual unit of production? For incremental costing decisions, it does nothing at all, since the variable cost of producing a single unit has not changed. It has, however, increased the total overhead cost of the production system, as well as (presumably) the ability of the system to produce more units.

For the purposes of analyzing the impact of a step cost on a product line, the main consideration for the analyst is to point out to management the existence of any impending step costs, their amount, and how they impact the production system. Management then needs to decide if it has a long-term need for the additional production capacity that the step cost represents, or whether it makes more sense to avoid the step cost by either turning away additional business or outsourcing the work.

The Sales Channel Cost Object

Management may need to consider the cost of its various sales channels, to see if they are being operated in a cost-effective manner that produces profits. If so, the analysis should certainly include the costs of all goods and services generated by that sales channel, as well as the support costs required to maintain the channel, which could involve any separate distribution infrastructure. Consider the assignable costs in the following table:

Additional Costs to Assign to a Sales Channel

+/-	Assignable Cost	Commentary
+	Product cost objects	This is the cost of any products sold through the sales channel
+	Marketing costs	If there is a separate budget for marketing through the sales channel, consider it a variable cost of the sales channel
+	Sales costs	If the sales staff is assigned solely to a sales channel, then they are a variable cost of that channel. If they sell through multiple sales channels, then do not assign their cost to this cost object.
+	Logistics costs	If the storage and distribution of goods is separate for the sales channel, consider logistics a variable cost of the sales channel

This is not a minor topic, for a chain of retail stores can be considered a sales channel cost object. It is not uncommon for management to evaluate an entire cluster of retail stores and their supporting regional warehouse and marketing budget to see if the cluster should be retained or shut down. The same analysis can be applied to Internet stores, distributors, and other sales channels. Thus, the proper analysis of sales channels can result in some of the largest decisions that a business can make – and those decisions must be supported by the correct information.

Cost Object Termination Issues

Much of the discussion surrounding cost objects tends to involve their termination. If it is considered necessary to actually terminate a cost object, there are several additional issues to be considered regarding how that termination is conducted. Consider the following issues:

- *Inventory reduction.* When a product or an entire product line is being terminated, the remaining inventory of raw materials and work-in-process should be converted into finished goods, and the finished goods completely sold off. Otherwise, the company will end up holding inventory that it will only be able to liquidate with difficulty. Thus, considerable planning regarding residual inventory levels must take place, which can impact the timing of a product or product line termination.
- *Inventory for warranties.* If a product is to be terminated and there is a warranty period associated with it, estimate the number of units to be held in reserve for warranty replacement purposes, and set them aside. Otherwise, production may have to be restarted at a later date to fulfill the company's warranty obligations.
- *Fixed asset maintenance.* If an entire production line is to be terminated, be sure to include fixed asset acquisition proposals in this decision. Ideally, maintenance of existing equipment should be enhanced during the final months of scheduled production, rather than spending funds on equipment that replaces worn-out machinery. This may mean that some production must be outsourced in order to sidestep production equipment that is no longer functional.
- *Severance costs.* If a product line or sales channel is being terminated, there will be associated severance costs for those employees impacted by the decision. Also, various laws may require that employees be given a certain amount of advance warning, which can delay the effective date of the shutdown.

These issues do not impact the decision to eliminate a cost object, but they can have an impact on the timing of the cancellation. Consequently, review these points on a regular basis as the termination date for a cost object approaches.

Which Cost Objects to Track

It is not necessary to track the cost of every conceivable cost object in a business. Some attract such a small amount of cost that there is no point in doing so, while there are no decisions that can be made in regard to other cost objects. The following table illustrates how to sort through the various cost objects in a business:

Tracking Concepts for Cost Objects

Cost Object	When to Track	When not to Track
Customers	When significant sales volume is concentrated with a small number of customers	When sales volume is widely dispersed among a large number of accounts
Employees	When specific sales can be traced back to an individual, or where pay levels are unusually high (examples: salespeople and engineers)	When there are a large number of employees whose pay is relatively low (example: retail clerks)
Products	When there is considerable pricing pressure that may drive product margins to zero	When product profitability is uniformly high
Product lines	When a product line is the sole focus of an entire production facility	When the product line has dispersed production and minimal targeted marketing or sales
Sales channels	When there is a large amount of supporting infrastructure, such as warehouses and a dedicated sales force	When the channel is incidental, with minimal ongoing costs

Summary

In essence, the study of cost objects is designed to focus attention on those aspects of a business that accumulate costs, and which therefore can interfere with profitability. This does not mean that the cost of all cost objects will be continually ground down over time to the bare minimum. On the contrary, management may conclude that *increased* spending on a cost object is needed in order to fulfill the corporate mission. However, these cases should be in the minority. In most situations, management should be made aware on a regular basis of how costs are concentrated throughout the business, and of any material changes in these costs over time.

Glossary

A

Accelerated filer. A company having an aggregate market value owned by investors who are not affiliated with the company of less than $700 million, but more than $75 million.

Accounting change. A change in an accounting principle, accounting estimate, or reporting entity.

Allowance for doubtful accounts. A reserve for bad debts that offsets the accounts receivable balance on the balance sheet.

Amortization. The write-off of an intangible asset over its expected period of use.

Available-for-sale securities. Investments that are not classified as held-to-maturity or trading securities.

B

Balance sheet. A report that summarizes all of an entity's assets, liabilities, and equity accounts as of a given point in time. It is also known as the statement of financial position.

Bank reconciliation. A comparison of the cash position recorded on an entity's books and the position noted on the records of its bank, usually resulting in some changes to the entity's book balance to account for transactions that are recorded on the bank's records but not the entity's.

Bargain purchase option. A lease clause allowing the lessee to purchase leased property for an amount below its expected fair value.

Bargain purchase. A business combination in which the fair value received by the acquirer exceeds the consideration paid.

Bargain renewal option. A lease clause allowing the lessee to renew a lease for an amount below its expected fair value.

Basic earnings per share. The earnings for an accounting period divided by the common stock outstanding during that period.

Bill and hold. A situation where the seller recognizes revenue from a sale, despite not shipping the related goods to the buyer.

Bill of materials. A record of the materials used to construct a product. It can include raw materials, sub-assemblies, and supplies, as well as an estimate of the amount of scrap that will be created during the manufacture of the product.

Book value. An asset's original cost, less any depreciation or impairment that has been subsequently incurred.

Boot. The cash paid as part of an exchange of assets between two parties.

Borrowing base. The ending balance of a company's accounts receivable and inventory, multiplied by the allowable percentage of each one against which the business is allowed to borrow by its lender.

Business combination. A transaction that results in an acquirer gaining control of an acquiree.

C

Capital expenditure. A payment made to acquire or upgrade an asset. It is recorded as a fixed asset, rather than being charged at once to expense.

Capital lease. A lease agreement that either shifts ownership of the leased asset to the lessee, contains a bargain purchase option, represents a long-term lease, or for which the present value of all lease payments represent nearly all of the fair value of the asset.

Capitalization limit. A minimum threshold, above which an expenditure is recorded as a long-term asset, and below which it is charged to expense.

Carrying amount. The recorded amount of an asset, net of any accumulated depreciation or accumulated impairment losses.

Cash equivalent. A short-term, very liquid investment that is easily convertible into a known amount of cash, and which is so near its maturity that it presents an insignificant risk of a change in value because of changes in interest rates.

Change in accounting estimate. A change that adjusts the carrying amount of an asset or liability, or the subsequent accounting for it.

Change in accounting principle. A change from one generally accepted accounting principle to another, or a change in the method of applying it.

Chart of accounts. A listing of all the accounts used in the general ledger, usually listed in order by account number.

Chief operating decision maker. A person who is responsible for making decisions about resource allocations to the segments of a business, and for evaluating those segments.

Class. A group of fixed assets having common characteristics and usage.

Collateral. An asset that a borrower has pledged as security for a loan. The lender has the legal right to seize the asset if the borrower is unable to pay back the loan by an agreed date.

Comprehensive income. The change in equity of a business during a period, not including investments by or distributions to owners.

Control. Having the power to direct the management and policies of an entity.

Cost to sell. The costs incurred in a sale transaction that would not have been incurred if there had been no sale. Examples of costs to sell are title transfer fees and brokerage commissions.

Current assets. Cash and other assets that are expected to be converted into cash during the normal operating cycle of a business.

Current liabilities. Those liabilities whose payment is expected to require the use of current assets or their replacement with other current liabilities.

Cycle counting. The process of counting a small proportion of the total inventory on a daily basis, adjusting the inventory records for errors found, and investigating the causes of those errors.

D

Debt security. A security that involves a creditor relationship with a borrower, such as bonds, commercial paper, and Treasury securities.

Debt. A contractual right to receive payment that is considered an asset by the lender and a liability by the borrower.

Depreciation. The gradual charging to expense of an asset's cost over its expected useful life.

Diluted earnings per share. The earnings for an accounting period divided by the common stock outstanding during that period and all potential common stock.

Dilution. When earnings per share is reduced by the assumption that all potential common stock is converted to common stock.

Direct method. A format of the statement of cash flows that presents specific cash flows in the operating activities section of the report.

Discrete view. The assumption that the results reported for a specific interim period are not associated with the revenues and expenses arising during other reporting periods within a fiscal year.

Disposal group. A group of assets that you expect to dispose of in a single transaction, along with any liabilities that might be transferred to another entity along with the assets.

E

Earnings per share. A company's net income divided by the weighted-average number of shares outstanding. This calculation is subject to a number of additional factors involving preferred shares, convertible instruments, and dividends.

Effective interest rate. The contractual interest rate of a loan, adjusted for discounts, premiums, and other costs.

Equity security. A security that represents an ownership interest in, or a right to acquire or dispose of an ownership interest in, an entity.

Exchange rate. The ratio at which a unit of one currency can be exchanged for another currency.

Extraordinary item. A highly unusual and infrequent event or transaction that is not expected to recur in the foreseeable future.

F

Fair value. The price paid for an asset or liability in an orderly transaction between market participants.

First in, first out method. A method of inventory valuation that operates under the assumption that the first goods purchased are also the first goods sold.

Foreign currency translation. The process of converting amounts stated in a foreign currency into the reporting currency of the parent entity.

Foreign currency. A currency other than the functional currency being used by an entity.

Form 10-K. A document that a publicly-held company must file with the Securities and Exchange Commission once a year, detailing its financial results for the preceding year.

Form 10-Q. A document that a publicly-held company must file with the Securities and Exchange Commission every quarter, detailing its financial results for the preceding quarter and the year-to-date.

Functional currency. The currency that an entity uses in the majority of its business transactions.

G

General ledger. The master set of accounts that summarize all transactions occurring within an entity.

Generally Accepted Accounting Principles. A set of authoritative accounting standards issued by several standard-setting bodies, which entities should follow in preparing their financial statements.

Goodwill. An intangible asset that represents the future benefits arising from assets acquired in a business combination that are not otherwise identified.

Grant date. The date on which an employer agrees to become contingently obligated to issue a payment to an employee once that person renders a service.

H

Held for sale. A designation given to assets that an entity intends to sell to a third party within one year.

Held-to-maturity securities. A debt security that the holder intends to hold to maturity, and who has the ability to do so.

Glossary

Historical cost. Costing based on measures of historical prices, without subsequent restatement.

Holding gain or loss. A change in the fair value of a security.

I

Impairment. A condition that arises when the carrying amount of an asset exceeds its fair value.

Imputed interest rate. The estimated interest rate used instead of the established interest rate associated with a debt.

Income statement. A financial report that summarizes an entity's revenue, cost of goods sold, gross margin, other expenses, taxes, and net income or loss. The income statement shows an entity's financial results over a specific time period, usually a month, quarter, or year.

Income taxes. Taxes that are based on the reported amount of income.

Indirect method. A format of the statement of cash flows that uses accrual-basis accounting as part of the presentation of cash flow information.

Intangible asset. A non-physical asset having a useful life greater than one year. Examples of intangible assets are trademarks, patents, and non-competition agreements.

Integral view. The concept that results reported in interim financial statements are an integral part of the full-year financial results.

Interim period. A financial reporting period that is shorter than a full fiscal year.

Intrinsic value. The excess amount of the fair value of a share over the exercise price of an underlying stock option.

Inventory. Tangible items held for routine sale, or which are being produced for sale, or which are consumed in the production of goods for sale. Depreciated assets are not considered inventory.

Investee. A business whose equity instruments are owned by an investor.

Investor. An entity that owns the voting stock of a business.

Item master. A record that lists the name, description, unit of measure, weight, dimensions, ordering quantity, and other key information for a component part.

L

Large accelerated filer. A company having an aggregate market value owned by investors who are not affiliated with the company of a minimum of $700 million.

Last in, first out method. A method of inventory valuation that operates under the assumption that the last goods purchased are the first goods sold.

Lease. An agreement that allows the lessee use of a fixed asset.

Lessee. The entity allowed use of a fixed asset under a lease agreement.

Lessor. The entity allowing use of its fixed asset to a third party under a lease agreement.

LIFO layer. A cost per unit ascribed to certain units of stock under the last in, first out method of inventory costing.

Local currency. The legal currency being used within a country.

Lower of cost or market. A rule requiring you to record the cost of inventory at the lower of its cost or the current market price.

N

Near term. A period not exceeding one year following the date of the financial statements.

Net income. Revenues and gains, less expenses and losses, not including items of other comprehensive income.

Net realizable value. The estimated selling price of an item in the ordinary course of business, not including any costs of completion and disposal.

Nonvested shares. Shares not yet issued, because the consideration that earns the shares has not yet been completed.

O

Operating lease. Any lease not designated as a capital lease.

Operating segment. A component of a public entity.

Other comprehensive income. A statement that contains all changes not permitted in the main part of the income statement. These items include unrealized gains and losses on available-for-sale securities, cash flow hedge gains and losses, and foreign currency translation adjustments.

P

Parent. A business that has a controlling interest in a subsidiary.

Payroll cycle. The length of time between payrolls. Thus, if a business pays its employees every Friday, that is a one-week payroll cycle.

Periodic inventory system. An inventory calculation method under which you only update the ending inventory balance when you conduct a physical inventory count.

Perpetual inventory system. The continual updating of inventory records to account for additions to and subtractions from inventory.

Potential common stock. Securities that can be converted to common stock, such as options, warrants, and convertible securities.

Preferred stock. A security that receives preferential treatment in comparison to common stock.

R

Reload feature. The automatic granting of additional options whenever previously granted options are exercised, in the amount used to exercise the previous option.

Remote deposit capture. The use of a check scanner to deposit checks from a remote location.

Reporting currency. The currency in which a business prepares its financial statements.

Reporting unit. An operating segment or one level below an operating segment. An operating segment is a component of a public entity that engages in business activities and whose results are reviewed by the chief operating decision maker, and for which discrete financial information is available.

Residual value. The estimated fair value of an intangible asset once an entity judges its useful life to be complete, minus disposal costs.

Restatement. The revision of prior financial statements to correct an error.

Restricted share. A share that cannot be sold for a certain period of time.

Retrospective application. The application of a different accounting principle to prior financial statements or the balance sheet at the beginning of the current period.

Reverse acquisition. A business combination in which the legal acquirer is the acquiree for accounting purposes.

S

Salvage value. The estimated value of an asset at the end of its useful life.

Security. An interest in an entity or an obligation of the issuer that is represented by an instrument that is a medium of investment, and which is divisible into a class of shares or other interests.

Segment reporting. A requirement to report the results of the operating segments of a publicly-held company.

Segment. A distinct component of a business that produces revenue, and for which the business produces separate financial information that is regularly reviewed internally by a chief operating decision maker.

Stock dividend. A common stock issuance to existing common shareholders that does not diminish corporate assets or increase the interests of shareholders.

Stock option. An instrument that gives the holder the right, but not the obligation, to buy or sell shares at a certain price, and for a certain period of time.

Stock split. A common stock issuance to existing common shareholders that causes a stock price reduction, with the intent of enhancing the marketability of the shares.

Subsidiary. A business in which a parent entity owns a controlling interest.

Suspense account. An account in the general ledger that is used to temporarily store any transactions for which there is some uncertainty about the account in which they should be recorded.

T

Trade receivables. Amounts billed by a business to its customers when it delivers goods or services to them in the ordinary course of business. These billings are typically documented on formal invoices.

Trading securities. Securities acquired with the intent of selling them in the near term to generate a profit.

Translation adjustment. An adjustment resulting from the translation of financial statements into the reporting currency of an entity.

Treasury stock. A company's stock that it has reacquired.

Trial balance. A report listing the ending debit and credit balances in all accounts as of the date of the report.

U

Useful life. The time period over which an asset is expected to be productive or enhance cash flows, or the number of units of production expected to be generated from it.

V

Variable interest entity. An entity in which an investor has a noncontrolling interest, and which may be subject to consolidation in some situations.

Vest. When rights have been earned, such as when the end of a service period required for the issuance of shares has been reached.

Volatility. The amount by which a variable fluctuates over time.

W

Warranty. A guarantee related to the performance of nonfinancial assets owned by the guaranteed party.

Weighted average method. A method of valuing ending inventory and the cost of goods sold, based on the average cost of materials in inventory.

Index

Index

Made in the USA
Middletown, DE
13 April 2018